John N Sevenngham

Dec 20, 2004

THE ENLIGHTENED JOSEPH PRIESTLEY

ROBERT E. SCHOFIELD

THE ENLIGHTENED
JOSEPH PRIESTLEY

---

*A Study of His Life
and Work from
1773 to 1804*

THE PENNSYLVANIA STATE UNIVERSITY PRESS
UNIVERSITY PARK, PENNSYLVANIA

Library of Congress Cataloging-in-Publication Data

Schofield, Robert E.
  The enlightened Joseph Priestley : a study of his life
  and work from 1773 to 1804 / Robert E. Schofield.
      p.   cm.
Includes bibliographical references and index.
ISBN 0-271-02459-3 (alk. paper)
1. Priestley, Joseph, 1733–1804.
2. Unitarian churches—Clergy—Biography.
3. Chemists—Biography.
I. Title.

BX9869 .P8S355 2004
540´.92—dc22   2004006338

Contents

List of Illustrations   vii

List of Abbreviations   ix

Preface   xi

PART I: CALNE, 1773–1780

I   Shelburne and Politics   3

II   Religion and Theology   25

III   "Common-Sense" and Associationism   43

IV   Matter and Spirit   59

V   Philosophical Necessity   77

VI   Observations on Air I and II: Oxygen   93

VII   Observations on Air III and Natural Philosophy I   121

PART II: BIRMINGHAM, 1780–1791

VIII   Science and the Lunar Society   147

IX   Science and the Chemical Revolution   169

X   Religion   195

XI   Theology   215

XII   Education, Metaphysics, History   241

XIII   Politics and the Birmingham Riots   263

Part III: Clapton/Hackney (1791–1794) and
        Northumberland, Pennsylvania (1794–1804)

XIV   Politics, Science, Education, Religion   293
XV   Emigration to the United States, Politics, and Education   317
XVI   Science   345
XVII Religion, Death   373

Appendix: Family   403
Bibliography   407
Index   447

Illustrations

Frontispiece: Portrait of the aged Priestley, by Rembrandt Peale. Photograph by permission of Dickinson College, Carlisle, Pennsylvania.

1. Joseph Priestley's house (1773–1780) on the Green, Calne
2. Plate of chemical apparatus, from *Experiments and Observations,* vol. 1, 2d ed. (1775)
3. Map of Birmingham, c. 1780
4. Gillray anti-Priestley cartoon, c. 1791
5. Lithograph print of the ruins of Priestley's Birmingham home after the riots
6. Lithograph print of New Meeting Chapel in ruins after riots of 1791
7. Priestley's House in Northumberland, Pennsylvania. Courtesy of the Pennsylvania Historical and Museum Commission.
8. Universalist Church, Philadelphia, in which Priestley preached in 1795, now owned by the Jewish congregation, Kersher Israel. This is the only building still standing in which Priestley preached.

Abbreviations

APS	Library of the American Philosophical Society, Philadelphia
Bolton, #	*Correspondence of Joseph Priestley.* Ed. Henry Carrington Bolton. New York: privately printed, 1892. Letter #.
Exp. & Obs.	Joseph Priestley, *Experiments and Observations on Different Kinds of Air.* London: J. Johnson, 1775, 1776, 1777.
Exp. & Obs. Nat. Phil.	Joseph Priestley, *Experiments and Observations relating to various Branches of Natural Philosophy . . .* London: J. Johnson, 1779, 1781, 1786.
SciAuto.	*A Scientific Autobiography of Joseph Priestley: Selected Scientific Correspondence.* Ed. Robert E. Schofield. Cambridge: MIT Press, 1966. Letters cited by number.
W x.x	*The Theological and Miscellaneous Works of Joseph Priestley, LL.D. F.R.S., &c.* Ed. John Towill Rutt. New York: Kraus Reprint Co., 1972. 25 vols. Vol. 1 in two parts.
Warr.	Warrington Municipal Library, Warrington, Cheshire, England
Wms.	Dr. Williams's Library, London

Preface

Nunc dimittis! A project begun some forty years ago is now completed. And if it is not the definitive biography (whatever that might be) of Joseph Priestley that I had originally intended, it is, in at least one sense, a complete one. So far as I have been able to do so, I have consulted and described every published writing of Joseph Priestley and attempted to place every bit of it in its historical context. I suggest that this is unique.

This is an intellectual biography, not a psychological personality study or a sociological history of middle-class Britain in the eighteenth century. That is partly in consequence of the materials available. Priestley was a man of the Enlightenment; he seems always to have maintained a decent reticence and did not display his emotions to public scrutiny. Only rarely, in correspondence or publications, did he express his feelings. Even his *Memoirs* dwell more on his friends, his benefactors, and his work than on himself. But intellectually is also how I see him. Priestley is important because of his ideas, and it is ideas that I chiefly describe and discuss.

There was a time when Francis Jeffrey's negative appraisal of Priestley's influence on posterity (in the review of his *Memoirs* with which this volume begins) seemed valid. As late as 1845, Henry, Lord Brougham, in his *Lives of Men of Letters and Science . . . in the time of George III*, found it necessary to devote a substantial part of his essay on Priestley to an attack on his personality, politics, and religious views. Brougham's rather unfriendly biographer for the *Dictionary of National Biography* described his work as "often superficial and his criticisms sometimes scandalously unjust," and this is clearly evident in this essay, where even his list of Priestley's publications is crudely distorted. Even worse was the portrait of Priestley in Leslie Stephen's *History of English Thought in the Eighteenth Century* (1876): a restless intellect incapable of confining itself to any single task, without force or originality, marked by hasty and superficial thought.[1]

---

1. Leslie Stephen, *History of English Thought in the Eighteenth Century* (London: Smith, Elder & Co., 1876), 1:430. There are equally critical statements in vol. 2. It is said that Stephen

It has been left to his science, primarily an avocation of his leisure, to have retained for Priestley a measure of general public recognition: "Oh yes, he discovered oxygen!" Even as a faulty tribute this is inadequate, for it is limited to his pneumatic experiments and, even there, neglects the eight other gases Priestley isolated and identified. The list of British scientists Priestley influenced includes Henry Cavendish, Humphry Davy, John Dalton, Thomas Graham, Michael Faraday, and Thomas Young, and conveys in part how meager that appreciation is. Apart from chemists who resisted Lavoisian chemistry, Priestley's prestige on the continent was less high. Most followed the scenario set for them by Lavoisier, epitomized by the phrase from Georges Cuvier's grudging éloge in 1805 for the Institut Royal de France: Priestley was the father of modern chemistry, who never acknowledged his daughter.[2]

In this biography of Priestley, I have attempted to show that he was more than a lucky empiricist in science, more than a naïve political liberal, more than an exhaustive compiler of superficial evidence in militant support of Unitarianism. It is past time for him to be recognized as a leading luminary of the Enlightenment in an extraordinary variety of subjects, from grammar, education, aesthetics, metaphysics, politics, and theology, to natural philosophy.

During my years of research on Priestley, I attempted, as a historian of science, to place the man and his work within the frame of contemporary science. It became increasingly obvious how little historians of chemistry had been aware of the issues involved in Priestley's discoveries and his disagreements with Lavoisian chemistry, while chemists tended to be entirely ignorant of them. I have tried to be fair, crediting Priestley with his achievements without concealing his faults. This has frequently involved putting the issues in modern terms, where they can be more easily understood, but the faults are to be seen in their context and against the achievements of his

---

later repudiated his *History* as marked more by immaturity than by judgment. Stephen was militantly agnostic and was offended by Priestley's support of miracles and prophecy, but his criticism still seems excessive. It is possible that some of his animosity stems from the drubbing Priestley had given his maternal grandfather, the Rev. Henry Venn, in 1769. In any event, Stephen's edited *Dictionary of National Biography* redressed the balance in 1896 with a perceptive sketch of Priestley by Alexander Gordon and Philip Hartog.

2. Cavendish, Davy, Dalton, Graham, and Faraday are cited in the text; Thomas Young, one of Britain's great physical scientists of the early nineteenth century, credited the reading of an odd volume of Priestley's chemical works, purchased at auction by his father, for turning his attention "to making chemical experiments." Young quoted in George Peacock, *Thomas Young* (London: John Murray, 1855), 7. Georges Cuvier, "Eulogy on Dr. Priestley," translated in the *Monthly Repository* 1 (1806): 216–19, 328–34.

contemporary critics. Given the emphasis of Joseph Black, Henry Cavendish, and Antoine Lavoisier on quantitative results of experiments, for example, Priestley's disinclination to do so *was* a failure, as was his ignoring of his own manipulative discoveries—though these were to be fully understood only within the nineteenth-century world of kinetic theory.

Although the creation of societies for eighteenth-century studies and the appearance of journals such as *Enlightenment and Dissent* have signaled a change in attitude toward that period, it is surprising how few persons (including historians) have assimilated the difference. As this is a biography intended for historians of science, chemists, and theologians, as well as intellectual and cultural historians, I have not assumed readers' familiarity with Priestley's historical environment. I have tried to encapsulate my reading in eighteenth-century English and American politics into an understanding of Priestley's place there. I do not pretend that my reading has been exhaustive, or that one can substitute Priestley's story for a general history of the period—though I should hope that it might be relevant to a revisionist history of eighteenth-century thought.

Being unable to find any modern consensual statement placing any part of Priestley's theology in context, I have attempted to do that myself by reference to near-contemporary and modern historians of theology and the church. As Priestley was primarily a theologian, this biography dwells, more than most readers may appreciate, on his theological writings. Historians of chemistry and chemists should observe that there was an immediate relationship between his theology and his science, while historians of the eighteenth century should note that the English Enlightenment contained far more religion than critics of the Enlightenment are wont to allow it.

In any event, I am done and shall leave it to others to mine my work for their own interpretations and for the popular biography of Priestley that he deserves.

Any project so long in gestation acquires baggage of obligations that must be acknowledged, starting with a Fulbright Fellowship, two John Simon Guggenheim Foundation fellowships, and two fruitful years at the Institute for Advanced Study, Princeton, New Jersey. I have enjoyed financial and intellectual support of the National Science Foundation and of the history faculties and administrations of the University of Kansas, Case Institute of Technology (later Case Western Reserve University), and Iowa State University. All historians owe gratitude to libraries and librarians; mine extend from those of the educational institutions with which I have been connected, either as a student or faculty member, to the libraries of the Royal Society of London, the American Philosophical Society, Dr. Williams's Library, and, most recently, to the Princeton, New Jersey, Public Library. And most specifically, for their patience and continued support, I acknowledge the help of my wife, Mary-Peale (especially for her splendid indexes), and son, Charles Stockton Peale.

And, finally, I thank the readers of the original text in draft for their suggestions, which led to substantial improvements. Neither they nor the many colleagues I have consulted are, of course, responsible for the errors, which are my very own. And my thanks and acknowledgments are also due the following institutions for permission to quote, or cite extensively, from manuscripts or copyrighted materials fully cited in footnotes:

The Birmingham City Council: Leisure and Culture, represented by the Central Library Manager, Archives, Local Studies and History, for Priestley correspondence, etc., held in the Central Library and Archives.

The Bodleian Library, Oxford, for letters from the Price correspondence: MS. Eng. Misc. c. 132; the Godwin letter from the Abinger collection, Condercet: MS. Eng., letter 140, fols. 27–28a; and William Priestley's MS, Montague d. 18, fols. 55–56.

The British Library, for Priestley correspondence, Sir Joseph Banks correspondence, and the Russell Papers.

Dickinson College, Waidner-Spahr Library, for materials related to Priestley and for the Rembrandt Peale portrait of Priestley used as the frontispiece.

The Harris Manchester College, Oxford, for Priestley manuscripts and letters.

The Historical Society of Pennsylvania, for Priestley correspondence from the Benjamin Smith Barton Papers, the Benjamin Rush Papers, and the Logan Papers, as well as separate letters to John Vaughan and Robert R. Livingston, from Benjamin Franklin to Richard Price, and items from its copy of the *Theological Repository,* vols. 4–6 (1784–88).

The Koninklijke Hollandsche Maatschappij der Wetenschappen, for correspondence of Martinus van Marum and archival references to Priestley.

The Library Company of Philadelphia, Correspondence of Dr. Benjamin Rush, for letters to Rush from Thomas Henry and John Bostock.

Lord Lansdowne, for Priestley papers in the Bowood Archives, Bowood, Calne.

The Massachusetts Historical Society, Adams Family Papers, for Priestley letters to John Adams, and the R. C. Waterston Autograph Collection, for Priestley letter to George Walker.

The MIT Press, for Priestley letters in the published version of my book *A Scientific Autobiography of Joseph Priestley* (1966).

The New York Historical Society, for Priestley and Robert R. Livingston correspondence.

The New York Public Library, Astor, Lenox, and Tilden Foundations, Manuscripts and Archives Division, for Misc. Papers (Joseph Priestley and Charles Nisbet).

Oxford University Press, for citations and quotations from my book *The Lunar Society of Birmingham* (1963) and from *Lichtenberg's Visits to England* (1938).

The Pennsylvania Historical and Museum Commission, 2002, for the photograph of the Joseph Priestley House, Northumberland, Pennsylvania.

The Royal Society for materials from Yates Priestleyana and from the Society's archives.

Warrington Borough Council, Warrington, Cheshire, England, Libraries Information Service, for correspondence with John Wilkinson.

The director of Dr. Williams's Library on behalf of the Trustees for Priestley's letters preserved there—primarily to Theophilus Lindsey and Thomas Belsham.

PART I

CALNE
(1773–1780)

I

SHELBURNE AND POLITICS

In 1806 Joseph Priestley was stigmatized as a presumptuous provincial who had prodigiously overrated himself.[1] Even the nominal part of this criticism was singularly ill conceived. Though Priestley had, it is true, lived more than 90 percent of his life in the provinces—or, worse, in the United States—he was cosmopolitan in a way that Francis Jeffrey, author of that critique, could never comprehend. By the time of his death in 1804, Priestley was a member of every major scientific society in the world and friend or correspondent of major scientific, intellectual, and political personages in many different countries. Author of more than 150 books, pamphlets, and articles, he had engaged successfully in controversy with theological, philosophical, and political opponents and participated in the founding of British Unitarianism, pneumatic chemistry, and the philosophical schools of utilitarianism and associationism. Most of these distinctions were achieved after 1773, when, at the age of forty, Priestley was thrust from a nominal provinciality onto the national scene.[2]

1. [Francis Jeffrey], "Memoirs of Dr. Joseph Priestley," *Edinburgh Review* 9 (1806): 147.
2. A substantial part of personal information about Priestley and his work is derived from the more than eight hundred letters he wrote, more than half of them to a circle of theological friends: Theophilus Lindsey and Thomas Belsham especially but also Joseph Bretland, Newcome Cappe, Richard Price, Caleb Rotheram, Joshua Toulmin, and William Turner. Originals of most of these, plus a scattering of similar letters, are preserved in Wms. and are transcribed

It was a role, however, for which his previous experiences had well prepared him. The opportunity to move from his post as Dissenting minister in Leeds to become companion to William Petty, Lord Shelburne, was merely recognition of a status his achievements had already earned.[3] Yet nothing in Priestley's background or experience could have prepared him for the social world of Lord Shelburne. Son of a lower middle-class cloth finisher, student and teacher at Dissenting academies, nonconformist minister at provincial chapels, he had spent his life in modest surroundings and moderate circumstances (at best). He had acquired cultured and sophisticated friends, Thomas Bentley, Benjamin Franklin, Theophilus Lindsey, Josiah Wedgwood, and others, but they too were of the middle class. William Petty, Earl of Shelburne and Baron Wycombe, by contrast, was one of the wealthiest members of the British aristocracy, with family estates at Bowood, Wiltshire and Wycome Abbey, Buckinghamshire, and other properties in England and Ireland.

But though Shelburne was, by title and wealth, in the English aristocracy, by background, education, and experience, he was not of it.[4] Born in Dublin in 1737 as William Fitzmaurice, cadet grandson of the Earl of Kerry, he had spent his early years in the cultural isolation of the family estate in south Ireland. In 1751 his situation was changed dramatically when his father inherited the estates and other property of a maternal uncle, Henry Petty, Earl of Shelburne, on condition that he adopt the Petty name and arms. On his father's death in 1761, William Fitzmaurice, now William Petty, became Earl of Shelburne in the Irish peerage and Baron Wycome in the English. Although he served with distinction as an officer in the British Army during the Seven Years' War, he had otherwise none of the social conditioning or family associations common to his peers. Not until his marriage, in 1765, to Lady Sophia Carteret, daughter of the late Lord Granville, can he have felt comfortable in his entrée into English society, and all of his life he was stigmatized for his affected, insinuating manner.

(more or less accurately) in John Towill Rutt's twenty-five-volume edition of *The Theological and Miscellaneous Works of Joseph Priestley, LL.D. F.R.S.* (London, 1817–31; reprint New York: Kraus Reprint Co., 1972), which will be cited throughout the text as *W.*, vol., page(s). Vol. 1 is in two parts and will be cited as *W.* 1.1:xx or 1.2:xx. Dated text references to these letters can be found there and will not be noted further.

3. For Priestley's career prior to his joining Lord Shelburne, see Robert E. Schofield, *The Enlightenment of Joseph Priestley: A Study of his Life and Work from 1733 to 1773* (University Park: Pennsylvania State University Press, 1997).

4. For biographical details of Shelburne's early life, see Edmund George Petty, Lord Fitzmaurice, *Life of William, Earl of Shelburne, afterwards first Marquess of Lansdowne: with Extracts from his Papers and Correspondence* (London: Macmillan, 1875–76), vol. 1, which includes an autobiographical memoir.

For many years Shelburne was to feel most comfortable in his role while traveling as an English "Milord" in France. When his wife died, in 1771, he escaped to France in the company of Isaac Barré. Barré, however, was not at ease in mixed polite society and Shelburne began to seek a companion. On the advice of Richard Price, and with the laudable ambition to serve also as a patron of learning, he selected Joseph Priestley, but there was a difficulty. Neither Shelburne nor Priestley was clear as to what Priestley's new duties were to be. In 1771 Shelburne had been looking for someone to combine the positions of companion and tutor. When, in 1772, he decided to become Priestley's patron, he employed Thomas Jervis as tutor; Priestley was to be companion and pensioner. Priestley's response to the offer frustrated Shelburne's good intentions: "I really think it would not be in my power to render his Lordship any services equivalent to the recompense which, in prudence, I ought to expect . . . and I could not satisfy myself with receiving a salary, without rendering what should appear to myself an equivalent service."[5]

As that salary was to be £250 per year, something more than flattering equivocation had to be offered to satisfy Priestley's bourgeois conscience. The result was the creation of a position as companion-librarian and supervisor of the tutor. Most of Priestley's labors directly in Shelburne's service occurred after he had demonstrated an incapacity to act in the role for which Shelburne had chiefly employed him. During the first year of their association, the novelty of the relationship may have concealed differences in temperament. Certainly Shelburne had no cause to regret his role as patron. Even before leaving Leeds, Priestley showed some experiments to a visitor recommended to him by Shelburne—a Mr. Fromond, who was to translate the "Observations" into Italian, c. 1774. In September 1773 Priestley was awarded the Copley Medal of the Royal Society for his 1772 papers on Pyrmont water and on airs. Shelburne's association with Benjamin Franklin was undoubtedly warmer in consequence of his employment of Priestley, and, throughout the period from late November 1772 through 1774, the Abbé Morellet, whom Shelburne had met in Paris and greatly admired, noted his respect and that of Trudaine de Montigny for Priestley and his enthusiasm for the establishing of Priestley at Bowood.[6]

5. Priestley to Richard Price, 21 July 1772; no. 50 in *SciAuto*.
6. Priestley to Shelburne, 20 May 1773, Bowood Papers III-C. Morellet visited London and Bowood late in 1772 and early in 1773. He wrote frequently to Shelburne, mentioning Priestley in his letters. See [Abbé Morellet], *Lettres de l'Abbé Morellet à Lord Shelburne* (Paris: E. Plon, Mourrit et Cie, 1898), nos. 2, 3, 5, 6, 9, 12, 13–16, 27, 31, 43, 57.

Then, in late autumn 1774, Shelburne traveled to the continent, taking Priestley with him as a companion. Shelburne's political career was then at a low ebb, leaving him at loose ends and frustrated by his inability to moderate ministerial coercion of the American colonies.[7] That surely was the major factor in Shelburne's desire to escape England again in travel, the recent death of Louis XV of France providing a convenient excuse to examine the new political situation there.[8] Priestley and Shelburne toured the low countries, along the Rhine, visiting Dusseldorf, Cologne, Bonn, Coblentz, and Mannheim, journeying on into Alsace and Lorraine and thence into France, where, finally, they spent a month in Paris. It was Priestley's first (and only) trip into Europe and he seems to have enjoyed most of it—as well he should have, for he saw it under the best of auspices.

> This little excursion made me more sensible than I should otherwise have been of the benefit of foreign travel. . . . The very sight of new countries, new buildings, new customs, &c., and the very hearing of an unintelligible new language [Priestley read, but did not speak, French and German], gives new ideas, and tends to enlarge the mind. . . . I saw every thing to the greatest advantage, and without any anxiety or trouble, and had an opportunity of seeing and conversing with every person of eminence, wherever we came; the political characters by his lordship's connexions, and the literary ones by my own.[9]

Priestley's journal of the trip, in the form of letters written to Shelburne's sons, reveals the insular middle-class Englishman, comparing the state of farming, the buildings, the appearance and manners of the people, the nature of the inns, to what he was familiar with in England. He dutifully accompanied Shelburne on state visits to dignitaries and to see paintings, cathedrals, and religious services. In Paris he went to salons with Shelburne, including

7. Shelburne had been secretary of state for the southern department (and thus in charge of colonial affairs) in the ministry of Lord Chatham, 23 July 1766. He was conciliatory toward the colonies and in conflict with colleagues in Chatham's cabinet, and Chatham was ill most of the time. When Chatham resigned on 5 Oct. 1768, Shelburne followed on the 19th.

8. On 20 Sept. 1774, G. Cressener wrote informing Williiam Knox that Shelburne and Priestley had visited Bonn the previous week, with Shelburne eloquent in favor of the Americans and on his way to Paris "to pick up matter for opposition next session." See *Historical Manuscripts Commission: Report on Manuscripts in Various Collections* (Dublin: H. M. Stationary Office, 1909), 6:116.

9. *W.* 1.1:198.

those of the Baron d'Holbach, Turgot, and Trudaine. Soon, however, he tired of public spectacles and assemblies, describing them as insipid and irksome. "I am quite tired of the idleness in which I spend my time here, and long exceedingly to be about my experiments or some composition."[10]

In fact, Priestley begged to be excused. Leaving Shelburne to attend the social activities by himself, he spent his evenings at the hotel with John Hycinth Magellan (Magelhaens) as his interpreter, entertaining people who came to see him. He even "chose to return" to England before Lord Shelburne and, once there, reported of France: "Upon the whole, I thought the country by no means a desireable one to live in, or to stay much in, and I wonder much at the taste of my countrymen, who spend so much of their time, and of their money, there." This is scarcely the behavior, or the attitude, of a companion, and it is not to be wondered at that this changed with Shelburne's return to England. Priestley performed his tasks and experiments at Bowood, or in London, as Shelburne moved from one to the other. Increasingly, though, the two did not seem to travel together. When next he went to Paris, Shelburne took James Townsend. The direction the relationship was taking is suggested in Richard Price's letter to Shelburne on his leaving London for Bowood, 31 October 1778: "Should your Lordship see Dr. Priestley, deliver my rememberances to him."[11]

When the relationship was finally dissolved, early in 1780, Samuel Vaughan wrote to Benjamin Franklin, "the two characters were such as did not understand the one the other. The one did not comprehend enough the nature & merit of a speculative scholar, nor the other the situation and difficulties of a political actor." The problem, however, was more subtle than that. Too many people are on record as having delighted in Priestley's company and conversation to dismiss his sociability in terms such as "speculative scholar." Though the majority of these friends, like Lindsey and Richard Price, were ministers, the number includes also such eminently "clubbable men" as Benjamin Franklin and John Lee. Nor was the problem simply that Shelburne was a politician. Throughout much of his life he displayed interest in religion, economics, art, literature, and music, as well as in politics. There is no reason to doubt that Priestley and Shelburne could find subjects for mutually satisfying conversation. But Shelburne did not want a conversation partner; he needed a companion with whom he could retreat from the

10. The journal is printed in W. 1.1:237–51; see also William Turner to Newcome Cappe, 22 May 1775, W. 1.1:257n; the quotation is from Priestley to Lindsey, 21 Oct. 1774, written from Paris, W. 1.1:251–54.

11. Price to Shelburne, 31 Oct. 1778, Price Letters, Bodleian Library, Oxford.

confusing world of English politics and the English upper-class life in which he had unexpectedly found himself, and he did not find this in Priestley.

There was, however, no immediate overt break between the two. Shelburne continued to behave with uniform politeness. An anteroom off the library at Bowood was set aside as a laboratory (still called the Laboratory, or Priestley's room) to be used in entertaining guests and especially foreigners (W. 1.1:210). When the Priestleys had their third son, on 24 May 1777, they named him Henry at Shelburne's request. Joseph Priestley lived at Shelburne House, London, during the winter season; the rest of the year he lived with his family in a house provided by Lord Shelburne in the village of Calne, two miles from Bowood. Calne was small, irregularly built along the banks of the Calne "river," with an old parish church, a "free school" directed by the vicar of Calne or his usher—so Priestley's sons were educated about six miles away, at Devizes—and a green around which the wealthier houses of Georgian Calne were built.[12]

The Priestley house was one of those on the green, but before the family could settle in substantial repairs had to be made, at a cost to Shelburne of £67.7.5 (see fig. 1).[13] Their move was begun in June 1773 and was not yet completed in July, when Priestley wrote that he was waiting for the arrival of his books and that the family was living in one room while the house was refitted. An early visit by Lord Shelburne is said to have caught Mary Priestley papering the walls. She responded to Priestley's apologies with an imperturbable, "Lord Shelburne is a statesman; and he knows that people are best employed in doing their duty."[14]

The Bowood property, during Priestley's years of service there, consisted of roughly a thousand acres, a "big house," a "little house," and a scattering

12. See Nikolaus Pevsner, *The Buildings of England: Wiltshire* (Hammondsworth: Penguin Books, 1963), 109–11, 140–43; see also A. E. W. Marsh, *A History of the Borough and Town of Calne and some Account of the Villages, etc. in its Vicinity* (Calne: Robert S. Heath; London, Castle, Lamb & Storr, 1907), 2–7, 31, 41, 169–72.

13. The house had gratings, shelving, cupboards, and baseboards removed, fencing gone, paving in the brewhouse missing, and garden wall undermined; see "Estimates of repairs at the Parsonage House" and "Estimates of Fixtures &c. in Doctor Priestley's House at Calne," Bowood Papers IV-P, IV-Q. The house, still standing, is marked by a plaque identifying it as Priestley's.

14. This comment may well have been directed at Priestley, who seems not to have been useful about a house; it was quoted by [Mary Anne Schimmelpennick (née Galton)] in *Life of Mary Anne Schimmelpennick*, ed. Christiana C. Hankin (London: Longman, Brown, Green, Longmans, & Roberts, 1853), 1:86. Mary Anne heard this story as a child and dictated it many years later, but she had greatly admired Mrs. Priestley and so there may be some truth in it.

Fig. 1   Joseph Priestley's house (1773–1780) on the Green, Calne

of wings and courts.[15] Landscaping and building continued during Priestley's years there, adding to the confusion and excitement of a shifting company of family, friends, and political visitors. Contemporary memoirs and correspondence refer to occasional visits from John Adams, David Garrick, Dr. Johnson, Joseph Banks, Benjamin Franklin, Richard Price, Daniel Solander, Joshua Reynolds, and the Abbé Morellet, among others.[16] Priestley had his own set of visitors: ministers such as Theophilus Lindsey, but particularly scientists, including Jan Ingenhousz, Jean DeLuc, and Georg Christoph

15. The buildings were so large and, eventually, unmanageable that the "big house" was demolished in 1955, still leaving ample space for family and guests, a picture gallery, and library. See John Cornforth, "Bowood, Wiltshire: The Seat of the Marquess of Lansdowne, Re-visited— I, II, III," *Country Life* 151 (8, 15, 22 June 1972): 1448–51, 1546–50, 1610–13; "The Making of the Bowood Landscape," *Country Life* 152 (Sept. 7 1972): 1546–49.

16. Petty, *Life of Shelburne;* [Abbé Morellet], *Mémoirs inedits de l'Abbé Morellet . . .* (Paris: De l'Advocat, 1872), 1:208–13.

Lichtenberg. Priestley often found himself engaged in social activities quite foreign to his former pattern of living.

Priestley attempted to compensate for his failure as companion by emphasizing the librarian and tutorial supervision part of his position. Shelburne had a large library at Bowood and at Shelburne House, a growing collection of important old manuscripts, and was compiling a set of papers on contemporary matters of state. Priestley bought books for the library, struggled with cataloguing books and manuscripts and indexing the private papers. As late as September 1776 he reported that he was making progress indexing the manuscripts but that there was no point in arranging or cataloguing books until the cases for them were completed.[17]

The tutor, Thomas Jervis, felt no need of supervision, however, and was later to insist that Shelburne had expressly determined to keep "the two departments [librarian and tutor] . . . distinct so as to avoid any interference which might prove detrimental to his views."[18] Either Shelburne did not make this distinction clear to Priestley (and some others) or he resisted it. Even before his move from Leeds, Priestley wrote Shelburne that he was, at his leisure, "putting down some thoughts on education . . . as they have a more immediate reference to the case of your Lordship's sons." The Abbé Morellet, visiting Bowood in 1773, found Priestley there "serving as the teacher of Shelburne's children." In 1776 Priestley wrote, "it often gives me concern, that I am of so little use to your Lordship, but I flatter myself I shall be of more use to your Lordship's children." Except when Jervis was on vacation and Priestley supplied his place at Bowood, Priestley seems not to have intruded on Jervis's general domain. He must have watched longingly over the familiar occupation from nearby, however, for he completed a number of education projects he had begun at Warrington. In 1777 the *Course of Lectures on Oratory and Criticism*, dedicated to "The Right Honourable Lord Viscount Fitzmaurice," was published, while the *Miscellaneous*

---

17. Priestley to Shelburne, 11 Sept. 1776, Bowood Papers III-D, Bowood Archives. The library was sold in 1806, the sale lasting 341 days; see *Biblioteca Lansdowniana: A Catalogue of the Entire Library of the late Most Noble William Marquis of Lansdowne, which will be sold by Auction* (London: Mundell and Sons, etc., 1806). The manuscript collection was described, in a detail perhaps derived from Priestley's cataloguing, in *Biblioteca Lansdowniana: A Catalogue of the Entire Collection of Manuscripts, on paper and vellum, of the late Most Noble William Marquis of Lansdowne which will be sold by Auction* (London: Mundell and Sons, etc., 1807). It was purchased by the nation in 1807 and re-catalogued by Henry Ellis and Francis Douce, *Catalogue of the Lansdowne Manuscripts in the British Museum* (London: British Museum, 1819).

18. [Thomas Jervis], "Veritas," "On Dr. Priestley's Connection with the Marquis of Lansdowne," *Monthly Repository* 6 (1811): 17–19.

Observations relating to Education appeared in 1778. In May 1779 Priestley wrote to Shelburne, "if your Lordship has no object to propose to my attention respecting yourself, I cannot employ my time better to Lord Fitzmaurice's improvement than by completing my Lectures on History."[19]

So long as there was no direct interference, Jervis was content, and the only subject on which Priestley approached his charges was science, where Jervis would not have attempted to compete. In September 1777 Priestley wrote Newcome Cappe that he had undertaken to teach philosophy (i.e., natural philosophy or science) to Shelburne's sons, having a "noble apparatus for that purpose." In October he informed Shelburne that John Warltire had given "two or three lectures at Bowood on such instruments as we have not," and hinted that more instruments ought to be acquired. "I flatter myself that I am providing for Ld. Fitzmaurice a source of *employment* and of *happiness* that will be inexhaustible and consequently invaluable."

As Shelburne had already spent more than £230 equipping Shelburne House and Bowood with apparatus, and as Fitzmaurice was not yet twelve, he may well have wondered what he had started in permitting science lessons for his son.[20] Priestley, however, was undaunted. By March 1778 he was attempting to teach "spherics" to Lord Fitzmaurice and had written George Walker asking what book on conic sections he should use for teaching "to one who will never make much of a mathematician, but must have a general knowledge of all the branches of mathematics." And, in December, he returned to the effort to get Shelburne "to establish and furnish a laboratory . . . to accustom Ld. Fitzmaurice, at an early age, to the use of philosophical instruments, and the sight of philosophical experiments and processes."

He also repeated his request, first made in October 1777, that Shelburne permit an explicit acknowledgment in the preface to the volume of experiments in the press, that "the experiments were made with your Lordship's encouragement, and at your Lordship's expense, in the course of Ld. Fitzmaurice's education." That permission was not granted, but the volume

19. Priestley to Shelburne, 20 May 1773, 11 Sept. 1776, 12 May 1779, Bowood Papers III-C, I, Bowood Archives; [Morellet], *Mémoires*, 212. *Oratory and Criticism* is discussed in Schofield, *Enlightenment of Priestley*, as is the *Miscellaneous Observations on Education*, though that, according to Priestley, was first written "for the use of Lord Shelburne" (*W.* 1.1:266). The *Lectures on History* were not published until Priestley had moved to Birmingham and no copy was listed in the catalogue of Shelburne's library.

20. Priestley to Shelburne, 8 Oct. 1777, Bowood Papers III-F. The Bowood Archives contain bills from various instrument makers dated as early as Dec. 1773 and continuing as late as Aug. 1779, for a cost of more than £250; see Bowood Papers IV-D, E, L, M.

in question, *Experiments and Observations relating to various Branches of Natural Philosophy*, does explain Priestley's intentions in his insistence on teaching science to Lord Fitzmaurice: "Scientific pursuits, having an advantage over most others, especially recommends them to persons of rank and fortune. They furnish materials for agreeable and active pursuits, and are, at the same time, useful, honourable, and particularly valuable to those with no talent or call to public affairs and their study."[21] Although Shelburne did not permit published acknowledgment of his financing of Priestley's experiments, or of the education in science being given to his son, he accepted some part of the argument of science's social value. He allowed Priestley to take Lord Fitzmaurice, as his guest, to meetings of the Royal Society in February 1779. This was nearly the last time that Priestley and Shelburne were in agreement.

During their negotiations of July and August 1772, there was mention of the possibility that Priestley might collect information for Shelburne "with respect to subjects of parliamentary discussion" (*W.* 1.1:179–92). Though he disclaimed expertise in political matters, he did have access to views of the Dissenting interest in the country. In 1774 he became a member of the General Body of Ministers of the Three Denominations in and about the cities of London and Westminster.[22] These connections might well interest Shelburne in a period in which Dissenters represented the most vocal part of the minority opposition to government action respecting the American colonies.[23] Priestley's first collection of political information was, however, in the completing of unfinished business.

21. Priestley to George Walker, 2 March 1778, MSS., Massachusetts Historical Society Library, Boston; Priestley to Shelburne, endorsed "30 December 1778," Bowood Papers III-H; Joseph Priestley, *Exp. & Obs. Nat. Phil.*, viii; the page is a cancel, suggesting that Priestley had made the acknowledgment and had to remove it. The emphasis on the study of natural philosophy for "persons of landed property or fortune" was repeated in the *Miscellaneous Observations on Education*, 15–19; possibly Priestley had the career of Henry Cavendish in mind.

22. Martin Fitzpatrick, "Joseph Priestley and the Cause of Universal Toleration," *Price-Priestley Newsletter* 1 (1977): 16. Priestley was well enough known to opposition political figures to have received "many personal civilities" from John Wilkes, to whom Priestley presented a copy of the *Essay on Government*, "more especially for what he owes him as a member of the same community, and a lover of liberty"; Priestley to Wilkes, British Library, Add. MSS. 30, 877.

23. There has been a recent revival of interest in the political role of eighteenth-century Dissenters; see particularly James E. Bradley, *Religion, Revolution, and English Radicalism: Nonconformity in Eighteenth-Century Politics and Society* (Cambridge: Cambridge University Press, 1990), and Knud Haakonssen, *Enlightenment and Religion: Rational Dissent in Eighteenth-century Britain* (Cambridge: Cambridge University Press, 1996). According to Bradley, Edmund Burke at one time believed that Dissenters formed the moral core of the Whig party (30).

Early in 1773, before taking residence in Calne, Priestley sent Shelburne "A short view of the state of opinions among Dissenters concerning the proposed test."[24] The bill, about to go to Parliament for the second time, to relieve the Dissenting minister or teacher from having to subscribe to Articles of the Established church, substituted a declaration of belief, as a Protestant Christian, in the Old and New Testaments as the rule for doctrine and practice. In three pages Priestley attempted to summarize Dissenting opinion respecting this declaration, or "test." All Dissenters, wrote Priestley, believed it none of the civil magistrates' business to interfere in matters of religion, any more than they do in medicine. If the magistrates favored one form of religion more than another and appropriated taxes to support it, those not sharing in its benefits should not be burdened with its creeds, and many disliked having to contribute support. Some thought it wrong even to declare themselves Christians, as a countenancing of the magistrates' right of interference, but most believed an honest declaration, in order to obtain civil privileges and immunities, was like giving a highwayman one's name. He had no right to demand it, but it was not wrong to comply. Finally, Priestley wrote, there were those who believed that the tacit exemption now enjoyed was preferable to a legal one that distressed any of their colleagues.

It is doubtful that the "short view" contained anything that Shelburne (who voted with the minority, 26–86, in the House of Lords to approve the bill) would not already have known through Richard Price, but Priestley went on to include that information in a longer treatise directed to a larger audience. *A Letter of Advice to those Dissenters who conduct the Application to Parliament for Relief from certain Penal Laws, with various Observations relating to similar Subjects* appeared late in 1773.[25] It was ostensibly anonymous (by the "Author of the *Free Address*"), but there can have been no serious effort to maintain secrecy. The author of the *Free Address to Protestant Dissenters* was widely known, at least among Dissenters, to be Priestley, the *Letter* was dated Calne, July 1773, and an early reference to "my Essay on Government" completed the exposure.

The rest of the *Letter of Advice* was as curious as the pretense of anonymity. Writing after the bill failed a second time to pass the House of Lords,

24. Priestley to Shelburne, "A short view . . . concerning the proposed test," Bowood Papers III-A, in Priestley's hand, no date. As the manuscript reflects the language of Priestley's published political writings of 1772 and 1773, it is unlikely to date from 1779. It must have been written after Dec. 1772, when the Priestley-Shelburne association was agreed upon, and before April 1773, when the relief bill was defeated in the House of Lords.

25. [Priestley], "Author of the Free Address to Protestant Dissenters, as such." *A Letter of Advice . . . [on] the Application to Parliament* (London: J. Johnson, 1773).

Priestley gratuitously commended the general committee of Dissenters who had pushed the bill and renewed the application after its first failure. For the committee had carefully distanced itself from Priestley and his fellow radicals and had drafted a bill that would have given them no legal relief. Was it political naiveté or irony, then, that prompted his suggestion that the next bill ask for more: "You have hitherto preferred your prayer as *Christians;* stand forth now in the character of *men,* and ask at once for the repeal of all the penal laws which respect matters of opinion." Such a bill, by its generality, would avoid the emphasis on differences (and antipathies) of Christian sects; surely the committee did not wish to exclude Arians and Socinians from "the circle of your toleration."

The greater part of the *Letter of Advice* is taken up by "various Observations" that have the miscellaneous character of *arrière-pensées* and pent-up resentments, to be discharged before commencing new duties. Some of Priestley's suggestions would have further impeded passage of any bill for relief of Dissenters by proposing all that "would be honourable in my country to grant, and desirable . . . to receive," including repeal of the Test Act and reform of the Established church. He would leave to the Feather's Tavern petitioners to suggest religious reform, but some reforms were simply matters of civil society: inequality in payment of clergy, for example, imposition of tithes, and participation of bishops in the legislature.[26]

Priestley noted that he had no more to do with the late applications to Parliament than did the bishops themselves, though they cited him in debate to kill the bills and most Dissenters disavowed him.[27] The charge of idolatry against the Church of England was not less true because some ingenious and good men believed in the Trinity, or because there was a legal declaration in its favor. Priestley would sooner have received a parliamentary system of philosophy than one of religion, for the plain and sufficient reason that, of the two, "our law-makers probably know rather more of *philosophy* than of *divinity.*"

---

26. The Feather's Tavern petitioners were Anglican clergymen, including Archdeacon Blackburne and Priestley's friend, Theophilus Lindsey, who met at Feather's Tavern, London, in 1771 to petition for relief from subscription to the Thirty-Nine Articles of the Church of England.

27. This had been noted in the newspapers, even in the colonies, where Ezra Stiles, soon to become president of Yale College, reported reading on 19 April 1772 that passages from Priestley's writings had been read in the House of Lords and the Bishop of London had declared that eminent Dissenting ministers were against the bill. See [Ezra Stiles], *The Literary Diary of Ezra Stiles, D.D. LL.D. President of Yale College,* ed. Franklin Bowditch Dexter (New York: Charles Scribner's Sons, 1901), 1:268.

Theophilus Lindsey begged Priestley to desist from attacking Benjamin Dawson, as such attacks would weaken the impact of the Feather's Tavern petitioners. But Dawson, a former Dissenting minister who had conformed, a friend of Archdeacon Blackburne and one of the petitioners, had publicly challenged Priestley's description of the Thirty-Nine Articles as something to which no intelligent and honest person could fully subscribe.[28] He rashly demanded that Priestley demonstrate that he, Dawson, did not honestly and fully subscribe—and so, of course, Priestley did so! Analyzing Dawson's published sermons, he showed that the interpretation of the Trinity in them was closer to the Socinian position than to the Athanasian Creed enjoined by the Articles.[29]

Priestley then repeated and expanded upon the arguments of the "Short View," sent earlier to Shelburne. The apostles and primitive Christians would have no scruples about declaring themselves Christians in order to avoid persecution and death. As religion is a concern affecting the temporal good of the state, a magistrate may reasonably think to interfere in it. Persuade him that interference does harm, not good. Dangerous principles are absurd and so easily refuted that they may be left to the common sense and reason of mankind. Important principles will guard themselves by their own evidence; the less important do not deserve to be guarded (83–88). Finally, Priestley denounced the so-called "orthodox dissenters" who had objected to the bill, not because it would hurt them, but because it would benefit others, and hinted at calamitous events coming to the states of Europe, when Established churches would be despoiled to pay the costs of wars they had encouraged. Perhaps on the ruin of these churches might rise something nearer to the Church of Christ than of Rome or England (98).

28. For Lindsey's objections concerning Dawson, see *W.* 1.1:167–68. Bentham was quite as severe as Priestley on the clergy and subscription to the Articles: "If the clergy are not the very worst body of the people, they have uncommon merit; for the tendency of their education is to make them so. Subscription begins what ordination finishes. . . . [A] character of hypocrisy and dissimulation—subscription traces in the young mind the character of imbecility and double-dealing." Mary Mack, *Jeremy Bentham: An Odyssey of Ideas, 1748–1792* (New York: Columbia University Press, 1963), 300. Note, however, that Bentham was more circumspect, for he did not publish these observations. William Paley, in his lectures on divinity at Christ's College, Cambridge, and in his *Moral Philosophy* (1785), maintained that the articles were merely "articles of peace, as they contained propositions so inconsistent with one another that it was impossible for any man to believe them all."

29. The Athanasian Creed, as a formula for the Trinity, is notoriously difficult to explain and interpret in any words other than those of the Creed itself, without falling into one or another of the heresies. See, for example, R. D. Richardson, "The Doctrine of the Trinity: Its Development, Difficulties, and Value," *Harvard Theological Review* 36 (1943): 109–34; and R. Nichol Cross, "The Blessed Trinity," *Hibbert Journal* 55 (1956–57): 231–40.

Priestley's next political work was an electioneering pamphlet, *An Address to Protestant Dissenters ... on the Approaching Election of Members of Parliament,* published anonymously in 1774 and the most outspoken of anything he ever wrote.[30] Priestley and his friends were angry that the committee of Dissenting ministers in London had decided not to renew (for the third time) their attempt to get the Dissenters' relief bill passed while the House of Commons was still friendly toward Dissent. They ascribed the decision to deceit and bribery with the *Regium Donum.* Priestley had observed the futile efforts of Lords Chatham and Shelburne and others to defeat the North ministry's response to the "Boston Tea Party."[31] He and his friends were disturbed at the "determined rancour and infatuated confidence" of members of Parliament regarding the American colonies.

The dissolution of Parliament and the new election set for October 1774 called, Priestley wrote, for all, and perhaps the last, efforts of the friends of civil and religious liberty (3). "[T]hose who actually guide the measures, which are now carrying on in this country, are equally enemies to civil liberty and to you" (4). Tricks and artifice were used to frustrate attempts to repeal laws that harmed Dissenters. Hopes had been blasted by the same throne that extended mercy to Papists and rebels, even to murderers, so long as they were friends of despotism and enemies of the constitution. "The painful memory of these proceedings should stimulate Dissenters to wipe off their disgrace. Our American brethren, disliked chiefly because they are mostly Dissenters and whigs, will probably be compelled to defend their liberties by taking arms. This would be improper and ineffectual for Dissenters in England who can, however, exert themselves to procure the return of men to parliament who are known to be friends to civil and religious liberty" (5).

Pay no heed to present professions of friendly zeal, Priestley wrote, but look to past conduct. Avoid as pestilence every man who voted against the repeal of oppressive laws. If you want your representatives to be uncorrupt and independent, be so yourselves. It was not surprising if members of Parliament sold what they were known to have bought. To restore the

---

30. Joseph Priestley, *An Address to Protestant Dissenters of all Denominations on the Approaching Election of Members of Parliament, with Respect to the State of Public Liberty in General, and of American Affairs in Particular* (London: J. Johnson, 1774). Bradley, *English Radicalism,* 191, describes the pamphlet as having attracted the most attention of any of the electioneering appeals.

31. He witnessed Wedderburn's invective against Benjamin Franklin at the Privy Council in Jan. 1774 and later wrote, on the authority of Silas Deane, that Franklin wore the suit of Manchester velvet at the signing of the treaty of assistance between France and the colonies that he had worn before the Privy Council. Joseph Priestley, "To the Editor," 10 Nov. 1802, *Monthly Magazine* 15 (1803): 1–2.

independence of Parliament from the Crown, it was necessary to reduce the multitude of places by which the court corrupted the members and to achieve a more equitable means of payment for civil services. Throughout Europe, he warned, states were losing their liberties as power settled in the hands of arbitrary princes—he pointed to the cases of Denmark and Sweden—while there was reason to fear that a partition of Switzerland and of the United Provinces would follow that of Poland (7–8).

Part II of *An Address* was written, at the request of Franklin and of the Quaker Dr. John Fothergill, on the American situation. It did not presume to offer any new arguments but hoped that a summary in different words might make the truth better understood. Different realms of English kings had always taxed themselves; Normandy, Scotland before the union, Wales, the Counties Palatine, and Ireland to this day. When the Puritans left England to escape persecution by prelates, they certainly had no intention of remaining subject to those laws. Their voluntary choice of the English king for their head did not make them his English subjects. Americans, like Englishmen, were subject to one king, "who is himself subject to the laws, and who is no longer our legal and rightful King, than he is so" (11).

Priestley also argued that taxation without consent deprived the people of proper liberty. It was true, he conceded, that Leeds, Manchester, and other large towns sent no representatives to Parliament, but those who taxed these towns taxed themselves; they taxed America to escape taxing themselves. The Crown had protected Americans, and they ought to pay? The Crown protected Ireland and Hanover without taxing them. Americans supported their own governments; such was their zeal at the end of the last war that Britain voted them large sums as recompense for their extraordinary exertions (13). The East India Company had suffered some losses by the action of a few people; did that justify the British government in punishing the innocent by blocking ports, abolishing charters, invading with troops, and denying jurisdiction to colonial courts? "If you help forge chains for America, can you suppose an enslaved America will scruple to bring you into the same condition?" (14). Priestley urged his readers to oppose, at the next election, every candidate who had joined the attempt to establish arbitrary powers in the British Empire, "to the imminent hazard of our most valuable commerce, and of that national strength, security, and felicity which depend upon UNION and on LIBERTY" (15).[32]

32. The phrase in quotation marks was added, in press, by Franklin, who supervised the printing, according to Priestley, because, as he mistakenly says, "I then lived at Leeds." See ibid., 1.

When the election was held, Priestley and Shelburne were in Europe. Though Priestley's *Address* attracted considerable national attention, it failed to produce practical results. The returning Parliament strongly supported the North ministry. When Shelburne returned to London in January 1775, he labored for conciliation with the colonies. In this endeavor, it is likely that Priestley and his associations were of some service. From his winter's residence at Shelburne House, Priestley resumed regular Sunday meetings with the Lindseys and with John Lee, who was a member of the Rockingham opposition. He saw Franklin frequently. He and Franklin were, in fact, members of the same club, meeting fortnightly at the London Coffeehouse, first in St. Paul's Churchyard and then at 24 Ludgate Hill, which Franklin was later to call the "Club of Honest Whigs."[33]

Some twenty members of this club have been identified, including James Burgh, John Canton, Franklin, Andrew Kippis, John Lee, Alderman Oliver, Richard Price, Priestley, and Samuel Vaughan. They held liberal political opinions, supported the American cause, and frequently entertained visitors from America. They had a wide range of correspondents and their information was often earlier and more accurate than that of the government. When Franklin left England in March 1775, having spent his last day there with Priestley, he continued writing to members of the club. Price and Priestley also wrote to other friends in America in spite of King George's Royal Proclamation of 23 August, which demanded information concerning "all persons who shall be found carrying on Correspondence with, or in any Manner of Degree aiding or abetting the persons now in open Arms and Rebellion against our Government."[34]

Throughout this period Shelburne could obtain from Price or Vaughan any information he might have learned from Priestley, and he had other

33. Verner W. Crane, "The Club of Honest Whigs: Friends of Science and Liberty," *William and Mary Quarterly* 23 (3d ser., 1966): 210–33. Josiah Quincy Jr. visited England in 1774–75 and was entertained by the "Honest Whigs," visited Priestley at Calne and Priestley and Shelburne in London, where he dined with Franklin, Price, Priestley, Lee, and others. See [Josiah Quincy Jr.], "Journal of Josiah Quincy, Jun., during his Voyage and Residence in England from September 28th 1774 to March 3d. 1775," *Proceedings of the Massachusetts Historical Society* 50 (1917): 433–70.

34. Proclamation quoted in Bradley, *English Radicalism,* 14. Richard Price believed (correctly) that his letters were intercepted and read by government agents; see Price to Chas. Chauncy, Dec. 1775; to John Winthrop, 15 June 1777, *Proceedings of the Massachusetts Historical Society* 17 (1903): 306–7, 311–12; and to Benjamin Franklin, 14 Oct. 1779, Franklin Papers 16, APS. Priestley wrote and received letters without caution, writing at least nine letters to Franklin between 1776 and late 1779, conveying one, of 13 Feb. 1776 (*SciAuto.,* 69), via Major Carleton. These letters had no information on military or political affairs that might have been useful to the Americans.

sources of news and gossip as well. Still, it must have been useful to have a leading member of the Dissenting interest living in his home. The Dissenters found it equally useful to have one of their number in so close an association with a major figure of the Chatham faction of the opposition. Neither the Dissenters nor the Chathamites were able to make any significant impact on political events over the next several years. One of the reasons was the unpopularity of their cause. Not until the colonists demonstrated the effectiveness of their resistance, declared their independence, and defeated Burgoyne at Saratoga did the country at large begin to feel that coercion of the Americans might, perhaps, be a mistake. The new Parliament of 1774 met for a month before hearing any reference to American affairs; Priestley and Lindsey witnessed the House of Lords treating the Duke of Grafton's motion of conciliation with levity in March 1776.

Even after attitudes began to change, serious divisions within the opposition to North's ministry made it impossible effectively to resist its decisions. The Rockingham Whigs, representative of the great Whig aristocratic families, were only secondarily concerned with events in America or with the desires of Dissenters. So far as they were concerned, all was well with the political system as a whole. All that was needed to end "the present discontents" was a change of leadership in which men of virtue (themselves) replaced wicked men. They favored reduction of ministerial placemen and of the influence of the king in order to weaken the North ministry. Only retrospectively, after the war with the colonies had begun, did they see their opposition to have been a support of the Americans' cause. Edmund Burke's *Thoughts on the Causes of the Present Discontent* (1770) had, in fact, failed to mention troubles in America.[35]

Chatham's group did take American troubles seriously, but it did not represent any significant family groupings and by its emphasis on "measures, not men" was unpopular with the Rockinghamites. Chatham, though once able to rally the population behind him, was ill and frequently incapacitated for effective leadership. His chief lieutenant, Lord Shelburne, was not a good manager of men and was one of the most widely distrusted figures in British politics. It is difficult to understand the depth of the dislike felt for him by so many of his contemporaries, except in the context of a transition in English politics from traditional family and country alignments to parties. Shelburne's Irish origins, his entry into politics under the aegis of Lord Bute, and the transfer of his allegiance to Chatham all had kept him from assimilation into

35. See Ian R. Christie, "Economic Reform and 'the Influence of the Crown,' 1780," *Cambridge Historical Journal* 12 (1956): 144–54.

any of the customary familial political combinations for which, indeed, he came to have outspoken contempt. He developed a set of economic and social principles as the basis of his political conduct, for which he would ignore personal associations. That, in the intensely personal world of eighteenth-century English politics, was regarded as unprincipled.[36]

Whether they liked him or not, all major political figures recognized the importance of gaining Shelburne's support, if possible, in the shifting coalitions of the period between 1775 and 1782. It was in this connection that Priestley probably made his most noteworthy political contributions during his years with Shelburne.[37] His publications had made little impact upon those not already aligned. His "philosophical" influence on Shelburne's ideas must have been small, for Shelburne's "stable" of advisors—Chatham, Samuel Garbett of Birmingham, Morellet, Price, Vaughan, and others—was already complete before Priestley joined him. There may have been some slight personal influence stemming from Priestley's utilitarianism, but this was in the naturalistic Christian-ethics mode. This held that moral law was imposed by God and, as the only law compatible with human nature, was deducible from nature by experience and right reason. Jeremy Bentham, who replaced Priestley as Shelburne's utilitarian associate, held a more directly applicable normative view.

Priestley, however, belonged to the major collective of political influence that was uncommitted to any of the groups contending for power, and its influence might be effectively applied, through Priestley, to persuade Shelburne to join in the formation of a workable coalition.[38] This Dissenting

36. Benjamin Disraeli later praised Shelburne as the most distinguished English politician of the eighteenth century; see his *Sybil, or the Two Nations* (1926; reprint Oxford: Oxford University Press, 1956), 16–19. See also Peter Brown, *The Chathamites: A Study in the Relationship Between Personalities and Ideas in the Second Half of the Eighteenth Century* (London: Macmillan; New York: St. Martin's Press, 1967), 433–38, and John Norris, *Shelburne and Reform* (London: Macmillan, 1963), esp. 5–6, 293–94. My interpretation is rather softer than that of Brown or Norris, as I look at him from the vantage point of the Dissenters rather than from that of revisionist Tory historians or the managerial ethics of Namier and his colleagues.

37. For the importance of Priestley in the political "Dissenting interest," see, for example, Colin Bonwick, *English Radicals and the American Revolution* (Chapel Hill: University of North Carolina Press, 1977), esp. 9–10, 45, 75, 107, 257. Bonwick called Priestley's 1768 pamphlet "the first substantial tract on the American question" in his "English Dissenters and the American Revolution," in *Contrast and Connection: Bicentennial Essays in Anglo-American History*, ed. H. C. Allen and Roger Thomson (Athens: Ohio University Press, 1976), 104. See also Bradley, *English Radicalism*, and Haakonssen, *Enlightenment and Religion*.

38. John Seed, "'A set of men powerful enough in many things': Rational Dissent and Political Opposition in England, 1770–1790," in Haakonssen, *Enlightenment and Religion*, quotes Edmund Burke: "Dr. Priestley is a very considerable leader among a set of men powerful

interest was generally sympathetic toward Shelburne. Priestley had described him to Price, in July 1772, as "the very first character, for ability and integrity together, in this kingdom" (*SciAuto.*, 50). There is no indication that he substantially changed his opinion, for all their differences, personal or political. Despite his publications, Priestley was not yet so notorious as to have become generally distrusted. As late as February 1779, when Priestley applied, through William Eden, for access to the Royal Library, it was his association with Shelburne that drew King George's chief rebuke: "If Doctor Priestley applies to my Librarian he will have permission to see the Library as other Men of Science have had, but I cannot think the Doctor's character as a Politician or Divine deserves my appearing at all in it. . . . I am sorry Mr. Eden has any intimacy with that Doctor as I am not over fond of those who frequent any Disciples or companions of the Jesuit in Berkeley Square."[39]

Priestley, therefore, could be used as an intermediary between Shelburne and other groups, and he could and did act to encourage or discourage Shelburne's acceptance of proposals. In October 1775 he approached Sir George Savile to see if an alliance could be arranged between Rockingham and Shelburne for the coming session of Parliament. Writing without Shelburne's knowledge, but knowing that he wanted Savile to know his thinking, Priestley declared:

> He is by no means that artful ambitious politician that he has been represented, and he is far from wishing to draw you from any connection you may have with the Marquis of Rockingham and his friends. . . . He would himself most cordially act with, and even under, the Marquis . . . provided his measures were more distinct and decisive, going to the bottom of the present disorders of the State. . . . I know Lord Shelburne wishes to explain himself to you upon these subjects, and would have no objections to do it in the presence of Lord Rockingham, or any of his friends. You will find him frank, plain, and open like yourself; and I shall think myself happy if I should be the means of bringing about such an interview.[40]

enough in many things, but most of all in elections; and I am quite sure that the good or ill humor of these men will be sensibly felt at the general election" (141).

39. King George III to Frederick, Lord North, 22 Feb. 1779, in [King George III], *Correspondence of King George the Third: From 1760 to December 1783*, ed. Sir John Fortescue (London: Frank Cass & Co., 1967), 4:2555, 2286.

40. Priestley to Sir George Savile, 28 Oct. 1775, from [F. J. Savile Foljambe], *The Manuscripts of the Right Honourable F. J. Savile Foljambe of Osberton* (London: H. M. Stationery Office, Historical Manuscripts Commission, 1897. Fifteenth Report, Appendix, Part 5), 149.

No formal arrangement followed from that letter. Though Rockinghamites and Chathamites joined in attacking North's policies, it was still too
early effectively to oppose them. In September 1776 Priestley sent some
news to Shelburne, then in Paris. The country at large was still indifferent
and the ministry, at least before the check at Charleston, was sanguine. General Howe was finding his enterprise more difficult than he had anticipated.
There was an irreconcilable difference between Lord Gower and Mr. Rigby.
"Whether this circumstance is likely to have any effect on public measures
your Lordship will be able to judge."[41]

By 1778 the situation had changed. France had entered the war, and
North, his resignation having been refused by the king, sent Eden to see if
Shelburne and Chatham would join the government. The national efforts
against the traditional enemy needed to be strengthened. On 15 March Eden
approached Priestley, who agreed to wait for him at Shelburne House:
"The conversation Mr. Eden wishes for may probably be obtained but Dr.
Priestley is intirely out of all political connection, and can form no conjecture about the issue."[42] The conversation took place, but Shelburne, speaking for himself and Chatham, declined to join any government without
Chatham at its head and without the Duke of Grafton and Lord Rockingham
included. The king rejected that arrangement, while the divided opposition
could not agree enough to justify negotiation—the Rockinghamites insisting
on American independence and Shelburne resisting.

On 17 March Shelburne spoke in the House of Lords on the treaty
between France and the colonies in a way that renewed Eden's hopes but
worried Priestley and his friends. Priestley wrote Shelburne that several persons, friends of liberty and of their country, including Price and the Bishop
of St. Asaph (Jonathan Shipley) were worried that the speech indicated an
intention to aid the king to evade his problems: War with France was unnecessary and unjust, acknowledgment of American independence would
detach them from their alliance. Shelburne should not abandon his determination for an inquiry into the conduct of the ministry, reformation of abuses
in government, and diminution of the enormous influence of the Crown.
This letter was probably unnecessary; Chatham had not changed his mind
about joining the government and his death shortly thereafter left North in
complete power.[43] Priestley, however, had begun to despair of Shelburne's

41. Priestley to Shelburne, 11 Sept. 1776, Bowood Papers III-D.
42. Priestley to William Eden, [15 March 1778], No. 349, Collection of Autograph Letters,
#67419, Reference Dept., Birmingham Public Library.
43. Priestley to Shelburne, 20 March 1778; Bowood Papers III-G.

agreeing to American independence. He began sending political news to other politicians. Writing in September 1779, he sent some news acquired from Boston, which he thought might be of service:

> If I had any intelligence of consequence, I should always chuse to dispose of it where it might be of use, rather than employ it to any factious purpose. You are not ignorant that I think very differently from Ld. Shelburne on the present state of Politics. . . . I wish for peace and think it would be cheaply purchased by granting the independence of America. . . . Whether I be right or wrong in my idea of your political connections, I shall always think myself happy in the esteem of such as you are. In or out of administration, I shall think them valuable.[44]

Two of the political developments for which Priestley had hoped had already occurred. With the war against France and political and economic unrest in Ireland, the North administration conceded a Catholic Relief Act in 1778 and, desiring to unite the country as much as possible, also pushed a Protestant Dissenters Relief Bill through both houses of Parliament in 1779.[45] Curiously, in view of Priestley's support for Catholic relief as early as 1768 and of the Dissenters' relief bills of 1772 and 1773, neither his extant correspondence nor his publications of 1778 or 1779 refer to the debates or to passage of either bill.[46]

For all his political activities behind the scenes, Priestley, in fact, published very little on politics during the time he was with Shelburne, though more than he was later prepared to admit. Much of the *Letter of Advice* of 1773 might have been written from Leeds as well as from Calne, and some of it might be called religious writing rather than political. The *Address to*

44. Priestley to unknown correspondent, Calne, 27 Sept. 1779, MS. Division, New York Public Library. This letter was perhaps to Thomas Howard, Earl of Suffolk, whose brother, Henry, Twelfth Earl of Suffolk, served as Lord Privy Seal and secretary of state for Lord North, and who died 6 March 1779. The letter refers to Lady Andover, and the title Viscount Andover was that of the son of the Earl of Suffolk.

45. The latter, 19 Geo. III, c. 44, exempted Dissenting ministers and teachers from subscription to the Articles of the Church on their making a declaration before a magistrate: "I A.B. do solemnly declare, in the presence of Almighty God, that I am a Christian and a protestant, and as such that I believe that the scriptures of the old and new testament, as commonly received among protestant churches, do contain the revealed will of God, and that I do receive the same as the rule of my doctrine and practice."

46. Priestley could not make that declaration and would have to continue under tacit toleration. Either that or the fact that his avowed support might have killed the bill may account for lack of published references, but this doesn't explain the silence of his extant correspondence.

Protestant Dissenters of 1774 was obviously political and could only have been written after he left Leeds, making the more remarkable his quite explicit statement, some nine years later from Birmingham: "As I find it has been supposed, much to my prejudice, that in my late situation I was engaged as a party writer, I shall take this opportunity of saying, that I never wrote a political pamphlet, or a political paragraph all the time that that connection subsisted, nor was I ever requested to do so."[47]

Why Priestley should have thought it important at this time to distance himself from politics under the aegis of Shelburne is far from clear. Perhaps he was attempting to circumvent his too-liberal reputation among the Birmingham populace. Maybe he wished to clear Shelburne from any onus attachable to the now infamous author of the *History of the Corruptions of Christianity* (1782). Perhaps, in retrospect, he felt the political activities of the Shelburne period unmemorable and chose simply to forget them, for his most substantial achievements of that period were in theology, metaphysics, and science, as he adjusted more fully to his role as protégé: "if, by your Lordship's generous encouragement, I be of use in promoting useful science, and rational knowledge of other kinds, your Lordship will not think your patronage ill bestowed." He recognized that though some of his work might make him "really useful to your Lordship's general fame and character . . . by some of my other publications, I may involve your Lordship in some part of the odium I bring upon myself with the ignorant and narrow minded."[48]

Probably the possibility that Priestley's work could directly affect Shelburne's reputation, positively or negatively, was exaggerated. The respect paid in England to the patron of arts or literature earlier in the century had diminished substantially. Certainly Shelburne was not then criticized for his support of the radical Priestley. Nor has he been given the credit due him for having financed Priestley during the period of his greatest scientific and philosophical creativity. In any event, whatever compensation Shelburne received for his expenditures on Priestley's behalf, it cannot have been in companionship or in enhancement of his reputation among his English contemporaries. It must have been in the personal satisfaction he derived from having generously encouraged, as Priestley suggested, his independent work in "useful science and rational knowledge of other kinds."

47. Joseph Priestley, *A Reply to the Animadversions on the History of the Corruptions of Christianity, in the Monthly Review for June 1783: with Additional Observations relating to the Doctrine of the Primitive Church, concerning the Person of Christ* (Birmingham: J. Johnson, 1783), ix; statement dated Birmingham, July 21, 1783. See also note 32 above for a compounding of this misinformation by referring the writing of the *Address* to Leeds.

48. Priestley to Shelburne, 11 Sept. 1776, 30 Dec. 1778; Bowood Papers III-D, III-H.

II

RELIGION AND THEOLOGY

Priestley's agreement with Shelburne had provided that he would be able to continue his own pursuits. Of these the most important were the religious and theological. He completed, at Calne, the publication of religious writing projects he had begun at Leeds: *An Address to Protestant Dissenters on . . . Giving the Lord's Supper to Children* (London, 1773) and the last volume of the *Institutes of Natural and Revealed Religion* (London, 1774).[1] Inevitably, as particular occasions arose, he also published occasional pieces on these and other religious subjects.

Shelburne had raised no objection to his preaching wherever he might have the opportunity. Priestley's irregular schedule precluded commitment to a single congregation, but there is evidence that he preached at least four times at Calne during his residence there and returned to preach at least once while living in Birmingham.[2] Not having a chapel of his own, Priestley was even more supportive than he might otherwise have been of the undertakings of

1. For analysis of the *Address* and of the *Institutes,* see Schofield, *Enlightenment of Priestley,* 177, 172–76.

2. Marginal notations on four of Priestley's manuscript sermons in the Library, Harris Manchester College, Oxford, and note on No. 8 of the sermons in Wms. Marsh, *History of Calne,* 169, 172, says Priestley was minister to the "Arian Chapel" on Bolling Lane, Calne, but there is nothing in Priestley's extant writings to support this claim. On 8 Dec. 1776 he wrote Joshua Toulmin from Calne, seeking a replacement for "our minister," and he may have filled in for a time.

his friend, Theophilus Lindsey. When Parliament rejected the "Feather's Tavern" petition in 1772, the majority of petitioning clergy found, as Archdeacon William Paley declared, that they "could not afford to keep a conscience."[3] They would not again subscribe to the Thirty-Nine Articles, but re-subscription was necessary only if one changed livings. It was possible to remain quietly in the same living, modifying the service to satisfy changes in religious sentiments, and leave any punitive action to the church authorities. This, in fact, is what Priestley had advised Lindsey to do, publicly justifying this behavior, in the *View of the Principles and Conduct of the Protestant Dissenters,* with the observation that some conscientious clergymen remained in their places, despite their disbelief, because of the good they actually did there, a good they probably could not match outside the church (20).

Lindsey, however, resigned his living and, openly adopting Unitarianism, seceded from the Established church.[4] He sold his library for living expenses and preached his farewell sermon at Catterick in November 1773. Moving to London, he resolved to gather a Unitarian chapel out of the Established church, as Priestley and others had done out of Presbyterian Dissent. For the next several months letters of Priestley and his friends were filled with references to Lindsey's proposed chapel. Priestley organized a subscription to defray the expenses (estimated at £200) of finding and furnishing a place of worship. Joseph Johnson, Priestley's publisher, located and rented a former auction room in Essex-house, Essex Street, for a chapel. John Lee overawed the magistrates of Westminster, who hesitated in granting it the registration necessary for a place of Dissenting worship, and Shelburne promised Priestley he would exert his influence to protect the chapel from legal difficulties. Mrs. Lindsey labored valiantly in redesigning the room and decorating it. The first avowedly Unitarian chapel in England opened for its first services on 17 April 1774.[5] Priestley attended those services and frequently

3. F. H. Amphlett Micklewright, "Some Prolegomena to the History of Protestant Dissent in England," *Notes and Queries* 187 (9 Sept. 1944): 117.

4. He had contemplated resigning since meeting Priestley. Catherine Cappe, a warm friend of the Lindseys, remembers Lindsey being envious of the "ease" of conscience of Priestley and William Turner in 1769. *Memoirs of the Life of the late Mrs. Catherine Cappe* (London: Longman, Hurst, Rees, Orme & Brown, 1822), 148–49.

5. See Thomas Belsham, *Memoirs of the late Reverend Theophilus Lindsey* (London: Johnson and Co., 1812), 100–120, 202, and passim. According to Herbert J. McLachlan, "More Letters of Theophilus Lindsey," *Transactions of the Unitarian Historical Society* 3 (1923–26): 363–64, Priestley and Price acted as acoustic consultants for the new chapel, discouraging Lindsey from placing a sounding board over the pulpit. The result was improved acoustics aided by the cupola over the room. Earl Morse Wilbur, *A History of Unitarianism in Transylvania, England, and America* (Cambridge: Harvard University Press, 1952), 291, states that from this

returned, sometimes preaching there. During the time he spent in London in Shelburne's service, he attended the chapel nearly every Sunday and usually spent that evening with the Lindseys and John Lee.

In keeping with the derivation of his chapel, Lindsey designed a worship service based on that of the Established church, using a version of the *Book of Common Prayer* that had been adapted to Arian beliefs by Dr. Samuel Clarke and further modified, slightly, for a more Unitarian service on the advice of Priestley. *The Book of Common Prayer Reformed for the Use of the Chapel in Essex Street* (London, 1774) and the plans of services at that chapel excited a great deal of negative comment. It was in response to this that Priestley published, anonymously, his *Letter to a Layman, on the Subject of the Rev. Mr. Lindsey's Proposal for a Reformed English Church, upon the Plan of the late Dr. Samuel Clarke.*[6]

The *Letter to a Layman* was addressed to just the sort of person that Lindsey hoped to attract to the Essex Street Chapel, the lay member of the Church of England unhappy with the doctrine but delighting in the society and the ceremony. Do not, Priestley declared, think to stay in the church and effect changes from within. The bishops would not, at danger to themselves, permit reforms. Priestley urged his readers to note the peremptory, rude, and insulting way in which petitioning clergy, and the Dissenters, were received (20–21). The argument that Lindsey's reformed church was yet another of those sects that constituted a danger to Christianity was a hackneyed attempt to oppose reform. "[The] only method of attaining to a truly valuable agreement is to promote the most perfect freedom of thinking and acting . . . in order that every point of difference may have an opportunity of being fully canvassed, not doubting but that . . . Truth will prevail, and that then a rational, firm, and truly valuable union will take place."[7]

Priestley pointed out that Lindsey advocated no new doctrine. His principles were "those of Christ and the Apostles, those on which others divided

---

beginning there had grown, by 1810, twenty avowedly Unitarian congregations and that growth was rapid thereafter.

6. [Joseph Priestley], *A Letter to a Layman . . .* (London: J. Wilkie, 1774). For revisions in the Prayer book, see A. E. Peaston, "The Revision of the Prayer Book by Dr. Samuel Clarke," and "Theophilus Lindsey's Prayer Book Revision Compared with Clarke's," *Transactions of the Unitarian Historical Society* 12 (1959–62): 27–38.

7. [Priestley], *Letter to a Layman*, 13. This is a variation on the emphasis of the Cambridge Platonists that religious differences were necessary as an instrument of religious knowledge. See Ernst Cassirer, *The Platonic Renaissance in England* (Austin: University of Texas Press, 1953), 36; it also continues Priestley's dialectical epistemology.

from the Churches of Rome and England." Adopting a liturgy was a difference in *form* but not *substance* from the worship of other Unitarians, and it
was substance that produced a truly Christian life. Reformation of the world
must begin with the individual (11). "Clergy persisting in doing wrong, in
order to do what is right and good, imagine that God stands in need of insin-
cerity, wickedness, and ruin to accomplish His designs" (19).

A major problem for true Christianity, Priestley continued, has always
been the pride of men, shocked at the mean appearance and ignominious circumstances of the life and death of Christ and captivated by external splen-
dor and reputable connections. Such persons would not attend Dissenting
chapels because their fashionable acquaintances did not. Many people who
approved Lindsey's conduct and proposals would not countenance him,
Priestley wrote, until their fashionable friends did so (22–24). "For such persons, affecting to be dissatisfied with the Church of England, but unable
to reconcile themselves to the method of worship among dissenters, here is
a reformed Church of England" (27).[8]

That Priestley's *Considerations for the Use of Young Man and the Parents
of Young Men* was another of his pieces originally written for a particular
occasion seems likely in view of the cryptic remarks in a letter to Lindsey
in March 1775: "I am at length, I thank God, got well home, and I find all
my family well. The girl was fully acquitted, and the young man will marry
her. . . . The Grand Jury did not find the bill, which, tho' it did not prevent
a public trial on the Inquest, made the favourable issue of it pretty certain."[9]

Just how Priestley became involved in what appears to have been a
domestic tragedy is hard to understand, for he had then no congregation
to which he was pastor. Nevertheless, he was clearly involved, perhaps as
a character witness, and appears successfully to have given pastoral advice.
Then, typically, Priestley turned that advice into a pamphlet, for the *Use of
Young Men*, to discourage premarital and extramarital sexual adventuring.

8. Subscribers to Lindsey's chapel in 1776 included Lord Shelburne (who apparently did not
pay his subscription), Sir George Savile, John Lee, and Charles James Fox. The pleasure of
Priestley and his friends that persons of fashion attended Lindsey's chapel shows that they too
were sensitive to opinion of the fashionable. It is unlikely that these people continued to attend,
but a congregation grew, sufficient to provide Lindsey with an income of more than £200 by
the 1780s.

9. [Joseph Priestley], *Considerations for the Use of Young Men . . .* (London: J. Johnson,
1775); I have used the second edition of 1776. The pamphlet was considered of sufficient usefulness to justify five editions in the space of sixteen years. Priestley made a curious reference
to this work that, he said, "I have printed," in a letter dated (probably incorrectly) 3 Aug. 1773
to Joshua Toulmin. The pamphlet is clearly dated 1775 on its title page and I chose that date, following the letter to Lindsey. W. 25:9 has another explanation for the writing of this pamphlet.

The pamphlet is surprisingly free of direct religious reference. Priestley said it was his intention to show, without appeal to the authority of God, that knowledge of human nature and human life leads to the maxims of purity and chastity recommended in Revelation (21). Of course his arguments reflected the views of a middle-class Dissenting minister and were directed to people of that class.

Many of his views seem stuffy and old-fashioned, but they also contain acute psychological and sociological perceptions, for all their presumed banality and conceptualization in associationist terms. The discussion was directed, successively, to young men, their parents, and the young women they might hope to marry. Premarital continence served society, the individual, and his future domestic happiness, Priestley argued. Early marriage was to be encouraged, with equality in education, understanding, and knowledge of the world more important than equality of fortune. Finally, though reason and philosophy might be twisted to support carnal inclinations, the Scriptures enforced proper rules of conduct and forbade irregular commerce between the sexes.

The last of Priestley's occasional religious publications of this period was also dictated by immediate circumstances. In July 1779 he preached at an ordination service for the brother of Thomas Jervis. His sermon, together with the charge by Andrew Kippis and a discourse on ordination, was to be published "by request." Then one of the attending ministers withdrew his approval, on grounds that the sermon supported the doctrine of necessity.

Now, this sermon, which Priestley had preached in Lindsey's chapel the previous spring, had, with his usual compositional economy, been rewritten from the unpublished treatise on divine influence he had prepared, circa 1756, at Needham Market. It can scarcely be supposed to have supported his recently published *Doctrine of Philosophical Necessity* (1777). But, the objection having been raised, the ordination service alone was published. Priestley decided that this made it the more necessary to publish his sermon, which he put to the press with an added preface. His *Doctrine of Divine Influence on the Human Mind* appeared in August 1779.[10] The *Doctrine of Divine Influence* supports the Arminian position that pardon for sin and ultimate salvation depend upon sincere, lasting repentance, the consequent

10. The sermon is, in fact, a variation on the "Pelagian heresy," that man has the ability to do the will of God without the immediate agency of God's actions. Joseph Priestley, *The Doctrine of Divine Influence on the Human Mind* . . . (Bath: R. Cruttwell, for J. Johnson, 1779). For events leading to publication, see Theophilus Lindsey to William Tayleur, 17 July 1779; Yates Collection of Priestleyana, no. 14, Library, Royal Society of London.

establishment of good moral character, and performance of good works by the sinner. Priestley explained in the preface that the doctrine of philosophical necessity must inevitably be involved in everything preached for the moral good of man, but that he was not explicitly putting that doctrine forward here. He mentioned it only because the sermon had been objected to on that ground (vi–x). What his sermon in fact argued was that no supernatural agency of the deity acted upon the minds of men to restrain them from evil or dispose them to good; there was only the influence of proper instruction and good motives (iv–v). The doctrine presented was not new, but "is here . . . more distinctly laid down, more largely illustrated, and urged with less caution and reserve, than . . . has been hitherto been done," and might therefore excite more attention (iii–iv). For the consequence of this argument was that notions of sovereign and irresistible grace, instantaneous conversion, new and miraculous birth, were incompatible with right reason. No inconvenience arose from a Christian's confounding primary with secondary causes and ascribing everything that is good immediately to God, so long as he did not leave himself out of the process of becoming established in virtue (xii–xiv).

During the same period, Priestley also had two major theological projects, one that had commenced in Leeds and was to continue into early days in Birmingham, the other conceived in Paris and carried into additional parts in the final years in the United States. To ease his boredom while on the European trip, he studied the Greek text of the New Testament and decided to print the Greek Gospels, rearranged to harmonize them (i.e., to bring them into the same chronological order), and prefixed by the rewritten dissertations from his *Theological Repository* papers of 1770 respecting Nicholas Mann's harmony of the Gospels.[11] *A Harmony of the Evangelists, in Greek; to which are prefixed Critical Dissertations in English* appeared in 1777 and was soon followed by a *Harmony of the Evangelists in English; with Critical Dissertations, an Occasional Paraphrase, and Notes for the Use of the Unlearned* (1780).[12]

11. ["Liberius"], "Essay on the Harmony of the Evangelists" and "Observations on the Harmony of the Evangelists," *Theological Repository* 2 (1770): 38–59, 98–122, 230–47, 313–27; and 3 (1771): 462–69.

12. Joseph Priestley, *A Harmony of the Evangelists, in Greek* . . . (London: J. Johnson, 1777); *A Harmony of the Evangelists in English* . . . (London: J. Johnson, 1780), includes "Observations." My remarks are taken from the English *Harmony,* having confirmed that the introductory materials and critical dissertations are the same as in the Greek. Each was reviewed favorably in the *Monthly Review: Greek* in 58 (1778): 89–95, *English* in 64 (1781): 81–90, 161–73.

The existence of four apparently independent and sometimes parallel accounts of the life and ministry of Jesus had early inspired attempts to bring them all into one chronological conformity, to reduce the sacred history, as Priestley wrote, to the order of time in which the events really happened (v). Tatian's *Diatessaron* is dated at 170 A.D.; early church scholars, such as Clemens Alexandrinus, Origen, Tertullian, Jerome, Augustine, and Eusebius made "harmonizing" efforts. Osiander, the Cambridge neo-Platonists, Samuel Craddock, and William Whiston were among those who brought harmonizing into modern times. William Newcome, Bishop of Ossary (later Bishop of Waterford and Archbishop of Armagh) published a harmony the year after Priestley's Greek *Harmony* appeared. These exercises continued until the mid-nineteenth century, when they were all but replaced by the "synoptic problem."[13]

Priestley's *Harmony* was, therefore, part of a long tradition and, like many of his other works, reflected prodigious scholarship. In addition to his easy familiarity with the received text of the Scriptures and his references to many writers of antiquity (some of which he seems to have derived from J. L. Mosheim's *Institutionum historiae ecclesiasticae*), he cited more than thirty modern authorities for the critical dissertations and notes, not counting his references to articles from the *Theological Repository* ("one of the most useful works I ever undertook," preface to the English *Harmony*, iv). These authorities ranged from men like Hugo Grotius, Nathaniel Lardner, John Lightfoot, and Johann David Michaelis, still cited in histories of commentary and criticism, to people almost impossible now to identify. They also include Adrian Reland on Jewish antiquities and Thomas Shaw on travels in the Near East, Isaac Newton's *Chronology*, the history of mathematics by Jean Etienne Montucla, and the astronomical tables of James Ferguson, "the ingenious author himself being so obliging as to give . . . his assistance in this work" (*Critical Dissertations*, 33).

Yet the work is so idiosyncratic as to bewilder and dismay modern biblical critics. The *Harmony* reveals the essentially reactionary nature of Priestley's

---

13. Note that "Harmonies" continue to be organized and published to the present day; see, for example, Frederick R. Coulter, *A Harmony of the Gospels in Modern English* (Los Angeles: York Publishing Co., 1974). It was not until 1835 that Karl K. F. W. Lachman showed, in principle, what became synoptic analysis, i.e., that variations and resemblances in chronology between the first three Gospels could be accounted for on the hypothesis that Matthew and Luke both used Mark as a source. There does not seem to be any good history of the transition from harmonizing into modern synoptic analysis; unfortunately for the historian, the title of Rudolf Bultmann's famous *History of the Synoptic Tradition*, trans. John Marsh (Oxford: Basil Blackwell, 1963) conceals an ambitious work in theology, not history.

religious radicalism. It illustrates one of the reasons why his quite cogent principles of criticism have seldom been taken seriously by historians of New Testament study.[14] On what sometimes seem the most arbitrary grounds, Priestley rejected the premises that have led scholars to adopt the same conclusions that he reached, while he achieved those conclusions from remarkably curious analyses of data that most scholars reject as spurious or irrelevant.[15]

Both *Harmonies* have the same dedication, dated Calne, January 1776, to Richard Price, acknowledging differences in some doctrines but knowing that he encourages freedom of writing in the search for truth (ii). The common preface observed that the intention of the Gospels did not require writers to adhere to an order of time. But so many references are chronological that it should be possible to arrange them ordinally (vii). This would strongly support the credibility of gospel history, Priestley wrote, but some authors had framed harmonies on such peculiar hypotheses that they discredited that history instead. To suppose the plenary inspiration of the Gospels, that they relate everything in strict chronological order and that different accounts of the same event must agree in every detail, was indefensible and unnecessary (vii–ix). Followed strictly, the results would provide multiple baptisms, institutions of the Lord's Supper, crucifixions, and resurrections.[16] Agreement on principal circumstances and disagreement on minute detail was, in fact, what one should expect in historical evidence. Some disagreement, indeed, seemed necessary to confirm that different accounts were truly independent (ix). Moreover, the Gospels had been transcribed and printed so many times that there were manifest errors in the versions now available. Yet one must not argue that the Gospels cannot be depended

14. The major reason is what might be called a "genealogical fallacy," ignoring a criticism because of its origin. Priestley's Unitarianism has discredited the value of his criticism.

15. A caveat is necessary here. The field of biblical criticism is and long has been hotly contested. Sectarian biases are strong; "schools" of criticism produce widely varying results. The conclusions of any professional will inevitably be denied by others. As a historian and not a critic, I have consulted standard Protestant biblical reference tools (e.g., *Dictionary of the Bible,* ed. James Hastings, revised by Frederick A. Grant and H. H. Rowley [New York: Charles Scribner's Sons, 1963]; *The International Standard Bible Encyclopedia,* ed. Geoffrey W. Bromiley et al. [Grand Rapids, Mich.: William B. Eerdmans, 1986]). In the section on Priestley's *Harmonies,* and later on his criticisms and commentaries, I have, to the best of my knowledge, adopted positions generally received by Protestant critics.

16. Yet Bible interpreters as early as St. Augustine declared that "it is a sacrilegious vanity to calumniate the gospels, rather than believe the same thing to have been twice performed, when no man can prove that it could not really be so." Augustine's *De consensu evangelistarum,* quoted in Robert Henry Lightfoot, *History and Interpretation in the Gospels* (London: Hodder and Stoughton, 1935), 5.

upon at all if they are not absolutely dependable, for that is not required of any other history that we know (xi–xii).

The core of Priestley's work is the harmony, which he achieved by blanking opposing pages of two copies of the four Greek Gospels, cutting the verses apart and placing the parts assumed to correspond opposite one another. He shuffled the order until he was satisfied that he had achieved the best sequence of events. "I will venture to say that, by the help of such mechanical contrivance as this, a person of a very moderate capacity, or critical skill, will have an advantage over a person of the greatest genius and comprehension of mind without it" (xvii). For the English *Harmony*, he corrected the common translation of the Greek text wherever it gave the wrong sense or used obsolete words or phrases (English preface, iii).[17]

It has been said that the "synoptic problem," the curious similarities in the order of events, style, wording, and content of the first three Gospels compared to those of John, is more obvious in parallel comparisons of the Greek text than of the English.[18] If one knows what to look for, it is clear enough in either. Yet Priestley missed it, as did all other critical analysts until the mid–nineteenth century.[19] Priestley's major problem was that his *Harmony* was designed to prove Nicholas Mann's hypothesis that the duration of the public ministry of Jesus was but a year and perhaps a few months. As Priestley complicated his task unnecessarily by adopting the contemporary orthodox view of the authorship of the various Gospels, he had to struggle to fit recalcitrant data to his predetermined scheme and missed what he might otherwise have seen without that bias.

17. The 1781 *Monthly Review* commended the "just and judicious" corrections of the "common version" of the English New Testament, and extracts from the Paraphrases and Notes, "in which are many things that do great credit to Dr. Priestley and his assistants, and which cannot fail to give pleasure to well-disposed, inquisitive Christians of all denominations."

18. Stephen Neill, *The Interpretation of the New Testament, 1861–1961* (London: Oxford University Press, 1964), 105, credits J. J. Griesbach for the first arrangement of the Gospels in parallel columns in 1774–80 and implies that the synopsis ("common view") is obvious in this arrangement. But Priestley, who knew of some of Griesbach's work in 1771 when he did his *Harmony*, clearly believed that his "mechanical contrivance" was original with him. Possibly he missed the synopsis because of the primary role he gives to the Gospel of John.

19. The common possession of the same materials, frequently in the same order and even the same words, has given the name synoptic gospels to Matthew, Mark, and Luke. Mark is supposed the earliest, Matthew and Luke are each composites dependent upon Mark and probably also upon a common source "Q" (for quellen), which each saw in a somewhat different form. A standard estimate is that less than 10 percent of the material in the synoptics coincides with that in John; more than 90 percent of Mark is paralleled in one or both of Matthew and Luke, while 50 percent of Matthew and about 40 percent of Luke are paralleled in the other two synoptics.

Most modern scholars agree that from none of the Gospels (even Mark) is it possible to obtain exact dates. General estimates now give about two and a half years to the public ministry of Jesus, whose date of birth is placed late in 7 or early in 6 B.C., baptism at 26–27 A.D., and crucifixion at 29–30 A.D., with 29 the most likely.[20] On most of the essentials of this summary, Priestley's position was the traditional one, close to that of his orthodox colleagues. Matthew and John were, in great measure, eyewitnesses of what they relate and show "more character of time and marks of orderly narrative." Mark and Luke were not eyewitnesses but appear to have been well informed concerning their subject. "None but the persons to whom they are ascribed, or . . . persons who enjoyed equal advantages for writing such histories, could have composed them. It is the more probable that they wrote from their memory and . . . actually heard and saw what they relate, as there is not, on the face of their writing, a single trace of imagination, or of an attention to any thing that might serve to embellish their narrative" (*Critical Dissertations*, 70).

Priestley noted "seemingly odd coincidences" in Mark and Luke, the arrangement of things "that appear to have little or no connection, in the same order" (87), but for his historical validation of Scripture he needed independent accounts. He would not even accept contemporary conjecture that Mark and Luke had copied or abridged Matthew. Parts of their Gospels were perhaps written in detached sections and collected by Mark and Luke. Matthew, knowing that they were authentic, might have adopted some parts. Then, each compiling "their histories independently of one another, they would, in some places, seem to have copied one another, or a common original" (72–73). Mark might have seen Matthew's Gospel after writing his own, and inserted into his account an incident found there (100). Having seen what the other evangelists had written, John differed, Priestley presumed, with design and in order to be more exact (101). For this reason, and because John was the beloved disciple and more directly involved in many critical episodes, his account was to be preferred, and then that of Matthew.[21]

20. Each item of this summary is controversial: many Roman Catholic scholars hold that Matthew's was the first gospel; Gnostic literature discovered at Qumran reheated arguments to date John's gospel earlier. Estimates of the duration of the ministry range from Guignebert's skeptical "possibly a few weeks only" to Zeitlin's five years. See Charles Guignebert, *Ancient, Medieval, and Modern Christianity: The Evolution of a Religion* (1927; New Hyde Park, N.Y.: University Books, 1961), 39n; Solomon Zeitlin, "The Duration of Jesus's Ministry," *Jewish Quarterly Review* 55 (1965): 181–200.

21. This choice was to cause major problems in Priestley's analysis, and later in his attack on Arianism, for it is now almost a commonplace in scriptural commentary that there is a

These rationalizations made Priestley's task of confirming the one-year ministry more difficult. It was from the synoptics that ancient scholars had argued for one year and from John that Eusebius and most later authorities had derived three and one-half years. With fearful ingenuity Priestley proceeded to argue himself out of the difficulty he had placed himself in. He rejected "insignificant" indications in Mark 6:39 of seasonal variations from which moderns had deduced a two-and-one-half year ministry (59). He followed Mann in declaring the word "passover" in John 6:4 to be an interpolation (43); and by inverting the order of John 5 and 6, arguing that the change was better also on literary grounds, he managed to fit more of John's chronological vagaries into synoptic arrangements.

Priestley also took up arguments about distances traveled and whether Herod could have been ignorant about Jesus had he been preaching as long as required by the usual hypothesis. There was some shifting of the order of events in the *Harmony,* to eliminate or to coalesce trips or events, and even an elaborate interpretation of a prophecy in Daniel, to show its agreement with the dates Priestley deduced from historical considerations (12–27). Those dates were Jesus' birth (late October of 7 B.C.); death (March 29 of A.D.), and, from arguments on events in the public ministry of Jesus, the baptism, he concluded, was some time in 28 A.D. Priestley had managed to achieve dates that conform more closely than those of most of his contemporaries to the results of modern scholarship, in spite of his primary reliance on the Gospel of John.[22]

Most modern commentators would declare that, having missed the significant conclusions to be derived from his *Harmony,* i.e., the synoptics, Priestley had wasted his time and considerable ingenuity. For chronological order, dates and durations are irrelevant to the real harmony of the Gospels — the mutual thrust of their message. For Priestley, however, as a historian,

---

substantial difference in intent between the synoptic gospels and the Gospel of John. See, e.g., George Holley Gilbert, "From John Mark to John the Theologian: The First Great Departure from Primitive Christianity," *Harvard Theological Review* 16 (1923): 235–58.

22. The standard orthodox determinations of Priestley's day, reflecting the King James Bible, are birth, late Dec., 5 B.C.; baptism, Jan., 27 A.D.; and crucifixion, 6 April, 30 A.D. Incidentally, F. J. A. Hort, the great nineteenth-century Anglican New Testament scholar, who also argued for a one-year ministry, also rejected "passover" in John 6:4 as an interpolation and inverted John 5 and John 6. The inversion has been adopted, on literary arguments similar to Priestley's, by many moderns. According to Neill, *New Testament,* 104, primary reliance on John was standard with conservative theologians who held to the theory of plenary inspiration, but Priestley clearly disagreed, yet gave himself additional problems trying to fit the synoptics to the Gospel of John.

rationalist, and Christian, it was important to establish the historical validity of the Gospels. Nor was he the only eighteenth-century commentator to treat the Gospels as historical data in a harmony, though most others used orthodox religious values in support of orthodox conclusions. Within a year of the publication of Priestley's Greek *Harmony,* William Newcome published a Greek harmony. He disagreed with Priestley's arguments and defended those for a three-and-one-half-year ministry. Priestley responded with a letter included in his English *Harmony,* to which Newcome replied. Priestley answered with another letter, reprinted with the first, in *Two Letters to Dr. Newcome.* Newcome rejoined, and Priestley replied in a *Third Letter to Dr. Newcome,* ending the debate with an extract from Newcome's letter of 19 April 1782, declaring that, each having had his full say, no point remained for continuing the discussion.[23]

These *Letters* primarily rehearsed, in different words, the arguments of the "Critical Dissertations" prefixed to the *Harmonies* and attempted to answer objections proposed by Newcome. The second letter apologized for Priestley's delayed response, due to a "tedious illness, from which I several times had little hope of recovery, and a total change in my situation and affairs" (27). Priestley refused to accept the "absurdity and embarrassment" of the one-year ministry being placed on "us poor moderns [i.e., Mann and himself] only," when that opinion had been held by most of the early Christian fathers and its origin in time was untraceable (29–30, 41–42). Leaving facts behind, conjecture may go where bias leads; the bishop had argued from what he supposed Jesus had to do, Priestley by what he could be shown, from actual references, actually to have done (87). And Priestley noted, "I think it very probable, that different discourses and transactions in the gospel history, were composed at different times by the writers, and put together afterwards" (72).

The only thing really new in Priestley's *Third Letter* was the introduction of examples, provided by some friends, of the transposition of paragraphs in printed editions of Virgil, the Old Testament, and Novatian, to support the transposing of verses in John (40–44). The debate ended as theological arguments generally did (and do), with each protagonist remaining of the same opinion still. There was, however, one singularity in this debate. It remained friendly throughout. There were no charges and countercharges between Trinitarian and Unitarian, no claims that one was an idolator and the other an atheist, no claim of churchly oppression or of willed destruction

23. Joseph Priestley, *Two Letters to Dr. Newcome, Bishop of Waterford. On the Duration of our Saviour's Ministry* (Birmingham: J. Johnson, 1780); *A Third Letter to Dr. Newcome, Bishop of Waterford, on the Duration of our Saviour's Ministry* (Birmingham: J. Johnson, 1781).

of the state. It was, as Priestley wrote, a contest for truth, not victory (38), and demonstrated that Priestley could, when addressed with respect and candor, respond in kind. Attending sufficiently to the great truths of religion, "we shall all love as brethren notwithstanding all lesser differences" (*Two Letters*, 129).[24]

The last major religious writing project that Priestley began at Calne was conceived on his visit to Paris in 1774. All the philosophical persons he met there were "unbelievers in Christianity and even profound atheists." One ingenious man and good writer (probably Baron d'Holbach) even "maintained seriously that man might arise, without any Maker, from the earth." Many of these unbelievers told him that he "was the only person they had ever met with, of whose understanding they had any opinion, who professed to believe in Christianity," but, on talking with them, Priestley discovered they did not really know what Christianity was. He concluded that he had some unique advantages for combatting the ignorance and prejudices of such people and began to compose his *Letters to a Philosophical Unbeliever*.[25] His attention was diverted, however, to a set of metaphysical treatises and concurrent scientific studies. Not until the posthumous publication of David Hume's *Dialogues concerning Natural Religion* (1779) did he return to this project. Once begun, however, and indefatigable in argument against named, unnamed, or imaginary opponents, he carried the series through three parts, an addition, and, with a change of title *(Letters to the Philosophers and Politicians of France)*, at least two more sections to as late as 1797. *Letters to a Philosophical Unbeliever, Part I* was sent to press when Priestley was still at Calne. Printing, however, must have been done after his leaving there but before he had settled in Birmingham, for it shows evidence of disruption in final press corrections.[26]

24. On 23 May 1782, Newcome wrote Priestley about their friendly controversy and added, "I was often struck with the learning, ingenuity, and liberal spirit of my antagonist, and . . . considered him as a diligent investigator and sincere lover of truth." As late as 1794, when Priestley was on the point of leaving England for the United States, he sent Newcome a copy of his sermons on the evidences of Revelation as a mark of esteem; see *W.* 20:121n.

25. *W.* 1.1:199; Priestley to Lindsey, 21 Oct. 1774; *W.* l.1:251–54; Joseph Priestley, *Letters to a Philosophical Unbeliever. Part I. Containing an Examination of the principal Objections to the Doctrines of Natural Religion, and especially those contained in the Writings of Mr. Hume* (Bath: R. Cruttwell, for J. Johnson, 1780). Note that this was published, and some of it, at least, written, after the publication of his *Disquisitions relating to Matter and Spirit*, the *Doctrine of Philosophical Necessity*, and *Free Discussion . . .* [with] *Dr. Price*, each of which will be discussed in detail in later chapters, though the commentary here can stand on its own.

26. The final "letter" is dated Calne, March 1780, and the work was being printed by 2 April, as Priestley was then hoping soon to send a copy to Joseph Bretland. In early May he was very

The form is that of fourteen letters ostensibly written to a person whose faith has been shaken by books and by "the company you have been obliged to keep, especially on your travels. . . . [I]t is always flattering to a person of a very speculative turn to be ranked with those whose mode of thinking is the most *fashionable,* being connected with ideas of liberality, courage, manliness, freedom from vulgar prejudices, &c." (1–2). But men of letters had a bias toward incredulity matching that of the vulgar toward credulity. There was an "insanity," i.e., a failure to assess things at their true value, that could be useful in particular arts or sciences. It did no great harm so long as it did not neglect important things like subsistence and support or the existence of a future life. Priestley hoped to exhibit here a Christianity to which men of letters could not object.

He began by treating the nature of proofs. Propositions of natural and revealed religion could seldom be demonstrated as true by definition. But the association of ideas in the unprejudiced mind could be as convincing as a mathematical demonstration, the difference between the two being, "as mathematicians say, less than any assignable quantity" (10).[27] Unfortunately, able and upright men disputed with so much rancor, it was no wonder sensible men took refuge in disbelief. "Had not mortality come in aid of the demonstrations on which the Newtonian system of the Universe is founded, it is not certain that it would even yet have supplanted the Aristotelian or Cartesian system. . . . But the old and incorrigibly bigoted abettors of former hypotheses leaving the stage, reason had a better chance with the younger, and the less biased" (5–6).

Provided that the moral purpose was attained, disputes using different modes of reasoning had advantages, some people being persuaded by one approach who could not be reached by another. An injudicious manner of defending the principles of religion neither overturned those principles nor convicted the defender of atheism (159–63). The best arguments for God's existence were to be adduced from man's experience and observations in the

---

ill, and Bretland had not yet received his copy by 23 June. When it appeared, a sheet with twenty-one "errata, corrections and improvements" had been added and there were even mistakes on that.

27. David Hartley's *Observations on Man* had a discussion of the "peculiar Characteristics of Truth." The process of association was essentially one of building by "mutual connexions" among three ascending orders of "agreement" of ideas: (1) "analogy," (2) partial "induction," and (3) perfect "coalescence." The first two corresponded roughly to "imperfect analogy between ideas of things in nature"; the third (also called "the highest Kind of Induction") was the sort of intuitive "coincidence" of ideas that only occurs in mathematics. Robert Marsh, "The Second Part of Hartley's System," *Journal of the History of Ideas* 20 (1959): 266.

Book of Nature. Priestley then developed the classic argument from design, in an almost geometrical form, leading from the necessary existence of a creator-designer to his self-comprehension, eternal existence, infinite power, omnipresence, and boundless benevolence. The "simple design" argument has been difficult to sustain since the development of evolutionary ideas, and though Priestley was always prepared to admit secondary causes while denying material primary ones, his examples of design do not now inspire conviction (101, 110). But in fact Priestley's arguments were only superficially logical and sometimes self-contradictory; their essence was a psychological certainty based upon analogy and associationism.

He dealt with the objection of infinite regress simply by dismissing it as absurd (22). The whole of a thing may have properties that its parts do not—as the vibration of a string may produce sound, though its separate parts cannot—but each part requires a cause, as does the arrangement and combination of those parts (26, 146). The notion that the intelligence, or soul, of the universe *is* the arrangement of the bodies in it revolted the imagination (28). Divine power might penetrate and fill all space without immediate perception by the senses. Other invisible powers, such as gravitation, repulsion, or magnetism, were known to do so (31–34). The intention of the creator must be determined not simply from the actual state of things but also from the tendencies of things in the future (58). And so it was with societies; increasing knowledge had decreased the evils of sickness, wars were less terrible, the folly of persecution for conscience' sake was generally acknowledged (59–61). And if the existence of man after death made the system more complete, making it possible that the righteous and the wicked meet with their just and full recompense, it was not impossible that that should happen, though we could not, from natural religion, know how or its proximate cause (84, 103).

Explicitly addressing the arguments of Holbach's *Système de la Nature* (a kind of "bible of atheism" abroad), Priestley answered the notion that the universe had come about through a "fortuitous concourse of atoms, in motion from all eternity." Atoms were solid particles, made of parts with powers of attraction and repulsion. Indeed, without such powers, as in the form of gravity, elasticity, electricity, and so on, matter could not exist, for take away all the powers, i.e., all the properties of matter, and the substance itself would vanish (31, 145). The powers, and their adjustment to one another—i.e., the matter itself—must have been the result of the comprehension of a superior power. The *Système* was the most plausible and seducing thing Priestley had yet met in support of atheism, but its author declaimed rather than argued, and seemed to be declaiming atheism in name only. He ascribed everything that exists to the "energy of nature" and, though he failed to give intelligence or purpose to "Nature," he otherwise used that term in just the way that others used the name God (154–57).

The crucial element in Priestley's description and defense of natural religion, however, came in his answer to Hume's *Dialogues concerning Natural Religion*. Throughout his *Letters*, Priestley reasserted arguments Hume had attacked and, in Letters IX, X, XIII, and XIV, he addressed the *Dialogues* and Hume's metaphysical writings in general. But Priestley basically did not understand Hume, and the objections he made in the *Letters* have generally been dismissed as typical of a chronic controversialist and theologian.[28] Now, Priestley understood quite well—better, certainly, than many an admiring commentator on Hume—the immediate intention of the *Dialogues*. At least, Priestley wrote, the author of the *Systèm de la Nature* has the honesty to write openly, unlike Hume. "[T]hough the debate [of the *Dialogues*] seemingly closes in favour of the theist, the victory is clearly on the side of the atheist" (158, 108–9).[29] But Priestley addressed Hume's work as he did Holbach's, simply as an attack on religion, while the *Dialogues* was, at base, a philosophical analysis of the grounds of belief. Whether a philosopher should be held accountable for the consequences (intended or unintended) of challenging those grounds has been debated at least since the days of Socrates.[30] Priestley's position, at least this time, seems clear in his criticism that Hume proposed doubts, yet left them unresolved, remaining altogether unconcerned about the results (107). Priestley was concerned about results, good results practically defining truth for him, independent of any rational proofs of the bases from which the truth was obtained. In this difference lies the classic conflict between the philosopher and the scientist.

28. One of the few seriously to discuss these objections is Richard H. Popkin, "Joseph Priestley's Criticism of David Hume's Philosophy," *Journal of the History of Philosophy* 15 (1977): 437–47. I have benefited from Popkin's study, though I disagree with some of his "facts" and conclusions. See also Leon Pearl, "Hume's Criticism of the Argument from Design," *The Monist* 54 (1970): 270–84, which suggests, on much the same inductive (associationist?) inference Priestley used, that Hume's criticism fails.

29. The efforts to interpret the *Dialogues* as other than an attack on any form of religion is exemplified in Bruce M'Ewen's introduction to his edition of Hume's *Dialogues concerning Natural Religion* (Edinburgh: William Blackwood and Sons, 1907). For a discussion of Hume's attitude toward religion and a cogent argument supporting Priestley, see Christopher J. Wheatley, "Polemical Aspects of Hume's Natural History of Religion," *Eighteenth-Century Studies* 19 (1986): 502–14.

30. Elsewhere, as in his letter to the Abbé Roger Joseph Boscovich, 19 Aug. 1778, Priestley absolved an author of the unintended consequences of his writing; *SciAuto.*, 79.

Hume did not help his cause by his manner of writing. Priestley acknowl-edged that "when the merits of any question were on his side, few men ever wrote with more perspicuity, the arrangement of his thoughts being natural, and his illustrations peculiarly happy" (106). Nevertheless, he could miscarry. Never responsive to whimsy, Priestley found the "supposition" of a universe created by an infant deity, a dependent inferior deity, or an elderly, superan-nuated deity in his dotage, to be "unworthy of a philosopher and miserably trifling on so serious a subject" (114–17).[31] Under the circumstances, it is scarcely surprising that Priestley should attempt to confute Hume, or that his arguments should appear to have the substance, if not the form, of Samuel Johnson's kicking a stone to refute Berkeley. For the most part Priestley sim-ply asserted that Hume was wrong, with no more analysis than Hume gave to support his initial assertions.

To one subject, however, that of cause and effect ("evidently a favourite topic" with Hume), Priestley gave substantial attention, for the whole struc-ture of his natural theology, of his doctrine of necessity, and of the develop-ment of natural laws rests on the validity of causal relationships. Hume declared that all we can pretend to know concerning cause and effect is the constant conjunction of two events, implying that the connection may be an arbitrary one and that effects may take place without causes (180–81). But the idea of cause was not simply the perception of the conjunction of appear-ances or events, Priestley argued. All men had an idea of power, or causation, and mankind had always acted upon that idea.[32] "Having found," Priestley declared, "in all such constant conjunction of ideas, with respect to which we have been able to make any discovery at all, that the conjunction was really necessary," we conclude that all conjunctions, if constant, are equally neces-sary, even when we are not able to perceive it (193, 183). Two events are necessarily connected if some more general law of nature must be violated before those events can be separated (194). "It is plain there could be little

---

31. For these two examples and others quite similar, see Hume, *Dialogues concerning Nat-ural Religion,* Part V, 76, 79–80, Part VII, 94, Part XII, 188.

32. For Hume, causal inferences were a consequence of the condition of mankind; constant conjunction giving the sense of cause and effect, but this did not mean that such beliefs were justified, i.e., that causality, having "explained" something, proved its validity. "Cause" here has no proper efficiency as causality; see John W. Lenz, "Hume's Defense of Causal Inference," *Journal of the History of Ideas* 19 (1958): 559–67. To Priestley, causality was not simply a belief but an explanation that determined truth. Kant declared it a "mortifying reflection" that Hume's opponents, "Reid, Beattie, Oswald, and lastly Priestley himself, totally misunderstood the tendency of his [Hume's] problems." Kant quoted in John Christopher Adelung, *Elements of the Critical Philosophy* (London: T. N. Longman, 1798), 11.

room for the exercise of wisdom, in God or man, if there had been no general laws. For the whole plan of nature, from which we infer design or wisdom, is admirable, chiefly on account of its being a system of wonderfully general and simple laws. . . . And the wisdom and foresight of man could have little scope, if there had been no invariable plan of nature to be the object of his investigation and study" (73–74). That nature operated according to "an invariable plan" meant that here God could not act other than he did; the world was subject to rational and deterministic analysis.

During the heyday of scientific positivism, when it was confidently expected that metaphysics could be excluded from science, the introduction of psychology and culture was regarded as irrelevant, even to theological argument. Hume was proclaimed the father of logical positivism. There was universal applicability of Hume's dictum, from the *Philosophical Essays,* that one should commit to flames any book that did not contain abstract reasonings concerning quantity or number, or experimental reasonings concerning matters of fact or existence. Priestley's charge that this meant Bible burning (207–8) was as malicious as his appeal to experience and custom was ignored. Recent studies of scientific creativity, imagination, cultural relativism, and gestalt psychology have cast doubts on the complete objectivity of experimental observations, and on the application of analysis to religion. Priestley's arguments with Hume now seem not so absurd as they long seemed.[33] But Priestley did not have the philosophical sophistication of a Kant for responding to Hume. Priestley was a theologian-scientist, not a formal philosopher, and his efforts at writing metaphysics made his religious arguments even more suspect than Hume's to the orthodox Establishment.

---

33. See W. W. Fenn, "Concerning Natural Religion," *Harvard Theological Review* 4 (1911): 460–76, for an analysis of natural religion as having continuing validity in theological argument.

III

"COMMON-SENSE" AND ASSOCIATIONISM

It is to be doubted that Priestley intended to write a metaphysical pentad when he started his *Examination of Scottish Common Sense Philosophy* (1774). As he wrote, on undertaking the fifth of the series, his *Free Discussion with Dr. Price* (1778), "It has been very insensibly and unexpectedly that I have been drawn into this course of publication; but being engaged, I am determined to see it out" (*W.* 1.1:315). Nor, during its writing, did Priestley ever claim that he was presenting a formal and coherent philosophical system. No more than most scientists, or writers on practical, applied issues (such as, in his opinion, theology), was he much interested in detailed, logical analyses of the grounds of his beliefs. He was inclined to be impatient with that kind of study, but when his beliefs were challenged, he was typically ready in their defense. Between 1774 and 1778 his defense was to result in five major metaphysical works.

He had, over the years, constructed for himself an implicit system of beliefs. It began with John Locke and Isaac Watts, added Philip Doddridge and David Hartley, the results of experience and experiments, and a gradual accommodation of the whole to fit a theology with which he felt secure. Attempting to communicate that security to the young people of his Leeds congregation, he had completed the *Institutes of Natural and Revealed Religion* (1772–74), which he began at Daventry Academy, where the formal elements of his metaphysics had first been brought together.[1] In the process, he was brought to consider an alternative system that seemed to challenge the basis of his beliefs.

He had looked into Thomas Reid's *Inquiry into the Human Mind, on the Principles of Common Sense* (1764) while at Warrington working on the *History of Electricity*. Because Reid's book was an attack on Locke, failed to mention David Hartley, and supported a type of innate ideas, he put it aside. As he was to write much later to George Walker, "I believe nothing of any original determination of the mind to objects of morality or any other objects, and though you and Mr. Hutchinson [Hutcheson?] say there must be such things, I do not see a shadow of proof for it" (*SciAuto.*, 63).

The year of its publication, he read James Beattie's *Essay on the Nature and Immutability of Truth* (1770). He reported to his friend, Samuel Merivale, "I like Beattie as you do, and am not afraid of its overturning the doctrine of necessity." It was James Oswald's *Appeal to Common Sense in Behalf of Religion* (1767) that excited his astonishment and indignation at Scottish Common Sense Philosophy. William Enfield had called Oswald to Priestley's attention in his *Remarks on Several Late Publications relative to Dissenters* (1770), and Beattie had cited Oswald favorably. On finishing the second volume of the *Institutes,* Priestley read Oswald carefully and felt compelled to answer his claim that common sense superseded almost all reasoning about religion.

Priestley's answer was to form part of the third volume of the *Institutes,* but, reading Reid as the source of Oswald's inspiration and rereading Beattie, Priestley did what he so often objected to in others. He imputed to Reid the consequences Oswald drew from the "system" of Common Sense and discovered the same unfortunate tendencies in Beattie. He therefore limited himself, in the *Institutes,* to some general remarks and extracts in the "Introduction," and developed a full scale attack on the system in a separate work.[2]

The *Examination of Dr. Reid's Inquiry . . . Dr. Beattie's Essay . . . and Dr. Oswald's Appeal* (1774) is a sustained polemic, for the tone of which Priestley afterward felt the need to apologize. Though the *Examination* was written with asperity, there was really little cause for regret at its tone.[3]

1. For his reading of Locke, Watts, Doddridge, and Hartley and his writing of the *Institutes,* see Schofield, *Enlightenment of Priestley,* chaps. 1 and 2.

2. See Joseph Priestley, *Institutes of Natural and Revealed Religion* (Birmingham: J. Johnson, 1782), 2d ed., vol. 2, "Introduction to Part III," 143–54.

3. Joseph Priestley, *An Examination of Dr. Reid's Inquiry into the Human Mind, on the Principles of Common Sense, Dr. Beattie's Essay on the Nature and Immutability of Truth,*

Oswald claimed that persons who disagreed with him were fools or mad, guilty of great stupidity or gross prevarication, talked nonsense, were, perhaps, "ideots." Beattie wrote with insolence of persons who differed from him, treated Berkeley as though he were a joke, and attacked Hume's character with singularly bad taste. Reid's *Inquiry* was blustering, patronizing, anti-intellectual, obscurantist; he wrote of philosophy as "a kind of metaphysical lunacy" when set in opposition to the *common sense* of mankind.[4] Priestley acknowledged the good intentions of Reid, Beattie, and Oswald in defense of religion; it was of their understanding and methods that he disapproved. Their manner justified that of Priestley's *Examination,* though his reviewer disagreed.[5]

Unfortunately, the *Examination* was also written in considerable haste. Priestley wrote to Caleb Rotherham, on 31 May 1774, of his intention to "consider the scheme of these writers more fully," while the dedication, jointly to Reid, Beattie, and Oswald, is dated 10 August 1774. During the same period, he was also preparing the three essays to accompany his edition of Hartley's *Observations on Man.* Priestley had a quick mind, but not a profound one. He could read nearly anything and immediately perceive its salient character and significance to his interests. Issues foreign to his concerns or sensibilities, however, he might never see. These "common sense philosophers" proposed a system of innate perceptive principles differing markedly from the doctrine of associationism. These principles had, he

---

and Dr. Oswald's *Appeal to Common Sense in Behalf of Religion,* 2d ed. (London: J. Johnson, 1775). See W. 1.1:202 for the semi-apology, which only appeared in his posthumously published *Memoirs.* Some remarks in his *Philosophical Unbeliever* might also be taken as something of an apology.

4. For Oswald, see Priestley's quotations in the *Examination,* e.g., 230, 246, 266, 278, 295. A biography of Oswald is not readily available; he appears to have been an evangelical Scottish Presbyterian. For Beattie and Reid, see Elmer Sprague, "James Beattie," and S. A. Grave, "Thomas Reid," in *The Encyclopedia of Philosophy,* ed. Paul Edwards (New York: Macmillan, 1967), and also the *Dictionary of National Biography.* Reid's *Inquiry* has been reprinted in *Thomas Reid's Inquiry into the Human Mind,* ed. Timothy Duggan (Chicago: University of Chicago Press, 1970). Note that Priestley was writing against the *Inquiry;* quotations from 76, 77. The later, more subdued and more carefully argued *Essays on the Intellectual Powers of Man* (1785) and *Essays on the Active Powers of the Human Mind* (1788) have been republished, with introductions by Baruch A. Brody (Cambridge: MIT Press, 1969). For an account of changes in Reid's work after writing the *Inquiry,* see J. H. Faurot, "The Development of Reid's Theory of Knowledge," *University of Toronto Quarterly* 21 (1951–52): 224–31.

5. The hostile review of the *Examination* in *Monthly Review* 52 (1775): 289–96, probably written by William Rose (1719–86), scarcely touches the substance of the book and spends its pages illustrating that Priestley's "manner of treating his antagonists is . . . extremely arrogant, contemptuous, and illiberal."

believed, serious religious and social consequences, but in so short a time for careful consideration, he never understood (if ever he could have) why they were proposed in the first place. Even for Oswald, the last to be treated in the *Examination* and the least subtle, there was a motivation that Priestley did not perceive.

Unlike Priestley, Oswald had been disturbed by inconclusive reasonings on the existence and attributes of God. Happily, he learned from Reid that absolute knowledge in religion was to be obtained not by reason but through the irresistible power of simple belief, i.e., common sense. To Priestley this set up every person, however biased or confused, as an expert and suggested the use of civil authority to enforce opinions. "Were it not for the dangers involved," Oswald wrote, he would have "wished that the civil magistrates were authorized to put a stigma on palpable absurdity in subjects where the honour of God and the interest of mankind are deeply concerned" (231). But for all his confidence that truth was achieved by an intuition that could not be denied, on its basis Oswald had been led to views on the nature of Christ that differed from those required by his subscription in the Church of Scotland (309).

The second of the Scots discussed in the *Examination,* after Reid and before Oswald, was James Beattie. Beattie had a fair reputation as a poet, was professor of moral philosophy and logic at Marischal College, Aberdeen, had an honorary doctorate of laws of Oxford and a pension from King George, who was much taken with the *Essay*. But he did not frighten a man willing to tangle with Blackstone. If Priestley treated him a bit more tenderly than he did Oswald, it was because he felt Beattie might be encouraged to change his mind. Beattie understood Reid better than Oswald had, and his *Essay* is more broadly directed than Oswald's *Appeal,* but Priestley did not hesitate to point out contradictions in Beattie's system and its bad consequences. Beattie's axioms of "self-evident truths" concerned unaccountable, instinctive persuasions, the power of the mind to perceive truth by an instantaneous and irresistible impulse from nature, independent of will (121, 127). Simple association of ideas, Priestley declared, would account for most of the actions Beattie cited as the mind's acting upon the laws of nature with which it is furnished prior to experience.

On Beattie's concept, Priestley claimed, all we can ever say is that certain maxims and propositions appear true to us. "Every man is taught to think himself authorized to pronounce decisively upon every question according to his present feeling" (121). Wanting to prove the immutability of truth, Beattie adopted principles that denied it and turned the search into a contest of sincerity. But "truth is a thing not relative, but absolute, and real, independent of any relation to this or that particular being, or this or that order of beings" (124). There was no defense in Beattie's system for a person's being wrong. Priestley concluded his *Examination* of Beattie with wonderment at his vehemence and his antipathy toward those who differed from him.[6] Oswald's and Beattie's arrogant assertions had their origin in Reid's *Inquiry*, to which these authors frequently turned as an authority. Priestley's refutation of each of them as frequently asserted his denial of that authority. The *Examination* ultimately rested, then, on the first section, the consideration of Reid's principles. Thomas Reid was professor of philosophy (regent) at King's College, Aberdeen, when he published his *Inquiry into the Human Mind,* and its success earned him the professorship of moral philosophy at Glasgow, in succession to Adam Smith. Although several persons, including the Scot Francis Hutcheson, might be regarded as his precursors, it was Reid's formulation of the doctrine of common sense that established it as a formal philosophical system. Scottish Common Sense Philosophy, as it came to be known, attracted the support of Dugald Stewart and, with variations, of Sir William Hamilton, as well as of philosophers on the continent and in the United States. It proposed solutions of human paradoxes, some of which were similar to (though less abstruse than) those of Kant, and provided guidance to philosophically minded people well into the nineteenth century. There has even been a recent, inexplicable revival of interest in Reid among philosophers.[7]

Clearly there were elements of Reid's concern that could not lightly be dismissed, whatever might be thought of his solutions to them. Priestley never comprehended the nature of that concern. Reid's starting point had been the skepticism of David Hume, specifically the panic he felt on reading Hume's *Treatise on Human Nature* (1739). Reid understood Hume to have proved that man cannot rationally demonstrate the existence of a world external to himself, nor the continuity of past, present, and future, nor even

6. John G. McEvoy and J. E. McGuire, in their "God and Nature: Priestley's Way of Rational Dissent," *Historical Studies in the Physical Sciences* 6 (1975): 325–404, assert that Priestley failed to credit Beattie's support of toleration in his *Essay,* but the statement they quote (p. 376) does not appear in the 1770 edition of the *Essay on the Nature and Immutability of Truth,* which Priestley read; see the 1983 facsimile reprint of the first edition of 1770. It appears in a "Postscript" dated Nov. 1770 and can be found in the 1773 edition, 513, the 1774 edition, 513, and the 1776 edition, 343, where McEvoy and McGuire found it.

7. Two separate issues of *The Monist*—61 (1978): 165–344, and 70 (1987): 382–526—are devoted to Reid, his philosophy, and friendly contemporaries. There is no significant reference to Priestley in either.

his own existence. The "proof" was, Reid understood, the necessary consequence of a system of philosophy that extended backward from Hume to Berkeley to Locke and finally to Descartes and the dualism of mind and matter. Unlike Priestley, Reid could not deny that dualism, but something was wrong with the system's explanation of how the mind perceived matter. Reid *knew* the external world existed, he *knew* cause-and-effect relations were valid, he *knew* that there was continuity in the universe.

Reid accepted Hume's assumption that sensations were absolute and immediate. Sensation was a simple and original affection of the mind, purely passive, had no object distinct from itself, could not be right or wrong. Here, as with Beattie, Priestley was strongly critical. Sensations *could* be wrong: sensory organs disordered, nerves malfunctional, brains injured or delirious. Moreover, their sense could be misunderstood. This was a point Priestley was to comment upon later in another context: "The force of prejudice . . . biases not only our *judgments . . .* but even the perceptions of our senses . . . [such] that even the plainest evidence of sense will not entirely change . . . our persuasions."[8]

What Reid denied was the concept of ideas. How, then, did one go from sensation to a knowledge of the external world? Sensations did not resemble qualities of bodies: the pain of running one's head against a pillar was unlike hardness, one smelled an odor, not a rose, heard a sound, not a coach. Nor were sensory processes disclosed by physiological analyses. Nothing in sensation could ever have led us to think of motions in nerves, animal spirits, or effluvia.[9] Sensation was translated directly into knowledge by immediate, independent, instinctive principles implanted by God in the minds of all persons of common understanding, i.e., the principles of common sense. By the nature of man's constitution, certain sensations suggested qualities to the mind and entailed a belief in them. We know nothing of the machinery by which impressions produce sensations, and sensations exhibit corresponding perceptions.[10]

Priestley found this entire doctrine of common sense so foolish as scarcely to be worthy of comment, save that it had attracted so much favorable attention and the refutation of it would give him an opportunity to bring Hartley's

    8. Priestley, *Exp. & Obs. II,* 2d ed., 30.
    9. Reid's *Inquiry,* 62, 22. For more detail, see Robert E. Schofield, "Joseph Priestley on Sensation and Perception," in *Studies in Perception: Interrelations in the History of Philosophy and Science,* ed. Peter K. Machamer and Robert G. Turnbull (Columbus: Ohio State University Press, 1978), 336–54.
    10. Reid's *Inquiry,* 66–67, 21.

associationism to the notice of the learned world. He had no problems with Hume's paradoxes, partly because he too depended upon a common sense, but his common sense involved a functional theory of knowledge based upon awareness of the purposes of knowing, and upon Hartley's physiological psychology. Most of what we know is by experience, not by conscious argument. Normally, man lives and acts without consciousness of thinking. Proof, truth, propositions, and syllogisms are all things of art and not of nature: Knowledge of the nature of vision is different from vision itself. "The philosopher only is acquainted with the structure of the eye and the theory of vision, but the clown sees as well as he does" (xliv–xlvii). In the normal course of living, man goes through the process of argument and obtains answers without conscious mental process, connecting subject to predicate through familiarity, suppressing the middle term of the syllogism. This is not a case of instinctive "original perceptions," but of the association of ideas.

Conceding that the efforts of Reid and his followers might be of service in checking too rapid a simplification of appearances, Priestley claimed that the system they proposed was so loose and incoherent as to violate the very purpose of philosophy. Instead of reducing the great variety of separate effects into fewer classes and these into still fewer causes, Reid proposed separate, arbitrary, instinctive principles to explain belief in the past and present, in personal existence, hardness, extension, place and change of place, veracity, credulity, and the validity of induction (9–18). And all these innate principles were unnecessary. Their number denied the agreeable simplicity shown in other parts of nature, and their character, as ultimate and primary, was such as necessarily to check all further inquiry into the operation of the mind (22). To accept this "vain multiplication" of separate faculties of the mind was intellectually offensive, and utterly unacceptable to the Unitarian monist that Priestley had become. And to offer, as proof of these "separate faculties," an appeal to common understanding was foolishness—as the coming Birmingham riots were so clearly to prove.[11] Reid's answer to Hume's skepticism was a worse skepticism. Instead of believing nothing, "these moderns believe every thing though they profess to understand nothing" (xxi).

11. In commenting on the difference between Reid and especially Oswald and Beattie and the transcendental philosophy of Kant, René Wellek writes that, in practice, the search for the a priori in Scottish Common Sense Philosophy "amounted to a simple declaration of bankruptcy, a complacent acceptance of the dicta of general untutored opinion. . . . It really became a defense of the intolerant orthodoxy of ordinary men." Wellek, *Immanuel Kant in England, 1793–1838* (Princeton: Princeton University Press, 1931), 26–27. Kant declared that neither the Common Sense philosophers nor Priestley had understood Hume; see chap. 2, note 33.

Reid abandoned the system of Locke because of a number of misconceptions that could have been avoided had he only read Hartley. Various sensations are associated in the mind over time to produce the perceptions of hardness, extension, relation, fear, belief, etc. The lack of resemblance between sensation and perception caused Reid to deny relationships. The same lack of resemblance between cause and effect should make Reid deny that the vibration of a string can produce a sound (31). Reid, the philosopher, insisted upon precise and complete details before he would assent to the "ideal system." Priestley, the practical, working scientist, found this an unnecessary requirement. A very high degree of probability, "not to be distinguished in feeling from absolute certainty," is attainable without the use of positive instinctive principles (46). "What evidence can we possibly have of any thing being necessarily connected with experience and derived from it, besides its never being prior to it, always consequent upon it and exactly in proportion to it?" (83). Priestley knew that the eye, retina, optic nerve, and brain are necessary to vision, because should any of them be injured, vision would be proportionally disturbed; it is not necessary to know how, to know that they work (36). To feel a thing, be affected by it, and to be influenced and directed by those feelings required no knowledge of the connections between feelings, perception, will, and act (73).

When we come to the end of Reid's negative arguments—all based, Priestley claimed, upon ignorance or misconceptions—what is left? Merely assertions, repeated over and over till one wearied of them, about Reid's sincere beliefs. But many beliefs we know to be founded upon prejudice and mistake; the fullest conviction of their truth is not enough. We know also that our sensations can fool us (49). Reid should have paid more attention to his idea of a gradual unfolding of the powers of the mind, for impressions other than the primary ones (40). One would think Reid could not admit this possibility, for it resembles the gradual acquisition of those powers by experience and can be extended, by association, to include all of the perceptions that concerned him.

Priestley described examples, drawn from his own experience and his observations of his children, to show how actions that appear immediately to follow sensations, were, in fact, learned over time, by experience: his learning to play the flute (68), his children's learning the fear of flame or distrust of others (89–90). He even broke down Reid's own example of "hearing" a coach, to show the steps by which a particular sound becomes associated with a particular object, or species of object, that makes the sound (79–80). And, at the end of this section, Priestley reverted, by implication, to

his concern that adopting the notion of a set of original and ultimate principles would forestall that further investigation of the operations of senses,
nerves, the brain, and the mind that the subject required.

Joseph Johnson, Priestley's publisher, said that the *Examination* sold well.
People as various as the zealous Calvinist Rev. Augustus M. Toplady and the
gentle Charles Lamb took delight in it. Toplady wrote Priestley, thanking
him for the "spirited (and for the most part just) animadversions on the three
Northern Doctors," and declaring that it was "the good providence of God,
which has raised up no less a man than yourself to contend so ably for the
great doctrine of necessity." Lamb recommended to Coleridge that "clear,
strong, humorous, most entertaining piece of reasoning." Lindsey heard, at
third hand, that William Robertson and David Hume had read the *Examination*, "and they declared that the manner of the work was proper, as the
argument was unanswerable."[12] Reid wrote to Richard Price, complaining of
Priestley's abuse, his lack of meekness, good manners, and candor, "what
Light with regard to the power of the Mind is to be expected from a Man
who has not yet Learned to distinguish vibrations from Ideas, nor Motion
from Sensation, nor simple Apprehension from Judgment, nor simple ideas
from complex, nor necessary truths from Contingent?" Nonetheless, it has
been suggested that Reid modified and strengthened his views as a consequence of Priestley's criticisms and that he retreated from the nativist position of the *Inquiry* when he wrote his *Essays*.[13]

Priestley's metaphysical task was, however, only begun. He had complained in the *Examination* of the lack of solid argument for Reid's principles,
but provided only the sketchiest information on the Hartleyan associationism he proposed as a substitute. Yet it was clear from the writings of the
"Northern Doctors," and also from those of other contemporaries, that
Hartley's *Observations on Man* was scarcely known or appreciated. While
writing the *Examination*, Priestley therefore undertook to prepare an edition of selections from the *Observations*, with introductory dissertations.

12. For Lindsey's report on Robertson and Hume, see *W.* 1.1:252n. There are echoes of the
Examination in Priestley's later *Philosophical Unbeliever.* There are also intimations in it of the
philosophical monism to which his Unitarianism and his material corpuscularity were explicitly
to lead him in his later *Disquisitions on Matter and Spirit.* See next chapter.

13. Thomas Reid to [Richard Price], 10 April 1775, Price Papers, Bodleian Library, Oxford.
J. H. Faurot, "Reid's Answer to Joseph Priestley," *Journal of the History of Ideas* 39 (1978):
285–92. Beattie apparently bore no grudges, for he wrote Thomas Percival on 24 Dec. 1786 of
Priestley's "laudable endeavours to convert the Jews," and referred to him as a Christian.
Thomas Percival, *The Works, Literary, Moral, and Medical of Thomas Percival. M.D.* (London:
J. Johnson, 1807), 1:cxiii.

Parts of that edition were printed at the same time as the *Examination,* while he was abroad. In October 1774 Lindsey was correcting proofs for the introductory "dissertations," but publication was delayed until Priestley's return from France. Priestley's *Hartley's Theory of the Human Mind, on the Principle of the Association of Ideas, with Essays relating to the subject of it* appeared early in 1775.[14]

It is probable that Hartley's *Observations* was a more significant work than all of Reid's works, but not in establishing a philosophical system. There were earlier statements of some associationist principles, most notably by John Locke and the Rev. John Gay, but the *Observations* was the first systematic elaboration of associationist theory and the first to add a physiological mechanism to parallel association of ideas in the mind. Hartley's work became a base from which late eighteenth- and nineteenth-century theories of aesthetics, learning, education, government, economics, psychology, neurophysiology, and even psychiatry were argued. Associationist theories influenced Erasmus Darwin, Coleridge, Wordsworth, James Mill, John Stuart Mill, Alexander Bain, and Herbert Spencer.[15]

Yet, it is generally agreed, but for Priestley's persistent advocacy of Hartley's *Observations,* it might have gone unnoticed. John Stuart Mill declared, "But for the accident of their [Hartley's Doctrines] being taken up by Priestley, who transmitted them as a kind of heirloom to his Unitarian followers, the name of Hartley might have perished, or survived only as that of a visionary physician, the author of an exploded physiological hypothesis."[16] Priestley had idolized Hartley since his student days at Daventry, publicly supporting associationism at least as early as his *Course of Lectures on the Theory of Language and Universal Grammar* (1762) and that on *Oratory*

14. Joseph Priestley, *Hartley's Theory of the Human Mind . . .* (London: J. Johnson, 1775). The text references to Hartley's propositions were not, in Priestley's absence, changed to conform to the new selection numbers as he had requested. A table was added to the Conclusions, relating Hartley's numbers to those of the selections. In the preface to the *Examination* Priestley claims to have obtained the approval of David Hartley Jr. for his editing of Hartley.

15. Robert M. Young, "Association of Ideas," in *Dictionary of the History of Ideas,* ed. Philip P. Weiner (New York: Charles Scribner's Sons, 1973), 1:111–18; see also Young's "David Hartley," in *Dictionary of Scientific Biography,* ed. Charles Coulston Gillispie (New York: Charles Scribner's Son's, 1972), 4:138–40.

16. [John Stuart Mill], *Collected Works of John Stuart Mill,* ed. F. E. L. Priestley (Toronto: University of Toronto Press, 1969), vol. 10, "Essays on Ethics, Religion and Society," 130. There are references to Priestley's *Hartley* scattered through Mill's *Works* and at least one favorable reference to his attack on Reid. After the 1749 edition of Hartley, the *Observations* was not printed in England until the second edition of Priestley's *Hartley* of 1790, but a sixth edition had appeared by 1834.

and Criticism (published in 1777).[17] But his *Hartley on the Human Mind* is not a general exposition of the whole of the *Observations on Man,* nor is it a selection of passages to illustrate the whole. Priestley ignored most of volume 2, the application of associationism to an understanding of man's religious duty and expectations. He also omitted nearly half of the propositions of volume 1.[18] Priestley did not disapprove of what he excluded. The volume on religion was what made Hartley's work second only to the Bible in Priestley's estimation. Nonetheless, it "clogged" the doctrine of associationism with material "in a great measure foreign to it," so far as understanding that doctrine was concerned.

The omitted propositions of volume 1 related to anatomy and the doctrine of vibrations and were excluded only because they made the book seem difficult and intricate (iii). So far as the concept of vibrations was concerned, Hartley had given as much evidence for it as the nature of the problem would admit. Though Priestley substituted, in the text, other expressions for vibrational ones, he included Hartley's own words in footnotes and his first prefatory essay described the general doctrine of vibrations. Fifty-one of the ninety-nine propositions, with their corollaries, of volume 1, were reprinted, including one (on language development from the divine gift of Hebrew to the Jews) that Priestley did not believe and included only because his edition of Hartley was to be an honest and scholarly edition of that part of the work dealing explicitly with the theory of association.

Nonetheless, as the purpose of the edition was to supply an alternative to the "original instinctive perceptions" of Reid, Beattie, and Oswald, Priestley included every proposition of the *Observations* that might do this. Propositions 11, 14, 20, 24, 38, and 42, for example, derive impression of hardness, roughness, magnitude, distance, position and change of position, single and upright vision, fear and trust, and assent and dissent from repeated and associated sensations.

Three introductory essays were intended to supplement and extend Hartley's text.[19] Essay 2, "A General View of the Doctrine of Association of

17. See Schofield, *Enlightenment of Priestley,* 56–60, 103, 107.

18. The entire table of contents of volume 1 is reprinted, with the items selected for republication distinguished by italic type. Sections 2, 3, and 4 of chap. 5 are taken from Part 2 of the *Observations.* Section 5, "On the practical Application of the Doctrine of Necessity," 365–67, appears to be Priestley's own summary of the remainder of Part 2; see Ronald B. Hatch, "Joseph Priestley: An Addition to Hartley's Observations," *Journal of the History of Ideas* 36 (1975): 548–50.

19. Priestley began collecting notes and hints for a volume of illustrations of Hartley's doctrine of association as early as 1765; "several volumes" of these were destroyed by "men of

Ideas," summarized Hartley's views so far as they concern ideas of sensation. It emphasized the greater simplicity of that system compared to "that seemingly operose and inelegant contrivance, of different original, independent instincts, adapted to a thousand different occasions" (xxxiii). "The admirable simplicity of this hypothesis ought certainly to recommend it to the attention of all philosophers as . . . it wears the face of that *simplicity in causes,* and *variety in effects,* which we discover in every other part of nature." As all varieties of languages are expressible by a short alphabet and we can reduce to simple and general laws the various and complex natural phenomena depending upon gravity, electricity, etc., "it does not appear impossible, but that, ultimately, one great comprehensive law shall be found to govern both the material and intellectual world" (xxv).

The third introductory essay, "Of Complex and Abstract Ideas," extended the summary to such abstract ideas as Locke included under the term "ideas of reflection" but that Hartley supposed also to result from association. Here Priestley contended implicitly with the Scots but also, explicitly, with his good friend Richard Price. Price, in his *Review of the Principal Questions of Morals,* did not go as far as Reid and the others in positing instinctive principles, but he maintained that abstract ideas of morality could not be deduced from experience. Priestley argued that ideas of morality vary too much among people to be original and innate. His own childhood training had given him an extreme repugnance for oaths, though "other persons, and men of strict virtue and honour in other respects . . . feel not the least moral impropriety in the greatest possible profaneness of speech" (xlv).

Only in the first essay, "A general view of the doctrine of Vibrations," did Priestley address anything not covered in the original text. Here, indeed, he not only summarized material he had excluded from his edition of *Hartley* but went significantly beyond it and beyond anything Hartley would have subscribed to. Newton, in the *Principia* and in the *Opticks,* first suggested that external objects excited light sensations in the optic nerves by vibrations that, transmitted to the brain, caused the sense of seeing. By analogy, and particularly relating to hearing and the vibrations of sound, it may be supposed that all sensations initially are in the form of vibrations in the brain. Such vibrations can differ in magnitude, frequency, place and direction of entry, and there may well be other forms and modifications of vibrations

---

common understanding" in the Birmingham Riots of 1791; see Priestley's *Appeal to the Public on the Subject of the Riots in Birmingham* . . . (Birmingham: J. Thompson, for J. Johnson, 1791), 38. Priestley's *Hartley* was the only published consequence of those studies, with the possible exception of an anonymous *Conclusion of the late Dr. Hartley's Observations* (London: J. Johnson, 1794), which just might be Priestley's.

such that their permutations and combinations result in complex ideas in the mind, as, unmixed, they make simple ideas of sensation (xiv). All particles of matter can vibrate about their static positions because they are kept from actual contact by a repulsive power, but solid substances tend to retain any form impressed upon them (as a bow when bent does not entirely restore itself to its original shape),[20] "in consequence of the spheres of attraction and repulsion belonging to the several particles having been altered by the change of their situation" (xvi).

One may suppose that the matter of the brain, having been made to vibrate in a particular way, will have a tendency to vibrate in that particular way again (a tendency or trace that Hartley called a vibratiuncle), the size of the tendency depending upon the intensity of the original sensation or the number of times it is repeated. And if two or more different vibrations occur at the same time, they will modify each other such that if any one takes place, another, or others, will be excited also, until finally one has a set of fixed vibrational tendencies that respond as triggered by any one of the set (xvii). Thus "all the sensations, ideas, and motions, of all animals, will be conducted according to the vibrations of the small medullary particles" (37). This vibrational mechanism was a physical analogue of Hartley's association of ideas, where ideas associated with one another sufficiently often induce one another (14). Hence simple ideas, by association, become complex, and these more complex still, to produce, with experience and over time, all of our ideas, pleasures, and passions.

Hartley was concerned lest the parallel he had drawn between vibrations in the brain and ideas in the mind be taken as support for materialism. In the *Life* of Hartley, written by his son and prefixed to the 1790 edition of the *Observations,* he is quoted as anxiously denying that he was a materialist and declaring that matter, as a passive thing whose essence was its *vis inertia,* was entirely incapable of sensation. If there were an element capable of sensation, the soul might consist of that element, but that introduced a new supposition.[21] Priestley saw no reason why Hartley's scheme should be burdened with such an encumbrance (xix). When matter was thought to be entirely inert, subject only to the five mechanical powers, the doctrine of vibrations was unacceptable. But now more subtle and important laws of matter in chemistry showed that "mere matter" was infinitely more complex than had been imagined. We

20. The example of the bent bow was probably derived from Hobbes's mechanical kinetic theory of elasticity, though he is not cited in this connection; see [Thomas Hobbes], *English Works of Thomas Hobbes* (London: John Bohn, 1839), 1:478, 7:34.

21. Quoted by Samuel Miller, *Brief Retrospect of the Eighteenth Century* (1805; reprint, London: J. Johnson, 1805), 2:192–93.

should admit the *possibility* of the brain's having been formed with powers with respect to vibrations, though the particulars of its constitution and mode of its disposition may still exceed our comprehension (xviii). "I am rather inclined to think that . . . man does not consist of two principles, so essentially different from one another as *matter* and *spirit* . . . described as having not one common property. . . . I rather think that the whole of man is of some *uniform composition,* and that the property of perception . . . is the result of such an organical structure as that of the brain" (xx).[22]

Hartley and Priestley each insisted that immateriality of the soul was unnecessary to a belief in the afterlife, which was founded upon Revelation and the doctrine of a resurrection from the dead (xix, 346). This caveat by Priestley satisfied some and intrigued others. Georg Christoph Lichtenberg, the Hanoverian physicist and literateur who had visited Priestley and seen some of his experiments, wrote from London:

> Dr. Priestley has hit upon some very fine subjects for investigation. In a preface to *Hartley's Theory of the Human Mind* he acknowledges openly that he believes that man ceases entirely at death; in the *London Review* . . . instead of contradicting him or warning the reader against him, they say: "Some, indeed, will find this strange and too daring, but we believe our thanks are due to Dr. Priestley for having had sufficient courage to make known to the world so important a truth."[23]

Others (and they outnumbered supporters) were incensed, and a clamor of abuse broke over Priestley. He was denounced as a materialist atheist, but Priestley was clearly not an atheist and the charge of materialism was, at least, imprecise. His real crime was to have taken the step, certainly suggested by Hartley, that provided materialists with a mechanism for directly relating material phenomena with mental activity.

It was a seductive step, not only for Priestley but for generations of physiopsychologists. That "exploded physiological hypothesis" about which John Stuart Mill wrote was to be one of the most enduring legacies of Hartley's

22. See Alan Tapper, "The Beginnings of Priestley's Materialism," *Enlightenment and Dissent* 1 (1982): 73–81.

23. G. C. Lichtenberg to Johann Andreas Schernhagen, 17 Oct. 1775, in [Georg Christoph Lichtenberg], *Lichtenberg's Visits to England: as described in his Letters and Diaries,* trans. and annot. Margaret L. Mare and W. H. Quarrell (Oxford: Clarendon Press, 1938), 104. There is a very hostile review, almost entirely devoted to Priestley's introductory essays, in the *Monthly Review* 53 (1776): 380–90; 54 (1776): 41–47.

Observations and of Priestley's advocacy of it. Herder referred to it. Johann A. H. Reimarus, professor of physics and natural history at Hamburg, wrote that Priestley's vibration theory clarified complicated psychological processes. Work by du Bois-Reymond, Helmholtz, and others in the electrical and biochemical activities of the nerves ultimately made the simple mechanism of vibrations seem naïve.[24] Yet long after references to associationism all but ceased, neurophysiologists continue to explore variations of the "traces" or "vibratiuncles" that sensations might leave in the substance of the brain.

Richard Wolfgang Semon's *Mnemic Psychology* (translated into English in 1923), for example, declared that every stimulus acting upon an organism leaves in it an "engram," a definite physiological trace. All the future reactions of the organism are dependent upon the chain of these engrams. Wallace Marshall, with explicit reference to Hartley and Priestley, declares in his *Immunological Psychology and Psychiatry* (1977) that "effects from sensory perception . . . are encoded or recorded in the recipient and cerebral centers. There they are stored as memory because of resultant neuro-electrochemical changes in the cerebal cells. . . . As the basis for learning since these encoded brain areas contain added brain potentials which can be released through one's recognition of associated . . . [afferent stimuli]." The concept has even become a part of modern science fiction. In one story, an artificial brain is created of masses of "superconductive tunnel-junction neuristors," super-cooled and surrounded with magnetized material: you pulse in data and let it establish its own preferential pathways, by means of the magnetic material's becoming increasingly magnetized each time the current passes through it, thus cutting the resistance. The material establishes its own route in a fashion analogous to the functions of the brain when it is learning something.[25]

24. Neither Hartley nor Priestley gets more than a perfunctory reference in Mary A. B. Brazier, *A History of Neurophysiology in the Seventeenth and Eighteenth Centuries: From Concept to Experiment* (New York: Raven Press, 1984).

25. For Herder and Reimarus, see H. B. Nisbet, *Herder and the Philosophy and History of Science* (Cambridge: Modern Humanities Research Assoc., 1970), 261–62. Semon references are due to Ernst Cassirer, *Essay on Man: An Introduction to a Philosophy of Human Culture* (New Haven: Yale University Press, 1944), 50. See also Herbert Marshall, *Immunological Psychology and Psychiatry* (Tuscaloosa: University of Alabama Press, 1977), 138–39, and Roger Zelazny, "Home Is the Hangman," in *My Name Is Legion* (New York: Ballantine Books, 1976), 149–50. For an overview of developments in neuropsychology and psychology that fails to mention contributions by Hartley or Priestley in its historical discussions, see Daniel N. Robinson, *The Enlightened Machine: An Analytical Introduction to Neuropsychology* (1973; reprint, New York: Columbia University Press, 1980).

IV

MATTER AND SPIRIT

Having so signally managed to shock large numbers of readers (and review-ers) by his initial doubts of body-spirit duality, one might suppose that Priestley's next metaphysical work would be extenuative, but this was not his style. He always prided himself on his willingness to change his mind, to exchange one theory or hypothesis for another, and it is true that he fre-quently did so. Unfortunately for his own dialectical theory of epistemology, rarely if ever did he change as the result of challenge and debate. When his ideas were attacked, he typically restudied his propositions and became more convinced of their general validity. This is what happened as a consequence of the monist suggestion in his *Hartley.* The "odium which I had thus unex-pectedly drawn upon myself, served to engage my more particular attention to the subject of it; and this at length terminated in a full conviction, that the doubt I had expressed was well founded." He wrote his *Disquisitions relat-ing to Matter and Spirit* to demonstrate the validity of his conviction.[1]

Knowing that he was dealing with an explosive issue, he did take steps to make the *Disquisitions* as inoffensive as possible. "That I might not obtrude on the public a crude and hasty performance on subjects of so much impor-tance . . . I put copies of the work after it was completely printed off, into the

1. Joseph Priestley, *Disquisitions relating to Matter and Spirit. . .* (London: J. Johnson, 1777), 2d ed., 1782, quotation at xiv.

hands of several of my friends, both well and ill affected to my general system, that I might have the benefit of their remarks" (349). From mid-1776 to mid-1778, he wrote his friends about the manner and content of the *Disquisitions.*

To Lindsey, in July 1776, he wrote, "I have done nothing yet about the soul; but I shall certainly write with my usual freedom, though not without such precautions as will, I hope, prevent my giving just offence to all truly sensible and candid persons." In December 1776 he informed Joshua Toulmin of the printing of the *Disquisitions,* of which "one great object . . . is to combat the doctrine of pre-existence, and especially that of our Saviour." In April 1777 he asked Newcome Cappe to read an early copy; he did not expect Cappe to approve of all of it, though Lindsey and Jebb, who had seen the whole work, agreed with him in everything. The copy was sent to Cappe in September and Priestley observed, "It is very probable that . . . you may find many things that you will disapprove, and I may not see reason to alter; but I hope by the help of such friends as you to send it out free from any *gross* mistakes, or passages needlessly offensive." As late as December 1777 he wrote Joseph Bretland that he was sending him a work "which I expect will rather shock and offend many of my friends, but I have some idea it will not much stagger *you.* . . . Be so good as to let me know freely what you think of it." In June 1778 he thanked Bretland for suggestions that he could use in his forthcoming controversy with Richard Price.[2]

Priestley also attempted to protect his flanks with a profusion of scholarship. More than half the *Disquisitions* was devoted to a discussion of early concepts of matter and soul and their relationship as treated in Scripture and in the church. For this Priestley listed nearly twenty primary authorities, including, for example, the works of Tertullian, Justin Martyr, Athanasius, Pope Gregory the Great, Bernard of Clairvaux, and Thomas Aquinas, but he particularly referred to Isaac de Beausobre's *Histoire Critique de Manichee et du Manicheism* (1734) and Louis Ellies Dupin's *History of Ecclesiastical Writers* (1696) for their summaries and interpretations. "Because these things have been very differently represented, I was confident that the opinion of these writers would be more respected than my own, their learning and exactness being universally acknowledged; and their views in writing being different from mine, they cannot be suspected of partiality to my hypothesis" (xxx).

2. Lindsey described the *Disquisitions* as Priestley's "great metaphysical work." Lindsey to Turner, 12 Nov. 1776, *W.* 1.1:294n.

Substantial parts of the rest of the treatise were presented in the same fashion. That "engagement of my particular attention to the subject" involved the assiduous collection of citations and quotations from a wide variety of authorities as the pieces from which to structure the appearance of a hypothesis that would not be unique to Priestley. Exclusive of passages from Scripture, he named more than fifty philosophers, theologians, historians, scientists, and antiquaries, including Descartes, Malebranche, Locke, Berkeley, Cudworth, Giordano Bruno, Toland, Samuel Clarke, Leibniz, Newton, Boscovich, and John Michell in his discussion.

Finally, not so much to deflect opposition as to channel it, Priestley promised to respond to any respectable answer to his arguments, provided the writers transmitted or properly announced their publications to him (xx). He did not agree with Hume in refusing to notice antagonists; so long as a reply was pertinent and decent, it required respectful notice. Not every attack was worthy of response, particularly when anonymous, but an able, or even plausible, answerer would not be neglected. "For, as in the controversy which I began with the Scotch writers, I really wish to have the subject freely and fully canvassed" (xix).

In fact, an anonymous writer (later identified as Joseph Berington) had already responded to the monistic suggestion of the *Hartley* with *Letters on Materialism*, and Priestley answered him in the *Disquisitions*. He continued his answer to Berington in a later work, along with responses to Samuel Horsley, William Kenrick, Richard Price, and John Whitehead. He thereby found himself contending with a Roman Catholic, an establishment clergyman, a hack writer without notable religious convictions, an Arian, and a Methodist turned Quaker soon to turn Methodist again. He had nearly achieved that position of Ishmael, about which he had earlier written to Lindsey, "My hand will be against every man and every man's hand against me" (*W.* 1.1:115). Yet he remained essentially unconcerned by the opposition of "professed christians." He was addressing "unbelievers, of a philosophical turn of mind" who might find "the true system of revelation to be quite another thing than they imagined it to be." The indignation of the converted "would do neither themselves, nor me, much harm; whereas the conviction of the *reasonableness* and *truth* of christianity, in a few really thinking and intelligent unbelievers, might do the greatest good; and even contribute to put a stop . . . to the infidelity of the philosophical part of the world" (xvi–xvii).

Priestley began the defense of his monism with an attack on "modern philosophical dualism," which had begun with Descartes though it had had the support of that pagan corruption of Christianity, the preexistence of souls. At once an issue arose: how can two substances—matter, solid, impenetrable, extendable, and inert (destitute of all powers), and Spirit, simple, unextended, properly immaterial, possessed of powers of perception, thought, and self-motion—act upon each other when they haven't a single property in common (60–62)? No one had yet proposed a satisfactory solution to this problem (63–65). The anonymous author of *Letters on Materialism* had suggested that spirit might have some properties of the inferior substance, but this was only a difference in degree between matter and spirit and essentially conceded the failure of dualism (68). Hartley had supposed an infinitesimal elementary substance, neither matter nor spirit, to link the two, but Priestley rejected this: "great as is my admiration of Dr. Hartley, it is very far from carrying me to adopt every thing in him" (79). But a solution to this problem was readily at hand, Priestley thought, if one adopted Newton's rules of philosophizing: Admit no more causes of things than are sufficient to explain appearances, and, to the same effects, as far as possible, assign the same causes (1–2).

The popularly accepted views of matter were based on vulgar, common appearances. In a remarkably unhistorical and unperceptive analysis, Priestley showed (*pace* Galileo and Newton) how the notion of inertia naturally follows from obvious, superficial observations of a billiard ball on a table (3–5). The concepts of solidity and impenetrability are also the results of superficial observation. Matter is not solid. Electrical experiments (by Priestley himself) showed how much weight was required to bring ordinary bodies into contact (13), while phenomena of temperature expansion and contraction showed that particles of bodies are themselves not in contact. The research of Newton, Thomas Melville, and others demonstrated how unfavorable the phenomena of light are to any hypothesis of solidity or impenetrability (14).

It was the opinion of modern philosophers that "all matter is ultimately the same thing, all kinds of bodies differing from one another only in the size or arrangement of their ultimate particles or atoms" (223). To this must be added, because of the discoveries of Newton, powers of attraction and repulsion. Locke, Andrew Baxter, and others asserted that these powers were the immediate agency of the deity, but the rules of philosophizing held that the constant effects of any substance be produced by powers properly belonging to it (8–9). As God can communicate powers, it is evident that he can produce such substances; this view also escaped the error of pantheism.

The apparent solidity and impenetrability of matter results from a power of repulsion of material particles from one another; extension, form, or shape equally require that the parts of bodies possess powers of mutual attraction (4–6). Matter is a substance possessed of such powers only as appearances prove, and appearances cannot be explained without supposing powers of attraction and repulsion, and of spheres of them, one within another (16). This was the opinion of Boscovich and Michell, who further supposed the ultimate particles to be physical points only, surrounded by these spheres of attraction and repulsion (19).

If it were argued that, on this hypothesis, matter is nothing because there is no substance if the powers are removed, one could answer only that we have no concept of substance except for its properties. As Priestley was later to write, in *Letters to a Philosophical Unbeliever* (26), "I know of no other definition of a substance than that which has properties. Take away all the properties of *any* thing, and nothing will be left." If those properties are fully explained by powers of attraction and repulsion, then substance vanishes when those powers are removed (351–52). How then does matter differ from spirit? True philosophy need not maintain that there is a difference (16). If you say, "on my hypothesis, there is no such thing as matter . . . every thing is spirit, I have no objection, provided . . . [you] make as great a difference in *spirit* as hitherto made in *substances*. The world has been too long amused with mere names" (353).

As the only reason that the principle of thought has been supposed incompatible with matter has been the belief in material impenetrability, the argument for an immaterial thinking principle dissolves (18). If the properties of sensation, perception, and thought are not logically impossible to matter, the rules of philosophizing require that no other substance is necessary. These properties are never found except in conjunction with that organized system of matter, the brain. The faculty of thought and the state of the brain accompany and correspond to each other; this is the only reason that any property is ever thought inherent in any substance (26–27). Any other hypothesis is not only without a fact to support it but contrary to all appearances.

How can material substances think? We cannot answer this question any more than we can answer how immaterial substance thinks. Persons prepared to accept an incomprehensible union of totally discrepant natures of mind and matter object with ill grace to the incomprehensibility of thinking matter (82–83). Once one accepts the possibility of simple perception in matter, all else follows on Hartley's doctrine of vibrations. There is no reason to believe that perception might not belong to a system of matter, though not to its component parts. (In *Letters to a Philosophical Unbeliever*, Priestley wrote that the faculty of thinking may be the result of an arrangement of the parts of the brain, which separately have no thought [26].) Sound proceeds from a mass of air, yet no single particle of air can sound (88–89). Materiality of the soul, and therefore its extension, does not mean divisibility into smaller souls, or intelligent systems. Systems of matter (e.g., a sphere) cannot be cut into two equivalent systems. To say, with the author of *Letters on Materialism,* that space is defined by the extensive order of coexisting bodies and therefore that space could not exist without matter is unthinkable (59).

No discussion of the nature of the soul, Priestley continued, has anything whatever to do with the nature of the divine essence. Too little is known of the essence of humanity and much less of that of God; indeed, we have no proper idea of any essence whatever (103–4). The divine nature must have properties so essentially different from everything else that we certainly deceive ourselves if we call things so different by any common name. On a subject so far above all human comprehension and, moreover, so irrelevant, toleration of differences of opinion is required. It is not the substance of God, but his properties that we revere. "[O]ur practical knowledge of God stands independent of any conception whatever concerning even the *divine essence*" (47).

The human body probably is the seat of all the powers exerted by man, but the marks of design in the constitution of man are superior to anything that man might achieve and must have a vastly superior cause (*Ltrs. Phil. Unbel.,* 148). Though neither reason nor appearance supports it, men still argue for immateriality, that some principle in man may subsist, resist corruption of the flesh, and be capable of sensation and action after death (35). But the incorruptibility of immaterial substance is by definition only, unsupported by evidence (101), while observations show a variety of mental affections that suggest alteration, depravation, and even corruption of the mind and the soul. For what are vicious habits, vices, and immorality but diseases of the mind? To suggest that freeing the soul from the body will purge the soul of sin is contrary to Christian doctrine (39–40), while the supposition of the mind's independence of the body absurdly suggests that disease or death would improve the quality of thought (29).

Priestley believed that every general system must be consistent and have all its parts properly filled in. This was not possible for the system of immaterialism, which left innumerable questions unanswered (43). When does the body become possessed of a soul? Is it created at the moment of sexual union, or, if it is preexistent, where was it prior to its embodiment and by what rule does it descend? "Must . . . unembodied spirits become embodied in *rotation,* according to some *rank,* and condition, or must it be determined by *lot,* &c?" (42). "Of what use is the body in this system? If the body impedes and clogs the soul, is this contagion of flesh and blood the 'blessed hope' promised by St. Peter in the resurrection of the body?" (43–48). What happens to the "immaterial soul" during the thousands of years between death of the body and the general resurrection (123)? The Bishop of Carlisle (Edmund Law), for example, and Archdeacon Blackburne supposed a "sleep of the soul" till the resurrection, but how was this better than a dissolution until that divinely revealed event (155)?[3]

None of these problems impeded the materialist system, according to Priestley. The soul is part of the system of the body and is created as that system is created. When the system dissolves, so does the soul, "till it shall please the Almighty Being who called it into existence to restore it to life again" (49). But if the system dissolves, how is personality retained? The identity of rivers remains, though their waters change. If, over time, every material particle of a *man* changes, the *person* remains the same (157–59). Some people (Watts and Charles Bonnet, for example) supposed the "germs" of all future identities were contained in the first germ of the species, but, Priestley pointed out, this was quite unnecessary. There is no reference to body-soul duality in Scripture, except "a few passages, ill translated, or ill understood, standing in manifest contradiction to the uniform tenor of the rest" (114). On a subject of such great importance, there surely would have been a discussion of this duality, yet no use is made, anywhere in the New Testament, of an argument about the separate and independent existence of the soul (130). There is no hint of the nature or the use of an intermediate state before the general resurrection, no reference to purgatory, and certainly nothing about the worship of the dead (50).

Now, truth is independent of the opinions of men (166), but a person had to wonder at the persistence of an opinion contrary to Scripture, to appearances, and to reason. Some ancient heathen authority must be its cause. In the infancy of the world, speculations about the nature of man and the moral government of God produced wild and extravagant systems of beliefs (244).

---

3. On the "sleep of the soul," note that Thomas Henry Huxley, in his address on dedicating a statue of Priestley raised in 1874, and published in his *Science and Education* (New York: D. Appleton & Co., 1897), 24–25, observed that Priestley's opinion was substantially upheld by Dr. Richard Whateley, Archbishop of Dublin in 1831, in his *Essay on some Peculiarities of the Christian Religion* (London, 1825), and by Dr. Courtenay, Bishop of Kingston in Jamaica, in *On the Future State* (1843).

Among these were the concepts of the Persians, Chaldeans, Egyptians, and Indians, which defined matter as evil and souls as preexisting intelligences, emanating from a world soul or supreme mind (250–51).

Priestley's information about non-Christian religions was, as he admitted, necessarily limited. Egyptian writing had yet to be translated and he relied on Greek accounts, the Old Testament, and Mosheim. For the Persians and the Chaldeans, he was dependent on Beausobre's *Manicheism* and on Thomas Stanley's *History of Chaldaick Philosophy* (1662). For the Sikhs, Buddhists, and Hindus, he was even less critically informed. Sanskrit had scarcely begun to be read in the West and Indian vernaculars were read primarily for administrative purposes. He used Andrew M. Ramsay's *Les Voyages de Cyrus* (1757), but his major sources were works of employees of the East India Company: John Z. Holwell's *Historical Events relative to the Provinces of Bengal* and Alexander Dow's *History of Hindostan.* In these, precise information had been curiously and variously transliterated and, at least in Priestley's summary, very little of the development, variations, or spirituality of Indian religions was conveyed. The concepts of metempsychosis and nirvana were reported, however. It was these that Priestley held had been assimilated into the philosophies of Greece and Rome.[4]

Owing to divine intervention, Jews and early Christians had escaped these mischievous tendencies (245), but in the spreading of Christianity, philosophically minded gentiles attempted to evade the fact and paradox of a crucified Savior by introducing the notion of his preexistence. They argued on the basis of Greek philosophy and concepts of emanations from a supreme being producing matter and a hierarchy of spirits. The lesser ones inhabited material bodies as a punishment for sin, from which they might eventually purge themselves and return to the supreme mind from

---

4. Priestley's main discussion of "Oriental religions" is to be found on 254–66. Isaac de Beausobre's work on the Manicheans was described by Edward Gibbon as "a treasure of ancient philosophy and theology." See *W.* 3:266n. Thomas Stanley compiled a *History of Oriental Philosophy;* the Chaldeans were the subject of vol. 4. Andrew Ramsay wrote his *Les Voyages de Cyrus, avec un Discours sur la Mythologie des Payens* (Paris, 1727) in imitation of Telemachus. For John Holwell and Alexander Dow, see Peter J. Marshall, ed. *British Discovery of Hinduism in the Eighteenth Century* (Cambridge: Cambridge University Press, 1970), especially the introduction, 1–44. Holwell studied some Indian languages and Arabic and is said to be the first Englishman to study Hindu antiquities; his *Historical Events relative to the Provinces of Bengal and the Empire of Indostan* (London, 1765), his *Mythology of the Gentoos* (London, 1766), and his *Dissertation on the Metempsychosis* (London, 1771) were early English studies of Hindu religions. Alexander Dow's *History of Hindostan* (1768, 1772) was supposedly a translation from one of the most trustworthy of Oriental historians, Mahommed Kasim Ferishta (c. 1578–1611), though the "translation" was very free and mixed with Dow's glosses.

which they issued (250–51). The first sign of this "oriental system" in the New Testament was found in Paul's Epistles to the Corinthians, where he warned against Greek "wisdom" and insisted on belief in resurrection of the body. The full flood of Platonism, Gnosticism, and hermeticism comes in post-apostolic commentaries. Such early church fathers as Origen, Clemens Alexandrinus, and even Augustine (all students of neo-Platonism) used Platonic and Pythagoric philosophy to illustrate mysteries (281–93). And by this easy channel, corruptions of the preexistence of souls, Arianism, Trinitarianism, worship of saints, etc., flowed into the Christian system (299). It was "a capital advantage of the doctrine of *Materialism,* that it leaves no shadow of support for the doctrine of *pre-existence*" (355).

In the Preface to the *Disquisitions,* Priestley claimed that his monism ("materialism") was of very recent adoption, that it was only while writing the *Examination* and preparing his edition of *Hartley* that he had had any serious doubts about the immateriality of the soul (xi–xiii). No doubt this is true, so far as an explicit, organized articulation of his thoughts was concerned, but even a cursory survey of its arguments reveals that the *Disquisitions* was the culmination of Priestley's reading and thinking over many years. It is singularly appropriate that the *Disquisitions* was dedicated to William Graham, whom he had met at his aunt's table in 1750 or 1751: "it was, in a great measure, by your example and encouragement, at my entrance on theological enquiries, that I adventured to think for myself on subjects of great importance" (vi).

Elements of the *Disquisitions* can be found in the books of Priestley's self-education before he went to Daventry. Man's necessary ignorance of any but a nominal essence of things he could first have learned from Locke; the continuance of matter only at the will of God from Watts; and the existence in matter of principles of attraction and repulsion from 'sGravesande, in whose *Mathematical Elements of Natural Philosophy* he might also first have read Isaac Newton's "Rules of Reasoning." From Watts he might also have learned that chemists regard all matter as the same, diversified only by its various shapes, quantities, motions, and situations.[5]

To this would have been added, when he read Rowning's *Compendious System of Natural Philosophy* at Daventry, those principles of gravitation, cohesive attraction, and elastic repulsion acting in concentric spheres about the particles of matter, providing an example of divine wisdom in the variety of effects produced by so short and easy a method. Newtonian forces are

5. For Priestley's early education, see Schofield, *Enlightenment of Priestley,* chaps. 1 and 2.

the physical evidences of an immanent God and the continued existence of matter, its solidity, gravity, and motion require the continued exertion of the will of God. Daventry, moreover, provided Priestley, via Doddridge's *Lectures on Pneumatology,* with a formal introduction to metaphysical problems and disputes. Against Locke's radical empiricism on real essences was opposed a radical idealism: we can have no conception of substance distinct from its properties. To Watt's denial of space independent of matter was opposed Henry More's indestructibility of space: if the whole material world were annihilated space would still remain what it was before. The *Pneumatology* confirmed Watt's distinction between spirit, defined by its power of thinking, and matter, defined by its solid extension ("solid extension cannot think"), but added the caution that man knows too little about his nature and existence to be dogmatic about them. Daventry also introduced Priestley to Hartley's *Observations on Man,* with its theory of vibrations. And, in the "Preliminary Dissertation" to a *Paraphrase of 1 Corinthians Chap. XV* (1766), by John Alexander, who had been his roommate at Daventry and remained a friend and correspondent until his death in 1765, Priestley would have found an argument for the sleep of the soul between death and the general resurrection (*W.* 1.1:25n.).

He had little time for metaphysical speculations at Needham Market, Nantwich, or Warrington, but his electrical studies at Warrington gave him experience with action-at-a-distance forces, suggested that electrical matter might be only a modification of ordinary substance, and, in the writing of Aepinus, reintroduced him to the concept of spheres of influence. At Leeds he read (or reread) Nathaniel Lardner's *Letter on the Logos,* in which he would find the citing of early church fathers to support theological arguments, the claim that learned converts from heathenism had introduced the concept of a preexisting inferior deity into Christianity, and the statement that, in Scripture, the word *body* was not understood as separate from the soul. This last opinion would find some confirmation in the words of Edward Elwall's *Trial,* which Priestley edited for republication in 1770: Man's spirit is not a person distinct from man; the word of a man and the spirit of a man are the man himself.

In Priestley's published writing of the Leeds period, there is also anticipation of the arguments of the *Disquisitions.* The *Free Address on Church Discipline* (1770) notes the debasing of the true system of Christianity by "Oriental, or more properly, Indian philosophy." His *Letters and Queries* of 1771 insists that nature was a gift of God and could not, therefore, be a malign principle. An article vindicating the Socinian hypothesis, in the

Theological Repository for 1771, traces the Arian position on the preexistence of Christ to Gnostics, discusses dependence of mind on body, and refers to Dr. Law and others on the "sleep of the soul." *Familiar Illustrations* (1772) argues for religious belief and practice based on the primitive church.

The *Vegetable Staticks,* which Priestley read in 1770 as he commenced "taking up some of Dr. Hales's inquiries concerning Air," employed the concept of attractive and repulsive powers of matter: "If all the parts of matter were only endued with a strongly attracting power, whole nature would then immediately become one unactive cohering lump; wherefore it was absolutely necessary, in order to the actuating and enlivening this vast mass of attracting matter, that there should be every where intermix'd with it a due proportion of strongly repelling elastick particles, which might enliven the whole mass."[6] These are the powers Priestley describes in *The History of Optics* (1772) in terms of the matter theory of Rowning, Boscovich, and Michell, with its spheres of attraction and repulsion.

The impression that this theory made on Priestley, clear enough in the *Disquisitions,* was earlier indicated in his letter of 7 March 1773 to Joseph Bretland:

> Mr. Michell supposes that wherever the properties or powers of any substance are, there is the substance itself, something that we call *substance* being necessary to the support of any properties; but what any substance is, devoid of all properties, we cannot, from the nature of the thing, have any idea whatever; since all the notices we receive of any substance are communicated to us by means of its properties. . . . And any property may be ascribed to any substance that does not suppose the absence of some other *known* property. Boscovich seems to suppose that matter consists of *powers* only, without any substance.

Clearly Priestley had already at hand major parts of the *Disquisitions* before his "particular attention to the subject . . . terminated in a full conviction." It is equally clear, from his reading both before and after he commenced explicitly to consider the subject, that there was some justice in the complaint of Priestley's critics that he had only revived an opinion long ago argued and as long ago refuted. Some justice, but only some. The arguments

6. Stephen Hales, *Vegetable Staticks . . .* (reprint, London: Oldbourne, 1961), 178. For detailed information on Priestley's reading and writing during his years at Warrington Academy and in Leeds, see Schofield, *Enlightenment of Priestley.*

of John Toland, Anthony Collins, and others had been insufficient to over-
come critics like Samuel Clarke and William Wollaston. Now, Priestley certainly knew the work of Hobbes and Collins. He cited Toland, Clarke,
Woolaston, and the Cambridge neo-Platonists (particularly Ralph Cudworth)
in the *Disquisitions*.[7] But his "materialism" was different from that argued in
the seventeenth and early eighteenth centuries, though he certainly adopted
some aspects of it.[8] He answered earlier refutations by combining a new
physiological theory of thought with a new theory of matter based on a
new science. Newton's *Principia* and *Opticks* had raised questions for which
extra-material forces of gravity and elasticity were introduced and the existence of other forces was suggested.

   The failure of force hypotheses satisfactorily to explain phenomena of electricity and magnetism, chemistry and biology, had, by Priestley's day, occasioned a return to explanations by what were in effect Aristotelian substantial
forms and qualities. "Orthodox" scientific theories posited substances of
heat, electricity, and magnetism and were even suggesting quality-carrying
chemical elements. Contemporary French "materialists," such as Mauper-
tuis, La Mettrie, Holbach, and Diderot, derived out of Leibniz's monads a
hylozoist argument that ultimate particles of matter possessed qualities of
sentience, emotion, and thought. Scottish Common Sense philosophers had
invested that immaterial substance, the mind, with multiple original principles, or qualities of perception. To these alternatives, bordering on rampant
pluralism, Priestley opposed his mechanistic monism, which held to the idea
of Newtonian forces, as elaborated by Michell and Boscovich, and to the
physiological mechanisms of Hartley's vibrational associationism.[9]

   7. Priestley's references to the literature of the neo-Platonists were considerable. He referred
to the writings of Theophilus Gale in the *Disquisitions* and in his article "An Essay on the One
Great End of the Life an Death of Christ," published under the name "Clemens" in *Theological
Repository* 1 (1769); he noted that of Cudworth and his *Intellectual System* in the *Disquisitions*
under the pseudonym "Josephus" in "Animadversions on the Preface to . . . Mordecai's Letters,"
Theological Repository 4 (1784), and *An History of Early Opinions Concerning Jesus Christ* (1786).

   8. F. H. Heinemann, "John Toland and the Age of Enlightenment," *Review of English Studies* 28 (1944): 125–46; James O'Higgins, *Anthony Collins: The Man and His Works* (The Hague:
Martinus Nijhoff, 1970), 69–75. Benjamin Franklin also once wrote on immateriality and
immortality of the soul, in a reply to William Woolaston's *Religion of Nature delineated* (Lon-
don, 1725); see Alfred Owen Aldridge, "Benjamin Franklin and Philosophical Necessity,"
Modern Language Quarterly 12 (1951): 292–309, esp. 307. See also John W. Yalton, *Thinking
Matter: Materialism in Eighteenth-Century Britain* (Minneapolis: University of Minnesota
Press, 1983), for materialism up to and including Priestley.

   9. For details of material-quality explanations in eighteenth-century science, see Robert E.
Schofield, *Mechanism and Materialism: British Natural Philosophy in an Age of Reason* (Princeton: Princeton University Press, 1970). French theories are discussed in Colm Kiernan, *The

That this was no traditional materialism is obvious; it was, to some people, obvious at the time. William Bewley, in reviewing the *Disquisitions*, wrote: "Having . . . spiritualized matter by . . . animating it . . . with powers, to the activity of which we owe all that we know concerning it;—the Author proceeds to shew that this substance may likewise possess the properties or powers of sensation or perception, and thought . . . in consequence of a certain organization, whatever that may be." Despite his lame description of it, Bewley recognized the immaterial aspects of "Priestley's" theory of matter; so also did William Whewell, who declared that a world in which Boscovichean atomism was true "would not be a material world."[10] For "Priestley's" theory of matter, essentially that of Rowning, Michell, and Boscovich, came increasingly to be identified with Boscovich.

Yet in Britain, at least, it might as fairly have been called that of Boscovich-Priestley. Although Priestley declared, in a letter to Joseph Bretland in December 1777, "Almost every body smiles at my notion of matter," the fascination of British scientists for Boscovichian atomism during the nineteenth century appears to stem from Priestley's advocacy of it. William Herschel's interest in Boscovich and that of William Rowan Hamilton certainly came from the reading of Priestley's *History of Optics*. A *Philosophical Magazine* article describing research of Ottaviano F. Mossotti on laws of molecular action was followed by a note calling attention to accounts of "similar theories of Father Boscovich and Mr. Michell, in Dr. Priestley's Disquisitions on Matter and Spirit and in his Correspondence with Dr. Price."[11]

The involvement of Lord Kelvin and James Clerk Maxwell (and of J. J. Thomson) with Boscovichianism may be said to begin with the interest of Michael Faraday, and this shows evidence of his having read Priestley. In "Speculations touching Electrical Conduction and the Nature of Matter"

Enlightenment and Science in Eighteenth-Century France (Banbury: Voltaire Foundation, Studies on Voltaire and the Eighteenth Century, No. 59A, 1973). French materialist explanations of life and mind in relation to theology are nicely described in H. W. Piper, *The Active Universe: Pantheism and the Concept of Imagination in English Romantic Poets* (London: Athlone Press, 1962), 16–21.

10. William Bewley, "Disquisitions relating to Matter and Spirit . . . ," *Monthly Review; or Literary Journal* 58 (1778): 347–53—a neutral, purely descriptive review, mildly approving of the work's ingenuity without accepting its conclusions. Whewell is quoted by David Knight, *Atoms and Elements: A Study of Theories of Matter in England in the Nineteenth Century* (London: Hutchinson, 1967), 13.

11. For Herschel, see Schofield, *Mechanism and Materialism*, 249–52; for Hamilton, see Robert Hugh Kargon, "William Rowan Hamilton and Boscovichean Atomism," *Journal of the History of Ideas* 26 (1965): 137–40. For the editorial notice of Priestley's *Disquisition*, etc., see *Philosophical Magazine* 10 (3d ser., 1837): 357.

(1844), Faraday criticized an atomic theory that defined the atom as "something material, having a certain volume, upon which those powers were impressed at the creation, which have given it . . . the capability of constituting . . . the different substances whose effects and properties we observe." He announced his partiality for the atoms of Boscovich as assuming the least amount possible. In a theory of material nuclei, surrounded by powers: "To my mind . . . the nucleus vanishes, and the substance consists of the powers . . . and indeed what notion can we form of a nucleus independent of its powers? . . . A mind just entering on the subject may consider it difficult to think of the powers of matter independent of a separate something to be called the matter, but it is certainly far more difficult, and indeed impossible, to think of or imagine that matter independent of the powers." This reads so much like a paraphrase of Priestley's *Disquisitions* that it has recently been argued that these ideas of Faraday on the nature of matter originally derive from Priestley's work. Whether or not one agrees, it is clear that, to scientists, Priestley's theory of matter was neither absurd nor distressing. Scientists, at least so far as their science was concerned, were more interested in the heuristic value of the theory than in its metaphysical problems.[12]

For the majority of Priestley's readers, however, the reaction was the reverse. Even Bewley disassociated himself from the "materialist" conclusions of the *Disquisitions,* Richard Price engaged Priestley in a published dispute about them, and Priestley's enemies, usually failing to understand and sometimes willfully misconstruing his theory, continued to insist that he must believe what they considered the atheistic consequences of any materialism. More than a dozen refutations of the *Disquisitions* were published by the date of its second edition (1782).

Boscovich was furious. He'd been told that Priestley represented him as a "favourer of the most extravagant materialism," and was not satisfied when Priestley assured him that it was only his theory of matter from which "materialism" had been developed, without any suggestion that Boscovich would approve that use of it. As he didn't read English, Boscovich may have overreacted to what others had told him, but he had been very careful to insist upon the difference between matter and spirit. He threatened to defend

12. P. M. Heimann, "Faraday's Theories of Matter and Electricity," *British Journal for the History of Science* 5 (1971): 235–57. The quotations from Faraday are from his paper "Speculations touching Electrical Conduction . . . ," *Philosophical Magazine* 24 (3d ser., 1844): 136–44, 136, 141. A discussion of Boscovich's attraction to British scientists can be found in Schofield, *Mechanism and Materialism,* 236–41.

himself against Priestley's inferences in the public journals—a threat that apparently was never carried out (*SciAuto.*, 79, 80).

Other responses varied. Augustus Toplady predictably approved its necessarian implications, but accepted no more than that part of the *Disquisitions*. He thought Priestley probably understood matter better than any philosopher on earth, but it was plain that his acquaintance with spirit had not been cultivated with equal assiduity. Publication of the *Disquisitions* had not lessened Toplady's respect and esteem, for he liked a person whose principles were openly acknowledged: "Give me the person whom I can hold up as I can a piece of crystal, and see through him. For this, among many other excellencies, I regard and admire Dr. Priestley" (*W.* 1.1:308). The Rev. David Davis, a Welsh Presbyterian, sent a *jeu d'esprit* to Richard Price, who read it to the amused Priestley: "Here lie at rest, \ In oaken chest, \ Together packed most nicely, \ The bones and brains, \ Flesh, blood and veins, \ And *soul* of Dr. Priestley."[13] Someone attempted to discredit Priestley by implying that he believed the claims of an eccentric Pembroke College student, John Henderson, to have called up spirits (Priestley denied it). Later, an otherwise liberal Whig clergyman, Richard Warner, attempted to include him in a story about precognition and a ghost, relating to the death of young William Petty in 1778. The story was not published until years after Priestley's death, and Thomas Jervis denied its validity indignantly and in detail.[14]

Not all of the responses were hostile. The Rev. Samuel Badcock, later a vicious critic of Priestley for the *Monthly Review,* defended Priestley's materialism from the charge of infidelity in *A Slight Sketch of the Controversy between Dr. Priestley and his Opponents on the Subject of his Disquisitions on Matter and Spirit* (1780). The majority of answers were bellicose, however. Brewster's *Edinburgh Encyclopaedia* (1830) declared that Priestley was "unworthy of notice as a metaphysician," but his views continued to be discussed well into the nineteenth century.[15] William Drummond had earlier

13. David Davis, "Obituary," *Monthly Repository* 1 (n.s., 1827): 693–95, 695. Note that Davis formally moved the resolution of "an Association of Dissenting Ministers," in Cardiganshire, deploring the Birmingham Riots of 1791.

14. See [John Henderson], "Two Letters from Mr. Henderson to Dr. Priestley, communicated by Dr. P. to the Gentleman's Magazine, April 1788," *Monthly Repository* 7 (1812): 286–92. Warner published his story in *Literary Recollections* (1830), the year before he published a tract, *Anti-Materialist.* Jervis categorically denied the story in *Remarks on some Passages in the Literary Recollections of the Rev. Richard Warner* (London: R. Hunter, 1831–32). See also Petty, *Life of Shelburne*, 2:330–31.

15. David Brewster, ed., *Edinburgh Encyclopaedia*, American ed. (Philadelphia: Joseph & Edward Parker, 1832), vol. 13, *Art: "Metaphysics,"* 107. The article was by James Esdaile, recently graduated from Edinburgh University, whose knowledge of metaphysics would have

been more gracious, in his *Academical Questions* (1805), where he described Priestley as "the ablest advocate of the Philosophy [of materialism], of which I am now speaking," though he thought to confute him with a jejune demonstration that matter would disappear in Priestley's definition of it.

Shortly afterward an American joined the fray, when Joseph Buchanan published his scarcely noticed *Philosophy of Human Nature* (1812). This was a thoroughly materialist work that failed to mention Priestley but adopted many of the same ideas and was heavily derivative from many of Priestley's sources. Naturally the book was vigorously denounced as atheistic by contemporary American clergy.[16] John Barclay's *An Inquiry into the Opinions, Ancient and Modern, concerning Life and Organization* (1822) is another example of the continuing criticism of Priestley's ideas, devoting fourteen pages to a critique of the *Disquisitions* and attacking Priestley's character, lack of prudence, strength of judgment, and reflection. This was immediately answered by Thomas Cooper's *Scripture Doctrine of Materialism,* together with a pamphlet on materialism first published in England in 1781, and an "Outline of the Association of Ideas," all republished as appendices to Cooper's translation of F. J. V. Broussais's *On Irritation and Insanity* (1831). Cooper had been a friend and disciple of Priestley and went to the United States about the same time as Priestley; his response was enlivened by an invective that finally matched that to which Priestley and his ideas had long been subjected: "I am aware of the 'faculties of the mind' the numberless brood of the Scotch metaphysicians. I cannot and will not condescend to reply to the dreadful nonsense on this subject assumed as true by Dr. Reid and Dr. Beattie, or the shallow sophisms of Dr. Gregory, or the prolix pages of inanity of Dr. Dugald Stewart, or the ignorant hardihood of assertion of Dr. Barclay in his late inquiry."[17]

---

been acquired from supporters of Scottish Common Sense, and his opinion is neither surprising nor unprejudiced; Esdaile also despised Hume and was merely confused by Kant.

16. William Drummond, *Academical Questions* (London: W. Bulmer and Co., 1805), 396. There have been two recent reprints of Joseph Buchanan, *The Philosophy of Human Nature* (Gainsville, Fla.: Scholars' Facsimiles & Reprints, 1969), intro. by Thom. Verhave; and (Weston, Mass.: M. & S. Press, 1970), intro. by James F. Adams. Neither introduction, nor the paper by James F. Adams and Arnold A. Hoberman, "Joseph Buchanan, 1785–1839, Pioneer American Psychologist," *Journal of the History of the Behavioral Sciences* 5 (1969): 340–48, seems aware of just how derivative Buchanan's work was.

17. John Barclay, *An Inquiry . . . concerning Life and Organization* (Edinburgh: Bell & Bradfute, Waugh and Innes; London: G. & W. B. Whittaker, 1822), 174–87, esp. 183, 187; Thomas Cooper, *Scripture Doctrine of Materialism* (Philadelphia: A. Small, 1823); Thomas Cooper, *A View of the Metaphysical and Physiological Arguments in Favor of Materialism* (first published at Warrington, England, 1781; reprinted in Philadelphia with some alterations by

By the 1850s the theological debate had nearly ceased. Unitarian leadership had become so romanticized, discreet, and genteel that it had repudiated Priestley; a major part of their gravamen was his "materialism."[18] Nor was Priestley's theological position helped by his *Disquisitions'* being cited by such notorious "free thinkers" as Robert Cooper and Charles Bradlaugh, though Bradlaugh, at least, understood Priestley's interpretation of matter as force or spirit.[19] It must, then, have been particularly satisfying to Thomas K. Cromwell to write, "Justice to Priestley—Dr. Scholten on Materialism—'The Soul and the Future Life,'" for the 1861 *Christian Reformer.* Cromwell had cited Priestley's *Disquisitions* favorably in *The Soul and the Future Life* (1859), though he ignored the transformation of substance into forces. Reviewers attacked the book, supporting orthodoxy and ignoring Cromwell's arguments. Now, he pointed out, Jan Hendrick Scholten, professor of theology at Leiden, had written "Modern Materialism and Its Causes," which adopted monism (denying that it was materialist) and conceded almost every position taken by Priestley's *Disquisitions,* without appearing to know of that work.

Dualism, said Scholten, is a worn-out conception and was denied by Kant. He declared that "we have no means to distinguish between matter and force." Spiritual force is not independent of the body, and mind separated from matter would be an empty abstraction. The notion of a soul existing independently of body had given rise to spectres, demonical possessions, transmigration of souls, preexistence of souls, a state intermediate between death and the resurrection. Did God create a soul for every new organism? This, as Cromwell observed, reads as though extracted from the *Disquisitions.* Scholten's "monadism" had caught up with the monism that Priestley, unfortunately for his argument, had persisted in calling "materialism."[20]

A. Small, 1823); and "Outline of the Association of Ideas," all as appendices to F. J. V. Broussais, *On Irritation and Insanity* (Columbia, S.C.: S. J. M'Morris, 1831), trans. Thomas Cooper, 342–43, and elsewhere.

18. That attitude was developing even earlier. See, for example, James Martineau, "The Life and Works of Dr. Priestley," in Martineau, *Essays, Reviews, and Addresses* (London: Longmans, Green and Co., 1890), 1:1–42. Originally published in the *Monthly Repository* as a review of J. T. Rutt's edition of Priestley's works, it includes, amid its pages of "faint praise," the remark that Priestley has been "misled by the plausible analogy which promises to explain the phenomena of mind by the changes of matter" (22).

19. See Edward Royle, *Victorian Infidels: The Origins of the British Secularist Movement 1792–1866* (Manchester: Manchester University Press, 1974), 117–18.

20. Thomas Cromwell, "Justice to Priestley," *Christian Reformer* 8 (n.s., 1861): 33–36; Thomas Cromwell, *The Soul and the Future Life* (London: Edward T. Whitfield, 1859); Jan Hendrik Scholten, "Modern Materialism and Its Causes," in *The Progress of Religious Thought*

Perhaps the adoption, by liberal continental theologians, of essentials from Priestley's thinking directed some of the animus toward "materialism" away from Priestley. Certainly, by 1861, conservative and orthodox Christians had, in Darwinism, more pressing concerns than the writings of someone who had been dead more than half a century. It was far easier to dismiss Priestley as a materialist without reading him than to face the possibility that here too he had been greatly wronged; and the memory of the *Disquisitions* was finally allowed to disappear in theological as well as scientific circles.[21]

---

as illustrated in the Protestant Church of France . . . , trans. and ed. John Relly Beard, transl. and edit. (London: Simpkin, Marshall & Co.; Boston: Walker, Wise & Co., 1861), 10–48.

21. Later monists, represented for example by Paul Carus, who edited the journal the *Monist* from 1890 to 1919 and published in it a host of articles favoring varieties of monism, fail to mention Priestley, as does Gilbert Ryle, *Concept of Mind* (New York: Barnes & Noble Books, 1949), 22. Ryle denies the "hallowed contrast between Mind and Matter," but also the "equally hallowed absorptions of Mind by Matter or of Matter by Mind," insisting that these are not terms of the same logical type.

V

PHILOSOPHICAL NECESSITY

Much the same thing, and for the same reasons, happened to Priestley's *Doctrine of Philosophical Necessity Illustrated*.[1] Priestley insisted that "The greatest difficulty in the consideration of the subject of liberty and necessity have arisen from ambiguities in the use of terms" (54). By his definition, the doctrine of philosophical necessity permits everything that is usually asserted of freedom of the will; so long as there are no external constraints, man has the power to do whatever he wills, turn his thoughts to whatever subject he pleases, consider the reasons for or against any proposition, reflect upon them as long as he pleases, suspend volition, and act upon his decisions (2, 4). "All the *liberty,* or rather *power,* that I say a man has not, is that *of doing several things when all the previous circumstances* (including the *state of his mind* and his *view of things*) are precisely the same" (7).

If there were no essential differences between the doctrine of philosophical necessity and the commonly understood concept of free will, why did Priestley choose to write a long and prolix treatise on the subject? Why

1. Joseph Priestley, *The Doctrine of Philosophical Necessity Illustrated: Being an Appendix to the Disquisitions relating to Matter and Spirit. To Which is added, An Answer to the Letters on Materialism, and on Hartley's Theory of the Mind* (London: J. Johnson, 1777). I have used the second (and last) edition (Birmingham: J. Johnson, 1782), for which the additions were increased and renamed *An Answer to several Persons who have controverted the Principles of it.* As these answers were also added to Priestley's *Free Discussion with Dr. Price* (1778), I have postponed treatment of them.

return to the subject over and over again, as he had done in the *Institutes of Natural Religion,* his *Examination* of the Scottish philosophers, his edition of *Hartley,* and the *Disquisitions?* And why argue in defense of his particular interpretation, as he was to do in at least four separate publications after the appearance of *Necessity Illustrated?* Part of the reason was that the subject followed naturally from the *Disquisitions.* Though philosophical necessity did not require the truth of the *Disquisitions,* the one supported the other. If man was material, his actions must be mechanical, and if they were mechanical, they must be subject to laws of nature—as required in Priestley's doctrine of philosophical necessity (xvii). More important, however, was the significance of an argument on free will and determinism to theologians in general and to Priestley in particular.

Priestley acknowledged that his doctrine of necessity was not original with him: Hobbes had stated its essentials, Cambridge neo-Platonists (especially John Norris and Ralph Cudworth) had argued for some parts of it, Spinoza and Locke had discussed it.[2] Anthony Collins's *Philosophical Inquiry concerning Human Liberty* (1717) had converted Priestley to the doctrine, and David Hartley had confirmed him in it. Jonathan Edwards had written supporting necessarian beliefs; David Hume, who called the question of liberty and necessity "the most contentious question of metaphysics," had tried to reconcile the two, Richard Price had questioned Hume's reconciliation, and, long after Priestley, into the twentieth century, the subject continued to generate vigorous philosophical debates.[3]

Nonetheless, Priestley did not write *Necessity Illustrated* to exploit some part of a popular philosophical debate. For persons who might want a complete treatise on philosophical necessity, he recommended the reading of Edwards, Hartley, Hume, Lord Kames, and especially Collins's *Philosophical*

2. Priestley cited Hobbes and Locke in his *Philosophical Necessity Illustrated;* the opinions of Cambridge neo-Platonists can be found in John H. Muirhead, *The Platonic Tradition in Anglo-Saxon Philosophy: Studies in the History of Idealism in England and America* (New York: Macmillan, 1931), esp. 30, 68, and 92; and in Mattoon Monroe Curtis, "Kantian Elements in Jonathan Edwards," in *Philosophische Abhandlungen: Max Heinze sum 70 Geburtstage* (Berlin: E.S. Mittler und Sohn, 1906), 34–62. Rosalie L. Colie, "Spinoza and the Early English Deists," *Journal of the History of Ideas* 20 (1959): 23–45, believed Priestley's necessarianism could be called Spinozist but that he probably derived it through Collins and Toland.

3. Collins, Hartley, Hume, and Price are cited in *Philosophical Necessity Illustrated;* the quotation from Hume is cited by William Bewley in his review of the *Doctrine of Philosophical Necessity Illustrated, Monthly Review; or, Literary Journal* 58 (1778): 354–62, 355. For a survey of continuing discussions in philosophy and theology, see Bernard Berofsky, "Free Will and Determinism," 236–42, and Austin Farrer, "Free Will in Theology," 242–48, in Weiner, *Dictionary of the History of Ideas,* vol. 2.

Inquiry, a small tract that, he said, he wished were reprinted and that he finally reprinted himself, with an introduction, in 1790 (xix, xxvii). For Priestley, the doctrine of philosophical necessity was a matter of continuing personal influence and concern. It represented the relationship of cause and effect, and therefore disclosed God: "if *one* effect might take place without a sufficient cause, another, and all effects, might have been without a cause; which entirely takes away the only argument for the being of a God" (16). It directly followed from the one aspect of his Calvinist heritage that he had retained: a belief in the omnipotence and omniscience of God.[4] He had given up his liberty with considerable reluctance (xxvii), but having done so, the conviction that "all things, past, present, and to come, are precisely what the Author of nature really intended them to be, and has made provision for" (9), and an unreserved confidence in the goodness and providential care of God, produced that serenity of mind and cheerful acceptance of circumstances that were such marked characteristics of Priestley throughout his life (120–21). This was the aspect of the doctrine of necessity that he wanted to share with others.

What he wrote was, in fact, an ingenious piece of sophistry. He insisted that the doctrine of necessity was more consistent with the expectations of most people than that of free will, if each was properly understood. Liberty and necessity were perfectly commensurate with each other. Voluntary was not opposed to necessary, but to involuntary; chance, or contingency, opposed to necessary (16). Nonetheless, there is an absolute determinism in Priestley's necessity: there is no distinction between moral and physical necessity (69). As, in the physical world, the connection between cause and effect is invariable and therefore necessary, so, in the mind, there is some fixed law of nature. The will is always determined by motive. With the same state of mind, and the same view of things, the motive remains the same, and man will always voluntarily make the same choice and come to the same determination (7–8, 10). Motives, or determinations of the will, are nothing more than particular cases of association of ideas (46) and are necessary links in the chain of causes and events. As Priestley wrote in his edition of Hartley's *Observations:* "each action results from previous circumstances of body and mind, in the same manner, and with the same certainty, as other effects do from their mechanical causes" (334).

4. He acknowledged having once been attached to the scheme of the Calvinists and, though he reflected with horror on what he felt when he tried conscientiously to think and act on their principles, conceded that many of them (including his aunt—"that person to whom in this world, I have been under the greatest obligation") were truly Christians (195–99).

Priestley argued that most people believe man always acts from motives and refuse to believe that motives are always determined because the presumed consequences have staggered them (xix). So determined are people to evade these consequences that some have even denied the prescience of the Divine Being, or left the problem as "a difficulty and a mystery," whereas it ought to be called an absurdity. It is not within the compass of knowledge to foresee a contingent event and, on the doctrine of philosophical liberty, God could not foresee what would happen in his creation, nor provide for it. Such a position removed divine providence, government, and revealed religion— involving, as they do, scriptural prophecies (28–33). Properly understood, the consequences of necessity are most agreeable to our concepts of reward and punishment. One can scarcely reward or punish a person for actions that had no intention (93). Punishment is proper to correct dispositions and habits that make virtuous behavior impossible. We thereby reform the sinner and warn others, which are the only just ends of punishment (76).

Yet, if God is the proper and sole cause of all things, no man can act other than he does, and God is the ultimate author of sin! Yes, said Priestley, this is true, but in a confined view only. There is no sin in God, for it is disposition of mind and design that constitute sinfulness of action (129). The Divine Being appears to determine vice, but only so that good may result to the whole system. Only an infinite mind is capable of comprehending entirety; individual men must shun vice and court virtue, for their present and future happiness depends upon it (128–30). The belief that *"whatever is, is right,"* provides the only sure anchor of the soul in time of adversity and distress (121). This confidence of necessarians was different from the fatalism of the ancients or the predestination of the Calvinists, for they supposed the Divine Being employed supernatural means in achieving ends (xxiii). Nor did the necessarian suppose any human would suffer eternally. The most vicious people would no doubt be reclaimed sooner or later; their sufferings, however (even after their resurrection), would be in proportion to their depravity (125–26).

Unlike the Calvinist, the believer in philosophical necessity knew that man could not relax his efforts toward virtue simply because the event is in the hands of God. He was at the same time both an instrument and an object in a system under unerring direction (vii), and though the chain of events was subject to the established laws of nature, his determinations were part of that chain. The success or failure of a farmer's crops was in the determination of God, but no farmer is thereby excused from sowing his fields (100). When man was persuaded that things have a necessary influence, good or evil, on his mind, he would be forced to consider more strongly those producing sensible, sympathetic, religious pleasure (such as exhortations of the Scriptures), which are motives impelling the will toward virtue. What then of the inevitable and natural chain of events that determine the will? God created the world and man such that, in the natural course of experience, vice and physical pleasures inevitably become less attractive and intellectual and spiritual pleasure more compelling. Though man will always, with the same inward disposition of mind and precisely the same view of things, act in exactly the same way, these circumstances do not, in fact, ever recur. For by acting, disposition of mind and view of things change and the new state of mind may operate to make the action differ in the future (99–100).[5]

It was this aspect of Priestley's necessarianism that made it so popular among nineteenth-century utilitarians such as James and John Stuart Mill and Herbert Spencer. Early nineteenth-century philosophers were well acquainted with scientific determinism. Pierre Simon Laplace had declared, in his *Essai Philosophique sur les Probabilités* (1814), that a supreme intelligence, knowing all the forces of nature and the situations of all things in it, could achieve complete understanding of the future. Immanuel Kant had applied determinism to will: "if it were possible to have so profound an insight into a man's mental character as to know all its motives, even the smallest, and likewise all the external occasions that can influence them, we could calculate a man's conduct for the future with as great certainty as a lunar or solar eclipse."[6]

Kant finishes this statement with the assertion that "nevertheless we may maintain that a man is free," but it was Priestley's *Philosophical Necessity* that explained to the English utilitarians how this might be so.[7] Man's actions are determined, but the determination is not merely mechanical. Man has a power of reason that, through experience, represents a change in circumstances and influences the motivation of his will. Priestley's doctrine of necessity thus became a philosophical justification for mutual improvement and moral activity.

5. Marsh, "Second Part of Hartley's System," notes how much of Priestley's arguments derive from Hartley.

6. Pierre Simon, Marquis de Laplace, *A Philosophical Essay on Probabilities*, trans. Frederick Wilson Truscott and Frederick Lincoln Emory (1902; 1917; reprint, New York: Dover Publications, 1951), 4; Immanuel Kant, *Critique of Practical Reason*, trans. T. K. Abbott (6th ed., 1927), quoted in Cassirer, *Essay on Man*, 193–94.

7. See Royle, *Victorian Infidels*, 21–22. In Herman Melville's *"Bartleby, the Scrivener,"* first published in 1853, the "employer" seeks solace by reading Priestley on necessity. Melville, *Great Short Works of Herman Melville* (New York: Harper & Row, 1969), 64.

Late eighteenth- and early nineteenth-century transitions from rationalism to transcendental romanticism shifted the arguments over determinism, and Kantian philosophy supported that shift. Priestley's commitment to reason and experiment, and his opposition to transcendental speculation, declared Kant, led him to reject the soul's liberty and immortality. The pious and zealous teacher of religion, obsessed with laws of material nature, had lost his way out of the field of physics.[8] Then, during the second half of the century, the emphasis on absolute physical determinism changed, and with that change Priestley's doctrine of philosophical necessity became increasingly irrelevant. Chance in Darwinian evolution, dependence on statistical methods and explanations in thermodynamics, and the culmination, early in the twentieth century, of antideterminism or indeterminism in relativity and quantum physics took the force out of arguments for philosophical necessity based on natural philosophy.

All of this, however, was well in the future, and Priestley was not to be relieved of defending his position by utilitarian acceptance, transcendental *Vernüft,* or existential neglect. He had promised, in the *Disquisitions,* to respond to responsible objections to his arguments. His "insensible and unexpected" foray into metaphysics was not to be completed until he had made some answer to his critics. The first and most extensive answer was that contained in his *Free Discussion of the Doctrines of Materialism and Philosophical Necessity. In a Correspondence between Dr. Price and Dr. Priestley.*[9] Price had been one of the persons to whom Priestley sent a prepublication copy of the *Disquisitions,* and Price's *Review of the Principles of Morals* had been mentioned and attacked in the *Examination* of the Scottish philosophers, the *Disquisitions,* and *Necessity Illustrated.* Price was also scientifically and theologically literate and was Priestley's friend. He served, therefore, as the best possible respectable opponent with whom Priestley might have a public discussion of metaphysical differences "without the mixture of any thing personal or foreign to the subject which . . . tends to divert the mind from attention to the real merits of the question in debate" (iii).

---

8. Immanuel Kant, *Critique of Pure Reason,* trans. Francis Haywood (London: William Pickering, 1848), part 2, 1st division, Section 2, 514. It should be noted that Kant did not read English and must therefore have depended on a German version of Priestley's *Philosophical Necessity.*

9. Joseph Priestley, *A Free Discussion of the Doctrines of Materialism, and Philosophical Necessity. In a Correspondence between Dr. Price and Dr. Priestley. To which are added, by Dr. Priestley, An Introduction, Explaining the Nature of the Controversy, and Letters to Several Writers who have animadverted on his Disquisitions relating to Matter and Spirit or his Treatise on Necessity* (London: J. Johnson and T. Cadell, 1778).

Most of Price's objections to the theory of matter in the *Disquisitions* reveal the prejudices of the mathematician educated in Newton's *Principia* and struggling to adapt seventeenth-century mechanical philosophy to late eighteenth-century scientific problems. These are displayed in detail in Price's contributions to the *Free Discussion* and the format of the work (the exchange of remarks, queries, and replies until it appeared useless to proceed further) reveal how clearly Priestley had been aware of just those problems that would most impede acceptance of his monism. Nothing in their repeated interchanges was able to make Price retreat from his initial position that solidity, inertness, figure, discerptibility, etc. are the properties that distinguish matter, and that sensation, perception, simplicity, self-determination, judgment, etc. are those that distinguish spirit (36).

Over and over, Price asserted, on the authority of Newton and Newton's laws, that matter is capable of acting only by impulse, on contact, and cannot act at a distance by its own proper agency (4, 6, 12, 24). "How does matter know *when,* and *where,* and with *what precise degree of force,* at different distances, to attract and repel other matter" (34)? Gravity is a power superadded to matter from without; it is not innate (28). Price saw matter only as a receptacle into which properties were poured. All power is the power of something; without solid extension, what is that something (15)? Attractions and repulsions cannot enter the idea of matter as matter (42). At the limit between attraction and repulsion, where no force acts, matter would not exist (12, 21).

It was in vain that Priestley rang the changes on his functional definition of matter. The word *substance* was nothing more than an expression, signifying that to which properties are ascribed; exclude the properties and the idea of substance is excluded. We know nothing of matter but what can be inferred from phenomena and this can be ascribed to attractions and repulsions (15, 20, 42–46, 244–45). Attraction and repulsion, rather than solidity or impenetrability, are what make matter what it is. The power of repulsion resists but does not prevent penetrability (5). The phenomena of optics, electricity, and magnetism, etc., demonstrate that there are spheres of attraction and repulsion within one another (47). The limits between spheres of attraction and repulsion are not places where there are no forces, but where forces balance each other as equal weights do in a balance. Parts of bodies remain at that limit, by which means bodies retain their form and texture (37, 46). All substances need not have the same modes of attraction and repulsion, nor need the properties of a compound be possessed by its parts, as the chemistry of alkalies and acids demonstrates (18, 364). For Priestley, Newton's

Opticks affirmed the existence of action at a distance. He could assume that everything was done by divine power operating according to certain laws relating to the structure of nature (7, 231–33, 251), but, he wrote, "I believe that it is possible . . . that God may endue substances with powers, which, when communicated, produce effects in a manner different from his immediate agency" (233).

It was not Priestley's primary concern to discuss the fundamental nature of matter, but to prove the uniform composition of man. He wished to demonstrate that mind, or the principle of perception and thought, is not a substance distinct from the body but the result of corporeal organization (240). This monistic assumption is independent of any consideration of the internal structure of matter, "about which we know very little, having few data to argue from" (243). But like Newton's speculations on the ether, which followed his declaration *Hypothesis non fingo,* Priestley could not resist a speculation on the internal structure of matter, based on the hypothesis of Rowning and Boscovich and Michell:

> Suppose . . . that the Divine Being, when he created *matter,* only fixed *certain centers of various attractions and repulsions* extending indefinitely in all directions, the whole effect of them to be upon each other; these centers approaching to, or receding from each other, and . . . carrying their peculiar spheres of attraction and repulsion along with them . . . these spheres may be diversified infinitely so as to correspond to all the kinds of bodies that we are acquainted with. . . . A compages of these centers placed within the sphere of each other's attraction will constitute a body that we term compact and two of these bodies will, on their approach meet with a repulsion, or resistance, sufficient to . . . appear perfectly hard. . . . Matter is, by this means, resolved into nothing but the *divine agency,* exerted according to certain rules. (247–48, 250)[10]

If his opponents chose to call this "matter" by the name of spirit, Priestley would not object; all he was contending for was a conjunction of powers in the same thing, or substance, such as experience shows always go together,

---

10. Jonathan Edwards had a similar view of the relation between God and matter: "So that this substance of bodies at last becomes either 'nothing' or nothing but the Deity acting in that particular manner in those parts of space where He thinks fit. So that speaking most strictly there is no proper substance but God Himself." Quoted in George Rupp, "The Idealism of Jonathan Edwards," *Harvard Theological Review* 62 (1969): 215.

so as not needlessly to multiply substances (23). It would be as possible, and as unnecessary, to imagine an immaterial substance for every operation in nature, the proximate cause of which we are not able to see (259).

At one point in this discussion, Price grudgingly admitted the possibility that there might be no such thing as the "matter" he had insisted upon, only to declare that it was not worth writing a book about matter and spirit if by matter was not meant solid extension (82, 56). So far as spirit was concerned, Price felt by an irresistible consciousness that it exists. Priestley agreed. If the belief that one possesses a single, thinking, feeling substance acting voluntarily through the senses and limbs was what Price contended for, then there was no argument (46). But that, of course, was not enough, for Price required that the spirit be distinct from the body. He agreed that it was contrary to reason and Scripture to suppose the body a calamity or a clog on the spirit; organization of the body is necessary for the exercise of the powers residing in the immaterial substance of the soul; but connection and dependence did not prove sameness (xvi, 4, 53, 89). What connection could possibly exist between attraction and repulsion on the one hand and perception, consciousness, and judgment on the other (19)?

Priestley answered that there was no reason why perception might not be a property of the material of the brain as easily as of some supposed immaterial substance, though the mode be as unknown as that supposed to connect the matter of the body to the immaterial soul (91). Hartley's *Observations* described a possible relationship between attraction, repulsion, and thought (20). The dependency might not be the result of the form, texture, or consistency of matter, but of a system of particles, the organization of matter, and the motions taking place within it (20, 18–19). On the connection between sensation and organization, Priestley's idea "now" was that sensation and thought "necessarily result from the organization of the brain, when the powers of mere life are given to the system," though he had no more idea of how this was done than he had on how the attraction of iron by a magnet was effected (256–57). Price would not accept this. A system of matter consists of many "beings" and, like matter, can be divided without loss of identity. If the soul, by contrast, were divided, it would lose its identity. Priestley repeated that a particular organization of matter may not be divisible and still retain its identity.

On the subject of philosophical necessity, there was relatively little argument in the *Discussions with Price*, though each protagonist had differences with the other. Priestley rested his case primarily on what he had said in *Necessity Illustrated* (145); Price rested his on the denial that any philosophic libertarian ever believed that actions were undetermined by motive. He thought it a greater achievement in God to have created man with the ability freely to choose between good and evil, and be accountable for his choices, than previously to determine all of man's actions (128, 158). He couldn't explain, but fully believed in, divine prescience (175–76). Priestley was impatient with pretended distinctions between certain determinations and necessary ones (146–47). He conceded a difference between physical and moral causes, but, the results being the same, the difference effectively vanished (147–48, 172). And he owned "an inexpressible satisfaction in the idea of that most intimate connection which . . . myself, and every thing in which I am concerned, have with the deity" (255).

Priestley hoped that having fairly engaged one worthy though friendly antagonist, he might be excused from encountering other opponents (vi). Yet he included letters to three others—William Kenrick, John Whitehead, and Samuel Horsley—in the *Discussion with Price* and later published a *Letter* and a *Second Letter* to John Palmer, and a *Letter to Jacob Bryant.*[11] Except as they indicated that the dominant concern of Priestley's respondents was philosophical necessity (most people were simply confused, though dismayed, by his theory of matter), these additional letters added very little to the substance of Priestley's arguments. It is not easy to find any substantial reason why he chose to answer this particular set of opponents.[12]

Kenrick's articles in the *London Review,* from 1775 to 1778, were but another of his journalist efforts to supplement his writing of plays, poems, political squibs, and so on in order to earn a precarious living. The article Priestley specifically answered related entirely to materialism, but Kenrick's object was to complain of Priestley's inadequate understanding of the knowledge he had supposedly derived from Kenrick's discussion of the question with Cadwallader Colden, and to quibble over Priestley's failure to acknowledge that source (a neglect "not so much real as affected"). Perhaps it was the eccentricity of the demand for credit for ideas about which Priestley was

11. The letters to Kenrick, Whitehead, and Horsley, from the *Discussion* with Price, and to Berrington (the "Author of Letters on Materialism and on Hartley's Theory of the Mind"), from the first edition of *Philosophical Necessity Illustrated* were reprinted together in the second edition of *Philosophical Necessity Illustrated* (1782). Joseph Priestley, *A Letter to the Rev. Mr. John Palmer, in Defence of the Illustrations of Philosophical Necessity* (Bath: R. Cruttwell, for J. Johnson, 1780); *A Second Letter to the Rev. Mr. John Palmer, in Defence of the Doctrine of Philosophical Necessity* (London: J. Johnson, 1780); *A Letter to Jacob Bryant Esq. in Defence of Philosophical Necessity* (London: J. Johnson, 1780).

12. Yalton, *Thinking Matter,* 115–25, discusses some of the other, and more interesting, opponents Priestley might have answered.

attacked, or maybe it was his implication of plagiarism (something which invariably incensed Priestley) that won Kenrick the notice he craved. In any case, Priestley denied ever having heard of Colden or knowing of Kenrick's writings on the subject, suggested that the lack of consistency between his "materialism" (based on Boscovich and Michell) and Kenrick's (which was hylozoic) proved that there was no plagiarism, and defended the scholarly principles on which he cited the editions of the references he used. Kenrick asked why Priestley had used the "obnoxious" term *matter* for something lacking solidity or impenetrability. Surely *spirit* would be better, he suggested. Priestley's response was that though both terms were equally "in his option," he chose to call everything by its *usual name*, it being a "mean subterfuge to impose upon mankind by words" (190–92).

Whitehead and Bryant were merely abusive and ignorant. Had he known that Whitehead was only transiently a Quaker between periods of evangelical Methodism, he might have treated him as savagely as he was to treat Bryant. Because he respected Quakers, Priestley simply pointed out that Whitehead was ignorant of ecclesiastical history and of the arguments of philosophers— e.g., Priestley's arguments did *not* support Arianism, but the reverse (201). Bryant's *Address* he noticed only because the author was distinguished in the republic of letters, and at the request of friends. Bryant, however, was not only ignorant of his subject, he wrote in such a tone of high authority that he needed a lesson in manners, syntax, and the art of reasoning. Priestley lectured Bryant as though he were an erring school boy. He should learn something about religion. He seemed to think all Dissenters were Calvinists, but it was the Church of England that was "strictly Calvinistical." The word "sincerity" did not mean what Bryant thought it did, nor was "involuntary" another word for "necessity"; the opposition to "involuntary" was voluntary, as "contingent" was to "necessary." Priestley had conceded Bryant's arguments for philosophical liberty in his *Philosophical Necessity*, but Bryant had confused the issues with fine words. "Every man . . . has his own weapons. . . . You have Oratory, I have Logic" (34). And Priestley ended by observing that Bryant's performance in this argument ("so little judgment, accompanying a boundless imagination") made him now suspect that there might be something wrong with Bryant's *System of Mythology*.[13]

13. Jacob Bryant's analysis of *Ancient Mythology* (1774) was once highly regarded, but Bryant knew no Oriental languages and had a puerile and misleading system of etymology. Though described as generally "temperate, courteous, and generous," he showed an inclination to enter upon disputes about which he knew little. Specific references to *Letter to Bryant* are to 1, 14, 17, 21, 34, and 64.

Of Priestley's short responses, only that to Samuel Horsley's sermon, *Providence and Free Agency*, was conciliatory. Perhaps this was because the context of a sermon did not allow Horsley to engage in personal abuse (his later disputes with Priestley were amply abusive) and therefore did not excite retaliation. Also, Horsley's status and knowledge as a mathematician, fellow of the Royal Society, lecturer at St. Martin's-in-the-Fields, and domestic chaplain to the Bishop of London, provided justification for treating his arguments seriously. Besides, Priestley believed that Horsley was a necessarian, though he used different words to describe his beliefs. He ought to acknowledge himself a believer in "the great and glorious, though unpopular doctrine of philosophical necessity" (227).

Horsley admitted the certainty of motives, arising from the operation of established laws of nature, and accepted the prescience of God (214). He objected to the term "physical necessity" applied to human activities, and Priestley was ready to disuse it if implied something other than the two agreed to maintain (220). But the term "physical" was derived from the Greek and merely meant agreeable to the laws of nature. Certainly the laws of the mind were very different from those of mechanics: "The compass of nature is great and comprizes very various things. *Chemistry*, for instance, and common *mechanics* are very different things; and accordingly we have different *kinds of laws*, or rules, by which to express, and explain their operations, but still they are equally branches of *Physics*" (221).

Though Horsley appeared to Priestley to be a necessarian, he did not agree. Events are certain because sufficient causes do act, but not because they must act to produce them. He knew intuitively that he was free because he felt it to be so. Priestley noted, in a postscript to his answer to Horsley in the *Free Discussion*, that Horsley evidently did not agree with the "system" of the *Disquisitions*. Their disagreements are made plain in manuscript notes in Hartley's copy of the *Disquisitions*.[14] Implications of the *Disquisitions* were injurious to true Christianity; forces are superadded to matter and there must be some substance to which they can be added. The divisibility of solid primordial atoms is a logical, not a physical, possibility, for the atom cannot be made less than the Creator made it, a monad.

There was, however, one response to Priestley's *Disquisitions*, and subsequently also to the *Free Discussion*, that suggests a more disturbing reason for Horsley's disagreement with Priestley. James Burnett, Lord Monboddo,

---

14. John Stephens, "Samuel Horsley and Joseph Priestley's *Disquisitions relating to Matter and Spirit*," *Enlightenment and Dissent* 3 (1984): 103–14.

took issue with Priestley in the second volume of his six-volume *Antient Metaphysics* (1773–91). Priestley never answered Monboddo's criticisms, though he is criticized throughout, frequently misquoted, and his name consistently misspelled: "I would seriously advise them not to philosophise without the assistance of the ancients, which has been most unsuccessfully attempted by so many moderns, from Des Cartes down to Dr. Priestly."[15] Possibly he was unaware of these criticisms, though Monboddo and Richard Price had a lengthy correspondence about the issues raised in the *Disquisitions* and *Free Discussion.*[16] Response would, in any event, have been useless, for Monboddo was an obdurate anti-Newtonian. "His study of Newton led him to believe that the metaphysical foundations of Newton's discoveries were not merely erroneous, but irrelevant, that the discoveries themselves had a validity which could be transferred to a different metaphysical foundation more consistent with both revealed religion and ancient philosophy." Philosophy had been brought to perfection in the writings of Plato and Aristotle; there was no such thing as vis inertia and Newton's "laws of motion" were untrue.[17] These ideas were not unique, but Monboddo's have a singular quality. "It should be pointed out that he did not reach these conclusions without help; Bishop Horsley, who had much the same interests, and maintained a copious correspondence with Monboddo, repeatedly urged this idea upon him." And the preface to volume 2 of the *Antient Metaphysics* specifically thanked Dr. Horsley, "without whose encouragement I should not . . . [have] written a second Volume of Metaphysics."[18]

The lack of more intensive debate on philosophical necessity disturbed some people, who thought Price was "too tender" and "made some imprudent concessions" in the *Free Discussion.* One of these persons was the Unitarian minister John Palmer, who wrote his *Observations in Defense of the Liberty of Man as a Moral Agent* (1779) in hopes of eliciting an answer from Priestley. As Palmer was an old and respected acquaintance, Priestley

15. James Burnett, Lord Monboddo, *Antient Metaphysics: or, The Science of Universals* (London: T. Adell; Edinburgh: J. Balfour and Co., 1782), 2:viii.

16. [Richard Price], *The Correspondence of Richard Price,* ed. D. O. Thomas and Bernard Peach (Durham: Duke University Press, 1983), 2:61–64, 65–68, 69–78, 87–90, 106–7.

17. E. L. Cloyd, *James Burnett: Lord Monboddo* (Oxford: Clarendon Press, 1972), 109; Monboddo, *Antient Metaphysics,* 2:2.

18. Cloyd, *Burnett,* 109; Monboddo, *Antient Metaphysics,* 2:xi. A notable aspect of Horsley's influence on Monboddo's anti-Newtonianism is that much of his scientific reputation was to be based on his edition of Newton's collected works (1785)—an edition that, not incidentally, did not include any of Newton's unpublished theological manuscripts, as they were not "fit to be published."

responded with a *Letter to the Rev. Mr. Palmer.* Palmer was unhappy with that answer, telling Price that he had been used roughly (*W.* 1.1:332). Nonetheless, he wrote a reply that Priestley answered with a *Second Letter to the Rev. Mr. Palmer.* Priestley was extraordinarily patient in his answers to Palmer. To fearful doubts about the doctrine of necessity, Priestley declared, "if the doctrine itself be true, we must take all the genuine consequences." Immaterial things are subject to laws other than those of matter. If a thing must be so, it must necessarily be so. Remorse for sin becomes a motive for future virtue. God claims prescience as a very test of divinity itself and the Scriptures assert it in numberless instances.[19]

Throughout this whole series of debates, Priestley retained his belief in dialectical epistemology, and Price agreed: "It is certain, that in the end, the interest of truth will be promoted by a free and open discussion of speculative points" (323). Each agreed that "truth not victory" was their object (v); each was punctilious in observance of their code for debates, and Palmer was scarcely less so: "All that candour requires is, that we never impute to our adversary a *bad intention,* or a *design to mislead* and also that we admit his *general good understanding,* though liable to be misled by unperceived biases and prejudices, from the influences of which the wisest and best of men are not exempt" (xxx). Yet the evidence is clear. Not one of the protagonists changed his mind, in any significant way, as a consequence of these arguments.

Part of the reason for continuing the arguments lay in that typical Enlightenment faith in "posterity." Priestley declared in the "Dedication" of the *Free Discussion,* "As truth will finally prevail over all opposition, time (though we may not live to see the issue) will discover whether my zeal in attacking, or his in defending, is better founded" (v). He was even more explicit in the *Letter to Palmer:* "Those who are younger than we are, and whose principles are not yet formed, are alone capable of judging between us, and of forming their opinions accordingly; and in that respect, they may derive an advantage from these publications that we cannot derive from them ourselves" (*Palmer,* 93).

Another reason for Priestley's repeated disputes of this variety was his conviction of the great importance of the subject. Certainly he could not avoid controversy by eschewing theology and metaphysics, by concentrating, as many of his friends suggested, on natural philosophy. He had not yet

19. Paraphrased answers are from Priestley's *Letter to Palmer,* 3, 13, 15, 21, 32, 59, 63, and 86. In June 1780 Priestley was attempting to find a better position for Palmer; see his letter to R. Scholefield.

become involved in his major scientific dispute (with Antoine Lavoisier), but, as he wrote in the preface to the *Disquisitions* (xxiv), "the most rancorous opposition, and the most unprovoked abuse that I have ever met with, has been from persons who never knew any thing of me but in the character of a philosopher [scientist]." His scientific work was not, then, an escape from disputes, but appears, as he was repeatedly to suggest, to be yet another way of exploring the nature of God, manifest in the physics that accompanied his metaphysics. It was also a useful mode of entertainment and relaxation, amid the pressures of social adjustment, political distress, and theological and metaphysical investigations during his years with Shelburne. This period of Priestley's most vigorous activities in metaphysics was also that of his most sustained achievement in science.

VI

OBSERVATIONS ON AIR I AND II

Oxygen

With the publication of his "Observations on different Kinds of Air," Priestley had completed the reporting of his pneumatic experiments through the summer and autumn months of 1772.[1] Winter was not a good time for his experiments on airs, and he had essentially given up experiments on anything else. Also, having committed himself to leaving Leeds, he was concerned to complete writing projects begun there (e.g., the *Institutes of Natural and Revealed Religion*); and there were the problems of packing and moving. It is unlikely that he had much time for science until the move was completed. Though his minerals and chemicals arrived at Calne with the household goods—Priestley had put them into boxes of clothing before closing—his apparatus had not yet arrived by 17 July 1773, but was expected the following week.[2] He had by then done little if any scientific work for more than half a year.

It is scarcely surprising, then, to learn that by 26 September he was doing little else (W. 1.1:220), and on that date he informed Benjamin Franklin of his

1. Priestley, "Observations on different kinds of Air," *Philosophical Transactions* 62 (1772): 147–264.
2. The story about the minerals and chemicals packed with clothing is another of Mary Anne Schimmelpennick's anecdotes, to which she adds that Priestley reassured his wife that the minerals had traveled perfectly well, though the clothing might be a little injured. [Schimmelpennick], *Life*, 1:85–86. Priestley to John Calder, 17 July 1773, Library, APS; misdated in W. 1.1:272–73.

identification of an alkaline air (ammonia, NH_3) obtained by heating volatile alkali (aqueous ammonia, or perhaps ammonium hydroxide, NH_4OH). On 14 October he informed the editors of (Rozier's) *Observations sur la Physique* of his new "air" and on 10 November he mentioned the new air in a letter to Volta. Private individuals in England, France, and Italy knew of Priestley's discovery before he made it public with a paper on alkaline air read to the Royal Society on 3 March 1774.[3] That paper was, however, not published. Priestley had agreed, after conferring with friends, including Sir John Pringle (then president of the Royal Society), to publish his major work in book form rather than burden the *Philosophical Transactions* with long papers.[4]

Priestley's first publication in science from Calne was instead a revealing letter to Pringle, sent after Pringle's Royal Society address of 30 November 1773 on giving Priestley the Copley Medal. Dated 7 December and read to the Royal Society on 16 December 1773, "On the noxious Quality of the Effluvia of putrid Marshes," was a response to treatises written by Dr. William Alexander of Edinburgh, contradicting Pringle on diseases of the army and maintaining that putrid matter would preserve other substances from putrefaction.[5] Priestley had evidence that putrid matter was dangerous. The pneumatic trough used at Calne was larger than that he had used in Leeds, and fresh water was not so conveniently at hand. He "neglected to change it, till it turned black, and became offensive, but by no means to such a degree as to deter me from making use of it" (92). Bubbles of air spontaneously rose from the water in this state; he collected them and found by nitrous air test that the air was highly noxious, while wholesome air agitated in the water soon became noxious as well!

Priestley's concern was to warn people against the air in putrid marshes. He did not apply the results to correcting his own experiments using that pneumatic trough. Indeed, for all the ambiguities in his first paper on airs, he appeared to regard the water of the pneumatic trough as purely instrumental in those experiments. In his letter to Pringle, he noted that different

3. Priestley to Franklin, *SciAuto.*, 57; Rozier's *Observations sur la Physique* 2 (1773): 389; Priestley to Volta, *SciAuto.*, 59.

4. The "Observations" had taken 118 pages when printed in the *Philosophical Transactions*. MS Journal Book of the Royal Society, vol. 23, 1774–77, 15, 18, notes the reading of the paper on alkaline air and adds that it was subsequently withdrawn. A manuscript copy of the paper can be found in the Royal Society archives, Decade 5, #67, vol. 52, 24 Feb.–23 June 1774.

5. Priestley, "On the noxious Quality of the Effluvia of putrid Marshes," *Philosophical Transactions* 64 (1774): 90–95; MS in the Archives of the Royal Society, "Effluvia of Putrid Marshes," Decade 5, #8, vol. 51, 11 Nov. 1773–17 Feb. 1774.

sources of water—from a deep well, rain, distilled, and spring—gave different results when used in his trough (93–94), but it did not occur to him that water and its impurities might play a constituent role in chemical experiments. One can only wonder how many of the curious results reported in his first paper and in the volumes of his *Experiments and Observations* were a consequence of using polluted water in his pneumatic troughs! The letter ends with a postscript recommending John Smeaton's air pump, giving details on how much better it was than the usual design. Perhaps the air pump he purchased from Nairne and Blunt on 2 December 1773 for Lord Shelburne was of that design. By the end of March 1774 he had also purchased a "condensing engine," an electrical machine, a large lens, and some prisms.[6] These may have been to stock new laboratories at Shelburne House, London, or Bowood, where he entertained visitors with experiments. Possibly the instruments were the beginning of the "cabinet" he was to purchase for the anticipated use of Shelburne's sons. But whether he performed his experiments at Calne, Bowood, or Shelburne House, by February 1774 he had put together enough of them for his first volume of pneumatic studies: *Experiments and Observations on Different Kinds of Air.*[7]

Experiments and Observations begins with one of those prefaces that had become characteristic of Priestley's scientific volumes, with their curious mixture of theology, politics, ontology, epistemology, and personal commentary. In this one, some of these can be traced to the influence of his chief mentors in natural philosophy, Benjamin Franklin and Stephen Hales, whose "various and valuable investigations" were "justly esteemed to be the solid foundation of all our knowledge of this subject" (viii, 4).[8] Surely Priestley's comparison of experimental philosophy to "the diversion of hunting," with its implication of chance discoveries (xi), echoes Hales's preface to the *Haemastaticks* and the remark that new experiments and discoveries owe

6. Bowood Papers, IV-D and IV-E.

7. Priestley, *Exp. & Obs.* I have used the second edition. Priestley's *Memoirs* (W. 1.1:201) states that he had the materials for this volume when he went to Calne, but its preface is dated February 1774, and it contains accounts of experiments of 1773 and early 1774. The volume was presented to the Royal Society on 12 May 1774. Magellan sent a copy to Lavoisier on 16 May (Lavoisier, *Oeuvres de Lavoisier: Correspondence,* 3:453–54, #242), and was favorably reviewed in the *Monthly Review* 51 (1774): 136ff.

8. There are other examples of Priestley's acknowledgment of this heritage: e.g., in *Exp. & Obs. II,* xvii–xviii ("It was Franklin's example and encouragement chiefly that led me to attempt philosophical investigations"), while he cited Hales as his authority in disagreement with opinions of Dr. John Hunter; see Priestley to Newcome Cappe, 13 April 1777. Note that Lavoisier also praised the work of Hales, writing to the Royal Society on 15 Jan. 1774 (Lavoisier, *Oeuvres de Lavoisier: Correspondence,* 3:398, 400).

their "first Rise only to lucky Guesses." And there are clearly parallels between Priestley's insistence on prompt publication and Franklin's that reputation for discovery was less important than "exciting the attention of the ingenious" to the subject.[9]

Other parts are pure, vintage Priestley—for example, his suggestion that encouragement of learning is dangerous to usurpers of authority: "the English hierarchy (if there be any thing unsound in its constitution) has . . . reason to tremble even at an air pump or an electrical machine" (xiv). The failure of men of high rank in England to participate in scientific activities was "made up [for] by men of leisure, spirit, and ingenuity, in the middle ranks of life" (xvi). Priestley sought "that greater command of the powers of nature, which can only be obtained by a more extensive and more accurate knowledge of them" (xii). His studies were necessarily incomplete, for the works of God "are infinite and inexhaustible" (vii).

Confirming that he had suspended, "for the present," writing a history of all branches of experimental philosophy, for want of a prospect of indemnification for his labor and expense, he hoped to write someday a history of discoveries on air. He commenced the introduction with a précis of such preceding discoveries as related to his own work, citing Boyle, van Helmont, Hales, Brownrigg, Black, McBride, Pringle, Lane, and Cavendish. This précis, however, owed more to Pringle's Copley Medal address than to any meaningful study on Priestley's part. He never understood the significance of Joseph Black's gravimetric techniques, for example, while he here ignored the understanding of Hales's work he had shown in the "Observations" and said, incorrectly, that Hales imagined "that the diminution of air was simply a taking away from the common mass, without any alteration in the properties of what remained" (4).[10]

The next section of the introduction is a detailed description of his apparatus, accompanied by two folding plates and instructions on how the various pieces were to be used. Most of this apparatus was very simple, readily

---

9. Stephen Hales, *Statical Essays: Containing Haemastaticks; or An Account of some Hydraulic and Hydrostatical Experiments made on the Blood and Blood Vessels of Animals*, vol. 2 (1773; reprint, New York: Hafner Publ. Co., N.Y. Academy of Medicine, 1964), xiv–xvi; Priestley probably knew this work in its third edition, 1769. Benjamin Franklin to Peter Collinson, Sept. 1753, in Franklin's *Experiments and Observations on Electricity*, 3d ed., where Priestley would have seen it (note the parallel in book titles with Priestley's); see [Benjamin Franklin], *The Papers of Benjamin Franklin* (New Haven: Yale University Press, 1962–), 5:72.

10. Hales had supposed that diminution was a consequence of the "elasticity of the whole mass being impaired," as Priestley said, and disproved, in the "Observations," reprinted in *Exp. & Obs.*, 46.

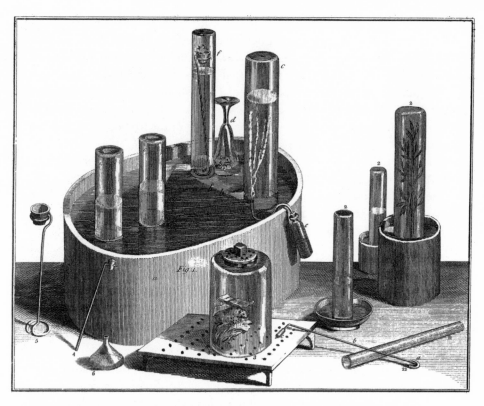

Fig. 2 Plate of chemical apparatus, from *Experiments and Observations,* vol. 1,
2d ed. (1775)

available in a kitchen, though he was later to obtain specialized glassware,
sometimes with ground stoppers, as gifts of W. Parker and Sons, glassmakers
of Fleet Street, London, and a variety of ceramic ware from his friend Josiah
Wedgwood.[11] The text proper begins with a republishing of the "Observations" paper from the *Philosophical Transactions* of 1772, "with such observations and corrections as subsequent experience has suggested to me" (xxi),
for persons who did not choose to purchase the whole volume for Priestley's
paper (v). There are few changes in these republished "Observations" and

11. See Lawrence Badash, "Joseph Priestley's Apparatus for Pneumatic Chemistry," *Journal
of the History of Medicine* 19 (l964): 139–55. Unlike Henry Cavendish, who was properly
obsessed with the design and operation of accurate apparatus and instruments, Priestley was
mostly perfunctory about apparatus; see Christa Jungnickel and Russell McCormmach, *Cavendish* (Philadelphia: American Philosophical Society, Memoir 220, 1996), 161–68.

some of these are differences between the first and second editions of the *Experiments and Observations*. Priestley clarified, though still with exaggeration, that it was experiments on *fixed air* he had been encouraged to make by living near a brewery (25); he omitted a note that fixed air prompted coagulation of blood, on the authority of Dr. William Falconer (appendix 4, Jan. 6, 1774); and the term "acid air" was replaced by "marine acid air," in consequence of the discovery, after the printing of the first edition, of other acid airs.

Part II of *Experiments and Observations* describes Priestley's work of 1773 and the beginning of 1774. In this part, also, there is a reprinting, in this case of the *Philosophical Transactions* letter to Pringle on effluvia from putrid marshes, but most of it relates to previously unpublished material. This volume is chiefly valued for its report of the identification of ammonia (163–77) and of nitrous oxide ("diminished," later "dephlogisticated nitrous air," N_2O) (215–22), but is most notable for its consistent, explicit application of theory to explain Priestley's experiments. His discovery of ammonia was a simple consequence of continuing Stephen Hales's technique of "distilling" or "fermenting" (i.e., heating or dissolving in liquids) every substance he could obtain, capturing, over mercury instead of the customary water, the "air" released. That of nitrous oxide followed the generalization of a curiosity about fixed air dissolving iron. The two are examples of the momentum of a research design and of Priestley's quite extraordinary powers of observation, but tell us very little more about what he thought he was doing. The discussions of theory in this volume, by contrast, reveal his opinions before his metaphysical writings on matter could have been explicitly reflected in his pneumatic studies.

Priestley wrote that he avoided hypotheses earlier in his work lest, in attaching too soon to any one, he might obstruct his further inquiries. Now, believing his conjectures confirmed by further experiments, he was prepared to speak with less diffidence (177). Besides, "theory and experiment necessarily go hand in hand, every process being intended to ascertain some particular hypothesis, which, in fact, is only a conjecture concerning the circumstances or cause of some natural operation" (259). He cited the "bold and eccentric thoughts" of Newton's Queries at the end of the *Opticks* in justification, for even wild, imaginative ideas may lead to capital discoveries not to be made by cautious, timid, sober, slow-thinking persons. Priestley never thought of himself as cautious, timid, sober, or slow; but it may also be doubted that he saw himself as indulging in wild ideas. His characteristic approach, throughout his career in science, was to recite what he thought of as "facts," deprecating the importance of any hypothesis used to explain them. Yet he had the words of David Hartley to warn him: "It is in vain to bid an inquirer form no hypothesis. Every phenomenon will suggest something of the kind; if he does not take care to state such as occur fully and fairly, and adjust them to one another, he may entertain a confused inconsistent mixture of all, of fictitious and real, possible and impossible; and become so persuaded of it, as that counter-associations shall not be able to break the unnatural bond."[12]

This is what Priestley had done (and was to continue doing) with respect to the action of water and his airs. It is notoriously difficult to describe a "fact" independent of any ordering theory, and when he states as "fact" that inflammable air stored over water for several months loses flammability, he was interpreting observations within a theory. What he saw was inflammable air placed in a jar over water; several months later the air was not inflammable. Priestley believed that the air had been transformed because he persisted in thinking that "agitation, or long standing in water" could alter the combination of the constituent principles of airs (261). None of his observations of what today would be called gaseous diffusion and ion exchange, not even his own damning description of the water in his pneumatic trough, was "able to break the unnatural bond" between his hypothesis and his observations. The reason for his interpretations of experience can be understood, but the consequence is such that no experiment reporting agitation or long standing over water can be deemed entirely meaningful.

The acknowledged theory in *Experiments and Observations* was the more inclusive doctrine of phlogiston, and that theory was widely understood, with well-known parameters.[13] But, for Priestley, phlogiston was to become something vastly different, assuming protean qualities. Though it was involved in combustions, it was not fire, for that term suggested the phenomenon of heat, and heat is a mode of vibration of the particles of the hot body, not a substance (282–83, 286). And phlogiston was a substance, whatever that came to mean in Priestley's monistic definition. He used the term in this case "to denote only one and the same *unknown cause* of certain well-known effects.[14]

12. Priestley, *Hartley's Theory of the Human Mind*, 180.

13. On phlogiston, as understood by Priestley's contemporaries, see James R. Partington and Douglas McKie, "Historical Studies on the Phlogiston Theory," parts 1–4, *Annals of Science* 2 (1937): 361–404; 3 (1938): 1–58; 4 (1938): 337–71; 5 (1939): 113–49.

14. Priestley, *Exp. & Obs.*, 282–83. The designation of phlogiston as "the unknown cause of known effects" is a significant one, for that is essentially the way Priestley was to regard phlogiston all of his life.

It was not capable of being exhibited alone, but could be transferred from one substance to another according to known laws, making a remarkable difference in those bodies (282–83). Variation in its presence changed the volume of airs, perhaps by a real contraction of an air when united to phlogiston. Its differing affinities for different substances helped him explain reactions of displacement and disassociation. Its presence did not change the weight of bodies. This could be easily explained by supposing that it might communicate absolute levity, but Priestley was "not willing to have recourse" to that idea (187, 267). Inflammability of a body usually involved removal of its phlogiston; lack of flammability may depend "upon some particular *mode of combination,* or degree of affinity, with which we are not yet acquainted" (140).[15] Water could imbibe great quantities of phlogiston and probably always contained an important portion of it, so that agitation in water of an air with high affinity for it could transfer phlogiston from the water to the air (261). Electric matter was, or contained, phlogiston, for a spark between a wire and water diminished the air over the water, deposited something of an acid nature, and formed a precipitate if the water was lime water.[16] Electric conductors contained phlogiston firmly united to some base; nonconductors possessed no phlogiston or held it lightly (182–86).[17]

Adapting the notion of phlogiston, Priestley was able to provide a single explanation for many of the phenomena he observed, especially in the nature of natural economy. His experiments, with their phlogistic explanations, led him to believe that the only distinct species of air were the fixed, alkaline, and acid. These, combined with phlogiston in different proportions, or different modes, constituted all other known kinds of air (260). It would not seem curious to "chemists" that mild (common) air should consist of acid

15. John G. McEvoy, "Joseph Priestley, 'Aerial Philosopher': Metaphysics and Methodology in Priestley's Chemical Thought, from 1772 to 1781," *Ambix* 25 (1978): 1–55, 93–116, 153–75, and 26 (1979): 16–38, 101, thinks the suggestion about mode of combination is derived from Pierre Joseph Macquer's *Elements of the Theory and Practice of Chemistry* (1758), 1:10, but Priestley did not mention Macquer in this connection, nor did he refer to the mode of combination on the referenced page in the edition of 1764 that Priestley possessed.

16. Note that Priestley had become so enamored of his new theory that he ignored, or quite forgot, his speculation of 1767 that there was no electric fluid, electrification being only a modification of the matter of the body being electrified. See Schofield, *Enlightenment of Priestley,* 234.

17. Many of the effects enumerated by Priestley were sufficient to suggest the concept of energy to some nineteenth-century historians of chemistry, without their supposing that Priestley himself was aware of it. See Alexander Crum Brown, "Note on the Phlogistic Theory," *Proceedings of the Royal Society of Edinburgh* 5 (1866): sec. 5, 328–30; and William Odling, "The Revived Theory of Phlogiston," *Popular Science Monthly* 9 (1870): 560–69.

vapor and phlogiston, considering the affinities and very different properties possessed by substances composed of them—e.g., sulphur is as mild as common air, yet one of its parts is oil of vitriol (264–65). Growing vegetation extracted phlogiston from the air and thus purified the air released, for example, from volcanoes, respiration, putrefaction, and combustion. It would not restore all noxious airs or, perhaps, any of them completely, but its effect was adequate to the purpose (269, 277). Animals ate materials containing phlogiston, transforming it, possibly by the vibrations Hartley supposed to occur in the brain, into the form of electric matter that was then directed by the nerves into the muscles, where it caused muscular motion (277–28, 286). Animals died in confined air, not for loss of a *pabulum vitae* but in convulsions, showing stimulus by excess freed phlogiston that could not be discharged into saturated air (194).

These sections of *Experiments and Observations* show Priestley's considerable explanatory ingenuity; they also come close to justifying the jaundiced view of James Partington (and many other historians of chemistry) that "A little more [chemical] knowledge would have saved Priestley from making many mistakes."[18] Now, these critics cannot mean (though sometimes they argue as though they do) the self-evident proposition that had he known nineteenth-century chemistry, he'd have escaped his eighteenth-century errors. Nor is the objection, strictly speaking, to the doctrine of phlogiston, for most chemists of Priestley's period believed in phlogiston at least until the late 1780s. In 1781, for example, Richard Watson, professor of chemistry at Cambridge University, wrote, "You do not surely expect that chemistry should be able to present you with a handful of phlogiston . . . you may just as reasonably demand a handful of magnetism, gravity, or electricity; there are powers in nature, which cannot otherwise become the objects of sense, than by the effects they produce, and of this kind is phlogiston."[19] Nor is it strictly true that Priestley was ignorant of chemistry, though what he knew best was dated. He had read Boerhaave (probably in a 1753 edition of the translation of a 1732 text) and Caspar Neumann (in the 1759 translation of papers dating from 1727 to 1735), joined a short course of chemistry at Warrington, and clearly had had access to the writings of a number of other chemists, including Joseph Black, Henry Cavendish, and P. J. Macquer.

18. James R. Partington, *A History of Chemistry*, vol. 3 (London: Macmillan, 1962), 246.

19. Richard Watson, *Chemical Essays* (Cambridge: J. Archdeacon for T. and J. Merrill et al., 1781), 1:167. Watson later became Bishop of Llandaff; he was never a major figure in chemistry, but his *Essays* reflect current accepted opinion.

Yet the criticism has a kernel of merit. From the way Priestley discussed phlogiston, as well as from experiments described in *Experiments and Observations,* he clearly found such chemistry works as he read to be irrelevant to his concerns. In 1777 the Swedish chemist Carl Wilhelm Scheele wrote that the "object and chief business of chemistry [was] skillfully to separate substances into their constituents, to discover their properties, and compound them in different ways."[20] But Priestley was not interested in compounds and their composition; indeed, one may doubt that he ever quite understood the concept of chemical compound.[21]

His focus was almost exclusively on gases. A chemist, examining the products of a reaction, might note changes occurring in all the ingredients involved. Priestley looked only at the gases and his attention was primarily on changes in their sensible properties. Chemists before Lavoisier and Dalton were limited in distinguishing between substances except by their sensible characteristics and their reactions; relative weights were not employed or employable. The handicap was increased with gases, and Priestley, seldom regarding any part of a reaction except in the airs he was studying, often missed significant variations in other parts of his processes.

In his new enthusiasm for the doctrine of phlogiston, he found a way to satisfy his philosophical concern to explain phenomena in terms of a few simple operations; it was to prove an inappropriate and premature simplification. By generalizing the case of carbon combustion to include all cases of air diminution and turbidity in lime water, Priestley equated the carbonate, sulphite, and nitrate or nitrite precipitates produced in his experiments. Another mistake occurred in an experiment perceptively described in the "Observations" (158–59) and reprinted in *Experiments and Observations* (38–39). In order to obtain fixed air by a method other than "digesting" chalk in acid, he "distilled" the chalk by heating it in an iron gun barrel. As he expected, much air was produced, but little more than half was fixed air; the remainder was inflammable. Now, inflammable air is produced from iron by acids, and some people supposed chalk to contain small quantities of sulphuric acid. But oil of vitriol must be diluted with water to produce inflammable air from iron, while this new air was unlike that procured by acid on metals. It burned blue and had the smell of air produced from vegetable

20. [Carl Wilhelm Scheele], "Chemical Treatise on Air and Fire," in *Collected Papers of Carl Wilhelm Scheele,* trans. and ed. Leonard Dobbin (London: G. Bell & Sons, 1931), 89.

21. An operational definition of a compound was one of the features of Lavoisier's "revolution" in chemistry; see Robert Siegfried and Betty Jo Dobbs, "Composition: A Neglected Aspect of the Chemical Revolution," *Annals of Science* 24 (1968): 275–93.

substances. Priestley had produced carbon monoxide by the action of carbon dioxide on hot iron. He described what are the standard, modern indications for carbon monoxide and correctly queried its production from iron and acid, but it did not occur to him that this might be a different kind of inflammable air, or that iron and fixed air might be included with heat and chalk as reactants in his experiment.

Carbon monoxide was not accepted as a species of gas by other "chemists" either until the late 1790s, and the inside of an iron barrel was not readily available for finding the ferric oxide produced in the reaction. Nonetheless, there is no indication that such an examination would have occurred to Priestley. He was confused when there seemed to be differences in airs with the same primary properties, or in the precipitates of lime water. He spent much ingenuity in attempting to account for these differences, but not to the extent of supposing them caused by different proportions or even different substances.

It is not entirely unreasonable to suppose that had Priestley been more of a "chemist," had he, that is, seen a chemical reaction as a system in which all reactants changed, he might not have made so many mistakes. Without his single-minded attention to airs, however, he might not have made so many discoveries, and it ill behooves those who are not discoverers retrospectively to criticize the methods of those who were. Notwithstanding the errors of interpretation, Priestley's description of the airs obtained in heating chalk in a gun barrel is acute. Even more so, because he did identify these as new airs, are his descriptions of ammonia and nitrous oxide.

His discovery of marine acid air by heating hydrochloric acid solution led him to heat volatile spirit of sal ammoniac (ammonia water), from which he obtained a great quantity of "vapour." Collected over mercury, the vapor did not condense when cold, proving it to be an "air," which he called alkaline air (163). He then went directly to the combination of sal ammoniac and slaked lime, heated with a water-trap between the reactants and the gas collector, a more direct production of the volatile spirit (166).[22] Alkaline air was heavier than common inflammable air but lighter than acid air; it dissolved

---

22. This set of experiments illustrates what John McEvoy has emphasized in his analysis of Priestley's work, i.e., Priestley's use of association and constant analogies to suggest further experiments. See McEvoy, "Priestley, 'Aerial Philosopher,'" *Ambix* 25 (1978): 101, 104–5, and *Ambix* 26 (1979): 27. He also points to Priestley's experiments with combinations of airs: fixed with noxious, fixed with inflammable, and alkaline with acid. Priestley hoped to produce common air, arguing by analogy and from a belief that the combination of opposites could result in a mean. A chemist would think that a combination of acid and alkali would produce (as it did) a salt; see ibid., 25, 109.

easily in water evolving heat and was slightly inflammable in the sense that a candle burned in it with an enlarged colored flame just before going out (175–77). His description of ammonia—its mode of production ($2NH_4Cl + Ca(OH)_2 = CaCl_2 + 2NH_3 + 2H_2O$), comparative specific gravity, exothermic solution in water, momentary enlargement of flame (decomposition of ammonia by heat) and various reactions with anhydrous hydrochloric acid, nitric oxide, carbon dioxide, and sulphuric acid—was accurate, containing those characteristics that many elementary texts list for its preparation and identification.

Priestley's description of depleted nitrous air (nitrous oxide, N_2O) was equally acute, though he did not here make a particular point of this new air. Because a solution of fixed air dissolved iron, he was curious to know whether fixed air alone would do so, and, as nitrous air had also an acid nature, he tried that as well. What he found in the latter case was the transformation of the nitrous air "into a species of air, with properties . . . I should not have hesitated to pronounce impossible" (215). This new air was highly noxious but supported combustion quite naturally and freely. Indeed, a candle would burn in it with an enlarged flame, sometimes not less than five or six times larger than in common air. The air dissolved freely in water and somewhat resembled that produced when nitrous air was diminished by a mixture of iron and brimstone. Priestley therefore substituted liver of sulphur (potassium sulphide) for iron in the reaction and found his diminished nitrous air produced more rapidly and in larger quantities (218). He concluded that the difference between these nitrous airs "depends upon some difference in the *mode of the combination* of its acid with phlogiston, or on the *proportion* between these two ingredients in its composition" (220). Indeed, the relationship between nitre, nitrous acid, and nitrous air, and their behavior respecting phlogiston is so curious as to promise a useful inquiry (271–73).[23]

This volume also contains some references to people and to experiments that would soon become of major significance to Priestley: Dr. Small and Mr. Boulton of Birmingham informed him that a paper soaked in a solution of copper in nitric acid and carefully dried would take fire with very little heat (254). Another future friend and fellow member of the Lunar Society of Birmingham, Dr. William Withering, then physician of Stafford,

---

23. As early as 25 Jan. 1774, before publication of this volume, J. H. Magellan had reported on these experiments with nitrous oxide to Gabriel de Bory, who communicated them to Lavoisier; Lavoisier, *Oeuvres de Lavoisier: Correspondence*, 2:421–24, #224.

is mentioned in a letter from Dr. Percival on the medicinal uses of fixed air (301). Mr. Thomas Henry, of Manchester, wrote to warn against the use of leaden pumps for water near large towns where nitre might be formed in the earth (323–24). And, in a portentous observation, Priestley noted that Hales and Hartley had observed that the calces of metals contained air that contributed to their added weights. He therefore heated a calx of lead (red lead) and obtained copious amounts of an air that was imbibed by water "exactly like fixed air." He added that he had since found that Mr. Lavoisier had discovered the same thing (192–93).[24]

The printed volume of *Experiments and Observations* was presented to the Royal Society in May 1774 and on 4 June Priestley wrote Lindsey that he had "just opened my experimental campaign with considerable success." As that new "campaign" was to result in his isolation and identification of dephlogisticated air (oxygen), Priestley's optimism was certainly justified. On Monday, 1 August 1774, he heated a sample of *mercurius calcinatus per se* (mercuric oxide, HgO) with a burning lens and obtained quantities of an air with curious properties. He repeated his experiments but did not have time to elaborate them in detail, for he was also working with other airs, writing his *Examination* of the Scottish philosophers, attempting to complete his edition of *Hartley*, and preparing for his continental tour. Only John Warltire, an itinerant lecturer who had visited him at Calne and Bowood early in August, was aware of this set of experiments when Priestley and Shelburne left for Europe.

They had reached Paris by October, where Priestley demonstrated many of his experiments, including the new ones resulting in the strange air, to Trudaine de Montigny, Lavoisier, LeRoy, and others, mentioning his surprise at the properties of the air obtained. He returned to England in late November, anxious to get to experimenting, but he had done nothing significant with the new air by late January 1775, when he wrote to Jacques Gibelin, who was translating the *Experiments and Observations* into French. He sent Gibelin a summary of his experiments performed since they had met in Paris. He had, for example, discovered vitriolic acid air (sulphur dioxide, SO_2) and obtained quantities of air from substances dissolved in nitric acid. Gibelin was free to add the summary to the translated volume, as Priestley was unsure whether he would prepare a supplement to *Experiments*

24. Red lead, or minium (plumbic oxide, Pb_3O_4), when heated, gives off oxygen, and this experiment marked the beginning of those leading to Priestley's discovery of that gas. Lavoisier's similar experiment is described in his *Opuscules Physiques et Chimiques*, published in Paris in January 1774; see Partington, *History of Chemistry*, 3:388, 390.

and Observations or communicate his results in a paper to the Royal Society.[25]

Not until 1 March 1775 did Priestley note anything additionally special about the air from mercuric oxide, but then experiment followed experiment, until he was able to write to Sir John Pringle on 15 March that he had discovered an air five to six times better than common air. That letter was read to the Royal Society on 23 March. On 25 March he wrote to Lindsey that he had found a cheap method of making his new air, but was "laid-up" with boils and could not pursue experiments as he wished. On 1 April Thomas Henry wrote to Benjamin Rush, in America, about Priestley's discovery, and on the same date Priestley wrote to Richard Price about "the pure air I discovered in London." An extract of that letter was read to the Royal Society on 6 April. Priestley wrote to William Turner on 6 April, mentioning the new air from mercurius calcinatus, red lead, etc., and stating his intention to prepare another volume of experiments, instead of a supplement, that winter. On 24 May Priestley wrote yet another letter to Pringle, describing other methods of obtaining the new air, and this letter, read to the Royal Society on 25 May, was combined with that of 15 March and the extract of 1 April into "An Account of further Discoveries in Air" and published in the *Philosophical Transactions.* By the time that paper was printed, therefore, Priestley's discovery had been revealed publicly three times to the Royal Society, his correspondents in England were aware of it, no doubt those in Europe had been informed, and word had even crossed to the colonies—though there the discovery would needs compete for attention with heated political events.

The "Account of further Discoveries" was not only an announcement of the discovery of dephlogisticated air.[26] Of the three letters that were joined to form the "Account," the first was intended as a summary of the materials to appear in the second volume of *Experiments and Observations.* There Priestley described the production of another new air, vitriolic acid air, a

25. Priestley to Jacques Gibelin, 19 Jan. 1775, in Gibelin's translation, *Experiences et Observations sur differentes Especes d'Air* (Paris: Nyon, 1777), vol. 1, appendix 8, 432–34.

26. Joseph Priestley, "An Account of further Discoveries in Air," *Philosophical Transactions* 65 (1775): 384–94. The paper was published as "Redde May 25, 1775," but the MS Journal Book of the Royal Society, 28, 1774–77, 221–24, 233–34, and 261–63, gives the proper dates for the reading of the separate letters. The last letter to Pringle is dated 25 May 1775 in the printed version, but the MS of the letter, in the Archives of the Royal Society, gives the date as 24 May. The 25 March letter to Lindsey is in Wms.; an extract is printed in W. 1.1:267. Thomas Henry to Benjamin Rush, 1 April 1775, Rush Papers, Series 7, No. 94, Library Company of Philadelphia.

vegetable acid air procured by heating concentrated acetic acid, and a nitrous acid air that could be observed only momentarily, as it could not be confined by any fluid he knew. Nitrous acid, indeed, provided a wonderful and inexhaustible subject, as it formed more kinds of air in combinations with phlogiston than all the airs formed by all the other acids (186).

Having obtained a burning lens, he had found a large variety of airs: inflammable, fixed, phlogisticated common, and nitrous, heating various substances in vacuo or over mercury with focused sunlight. The most remarkable of these airs was that first obtained by heating *mercurius calcinatus per se*.[27] This new air was "five or six times better than common air for the purpose of respiration, inflammation, and, I believe, every other use of common atmospherical air" (387), and might properly be called dephlogisticated air. The air could also be obtained from red precipitate of mercury (actually the same substance, HgO, as *mercurius calcinatus per se*) and red lead, though that from the latter was mixed with fixed air. The new air vigorously supported combustion and the respiration of mice. Priestley then thought it likely that nitrous acid was the basis of common air, but he added, "it is possible that I may think otherwise tomorrow. It is happy, when with a fertility of invention sufficient to raise hypotheses, a person is not apt to acquire too great attachment to them. By this means they lead to the discovery of new facts, and from a sufficient number of these the true theory of nature will easily result" (259).

The extracts from the letter to Richard Price extended the method of producing "that pure air I discovered in London" to the heating of substances moistened with spirit of nitre and added a speculation (withdrawn in the third part) that fixed air was a modification of nitrous acid, because the air from acid-moistened clay was fixed—the first instance of the proper generation of fixed air. "What we have got of it hitherto has been by dislodging it from substances, that contain it" (391). The third letter to Pringle repeated the information of the second on production of dephlogisticated air and speculated that there was a continuum of purity in airs from dephlogisticated, containing the least phlogiston, to nitrous, containing the most. Nitrous acid, Priestley thought, was the basis of all airs, each differing by its quantity of phlogiston and, perhaps, in the mode of combination. Priestley also announced the beginning of his study of the new mineral acid, first discovered in Sweden (probably hydrated hydrofluoric acid, HF).

27. This is the first printed reference to the gas that was ultimately to be called oxygen, while the reading of the letter to the Royal Society on 23 March 1775 gave the "publication" date for the discovery. It is generally agreed that Carl Wilhelm Scheele had discovered the gas sometime between 1771 and 1773, but he lost credit for the discovery as his work was not published until after Priestley's account; see Partington, *History of Chemistry*, 3:219–21.

Although Priestley informed Dr. John Calder in July 1775 that the second volume of *Experiments and Observations on Air* had been sent to the press, it was still possible, in late September, to add a letter to its appendix. The dedication to Sir John Pringle is dated November 1775.[28] On 6 November Priestley wrote to Trudaine de Montigny, sending printed sheets of the volume for transmitting to the French translator, Jacques Gibelin, with duplicate sheets for himself—and compliments to Lavoisier, but the printed volume was not presented to the Royal Society until February 1776.[29] By that time, everyone in the European and British scientific world had, no doubt, heard something of dephlogisticated air. In the preface to *Experiments and Observations II*, Priestley wrote that he was but an "instrument in the hands of divine providence" and had no merit but that of patient industry and unprejudiced attention, but he prided himself that he was responsible for having gained for airs an attention almost universal among philosophers in every part of Europe, greater perhaps than even that for electricity.[30] And certainly the information in this new volume, and especially the details about dephlogisticated air, was to command the attention of "philosophers."

Yet the volume does not make a point of that discovery. In format it is very like the first volume, with its idiosyncratic preface and ingenuous narrative style, with reprintings of the *Transactions* paper ("Experiments and Observations on Charcoal" of 1770 [241–62]), and the substance of the pamphlet on artificial Pyrmont water, "having no intention to publish it any more separately" (xii). The preface suggests an influence from the metaphysical writings on Common Sense Philosophy and Hartley's theory of the mind, on which he had been working while experimenting for this volume. "This is not now a business of *air* only . . . but appears to be of much greater

28. Priestley, *Exp. & Obs. II.* I have used the second edition (London: J. Johnson, 1776), which was a reissue of the sheets for the second issue of the first edition with a new title page. There was a third edition, in 1784, and the same translations as for vol. 1.

29. Priestley to Trudaine de Montigny, 6 Nov. 1775, Lyman C. Newell Collection, Boston University Library. See Ralph E. Oesper, "Priestley, Lavoisier, and Trudaine de Montigny," *Journal of Chemical Education* 13 (1936): 403–12. J. H. Magellan informed Lavoisier on 13 Nov. that the sheets had been sent. Lavoisier, *Oeuvres de Lavoisier: Correspondence*, 2:504–6, #278; MS Journal Book of the Royal Society 28, 1774–77, 22 Feb. 1776, 387.

30. Priestley, *Exp. & Obs. II*, ix, v. Antoine François de Fourcroy described Priestley's "Observations" paper as having "opened out a wholly new vista of fresh fields of scientific inquiry on a scale that had never been known before." Quoted in F. W. Gibbs, *Joseph Priestley: Adventurer in Science and Champion of Truth* (London: Thomas Nelson and Sons, 1965), 68. The laudatory review of *Exp. & Obs. II* in *Monthly Review* 54 (1776): 107–14, 425–35, ends with the statement that "Experimental philosophy has, perhaps, never been enriched, in so short a space of time, and by a single individual, with so great a number of new and important facts, as are contained in the present publication and that which preceded it."

magnitude and extent, so as to diffuse light upon the most *general principles* of natural knowledge, and especially those about which *chymistry* is particularly conversant. And it will not now be thought very assuming to say that... we may perhaps discover principles of more extensive influence than even that of *gravity* itself" (vii–viii).[31]

Many persons in many countries, he wrote, were now engaged in study of this subject, "allied to most general and comprehensive laws of nature with which we are acquainted," but we must not suppose that progress will continue to be made at the recent rate (xxiv). The most that could be said was that the subject was "well-opened." A section of the preface (and another in the text) refers to mistakes respecting his work made principally by foreign philosophers, due probably to poor translations. These should now be corrected by the work of Landriani in Italy, Gibelin in France, and Ludewig in Germany. In England, however, Benjamin Wilson had chosen to cavil pettily at the *History of Optics*, criticizing a mistake that was corrected in the errata; and there had been a "wilful and wicked perversion" of his writing in *Hartley*, from which a sentence had been truncated in quotation to give an impression that he did not believe in a future state (xiv–xx).[32] Priestley defended his religious views and called upon philosophers to attend to Christianity—not invented by priests and magistrates but opposed by them and established by extraordinary circumstances (xxiii). The preface ended with a curious Newtonesque denial that there were conjectures or speculations in this volume, followed immediately by a speculation on the "mutual convertibility, and ultimate identity" of all the aerial acids when combined with substances (xxvii).[33]

The introduction to the volume describes apparatus additional to that described in the first volume. Priestley made it clear that he did not intend the work as an elementary treatise and that no one could hope to understand the manipulation of apparatus except by actual practice (xxxiii). Practice

---

31. Perhaps he had in mind his statement in *Hartley*, xxv, "it does not appear impossible, but that, ultimately, one great comprehensive law shall be found to govern both the material and intellectual world."

32. Benjamin Wilson had a particular animus against Priestley, a friend of Benjamin Franklin and defender of the pointed lightning rods, while he favored blunt ones. The force of his sometimes perfectly correct criticisms of Priestley was diminished by the perversity of some of his other criticism.

33. It was a common belief among eighteenth-century chemists that there was but one acid, of which all others were supposed modifications. That the acid was vitriolic originated with Georg Ernst Stahl and his "saline principle," but Priestley was becoming convinced that it was nitric.

had made Priestley himself more skilled, and more cautious, in experimental operation and interpretation. He found airs and vapors were affected by the lutes he used for closing phials and tubes. Thanks to a suggestion of his friend and former pupil Benjamin Vaughan, and the generosity of Mr. Parker, he now used ground-glass stoppers variously perforated. He also discovered that gun barrels became corroded when used in generating airs and noted (57–58) that phlogiston was disengaged from the iron, infecting the airs, while it was not easy to clean the barrel from materials of previous experiments.

The text characteristically follows the pattern of chronological narrative. Part 1 describes the production of vitriolic acid air. The discovery of anhydrous gaseous marine acid had prompted him to search for other such airs. He tried to obtain "volatile vitriolic acid" to capture the air given off but, "not being a practical chemist" (1), he had trouble obtaining a supply. Timothy Lane then informed him that heating vitriolic acid with any oily substance would yield what he needed, but the experiments were interrupted by his trip to France. There he resumed his inquiries, boiling the acid with oil of turpentine at the suggestion of Trudaine de Montigney's brother, and obtained so many fumes so rapidly that he was unable to capture any. Returning to England, he repeated the experiments with olive oil and then with mercury, obtaining so much air that the apparatus once exploded, burning him severely. He concluded that phlogiston provided the volatility and elasticity in all substances.[34] As all bodies are somewhat elastic, the difference between airs and vapors appeared to be one of degree only; all substances, even water, at a sufficient degree of heat, might be exhibited in the form of air (6, 8). More cautious proceedings produced quantities that Priestley could capture and examine. Vitriolic acid air was transparent, did not affect mercury but readily dissolved in water, neither burned nor supported combustion, and was heavier than common and alkaline airs. He noted, but did not understand, the decomposition of the air by light, observed and reported the phenomenon of adsorption on charcoal.[35]

34. Recall that Priestley had once thought that phlogiston might cause the diminution of air in combustion, etc. Now he reversed himself, for if phlogiston was responsible for the elasticity of air, its presence could hardly cause diminution.

35. The top of the container in which SO_2 was generated or the glass tube through which it passed was filled with a white vapor (6), transparent sulfur dioxide having been decomposed by light into the solid forms of sulfur trioxide and sulfur, as a whitish cloud [$3SO_2 = 2SO_3 + S$]. The phenomenon of adsorption was also discovered, independently, by Scheele, but not described publicly until 1777. Priestley later, around 1779, curiously ascribed the discovery to Fontana in 1777.

Section 2 contains a description of what Priestley thought was a vegetable acid air. Obtained from a sample of concentrated acetic acid supplied by the London practical chemist Bryan Higgins, the air had many of the properties of vitriolic acid air (24). Later in the text (324), Priestley expressed suspicion of this "discovery," thinking that the sample might be contaminated by the vitriolic acid used in its manufacture; and he disavowed the "discovery" in 1779. Not until section 3 (29) did Priestley get to the discussion of dephlogisticated air, for which so many people had been waiting. There he provided a detailed description of the discovery and of the properties of the new air, taking some seventy-five pages of the text on that subject alone.

These experiments had also begun in England, where an air obtained on 1 August 1774, by heating *mercurius calcinatus per se,* vigorously supported combustion, resembling diminished nitrous air, but was only sparingly soluble in water. Priestley compared the air from *mercurius calcinatus* to that obtained by heating common red precipitate of mercury, which involved nitrous acid in its manufacture. (Each is mercuric oxide, the former obtained by heating mercury in air, the latter by heating the mercuric nitrate formed from mercury and nitric acid.) The airs were the same and Priestley had concluded that the *mercurius calcinatus* had collected nitre from the atmosphere, "though had I been any thing of a practical chemist, I could not have entertained any such suspicion" (36).

In this state of confusion Priestley visited France, where he repeated his experiments with a guaranteed-pure sample of *mercurius calcinatus.* The air obtained was the same as that previously found and when, on heating a similarly pure sample of red lead, or minium, he procured the same air, he concluded that the new air was acquired from the atmosphere. He insisted that the air supported combustion better than common air, but the Parisians remained doubtful. Lavoisier, in fact, concluded that the *mercurius calcinatus* "had, during the process of calcination, imbibed atmospheric air, not in part, but in whole" (320).[36]

Resuming his experiments on his return to England, Priestley found again that agitation in water did not deprive the new air of its property of supporting combustion. It was, therefore, not diminished nitrous air. At this point his experiments on this air were interrupted for those on vitriolic acid air (sulphur dioxide) and what he thought was a nitrous acid air. Not until

---

36. In a "Pli cacheté" of 24 March 1775 Lavoisier described experiments with *precipitate per se.* As a candle flame will burn in the released air ("a part of these facts have already been published by Mr. Priestley"), "it follows . . . that the elastic fluid fixed in mercury precipitate per se is common air." Lavoisier, *Oeuvres de Lavoisier: Correspondence,* 2:474–77.

1 March 1775 did he return to work on the air from mercuric oxide, and then, for the first time, he applied the nitrous air test. Finding it diminished "quite as much as common air" (41), for one day he concluded that all parts of common air were involved in making mercuric oxide, but the following day he found the air remaining after the nitrous air test still supported combustion. It could not, therefore, be diminished common air. Not until 8 March, however, did he completely withdraw his notion that the air from mercuric oxide might simply be common air. On that day he found that a mouse lived comfortably in the air for twice as long as it would have lived at all in common air. The next day he tested the air in which the mouse had lived, to find that residue still better than common air. On 10 March a nitrous air test found the residue of the residue still further diminishable, a mouse could still live in what remained, and that was then further diminished by nitrous air. Finally, he determined to find out just how good the new air was and discovered that five times as much nitrous air was required to saturate it as to saturate common air (47–48). This was something new, deserving of the name "dephlogisticated air."

This circumstantial account of his work on dephlogisticated air serves only to confuse the issue of when "exactly" Priestley "discovered oxygen." The "Observations" paper shows that he had produced an air, later identified as oxygen, from saltpetre sometime between the end of March and November 1772. He recognized the "extraordinary and important" nature of this air but did not pursue the matter. On 1 August 1774 he procured the air from mercuric oxide and noted some of its quality, but did not distinguish it as a unique species of air. Not until 12 March 1775 did he commence the task of discriminating between it and other airs, and it appears to have been sometime between 10th of March and the 15th, when he first wrote to Pringle, that he concluded that he had found a different kind of air. As he called it dephlogisticated air and never conceded to it all of the properties Lavoisier gave to "oxygen," it may be argued that he never quite did discover oxygen. Of course, in that sense, Scheele did not discover it either. Certainly there is no reason to doubt Priestley's claim: "especially (in) the Section on the discovery of dephlogisticated air . . . I am not conscious to myself of having concealed the least hint that was suggested to me . . . any kind of assistance . . . given me, or any views or hypotheses by which the experiments were directed, whether they were verified by the result, or not" (x). The discovery was, as Priestley insisted, accidental in the sense that he had not expected that the air he obtained would have the properties that it had (29–30). Scheele's work, on the other hand, appears, at least as he presented it to the public, to have been a deliberate effort to uncover a gas with the particular properties represented by his name for it, "fire air."[37]

Having finally determined that the air from heated mercuric oxide was a new kind of air, Priestley tried the same experiments with the air from red lead. Now both dephlogisticated and fixed air were obtained by heating. Attempting to determine the circumstances in the preparation or keeping of red lead on which the differences depended, he acquired a range of lead calces: minium, litharge, massicot, etc., fresh and kept for different periods under different circumstances. As the "pure" sample of red lead was in fact not pure (it ranged in color from red to yellow, containing PbO, plumbous oxide, as well as plumbic oxide, Pb_3O_4), the attempt failed. (Powdered plumbous oxide will take up carbon dioxide and moisture from the atmosphere, becoming lead carbonate, which, when heated, will release "fixed air.") But convinced that red lead acquired nitrous acid from the air, he moistened various non-phlogistic earths with the acid, and, heating them, now obtained dephlogisticated air from these substances. These results convinced him that atmospheric air consists of nitrous acid (nitric acid, HNO_3) plus an earth with phlogiston enough to make it elastic. This hypothesis was, he believed, consistent with the natural production of nitre. The determination of which earths, moistened with "nitrous acid," were most productive of the new air reminded Priestley of his earlier experiments on the air released by heating saltpetre ($2KNO_3$ + heat = $2KNO_2 + O_2$), now recognizing it to be dephlogisticated air (63–90).

The next section relates experiments on some miscellaneous properties of dephlogisticated air, starting with attempts to find its specific gravity. Determination by measuring the volume of air released from red lead and the difference of weight of the lead compound, before and after heating, gave a value "beyond all proportion" (91), an erroneous result Priestley explained as due partly to the fixed air also emitted in the process. He then adopted the method of "Mr. [Henry] Cavendish," weighing a bladder filled with the air. Priestley listed values, in order of increasing weight, for phlogisticated, nitrous, common, and dephlogisticated airs (94), giving total weights. It is possible from his data to determine comparative weights, and, though he has inverted the order of common and nitrous air, his determinations are reasonably good, given the basic crudity of method. He suspected that the less phlogiston there was in an air, the heavier it would be. The rule did not hold

37. For Priestley's experiments of 1772, see Schofield, *Enlightenment of Priestley*, 269. For the work of Scheele, see Partington, *History of Chemistry*, 3:219–25.

for solids or for nitrous air, which should then be heavier than dephlogisticated air. The failure of the rule in the latter case might, he thought, lie in the mode in which phlogiston was combined with the nitrous acid in the constitution of nitrous air (95).

He did not perform many experiments mixing dephlogisticated air with other airs, as the analogy between it and common air was so great that the results could be known beforehand. Precise combination with phlogisticated air, for example, could accurately produce air corresponding to common air. This observation might be useful, he thought, in improving the air in crowded rooms (97–98). A combination of inflammable air with dephlogisticated air exploded with more violence than that with common air; the loudest explosion occurred when the proportions were two to one (99). The "force of fire" was so augmented by dephlogisticated air that Mr. Michell suggested that platinum might be melted with its use, while it must surely be salutary to morbid lungs, though healthy persons might do well to avoid it, lest they "live out too fast."[38] Priestley closed the section with a curious speculation, based on comparative lengths of human life, that the atmosphere must have remained at about the same purity over many ages. "A moralist . . . may say, that the air which nature has provided for us is as good as we deserve" (101).

The discovery of dephlogisticated air by heating mercuric oxide (or red lead) with his new burning lens was part of a program of testing airs released from substances by heating. Section 6 reports results of the rest of that project, subjecting a variety of other materials—iron and steel filings, other metals, metallic compounds, a range of salts and earths—to the heat of his lens. In no case did he find another new air; in most instances he found no air at all, or fixed or nitrous. As most of these experiments (except those on iron and steel) were performed with the sample in the vacuum of Smeaton's air pump, he could not have observed, even if he had wanted to, any depletion of air with calcination. Curiously, he reported that inflammable air was produced from "all the metals that yield inflammable air, when dissolved in acids" (109). Priestley felt that air produced from heated iron or steel was like that from acids, but it probably was carbon monoxide. The inflammable air from the other metals was probably from organic impurities, "hardly discoverable by the eye," yielding more inflammable air than a considerable

38. This observation was subsequently the basis of a therapy recommended for consumption by Dr. Thomas Beddoes, at his Pneumatic Medical Institute of Bristol. There he treated consumptive patients, including Priestley's daughter, by having them inhale gases deficient in oxygen, reasoning the disease was one of a too-rapid metabolism, consuming the patient's body.

quantity of iron filings (107–8).[39] The questionable "discovery" of inflammable air from metals by heat only had at least the merit of destroying his hypothesis that inflammable air consisted of marine acid air and phlogiston. That conclusion might still be right, "for the chymical principles are so altered, by combination, that many of them are known to exist where their presence is least of all suspected" (106), and metals might contain marine acid, but the facts seemed against it.

As some continental chemists, including Lavoisier, questioned Joseph Black's assertion that the air from heated chalk was fixed air, Priestley also heated chalk in the focus of his burning lens. Strangely, he reported that little air was obtained from chalk by heating (production of quicklime by heating chalk, $CaCO_3 = CaO + CO_2$, was standard practice), but the air he got was fixed, supporting Black's contention. He repeated his experiments on heating chalk in a gun barrel, this time substituting iron filings for the iron of the barrel. Again he obtained inflammable air and again missed the discovery of carbon monoxide, concluding that the blue flame of this burning inflammable air was a result of its mixing with fixed air (110–11).

Two sections pursue the implications of an experiment Priestley had seen "at Paris, in the laboratory of Mr. Lavoisier, my excellent fellow-labourer in these inquiries" and to whom "the philosophical part of the world has very great obligations" (121). William Bewley had first noted the production of nitrous air in the preparation of nitrous ether and Lavoisier had demonstrated the production of great quantities of air from a mixture of nitric acid and alcohol. Priestley examined the airs produced by combinations of nitric acid, first with vegetable substances and then with animal, with the hope that light might be thrown upon the processes of vegetation and animalization by striking differences between the products of the experiments (146–47). The results were, inevitably, confusing. Fundamental uncertainties of primitive organic chemistry were multiplied by the facile variations in nitrogen-oxygen combinations, their permutations, and their ease of transformation into one another. The possible combinations of vegetable and animal substances with acids other than nitric would have been difficult enough to unravel; those with nitric were, at this stage, impossible.[40]

39. This comment underlines the many problems with impurities experienced by Priestley and his contemporary pneumatic chemists. Morris W. Travers, *The Experimental Study of Gases* (London: Macmillan, 1901), for example, provided instructions for elaborate washing of apparatus and freeing receiving tubes of air bubbles.

40. A. N. Meldrum, who had a most extensive discussion of Priestley's experiments with nitric acid and the oxides of nitrogen, wrote, "Let me remark that what is labelled 'nitric acid' is not always the same thing: it must contain water and nitric acid, it may contain nitrous acid

But this only made these experiments all the more alluring to Priestley: "the nitrous acid is of a most wonderful nature; the more I consider it, the more it excites my imagination, and the more unfathomable the subject appears" (123). And he addressed the problem in section 9, "Miscellaneous Experiments relating to Nitre, the Nitrous Acid, and Nitrous Air." Study of the subject promised "a fund of valuable discoveries, looking far into the constitution of nature" (160); but this set of experiments did not deliver on its promise—especially as it involved Priestley's perpetual experimental fallacies: agitation in, and long standing over, water. It did produce one methodological insight: If an experiment apparently produces different results from "what we *imagine* to be the same circumstances," consider how difficult it is exactly to reproduce the same circumstances (176–77).

Section 10 described a set of observations on common air, which chiefly involved processes for its depletion, or restoration, with corrections and amplifications of comments of earlier publications. Priestley was now convinced that depletion processes always involved mixing with phlogiston, the source being a "matter of indifference." That air, injured by respiration or putrefaction, could be restored by vegetation was confirmed by a curious fact, communicated by Mr. Garrick, that the green matter growing in a reservoir preserved the water's sweetness, "imbibing the phlogistic matter that was discharged in its tendency to putrefaction" (186).

Turning to the experiments performed with the "new mineral acid" discovered by Scheele in Sweden, Priestley did not doubt that he could obtain this acid in the form of air, as he had done with others. It is apparent from the description of his experiments that he did not examine anhydrous hydrofluoric acid (HF), but rather the gaseous product of the reaction of hydrofluoric acid with the glass containers in which it was generated or stored (silicon tetrafluoride separated from the water formed with it, $4\,HF + SiO_2 = SiF_4 + 2H_2O$), which he named fluor acid air. Priestley supposed himself unique in having exhibited silicon tetrafluoride in the form of air, though many of his experiments were admittedly similar to those performed by others.[41] He also observed incrustation of gelatinous silica, formed as silicon

---

and oxides of nitrogen. Moreover, these substances act together so as to produce others that are not well understood even at this stage of the 20th century." Sir Philip Hartog, A. N. Meldrum, and Sir Harold Hartley, "The Bicentenary of Joseph Priestley," *Journal of the Chemical Society* (July 1933): 896–920, 907.

41. He did not mention his sources for Scheele's discovery, though he did refer to the work of an "M. Boulanger" (the Duc Rochefoucauld de Liancourt), who published an account of the acid in 1773. An English abstract of Scheele's experiments was published in 1772 and an account

tetrafluoride came in contact with water ($3SiF_4 + 2H_2O = SiO_2 + 2H_2SiF_6$), diversifying the process to entertain his visitors, and subjected the air to his usual battery of tests: with a flame, with nitrous and alkaline airs (where he got an insoluble white cloud), in contact with charcoal and salts, and for solubility.

Priestley early conceived the acid air to be "acid of vitriol, charged with so much phlogiston as is necessary to its taking the form of air, with much of the earthly matter of the spar" (188). He explained the characteristic production of gelatinous silica in water as the acid dissolving in water, leaving the earth behind as a precipitate (195). When he heated the acidulous water left after the silica was removed, he was convinced that he would find vitriolic acid air—and so he did! He was too accurate an observer and too honest not to be believed when he reported, "I . . . got from it great plenty of air, which . . . appeared to have the very same properties with the vitriolic air" (207). But hydrofluorsilic acid evaporated to dryness does not yield sulphur dioxide. Bemused by theory, he appears to have misconceived an experiment, or wrongly interpreted results, failed to identify hydrogen fluoride, and initially (he later, in 1777, expressed some minor doubts) misidentified his fluor acid air.

Neither of the two sections on fixed air and miscellaneous observations reports anything of much significance. Many of these experiments are vitiated by his continued assumption that any air that forms a precipitate in lime water must be fixed air. Experiments (made at the suggestion of John Hunter) with the air from fish bladders and on live fish put into carbonated water or nitrous air indicated that bladders perform some function other than maintaining the position of the fish in water (230). Alkaline air cannot be obtained from caustic fixed alkali (KOH), though it is known that the fixed and volatile alkalies (NH_4OH) differ only in their combinations (232). Experiments on the indices of refraction of various airs had not yet met with success, but those on taking a series of electric sparks through airs confined over mercury have furnished "matter for much speculation and further experimental inquiry" (240).

---

of the "Swedish Acid" was published by John Hill in 1774, while Priestley borrowed the *Transactions of the Royal Academy of Sciences at Stockholm*, in which Scheele published, from the Royal Society on 14 April 1774. See MS Journal Book of the Royal Society vol. 28, 1774–77, 50. If any one of these sources mentioned that Scheele had identified an anhydrous form of silicon tetrafluoride, it was not done in such a way that Priestley recognized it. His claim to independent discovery of gaseous silicon tetrafluoride was, therefore, not entirely erroneous. See Partington, *History of Chemistry*, 3:213–15, 267; Gibbs, *Joseph Priestley*, 110–11.

There follow the two reprinted sections, on charcoal and on Pyrmont water, in which there is little new except an injunction to historians not to assert as facts things that are only imagined to have been necessary. Although Dr. Nooth supposed that people must have developed methods for impregnating water with fixed air as soon as it was found that that could be done, there is, in fact, no evidence that anyone had done so prior to Priestley's work (264–65). Section 16 deals with misrepresentations of Priestley's "sentiments" that had appeared in the writings of others. Priestley was seldom gentle with people who distorted his writings and he had particular reasons to be savage at this time, but he was surprisingly mild in his corrections. There is a characteristic bite in his comment: "I hope he [Mr. Lavoisier] has been more exact with respect to others, than he has been with respect to me" (310). On the whole, however, he corrected without commentary. To discuss all the errors would require a book, he wrote, but he would consider only those of a few writers of reputation, whose works went into many hands, lest readers be misled (305).

Priestley believed that he wrote clearly and could only assume that mistakes of translation into other languages had been responsible for most of the errors. Examination of the twenty pages of corrections suggests, however, that the problem was chiefly one of fixing upon a casual passing suggestion as though it were a formal proposition or of generalizing from a single reported instance as though it represented a fixed conviction. Even in the 1770s Priestley's discursive writing style was confusing to people who had already begun the process of reconstructing experimental experience into posterior rationalization, so common in modern scientific practice. Equally confusing was his willingness to print, in appendices, opinions different from his own, "in order to promote a farther investigation of the subject" (325).[42]

Priestley did attempt to clarify a basic difference between himself and his contemporaries. "Mr. Lavoisier, . . . Sig. Landriani, Sig. F. Fontana, and indeed all other writers except myself, . . . [seem] to consider common air (divested of the effluvia that float in it, and various substances that are dissolved in it . . .) as a simple elementary body; whereas I have, for a long time, considered it as a compound" (322). Indeed, he later justified his continued use of

---

42. This, of course, is consistent with Priestley's belief in the free exchange of ideas, with truth winning out in the end. He continued this practice throughout his scientific activities. See, e.g., his letter to Thos. Henry, 5 Jan. 1777, where he asks permission to publish, in an appendix, Henry's determination, which differed from his own at the time, that CO_2 was favorable to vegetation. Priestley wished, he said, to present the evidence for both sides of the dispute. See William Henry, "Tribute to the Memory of the late President of the Literary and Philosophical Society of Manchester," *Memoirs of the Literary and Philosophical Society of Manchester* 3 (2d ser., 1819): 215.

the term "air" on the same grounds. "Air" was a designation of form, not substance, and an extension of common usage—as in common, atmospheric, fixed, and inflammable airs, all in use before Priestley's time. He demanded proof that there was an elementary substance "common air," which might become confused with other substances by his terminology (334–35).

There is a final text section on experiments relating to previous sections "since they were printed" (324–35), which adds nothing significant to what has already been remarked upon, and an appendix in six parts. An index to "both of the Volumes" concludes the work. The appendix, including material dated as late as 29 November 1775, mostly relates to supposed medical applications of fixed air (he had earlier "confirmed" Percival's contention that consumption of carbonated water was a treatment for bladder stones [216–17]), or to William Bewley's repeated experiments demonstrating the acid nature of that gas. The general impression of the whole is that of a stage in a continuing process of investigation.

VII

Observations on Air III and Natural Philosophy I

During the time that he was working on the experiments, writing, and publication of *Experiments and Observations II*, Priestley's other activities in science continued. He had essentially given up original investigation on all subjects other than airs, as the sale of his achromatic telescope to Caleb Rotherham in March 1774 attests (*W.* 1.1:229–33), but he remained interested in electricity and still had the commitment entailed by his writing of the *History of Electricity* in its many editions (3d and 4th, 1775). On 14 April 1774 he delivered to the Royal Society a letter from William Nicholson on a lightning storm. In May 1775 he visited Cavendish in his laboratory to view the discharge of the artificial electric torpedo (fish). On 14 December 1775 he forwarded to the secretary of the Royal Society, with a brief cover letter, a long report from Mr. Richard Arden and another from Adam Walker (subsequently published together in the *Philosophical Transactions*) on electrical phenomena. As late as 1778 he was still active in the Royal Society committee appointed to compare pointed to blunt-ended lightning rods for the Board of Ordinance. And the connection between Priestley and electricity was kept alive abroad by the publication, in the *Scelti d' Opusculi Interessanti*, of Italian translations of extracts from the *History of Electricity*.[1]

1. Journal Book of the Royal Society, vols. 27, 52, xxix; Jungnickel and McCormmach, *Cavendish*, 190n29; "Colori dell' esplosione electrica, "Elettricità e flogisto," *Scelti d'Opuscoli Interessanti* 1 (1775): 253ff., 365ff.

He had also the citizenship responsibilities of a member of the "republic of science." He had been elected a fellow of the Royal Society in 1766 and he took his membership seriously. Although he now published most of his scientific studies in separate books, he continued to send some papers to be read at the Society and, during the season when in residence in London, he regularly attended meetings, occasionally bringing guests with him. He also joined with other fellows in proposing new fellows.[2] He now also sent copies of his scientific work to the secretaries of foreign societies, which frequently led to exchange of letters, and J. H. Magellan (Magelhaens) routinely reported to French scientists, including Antoine Lavoisier, on Priestley's work.[3]

This further increased his already extensive correspondence with people in Britain and abroad. Some of the letters, particularly those from physicians, were appended to the volumes of his *Experiments and Observations*.[4] His letters to Tobern Bergman had begun with the subject of electricity and continued with his work on airs. So also had those with Alessandro Volta. As late as April 1776 he was still writing on electricity to Volta, acknowledging the latter's published letter to him on the discovery of the electrophorous (*SciAuto.*, 70, 72). The trip to France added Trudaine de Montigny and Jacques Gibelin, at least, and perhaps others, to his list of correspondents, while visitors from Italy resulted in the addition of Giambatista Beccaria and P. Moscoti to the list. A letter of August 1775 to Marsilio Landriani gave details on the making of dephlogisticated air. In February 1775 he wrote to Andrew Oliver in America, commenting on Oliver's *Essay on Comets* and the causes of electricity in the atmosphere.

In July he wrote to John Calder, sending an article on airs for Calder's revision of Chambers' *Dictionary*. In October and again in November he

---

2. He took John Calder, Adair Crawford, Matthew Dobson, young Ld. Fitzmaurice, Samuel Heywood, Joseph Johnson, Theophilus Lindsey, Thomas Jervis, and William Wood as his guests between 1774 and 1780. See MS Journal Book of the Royal Society, vols. 27–30. And he signed certificates for Thomas Blackburne, Tiberious Cavallo, Jeremiah Dixon, Matthew Dobson, William Enfield, Samuel Farr, William Henley, Thomas Henry, William Hey, John Jebb, Andrew Kippis, J. H. Magelhaens, Edward Nairne, and Abraham Rees between 1773 and 1782; see Certificate Books, Archives, Royal Society of London.

3. Lavoisier, *Oeuvres de Lavoisier: Correspondence*, fasicule 2:291, fasicule 3:312, 335.

4. They also included letters from Benjamin Franklin, Thomas Henry, Jan Ingenhousz, Marsilio Landriani, J. H. Magellan, Adam Walker, and John Warltire. Priestley was also the path by which many persons communicated with the Royal Society—e.g., Giambatista Beccaria on phosphorescent light, Felice Fontana on air, Matthew Guthrie on Russian sanitary practices, a Mr. Hayes, surgeon, on "size" of blood, Joseph Huddart on color blindness, Thomas Percival on medicine, and a Mr. Roger on resistance of fluids. See Journal Book of the Royal Society, vols. 27, 28, and 30.

wrote to Matthew Boulton, first asking for some pieces of the "Derbyshire Spar" ("Blue John") that he had seen on a visit to Boulton's manufactory at Soho, Birmingham, to use in his fluorspar experiments, and then with thanks for the gift of spar and a comment on their differences in sentiments respecting events in America. Late in December 1775 he sent William Turner a copy of *Experiments and Observations II* with another copy for John Michell, and the last of December he wrote to Thomas Henry, at Manchester, regarding Lavoisier, who "has much public business, but finds leisure for various philosophical pursuits for which he is exceedingly well qualified. He ought to have acknowledged that my giving him an account of the air I had got from *Mercurius Calcinatus* . . . led him to try what air it yielded, which he did presently after I left. I have, however, barely hinted at this in my second volume."[5]

Priestley's most surprising new correspondent of this period was probably Jeremy Bentham. The exchange was begun by Bentham early in November 1774, with the transmission of a friend's (Dr. John Simmons's) pamphlet on the cause of atmospheric electricity. There was a cover letter and a note on an apparatus for generating airs, with a Benthamite discussion on the reformation of chemical nomenclature. Priestley responded in December, acknowledging the ingenuity of the apparatus, adding that it must be troublesome in practice, and denying the necessity of nitrous air being "very pure" in a nitrous-air test, as that always involved immediate comparison with samples of nitrous air from the same container. He also asserted that he had already changed acid air to marine acid air, now that other acid airs had been procured, and gently rejected Simmons's ("Symond's") theory of atmospheric electricity.

In March 1775 Priestley returned Simmons's paper to Bentham, apologizing because illness had prevented their meeting and offering to show him Andrew Oliver's pamphlet. In August the correspondence appears to close with Priestley's letter returning a paper of "hints" by Bentham, encouraging him to "go to work in good earnest" and announcing that he was, after publication of *Experiments and Observations II*, going to attend to other things in which he found more satisfaction. Curiously, for all Bentham's presumed

5. Priestley to Landriani, 29 Aug. 1775: Autografoteca Campari, MS Biblioteca Estense, Modena, Italy; Priestley to Trudaine du Montigny, 6 Nov. 1775, Lyman C. Newell Autograph Collection, Boston University Library. Priestley to Oliver, 12 Feb. 1775, *SciAuto.*, 62; Priestley to John Calder, 7 and 17 July 1773, Library, APS; both letters in the *Works* have wrong dates; Priestley to Matthew Boulton, 22 Oct., 6 Nov. 1775, *SciAuto.*, 65, 66; Priestley to Henry, 31 Dec. 1775, *SciAuto.*, 67.

interest since 1768 in Priestley's political philosophy, there is no reference to politics in this exchange of letters; it is all on science.[6]

His letters to Franklin refer to politics but also send news of scientific investigations. A letter of 13 February 1776 discusses his observations on blood and respiration and experiments on metals dissolved in nitric acid: "You will smile when I tell you, that I do not absolutely despair of the transmutation of metals." Franklin responded on 27 January 1777 that should he find the philosopher's stone, Priestley should take care to lose it: "Mankind are wicked enough to continue slaughtring one another as long as they can find Money to pay the Butchers."[7]

The most demanding of Priestley's peripheral "scientific" activities during this period was, however, the writing of a vigorous defense against a charge of plagiarism, his *Philosophical Empiricism*.[8] Primary culprits in this unpleasant business were Bryan Higgins (1737/41–1818) a paranoid Irish physician, and Richard Brocklesby (1722–97), Higgins's principal dupe. Throughout his life, Higgins, who had opened a school of practical chemistry in London in July 1774, enlivened his lectures and printed syllabi with vague references to his own discoveries, the many people who had exploited him without acknowledgment, and the many errors of other chemists. Brocklesby, a subscriber to an early set of Higgins's lectures, was much impressed and, wanting to help the struggling lecturer, urged Priestley to meet him. Against the advice of a "respectable friend," who warned him to have nothing to do with Higgins, Priestley agreed, and the two met for the first time early in February 1775.

"Not being a practical chemist, having never had a proper laboratory, or seen much of the usual processes" (26), Priestley thought he might observe

---

6. Bentham to Priestley, Nov. 1774, [Jeremy Bentham], *Correspondence of Jeremy Bentham*, ed. Timothy L. S. Sprigge (London: University of London Press, 1968), vol. 1, nos. 123–124: 208–9, 210–16; Priestley to Bentham, 16 Dec. 1774, *SciAuto.*, 61; 19 March 1775, Priestley-Button Collection, Dickinson College Library, Carlisle, Pa.; 23 Aug. 1775, [Bentham], *Correspondence*, vol. 1, no. 142: 260–66. Bentham typically did not take kindly to what might have seemed condescension and as late as 1827 wrote: "Dr. Priestley assumed that he had made discoveries which were no discoveries; for example the muriatic acid in a gaseous shape. He professed to have found it, but it was found by van Hamel [van Helmont?] two hundred years ago." [Jeremy Bentham], *Collected Works of Jeremy Bentham*, ed. John Bowring (London: Simkin, Marshall Co., 1838–43), 10:571.

7. Priestley to Franklin, 13 Feb. 1776, *SciAuto.*, 69; Franklin to Priestley, 27 Jan. 1777, [Franklin], *Papers*, 23:237–38.

8. Joseph Priestley, *Philosophical Empiricism: Containing Remarks on a Charge of Plagiarism respecting Dr. H——s, interspersed with various Observations relating to Different Kinds of Air* (London: J. Johnson, 1775). He did not publish the name of the accuser, lest he do injury beyond a necessary refutation of an "absurd and ridiculous accusation."

some of them and also obtain some chemicals not readily available in shops. He visited Higgins several times, purchasing chemicals and chatting, but seldom stayed for more than a quarter of an hour. He also attended two of Higgins's lectures, the first an introduction for beginners, where he was embarrassed by Higgins's fulsome praise, and a second, where he was chagrined at the failure correctly to exhibit the alkaline-air experiments (40–41). The two men saw each other for a total of perhaps four to five hours, and then—Higgins says in March, Priestley thinks perhaps as late as May 1775 (a three-month period during which he was mostly in the country)—Higgins rudely broke off the connection.

He had tried several times to get Priestley to enroll in his course of lectures and, when finally convinced that this was not to be, informed Priestley that "his time was so much taken up with necessary business, that, without meaning any person in particular, he was obliged to come to a general resolution, to answer no questions but such as he was paid for" (32). It is not entirely clear why Higgins wanted Priestley's enrollment. It may have been for the subscription money; though he always spoke contemptuously of money, there remains, as Priestley said, "some little doubt whether in this, he had a view to his own money, or to mine" (39). Perhaps, Priestley speculated, Higgins "meant to engage my attendancy upon his lectures with a view to something further . . . viz. that he might have the honour of being my instructor, and thereby have a pretence for laying claim to all my experiments" (34). For by the ending of their personal connection, Priestley's view of Higgins had changed.

He had at first thought him a modest and diffident man who had "wasted his constitution as well as his fortune" in philosophical pursuits and actually recommended him to acquaintances as a sensible lecturer (25). Soon, however, Higgins revealed his conceit and self-importance, boasting of his discoveries and complaining of people who had stolen them from him. Before leaving for Calne in the spring of 1775, Priestley heard reports that some of his experiments were the result of Higgins's general principles concerning air, while Brocklesby was claiming that all of the experiments he had witnessed Priestley perform in May at Shelburne House, in company with Dr. Fothergill, the two Drs. Watson, Dr. and Mr. Hunter, were those of Higgins.[9]

9. Whether at Shelburne House in London or at Bowood, Priestley frequently had spectators when he performed experiments; in addition to Fothergill, the Watsons, and the Hunters named above, there are references to visits from the itinerant lecturers Richard Arden and John Warltire; the instrument maker Edward Nairne; the physician William Hey, and scientists Jan Ingenhousz, G. C. Lichtenberg, and J. H. Magellan.

Sharing no principles concerning air with Higgins and Brocklesby being incompetent to judge, Priestley thought his character sufficient defense against such insinuations. He was informed, however, that the claim of his having plagiarized Higgins was gaining ground and, on his return to London, he found people saying that all his discoveries had been taken from Higgins. As neither the publication of *Experiments and Observations II* nor a reference to times and dates of his work seemed sufficient to halt the calumnies, and as friends and acquaintances urged Priestley to intervene to stop the nonsense, he wrote to Brocklesby and to Higgins on 30 November 1775. He demanded that Brocklesby give details of the experiments he had seen that were common with those of Higgins. He asked Higgins to particularize the charge that Priestley had published Higgins's discoveries as his own. Brocklesby responded the next day that the experiments shown at Shelburne House were "so nearly the same" as a variety of those he had seen in Higgins's course that justice to his friend required his declaring that none was new, save those on fluor acid. Higgins replied on 3 December with an insolent and abusive letter. As their connection had ended nine months previously, he could not be expected to enumerate all of Priestley's thefts. He might, were it necessary, "commence . . . with comparisons of the dates of Dr. Priestley's rapid publications, with the dates of my courses of chemistry. . . . I will add . . . that you have treated others as you have treated me; and that your originality in experiments consists chiefly in the knack of rendering the phenomena, which all practical chemists have observed and understood, perfectly mysterious and surprising to others" (9).

Priestley tried once more to obtain some satisfaction from Brocklesby, demanding that he explain the similarities in the challenged experiments. Some of these were of the nitrous air test and others were taken from *Experiments and Observations,* which had been published before Priestley had met Higgins and indeed before Higgins's first course of chemical lectures had begun. Another was the firing of inflammable air, adopted from Henry Cavendish; still another was that with fluor acid, which Brocklesby admitted he had not previously seen. The only experiments remaining were those on dephlogisticated air. Therefore, Priestley asked, can you tell me what the experiments were, what materials were used, what air was obtained, what were its properties, and how were they demonstrated? Finally, how long before Priestley's demonstration in May had they been seen at Higgins's lectures?

Brocklesby's response exhibits his ignorance. He could not answer any of the questions about the dephlogisticated air experiments and could only declare that as early as June 1774 Higgins was demonstrating the combination of air with "nitrous vapour" by unstopping a bottle of the strongest nitrous acid and illustrating his beliefs that there were elastic fluids distinct from air, that acid was one of these, and that it formed a combustible vapour and became fixable air when exploded. He then declined to write any further and advised Priestley to emulate Sir Isaac Newton in avoiding controversy! Failing to settle the matter privately, Priestley then went public with his defense by writing the *Philosophical Empiricism,* the title being derived from the quaint manner and phrases, the solemn and authoritative tone, in which Higgins delivered himself of long-exploded and crude notions (59).

Philosophical Empiricism begins with an "advertisement" that is essentially an apology for its length. It might well seem that an eighty-six page answer to a charge of plagiarism from a mediocrity was overkill, the swatting of a fly with a club.[10] But Priestley rightly prided himself on the care he took in giving credit to anyone who had been the least helpful and he bitterly resented the charge of plagiarism. This was the rancorous opposition and abuse of which he was to write two years later in the preface to the *Disquisitions.* Moreover, it appears that Higgins was attempting to establish himself as a rival to Priestley by attacking him and was, at least early in 1775, being taken seriously. In April 1775 J. H. Magellan, who was employed to inform Europeans of scientific activities in England, wrote Pierre J. Macquer, then the foremost of French chemists, praising Higgins as a skillful chemist, distinguished for his talents. In November 1775, after reading Priestley's *Experiments and Observations II,* Magellan wrote Macquer that Higgins was a charlatan and his declarations sophisms. Even so detailed a defense did not convince everyone. In 1787 Dr. Eason wrote Joseph Black: "Docr. Priestley, not having any one to steal from at present, I believe is quiet, unless it is to trouble the world with his religious nonsense." But whatever might be said of him privately, Priestley was never again, when he could respond, subjected publicly to charges against his scientific originality. In science as in theology and metaphysics, the provincial schoolmaster and minister had shown that he had sharp teeth.[11]

10. The reviewer observed that, in his opinion, the whole was "much more than was necessary to a complete refutation of the charge." *Monthly Review* 54 (1776): 411–12.

11. J. H. Magellan to J. Macquer, 7 April, 24 Nov. 1775, MN. Dept. Bibliotheque National, Paris. Magellan also described Higgins as a charlatan in a letter of 13 Nov. 1775 to Lavoisier and sometime that year sent him a copy of *Philosophical Empiricism.* Lavoisier, *Oeuvres de Lavoisier: Lavoisier Correspondence,* fasicule 2:278–79, 504–8. Eason letter in Sir Wm. Ramsey, *Life and Letters of Joseph Black, M.D.* (London: Constable and Co. 1918), 87. On at least two other occasions Priestley was charged with plagiarism, but in each case he may not even have been aware of it—one on the eve of his sailing for the United States and the other while living there.

The introduction to *Philosophical Empiricism* sets the stage with the letters exchanged by Priestley, Brocklesby, and "H——s," with accompanying commentary. There follows a section describing incidents of his association with H——s and the occasion of its termination. Priestley then recounted what he had seen and heard from H——s, with particular reference to their differences over the nature of fixed air. Common air plus phlogiston could not be fixed air; phlogisticated air lacked almost all the distinguishing properties of fixed air: it was not water soluble, not acid, did not precipitate lime from lime water, and "lastly, which makes as manifest a distinction between these two airs as any, they differ very greatly in specific gravity" (42). Priestley had described to H——s, in the presence of Brocklesby, his experiments on marine acid and vitriolic acid airs and declared his expectations of finding other acid airs. H——s had denied that air could be obtained from red lead or earths moistened with spirit of nitre (47).

The next section (52–59) discusses the oddities to be found in the *Syllabus* of Higgins's lectures. Priestley's views and those of Higgins were totally opposed. Higgins called acid air, alkaline air, and nitrous air "conceits"; he believed that there were seven primary elements of matter: earth, water, alkali, acid, air, phlogiston (having the power to counteract gravity), and light (which, combined with phlogiston, constituted fire). These were all, in Higgins's words, "impenetrable, immutable, and inconvertible." To which Priestley responded, "We are far from being sufficiently advanced in the knowledge of nature to pronounce concerning its primary constituent parts" (56). Higgins said that nitrous acid prevented the formation of inflammable air despite Priestley's discovery of depleted nitrous air, which burns. He supported a vibration theory of light and declared that gravity depended on the species of gravitating matter (57). Given these opinions, how could anyone suppose that he had derived anything of consequence from Higgins's ideas?

Finally, there is a section of miscellaneous observations, with particular attention to dates of association and dates of Priestley's published writings, along with wonder that Higgins should be so anxious to claim the discovery of what he had termed mere conceits. There follows a rhetorical letter to Higgins demanding that he specify the discoveries he claimed Priestley had stolen, that he prove he made them public and that Priestley knew of them before publishing, that he prove Priestley's plagiarism from others besides Higgins, that he validate the opinions expressed in his "extraordinary *Syllabus*," and that he specify the names of the many persons who had behaved toward him with the baseness and ingratitude he ascribed to Priestley, so that the company might unite in comparing notes. A rhetorical letter

to Brocklesby rather heavy-handedly warned him against mistaking superficial appearances for fundamental similarities.

Scarcely had Priestley completed the chore of his *Philosophical Empiricism* than he began the more congenial task of writing a paper for the Royal
Society. Read to the Society on 25 January 1776 and published the same year,
his "Observations on Respiration and the Use of the Blood" describes his
last significant independent discovery.[12] So important did Priestley think this
paper that he returned to his favorite historical mode of exposition, outlining the previous theories on the physiological function of respiration and
the blood before presenting his own conclusions. His major source for historical information was von Haller's *System of Physiology*, from which he
derived the opinions of Hippocrates, Galen, and other "ancients," Descartes,
Malphigi, Lister, Boerhaave, and Albrecht von Haller himself. None of these
"philosophers," not even Stephen Hales, who has "thrown much more
light upon the doctrine of air than all his predecessors" (230), had been able
to arrive at the answer that Priestley discovered "without any trouble or
thought, in the course of my researches into the properties of different kinds
of air" (226).

Once again Priestley was too modest. It is true that the discovery seems
not to have resulted from experiments deliberately conceived to bring an
answer to this ancient problem. On the other hand (and his long list of
predecessors and contemporaries who had addressed the question supports
this contention), Priestley alone was able to put together a series of observations to achieve a solution that led for the first time in a promising direction. He thought it clear that respiration was a phlogistic process, affecting
air like other such processes by diminishing its quantity, lessening its specific gravity, and rendering it unfit for respiration or the support of combustion (227). It appeared that this was effected by means of blood coming in
contact with air in the lungs, where it parted with the phlogiston it had
imbibed in the course of its circulation (238). Venous blood becomes arte-
rial in passing through the lungs, changing color in the process, while the air
in the lungs is phlogisticated. Experiments *in vitrio* confirmed the theory,
dark blood becoming bright and florid when placed in contact with atmospheric or dephlogisticated air, phlogisticating the air in the process, bright
red blood darkening in contact with air unfit for respiration. And although
the blood and air in the lungs never came into actual contact, black blood

---

12. Priestley, "Observations on Respiration and the Use of the Blood," *Philosophical Transactions* 66 (1776): 226–48; MS Decade VI, #153, vol. 56 (9 Nov. 1775–1 Feb. 1776), Archives,
Royal Society.

placed in a bladder and hung in the air overnight acquired a coating of florid red (243–44).[13]

Understandably elated over his new discovery, Priestley quickly wrote his correspondents. In February, for example, he sent the news to Caleb Rotheram, Benjamin Franklin, and Jacques Gibelin; Gibelin abridged the Royal Society paper in an appendix to the French translation of *Experiments and Observations II* (Paris, 1777).[14] The claim that respiration was a phlogistic process involving blood as a transfer medium quickly attracted attention. In May 1777 Lavoisier read the first of a series of papers on respiration to the Académie des Sciences. These papers are frequently cited as beginning the understanding of respiration as an oxidation phenomenon. In fact, Lavoisier's interpretation was almost the inversion of Priestley's, and it is clear that Priestley's paper was the starting point. Lavoisier had already begun to question the concept of phlogiston, and the work of Adair Crawford on animal heat (1779), also strongly influenced by Priestley, led to the oxidation-respiration papers by Lavoisier and his collaborators, Laplace and Seguin. Priestley had again been catalyst for others' discoveries.[15]

This was, however, the last time his scientific work was to have the creative quality that had characterized so much of it from the time of his electrical experiments roughly ten years earlier. Seventeen-seventy-six was not a happy year for British Dissenter-friends of Americans and Priestley's attention may well have been diverted from his work to the stirring events in the colonies. Nonetheless, the root cause of the lack of excitement in his next published work on airs was his turning toward metaphysics. In August 1775 he had informed Bentham that he was going to quit science for a while

13. Priestley here confirmed his own earlier comments, in the 1772 "Observations" paper, that bladders did not prevent the airs in them from mixing with external air. See Schofield, *Enlightenment of Priestley*, 265.

14. Priestley to Franklin, 13 Feb. 1776: *SciAuto.*, 69; and to Gibelin, 9 Feb. 1776, *Exp. & Obs.* (Paris, 1777), trans. Gibelin, appendix 6, vol. 3.

15. The Lavoisier paper of 1777, "Expérience sur la Respiration des Animaux et sur les Changements qui arrive à l'Air en passant par leur Poumons," was published in the *Mémoires* of the Académie in 1780; Lavoisier's debt to Priestley was, as usual, scarcely admitted. Later papers were dated 1784, 1785, and 1791. For this work by Lavoisier et al., see Partington, *History of Chemistry*, 3:416–18, 471–75. Crawford published a paper, "Experiments on the Power that Animals when placed in certain Circumstances possess of Producing Cold" in *Philosophical Transactions* 71 (1781): 479–91, which cites Priestley's work to support his own. The second edition of his *Experiments and Observations on Animal Heat* (1788) was revised in light of Lavoisier's oxidation theory, but retains references to Priestley and some of the concept of phlogiston. Still, Robert Fox, *The Caloric Theory of Gases from Lavoisier to Regnault* (Oxford: Clarendon Press, 1971), 38n†, feels that "Crawford's debt to Priestley is obvious, though unacknowledged."

for more satisfying studies. The following year he became involved in writing the *Disquisitions* and preparing to write *Necessity Illustrated*. Although he wrote to Volta in April 1776 that he hoped to have a third volume on air ready by winter, and to Lindsey in July that he was experimenting every day, *Experiments and Observations III* was not published until the spring of 1777, and when it appeared it had the character of a termination, a tying up of loose ends.[16]

Even the preface has an elegiac tone. Priestley had not expected to have another volume so soon, but materials had accumulated to justify it. Now he would give himself and his readers some respite, as his attention would "be sufficiently engaged by speculations of a very different sort" (vii). He had the satisfaction of being a spectator of the progress made with research left in such good hands, he said, listing several German, Italian, English, and French chemists (including Lavoisier) who were investigating airs with ardor and ability (viii–ix). This volume was not as "brilliant" as previous volumes, he acknowledged, but there were more "new facts," sure to be valuable to "philosophers and chemists" (vi). He had hoped to conclude his work with a general theory of different kinds of air but had decided that his investigations were not advanced sufficiently for that. He did, however, reveal a cause of his enthusiasm for pneumatic studies as a means of unfolding "some of the most curious secrets of nature," a cause that may also reflect some of the matter theory of the *Disquisitions*: "The reason of my great expectations from this mode of experimenting is simply this, that, by exhibiting substances *in the form of air,* we have an opportunity of examining them in a less compounded state, and are advanced one step nearer to their primitive elements" (ix).[17]

Priestley described the "form of air" as "exceedingly convenient for a chymical examination and analysis" (174). He supposed that all substances, "in a *certain degree of heat,*" were capable of becoming permanent vapors, though he was unable to exhibit the fact (324) and suspected the rate of

16. Priestley to Bentham, 23 Aug. 1775, [Bentham], *Correspondence*, vol. 1, no. 142; to Volta, 25 April 1776, *SciAuto.*, 70; Priestley, *Exp. & Obs. III* (London: J. Johnson, 1777). The dedication is dated 3 Feb. 1777 and a copy was given to the Royal Society Library on 17 April 1777. Journal Book of the Royal Society, vol. 29, 1777–78, 39. In contrast with previous reviews, that for this volume (*Monthly Review* 58 [1778]: 60–68) is primarily descriptive and confines its praise to: "The present volume contains such a variety of curious matter, that we find it most proper and convenient to confine our extracts to a few subjects."

17. This sentiment was a reflection of an intention revealed as early as 1767 when, in his *History of Electricity*, he spoke of chemistry as being "conversant about the latent and less obvious properties of bodies"; see Schofield, *Enlightenment of Priestley*, 155–56.

heating was a factor. "I imagine . . . when the heat is applied slowly, some parts of the substances . . . become, by degrees, accustomed . . . to bear a force, which, if it had been applied suddenly, would have inevitably broke their cohesion with the rest" (337). His belief that elastic vapors, once achieved at some high temperature, would be permanent when the temperature fell might be argued on the principles of Newton, Boscovich, Michell, and Hales, that once the particles of a substance were repelled out of their spheres of attraction, they would be in a state of permanent repulsion, i.e., an elastic fluid. Experiments over the next century showed this theory to be untenable, but specific heat and atomic weight studies confirmed that substances in gaseous form provided unique opportunities for study. As the distinguished chemist Thomas Graham wrote in 1863, "In the condition of a gas, matter is deprived of numerous and varying properties with which it appears invested when in the form of a liquid or solid. The gas exhibits only a few grand and simple features."[18]

The difference between an elastic vapor and a permanent elastic fluid also provided Priestley with a further opportunity to address charges made during the *Philosophical Empiricism* affair. Still smarting from the accusations of Higgins and Brocklesby, he refuted the claim that practical chemists had previously observed and understood his claimed discoveries. Van Helmont, Boyle, Hales, and others were aware of the effluvia of spirit of salt and of volatile alkali, but not that these could be exhibited as permanent elastic fluids, or airs (325–27). They had not discovered marine acid or alkaline airs before he had.

Priestley's summary of the contents of *Experiments and Observations III*, contained in the preface and some sections of the text, including parts of the introduction, suggest that he was attempting, not entirely successfully, to come to terms with contemporary developments in chemistry, including the increasing role of gravimetric considerations. An example was his "disproof" of experiments by Felice Fontana that indicated that dephlogisticated air contained no "earth" and found that the weight of mercury was unchanged by experiments making and expelling dephlogisticated air. When Priestley repeated the experiments, he always found a loss of mercury weight—a loss of more than one-third in one case. He was unpracticed in weight experiments,

---

18. Priestley's speculations here expanded on those of *Exp. & Obs. II*, 6, 8. See Thomas Graham, "Speculative Ideas respecting the Constitution of Matter," *Proceedings of the Royal Society* 12 (1863): 620–23. Graham may have arrived at these ideas independently, but he knew Priestley's work; see, e.g., Thomas Graham, *Elements of Chemistry, including the Applications of the Science in the Arts* (London: Hippolyte Bailliere, 1842), 70.

but the wide variations in his results might well have disturbed him had he taken such experiments seriously.[19]

That he did not do so may partially have been the result of uncertainty as to the pertinence of weight relationships in experiments with phlogiston. When he described his attempt to determine the quantity of spirit of nitre in dephlogisticated air, he complained that he was unable to ascertain the amount of phlogiston involved by circumstances of weight (41–54). More important, however, was his indifference to the role of weight in chemistry, and this was a part of his general indifference to quantitative considerations in science. When performing a quantitative experiment, Priestley would typically mix parameters, reporting, for example, the weight of iron, the volume of gas, and no measure at all of the liquid, when he "extracted" the inflammable air from iron with acid (165–73).

He had an understandable confidence in his own experiments and doubts about those of others, but he was beginning to feel pressured by interpretations of his experiments that differed from his own. He always minimized the importance of interpretation: "Let the new facts, from which I deduce . . . [my opinions] be considered as my discoveries and let other persons draw better inferences from them if they can" (xvii). But a complete and accurate description of an experiment and its results that in no way involves theory is nearly impossible. Priestley frequently defended as fact what was, in the end, demonstrably theory. For all his protestations of open-mindedness, he regularly defended his opinions with considerable vigor when they came under attack, and he clearly resented Lavoisier's suggestion that he was propagating "dangerous errors" (xxix, xxxiv).

This was the first intimation of Priestley's response to what was to be a full-scale attack on his theoretical position. Previously he had known Lavoisier as an enthusiastic experimenter, not overly scrupulous about publicly crediting the originators of his experimental designs.[20] Now he began to see him as a theoretician, denying or even inverting Priestley's interpretations of his experiments. It is scarcely surprising, then, that Priestley could not confirm Lavoisier's experiments, particularly when they were coupled

19. He corrected this in his next volume, *Exp. & Obs. Nat. Phil.,* 260, where he still found a small loss of weight in the mercury but concluded that earth can be but a very small proportion of the weight of dephlogisticated air.

20. Yet, on 8 June 1777, Lavoisier invited Franklin to join him in repeating experiments explicitly credited to Priestley. Franklin Papers 5.1:551–2, APS. The experiments were perhaps those of *Exp. & Obs. III,* from the copy Priestley had sent to Lavoisier. See Memo, Wellcome Medical Historical Library, London.

with declarations—e.g., that it was the air previously contained in nitrous acid that combined with mercury to make red precipitate; that pure air entered the composition of all acids without exception, causing their acidity; and that all metallic calces contained common air (xxvii, xxxii). Priestley's responses included a defense of the concept of phlogiston and a return to the process of agitating airs in water to refute the contention that there was no "proper air" in nitrous air (xxx). And they criticized Lavoisier's belief that dephlogisticated air was the acidifying principle (i.e., oxygen). This error, Priestley thought, was based on the mistaken "opinion of the ablest chymists" that all acids were ultimately the same, with modifications and different combinations (28).

As Priestley tried to bring an end to several sets of uncompleted experimental investigations—e.g., miscellaneous experiments on dephlogisticated air (5–40, 85–91), or the influence of paints, oils, and alcohol on common air (92–99)—he repeated many of the errors in technique or interpretation that he had earlier made. Some of these are scarcely surprising. He persisted, for example, in identifying any air that produced a precipitate in limewater as fixed air (5–20), but analytical principles were not yet fully developed and he had no reason to change his mind. Other instances display what he was to call his "humbling failure of recollection." In the introduction, where as usual he described new apparatus and variations on old, Priestley included the recipe for a new lute, though he had earlier discovered that lutes introduced impurities into chemical operations (4). He continued agitating airs in water and storing them over water for weeks, or even months, though he had noticed earlier the *results* of molecular transport and diffusion (100–103).[21] He described the "diminishing" of nitrous air confined in a bladder, despite an earlier declaration that bladders could not hold airs unchanged (151–58). He again noted the discoloration of the water in his pneumatic trough, but he still regarded water as only an instrument.[22] Assessing his career, one must take account of a "defect" in the "constitution" of his mind: "I have so completely forgotten what I have myself published, that in

21. He also noted, however, the "purification" of air by agitation in salt water. Philip Hartog, "Joseph Priestley and His Place in the History of Science," *Proceedings of the Royal Institution* 26 (1931): 395–430, 413, noted an observation in *Comptes Rendus* 90 (1880): 1410, that agitation of air over the sea helped keep the partial pressure of carbon dioxide in the air constant.

22. Note, for example, the "extraction" of nitrous acid from nitrous air by decomposition with common or dephlogisticated air (159–64), for he was convinced that HNO_3 was in NO, which is decomposed by the addition of O_2. Actually the process takes place over, and includes, water, as: $4NO + 3O_2 + 2H_2O = 4HNO_3$.

reading my own writings, what I find in them often appears perfectly new to me, and I have more than once made experiments, the results of which had been published by me."[23]

Not everything in *Experiments and Observations III* is repetition (though there is the usual reprinting, this time of "Observations on Respiration" [55–84]), nor does "failure of recollection" or misconception mar the entire work. Priestley's extraordinary powers of observation are still evident in his identification of a "black matter" (Hg) produced when taking an electric spark through vitriolic acid air, confined over mercury (279, xxiv);[24] his description of the various colors of iron salts; his report of the anomalous behavior of tin with nitric acid; and his observations on color changes in nitrogen-oxygen gases as he pursued his conviction that nitric acid and the nitrogen oxides afford the most promising investigations concerning airs (103–31). His continuing efforts to procure an anhydrous nitric acid in the form of air failed, for his experiments with "nitrous acid vapour" (174–233) were inevitably confused by the widely varying products of dissociation with but slight differences of temperature, pressure, concentration, and so on.[25] He described the manufacture of nitrosyl chloride, and commented on, without entirely understanding, the problem of deliquescence in his reactions.

He had also begun to recognize the necessity of observing all the changes in a chemical reaction, reporting, e.g., that in making nitrous air by combining a metal with nitrous acid, not all the phlogiston from the metal goes into the air. Some of it must remain in the saline substance formed by the union of acid and metal (165). Nor did the inflammable air generated by marine acid air and iron filings replace all of the acid air, "part of the acid no doubt being requisite to form the salt formed by the union of the acid and the iron" (268). The quantitative implications of these qualitative observations were not pursued, for they required a recognition of gravimetrically balanced equations, not to be fully acknowledged by chemists until Lavoisier's operational definition of chemical compounding was ratified by Dalton.

It is true, however, that the startling phenomenological changes in pneumatic chemistry are those in volume, while changes in mass are less obvious.

---

23. *W.* 1.1:345. He repeated the same appraisal of himself in a letter to Newcome Cappe, 13 April 1777: "I hardly ever look into any thing I have published, and when I do, it sometimes appears quite new to me."

24. On 4 Feb. 1778 he wrote James Keir, noting that in a pneumatic trough with air confined over mercury, the "mercurial vapour is diffused thro the mass of air even when cold"; he repeated the same observation in June 1779 in a letter to Fabrioni (*SciAuto.*, 77, 81).

25. Anhydrous nitric acid (dinitrogen pentoxide, N_2O_5) was not to be isolated until Deville's success of 1849; but note: $2HNO_3 - H_2O = N_2O_5$.

And there is, in Priestley's work, some recognition of quantitative changes of volume, e.g., "in every complete diminution of air by a phlogistic process, there is a real absorption of one fourth part of it" (98).

His most intriguing change of "volume" experiments were not chemical, however, but physical and philosophical. These represent an aspect of Priestley's work that was soon to be acknowledged in a change of title of his series of science volumes—to *Experiments and Observations, relating to Various Branches of Natural Philosophy*. Having noted, in *Experiments and Observations I* (1774, p. 250) that common and fixed airs expanded equally in equal degrees of heat, he now resolved to determine more carefully the heat expansion of a number of different gases (343–48). The experiments were primitive and Priestley recognized that the results were not entirely dependable (345). In fact, they were not at all dependable, for they showed that gases (including common and fixed airs) expand quite differently with the same degree of heat.[26]

His experiments on mixing nonreacting gases were also experiments in "physics." He expected that mixtures of airs with different specific gravities—of fixed and common airs, for example, or inflammable and nitrous—would separate themselves. The airs diffused through one another, however, and could not be separated by any method he tried (301–5).[27] His attempts to measure indices of refraction of different gases were also inconclusive, only inflammable air (surely hydrogen in this instance) having an index substantially different from that of common air. Priestley did not specify which of his gases he chose to examine, but of the ten he might have tested only hydrogen, sulphur dioxide (his vitriolic acid air), and nitrous oxide (his phlogisticated nitrous air) have indices differing from that of common air by as much as two hundredths of a percent. His techniques were incapable of measuring so small a difference, but it is significant that he thought to try. As earlier, when he had attempted to measure change in refractive index

26. His measurements of the expansion of airs, *Exp. & Obs.* (1:250; 3:345–48), and their continuation in *Exp. & Obs. Nat. Phil.* (2:359), were rightly ignored when John Dalton and Joseph Louis Gay-Lussac published their work on what became known as Charles's Law in 1802. Priestley's results and those of other experimenters, being so varied, were explained by Dalton as due to want of care in keeping apparatus free from moisture. See Partington, *History of Chemistry*, 3:769–71.

27. John Dalton cited Priestley in three works: *Meteorological Observations and Essays* (London: W. Richardson, 1793), 104–5; "On the Tendency of Elastic Fluids to Diffusion through Each Other," *Memoirs of the Literary and Philosophical Society of Manchester* 1 (2d ser., 1805): 259–70, 259–60; and his Lecture 17, 27 Jan. 1810, of a series at the Royal Institution. See Henry E. Roscoe and Arthur Harden, *A New View of the Origin of Dalton's Atomic Theory* (1896; reprint New York: Johnson Reprint Corp., 1970), 13–14.

with electrification, Priestley was again following the Newtonian injunction to combine optics with chemistry to gain "an inlet into . . . [the] internal structure of matter."[28]

Given the tone of *Experiments and Observations III* and its promise of "respite" from more volumes "on the same subject," it is surprising to find yet another volume within two years.[29] Priestley explained that the speculations that were to entice his attention were of a "metaphysical nature" and had not taken as much time as expected; single sections of this new volume cost more in labor, patience, time and expense than whole volumes of his metaphysical writings! Besides, he liked experimenting, though scientific studies ranked less high than others (e.g., theology). Still, they needed no apology, being useful and honorable, especially for persons of rank and fortune, who should become accustomed to the sight of experiments in early life if they were to lay a good foundation for philosophical pursuits.[30]

The difference in title—*Experiments and Observations relating to Various Branches of Natural Philosophy, with a Continuation of the Observations on Air*—raised expectations of a change in subject. The emphasis in the new title perhaps followed from several years of metaphysical speculation, and there was some slight shift toward greater emphasis on physical phenomena. The shift was, however, so slight that it is customary to treat the "new series" as a continuation of the old, with standard abbreviations as *Experiments and Observations IV, V,* and *VI.* The general impression of the new volume was much the same as that of the previous volumes; there was still the idiosyncratic preface, the introduction dealing with apparatus, and the text describing series of experiments. The introduction on apparatus added little more than minor improvements to previous discussions. Priestley included an illustration of the device used in taking an electric spark through airs confined over mercury and a description of the way in which he mixed airs in the nitrous air test, "though it has nothing to boast of with respect to ingenuity" (xxx).[31]

28. Sulfur dioxide has twice the difference from common air that hydrogen has and this would surely have been detected if that gas were tested and the technique were sound. John Warltire to Priestley, 3 Jan. 1777; see *Exp. & Obs. III,* 363–68, for the refraction experiments. For the Newtonian suggestion and the electrical/refraction experiments, see Schofield, *Enlightenment of Priestley,* chap. 6.

29. Priestley, *Exp. & Obs. Nat. Phil.* The preface is dated 1 March and a copy was presented to the Royal Society on 20 May 1779; see Journal Book of the Royal Society, vol. 30, 1778–80, 440.

30. *Exp. & Obs. Nat. Phil.,* v–viii. This last comment clearly had reference to the campaign Priestley had been carrying on for the scientific education of Shelburne's sons.

31. In fact, the method of mixing was important enough to justify a publication by Cavendish, who concluded that the only way to ensure uniform results was to establish a standard

The text of this volume illustrates the qualities of Priestley's work so often criticized by chemists and historians. It is prolix and rambling, without apparent design or intent. In fact, Priestley was doing exactly what he so frequently recommended to others. He was being empirical; he did not understand exactly what he was doing or why, and had therefore to try to describe everything he did and saw. Given the particular gestalt within which he was working, his observations were extraordinarily perceptive, even to modern eyes, despite his wayward commentaries. Consider, for example, his experiment with his new "sand heat," which he enthusiastically employed in diversifying previous experiments involving heat. Continued sandbath, heating of vitriolic acid air and water in a confined state changed the air into sulphur ($3SO_2 + 3H_2O$, in a heated hermetically sealed tube $= 3H_2SO_3 = 2H_2SO_4 + H_2O + S$) (124–25, 259); on marine acid (HCl) in a sealed glass tube dissolved the lead in the glass. And he appears to have obtained phosphorous acid and repeated Robert Boyle's discovery that, in a sandbath-heated sealed tube, it becomes a solid crust sometimes exhibiting flashes of light extending the whole length of the tube ($4H_3PO_3 + heat = 3H_3PO_4 + PH_3$ [phosphine] which can spontaneously ignite) (135). Yet he also reported that inflammable air from metals, long heated in a hermetically sealed tube, is decomposed to a black substance coating the tube and phlogisticated air (367–68)!

As his preface implies, the text essentially consists of a systematic extension of processes previously examined, starting with seven sections (seventy-seven pages) on his obsession: nitric acid and the oxides of nitrogen. Priestley noted first that the constitution of "nitrous and inflammable air" were very different as the phlogiston must be combined in them in a very different manner (45). He noted (but did nothing about it) that "when the water in my trough had got impregnated with various metallic substances, that which was contiguous to the nitrous air, in jars standing in it, would be of a darker colour than the rest of the water" (54).[32] In a series of experiments that compel amazement, if not admiration, he tested the preservation of animal substances in nitrous air (NO). A pigeon carcass preserved in nitrous air from April to September was cooked! "Mr. Magellan . . . had not so bad an opinion of this piece of cookery as I had" (71).

---

procedure. Cavendish, "An Account of a New Eudiometer," *Philosophical Transactions* 73 (1783): 106–35. See Jungnickel and McCormmach, *Cavendish*, 260. Lavoisier criticized the test because its results were susceptible to temperature, pressure, rapidity of experiment, size of vessel, and amount of nitric oxide used.

32. He later observed (291–92) that the "water [of his pneumatic trough] permits phlogiston to pass from . . . [a] precipitated calx to the air."

In the section on marine acid (HCl), he found that common salt "contains" marine acid (106), and that marine acid differs essentially from vitriolic and nitric acids in that "it cannot . . . be made to yield dephlogisticated air" (244). In that on dephlogisticated air, he noted that, as his "Observations" paper showed, he must have possessed it, unrecognized, before November 1771 (193), and that iron behaves anomalously in the processes of rusting (253). He was disappointed that samples of common air taken from cities, factories, the seaside, dining rooms, hot houses, and mountain tops differed so little in nitrous air tests (269–81).[33] A spark taken in common air confined over water diminished the air and turned the water acid; this could not result from the mere *concussion* given to the air by the spark, because the spark had no effect when the air was completely diminished (284–87).

Six sections (296–359) relate to the confusing interaction of plants and airs. Priestley had worked on this problem for many years, with contradictory results. His experiments are notable for demonstrating that plants do not live as well in dephlogisticated air as in common and for the discovery of a "green matter" that appeared spontaneously on the sides of containers filled with pump water, from which bubbles of dephlogisticated air streamed. This green matter "can neither be of an animal or vegetable nature [as it appeared in containers which were "closely corked"], but a thing *sui generis* . . . extraordinary as it will seem . . . *light* is necessary to the formation of this substance" (342).[34] Only in September did Priestley discover that the "green matter" was a vegetable, and even then he did not understand its action (*SciAuto.* 83–85). The complicated processes of photosynthesis, hinted at by Priestley in his "Observations" paper of 1772, were not yet finally unraveled; it took the combined efforts of Jan Ingenhousz, Priestley, Jean Senebier, and Nicolas T. De Saussure to demonstrate, against much hostile criticism, that green vegetation, under the action of sunlight, absorbed carbon dioxide and released oxygen to the air.[35]

His experiments on "exposing substances to a long continued heat were begun, principally, with a view to ascertain the conversion of water into earth" (406). Although he succeeded in turning an air (vitriolic acid air) into

33. In 1777 he had written to Matthew Boulton for air samples from Birmingham (*SciAuto.*, 75, 76). The dining room section (278–81) was reprinted in *Weekly Entertainer* 18 (1791): 145–46.

34. In writing about this "green matter" to Landriani in July 1778, he failed to relate it to that mentioned by Mr. Walker, which grew on the sides of the reservoir of an inn and kept the water sweet (*SciAuto.*, 78; *Exp. & Obs. II*, 185–86), though they must have been the same.

35. The demonstration was not complete until after 1807; see Partington, *History of Chemistry*, 3:277–84.

a solid, despite the successes of Woulfe and Godfrey, he failed with water. "I went upon the idea, that the change of consistence in water was brought about by extending the bounds of the repulsion of its particles, and at the same time preventing their actually receding from each other, till the spheres of attraction within those of repulsion should reach them. The hypothesis may still be not much amiss, though I did not properly act upon it."[36]

The implied physicality of this operation fits the *Natural Philosophy* part of the volume title, as does the section on electricity (425–29), where, for the first time, we are given sufficient information about his charged tubes (i.e., both area coated and thickness of glass) to allow determination of capacitance. Perhaps, also, Priestley's comments on the article "Gas," in James Keir's translation of P. J. Macquer's *Dictionary of Chemistry* (2d ed., 1777) imply a retreat from chemistry:

> Not being a professed chemist, and attending only to such articles in that branch of knowledge as my own pursuits are particularly connected with . . . illustrations of chemical processes are not likely to occur to me as they are to others [39]. . . . Having, in some parts of this volume, ventured to launch beyond the bounds of the doctrine concerning air into the region of a more extensive chemistry, in which I profess myself to be but a novice, and being unwilling to advance any trite observations as discoveries of my own . . . I begged the favour of my chemical friends, Mr. Bewley, Mr. Keir, and Mr. Hey, to peruse the work . . . and to communicate such observations as might enable me to make it, in any respect more correct. (486)

His letter to James Keir, dated 4 February 1778, further explains this paragraph. His work was then so large as to justify two volumes, but had yet to be transcribed. When a volume was finished, he proposed sending it to Keir for remarks, "for I am afraid of tripping on chemical ground. My walk is between what is call'd *chemistry*, and other branches of Natural Philosophy. On this side I am pretty well received, but on the other there are some that

---

36. *Exp. & Obs. Nat. Phil.*, 408. This is the only explicit intimation in his published scientific work that Priestley followed suggestions of the Newton, Rowning, Boscovich, Hales, and Michell matter theory, though many processes he adopted may be so interpreted. According to Jungnickel and McCormmach, *Cavendish*, 170, Cavendish also "had theoretical notions about chemical reactions at the level of particles and forces," but was unable to develop this approach.

show a willingness to peck at me, and therefore it behooves me to be on my guard and secure as able seconds as I can."[37]

There is a hint here of a difference in the direction of his research, which supports the impression given by the *Natural Philosophy* part of the volume's title. Any continuation of a new direction would, however, needs be postponed for a major shift in location and occupation. During the last year covered by that volume, the tenuous connection with Lord Shelburne came unglued. Priestley suggests that the situation developed "about two years before I left him," that is, around 1778, but the nature of their association had been something other than the companionship Shelburne had originally intended, since Priestley had returned from Paris alone in 1774. There is no suggestion in the record of a positive break in the relationship, however, until early in 1779. In a letter to Franklin of March 1779 Priestley hinted at "a scheme you once had in my favour," and before mid-May he made some kind of financial appeal to Shelburne, eliciting an "obliging and liberal proposal," which Mrs. Priestley rejected. A more "rigid oeconomy to bring our expenses within our income" would obviate any need to improve "our circumstances, either at Calne, or any other place." Priestley was still purchasing books and apparatus for Shelburne as late as September 1779.[38] But sometime between 27 September 1779 and 8 February 1780 he wrote again to Franklin, complaining that his expenses exceeded his salary and expressing doubts about continuation of the Shelburne relationship. On 8 February 1780 Franklin wrote Priestley about his leaving Shelburne.

On 21 March, the night before his duel with William Fullarton, Shelburne arranged details of the break via Richard Price.[39] "He intimated to Dr. Price that he wished to give me an establishment in Ireland, where he had large property. This gave me an opportunity of acquainting him that if he chose to dissolve the connexion, it should be on the terms . . . [in] which I should be entitled to an annuity of an hundred and fifty pounds, and then I would

37. *SciAuto.*, 77. There are undertones here of the plagiarism criticism, but Priestley also wrote of his inadequacies as a chemist to Giovanni Fabroni, 17 Oct. 1779 (*SciAuto.*, 86).
38. See Priestley's discussion of the break in *W.* 1.1:206. The return from Paris is discussed in Chapter 1 (see note 11 to Chapter 1 above). Priestley to Franklin, 11 March 1779, Franklin Papers 13:186, APS; to Shelburne, 12 May 1779; to instrument makers Nairne and Blunt, 2 Aug. 1779; to Shelburne's agent, 3 Sept. 1779, all in Bowood Papers III-i, IV-M, III-j.
39. Priestley to Franklin, "before February 8, 1780"; Franklin to Priestley, 8 Feb. 1780, [Franklin], *Papers*, 31:454–55, 455–57; also *W.* 1.1:330, but Rutt fails to note that this part of the letter is separate from that which refers to Priestley's letter of 27 Sept. 1779. Samuel Vaughan to Franklin, 26 June 1780, Franklin Papers, APS. Priestley reported the end of the connection to Franklin from Birmingham, 21 Dec. 1780, APS.

provide for myself" (*W.* 1.1:206–7). The formal ending of the "connexion" was to take place on Michaelmas (29 September), but the situation was complicated by Priestley's serious illness with gallstones during the late spring of 1780.[40] By mid-June Priestley had, at the urging of his brother-in-law, John Wilkinson, taken a house in Birmingham. Late in July he was packing his books and had accepted a gift of moving expenses from Mrs. Elizabeth Rayner, to whom he was introduced by Theophilus Lindsey and his wife. The Priestleys were completely installed in their new home, "Fairhill," on the edge of Birmingham, by December.

Reasons for the final break can only be conjectural. Shelburne told people it was because of Priestley's health. Priestley complained that although Shelburne had found no fault in his conduct, he had "no farther use in him," which Lindsey explained by emphasizing Priestley's stubborn political independence. Possibly the financial panic of 1778–79 was involved, though Shelburne's financial position should have cushioned him from major problems. Samuel Vaughan explained to Franklin that the two simply did not understand each other; some mutual friends thought that Priestley's publications, perhaps on politics but especially the *Disquisitions,* were an embarrassment to Shelburne's political career, on ascendency again as he assumed leadership of the Chathamites with the death of Lord Chatham in May 1778.

None of these reasons is entirely convincing by itself, especially as there exists another probable contributing cause. On 9 July 1779 Shelburne married Louisa Fitzpatrick. She was the daughter of the Earl of Upper Ossory, an Irish peer and a Member of Parliament for Bedfordshire; she was also, with her brother Richard, an active participant in the tonish social life of the last half of the eighteenth century. As Shelburne's wife, she became a notable political hostess—and some of Priestley's friends reported that she did not like the Priestleys! That would hardly be surprising, considering their unabashed middle-class outlook. On one occasion in 1776, after witnessing a trial at the House of Lords, Mrs. Priestley reported that "the conduct of the upper [class was] so exactly like that of the lower classes, that I was thankful I was born in middle life."[41] Priestley wrote, "I used to make no scruple of maintaining, that there is not only most virtue, and most happiness, but even most true politeness, in the middle classes of life" (*W.* 1.1:205).

40. See letter of Sarah Vaughan to her son, Samuel, 14 May 1780, Library, Franklin Institute, Philadelphia.
41. Quoted in Gibbs, *Joseph Priestley,* 87–88.

Shelburne said he wished the separation to be amicable, but he subsequently declined to receive Priestley in London.[42] Yet, Priestley wrote, "when I had been some years settled at Birmingham, he sent an especial messenger, and common friend, to engage me again in his service, having, as that friend assured me, a deep sense of the loss of Lord Ashburton (Mr. Dunning) by death, and of Colonel Barré, by his becoming almost blind, and his want of some able and faithful friend, such as he had experienced in me. . . . I did not choose, however, on any consideration, to leave the very eligible situation in which I now am" (W. 1.1:207).[43] It is suggestive to note that the second Lady Shelburne died in August 1789, but whatever the reason for the split, Priestley was, at least till 1791, supremely happy in Birmingham.

42. This according to Priestley. Talleyrand declared that he found Priestley visiting at Lansdowne House after the Birmingham Riots of 1791. [Charles M. de Talleyrand], *Memoirs of the Prince de Talleyrand* (New York: G. Putnam's Sons, 1891), 1:170, 170n3; but he was wrong about meeting Price then, so perhaps he was also about Priestley.

43. J. T. Rutt added a note in his edition of the *Works* dating this reference to 1787; a letter of Price to Lansdowne (Shelburne), 29 Oct. 1785, Price Papers, Bodleian Library, suggests that date, but a 1789 suggestion makes more sense to me.

PART II

BIRMINGHAM
(1780–1791)

VIII

SCIENCE AND THE
LUNAR SOCIETY

The Priestleys' move, begun in July 1780, was not completed until the end of the year. By that time Priestley had resumed his pre-Shelburne life in religion and in science. He had accepted a position as preacher in New Meeting and begun again to write and experiment. On 13 October 1780 he informed Adam Walker that he was still settling in and that his laboratory was not yet finished; on 30 November he wrote Wedgwood that he was finally established, with his laboratory in place.[1] Priestley wrote of his move: "I consider my settlement at Birmingham as the happiest event in my life, being highly favourable to every object I had in view, philosophical or theological" (W. 1.1:338). Offered a position late in 1785 to teach the son of Lord Bristol, and invited again to return to Shelburne's service, probably in 1789, he turned down both offers. He was, wrote Richard Price, "so well satisfy'd with his situation at Birmingham that nothing can induce him to quit it."[2]

This is hardly surprising. Most of his life had prepared him to welcome and be welcomed by the Birmingham of the 1780s. John Alexander (1736–65), his roommate and fellow in self-improvement at Daventry Academy,

1. Priestley to Walker, Wellcome Library of Historical Medicine; Priestley to Wedgwood, Bolton, #2. The laboratory is briefly described as consisting of several apartments on a ground floor, detached from the house to avoid fire, in B. Faujas de Saint-Fond, *Travels in England, Scotland, and the Hebredes* (London, James Ridgway, 1799), 2:338.
2. Richard Price to Shelburne, 29 Oct. 1785, Price Papers, Bodleian Library, Oxford.

had gone to Longdon, near Birmingham, as Presbyterian minister; another fellow student and correspondent, Radcliffe Scholefield, became minister of Old Meeting, Birmingham, in 1772 until his retirement in 1799. Priestley's favorite tutor, Samuel Clark, had gone from Daventry to a Dissenting ministry at Old Meeting from 1756 till his death in 1769, and John Palmer, who had been one of his students at Warrington, had settled in Birmingham in 1779. One of Lord Shelburne's advisors among midland manufacturers was Samuel Garbett of Birmingham, and Shelburne visited there several times, accompanied at least once by Priestley.

Although it had been noteworthy for its concentration of workshops and forges by the early sixteenth century, Birmingham was still more town than city in 1780, when its population was approximately fifty thousand, with 8,500 houses. There was a hospital, two Establishment charity schools, six churches, three Dissenting (Presbyterian) meeting houses, a Quaker, a Baptist, and a Methodist chapel, a Roman Catholic church, and a synagogue. Twelve public roads led out from Birmingham, and two turnpikes—to Dudley and to Wolverhampton, near Bradley, where Priestley's wealthy brother-in-law, John Wilkinson, had an iron foundry. There were also two canals, joining the town to the Staffordshire and Worcester and the Coventry canals. Some of the streets were paved and lighted, there was a subscription library (reformed by Priestley on his move there), five bookseller-printers—Myles Swinney, James Belcher, Piercy and Jones, Pearson and Rollason, and John Thompson—each of which was to print books by Priestley, two theaters, at least one coffeehouse, and an assembly room. And yet, according to advertisements in *Aris's Birmingham Gazette* (established in 1741), it was still possible easily to walk to gardens and green fields, as Priestley was to do, in reverse, from his new home, Fairhill, a mile and a half from town.[3]

It was, however, the people and their spirit that were most attractive. William Hutton had observed on his arrival at Birmingham in 1741, "I was surprised at the place, but more so at the people: They were a species I had never seen: They possessed a vivacity I had never beheld: I had been among dreamers, but now I saw men awake."[4] Uniquely characteristic of these

3. For details about Birmingham, see W. Hutton, *An History of Birmingham, to the End of the Year 1780* (Birmingham: Pearson and Rollason, 1781), with folding map dated 1781; John Alfred Langford, ed., *A Century of Birmingham Life: or, A Chronicle of Local Events, from 1741 to 1841* (Birmingham: E. C. Osborne; London: Simkin, Marshall & Co., 1868); John Money, *Experience and Identity: Birmingham and the West Midlands, 1760–1800* (Montreal: McGill-Queens's University Press, 1977); and Joseph Hill, *Bookmakers of Old Birmingham: Authors, Printers, and Booksellers* (Birmingham: Cornish Bros. Ltd., 1907).

4. Hutton, *History of Birmingham*, 63.

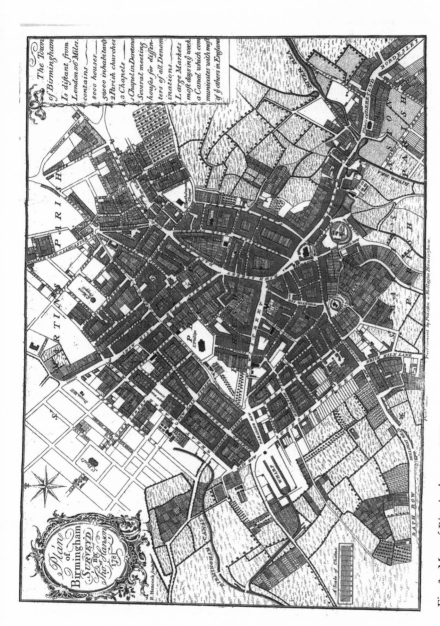

Fig. 3 Map of Birmingham, c. 1780

people, since about 1765, were the members of the Lunar Society of Birmingham. Initially meeting once a month on the Sunday nearest the full moon (the better for members to see their ways home), the Society never numbered more than fourteen members during its short history. It published nothing of its own and kept no explicit records; yet it has come to represent the coming of the Industrial Revolution in Britain.[5] Six of the pre-1780 members were still active in the Society when Priestley arrived: Matthew Boulton, Erasmus Darwin (who soon left), James Keir, James Watt, Josiah Wedgwood, and William Withering. Priestley had known of each of them before coming to Birmingham, and they as certainly had known of him.

Boulton had supplied John Seddon of Warrington Academy with thermometers, circa 1761, and, with William Small, had corresponded with Priestley about chemistry in 1774. In 1775, referring to a visit to Birmingham, Priestley wrote Boulton requesting fluorspar samples, as he requested samples of Birmingham air in 1777. In 1776 Boulton had ordered glass chemical apparatus from "Parker, the glass man," on Priestley's recommendation. Priestley twice cited the work of Darwin in his *History of Electricity,* and Darwin had corresponded with Benjamin Franklin in 1772 about Priestley's Pyrmont water paper and cited Priestley's *Optics* in a *Philosophical Transactions* paper of 1778. Priestley knew of Keir in connection with Keir's translation of Pierre Joseph Macquer's *Dictionary of Chemistry* (1771). He called him, in a letter to Boulton of 1777, "a very able chymist and useful writer." By February 1778 Priestley was writing Keir about his experiments and asking for advice on chemistry. Watt and William Small had corresponded in 1773 about Priestley's discovery of nitrous oxide and his observations relating to photosynthesis. Wedgwood was known to Priestley first through Priestley's Nantwich friend, the Rev. William Willets, one of Wedgwood's brothers-in-law, and then because of Thomas Bentley, a Warrington Academy trustee. Wedgwood bought Priestley's *History of Electricity,* subscribed to that of *Optics,* purchased volumes of *Experiments and Observations* as they came out, corresponded with him on ceramic chemistry, and by 1780 was supplying him with chemical apparatus. The first volume of *Experiments and Observations* referred, via Percival, to Withering, while a Withering *Philosophical Transactions* paper of 1773 showed an awareness of Priestley's experiments of 1772 on the influence of fixed air in plant growth.[6]

5. See Robert E. Schofield, *The Lunar Society of Birmingham: A Social History of Provincial Science and Industry in Eighteenth-Century England* (Oxford: Clarendon Press, 1963); uncited text references to the Lunar Society are drawn from this work.

6. For these pre-1780 intersections of Priestley with Lunar Society members, see ibid., 92–100 and elsewhere.

Little wonder, then, that Priestley was delighted when, by early March 1781, he was invited to become a member of the Lunar Society. He wrote in his *Memoirs,* "I had . . . the society of persons eminent for their knowledge of chemistry, particularly Mr. Watt, Mr. Keir, and Dr. Withering. These with Mr. Boulton, and Dr. Darwin (who soon left us . . .) Mr. Galton [Samuel Galton Jr., Lunar Society member in 1781], and afterwards Mr. Johnson of Kenilworth [Robert Augustus Johnson, Lunar Society member in 1787), and myself, dined together every month, calling ourselves the *Lunar society,* because the time of our meeting was near the full moon" (*W.* 1.1:338–39).[7]

Priestley was the only member ever to refer to the Society in print while it was still active. He was also the only member publicly and repeatedly to express his indebtedness to the Society. Some of that was financial. From early in his career, Priestley's work (scientific and theological) had been subsidized by grants from friends and admirers. "Without assistance," Priestley wrote, "I could not have carried on my experiments except on a very small scale, and under great disadvantages." Dr. John Fothergill had, till his death in December 1780, promoted and managed the subscription, amounting to £40 to £50 a year. The subscription (increased on Priestley's leaving Shelburne) was then managed by Mr. Samuel Salte: "It is nearly 100£ per annum, which, if it be kept up, will be very well, though it is necessarily a very expensive business" (*W.* 1.1:353–54). Some subscribers dropped off the list, offended by Priestley's theological or political writings, but Boulton, Darwin, Galton, Wedgwood (and later Wedgwood's son Thomas) continued throughout Priestley's residence in Birmingham, and Watt and Wedgwood, at least, continued with gifts of apparatus into his exile in the United States.[8]

Members of the Lunar Society also joined in the science community activities that occupied much of Priestley's "social" life. On 26 February 1784 Priestley became a foreign member of the Académie Royale des Sciences;

---

7. In fact, according to Jonathan Stokes (another new member, 1783–86?), the Society changed its meeting day to Monday to accommodate Priestley. Ibid., 145.

8. *W.* 1.1:217; the following list (of regular or occasional non-Lunar benefactors) is derived from ibid., 214–17: Mr. Constable, Dr. Fothergill, Dr. Heberden, Sir Theodore Jansen, Mr. Jeffries, John Lee, Mr. Moseley, Richard Price, Mr. Radcliffe, Mrs. Rayner, Mr. Remington, Mr. Reynolds, William Russell, Sir George Savile, Samuel Salte, Samuel Shore, Rev. Mr. Simpson, Mr. Strutt, Mr. Tayleur, and Dr. William Watson and his son. There is a document in the Hunterian Museum, Glasgow, citing Constable, Fothergill, and Price as subscribing. In 1785, at the initiative of Thomas Percival, the Manchester Literary and Philosophical Society resolved to subscribe £50; see Percival, *Works,* 1:c–ciii. Priestley twice refused tentative offers of government pensions (one made, via John Lee, from the Rockingham administration and the other, via a bishop, perhaps Edmund Law, Bishop of Carlisle, early in the administration of the younger Pitt), thinking it safer to avoid any dependence upon the court.

on 22 January 1785 he was elected to the American Philosophical Society, Philadelphia, and by 23 June he was a member also of the American Academy of Arts and Sciences, Boston. On 12 May he acknowledged his election to the Philosophical Society at Orléans; on 9 May 1786 he acknowledged that to the Philosophical Society at Haarlem. In 1786–87 he was elected an honorary member of the Medical Society of Edinburgh and became a member of the philosophical/literary society, meeting at the Chapter Coffee house and then at Walker's lecture room, which included most members of the Lunar Society. He was also an honorary member of the Literary and Philosophical Society of Manchester, with Darwin and Wedgwood, of which James Watt Jr. and Joseph Priestley Jr. became active members.[9]

By 1790 Priestley could, with pardonable pride, list himself as: "LL.D., F.R.S. Ac. Imp. Petrop. R. Paris. Holm., Taurin. Ital. Harlem. Aurel. Med. Paris. Cantab. Americ. et Philad. Socius." on the title page of his collected edition of *Experiments and Observations*. But there was more to this listing than a little innocent vanity. When he wrote to Charles Blagden in May 1785, asking that his membership in the Societé Royale du Physique, d'Histoire Naturelle, et des Arts, D'Orléans, and of the Society at Stockholm be annexed to his name in the list kept at the Royal Society, he added: "As several of these papers [by Priestley, just published in the *Philosophical Transactions* of the Royal Society] will be sent abroad, and to members of these Societies, perhaps it will be right to annex the titles to my name in the title page. I know no good end that foreign titles answer, but I would do what will be thought right."[10] Being a prominent member of the science community carried with it, apparently, a considerable burden of formal civilities.

9. Institut de France, *Index Biographique des Membres et Correspondants de L'Académie des Sciences du 22 Décembre 1666 au 15 Décembre 1954* (Paris: Gauthier, Villars, 1954); Benjamin Franklin wrote Richard Price that he had recommended Priestley at every vacancy and thought foreign membership had "never been bestowed more worthily," 16 Aug. 1784, Historical Society of Pennsylvania (*SciAuto.*, 124, 125, 126, 129). The minutes of the Koninklijke Hollandsche Maatschappij der Wettenschappen, Haarlem, for early 1787 note a protest (rejected by the council) to Priestley's election because of his theology, while van Marum, its secretary, called Priestley "the famous and venerable christian philosopher" in his "autobiographical notes." [Martinus van Marum], *Martinus van Marum: Life and Work*, ed. E. Lefebvre and J. G. De Bruijn (Leyden: Noordhoff International Publishing, 1969–76), 4:390. See also Schofield, *Lunar Society*, 232–35.

10. Quoted, by permission, from a letter in the personal collection of David Richardson, Washington, D.C. On 27 March 1784, John Vaughan transmitted to David Rittenhouse, for the American Philosophical Society, a thirty-three-volume set of Priestley's works; Archives, APS.

It also carried with it the opportunity of meeting or corresponding with people with similar interests. Darwin was already a fellow of the Royal Society and Wedgwood became a fellow in 1783. In 1785 Priestley signed fellowship nominations for Boulton, Galton, Keir, Watt, and Withering; in 1788 he joined Boulton, Galton, Keir, and Withering in nominating Robert Augustus Johnson. During the 1780s he joined other members of the Lunar Society in nominating several other fellows.[11] Priestley and other Lunar Society members entertained and introduced to the others Aimé Argand, Adam Afzelius, Claude Louis Berthollet, Pietr Camper, Henry Cavendish, Jean André DeLuc, Edmond C. Genet (probably a French industrial spy), Johann F. A. Göttling, Marsilio Landriani (suspected by Wedgwood to be also an industrial spy), Martinus van Marum, Joseph de Montgolfier, Rudolf Eric Raspe (a geologist as well as creator of Baron Münchausen), Faujas de St. Fond, and Francis Swediaur. Visitors also became correspondents, and to their names can be added others who were correspondents only—for example, Jean Claude De La Métherie, who sent his best wishes to "all the members of your Society" in a letter of 9 January 1789 to James Keir.[12] Many visitors attended meetings of the Society. An extraordinary meeting of the Lunar Society was organized to meet William Bewley in 1783; he and John Wilkinson, Priestley's brother-in-law, attended a meeting in October 1787.[13]

More important to Priestley, however, was the contribution of the Lunar Society to his scientific endeavors, though its members cannot have had much influence in the production of *Experiments and Observations on Natural Philosophy II,* which essentially represents work done before the move to Birmingham. Dated references in the volume cover the period from May 1779 to 20 July 1780, and he notes that he "removed my habitation on the 21st of July, 1780." He wrote Franklin on 21 December that he had just sent another volume of experiments to the press, and on 19 March 1781 that the volume was "nearly printed." The preface is dated 24 March 1781, and in it he declared that he was "entering, as I may say, upon *a new period of life,* . . . [and] was willing to close my philosophical accompts as they stand

11. For Lunar Society participation in nominations, see Schofield, *Lunar Society,* 236, and for all nominations, Royal Society Certificate Books, Archives, Royal Society of London.

12. Schofield, *Lunar Society,* 237–39 and elsewhere; A. Moillet, *Sketch of the Life of James Keir* (London: Robert Taylor, 1868?), 90–91.

13. Bewley, who wrote so many flattering reviews of Priestley's scientific works for the *Monthly Review,* visited Birmingham to meet Priestley during his last illness. Priestley wrote of him: "His letters to me would have made several volumes and mine to him still more." These letters have never been found, and it is believed that Bewley destroyed his correspondence file before his last trip. The Wilkinson meeting is noted in Bolton, #43.

at present, before I open a new one" (x). This volume represented his old period of life.[14]

The work begins with a shorter than usual discursive preface in which Priestley suggests that the most important material in the volume related to experiments on vegetable green matter, which "purify noxious air by action of light, only, not heat," by which he had been led to "other important circumstances relating to the general oeconomy of nature." He had hoped to lay out a general theory of all kinds of air and tables of affinity but deferred that till further progress had been made in his inquiries (v–vi). "All that is meant by theory, exclusive of *hypothesis*, is a number of general propositions, comprehending all the particular ones." Many experiments in the volume were left imperfect (owing to "a tedious and dangerous illness" followed by his move), but in any event imperfection was unavoidable, it being in the nature of philosophical investigation. "Did Dr. Hales excite no wish that he did not satisfy with respect to *air*? And did Newton himself solve every query concerning *light*?" (vii–ix).

Following a short introduction that described the earthenware jar with which his plant experiments were made, the text commenced with eighty-three pages of observations ultimately relating to photosynthesis. Priestley had introduced the topic in his "Observations" paper of 1772, and he had returned to the subject in *Exp. & Obs. Nat. Phil.* (1779), with special reference to a green matter, for the formation of which *"light* is necessary," for it purified the air in water. The new experiments began with a curious section on the absorption of inflammable air by willow plants, changing what remained into phlogisticated air (N_2) and sometimes into air as good as, or better than, common. "In this there could not possibly be any mistake, unless we suppose the water to have absorbed the air, which it has never been known to do in any similar circumstances" (1). Possibly it helps our understanding that the inflammable air used in this experiment appears to have been marsh gas (methane and carbon dioxide).

He then described work with the "green matter" discussed in 1779 and now definitely identified as vegetative. Plants will not thrive without light (18) and, despite his earlier opinion, it was the green matter in the water, not merely the action of light on water, that yielded air (21). He disagreed with Jan Ingenhousz, who seemed to believe that the process was an "operation of the wonderful power of nature" entirely within the plant (24n.). The plant

14. To Franklin, B/F85.ba, Franklin Papers, APS; Priestley, *Exp. & Obs. Nat. Phil. II.* The volume was presented to the Royal Society on 17 June 1781, Journal Book of the Royal Society, vol. 31, 325.

and light were only agents to produce the effect of *depuration* or dephlogisti-cation of the air in the water (though he was not entirely clear what kind of air, or airs, were purified). But "it is agreeable to analogy that plants growing in air should depurate that air to which they are exposed" (29). Before read-ing Ingenhousz, he had not suspected that leaves alone would do the job—though he might have suspected it from reading Bonnet (Charles Bonnet, *Recherches sur l'usage des feuilles dans les plantes* [1754)])—and he discon-tinued his trials with other plants when "I was informed of the experiments of Dr. Ingenhousz, whose assiduous attention to this subject gave me the greatest satisfaction, and entirely superseded what I might otherwise have thought of doing in the same way" (30).

The politeness of this gesture toward Ingenhousz notwithstanding, a dis-pute over priorities began. Ingenhousz complained to Benjamin Franklin on 24 April 1782 and again on 27 November 1782, to Sir Joseph Banks on 6 May 1782, and was complaining to English visitors in Vienna in December 1783 about Priestley's treatment of him. The complaint dealt first with Priestley's failure, in *Exp. & Obs. Nat. Phil. II*, to credit Ingenhousz with the discov-ery that it was light that causes plants to mend air, but also with the declara-tion that it was the air in water that was acted upon, not pure air produced by the plants.[15] Priestley wrote to Ingenhousz late in 1782 without any indi-cation of Ingenhousz's unhappiness with him, but in November 1787 he wrote that he was sorry to learn that Ingenhousz thought he was attempting to detract from his achievement, "which is very far from being my disposi-tion." "That plants restore vitiated air, I discovered at a very early period. Afterwards I found . . . that the green matter . . . produced pure air by means of light. . . . What you did with *leaves* was altogether independent of what I was doing with *whole plants*. The same summer, and the same sun, operated for us both, and you certainly published before me."[16]

But this hardly settles the matter, and there is some evidence that Priestley's work *was* independent. Ingenhousz's book, *Experiments upon Vegetables, discovering their great Power of purifying the Common Air in the Sunshine, and of Injuring it in the Shade and at Night,* was published in London with a dedication to Sir John Pringle dated 12 October 1779. Assuming some time between the dedication and the appearance of the printed volume, it is pos-sible that Priestley had not seen it when, as he later wrote Caleb Rotheram,

15. Ingenhousz to Franklin, Franklin Papers 25:40 and 26:74, APS; Ingenhousz to Banks, Add MS 8095.84–85, British Library; and James Hall to William Hall, from Vienna, in V. A. Eyles, "The Evolution of a Chemist: Sir James Hall," *Annals of Science* 19 (1963): 153–82, 159–61.

16. Priestley to Ingenhousz, 4 Dec. 1782, extract, in *Opuscoli Scelti* 6 (1783): 160; Priestley to Ingenhousz, 24 Nov. 1787, *SciAuto.,* 130.

"I soon discovered that the 'green matter' I speak of in my last volume is a vegetable substance, and that all other water plants do the same, converting the impure air contained in water into pure air, and therefore I conclude that all plants do the same in the light." By the time he wrote that letter, 12 December, he had at least heard of Ingenhousz's work, but merely added that Ingenhousz had found leaves did the same even separated when from the tree. He reaffirmed his independence in a letter to Richard Kirwan, in August 1780, writing, "of what I had observed before the publication of Dr. Ingenhousz's book . . . that a *green matter,* which I then supposed to have been deposited by the water, yielded a great quantity of very pure Air, when exposed to *light,* but that mere *warmth,* had no such effect upon it" (*SciAuto.,* 88).

Priestley refused to concede that it was not air in the water that was acted upon by the green vegetable matter, though he admitted that water must be saturated with air before it will readily part with it without heat or agitation. He demonstrated that the effect was dependent upon the capacity of the water for dissolved air and would cease when all the air was acted upon. (27–29).[17] Nor was Priestley inclined to accept Ingenhousz's suggestion that the green matter appearing in water was the result of equivocal or spontaneous generation, noting his belief that it must come from seeds floating invisibly in the air and insinuating themselves through the smallest apertures to produce plants upon meeting with water (34).[18]

Later sections deal with putrefaction and the growth of green matter on plant and animal substances, noting that inflammable air is produced by putrefaction. It was an "admirable provision" of the system of nature that putrefaction of animal and vegetable substances, in air or water, should be a "pabulum" for green matter, which produces from it the purest of air (52–63). He had hoped, from these experiments, to discover the principle of nutrition in plants and animals and concluded, as he had hinted earlier, that the principle was phlogiston or the principle of inflammability, "in such a state as to be capable of becoming, by putrefaction, a true inflammable air, but not generally such as to burn with explosions but rather with a blue and

17. According to James Hall, Ingenhousz was still asserting in December 1783 that airless water initially absorbed the air produced by plants and only began to collect on the plants after the water was saturated. Eyles, "Evolution of a Chemist," 161.

18. He quoted Ingenhousz's idea, 33n, and persisted in his disbelief in spontaneous generation as late as 1804, when his paper disagreeing with the suggestion by Erasmus Darwin was published in the *Transactions of the American Philosophical Society.* As late as 1784 Ingenhousz was also insisting that Priestley's "green matter" was of animalcule, not vegetative, origin. See his "Remarques sur l'Origine et la Nature de la Matière verte de M. Priestley," *Journal de Physique théorique et appliquée* 25 (1784): 3–12.

lambent flame, mixed with . . . fixed air" (64). In nutrition, he wrote, phlogiston was held in solution by gastric juice and the chyle formed by it, and, entering the circulation with chyle, "after answering purposes of animal oeconomy which are yet very imperfectly known to us, is thrown out again by means of the blood in the lungs, and communicated to the air, which is phlogisticated by it" (64–65).

The remaining sections are, as usual, miscellaneous and frequently repeat material from earlier volumes. The air produced in the exothermic production of ferrous sulphide from iron filings and brimstone paste was inconsistently inflammable; "what may appear to be the *same materials* and the *same preparation* of them, may have different results, in consequence of there having been some circumstance, respecting either the materials or the process, that was unnoticed, but which was the secret cause of the unexpected results" (85–86). Neither heat short of ignition nor passage of time succeeded in causing inflammable air to part with its phlogiston. Priestley disproved the contentions of Ingenhousz and of William C. Cruickshank, via P. Moscati, that air was phlogisticated by perspiration or that air continuously issued from human skin (100–107). The air contained in water was necessary to the life of fish (136–41). He had frequently found the air expelled from water to be much better than common air (166–70). (Note that oxygen is about twice as water soluble as nitrogen.)

On the production of dephlogisticated air, particularly by heating minium moistened with spirit of nitre, he wrote, "being a little more conversant than I then was in the common operations of chemistry (though I still have little to boast of in that respect) I find Mr. Scheele's method of procuring it (and indeed that in which it will be found that I myself first of all procured it, but without knowing what I had got) viz. from *nitre alone,* much preferable" (142). His curiosity was roused by an air (dephlogisticated nitrous, N_2O) fatal to breath but supporting combustion (192–202). His experiments on it were done with the gas "confined so as not to be exposed through the medium of water to the common atmosphere" (215). He conjectured that phlogiston might be weightless, though in the decomposition of alkaline air it enabled the alkaline base to occupy more space than before the experiment (221). The volatility of mercury involved a "proper *evaporation,* that is . . . the repulsion of its particles, whereby it is made to assume an elastic form" (231). He found that marine acid, deprived of its phlogiston, was incapable of being exhibited as air confined by mercury, as it immediately formed with it a white powder (251). In fact, he had generated chlorine, which instantly combines with mercury to form mercurous chloride.

Section 27 (258–86) was a reprint of his article on lateral explosion in electricity, from *Philosophical Transactions* 60 (1770), and was followed by another section of electrical experiments that included the observation that he had never succeeded in mending thin glass jars cracked by electrical explosions (not even with the amber varnish recommended by "my then tutor in chemistry, Mr. Turner of Liverpool"), for the jars always broke again and always where the cement terminated. Intensity of sound in airs depended solely upon their densities (in inflammable air, the sound of a bell was hardly distinguishable from that in a good vacuum) and not upon any chemical principle in their constitutions (295–99).

He again noted the use of foul water in his pneumatic trough, "it not having been convenient to change the water" (300), but this did not lead him to any corrections for such experiments in the section "explaining or correcting" passages in previous volumes. In this section, and again in that which follows, summarizing the most remarkable facts in those volumes, he returned to his experiments on heat expansion of airs (316–17, 358–59) with the same greatly differing values, including an anomalous value for alkaline air, which must have come from disassociation.[19] He noted that, in his first volume, he had "supposed heat to consist in a vibratory motion of the particles of bodies." This he reaffirmed for sensible heat, "But there may be a *principle of heat* latent in bodies, and not manifest by any sensible effect. Heat may therefore be what is usually termed *a substance*, whether it be subject to the action of gravity, or not" (317).[20] He did not believe that there was acidity in dephlogisticated air (329); compared (correctly) specific gravities of common, nitrous, marine acid, vitriolic, and alkaline airs; and noted again that "Different kinds of airs that have no affinity do not, when mixed together, separate spontaneously, but continue diffused through each other" (358).[21]

Priestley added a final section (33) of "Experiments and Observations made after the preceding sections were sent to press"—i.e., work done in Birmingham—and an appendix. The first is of little consequence, as Priestley

19. On 26 March 1780 Priestley wrote Benjamin Vaughan, "Mr. Arden has observed, and I saw the experiment fairly tried, that *air* parts with its heat in *condensation*. I intend to repeat the experiment with different kinds of air," *SciAuto.*, 87. It is unclear what he meant by "condensation" of air, as there was certainly no liquidization involved. Perhaps he meant the inverse of heat expansion experiments, but there is no later evidence of gas compression experiments.

20. There are inferences here of the "energetic" characteristics of phlogiston, a "substance," though weightless.

21. He had previously observed this phenomenon in *Exp. & Obs. III*, 301, and *IV*, 432; see Chapter 7, n. 27, which mentions John Dalton's notice of Priestley's work.

really had had very little time for experimenting between reestablishment of his laboratory and the sending to press materials for the volume. There is an account of inconclusive experiments to determine what he thought was the heat conductivity of different gases, a topic of interest since his days in Leeds to which he now returned after reading Adair Crawford's book (*Experiments and Observations on Animal Heat, and the Inflammation of Combustible Bodies,* 1779). Priestley's experiments are described in sufficient detail (375–78) to show that he was not measuring what he thought he was, but rather the rate of temperature change in a thermometer enclosed in a gas. That convection was also involved in his experiments Priestley could not have known until after the work of Benjamin Thompson (Count Rumford), John Leslie, and William Prout.[22]

The appendix contains letters from several persons, including William Bewley, James Watt, and William Withering, with minor comments on the material in the volume, and one letter, from John Warltire, reflecting perhaps the text's comment on the possible weightlessness of heat, but certainly introducing a set of experiments of considerable importance. Warltire had passed an electric spark through a mixture of inflammable and common air— first as contained in a closed copper ball and then in glass vessels—to determine if there was a change in weight between the explosion-heated container and its later cooled condition. His weight results were inconclusive, but he noted that though the glass container had been clean and dry prior to firing the air, "it became dewy and . . . lined with a sooty substance" after firing. Warltire believed that this experiment proved that common air deposited its moisture when phlogisticated.

Priestley added that he and Withering had observed the experiment with the copper vessel, which weighed less after the explosion than before, and that he had then fired inflammable and dephlogisticated airs in glass. "With me it was a mere random experiment, made to entertain a few philosophical

22. See Alex C. Burr, "Notes on the History of the Experimental Determination of the Thermal Conductivity of Gases," *Isis* 21 (1934): 169, 171. Burr credits Priestley for being the first person to undertake a "systematic study of the thermal conducting power of gases" and the first to note that hydrogen "possessed markedly different thermal properties" than other gases. Leo L. Beranek lists conductivities for common air, carbon dioxide (fixed air), nitrogen, oxygen, and hydrogen, showing the last with roughly eight times the values for the others, in "Acoustic Properties of Gases," *American Institute of Physics Handbook* (New York: McGraw-Hill, 1957), table 3d-5, "Thermal Conductivity of Gases." Thomas Young notes Priestley's experiments on heat conductivity, as well as those on heat expansion of gases, in his *Course of Lectures on Natural Philosophy and the Mechanical Arts,* 2d ed. (London: Taylor and Walton, 1845), 2:507.

friends, who had formed themselves into a private society, of which they had done me the honour to make me a member" (397–398).[23] What a portentous way of introducing himself to the Lunar Society! This "mere random experiment" was to lead to the discovery of the composition of water and to fuel the controversy with Lavoisier over the existence of phlogiston. But members of the Society hardly needed such an auspicious beginning to further their relationships with Priestley, for they were finding him not merely a charming and interesting friend but also a consultant for their varied industrial and scientific activities.

The 1780s were, for almost every member of the Lunar Society, a period of personal and financial success, but the greater part of Priestley's scientific success had already been achieved. There remained, however, much to be done in the practical areas of science. While Priestley held that "the greatest and noblest use of philosophical speculation" was the religious discipline it inspired, he had also believed from very early that "speculation is only of use if it leads to practise," and that the "immediate use of natural science is the power it gives us over nature, by means of the knowledge we acquire of its laws; whereby human life is, in its present state, made more comfortable and happy."[24] He welcomed the opportunity to lend his efforts to the activities of his fellow Society members.

As early as 1767 Erasmus Darwin had written Boulton that he was trying experiments on vapors other than steam as "food for fire-engines," and in July 1781 Watt wrote in a panic about the possibility that some of Priestley's new gases might substitute for steam in engines. Boulton responded on 21 July 1781 that experiments would be tried, "as I have raised a confidence in Dr. Priestley who had seriously promised me to keep the secret & to give me all the facts and all he can discover in that line." By 26 July Boulton could assure Watt that he and Dr. P. were persuaded that none of his airs could produce mechanical power as cheaply as steam. In 1784 Baron Kempelen wrote Boulton that he had patented a rotative steam engine, which Priestley had seen and approved. Watt wrote Boulton on 11 May that Priestley was misrepresented; Kempelen's engine was only a "Barker's Mill" that exerted

---

23. Everett Mendelsohn, *Heat and Life* (Cambridge: Harvard University Press, 1964), 157, citing the second edition of Adair Crawford's *Experiments and Observations on Animal Heat, and the Inflammation of Combustible Bodies* (1788), notes that at Priestley's suggestion Crawford attempted to determine the heat of combustion of inflammable air by igniting it and pure air in a brass chamber arranged so that increase of heat might be measured.

24. Joseph Priestley, *History and Present State of Electricity* (London: Joseph Johnson et al., 1767), xix.

no force. It has been suggested that Priestley gave Watt hints on perfecting the ink and presses for Watt's copying machines, and certainly Priestley joined Watt and Jean André DeLuc in experiments on heat, steam, and evaporation and recommended a glass-grinder to Watt for the making of lenses.[25]

Josiah Wedgwood, comparing two samples of clay and finding that the glaze on one was prevented from vitrifying by, he supposed, an acid in one absent in the other, wrote, "Send some of each to Docr. Priestley to extract the air from them and examine the difference." In a letter of 26 May 1781 Priestley wrote, "If there be any earthy substance that you wish me to examine in my way, especially such as you may suspect to be found in places where volcanoes abound, and that have not been exposed to heat already, I shall be much obliged to you if you will send specimens of them along with the [earthen] retorts." Priestley acknowledged receipt on 22 July 1781 of retorts and of clay and flint from "the Appalachian mountains," on 8 August of specimens of basalte, lava from Vesuvius, and toadstone, all becoming black glass under intense heat, and on 18 August he wrote, "Whatever the *basaltes* is, the same is the *Rowley rag*, and similar to it *may* be the *toadstone*, and perhaps as you conjecture even *granate*, and many other substances." Wedgwood wrote to Boulton on 8 April 1782 that Priestley had approved his pyrometer, described in "An Attempt to make a thermometer for measuring the higher degrees of Heat," published in *Philosophical Transactions* 72 (1782).

When sent retorts, Priestley returned reports on their behavior and made sure that chemists learned of their properties by explicitly praising the retorts in his published papers. He wrote Wedgwood on 8 November 1784 (and repeated the news to Cavendish on 30 December) that he had made a discovery relating to hot copper and alcohol and intended to explore the process with lead and silver. He appears to have turned the alcohol into acetylene and, from that, produced what he was to call, in a letter to Wedgwood of May 1785, "charcoal of metals," i.e., copper and silver acetylides. Wedgwood was not always equally forthcoming to Priestley, for when the latter requested samples of those "scarce materials, *terra ponderosa aerata* [barium carbonate] and calk [barium sulphate]," Wedgwood responded that he was sending some calk, but had no terra ponderosa in his possession—

without revealing that he used both regularly in his jasperware. Early in 1791 Josiah's son, Thomas Wedgwood, commenced a correspondence with Priestley that lasted at least into 1792. Thomas was interested in the relations of heat and light and Priestley encouraged him in his experiments. As late as 2 September 1791, after the Birmingham Riots and Priestley's resettlement at Hackney, Wedgwood asked Priestley his opinion on refractory clays for furnaces, which Antoine Lavoisier and Armand Séquin had requested he make for them.[26]

There is no evidence that Priestley was involved with James Keir's chemical manufactories, though mutual interest in chemical operations might, in the course of conversation, have been useful to Keir. The two exchanged correspondence about chemical subjects as late as Keir's *First Part of a Chemical Dictionary* (Birmingham, 1789). Moreover, Priestley's work on basaltes, lava, and obsidian (described to Wedgwood and Withering) paralleled Keir's *Philosophical Transactions* paper "On the Crystallizations Observed on Glass" (1776), while, as Priestley wrote Wedgwood on 18 August 1781, "I can have the use of a glass-house [surely Keir's] for the purpose."[27]

Priestley did not join Withering in either of the areas of his chief interests: medicine and successive editions of his *Botanical Arrangement of British Plants,* though their first contact was through claims for the medicinal value of Priestley's artificial Pyrmont water. Their primary shared concerns were in chemistry, though Priestley's correspondence with Joseph Johnson in 1783 reveals that he was reading Buffon and other books on botany. Withering sent, via Priestley, a paper to the Royal Society, "An Analysis of two Mineral Substances, viz. The Rowley Rag-Stone and the Toad-Stone," *Philosophical Transactions* 72 (1782). The paper was accompanied by Priestley's letter of 1 April 1782 to the president of the Society, as an appendix to Withering's paper: Rowley-Rag appeared to be the same thing as basalt and toadstone resembled some species of lava.[28] His inference was correct—"Rowley-Rag" is a basaltic intrusion rock and toadstone is volcanic. Unfortunately, Priestley was to negate his inference in his 1786 volume of *Experiments and Observations,* where he declared that basalt yielded too much air to have

26. Wedgwood references are from Schofield, *Lunar Society,* 210, 267, 378, 420–22; *SciAuto.,* 90, 91, 121, 123, 139; and Bolton, #6, 8, 28, 34, 41, 42, 59, 76.

27. A selection of Keir-Priestley correspondence was published in Moillet, *James Keir;* see also Bolton, #8.

28. Priestley to Joseph Johnson, 24 May and 27 May 1783, Birmingham University Library, L.Add 2447, and personal collection of Sidney M. Edelstein, now in the Edelstein Collection in Israel; Journal Book of the Royal Society, vol. 31, 16 and 30 May 1782, 575–77, 580; and Priestley, *Exp. & Obs. Nat. Phil. III,* 215–22.

been volcanic. It and granite were probably crystallizations "of a mass of matter in a fluid form." In this "Neptunist" conclusion, he disagreed with his Lunar Society friends, for most appear to have been "Plutonists.

There were other occasions of joint operations with Lunar Society members. In 1782 Sir Joseph Banks sent Priestley (and Withering via Priestley) and Wedgwood samples of "Black Wadd," or "Derbyshire Mineral," (native manganese dioxide, pyrolousite) to determine the cause of the spontaneous combustion occurring when it was substituted for lamp-black in linseed oil paints. Priestley responded on 28 December with a report that the substance contained "a considerable quantity of . . . dephlogisticated air," so easily released that it would encourage combustion. On 29 December John Kennick wrote for the Board of Ordinance, thanking Withering for his warning about the dangers of using the substance, and Wedgwood wrote a paper, "Some Experiments upon the ochra friabilis nigro fusco . . . called by the Miners of Derbyshire, Black Wadd," published in *Philosophical Transactions* 73 (1783). In 1784 the Lunar Society went balloon mad. Priestley demonstrated a simple, inexpensive method of making inflammable air for balloons (steam passed over hot iron) to Faujas de St. Fond. And in January 1785 Withering assisted a Mr. Harper in filling a gas balloon for a flight in which "several bottles of Dr. Priestley's philosophical experiments, were broken by its striking a tree."[29]

The standardization of weights and measures was also a concern of Lunar Society members, particularly those involved in commerce.[30] Establishing "natural" standards provided a topic of correspondence for John Whitehurst (a pre-1780 member of the Society till his move to London), Boulton, Keir, Priestley, Watt, and Withering.

Lesser members of the Lunar Society and people only peripherally associated were involved in aiding or suggesting research. With the letter of 1 April 1782 to the Royal Society accompanying Withering's Rowley-Rag, Priestley also sent a short paper— "Experiments on the prismatic Colours," written by Samuel Galton Jr. Galton's primary scientific interest was in natural history, and this one public foray into the physical sciences was not published by the

29. See Schofield, *Lunar Society,* 302–3, 250–54. Priestley permitted Saint-Fond to make drawings of his inflammable air apparatus "for the purpose of communicating it to the French chymists," Saint-Fond, *Travels in England,* 2:339. James Glaiser, "On Scientific Experiments in Balloons," *Proceedings of the Royal Institution of Great Britain* 39 (1962–63): 641–50, was unaware of these experiments with balloons, or of those of Henry Cavendish, the preceding year, as anticipating those of Joseph Louis Gay-Lussac and Jean-Baptiste Biot of 1804–6 and of himself some forty-five years later.

30. Schofield, *Lunar Society,* 255–61.

Royal Society. Robert Augustus Johnson, Lunar Society member in 1787, scarcely enters the science picture but is mentioned in a letter of 1788 from Keir to Priestley as "our ingenious philosophical friend" who reminds them of a chemical process. Johnson wrote to Wedgwood in 1789 for some earthenware tubes "similar to those used by Dr. Priestley."[31] Priestley attempted to do something that might appeal to his iron-master brother-in law, John Wilkinson. At a Lunar Society meeting in July 1781 Priestley demonstrated that some of Boulton's "white spathos iron ore" (ferrous carbonate) contained more air than any ore he had ever tried and that this air was part fixed and part inflammable. He later wrote a set of observations on the "Conversion of Iron into Steel."[32] A "black substance" sent to Priestley for analysis by Joseph Bretland in 1789 was examined when "a number of my philosophical friends . . . dined with me yesterday. . . . It appears to be real coal, of that kind which burns without smoke or smell."

There are five letters from Priestley to the agricultural journalist and experimenter Arthur Young from July 1782 to November 1785. Priestley admired the work Young was doing and agreed to send him any experimental results that might be useful. He analyzed airs from samples of water sent by Young from a spring that seemed to promote fertile growth—though "it is very possible that fitness of water for meadows may depend upon something besides the phlogiston it contains." Priestley disclaimed any particular knowledge of agriculture and insisted that his observations were impractical, as most ways of administering phlogiston (the essence of plant food) killed rather than aided growth. Young reported his own experiments in his journal *Annals of Agriculture,* guided by Priestley, "our great philosopher . . . that truly great man."[33]

Among Priestley's miscellaneous science references can be found those returning to his first love, electricity. In 1781 he recommended electric shock as a means of recovering the loss of voice; in 1784, with Jean DeLuc, he was retesting the conductivity of fixed air. In 1785 he wrote twice to John Canton's son, William, supporting John's claim to a method for making

31. Galton's paper on colors is recorded in the Journal Book of the Royal Society, vol. 31, 615–18; it was finally published, as "Experiments on Colors," in the *Monthly Magazine* 8 (1799): 509–13. The peculiar status of Johnson in the Lunar Society is discussed in Schofield, *Lunar Society,* 227–29.

32. Schofield, *Lunar Society,* 245, 302. The "Observations on the Conversion of Iron into Steel," are found in Nicholson's *Journal of Natural Philosophy* 2 (1802): 233–34; repeated in *New York Medical Repository* 6 (1803) and *Medical and Physical Journal* 20 (1808): 347.

33. Schofield, *Lunar Society,* 325–26; Priestley to Young, 1 July, 12 Dec. 1782; 27 Jan., 31 March 1783; 11 Nov. 1785, *SciAuto.,* 96, 104, 108, 110, 128.

artificial magnets.[34] On 14 September 1785 he acknowledged a letter and book on electrical experiments received from Martinus van Marum. He praised van Marum's Tylerian Museum and his large-scale electrical experiments. Responding to a request for research suggestions, Priestley could only propose a repetition of his early experiments, but he passed along Withering's six queries on the chemical and physiological effects of electricity. On 9 June 1786 Priestley wrote van Marum of his great pleasure with the second volume, which reported the results of electrical experiments made with the great Tylerian electrical machine.[35] On 20 November 1786 Priestley wrote to Charles Blagden, forwarding an account of Abraham Bennet's electrometer, its value exceeding "any thing I have seen of the kind." He acquired new plates for his electrical machine from John Parker, his supplier of glass apparatus, and joined Erasmus Darwin, John Southern (of Boulton's Soho Works), and Wedgwood in assisting Bennet in experiments for Bennet's *New Experiments on Electricity* (1789). Along with Boulton, Darwin, Galton, Johnson, Keir, Watt, and Withering, he also subscribed to its publication.[36] He even found himself peripherally involved in the ephemeral excitement over animal magnetism, viewing an attempt to "magnetize," conversing with several believers, and reading a pamphlet on the subject before responding, on 26 June 1791, to a query from Bretland that he found nothing that could be confirmed and that reports from France were unfavorable.[37]

Priestley's most important research of the period, for him personally and for the history of science, was that first reported in his *Philosophical Transactions* paper for 1783, "Experiments relating to Phlogiston, and the seeming Conversion of Water into Air."[38] It is a paper of two distinct parts, related

34. Priestley, 7 June 1781, to unknown correspondent, Birmingham Reference Library. There is no reference to Priestley in Ernest Harms, "The Origin and Early History of Electrotherapy and Electroshock," *American Journal of Psychiatry* 111 (1955): 933–34, but Harms takes seriously the possibility that some eighteenth-century treatments were successful as a psychiatric tool. Note that Priestley once described successfully giving shock treatment to a poor woman who thought herself possessed by the devil. W. 1.1:111n–112n; *SciAuto.*, 120; Canton Papers, Archives, Royal Society of London.

35. *SciAuto.*, 127, 129. Van Marum wrote a letter in April 1787, acknowledging the suggestions from Priestley and Withering. A near-illegible draft is in Archives, Koninklijke Hollandsche Maatschappij der Wetenschappen, Haarlem.

36. *SciAuto.*, 135; Priestley to Blagden, quoted by permission from the private collection of David Richardson, Washington, D.C.

37. Schofield, *Lunar Society*, 255.

38. Joseph Priestley, "Experiments relating to Phlogiston, and the seeming Conversion of Water into Air," *Philosophical Transactions* 73 (1783): 398–434, dated 21 April 1783 and read to the Royal Society on 26 June. An incomplete MS copy, with letter to Sir Joseph Banks, can be found in Decade VIII, #31, vol. 72 (6 March–10 July 1783), Archives, Royal Society.

only by the apparent conjunction of water and air. Part I (398–413) contains his first published response to Lavoisier's attacks on phlogiston—a subject that, in the form of "the Chemical Revolution," was to dominate his research for the rest of his life. Part II (414–34) on "the seeming Conversion of Water into Air," describes experiments in which water heated to steam in closed containers was "converted" into air that then passed out a delivery tube and was collected. This air was almost as good as common air and nearly equal in weight to the water from which it had been converted.

The experiments were suggested, in part, by Priestley's "general idea," as he told Wedgwood on 8 December 1782, "that if the parts of any bodies be rarefied beyond the sphere of *attraction* they will be in a sphere of repulsion to each other." The initial technique, in which the water was soaked into calcereous matter, was adopted, he wrote Watt on the same date, by analogy with the conversion of acids into air when combined with metal calces. Watt wrote Boulton on 10 December 1782 that Priestley had confirmed Watt's opinion that "if water could be heated red hot or something more, it would probably be converted into some kind of air, because steam would in that case have lost all its latent heat and that would have been turned solely into sensible heat, and probably a total change of the nature of the fluid would ensue."[39]

Priestley and Watt were very excited by this "conversion." Watt wrote Wedgwood, DeLuc, and Joseph Black. Priestley also wrote Banks, DeLuc, and Franklin, and to Bretland he speculated that air from heating water with calcereous matter was of the type possibly emitted from volcanoes, best for plants and like that of the original atmosphere of the earth, as Moses had written that there were plants on earth before animals.[40] On 8 January 1783 Priestley wrote Wedgwood that calcereous materials were not necessary to the experiment, but that it did not work with glass retorts. He asked Wedgwood on 16 January for retorts glazed on the outside, and his response of 23 January to a Wedgwood letter shows that Wedgwood was beginning to suspect the "conversion" interpretation of the experiments. DeLuc, in Paris, and Watt were also informed that the experiments worked with earthenware retorts but not with glass. Finally, on 29 April, he wrote to Watt, and on 6 May to Wedgwood, with a diagram revealing the error in interpretation of his water-to-air experiments: air outside the retort diffused in through the walls of the earthen retort and passed out the delivery tube, while the

---

39. Priestley to Wedgwood and Watt, 8 Dec. 1782, *SciAuto.*, 100, 101; Bolton, #45n1.
40. *SciAuto.*, 100, 103, 105; Franklin Papers 26:95, APS; *W.* 1.1:366–68.

steam passed out through the walls.[41] The letter to Watt asked that the "Club" be told.

This late activity required changes in the paper sent to the Royal Society. Priestley's cover letter of 21 April to Banks declared that the paper had been sent "at the persuasion of *my friends,*" though he had still many things to do on the subject. Before the paper was read, on 26 June, the word "seeming" had been inserted into the original title and the second part had been completely rewritten. As now presented, this part of the paper commences with an oblique reference to his previous desire to exhibit substances "*in the form of air*" and a conclusion that it would be necessary to heat some of them "in a state of confinement."[42] He had imagined, he wrote, that "when substances consisting of parts so volatile as to fly off before they attained any considerable degree of heat, in the usual pressure of the atmosphere, were compelled to bear great heat under a greater pressure, they might assume new forms, and undergo remarkable changes, similar to what we may suppose to be the case within the bowels of the earth."

Supposing that giving red heat to calcined lime with which water was combined "might have the same effect as making water itself red hot," and not imagining that the nature of the retort would make any difference, he found that nothing came over in the form of steam but rather a great quantity of air, and "on some of the processes, the weight of the air . . . was very nearly, if not quite equal to that of the water" (416–17).

He concluded that he had converted water into air but then was "utterly disconcerted" to discover that the process worked without the lime but did not work when a coated glass retort, gun-barrel, porcelain, or glazed earthenware, was substituted for ordinary earthenware. He then placed the earthen retort inside a glass receiver over water and found that water rose in the receiver, filling space roughly equal to that of the air supposedly generated by conversion of water. This experiment made it probable that air on the outside of the retort passed through it, "yet it was contrary to all the known principles of hydrostatics . . . that air should be transmitted through a vessel of this kind and in a direction contrary to that which would have been forced by the pressure of the atmosphere; while water went the other way" (431–32).

41. Bolton, #18, 19, 20, 23, 25, 26; *SciAuto.,* 111; W. A. Smeaton, "Is Water Converted into Air? Guyton de Morveau Acts as Arbiter Between Priestley and Kirwan," *Ambix* 1 (1968): 73–83.

42. For reference to exhibiting substances in the form of air, and with the idea of compressing steam to turn it into a solid, see Chapter 7, n. 36. The quotation is from "Experiments relating to the seeming Conversion . . ." (415). Note that James Hutton used the notion of high pressure and heat in his *Theory of the Earth* (1795). See Patsy A. Gerstner, "James Hutton's Theory of the Earth and His Theory of Matter," *Isis* 59 (1968): 26–31.

This discovery, "contrary to all the known principles of hydrostatics," and his previous discovery of the diffusion of gases through one another, would, half a century later, find explanation in the kinetic theory of gases.[43] These discoveries were instrumental in the introduction of that concept by John Dalton and Thomas Graham.[44] The physical imagination and experimental creativity of Priestley were, once again, to lead to important work by others.

43. It is hardly surprising that Priestley's observations were not immediately taken up by others. Chemists were soon obsessed by the compositional problems associated with the "Chemical Revolution" and, for all Lavoisier's claim to be a physicist, there was little interest in the physics of gases. Dalton, it should be noted, came to the problem through meteorology.

44. To Dalton's references to Priestley's work cited previously can be added a reference, in "Elastic fluids," 269–70; for Graham, see "A Short Account of Experimental Researches on the Diffusion of Gases through each other, and their Separation by mechanical Means," *Quarterly Journal of Science and the Arts* 28 (1829): 82, and "On the Law of the Diffusion of Gases," *Philosophical Magazine* 2 (1833): 176, 178. See also Annette Ruckstuhl, "Thomas Graham's Study of the Diffusion of Gases,' *Journal of Chemical Education* 28 (1951): 594–96.

IX

SCIENCE AND THE CHEMICAL REVOLUTION

One of the most important persons whose work was thus led by Priestley was undoubtedly Antoine Laurent Lavoisier. Lavoisier was the architect and chief publicist of the "Chemical Revolution." He defined a new theory of combustion in opposition to that of phlogiston, established an operational definition for chemical elements and compounds based on weight, and participated in the creation of a new chemical nomenclature. For none of these achievements did he open the paths leading to his conclusions. Lavoisier was an interpretive genius, a masterly promoter with a capacity for detailed and tedious examination of other people's experiments. But he was not an original, creative experimenter, nor was he always scrupulous in reporting the origin of the clumsy ideas that he perfected.[1]

1. The literature on Lavoisier, especially by his acolytes, is extensive. See Edouard Grimaux, *Lavoisier, 1743–1794* (Paris: Felix Alcan, 1896), and Douglas McKie, *Antoine Lavoisier: The Father of Modern Chemistry* (Philadelphia: J. B. Lippincott, 1935). For more balanced accounts in English, see Henry Guerlac, "Lavoisier, Antoine-Laurent," in *Dictionary of Scientific Biography*, 8:66–91, and Arthur Donovan, *Antoine Lavoisier: Science, Administration, and Revolution* (Oxford: Blackwell Publishers, 1993). My account, from Priestley's point of view, will not be as favorable. Grimaux, *Lavoisier*, 57, insists that taking credit for another's work would be contrary to Lavoisier's whole life, that he always gave credit, and in a way this is true. But the credit he gave seemed to many of his contemporaries (including Priestley) and to later historians to be so oblique as to appear that his adoption of another person's work was almost incidental to his own achievement. His declaration, in the preface to his *Traité Élémentaire de Chimie*, "that, in the first part of my work, I make very little use of any experiments but those

The origin of his new theory of combustion had its basis in the familiar observation that many substances, when burned, increased in weight. Lavoisier thought this incompatible with Stahl's theory that substances lost phlogiston in combustion. Influenced by the work of Hales (as Priestley was at about the same time), Lavoisier decided that air was fixed in the calces and commenced experimenting to test his hypothesis. He reported a calcination intake of air in a "pli cacheté" deposited with the secretary of the Académie Royale in early autumn of 1772. A 20 February 1773 entry in his research notebook declared his intention to bring about a "revolution in physics and chemistry." His "pli" was opened on 5 May 1773 and the experiments reported there and subsequently formed the substance of his first book, *Opuscules physiques et chimiques* (1774).[2]

Early in 1774 Pierre Bayen and Cadet de Gassicourt reported the peculiar behavior of mercurius calcinatus per se under heat—i.e., that it regenerated without the addition of a phlogistic agent—and Lavoisier was made a member of the committee to investigate. At this point, October 1774, Joseph Priestley visited Paris and told French scientists, including Lavoisier, about the air released in heating mercurius calcinatus. Lavoisier repeated and confirmed Priestley's verbal report of 1774, assuming, however, that the gas released on heating the calcinatus was common air. Priestley's identification of dephlogisticated air was reported in Rozier's *Observations* in May 1775, and, after the publication of Priestley's *Experiments and Observations II*, Lavoisier initially called that air the "dephlogisticated air of M. Presley." His "Mémoire sur la nature du principe qui se combine avec les métaux pendant leur calcination, et qui en augmente le poids" (1775, 1778), asserted that this was the air fixed in calcination.[3]

---

which were made by myself" is an example of a failure to make acknowledgments when he might have done so. Lavoisier, *Elements of Chemistry, in a New systematic Order, containing all the modern Discoveries*, trans. Robert Kerr (1790; reprint, New York: Dover Publications, 1965), xxxiii. As he had so extended, modified, or even inverted the nature of his borrowings, however, his attitude has some merit.

2. Increase in weight was not a new discovery. Jean Rey, as early as 1630, had observed that the calces of lead and tin were heavier than these metals before calcination. Early in 1772, Louis Bernard Guyton de Morveau published a book proving that "the well-known gain in weight of lead and tin when they are calcined is not a peculiarity of those metals, but that all calcinable metals become heavier when transformed into a calx," and that the increase in weight was differently limited for each metal.

3. The first (incorrect) version of this paper was read to the Academy in April 1775 and was published in Rozier's *Observations* in May; it was corrected after Priestley's designation of dephlogisticated air, and the revised version was read to the Academy in 1778 and published in its *Mémoires* for that year.

Lavoisier's "Mémoire sur la combustion en général"—the first announcement of his theory of combustion and first cautious assault on the theory of phlogiston—was presented to the Académie Royale in November 1777 and published in its *Mémoires* (for 1777) in 1780. It was this paper that Priestley felt compelled to answer in the first part of his *Philosophical Transactions* paper of 1783.[4] The paper is dated 21 April 1783 and was read to the Royal Society on 26 June, but its basic contents were already known. Priestley informed Wedgwood, the Lunar Society, and Landriani in March 1782; wrote to Landriani again and to Franklin in Paris (with a request that the Duc de Rochefoucauld be informed) in June 1782; wrote to Wedgwood again in September 1782 and March 1783; and wrote Arthur Young and DeLuc (in Paris) in January 1783—all before the paper was sent to London.[5]

These communications reflected the experiments Priestley was making in response to Lavoisier's denial of phlogiston. True, metallic calces did usually contain air that could be expelled by heat, but this did not generally regenerate the metals; regeneration required the addition of phlogiston. As a source of phlogiston, Priestley generally used inflammable air, though alkaline air worked as well, except that the residue, after the calx had "absorbed" all the air it could, was phlogisticated air rather than being still inflammable. He thought that phlogiston might well be the same thing as inflammable air "in a state of combination with other bodies, as fixed air is contained in chalk."

The published paper summarized the phlogiston theory and recited the evidence for Priestley's refusal to accept Lavoisier's rejection of it. "Many celebrated chemists, Mr. Lavoisier among others," believed that in all cases in which it had been thought that bodies parted with the principle of phlogiston, they lost nothing, but acquired something, in most cases an addition of some kind of air (399). In this view, a metal was not a combination of an earth and phlogiston but was probably a simple substance and became a calx by acquisition of air, not loss of phlogiston. These arguments were so

4. Priestley, "Experiments relating to Phlogiston." This was his first published response to Lavoisier's attacks on phlogiston. There were at least three published attacks prior to Lavoisier's, one by the Compte de Buffon in the introduction to his *Histoire des Minerales* (Paris, 1774) and, more pertinently, the anonymous "Précis de la doctrine de M. DeMorveau" and "Discours sur la phlogistique," Rozier's *Observations sur la Physique* 2 (1773): 281–91 and 3 (1774): 185–291. Carleton Perrin, "Early Opposition to the Phlogiston Theory: Two Anonymous Attacks," *British Journal for the History of Science* 59 (1970): 128–44, has concluded that these were probably written by Pierre Bayen.

5. *SciAuto.*, 92, 93, 95, 106, 108, 109; Schofield, *Lunar Society,* 290; *Opuscoli Scelti* 5 (1787): 71–72, 350–51; Bolton, #24. There was even a published extract from a letter to "one of his friends in London," *London Medical Journal* 3 (1782): 87–88.

plausible that he was inclined to accept them. But experiments based on Kirwan's belief that phlogiston and inflammable air were the same showed that calxes actually imbibed something from the air *in toto*, leaving nothing behind; "that something must be *phlogiston*" (401). Priestley tried his experiments with other kinds of air than the inflammable, but only alkaline also worked. Inflammable air from wood worked only with difficulty, leaving residue air still inflammable but with a mixture of fixed air. He provided some incongruous quantitative data of weights of metals and volumes of airs.

The answer to the major problem posed by Priestley's response to Lavoisier's paper on combustion in general—the disappearance of inflammable air without residue in reconstituting metals from calces—was soon found, and partly through Priestley's agency. Warltire's letter on igniting inflammable and common airs in a glass vessel, published in the appendix to Priestley's *Experiments and Observations on Natural Philosophy* of 1781, was followed by experiments by Priestley and Withering and by Cavendish. Late in 1782 DeLuc visited Priestley in Birmingham, where he learned that Cavendish had found that igniting inflammable and dephlogisticated airs left a residue of water. In January 1783 Priestley wrote DeLuc in Paris about his "seeming conversion" experiments, but also mentioned that decomposing dephlogisticated and inflammable air by electric spark, he too got much water. DeLuc communicated this information to several members of the Academy of Sciences, but he viewed the experiments as revealing that air could contain dissolved water. On 23 March Priestley informed Wedgwood that the weight of the water obtained equaled that of the two airs.

The paper on the seeming conversion of water into air, sent by Priestley to the Royal Society in April 1783, had originally included a letter by James Watt that described Priestley's experiments on firing "quite dry inflammable air, and quite dry Dephlogisticated air," finding a quantity of water "very nearly, or quite equal in weight to the whole air." Watt's letter asked, "Are we not then Authorized to Conclude that Water is composed of Dephlogisticated Air, and Inflammable Air, or phlogiston, deprived of part of their Latent or elementary heat, and that Dephlogisticated or pure air is composed of Water deprived of its phlogiston . . . ?" Unfortunately for Watt, the discovery of Priestley's error in the conversion of water to air led him to request that the letter be withdrawn. On 15 January 1784 Henry Cavendish read his paper "Experiments on Air," subsequently published in *Philosophical Transactions*, which included descriptions of his experiments on firing inflammable and dephlogisticated air and obtaining water, which concluded: "I think we must allow that dephlogisticated air is in reality nothing but dephlogisticated water, or water deprived of its phlogiston; or in other words, that water consists of dephlogisticated air united to phlogiston; and that inflammable air is either pure phlogiston, as Dr. Priestley and Mr. Kirwan suppose, or else water united to phlogiston."[6]

In June 1783, before Cavendish's paper was published, Charles Blagden reported on his experiments to Lavoisier. Almost at once Lavoisier grasped that experiments previously discrediting his hypothesis of combustion could now be explained by the hypothesis that water was a compound: inflammable air used in regenerating metals from calces combined with dephlogisticated air in the calces to form water.[7] Lavoisier and Laplace repeated the experiments, burning substantial amounts of inflammable and dephlogisticated airs in a slow-combustion apparatus Lavoisier had designed. They found enough liquid to be tested and concluded that the liquid was water: "it was not possible to be certain of the exact quantity of the gases that burned, but since in physics as in mathematics, the whole is equal to the sum of its parts, and since only water and nothing else was formed, it seems safe to conclude that the weight of the water was the sum of the weights of the two gases from which it was produced." Lavoisier reported on his experiments to the Royal Academy the next day, 24 June 1783. A summary of Lavoisier and Laplace's work and Lavoisier's interpretations was published (without acknowledgment to Cavendish) in two papers in Rozier's *Observations* in 1783, with a fuller account in the *Mémoires* of 1784.

Early in 1784 Priestley began reporting the various, and sometimes contradictory, results of his experiments on combustion, regeneration, and the decomposition of water.[8] Talking with Faujas de St. Fond, he declared that

6. Jean André DeLuc, *Idées sur la Météorologie* (Paris: Veuve Duchesne, 1786), "Anecdotes relative à la découverte de l'EAU sous la forme d'Air," chap. 4, sec. 1, 206–24; *SciAuto.*, 106; Bolton, #24. This led to the so-called "Water Controversy" between supporters of claims by Watt and supporters of Cavendish to the discovery of the composition of water. In each case, the relevant statement is ambiguous. Cavendish clearly published first, and Lavoisier first clearly stated, and used, the correct conclusion. For more details, see [James Watt], "James Watt's Letter to Joseph Priestley, 26 April 1783," *Annals of Science* 10 (1954): 294–300. The letter was subsequently read to the Royal Society in April 1784, but not published. See Robert E. Schofield, "Still More on the Water Controversy," *Chymia* 9 (1964): 71–76.

7. When performed in air, the water had dissipated in the atmosphere; in containers isolated by pneumatic troughs, the water merged with the trough water.

8. Saint-Fond, *Travels in England;* Priestley to Wedgwood, 16, 23 Jan., 8 Nov. 1784, Bolton, #29, 30; *SciAuto.*, 121; to Cavendish, 16 June, 30 Dec., Cavendish to Priestley, 20 Dec. 1784, *SciAuto.*, 118, 122, 123; Priestley to DeLuc, 9 Sept. 1784, *SciAuto.*, 120; Watt to DeLuc, 9 Sept. 1784, Dibner Library, Smithsonian Institution Libraries; Priestley to Wilkinson, 16 June 1784, *SciAuto.*, 119; Vaughan to Benjamin Rush, MS communic. to APS, vol. 1, #13, APS; Thomas Henry to Rush, Rush Papers, Library Company of Philadelphia.

the decomposition of water was of such great importance that all objections that might be made against the theory should be completely refuted. He communicated, in correspondence or discussion, with Cavendish, De Luc, Watt, and Wedgwood. Sending an account on 16 June 1784 to William Wilkinson, then in Paris with Joseph Priestley Jr., he suggested that Joseph report it to Senebier or any other philosophical person he met with, including particularly Landriani at Milan. Benjamin Vaughan reported Priestley's work to Benjamin Rush in the United States late in 1784, as Thomas Henry did early in 1785.

The rationalized results of those experiments were published in Priestley's paper "Experiments and Observations relating to Air and Water," read to the Royal Society on 24 February 1785 and published in *Philosophical Transactions*.[9] For the historian, this is one of the most frustrating of Priestley's publications, for he repeated Lavoisier's experiments, confirmed many of the results, and then interpreted them differently. Analysis of the paper, however, reveals that the problem lay in one of the unacknowledged anomalies of Lavoisier's combustion theory, unresolved until the identification, in 1800, of carbon monoxide as an inflammable air different from hydrogen. Throughout this long paper, Priestley treated the two airs as though they were the same, and of course got results that conflicted with each other and with Lavoisier's. The situation was further complicated by Priestley's frequent use of iron in his experiments. Although he recognized a difference in the chemical behavior of cast iron and of "cast iron . . . kept red-hot in charcoal [steel?]" (304), and periodically referred to the "plumbago" (carbon) in the iron he used, he was regularly misled by the appearance of fixed air in "phlogisticating" iron calces.[10]

From these experiments, however, Priestley initially concluded that water, with or without fixed air, was the product of the inflammable air and the pure air let loose from the iron, "though afterwards I was taught by Mr. Watt . . . to account for this result in a different manner" (286).

That is, the water was previously contained in the iron scales and was replaced by the introduction of phlogiston from the inflammable air (308).

9. Joseph Priestley, "Experiments and Observations relating to Air and Water," *Philosophical Transactions* 75 (1785): 279–309.

10. Note that Priestley was not alone in his confusion over inflammable airs or over the carbon in the iron he used in his experiments. One cannot explain his failure to accept Lavoisian chemistry either by inept experimental procedures or by impure chemicals, for his opponents found the same things he did but chose to ignore them because of the overall coherence and beauty of the new chemistry. See F. Verbruggen, "How to Explain Priestley's Defense of Phlogiston," *Janus* 59 (1972): 47–69.

Iron plus steam yielded more inflammable air than iron plus acid, and more rapidly. It gained the same weight as by combustion and became the same substance. In combustion, part of the iron's phlogiston entered into the small quantity of fixed air produced, and the remainder formed water with the dephlogisticated air imbibed by the iron. There was a remarkable difference between the inflammable airs from metals and from charcoal, in their combination with dephlogisticated air. The air from metals gave neither water nor fixed air but an acid, while the air from carbon gave water and fixed air. To Cavendish's report that a spark taken in impure dephlogisticated air formed an acid, Priestley responded with pleasure at the discovery that nitrous acid was contained in phlogisticated air. Alkaline air revived more lead than inflammable air, leaving a residue that was one-quarter phlogisticated air. The French experiments with inflammable air from iron were suspect, as iron was itself inflammable; those with steam over iron or charcoal did not prove that inflammable air came from water.[11]

Priestley's next scientific publication was his *Experiments and Observations relating to Various Branches of Natural Philosophy III*.[12] The last volume in the *Experiments and Observations* series, it was dedicated to William Constable, a longtime contributor to Priestley's research fund, but it owed its return to something of the exuberance of the earlier volumes to the inspiration of Priestley's Lunar Society activities. It owed its size to previous publications and direct extensions of them, which together take up roughly 70 percent of the volume.

It begins with one of Priestley's usual personal, philosophical, theological prefaces. In this one he apologized to his "philosophic friends," especially those by whose assistance he was able to perform his experiments, for spending so much time on other pursuits—especially those leading to his *History of the Corruptions of Christianity* and the *Opinions concerning Christ*. He assured those friends that more time was spent on a single volume of experiments than on those six volumes and the works defending them. Besides, he insisted, the really important studies, those from which mankind would finally derive the greatest good, were those in theology—"my original and proper province" (viii–ix).

The first part of the text is taken from the phlogiston half of his *Philosophical Transitions* paper of 1783, to which some notes were added, though

11. Priestley to Wedgwood, 16 Jan. 1784, Bolton, #29; Cavendish to Priestley, 20 Dec. 1784, *SciAuto.*, 122; Priestley to Cavendish, 30 Dec. 1784, *SciAuto.*, 123.
12. Priestley, *Exp. & Obs. Nat. Phil. III* (Birmingham: by Pearson and Rullason, for J. Johnson, 1786). No further English edition save in the collected edition of 1790; trans. French and German.

nothing on the composition of water. Section 2 added the "conversion of water into air," with notes that "there is no acid in dephlogisticated air" (54) and that there were powers in chemistry, such as the attraction of cohesion, greater than that of an air pump that could draw air through the small pores of unglazed earthenware (64–69). An attempt to measure the force required had ambiguous results. Section 3 was taken from the *Philosophical Transactions* paper of 1785, on air and water with added experiments. These disproved the hypothesis of Lavoisier that "neither the scales of iron, nor the charcoal, contain phlogiston, or any thing from which inflammable air can be made, but are merely substances capable of imbibing pure air, and thereby setting at liberty the inflammable air contained in water" (111). Section 4 continued observations on the composition of water, noting that inflammable air from iron (and acid) seemed to confirm that water consists of dephlogisticated air and inflammable, but fixed air resulted when the inflammable air came from wood and produced no water when red precipitate was revived in it (125–30). Sections 5–10 involve different kinds of inflammable air. Inflammable air showed a great variety of modifications because its chief ingredient, phlogiston, entered a great variety of combinations with solid substances, including sulphur, which, with water, forms sulphurated inflammable air (145–62). The purest inflammable air was that obtained from metals in acids. Its constitution was uncertain, "But [as] we are as yet ignorant of the principles of combination and cohesion in the parts which compose natural substances, how much more are we with respect to the constituent parts themselves?" (164). Many people had observed that there were different kinds of inflammable air, noting, for example, different colors of flame or explosion, and different specific gravities (167). The differences did not, however, suggest to Priestley (or to most of his contemporaries) any difference in the substance itself.

Sections 14 and 15 (on fixed air), 17 (on dephlogisticated air), and 18–20 (on various nitrous airs) continued Priestley's investigation of air and water that he had reported in his paper of 1785, while section 23, on steam passed over heated substances, continued that of the "apparent conversion" part of the 1783 paper. This last section also echoed the Lunar Society concern with filling balloons. Other echoes of that kind are to be found in section 11, on the "charcoal of metals," and in sections 12, 13, and 16, on the air expelled from heating substances, on which Priestley had written to Wedgwood as early as 1781 and had prefixed to Withering's *Philosophical Transactions* paper of 1782. That on mineral substances included a repetition of his remarks on "black woad" (232), while that on charcoal (237–48) also reported on the phenomenon of adsorption, and observed, correctly, that there is preferential adsorption of "pure air" over phlogisticated.[13]

Section 21, on electricity and chemistry, recalled the late electrical experiments of Lunar Society members and the correspondence of Priestley and Withering with van Marum, but also was reminiscent of Priestley's declaration, as early as 1767, about combining electricity and chemistry. The observations "Of the Influence of Light on Vapour of Spirit of Nitre," offered nothing new (except perhaps the note that heat does not produce the same result, 342–46), but may be responsible for beginning his correspondence with Thomas Wedgwood on similar subjects. Experiments on iron (355–76) revealed Priestley's awareness of manufacturing practices, including the differences between cast and malleable iron and of "cementing" the latter with charcoal, called "annealing" in Birmingham. Those on "finery cinder" explicitly referred to his brother-in-law, John Wilkinson, but here served only as an introduction to a subject that would occupy Priestley's attention well into his exile in the United States.

There are two curious and overdue sections: one on "air acting through bladders" (374–76), in which Priestley explicitly acknowledged what he had only indifferently remarked before, that air inside a bladder could act upon that outside and vice versa; and the other, "Of the Influence of Water on Phlogisticated Air" (385–86). He had early thought that agitation in water brought all kinds of air to the same state, "never imagining that when the air in my jar was separated from the common air by a body of water ... they could have any influence on each other. I have, however, been long convinced that, improbable as it then appeared to me, this is actually the case, though a fact so remarkable well deserves to be farther attended to" (385–86). However long he had held that conviction, it did not preclude his continued experimenting with air kept for long periods of time (as much as a year) in a phial with its mouth immersed in water (section 10, 203–7) nor did it encourage any corrections about previously reported results.[14]

13. If, by "charcoal of metals," Priestley did indeed intend the acetylides—and his description to Wedgwood and Cavendish of their formation (*SciAuto.*, 121, 123), makes it appear so, it is curious that he failed to note their explosive character. This part of the book, 207–14, was separately translated for Rozier's *Observations*, "Du Carbon des Metaux," 30 (1787): 81–83, and, probably from that source, "Memoria del Sig. Priestley Sul Carbone de Metalli," *Opuscoli Scelti* 10 (1787): 288–90. See Chapter 8, n. 25, above; Schofield, *Lunar Society*, 278–79, 302–4. The observations on adsorption continue those started in *Exp. & Obs. II*. See Chapter 6, n. 35, above.

14. He expressed doubts about bladders and about failure of water to separate airs as early as his first experiments in pneumatic chemistry. See Schofield, *Enlightenment of Priestley*, 265, and repeated observations relating to the same doubts through early volumes of *Exp. & Obs.*; see chap. 6, 149, chap. 7, 199, and n. 13 above.

"Observations on Theory" (400–426)" essentially brought this volume to an end.[15] It revealed, even more than earlier parts of the text, how little comprehension Priestley brought to understanding the implications of Lavoisier's "Considérations Générales sur la Nature des Acides, et sur les Principles dont ils sont composés" (submitted to the Academy in 1777, read in November 1779, and published in the Mémoires [for 1778] in 1781). "Sur la Nature des Acides" concluded that the "purest part" of air, i.e., dephlogisticated air, which Lavoisier renamed oxygine, was in all acids and necessary to their acidity. Priestley temporarily accepted this erroneous conclusion (300, 403), but he missed the significance of the enumeration of the number of elements Lavoisier supposed "necessary to constitute all substances we are acquainted with" (401).

It was in this paper of 1781 that Lavoisier first significantly showed his interest in the nature of a chemical compound.[16] The paper confirmed his views on the order of simplicity between the combustibles and their products, which in turn required that metals and the acidifiable bases be classed as simple bodies. This marked the first real progress toward definition of the chemical elements, and an aspect of this progress was tracking changes in weight. It was just this aspect that Priestley missed. That he had become aware that weights had some significance in chemistry is clear from his grudging use of weight measurements in his late experiments, but what that significance might be was obscure—to Priestley and to many of his contemporaries.

In an age that had accepted imponderable fluids of electricity, magnetism, and even of vitality, attachment to ponderability was not an essential.[17] When Priestley, declining to give any general theory, proposed to supply some observations on "the constituent parts of all the kinds of air with which we are acquainted," he included latent heat as a necessary ingredient in every kind of air. We know very little of that principle, he wrote, and "as it is not probable that this adds any thing to the weight of bodies, it can hardly be called an element in their composition" (411, 403). "The term principle may be applied to any cause of a known effect, whether it be what logicians call a

15. There was a subsequent section of trivial late experiments (427–38) and an appendix of two irrelevant letters, from James Keir, 31 March 1786, and Thomas Henry, 22 March 1786 (439–48).

16. See Robert Siegfried, "Lavoisier's Table of Simple Substances: Its Origin and Interpretation," Ambix 29 (1982): 29–48; also Siegfried and Dobbs, "Composition." The argument that it was his work on acids that confirmed Lavoisier's move to definition of simple substances is that of Siegfried, "Lavoisier's Table," 39–40.

17. For the role of imponderable fluids in eighteenth-century science, see Schofield, Mechanism and Materialism.

substance, or a property." Thus, where there is such a thing as heat, there must exist a principle or cause of heat, whether that be a change of state of the parts of the heated body (e.g., vibratory motion) or a substance, such as air or water, infused into a body when heated and withdrawn when cold (418).

With so little understanding of the new role of comparative weights, it comes as no surprise that in Priestley's details of the specific constitution of a number of different airs, some should be found to "contain" compounds heavier than themselves. Phlogisticated air, for example, was nitrous acid plus phlogiston (403), as the composition of sulphur consists of vitriolic acid and phlogiston (405). Fixed air seemed a compound of phlogiston and dephlogisticated air. "It is something remarkable that two substances, so different from each other as *fixed air* and *water* should be analyzed into the same principles" (405). Alkaline air was a combination of inflammable air and phlogisticated air, "but the mode of combination and the proportion of the ingredients, remain to be investigated" (408–9).[18]

The brilliance, and partial cause, of Priestley's intransigence can be seen in the part of "relating to Theory," dealing particularly with phlogiston. Priestley believed that winning the argument depended upon experimental evidence. He was wrong—or wrong in believing that raw experimental results were sufficient. For experiments must be interpreted, and interpretation always lies within a system of beliefs. If, in his interpretations, Priestley tended to ignore the evidence of the balance as not required in his system, so his opponents ignored such anomalies as different inflammable airs as not fitting their system. But such anomalies there were, and Priestley focused on them in his discussion of phlogiston.

Giving details of Stahl's interpretations of acids and calces, Priestley noted that there were differences of interpretation, "and did facts correspond to this [new] theory, it would certainly be preferable . . . as being more simple. . . . But I do not know of any case in which phlogiston has been supposed to enter into a body, but there is room to suppose, that something does enter into it; and . . . especially [in] some of my own late experiments, something certainly does" (419). The regeneration of mercury from its calx, without

---

18. I have deliberately avoided adding modern notations to these conclusions, as this would only have made a historically confused issue seem simpler than it was, but for purposes of understanding the anomalies, I add them here: phlogisticated air (N_2) composed of nitrous acid (HNO_3) plus phlogiston (probably H_2). Sulfur (S) consisting of vitriolic acid (H_2SO_4) plus phlogiston (H_2). Fixed air (CO_2) a compound of phlogiston (in this case, probably CO) and dephlogisticated air (O_2), while water (H_2O) is a compound of phlogiston (H_2, this time) and dephlogisticated air. Alkaline air (NH_3) a combination of inflammable air (H_2, in this instance) and phlogisticated air (N_2).

addition of any other substance, had been a chief example for anti-phlogiston, but that could, as Kirwan showed, be explained in a way consistent with phlogiston theory. When the calx was formed, phlogiston belonging to the metal united with imbibed air to form fixed air, which, with the metal, constitutes the calx. In greater heat, the factitious fixed air is decomposed, its phlogiston reviving the metal and loosening the pure air. "Since, therefore, this *fact* can be accounted for without excluding phlogiston, the supposition of which is exceedingly convenient, if not absolutely necessary, to the explanation of many other facts in chemistry, it is at least adviseable not to abandon it. Besides *light* contains phlogiston, if there be any such thing, and there can be no *red heat* without light . . . all the phlogiston that is necessary to the revival of this particular metal may enter into the heated calx, notwithstanding all our endeavours to exclude it" (421–22).

For Priestley, the most convincing of his experiments demonstrating that phlogiston is a real substance, even adding to the weight of bodies, was that of the decomposition of charcoal by heat of a lens in vacuo. Lavoisier said charcoal was a simple substance, capable of decomposing water heated with it but contributing nothing to the inflammable air procured in the process. But the whole of the charcoal disappeared, leaving nothing but inflammable air ("though not of the most simple kind") and an inconsiderable portion of white ashes that could not have imbibed the dephlogisticated air of the water, setting inflammable air at liberty. What became of the substance of the charcoal, if it did not supply something which might be termed phlogiston, from which inflammable air is made (422–23)? "If this hypothesis of Mr. Lavoisier cannot explain the present known facts, and the doctrine of phlogiston *can* do it, the latter ought as yet to be retained, in preference to his, or any other that has yet been proposed" (425).

Even while Priestley was publishing this defense of phlogiston, Lavoisier's *Réflexions sur le Phlogistique pour servir de Dévelopement à la Théorie de la Combustion et de Respiration* was being published in the Academie's *Mémoires.* This "rhetorical masterpiece," in the words of Arthur Donovan, drafted after 1777 and first read to the Academy in 1785, was the beginning of a sustained, coordinated, and successful attack on the whole of the old chemistry.[19] The essentials of the new theory of combustion can be summarized

19. Donovan, *Antoine Lavoisier,* 135. The term "rhetorical" suggests argument for the sake of winning, and I intend that here. Lavoisier's arguments, and those of his supporters, made skillful use of the advantages of their new chemistry while concealing some of its flaws. That the new chemistry, for all its deficiencies, was superior to the old does not entirely justify ignoring those deficiencies when judging Priestley's career.

as: (1) combustion occurs only in "pure air," now to be called *oxygine*, and is accompanied by release of the matter of fire and/or light; (2) during combustion, pure air is decomposed and the weight of the burning substance increases in proportion to the amount of the air decomposed; (3) the substance burned is changed into an acid by the addition of the substance that increases its weight; (4) pure air ("oxygine" or acid-former) is a compound of a base plus the matter of heat or fire. It mattered little, in the long run, that only the second of these "essentials" has survived. The emphasis on change in weight of the burned substance, and the reason for it, was to become the basis for distinguishing between elements and compounds and for the major direction of chemical research for the next half century. In the short run, these explicitly stated "essentials" opened the new combustion theory to explicit attacks.[20] And Priestley quickly took advantage of that opening. He did not, of course, attack those essentials on any metaphysical ground, though his persistence in opposition suggests that he had metaphysical doubts. He focused his attention on the experiments said to support the theory and here, he found, there was a paradoxical error.

The combustion of inflammable air in *oxygine* did not, to Lavoisier, produce an acid (*pace* essential no. 3), but water. Yet production of water was a necessary consequence of Lavoisier's theory! If the product of combustion was a combination of pure air and the substance burned, then regeneration of that substance by inflammable air must be the extraction of the pure air and its combination with the inflammable, and that combination, whether in regeneration or combustion, must be water. At once composition of water became a major issue. As early as 17 July 1786, Faujas de St. Fond wrote to Sir Joseph Banks from Paris, asking for the opinions of Cavendish, Priestley, and Watt on the conversion of air to water, and vice versa. Through the remainder of 1786, 1787, and early 1788, Priestley corresponded with Ingenhousz, Price, Wedgwood, Withering, and James Keir, reporting that his experiments showed the combination of dephlogisticated air and inflammable air produced not water but an acid.[21] These experiments were at length published as "Experiments and Observations relating to the Principle of Acidity, the Composition of Water, and Phlogiston."

Read to the Royal Society on 7 February 1788, the paper began by admitting that Priestley had not, at first, found acid in the "pretty large quantities"

20. Combustion can occur, for example, in chlorine or sulfur; oxygen is not an acid former nor is it present in all acids; neither heat nor light is, in a chemical sense, a material substance.
21. Faujas to Banks, Add. mss 8096.306–7, British Library; Priestley to Ingenhousz, 24 Nov. 1787, *SciAuto.*, 130; to Price, 4 Dec. 1787, Price Papers, Bodleian Library; to Wedgwood, 8 Jan. 1788, *SciAuto.*, 131; to Keir, 10 Jan. 1788; Moillet, *James Keir*, 92; Bolton, #45.

of water he had produced, though he had accepted the doctrine of dephlogisticated air being or containing the principle of universal acidity (147). Then experiments with inflammable air (from iron with steam) and dephlogisticated air (from manganese, red precipitate, or red lead), in a vessel exhausted of its contained air, formed acidified water (149–50). Keir and Withering had identified the acid as nitrous.[22] That paper was quickly followed by "Additional Experiments and Observations relating to the Principle of Acidity, the Decomposition of Water, and Phlogiston. With Letters . . . on the Subject by Dr. Withering and James Keir, Esq."[23] Read to the Royal Society on 1 May 1788, it repeated some of the experiments, with Keir's determination of the amount of "nitre" contained in the acidified water (313–14). Priestley suspected that there might be other acids as well (e.g., carbonic) produced in the decomposition of dephlogisticated and inflammable airs. Antiphlogistians might argue that when a metallic calx was revived in inflammable air, air joined dephlogisticated air in the calx, the metal resuming its form and qualities without addition. But when red-hot iron in steam became a calx by emitting inflammable air, it could not become a metal again without absorbing the inflammable air whose loss had made it a calx (315). What became of the dephlogisticated air expelled from red precipitate when heated in inflammable air, if that air entered the regenerating calx? It united with part of the inflammable air to form nitrous acid (316). Withering's letter gave details of his identifying the acid as nitrous, and Keir's of his determination of the kind and quantity of the acid.

These papers drew immediate protests, for Henry Cavendish had already argued, in his "Experiments on Air" in the *Philosophical Transactions* of 1784, and had "confirmed" that argument in a paper of 1785, that acid produced in the combination of dephlogisticated and inflammable airs was an effect of phlogisticated air impurity in one or both the airs.[24] Priestley addressed those protests in letters to DelaMétherie, Banks, Watt, and Wedgwood between July and late October 1788, before publishing his responses in "Objections to the Experiments and Observations relating to the Principle of Acidity, the Composition of Water, and Phlogiston, considered; with farther Experiments and Observations on the same Subject," read to the Royal

---

22. Joseph Priestley, "Experiments and Observations relating to the Principle of Acidity, the Composition of Water, and Phlogiston," *Philosophical Transactions* 78 (1788): 147–57.

23. Joseph Priestley, "Additional Experiments and Observations relating to the Principle of Acidity, the Decomposition of Water, and Phlogiston. With Letters . . . on the Subject by Dr. Withering and James Keir, Esq.," *Philosophical Transactions* 78 (1788): 313–30.

24. See Partington, *History of Chemistry* 3:338–39, for this work by Cavendish.

Society on 17 November 1788 and published in *Philosophical Transactions* 79 (1789).[25]

In correspondence, and in the published paper, Priestley answered that the more phlogisticated air he added to the pure and inflammable airs, the less acid he obtained (9–10). Claude Louis Berthollet had objected to his experiments, but the use of precipitate per se of guaranteed purity sent him by Berthollet gave the same results, including the production of some fixed air. It had been claimed that the fixed air came from plumbago in the hot iron from which inflammable air had been obtained (driving out any contained water), but the antiphlogistians claimed that water was the only source of inflammable air (11–12). After describing his experiments, Priestley repeated some considerations of the allegations of Lavoisier, Berthollet, and Fourcroy, in their report on the New *Nomenclature*.

The conflict between Priestley and the antiphlogistians was now joined in earnest. Although he was to publish four more scientific papers during his stay in Birmingham, only the last of them dealing explicitly with the problem of composition of water, the other papers each referred to phlogiston, his scientific correspondence was almost exclusively on the problem, and his research for the remainder of his life centered on phlogiston and the composition of water. His paper on the "Phlogistication of Spirit of Nitre" is a case in point.[26] Read to the Royal Society on 26 March 1789 and published the same year, the paper may have had its immediate origins in a correspondence with Isaac Milner. Milner, temporarily Jacksonian Professor of Chemistry at Cambridge (1783–92) on his way to becoming evangelical president of Queens College, had written to Priestley about his method of making nitric acid from ammonia. Priestley responded that he wished Milner to follow up these experiments himself, "as I am not fond of putting my sickle into another man's harvest."[27] He had, however, scarcely any need for a reason to return to experiments on nitre itself.

25. Priestley to de la Mètherie, July 1788, appended to the Italian translation of the first *Philosophical Transactions* paper of 1788, *Opuscoli Scelti* 12 (1789): 93–94; Priestley to Banks, 18 Aug. 1788, Dibner Library, Smithsonian Institution Libraries; Bolton, #48; Priestley to Watt, 20 Aug. 1788, JWP/W/ 13/13, Birmingham City Archives; to Wedgwood, July, 18 Aug., 9 Oct. 1788, Bolton, #46, *SciAuto.*, 132, Bolton, #49; Joseph Priestley, "Objections to the Experiments and Observations . . . ," *Philosophical Transactions* 79 (1789): 7–20.

26. Joseph Priestley, "Experiments on the Phlogistication of Spirit of Nitre," *Philosophical Transactions* 79 (1789): 139–49.

27. Priestley to Isaac Milner, 24 June 1788, in Mary Milner, *Life of Isaac Milner, D.D. F.R.S.* (London: John W. Parker; Cambridge: J. and J. J. Deighton, 1843), 35. Partington, *History of Chemistry*, 3:343, describes Milner's discovery, published in the *Philosophical Transactions* of 1789, as the basis of the modern process for making nitric acid.

The paper related the doctrine of phlogiston with the coloring of spirit of nitre. Experiments on its coloration persuaded Priestley that neither heat nor light was, by itself, capable of changing the colorless acid to reddish-orange. It appeared that air over the acid must be involved, and he finally asserted that the process involved the emission of dephlogisticated air and the addition of phlogiston, imbibed from the common air in which the experiment was performed (146). Priestley believed that these experiments favored the doctrine of phlogiston, as the red vapor of spirit of nitre contained the principle called phlogiston, or that in the constitution of inflammable air, and antiphlogistians must then suppose that the water in the acid was decomposed by an extraordinarily moderate degree of heat (146–47).

Roughly three months later Priestley read his paper on the transmission of acid vapor through a hot tube.[28] A continuation of the earlier paper, for it examined oil of vitriol as well as spirit of nitre when pure air had been expelled from them by passage through a hot earthen tube, it concluded that the acids were left super-phlogisticated (289). This, somehow, related to phlogiston, for Priestley then reasserted his claim that in the calcination of iron in dephlogisticated air, something was emitted from the iron as the dephlogisticated air was imbibed. More fixed air was found in the vessel in which the iron was melted with dephlogisticated air than could be accounted for by supposing it came from plumbago. Priestley concluded that it must have come from phlogiston in the iron combining with pure air in the vessel (295–96).

In "Observations on Respiration," read to the Society on 25 February 1790, Priestley emended his paper of 1776 on the subject, after observing the transmission of dephlogisticated, inflammable, and nitrous airs through a moist bladder.[29] Besides the emission of phlogiston from the blood, dephlogisticated air, or the acidifying principle of it, was received into it at the same

---

28. Joseph Priestley, "Experiments on the Transmission of the Vapour of Acids through an hot Earthen Tube, and further Observations relating to Phlogiston," *Philosophical Transactions* 79 (1789): 289–99.

29. Joseph Priestley, "Observations on Respiration," *Philosophical Transactions* 80 (1790): 106–10, emending *Philosophical Transactions* 66 (1776): 226–38. This return to the study of respiration commenced at least as early as 22 July 1789, when Priestley wrote about it to Theophilus Lindsey, and cannot have been prompted by word of the first part of Lavoisier and Sequin's *Mémoire* on the respiration of animals, read (according to Grimaux, *Lavoisier,* 332) on 17 Nov. 1789 and published in the academy's memoirs for that year, in 1793. Partington, *History of Chemistry,* 3:473n1, reports that Maurice Daumas claimed this *Mémoire* was, in fact, read 17 Nov. 1791, which would reverse the order of influence. These observations and those leading to them about plant and animal affects on air are frequently cited in Daniel Ellis, *An Inquiry into the Changes induced on Atmospheric Air by the Germination of Seeds, the Vegetation of Plants, and the Respiration of Animals* (Edinburgh: Wm. Creech; London: J. Murray, 1807).

time. But some of the latter united with the phlogiston to form the fixed air that was the product of respiration (106). After experiments on breathing and measuring the fixed air, he concluded that three times as much dephlogisticated air entered the blood as was used in forming fixed air. Some phlogisticated air must be inhaled in respiration; and Charles Blagden suggested that there was a greater proportion of it in the lungs after respiration than before it (108–9).

Between November 1788, when he read his paper answering objections to his experiments on acidity, and early 1790, in addition to extensive nonscientific activities, Priestley was "working like a horse" editing a three-volume abridged and methodized edition of the six-volume series of *Experiments and Observations* and obtaining permission to dedicate it to the Prince of Wales.[30] A reading of the three volumes shows them primarily to be a reordering of the material that has already been discussed in its previous distributions among six volumes.[31]

Nonetheless, the abridged edition, summarizing a nineteen-year distinguished career in pneumatic chemistry, must command some attention, even without the admonition that there were "many additions." In fact there are very few of these, and analysis will therefore focus on the incongruities newly displayed, as this edition placed Priestley's work into a scientific ambience he had done much to change but that was making him irrelevant.

Priestley explained that the six volumes, "being at present so far out of print," it was more advisable to "new model" the whole than to reprint. But even the dedication to "His Royal Highness George Prince of Wales" and the preface primarily reprint what he thought worth preserving of the prefaces to the previous six volumes (xv, xvn). The dedication does add the hope of "a person whose deliberate judgment has led him to dissent from the mode of religion by law established in this country" that "as future sovereign of Great Britain you will be the equal father of all your subjects; and . . . every man will meet with encouragement and favour in proportion to the services he renders his country, and the credit he is to it" (xi–xii).

---

30. Joseph Priestley, *Experiments and Observations on Different Kinds of Air, and other Branches of Natural Philosophy, connected with the Subject. . . . Being the former Six Volumes abridged and methodized, with many additions* (Birmingham: J. Johnson, 1790). Priestley to Keir, Bolton, #50; to Lindsey, 22 July, 29 Oct. 1789, 22 March 1790.

31. Truly to appraise this three-volume edition, one should carefully compare each section in it to the relevant sections from each of the former six volumes. Having previously analyzed each of the six, I think I could detect significant changes and additions without such detailed a comparison, but cannot guarantee that subtle variations may not have escaped me.

The introduction repeated Priestley's praise of Stephen Hales, who, though he "had no idea of there being more than *one kind of air,*" provided so many and various experiments "that they are justly esteemed to be the solid foundation of all our knowledge of this subject" (5). There is, perhaps, a criticism of the New Nomenclature in his statement that "The language that I adopt . . . implies no attachment to any hypothesis whatever, and may still be used though I should change my opinion . . . which is certainly a very great advantage in philosophical language" (10). Priestley organized the volumes in "books" relating to experiments on different airs. Book 1, for example, is on fixed air. In it, Priestley continued misleading on the origin of his experimenting on fixed air, conceding, on the advice of James Keir, that the amount of air released from mineral substances was not a decisive test of that substance's volcanic origin (64), and included experiments showing the passage of various kinds of air through a bladder (174–81).[32]

Book 2 related experiments and observations on inflammable air, noting that every substance containing phlogiston will yield inflammable air, their respective natures requiring different modes of treatment (200). Communication of the experimental airs with external air, through water, might produce changes in the airs, but Priestley still reported experiments in which air was "changed" by long holding, or agitation, in water (227, 230). A footnote (353n) added a late comment that water might be the basis of inflammable air. Kinds of inflammable air were enumerated and distinguished by color of flame, production of explosions, source (extracted from metals by acids or expelled from wood, coal, and other substances by heat), and specific gravities (311). But the advantage one might suppose gained by bringing together these observations did not lead to the conclusion that they were indeed different substances (311).[33]

Book 3 (328–411, continuing into the second volume, 1–102) was on nitrous air and had only one addition (367n) noting that nitrous air escaped from water impregnated with it by long exposure to the open air. Experiments involving long storage of airs over water were repeated (2–3, 18) without the concern just suggested and repeated from the 1786 *Exp. & Obs. III* that such

32. These observations do not preclude repeated instances of experiments making use of bladders, either as holding devices or in transference of airs from one receptacle to another; see e.g., vol. 2, 30, 196.

33. Section 5, Book 2, 308–27. Priestley did suggest that some of the heavier inflammable airs may contain *combined fixed air,* but he also observed that burning inflammable air in dephlogisticated air must have *generated* the fixed air found after combustion (311). Note that Lavoisier did not distinguish between different inflammable airs but subsumed them all as "Hydrogen"; see Lavoisier, *Elements of Chemistry,* 175.

airs communicated with common air through the water; he even proposed that there was "a change in the constitution of a body depending upon *time* only" (3). Later he noted that water in his pneumatic trough, fouled by various metallic substances, in contact with nitrous air in jars standing in it, "would be of a darker colour than the rest of the water," again without apparent concern that this might vitiate the results of some of his experiments (13).

Book 4 (102–87) concerned dephlogisticated air. Priestley repeated his observation that more was due to chance, in philosophical investigations, than to design, regardless of the appearance of work written "synthetically" (102–3). Yet, retrospectively considering his discoveries relating to the constitution of the atmosphere, he saw the closest and easiest connection between those discoveries and that of dephlogisticated air and wondered that he was not led immediately from one to the other. He attributed this to prejudice, which had biased even his perceptions to the point that the plainest evidence could not change his persuasion that atmospheric air was a simple elementary substance (103–4).

Book 5 (188–274) related to phlogisticated air and began with an added note that the name originated with the supposition that the air was atmospheric, affected by phlogiston. But the term still applied if the air of the atmosphere consisted of two distinct parts, and substances containing phlogiston attracted the dephlogisticated and left the other phlogisticated (188n). Book 6 dealt with the various airs that were readily absorbed by water: marine acid air, vitriolic acid air, fluor acid air, and alkaline air (275–376). Each of these was an air that Priestley believed he had first identified. He was perhaps mistaken in the case of fluor acid air, but his discussion treated it as a logical step from Scheele's discovery of fluor acid, which, heated in analogy with vitriolic acid or marine acid, should and did release an acid air.[34] He had once suspected the new acid air to be merely vitriolic acid air with added silicon impurity, but subsequent experiments had demonstrated that the acid, and therefore the air, was of a different nature (351–55).

"Miscellaneous experiments and observations relating to air" (402–72) began with the assertion that there was no substance in nature but what is capable of becoming a "dry and permanently elastic vapour" in a certain degree of heat (403). To the reprinted *Philosophical Transactions* paper on the seeming conversion of water into air, he added that air must have entered

34. Vol. 2, 340–42. Partington, *History of Chemistry*, 3:214, has no doubt that Carl Wilhelm Scheele discovered the gas before Priestley, but Priestley, who gives Scheele complete credit for discovering the acid, did not recognize that he had observed and distinguished the gas from a vapor.

pores in his retorts, while steam escaped, "by means of a power very different from that of *pressure,* and able to counteract it," and he insisted that the phenomenon was not a double transformation of air to combination with clay and then back again (415n, 430n). There were sections on rapid and slow productions of airs; diffusion of airs through one another; heat expansion of airs (small differences except for alkaline air); specific gravities; and intensities of sound in different airs and their refractive powers—where his experiments were inconclusive.

Volume 3 considered the different acids, that on nitrous acid being the longest (1–207). A note added to a recapping of *Philosophical Transactions* papers of 1788 (52n) declared that subsequent experiments suggested that dephlogisticated air contained more of the acidifying principle and less water than supposed, as its combination with inflammable air produced more acid than initially determined. Book 10 (247–394), on vegetation and respiration, again invoked the economy of nature and included an extract from Benjamin Franklin's letter on the rational system in which vegetables restore air that animals spoil (269–70). It added (260n) that his first finding of dephlogisticated air was a consequence of the hope that nitrous acid might restore tainted air. He again quarreled with Ingenhousz's beliefs that plants possessed the power to transform their substance into air and that the "green matter" was an example of "equivocal" or "spontaneous generation" (299n–300, 307n). The part reprinting material from the *Philosophical Transactions* respirations papers of 1776 and 1790 began with a note (348n) that in the 1776 paper there was no recognition that breathing involved the absorption of dephlogisticated air (Lavoisier's discovery) as well as the emission of phlogiston.

Book 10 related to substances containing phlogiston. Part 1, on carbon (395–431), reprinted the *Philosophical Transactions* paper of 1770. Part 2, on mercury, noted (441n) a meniscus/adhesion test for the purity of mercury. The part on iron declared (482n, 485n), partly on the authority of Watt, that iron absorbed water in becoming a calx and resisted all effects of heat to separate them. A note in Book 11 (519n) observed that long heating with steam eroded copper.

The book relating to theory contained the only material that was obviously new, though most of it was derived from the section on theory of the third volume of his *Experiments and Observations on Natural Philosophy* (1786). Inflammable air was added to dephlogisticated as the most simple of airs, and fixed air was now half water and half phlogiston (537). "[S]ubstances possessed of very different properties, may . . . be composed of the same elements in different proportions, and different modes of combination" (543).

The experiments of the Dutch chemists Paets van Troostwyck and J. R. Deiman on the composition of water were noted (544), and there was added a long and repetitive answer to Berthollet's memoir in the *Annales de Chymie III* (556–63).

It is customary to bemoan the prolixity of Priestley's scientific writing, and he himself pointed to the apparent advantages of work written "synthetically" (II, 103). But the appearance of this "methodized" edition did nothing to enhance Priestley's scientific reputation. James Keir wrote to Erasmus Darwin that the new edition displayed more clearly Priestley's discoveries— dephlogisticated air, eudiometry, effect of vegetation, acid in combination of inflammable and dephlogisticated air, diffusion of air through a membrane, and the acid and alkaline airs—but it was the "six volumes on air" that Sir Humphry Davy thought the most "likely to lead a student into the path of discovery."[35] What this edition illustrates most clearly is that the direction of chemistry had, for a time, left Priestley behind. Given the heavy burden of theological writing that he had recently assumed, one might regard the edition as a deliberate closure of his career in science. This was, perhaps unfortunately, not the case! Priestley would continue to publish papers against the new chemistry, long after most other nonbelievers had been silenced. His last scientific paper from Birmingham is the first case in point.

Between November 1788, when his paper answering objections to his experiments on acidity, etc., was read, and April 1791, Priestley was continuing those experiments and his correspondence related to them. To van Marum, in December 1788, he claimed that he obtained either nitrous acid or fixed air from the decomposition of dephlogisticated and inflammable airs, depending on whether the airs were already formed or in the act of formation when decomposed. Thomas Hope, lecturer in chemistry at Glasgow, wrote to Joseph Black from Paris in March 1789, reporting French reaction to Priestley's last paper. An early imperfect account had "excited a little the alarms of the anti-phlogistians," but the small scale of his experiments could not shake the belief of those who conducted their experiments on so grand a scale as to procure many ounces of water. Nor was the appearance of nitrous acid more conclusive to those who obtained none when the airs were united by gradual inflammation and had been warned by Cavendish to expect its occasional occurrence.[36]

35. James Keir to Erasmus Darwin, c. 15 Dec. 1789, Moillet, *James Keir,* 96–97; [Humphry Davy], *Collected Works of Sir Humphry Davy* (London: Smith, Elder & Co., 1839–40), 6:117.

36. Priestley to van Marum, 12 Dec. 1788, *SciAuto.,* 133; Dr. Hope to Joseph Black, 22 March 1789, Ramsey, *Life and Letters of Joseph Black,* 91–92. Large-scale experiments on

Claude Louis Berthollet wrote Keir in May 1789, declaring that the French were anxious for details of Keir's and Priestley's experiments on the nitric acid produced when dephlogisticated and inflammable airs were united; and Keir wrote Priestley, sometime late in 1789 or early 1790, "I long to know what acids you get with other inflammable airs. If you get different acids . . . then will you not be obliged to admit that there is not one inflammable but many inflammables, which opinion you now think as heterodox as the Athanasion system?" But Priestley did not admit that, any more than he conceded, in correspondence with van Marum, that the French experiments were decisive. Repeating Berthollet's experiments before "our little philosophical society," he failed to confirm Berthollet's results. In his experiments, the purer the dephlogisticated air, the more acid he found. "I imagine more than we were aware depends on the different methods of combining the two kinds of air." Lindsey, Price, Wedgwood, even the Duc de Rochefoucald all heard from him about his experiments: he could make water or acid at will; no doubt the French got purest water with slow combustion, different modes of combining the same elements giving different results.[37]

On 7 April 1791 Priestley read "Farther Experiments relating to the Decomposition of dephlogisticated and inflammable air" to the Royal Society, summarizing these results.[38] He was uncertain about how he wished the controversy about phlogiston to end, "notwithstanding the part that I have taken in it," but believed that the experiments described in the paper would prove decisively that acid results from the combination of dephlogisticated and inflammable airs (213). As they also composed fixed air, it was not

production and decomposition of water had been performed before witnesses in Paris on 27 and 28 Feb. 1785, but the official reports neglect to say that all the water produced was acidic; see Maurice Daumas and Denis Duveen, "Lavoisier's Relatively Unknown Large-Scale Decomposition and Synthesis of Water, February 27 and 28, 1785," *Chymia* 5 (1959): 113–29; but also Verbruggen, "Priestley's Defense of Phlogiston," 50–54.

37. Berthollet to Keir, 19 May 1789, Moillet, *James Keir*, 88–89; Priestley to Keir and Keir's response, n.d. but before 25 Feb. 1790, ibid., 93–94, Bolton, #51, #52; Van Marum to Priestley and reply, 5 Dec. 1789, 21 Aug. 1790, Archives, Koninklijke Hollandsche Maatschjappij der Wetenschappen, *SciAuto.*, 136; Priestley to Price, 16 Feb. 1791, Price Papers, Bodleian Library; Priestley to Wedgwood, [Oct.] 1790, 16 Feb. 1791, 26 Feb. 1791, Bolton, #55, 57, 58; Priestley to Rochefoucault, 28 April 1791, *SciAuto.*, 138.

38. Priestley, "Farther Experiments relating to the Decomposition of dephlogisticated and inflammable air," *Philosophical Transactions* 81 (1791): 213–22. The French translation—"Dernières Expériences relatives à la Decomposition de l'Air déphlogistique et de l'Air inflammable"—appeared in Rozier's *Observations sur la Physique* 40 (1792): 91–97; this was probably the source of the Italian "Sperienze Relative alla Decomposizione dell' Aria Deflogisticata dell' Aria Infiammablile," *Opuscoli Scelti* (1792): 283–88. Keir summarized Priestley's experiments for de la Métherie in a letter abstracted in *Opuscoli Scelti* 14 (1791): 216.

surprising that they should compose another acid. The doctrine of phlogiston would not be affected by the most decisive proof of the composition of water, as that would only prove Priestley's earlier suggestion that phlogiston was a constituent part of water—hardly surprising, given water's resemblance to metals in conductivity of electricity (214).

He answered objections that his acid had come from impurities in the dephlogisticated air with his usual argument that he got less acid after deliberately introducing phlogisticated air, while he had demonstrated the purity of airs used in recent experiments (215–16). He could now produce either acid or pure water from the same materials by varying the proportions of the airs—acid if dephlogisticated air was surplus, water if inflammable air. He could not explain why these variations produced different results, but explained the results of Lavoisier's slow combustion process by supposing that this gave the principle of acidity in the dephlogisticated air, and the phlogiston in the inflammable air, a better opportunity to escape, forming phlogisticated air in their residuum (221).

This paper had little influence on the growing acceptance of the "New Chemistry," nor did any paper by Priestley from this time on. Events in France had already overtaken any possibility that Priestley's experimental "disproofs" could affect the new chemistry. In 1787 Guyton de Morveau, Berthollet, Antoine François de Fourcroy, and Lavoisier published their collaborative *Méthode de nomenclature chimique*, with an introduction by Lavoisier. Lavoisier's *Traité élémentaire de chimie* appeared in 1789, presenting the new combustion and oxygen-acid theory, an elaboration and justification of the New Nomenclature, and a treatment of the instruments and operations of chemistry.[39] Also in 1789 Lavoisier and his colleagues founded the *Annales de Chimie*, a journal intended to promote the new chemistry. Whatever opposition there might be, the new chemistry was established.

And there was plenty of opposition, besides that of Priestley. The Académie Royale allowed the New Nomenclature to be published only with reluctance.[40] Many persons objected to the implications of the nomenclature. Their objections were irrelevant. About the individual names there might be errors—oxygen gas was not the acid former, azote (for nitrogen), meaning privation of life, was not unique in that quality, but a system that defined

39. The Paris edition of 1789 was quickly followed by an English translation in 1790. I have used that version.

40. See Donovan, *Antoine Lavoisier*, 158. Partington and McKie, in "Historical Studies on the Phlogiston Theory" (part 4, "Last Phases of the Theory") list many persons who continued, like Priestley, to support the notion of phlogiston.

substances by constituents could not be overturned, for it greatly eased the teaching and the apprehension of chemical knowledge. For this reason, the concept "element" played a pivotal role in the new chemistry. Definitions of the element were not new. The term was defined, in almost the same way as Lavoisier's, at least as early as Robert Boyle's *Skeptical Chymist* (1661), Stahl had repeated it, and P. J. Macquer, whose work Lavoisier knew, had defined it again, in roughly the same way, in 1749. But to declare that the chemical element was that substance that could not further be broken down in chemical analysis was useless without defining the term "broken down." In combustion, for example, was the calx an example of a "broken-down" constituent of the burnt metal? Lavoisier added what was, in effect, an operational definition of "broken down," which assumed that weight was the basic parameter of chemical analysis.[41] If one performed a chemical operation on a substance and obtained only substances of greater weight, then the initial substance was, by definition, an element, subject always to the possibility that someone might later succeed in breaking that one down as well. Priestley's careful changes-of-volume measurements (implying changes in elasticity and therefore in force relationships) became irrelevant, as did elective attractions, color, shape of ultimate particles, or any other parameter that might have been employed.

Not that this principle, or any of the others stated in the *Méthode nomenclature* or the *Traité*, was invariably adopted by the antiphlogistians. The purpose of their publications was essentially propagandistic and educational, the introduction of a clearer and more consistent set of chemical ideas not to be overturned by a few inconvenient experimental anomalies or internal inconsistencies. The concept of phlogiston was, for example, attacked partly because of its lack of weight, but Lavoisier's table of elements included heat (calorique) and light, neither possessing weight. Consistently applied, nomenclature and weight criteria together might have identified the differences between inflammable airs (carbon monoxide, hydrogen, water gas, and organic gases such as methane), which were to persist as experimental confusions in the new chemistry.

Nothing in the new chemistry was applicable in resolving the appearance of acid in Priestley's experiments combining oxygen and hydrogen. Knowing that this combination "cannot" produce acid; knowing, as Lavoisians did, that the acid that persistently appeared was caused by nitrogen impurities in one or both of the airs, one can readily explain the ignoring of Priestley's

41. Lavoisier, *Elements of Chemistry*, xxiv, 130–31.

experiments. But failure to take those experiments seriously reveals a major flaw in the new chemistry, for the experiments did not simply reveal an acid, they showed that the amount of the acid was to be controlled not by elimination of an impurity but by its deliberate introduction (in common air or in varied measured amounts), or by slow combustion rather than explosion. The explanation is to be found in the heats required for formation of the water and of the nitric acid, the heat required for that of nitric acid being dissipated through excess nitrogen or not supplied in slow combustion of oxygen and hydrogen. But this solution was unavailable to the new chemistry, which ignored problems to be solved by the nineteenth-century invention of energy.[42]

Priestley was, unfortunately perhaps, to continue research and opposition to Lavoisier into his final years in the United States, but nothing would change the orthodox, and anomalous, assessment of his work. Before Lavoisier, Priestley was a brilliant experimenter, afterward, a bumbler. Douglas McKie denounced that view in 1933, but the standard approach has until recently remained much the same. This picture has changed thanks to more serious attention to the breadth of Priestley's activities and how this has related to his chemical ideas in the work of John McEvoy, J. E. McGuire, and myself.[43] Frederic Holmes suggests that Priestley differed from Lavoisier not because he was supporting Georg Stahl's discredited chemical theory of phlogiston, but because he was defending his own incoherent collection of phlogiston explanations for a number of phenomena that Stahl never considered. Holmes is certainly on the right track here, but he could go further. As John McEvoy declares, Priestley's scientific thought will be found wanting as long as "science" is viewed in isolation from its cultural context.[44] Priestley was never a chemist; in a modern, and even a Lavoisian, sense, he was never a scientist. He was a natural philosopher, concerned with the economy of nature and obsessed with an idea of unity, in theology and in nature.

42. (1) $3H_2 + 4 O_2$ (with N_2 impurity) $= 2H_2O + 2HNO_3$ if heat of combination of H_2 and O_2 is kept high enough; (2) with other inflammable air: $2CO + O_2$ (again with N_2 impurity) $= 2CO_2$, where heat of combustion is insufficient to permit formation of nitric acid. Lavoisier did use transfer of caloric among substances as a kind of *deus ex machina*.
43. Douglas McKie, "Joseph Priestley (1733–1804), Chemist," *Science Progress* 109 (1933): 17. A good general reference to this problem is Simon Schaffer, "Priestley Questions: An Historiographic Survey," *History of Science* 22 (1984): 151–83. See especially McEvoy and McGuire, "God and Nature." Although I suspect they would object, I'm inclined to believe that our disagreements are mostly semantic.
44. Frederic L. Holmes, "The 'Revolution in Chemistry and Physics': Overthrow of a Reigning Paradigm or Competition Between Contemporary Research Programs?" *Isis* 91 (2000): 735–53; McEvoy, "Priestley, 'Aerial Philosopher,'" *Ambix* 26: 34–35.

He attempted, prematurely, to conflate phenomena and give reasons for the reactions he observed.

Under the influence of the dynamic corpuscularity of Newton, Locke, Hartley, Hales, and Isaac Watts, he was periodically persuaded that the explanation for most material differences could be found in arrangements of the matter of which things were made. And phlogiston was, at least partially, the principle behind the ordering and disordering of particulate nature. It has been suggested that phlogiston had, in its late manifestations, many of the characteristics of energy. It would be absurd to suggest that Priestley foreshadowed the concept of energy, but he clearly felt the lack of such a concept.

His "materialist" view of matter as spirit, or powers, the physical evidence of an immanent God (*Disquisitions*, 1777), his repeated appeal to Boscovich and Michell, his insistence that time and temperature were involved in differentiating chemical processes, and his repeated denials, in theological works, of any distinction between body and soul link various aspects of his work. To quote McEvoy again, "Order informs apparent chaos when . . . methodology is located in the overall programme of an earnest study of nature that promised to reveal the greater glory of God." Demonstration of the glory of God and of his loving care for mankind was, after all, Priestley's major concern, and to this subject, and to the confrontations into which it led him, he was increasingly to devote substantial time and effort.

X

RELIGION

Within a month of his arrival, Priestley was invited to join Samuel Blyth as one of the two ministers to the New Meeting congregation, Birmingham. It is said that William Hawkes, Blyth's colleague for twenty-six years, resigned in order to create a place for Priestley. The salary was only £100, inadequate to maintain a man and his family in the middle-class rank of the majority of his congregation, but he had in addition the pension from Lord Shelburne. Besides, the position allowed Priestley to fill again "the capacity of a public teacher of Christianity (which I deem to be the most truly honourable of any character, office, or employment, in this world)."[1]

As Birmingham was not a corporate town, it was exempt from the "Five Mile Act" of 1665 and became a residence for "divines" ejected from their livings by the Act of Uniformity (1662), so long as they had not previously preached there. A settled Dissenting congregation was gathered there at least as early as 1687 and the Act of Indulgence of James II. By 1692, shortly after the Toleration Act of William and Mary, it had grown large enough to split

---

1. Joseph Priestley, *Discourses on Various Subjects, including Several on Particular Occasions* (Birmingham: J. Johnson, 1787), quotation from preface, ix. There was a positive notice in the *Monthly Review* 78 (1788): 266, describing them as five sermons "upon subjects of general utility" that "may be read with pleasure and profit even by those who do not follow the Author in his peculiar tenets."

off the New Meeting Society. Like Mill Hill, Leeds, the New Meeting chapel was "proprietary," built, paid for, and owned by members of the congregation. Originally controlled by the first investors and signers of its trust deeds, by 1778 the Society's internal affairs were managed by the vestry, a committee of subscribers that was essentially self-perpetuating. In November 1782, at Priestley's suggestion (made first in his sermon on the constitution of a Christian church), the vestry was elected annually from a list of subscribers of one guinea or more. The vestry was the employer of the "servants" of New Meeting: ministers, treasurer, clerk (responsible for conduct of Sunday services), beadle (caretaker of building), and singing master, and (again at Priestley's suggestion) shared duties of services, organized the young people's classes (the minister taught them, but was not responsible for finding pupils), and maintained moral discipline.[2]

Although Priestley seems to have been the first Unitarian minister at New Meeting (Samuel Bourn, minister from 1732 to 1754, had adopted high Arian views and Samuel Blyth, senior minister from 1747 to 1791, was Arian), he was later to declare: "It has been my boast that no Congregation that I have been acquainted with was so candid, so well-informed, and so ready to adopt whatever their Ministers recommended for their edification. . . . I had also perfect Liberty which few Dissenting Ministers have, to follow all my favourite pursuits of every kind, and to write and preach without the least hazard of giving offence, whatever I thought proper."[3] He had, in fact, accepted the call on condition that he would preach and teach on Sundays but otherwise be free for other activities.

Some of those other activities were in pneumatic studies, others in civic and political concerns, but the majority, while related to religion and theology, did not always immediately involve New Meeting. Occasionally Priestley could be found acting as pastor as well as preacher and teacher. He interceded with Matthew Boulton, for example, for a job change for a disabled member of his congregation and he consoled Miss Martha Russell on the sudden death of her mother, recommending the therapy of caring for her

---

2. Information about New Meeting Society and its chapel is derived chiefly from Emily Bushrod, "The History of Unitarianism in Birmingham from the Middle of the Eighteenth Century to 1893," Master's thesis, University of Birmingham, 1954. See also Joshua Toulmin, *Memoirs of the Revd. Samuel Bourn, for many years, one of the Pastors . . . of the New Meeting in Birmingham . . .* (Birmingham: J. Johnson, 1808).

3. To New Meeting Congregation, 8 Oct. 1791, in *An Appeal to the Public on the Subject of the Riots in Birmingham*, appendix, "Answer to address from New Meeting congregation," 167–69; also W. 1.2:165.

bereaved father. Generally, however, these duties were left to Samuel Blyth until his resignation in 1791.[4]

Priestley was conscientious in teaching his religious classes and in fulfilling his duties of officiating on most Sundays. He generally began by expounding the Scriptures, beginning with a "Harmony of the Gospels," then the Book of Acts and the Epistles in the order in which they were written, remarking on everything favorable to evidences of Christianity and the humanity of Christ. This would be followed by hymns and prayers (for which he would soon provide set forms) and then by a sermon, kept "almost entirely sacred to the . . . important business of inculcating just maxims of conduct."[5] During Radcliffe Scholefield's illness in 1786, Priestley and Blyth preached for him at Old Meeting. Priestley periodically preached for Lindsey at Essex House, London, as Lindsey occasionally preached for him at New Meeting. He annually preached a sermon for Richard Price at the Gravel-Pit Meeting, Hackney, returned to Leeds and Calne for an occasional sermon, and, as he became famous (or notorious), would occasionally be invited to preach elsewhere. He was even invited (and declined) to be the preacher at a "Double Lecture" at Dudley and Oldbury in 1782, with his brother Timothy to be the "supporter" half of the double![6]

Most of his sermons preached at New Meeting and elsewhere were unpublished.[7] One of those published was blatantly political and will be discussed in a later chapter; other sermons were published (or republished) in collections, such as his *Discourses on Various Subjects*. In most of his sermons, there is ample evidence to support the claim by R. K. Webb: "Whatever theological issues divided the orthodox from Unitarians . . . it is a serious

4. Priestley to Matthew Boulton, [June 1785], Bolton, #36; to Miss [Martha] Russell, Oct. 1790, W. 1.2:86–87. The Russells were something of an exception, as William Russell was a vestryman, personal friend, and right-hand man to Priestley at New Meeting. For Blyth, see Toulmin, *Memoirs of the Revd. Bourn*, 274.

5. His method of exposition is paraphrased from a description to Joseph Bretland, 5 July 1786. The general nature of his sermons was declared in his letter to the Mill-Hill, Leeds congregation, 20 Dec. 1772, published in *Discourses on Various Subjects*, vi.

6. Lindsey preached for Priestley during Sept. 1789, when he went on a visit to Leeds (no reference to a family visit, though they still lived just outside Leeds). For the "Double Lecture" invitation, see Alexander Gordon, *Cheshire Classis Minutes* (London: Chiswick Press, 1919), 135. It seems to have been a malicious invitation, as Joseph and Timothy were theologically at odds, though Priestley was interested enough in Timothy's well-being to ask Lindsey to obtain a pamphlet written against him, 7 March 1791.

7. See Chapter 2, n. 2, above, for reference to manuscript copies of some of his sermons. Another, the annual New Meeting Sunday School Charity Sermon, on 1 Corinthians 12:21, preached 29 Nov. 1789, we know of only because it is recorded in the MS Records, New Meeting Sunday School. Incidentally, the charity collection raised £26 18s 2 1/4d.

historical error to overlook or deny the possibility of rational piety, as in its main outlines the eighteenth century would have understood the term."[8] The first of Priestley's separately published Birmingham sermons was that of 31 December 1780, on accepting the invitation to New Meeting.[9] Printed at the request of the congregation to show that there were respectable Christians willing to hear Unitarian doctrine (28–29), the sermon dealt with the "proper *end and use of Christian societies*" and with their duties. He generally preached on doctrines and duties on which "all christians are agreed, but "I shall not fail . . . to hold up to your views . . . this great doctrine of the *proper unity of God*. . . . I choose to deliver myself in this explicit manner, at this time . . . as a specimen of the perfect freedom with which I shall always lay before you my real sentiments. . . . I do this both that you may not be deceived in me, and I may not be deceived in you" (42).

Mankind could not, unfortunately, do without forms of civil or ecclesiastical government (37). Priestley recommended the structured discipline, involving church elders, on which he had written in his 1770 *Essay on Church Discipline* and would again describe in his 1782 sermon *The Proper Constitution of a Christian Church*.[10] There Priestley declared that rational Christian societies failed to flourish because members lacked the zeal of converts. There was need to instruct children, and to restore the office of elders, chosen annually, to lead the congregation in moral discipline.

One of the few instances of cooperation between clergy and Dissenting ministers during Priestley's Birmingham years involved a Committee of Correspondence for abolishing the slave trade. A Sunday was set aside in January 1788 for antislavery sermons at churches and meeting houses. Priestley's sermon was published later that year.[11] The preface exulted in the agreement

---

8. R. K. Webb, "Rational Piety," in Haakonssen, *Enlightenment and Religion*, 311.

9. Joseph Priestley, *A Sermon* [on John 17:16] *preached December the 31st, 1780, at the New Meeting in Birmingham, on undertaking the Pastoral Office in that Place* (Birmingham: Pearson and Rollason, for J. Johnson, 1781). I have used the version in W. 15:28–35. The sermon had just been printed by 19 March 1781.

10. Joseph Priestley, *The Proper Constitution of a Christian Church, considered in A Sermon* [on Revelation 3:2], *preached at the New Meeting in Birmingham, November 3, 1782, &c.* (Birmingham: Pearson and Rollason, 1782). I have used the version in W. 15:45–69. Noticed, summarized, and quoted, but hardly reviewed, in *Monthly Review* 68 (1783): 462–63.

11. Priestley wrote Newcome Cappe, 23 Jan. 1788, about his membership in this committee of correspondence and of citywide cooperation. Joseph Priestley, *A Sermon* [on Luke 10:36–37] *on the Subject of the Slave Trade; delivered to a Society of Protestant Dissenters, at the New Meeting, in Birmingham: and published at their Request* (Birmingham: for the author, sold by J. Johnson, 1788). I have used the version in W. 15:363–89. The sermon was favorably reviewed, anonymously, as 2 of 5 in "Single Sermons on the Slave Trade," *Monthly Review* 78 (1788):

on this subject of all Christians, regardless of doctrinal differences, and hoped that similar tolerance would eventually be achieved for other subjects. The sermon declared that we should exert ourselves to relieve the distresses of all Christians, and of Jews, Mahometans, and "Infidels," but especially of African Negroes, because we had gained in oppressing them (368). Priestley believed that an application to Parliament was assured once people were made aware of the shocking facts of the treatment of slaves, the gross abuses, numbers callously destroyed, cruel and brutal treatment to which they were subjected, confirmed by notes to sources that showed that even being master of a slave was degrading (369).[12] Britain was a major European slaveholding nation and its treatment of slaves was the worst in not even encouraging their Christianization (372). Modern beliefs disavowed many things permitted by Scripture, and the spirit of Christianity recommended teaching slaves to make proper use of their freedom that could then be granted (376, 383).

Early in 1790 Priestley invited the Rev. Robert Robinson, an admired Baptist minister of Cambridge, to preach an annual charity sermon at New Meeting. After preaching two rambling and incoherent sermons on 6 June, he died of angina pectoris on the 9th. Priestley preached a sermon on Robinson's death on 13 June. This was not a funeral sermon but rather a tribute to a worthy and extraordinary man (404). Robinson's death was a warning that we must be always ready to be called to give an account of our conduct (408). To Christians *death* has no *sting,* and the *grave* no *victory*," but is a gate to a new and better life (423–24).[13]

In March, Richard Price became alarmingly ill and, despite hopes for his recovery, died on 19 April. Priestley preached a memorial sermon on the

---

269–70, was praised for its "manly freedom" and "arguments irrefragable," and ended quoting: "'all the articles on which we differ are trifling, compared to those with respect to which all christians are, and ever have been, agreed.'—Echo—*agreed.*" Priestley sent a copy to Thomas Percival, who compared it to a poem by Thomas Day, "The Dying Negro": "The composition of the former is careless to an extreme, in point of style and language; but with respect to matter, is judicious and full of information; the work of the latter is polished and brilliant inanity," Thomas Percival to Dr. [William] Robertson, 2 March 1788, Percival, *W.* 1.1:cxxxix.

12. It is not easy to distinguish between Priestley's notes (sometimes signed "P") and those added by Rutt. The letter to Cappe of 23 Jan. 1788 mentions "a few tracts," and it seems reasonable to suppose that references to Granville Sharpe, "Porteus," the Bishop of London, John Newton, and Richard Oswald are to Priestley's sources.

13. Joseph Priestley, *Reflection on Death: A Sermon* [on Matthew 24:46], *on Occasion of the Death of the Rev. Robert Robinson* ... (Birmingham: J. Johnson, 1790); I have used *W.* 15:404–19. Robinson's family was not entirely happy about the sermon and required the cancellation of a leaf and substitution of another prior to publication; see Priestley to Lindsey, 11 June and 2 July 1790.

Sunday following Price's funeral. Listeners had gathered to mourn the decease of a man truly excellent to his congregation, and more to his country and the world (1). Dr. Price's virtues would live for generations for his studies into the doctrine of annuities and his zeal for the natural rights of man (8). Price had warned about the dangers of the national debt, opposed the "cruel, unjust, and impolitic war with our brethren across the Atlantic," exalted at the emancipation of the French from their arbitrary government (13). He had earned honor by his enemies, was exemplary in his duties as minister of the gospel; his unstudied eloquence had gained universal attention. "Let us acquiesce in the will of God and be thankful for the instruction and example we received" (34).[14]

For the use of his classes, Priestley had new editions printed of devotional pieces written at Leeds—including 1781 and 1782 editions of his *Scripture Catechism*. In 1783 he published his *Forms of Prayer and other Offices*.[15] This is a substantial elaboration of his *Serious Address to Masters of Families* (1769), in which he wrote that no one should affirm what he does not believe, though enjoined by the civil powers (475–76). He also argued for more Unitarian societies, and *Forms* was intended to make their creation easier. He repeated material from his sermon on the constitution of a Christian church, with the more explicit statement that the laity, especially selected elders, could perform every one of the normal offices, including baptism and administration of the Lord's Supper (481–82).[16]

If the society wanted a liturgy, it could use that modified by Lindsey; others could use the forms provided here. Public worship should begin with singing of an appropriate psalm, to give the congregation an opportunity of settling (500). This should be followed with exposition of the Scriptures, recitation of the Apostle's Creed (as corrected by Lindsey), the singing of

14. Letters from Priestley to Lindsey in March and early April attest to Priestley's concern over Price. See *A Discourse on Occasion of the Death of Dr. Price; delivered at Hackney, on Sunday, May 1, 1791* (London: J. Johnson, 1791). In his *Memoirs* of Price (1815), Price's nephew, William Morgan, wrote that Priestley was the most qualified to pay tribute to Price; see W. 15:441n†.

15. Joseph Priestley, *Forms of Prayer and other Offices for the Use of Unitarian Societies* (Birmingham: J. Johnson, 1783). I have used W. 21:474–558. *Forms of Prayer* was translated into German in 1796 by the Lutheran pastor Hermann Andreas Pistorius, who also published a German translation of David Hartley's *Observations on Man*. Priestley wrote his publisher, Joseph Johnson, on 26 Oct. 1783, Birmingham City Archives, on advertising the *Forms of Prayer.*

16. This was particularly necessary, as Priestley wrote to Rotheram, 12 Oct. 1782, because many congregations could not afford to (or would not) maintain a minister without resources of his own. "I have some thoughts of writing something on the subject, with proper forms for all the occasions of a Christian society."

select psalms or hymns, and then a sermon. Satisfactory sermons could be read and adapted from preachers such as those in named in Enfield's collection *English Preaching* (492). And services should end with a unison prayer and a benediction. Priestley suggested modifications for particular services ("offices"): baptism, Lord's Supper, funeral service, and public fasting and thanksgiving. There was no office for marriage, as only Quakers and Establishment ministers were allowed to perform that service (499). There followed sample addresses for these particular services, with fourteen examples of prayers for ordinary and extraordinary occasions (500–558). He had had published in addition "A Prayer respecting the present State of Christianity" in William Christie's *Discourses on the Divine Unity*.[17] It was, of course, Unitarian, Pelagian, and against the "corruptions" of Christianity.

In 1787 Priestley determined to compile a set of psalms for use in his services, and by 1790, with the help of William Hawkes, this had grown to *Psalms and Hymns for the Use of the New Meeting, Birmingham*.[18] The hymnbook included 176 hymns, sixty-nine by Watts, twenty-six by Doddridge, others by Addison, Enfield, and Mrs. Barbauld, two by Toplady, and three by the Wesley brothers, with some variations in the words. Priestley wrote in the preface, "Most of the variations from Dr. Watt's compositions are made for the sake of rendering the sentiments unexceptionable to Unitarian Christians ... [while] his versification is often extremely negligent and the grammatical construction incorrect. It is hoped, therefore, that many of the variations will be found to be improvements." The stock in Birmingham was destroyed in the riots of 1791, and John Edwards, Priestley's successor, compiled a smaller version of the collection in 1798.

The devotional literature that concerned Protestants most was the Scriptures, and rational Dissenters, at least, were aware of flaws in the English version most in use. Modern Anglican critics are prone to ignore the activities of late eighteenth-century Dissenters in biblical criticism, skipping from the contributions of Locke and the Deists directly to the Germans and maintaining that "the Church of England allowed ... the flourishing of biblical

17. William Christie, *Discourses on the Divine Unity, or, A Scriptural Proof and Demonstration of the One Supreme Deity . . .* , 2d ed. (Montrose: David Buchanan, 1790), 303–8.
18. Priestley discussed the beginning of the project in a letter of 17 March 1787 to Bretland and its progress to printing in letters to Lindsey, 22 March, 21 June, and 24 June 1790. See *Psalms and Hymns for the Use of the New Meeting in Birmingham*, comp. William Hawkes and Joseph Priestley (Birmingham: J. Thompson, 1790). Bushrod, *Unitarianism in Birmingham*, 65–67, asserts that it was sufficiently popular for other societies to buy it. H. L. Short, "From Watts to Martineau," *Transactions of the Unitarian Historical Society* 10 (1951–54), discusses this and other Unitarian hymn books.

criticism. Its tolerant norms were hospitable toward it."[19] There was, in fact, little indication in the late 1780s that the Established church was interested in correcting even the most obvious flaws in the English version then in use or that it was tolerant of criticism by Unitarians. One modern scholar has noted:

> The Unitarian movement had a special affinity for Biblical criticism that needs exploration against the background of its well-charted contributions to social and political liberty. . . . This was connected with the struggle against priestcraft and obscurantism and increasingly against political oppression, the state and ecclesiastical authorities who had concealed the true nature of the text. . . . Knowledge of the most advanced Continental scholarship was a stick to beat the Anglican academic Establishment, pictured by Unitarian journals as sunk in parochial ignorance, sloth, and obscurantism.[20]

Late in 1783 a Society for Promoting the Knowledge of the Scriptures was organized to publish *Commentaries and Essays* on various parts of the Old and New Testaments. Priestley was a member of this Society (composed mostly of varieties of Unitarians, though it included the Bishop of Carlisle), but as it held its monthly meetings at Essex House, London, he was not an active participant and wrote none of the articles in the *Commentaries and Essays.* Instead, he revived the *Theological Repository* in late 1784.[21] As late as December 1782 Priestley had declared that he had no thoughts of reviving the *Repository*, but by August 1784 he was sending proposals for its

19. John Drury, *Critics of the Bible, 1724–1873* (Cambridge: Cambridge University Press, 1989). Donald Wayne Riddle, "Factors in the Development of Modern Biblical Study," *Church History* 23 (1933): 211–26, claims that nonconformist churches were slow in developing educational institutions and pursuing scholarship, though they "now" were doing good, but on the whole conservative, work! And Henry S. Nash, *History of the Higher Criticism of the New Testament* (New York: Macmillan, 1900), 95, earlier allowed that Dissenters "lacked, in the eighteenth century, both the culture and the standing in the universities that was necessary, if men were to feel the full force of the mental movements of the epoch."

20. E. S. Shaffer, *"Kubla Khan" and the Fall of Jerusalem: The Mythological School in Biblical Criticism and Secular Literature, 1770–1880* (Cambridge: Cambridge University Press, 1975), 24–25.

21. Joseph Priestley, ed., *The Theological Repository; Consisting of Original Essays, Hints, Queries, &c. calculated to Promote Religious Knowledge,* vols. 4, 5, 6 (Birmingham: J. Johnson, 1784, 1786, 1788). Herbert J. McLachlan, *The Unitarian Movement in the Religious Life of England: Its Contributions to Thought and Learning, 1700–1900* (London: George Allen and Unwin, 1934), 168, notes of the *Repository:* "Of the forty-one names of contributors that have been identified, twenty have been deemed worthy of a place in the Dictionary of National Biography." For the earlier volumes, see Schofield, *Enlightenment of Priestley*, 193–201.

resumption and early in 1785 announced to the editor of the *Critical Review* that the first number had been published, a second was due in February, and submissions on "any *query* or *difficulty* relating to religion," were solicited. From then till 1788, when it was again "suspended" (never again to be resumed), the *Repository* was a constant factor in Priestley's correspondence. Although the *Repository* was open to any respectable writer, including even atheists, the majority were Unitarians and Arians. Priestley contributed some five hundred pages—slightly more than one-third of the whole. Much of what he wrote in the *Repository* was an expanded version of his writing in more famous polemical pieces, but the *Repository* gave him a less belligerent audience. Priestley's introduction to volume 4, dated 1 November 1784, noted that the *Repository* was discontinued in 1771 for want of sufficient (financial) encouragement, though publication had been of use for the free discussion of theological questions of importance (iii): "truth never has, and . . . never can suffer, but, on the contrary must gain, by the freest investigation" (v). The discoveries of Galileo, Copernicus, and Newton were debated amid much controversy before being received, and Christianity must necessarily go through the same trial (x). As editor he announced that he would publish opinion papers "on anything within the general character of *religious knowledge*" and thus was not in competition with the Society for Promoting the Knowledge of the Scriptures, which he wished well (iv).

Of the forty papers in volume 4, Priestley wrote more than half. Among these were five, signed "Pamphilus," on inspiration in general, and on the inspiration of Moses, the prophets, the apostles, and Christ. "Every thing which is really valuable in the system of revelation may be retained without that doctrine of inspiration which . . . lays it open to so many embarrassing objections," Priestley wrote (22). There is no inspiration unless the messenger claims it, the object of his mission requires it, and his ability to work miracles confirms it.

Only when Moses claimed to have received the word of God did one need to believe him inspired; and Christians did not need to believe his account of the creation or early human history, while his outline of the history of the Jews could not have escaped adulteration as the story passed through generations (23–24, 31–37). His credibility no more depended on these things than Livy's history of Rome required belief in twins suckled by a wolf. The inspiration of the prophets was limited. If we adopted their interpretation of Scripture, then everything might be prophecy and we might as well indulge our imaginations without bounds (97–122). The apostles did not always claim divine inspiration, and their writings occasioned speculation, dispute, and offense. "Supernatural communications are never imparted unnecessarily, there being infinitely more wisdom in acting by general laws" (189–210).

"Pamphilus" submitted the inspiration of Christ to the same maxims. Constant "*immediate* divine *suggestions*" were unnecessary. We lost the benefit of Christ's example if we never regarded him as thinking, speaking, or acting like other men. A propensity to give Christ superior endowments was the root cause of almost all the corruptions of Christianity (433–61). As "Biblicus," "Scrutator," and "Pamphilus," Priestley also wrote a series of papers on the prophecy of Abraham, on Shiloh, on Old Testament quotations in the New, on Isaiah, on the Messiah and the House of David, and on some prophecies not yet fulfilled. Six of these papers relate to supposed predictions of the coming of Christ. Great difficulties arose from applying more prophecies to Jesus than were warranted. Bad transcriptions or translations, the allegorical and poetic character of the language, and even the wishful thinking of the Jewish nation had led people astray.[22] Only three prophecies seemed clearly to refer to Jesus — Isaiah (52:13–15, 53:1–12), Zechariah (12:10–13), and Malachi (3:1–4, 4:1–3) (*TR* 5:226, 302, 307–8). "Pamphilus" considered prophecies not yet fulfilled. It did no harm to speculate, although they were never intended to give exact verified knowledge of future events (*TR* 6:203–8).

"Beryllus," "Photinus," and "Josephus" argued against Arians with five papers in volume 4 and two in volume 6; and the pernicious influence of Greek philosophy was argued by "Josephus" and "Pelagius" in four papers in volume 4. These are all of a piece, for Priestley believed that Arianism arose by transpositions of obscure and enigmatic passages of Plato and his followers. "Beryllus," (*TR* 4:70–72), queried the first rise of high Arian doctrine. The opinion of Christ as a man was the general opinion of "*unlearned christians*" till the Council of Nicaea (71). The common people for whom the Scriptures were written were better qualified to understand them than the "*learned* and *philosophizing* Arians," who had an undue veneration for Plato (72).

"Beryllus" then provided a view of the rise of Arianism, with arguments verified by quotations from eighteen early church fathers. Ancient Arians generally held that Christ was voluntarily created by God out of nothing before the creation of the universe. The "orthodox" considered this view heretical, saying that Christ could not have been created of nothing and must

---

22. Note the reappearance of an argument from language that Priestley had earlier derived from Locke and used in his earliest theological publication, the *Doctrine of Remission;* see Schofield, *Enlightenment of Priestley,* 70–72.

have existed from eternity as consubstantial with God. Everyone interpreted Scripture to favor his own opinions, but those who lived nearest the age of the apostles and shared their language, customs, and idioms understood better than we, and the great body of these people were Unitarians (*TR* 4:306–37). "Photius" explained why Socinians excluded Arians as "proper unitarians": belief in two omnipresent powers was polytheistic (*TR* 4:338–44).

"Josephus" objected to the *ad hominum* attacks of Dr. (Henry) Taylor's preface to Ben Mordecai's *Letters*. Athanasianism and Socinianism *were* opposite extremes, but it did not follow that Arianism was the proper compromise between them. The edition of Ben Mordecai's *Letters*, supported by arguments of Bishop Pearson and quotations from the Sepher Ikkarim and the Midrash, said that Jewish Cabbalists believed in the preexistence of the Messiah. "Josephus" objected to this (*TR* 4:180–86, 477–83). Jews in all ages considered the Messiah a mere man. Though Justin Martyr, Tertullian, and Eusebius believed in the preexistence of Christ (*TR* 486), they declared that the apostles did not teach the Platonic logos because it would have given too much offense to a Unitarian majority. He asked about the origin of "low Arian Doctrine," which had evolved in the past twenty years or so, but answered the criticism of neither Unitarians nor orthodox (*TR* 6:376–82).

"Josephus" also asked where Plato ever referred to a Trinity, as claimed by Philo and some Christian fathers (*TR* 4:76), and "Pelagius" responded that the personification of the logos was introduced by Platonists and adopted by Christian fathers, but that it did not come from Plato (*TR* 4:77–97).[23] "Pelagius" then described the work of Platonists; they adopted the general principles of Plato but incorporated these with those of other philosophers, pretending only to interpret their master. "Pelagius" attended only to the absurdities of Platonists as they involved the concepts of later philosophic Christians. Because Julian was as inextricably confused in his ideas as the rest of them, he was a Platonist.

"Pelagius" quoted Hermetic ("Egyptian") doctrine as a possible source of Plato's mistakes — an idea popular with seventeenth- and eighteenth-century Christian Kabbalists. The intellectual powers of the Platonists were equal to those of any other early metaphysicians (including Aquinas), but men had not acquired the first elements of the greater (if still imperfect) light of true metaphysical knowledge of the present day (*TR* 4:381–407). Finally "Pelagius" considered the Platonism of Philo, who most nearly approached

23. There follow many translated quotations from Plato and Platonists, with the Greek originals footnoted.

a personification of the logos, though he never imagined the logos to be related to the Messiah. The first learned Christians believed that this logos-emission from God could, at his pleasure, be drawn back into himself. They were, properly speaking, philosophical Unitarians (*TR* 4:408–20).

Of the smaller sets of Priestley's writing in the *Repository*, "Hermas" argued for the tradition that Paul was wrecked on Malta (modern assessments agree). "Hermas" also believed that the unique covenant of God with the Jews, not possessed by Gentiles, still held. "Ebionita" cast doubt on the miraculous conception, an unnecessary and potentially embarrassing miracle to no good purpose. No testimony survives from any of the few persons who could have known of it. Christ's near contemporaries did not believe it, not even the Gnostics or numbers of Jewish Christians called Ebionites (or Nazarenes). There should exist considerable evidence to support the doubtful case—yet the "facts" cited were implausible and inconsistent. Genealogies in Matthew and Luke were contradictory and irrelevant. There were grave questions about the census that Luke mentions, and Joseph would not, in any event, be obliged to go to Bethlehem for it or to take Mary with him. No general notice was taken of any such momentous events as visits of shepherds or wise men.[24] "When once it is taken for granted that any religious tenet is true, it is remarkable how readily the proof is found in the scriptures."

"Pelagius" would rather that Paul "sometimes expressed himself unguardedly and improperly" than adopt Dr. Taylor's suggestion that he used "*election, justification*, and *salvation* in two different senses." "Biblicus" proposed a slight change in the translation of a Hebrew letter in Exodus, which would transform "poor" into "great," making more sense. This must have been the original reading, according to "Biblicus," though it has not appeared in any manuscipt or ancient version. "Pamphilus" continued the consideration of "Clemens," from the *Theological Repository*, volume 3, of 1771, on Christ's agony in the garden. It was a better example to mankind to know that Christ suffered agony and was "made perfect through suffering" than to suppose that he was able rise above pain and the evil of the cross (*TR* 3:314). Priestley

---

24. J. Estlin Carpenter, *The Bible in the Nineteenth Century* (New York: Longmans, Green, & Co., 1903) 482n1, claims that Priestley was the first English critic to oppose the story of the Virgin Birth. Modern analysis confirms the introductions to Matthew and Luke, Ebionite and Marconite versions being truncated. Neither James L. Price, *Interpreting the New Testament* (New York: Holt, Rinehart and Winston, 1961), 302–4, nor Robert M. Grant, *Historical Introduction to the New Testament* (New York: Simon & Schuster, 1972), 302–8, is as iconoclastic as G. A. Wells, *Who Was Jesus: A Critique of the New Testament Record* (LaSalle, Ill.: Open Court, 1989), 53–81. Yet all agree that the origin of the story lies in the desire of Matthew and Luke to join Mark's account of the career of Jesus to Old Testament prophecy.

inserted a note supporting "Clemens" with another secular example of a bloody sweat (*TR* 4:57–69, 73–74, 302–22, 347–48).

"Scrutator" referred to Priestley's *Letters to Philosophical Unbelievers, Part II* about the difference in evidence for the works of Moses and of the religion of the "Hindoos." Queries were sent to the "most intelligent of our countrymen residing in Indostan" (probably Sir William Jones) and also to a gentleman who had resided in the East (probably Nathaniel Brassey Halhed, who referred to his friend, Sir Charles Wilkins). The latter responded, in an anonymous letter of 8 November 1787, revealing how little was then known of the Vedas (*TR* 6:408–14). "Hermas" responded to a paper by "Ebulus," "Objections to a weekly Day of Rest," citing evidence from Acts and the Epistles, and also of some ten authorities (Greek and Latin) on the second- and third-century practice by which primitive Christians set aside one day each week for worship (*TR* 473). While it was all right to do "work of necessity," a day of rest was otherwise a pleasing and useful distinction" (*TR* 474, 482).

Deploring the sudden death of his friend and former Warrington pupil, the Rev. John Palmer, Priestley thought himself able to finish, from conversations and a few extant notes, an article that Palmer had started on the mission of John the Baptist (*TR* 6:221). A postscript to volume 6, dated 21 July 1788, regrets the discontinuation of the *Repository*, not for want of materials but because of its expense (491). Priestley hoped to resume in a year or two, as the articles had been valuable to theology and free inquiry. No paper had ever been rejected for its opinions, and he had solicited, without success, papers from "*serious unbelievers*"—including Mr. Gibbon, who would have been more consistent and manly had he contributed (493).

In the fourth volume, Priestley published "A Proposal for correcting the English Translation of the Scriptures."[25] There being no steps by authority to correct the "many errors and imperfections" in the present translation (187), learned friends of free enquiry should transmit to the *Repository* whatever corrections that had occurred to them. Priestley promised a new edition once a sufficient number of corrections had been received; he considered this a more advisable approach than an entirely new translation. Neither the *Repository* nor the *Commentaries and Essays*, however, solicited a sufficient number of corrections, and it became clear that an entirely new translation was called for.

25. [Editor], "A Proposal for correcting the English Translation of the Scriptures," *Theological Repository* 4 (1784): 187–88. He had noted the need for a new translation as early as 1772 in his *Familiar Illustrations of Scripture*. See Schofield, *Enlightenment of Priestley*, 187.

Late in 1787 Priestley began thinking of a new translation, he to do the Old Testament and Lindsey the New. He (and possibly the Society for Promoting Knowledge of the Scriptures) issued a prospectus for a new translation in 1788.[26] Three principals were to be chosen, each of whom would recruit learned friends to undertake the translation of a portion of the whole "in the space of a year." Constant attention would be given to all other new translations and other sources of information. After the principals approved the translation, it was to be published in a single volume, with any profits to go to some public institution. No change would be adopted in the received version without some improvement, and notes would be restricted to citing authorities (old versions or manuscripts) for changes in text or phraseology. Joseph Johnson had been asked to obtain a copy of Johann David Michaelis's new translation.

From 1789 to early 1791 Priestley's correspondence with Lindsey, Thomas Belsham, Joseph Bretland, William Frend, and Joshua Toulmin was strewn with references to a new translation.[27] Priestley was to do the hagiography and later proposed to undertake Daniel and the minor prophets (though he worried about his Hebrew), or Michael Dodson might do the minor prophets. One of the aims of the new translation was to demonstrate that the chief enemies of corruptions of Christianity were its most strenuous and able defenders. Whatever materials were collected for publication of a new translation, they were among the manuscripts destroyed with Priestley's library in the Birmingham Riots of 1791. When a "Unitarian Bible" was finally published as the "Improved Version" of the New Testament, it was that edited by Thomas Belsham in 1808, based on Bishop Newcome's translation of Johann Jacob Griesbach's text (1774–75). Belsham added corrections and improvements from the second edition of Griesbach, with some minor additions of his own. Priestley's *History of Early Opinions* was cited on the doubtful authority of the story of the miraculous conception.[28]

The elaborate organization of potential translators, though dispersed in 1791, may however have aided in the prior publication of Priestley's 1788–89 "edition" of the Baskerville-printed Bible. The preface, clearly by Priestley,

26. "A Plan to Procure a Continually Improving Translation of the Scriptures," W. 17, appendix 6, 532.

27. In addition to W. 1.2, see Priestley to Lindsey, 13 July 1790, Reference Library, Birmingham; Priestley to Frend, 2 Nov. 1790, Dickinson College Library, Carlisle, Pa. See also Frida Knight, *University Rebel: The Life of William Frend (1757–1841)* (London: Victor Gollancz, 1971), 97–102.

28. See Priestley, *Appeal to the Public*, 37; Shaffer, *"Kubla Khan" and the Fall of Jerusalem*, 24–25, 6.

indicates that the notes of the Baskerville edition had been retained and that notes had been added from collations of Hebrew manuscripts by Dr. Kennicott and Mr. Rossi, with additions from the Samaritan Pentateuch and "of the conjectures of many learned men for restoring passages . . . [and] the principal variations from the common translation by Bishop Lowth and others." Some notes were added by Priestley, and his 1789 letter to Joseph Bretland read in part: "All the notes in Baskerville's Bible, distinguished by *asterisms* [*sic*], which are very numerous, are mine."[29]

In a late note "To the Purchasers," Priestley identified the writers and works from which the new notes were collected, and some few sources were identified *in situ*. His notes to the New Testament, critical to arguments for Unitarianism, numbered nearly three hundred. Most of these were simply glosses on marked verses, but there were occasional proposals for variations on translation from the Greek, occasional omissions, interpolations, and transpositions. Sometimes Priestley explained an omission—for example, in Acts 2:30 ("not in 3 or 4 principal MSS and several ancient versions")—or a substitution (in Acts 18:17, the "latter not in Cambridge MS and three other MSS"), an omission in Acts 22.29, which seemed "plainly to be the remark of some unskilled reader," in 1 Corinthians 10:28, "the last clause . . . omitted in many MSS and seems improper here." He cited Newton for a variation in 1 Timothy 3:16 and, of course, for the comma Johanneum, 1 John, verse 7; the three witnesses verse was omitted, "as in no Greek MS except one in Berlin, which is a transcription from the Complutensian Bible, even to the errata."

Compared to those recommended by respected modern biblical critics, Priestley's changes were few and conservative.[30] The notes were derived from some thirty different sources, many of them from *Commentaries and Essays* and the *Theological Repository*, most of the others from William Bowyer's 1763 critical edition of the New Testament (Bowyer, in turn, had followed the text of Johann Jakob Wettstein's 1751–52 edition). Additionally, Priestley

---

29. *The Holy Bible, containing the Old and New Testaments; and also the Apocrypha: translated out of the Original Tongues, with Annotations* (Birmingham: by Pearson and Rollason, 1788); my copy is in three volumes, with the New Testament in one, clearly published in parts, into 1789. Noted in A. S. Herbert, *Historical Catalogue of Printed Editions of the English Bible: 1525–1961* (London: British and Foreign Bible Society; New York: American Bible Society, 1968), #1324, 303, with no reference to the fact that the edition was Priestley's, but his letter to Bretland, 7 May 1789, is supplemented by a letter of 28 Oct. 1787 to Lindsey, sending sheets of a Bible he had been working on.

30. See, e.g., Bruce M. Metzger, *The Text of the New Testament: Its Transmission, Corruptions, and Restoration* (New York: Oxford University Press, 1968).

explicitly referred to Johann Albrecht Bengel, Johann Jacob Griesbach's "late and much admired edition of the New Testament," Hugo Grotius, Johann David Michaelis, and Wettstein—almost every one of the pioneer critics of the New Testament text.

The articles on prophecy in the *Repository* and those establishing the correct text of the Scriptures combined, in Priestley, to feed another enthusiasm that was increasingly to haunt him—the Christian millennium. He had great sympathy for Jews, whose plight he thought resembled that of Dissenters oppressed by a corrupt and discriminatory religious and civil Establishment. Moreover, his theology was strongly based in the Old Testament and even his monism had Hebrew roots: "To the Hebrew man has not a body, he *is* a body."[31] But more important yet were his visions of Millenarian Restorationism, derived from the Books of Daniel and Revelation, which claimed that the Christian millennium must be immediately preceded by the conversion and restoration of the Jews to their homeland and glory. Priestley was hopeful that the "last days" were portended by contemporary events: the American Revolution, developments in places with key providential implications (e.g., the papal territories, Turkey and Palestine). He had long thought of writing to the Jews, and by July 1786 had finished *Letters to the Jews,* which were to be printed first in English and then translated into Hebrew.[32] Unlike the painful and impudent challenge of the Swiss pastor and physiognomist J. K Lavater to Moses Mendessohn in 1769, Priestley aimed less to convert Jews than to eliminate needless obstacles preventing a convergence between a purified Christianity and an enlightened Judaism.

Addressed to the heirs of the promises of God, to *"his peculiar people,"* the *Letters* argue that Christ's mission was perfectly compatible with Jewish belief. Jews and true Christians agreed on articles of faith (see his *History of the Corruptions of Christianity* and *History of Early Opinions concerning Jesus Christ*). The New Testament represented the fulfillment of prophecy begun in the Old. Priestley had sent a manuscript copy of the *Letters* to a Jewish friend before publication and heard that many Jews read the printed

31. J. G. Davies, *The Early Christian Church* (New York: Holt, Rinehart and Winston, 1965), 58.

32. Iain McCalman, "New Jerusalems: Prophecy, Dissent, and Radical Culture in England, 1786–1830," in Haakonssen, *Enlightenment and Religion,* 315–16. See also Jack Fructman Jr., "The Apocalyptic Politics of Richard Price and Joseph Priestley: A Study in Late Eighteenth-Century English Republican Millennialism," *Transactions of the American Philosophical Society* 73 (1983): pt. 4; Priestley to Lindsey, 20 July 1786. Joseph Priestley, *Letters to the Jews; inviting them to an Amicable Discussion of the Evidence of Christianity. (Part I)* (Birmingham: J. Johnson, 1786); I have used *W.* 20:227–50.

version. Though he did not expect to make many converts, he hoped for a formal answer. He heard that a Jew in Vienna might possibly publish an answer, then that a "Dr. Levi" was to answer. When he received an answer by David Levi, a Jewish hat dresser, he thought it not worthy of notice but used it as an excuse to address the Jews again. His *Letters to the Jews, Part II* was ready for publication by mid-July 1787.[33] In Part II he expressed his pleasure that his *Letters* had been noticed by Jews, but wished that the answer had been written by a person with more candor, more knowledge of "profane" literature and of the New Testament. He even criticized Levi's interpretation of Hebrew passages in the Old Testament (252–53, 258, 263, 265). *Letters, Part II* was followed in 1791 with a short "Address to the Jews."[34] Priestley again emphasized the similarity between Unitarianism and Judaism and reiterated his previous arguments. Jews could proclaim themselves Christians without ceasing to be Jews (404). Together, Unitarians and Jews, united in worship of the one Judeo-Christian God, could lead the rational inhabitants of the civilized world in preparation for the devoutly anticipated second coming of Christ.

Having addressed Christian persecution of Jews, Priestley next edited, with introductions, two tracts relating to persecution by Christians of other Christians: *An History of the Sufferings of Mr. Lewis de Marolles, and Mr. Isaac Le Fevre* (1788) and a new edition of Edward Elwall's *Triumph of Truth* (1789).[35] The preface to *Sufferings* declared his chief purpose: to prepare readers to act with the same fortitude should they be called to it (v, viii).

33. Joseph Priestley, *Letters to the Jews. Part II. Occasioned by Mr. David Levi's Reply to the Former Letters* (Birmingham: for the author, 1787); I have used *W.* 20:251–74. Priestley heard (letter to Cappe, 23 Jan. 1788) that a learned Jew of Konigsburg was translating the *Letters* into Hebrew to be printed in England, but no record of a Hebrew edition has been found. According to Harold J. Abrahams and Wyndham D. Miles, "The Priestley-Levi Debates," *Transactions of the Unitarian Historical Society* 12 (1959–62): 111–29, 112, David Levi was an "intellectual giant" and "dominated Anglo-Hebrew learning for two decades." Priestley told Lindsey, 3 April 1789, that Levi was not worthy of notice and wrote to Bretland, 7 May 1789, that he would take no notice of Mr. Levi, but of course he did.

34. Joseph Priestley, "Address to the Jews," annexed to *Discourses relating to the Evidences of Revealed Religion* (London: J. Johnson, 1794), 398–408. He wrote of this address to Lindsey, 2 June 1791.

35. Joseph Priestley, ed., *An History of the Sufferings of Mr. Lewis de Marolles, and Mr. Isaac LeFevre, upon the Revocation of the Edict of Nantz. To which is Prefixed, A General Account of the Treatment of the Protestants in the Gallies of France* (Birmingham: J. Johnson, 1788); he was still working on his preface as late as 20 Oct. 1788. He had first edited Elwall's *Triumph* in 1770; see Schofield, *Enlightenment of Priestley*, 183–84; according to a letter to Lindsey, Nov. 1788, he was adding to the preface, but this appears to be no more than references to the memories of Elway's friends who had attended his trial. *W.* 2:419.

The text described Catholic persecution of Protestants after revocation of the Edict of Nantes, but Priestley implied that Protestants and even Dissenters who condemned other views without thinking were as bad as a popish inquisition. Demanding toleration for his religious views, Priestley set an example by his toleration of others. He had been criticized as early as 1768 for advocating toleration of Roman Catholics and he continued this attitude. In October 1790 Joseph Berington, a priest from nearby Oscott, was invited at Priestley's urging to preach the annual New Meeting Sunday School charity sermon. He was something of a Gallican minimalist and was several times censured and suspended by the vicars-apostolic, but he had the sense to decline this invitation, knowing the trouble it would cause with his co-religionists.[36] Establishment "colleagues" in Birmingham were unfriendly from the date of Priestley's arrival, but he had Anglican friends and friendly correspondents (mostly higher clergy, such as Richard Watson, Bishop of Llandaff; Edmund Law, Bishop of Carlisle; and John Law, Bishop of Elphin), and a friendly correspondence with Bishop Newcome. He met and became friendly with Rev. Samuel Parr of Hatton, the "Whig Dr. Johnson," in 1790, and the same year preached a sermon at Buxton at the request of Anglican laity and impressed most of his hearers, including the provost of the University of Dublin.[37] His Lunar Society friend Samuel Galton Jr. was a Quaker, and though he differed with both Methodists and the Swedenborgians, he published what he regarded as friendly letters to each of them.

As he desired a rapprochement with the Jews, so Priestley hoped for a dialogue, at least, with two fringe Dissenting sects: the Methodists of John Wesley and the Church of the New Jerusalem of Emanuel Swedenborg. He published "An Address to the Methodists" in 1791, prefixed as a preface to his edition of *Original Letters by the Rev. John Wesley*. The letters had been given to Priestley by Samuel Badcock (when they were still friends), who had been given them by the granddaughter of John Wesley's elder brother.[38]

36. Discussion and copies of letters to and from Berington about the invitation, 17, 18, and 24 Oct. 1790, MS. Minutes, New Meeting Sunday School, Birmingham City Archives; letters are also printed in an appendix to *Discourses relating to the Evidences of Revealed Religion* (1794). For the earlier controversy see Chapter 4.

37. For Newcome, see Chapter 2, nn. 24, 25; for Parr, see Priestley to Lindsey, 13 July, 16 July 1790; for the Buxton sermon, see Priestley to Lindsey, 22 Sept. 1790. The sermon "Discourse on the Resurrection of Jesus" was printed as Discourse 11 in Priestley, *Discourses relating to the Evidences of Revealed Religion* (London: J. Johnson, 1794); an appendix described the circumstances of this sermon, including the invective from "a dignitary of the Church of England."

38. Strictly speaking, Wesley's Methodists were not Dissenters until after his death (1791) and the Church of England claimed property rights to Wesleyan lay-chapels. Joseph Priestley,

The letters were private and Priestley's preface began with what was, in effect, an apology for publishing them: "Mr. Wesley being the founder of a numerous sect of Christians . . . the public is interested in every thing that can throw light upon his character and principles" (326). The letters showed a desire for miraculous and supernatural divine influences. They demonstrated that honesty, good natural understanding, acquired knowledge, and disposition were insufficient against enthusiasm (330).

Priestley's "Address to the Methodists," illustrated that unconscious arrogance which so annoyed his opponents.[39] Addressed to his "Christian Brethren," though aware that most of them would refuse the title, he praised their preaching to the poor and laboring classes neglected by the government (331). Because of this great good, Priestley ignored their dislike of him, knowing that as they had added knowledge to zeal they had become more rational (332). Given Wesley's declaration that the end of religion was good morals, not particular opinions, Priestley suggested that they should think better of those taking a different road to a common Christianity (333).

When Swedenborgians approached Priestley in late 1790, he responded that "what they had to propose (which related to natural philosophy) was so wild and absurd, that I could not treat it with much respect." In June 1791 they opened an "elegant place of worship" in Birmingham and he attended a service, they having claimed to be Unitarian. He then wrote his address to the Swedenborgian Society.[40] He arranged to read the manuscript to the minister and heads of the Society on 15 July but, the riots intervening, his books and manuscripts were destroyed and he had to recompose the letters published here—they are signed London, 1 October 1791 (43).

Three pages, reprinted in his *Appeal to the Public on the Subject of the Riots in Birmingham,* described how far resentment of differences in politics

---

ed., *Original Letters by the Rev. John Wesley and his Friends, illustrative of his Early History, with other curious Papers, communicated by the late Rev. S. Badcock. To which is Prefixed an Address to the Methodists* (Birmingham: J. Johnson, 1791). The "Address" (and presumably the edition) is dated 1 June 1791; Wesley had died in early March. I have used *W.* 25:325–36.

39. He wrote Joshua Toulmin, 25 June 1791, *W.* 1.2:111, that the "Address" was well meant, whether it would be well received or not. Needless to say, it was not well received. It was answered and controverted, 6 Sept. 1791, in the *Arminian Magazine.* Wesley had once returned Priestley's "regard," describing him as "one of the most dangerous enemies of Christianity," in a letter of 3 April 1785; see [John Wesley], *Journal of the Rev. John Wesley, A.M.,* ed. Nehemiah Curnock (London: Robert Culley/Chas. H. Kelly, 1909–16), 7:64n3.

40. Priestley to Lindsey, 17 Oct. 1790; Priestley to Bretland, 26 June 1791; *Memoirs, W.* 1.2:121; Joseph Priestley, *Letters to the Members of the New Jerusalem Church, formed by Baron Swedenborg* (Birmingham: J. Johnson, 1791). I have used *W.* 21:43–86. Priestley subjoined large extracts from Swedenborg's writings, printed as appendix 1 in *W.* 21:591–93.

or religion prevented normal compassion at the destruction of a man's labors, just because he held obnoxious opinions.[41] Rejecting the respect due his works in natural philosophy, Swedenborg had submitted his theological works (a list of forty-three of these is appended to the preface) to critical examination, an invitation Priestley accepted in a series of eight letters addressed to "Fellow Christians." Differing so much from all other faiths, Swedenborg's system required proportionally strong (and missing) evidence. Lacking miracles, Swedenborg could not be a messenger from God (54–55). His "prophetic" visions of the religious nature of Africans were disproved by the proceedings of the *Association* for promoting the discovery of the interior parts of that country (57).

Swedenborg's "plain and literal" sense of Scripture involved a few passages differently and obscurely interpreted (66). That the second coming and future judgment was emblematic and was accomplished in 1757 was obviously unscriptural. Swedenborgian natural philosophy was in error (74–78): "All we know of any thing is its properties. . . . But these properties, we say, belong to something to which we give the name of *substance,* without having any idea of its nature" (74). But Swedenborg made property into substance. Perhaps, Priestley suggested, the explanation lay in a baffling distinction drawn by Swedenborg between the *esse* and the *essence* of God (77). He acquired no new ideas in his "conversations" in the world of spirits (with apostles, departed popes, emperors and kings, Luther, Calvin, and Malancthon), only such combinations of old ideas common to reveries or dreams, commonly found in enthusiasm mixed with imposture (78). His system failed to simplify the idea of God, gave no closer access to God, and rivaled the Catholics for lack of tolerance.

Priestley wrote, he insisted, in the "*spirit of love* from a *sound mind,* with sincere prayers to the true *Fountain of light,* that we may all be led into real truth" (86). And he clearly intended that truth to be his Unitarianism, as his previous letters to Jews and Methodists also argued. For Priestley was becoming chief missionary for a developing Unitarian Church association.

---

41. Printed as section 1 of "Reflections," 45–50 in *Appeal to the Public,* 1791; there is a note on a sheet of "Errata et Corigenda," pasted, in my copy, to the verso of xxxix, to the effect that this article was copied from the preface of his *Letters* to the Swedenborgians, his first publication after the riots.

XI

THEOLOGY

Dutiful as were Priestley's Sunday ministrations, his other preaching, and a great part of his weekday religious activities, these were soon subsumed under a related vocation: acting as communication link, suggesting candidates for church positions, and leading in propaganda and political agitation for Unitarianism. Theophilus Lindsey, minister to the only avowedly English Unitarian chapel, Essex House, London, whose activities in church building tended to be less obtrusive, generally read, criticized, and sometimes suppressed Priestley's writing prior to publication.[1]

Priestley had engaged Lindsey in the cause in 1773, and was to assist in enlisting Lindsey's brother-in-law, John Disney, in 1782, Disney's nephew-in-law, William Frend, in 1787, and Lindsey's eventual successor, Thomas Belsham, in 1789. William Christie, on the recommendation of Priestley, founded the first Unitarian Church in Scotland in 1781.[2] In 1789 Priestley met and encouraged some Unitarian Baptist street preachers in Manchester. Though bigotry had increased, things looked promising early in 1790, with

---

1. See, for example, Priestley's letters to Lindsey from late 1787 to 1789, when he submitted to Lindsey's judgment, declaring Lindsey "almost a part of myself." In a letter of 31 Aug. 1789 Priestley claimed he could do twice as much as he was doing, while urging Lindsey to relax!

2. Christie, who emigrated to the United States in 1795, claimed in a sermon preached at Priestley's burial that it was Priestley's *Free-Address to Protestant Dissenters* (1769) that most influenced him; see L. Baker Short, "William Christie and the First Unitarian Church in Scotland," *Transactions of the Unitarian Historical Society* 14 (1967–70): 10–27, 78–92.

the acquisition of Unitarian ministers and talk of opening an avowedly Unitarian chapel in Birmingham. The search for a Unitarian replacement for the Arian Samuel Blyth pervaded Priestley's correspondence with Lindsey, Bretland, and Price in 1790 and early 1791—Price was anxious lest Thomas Belsham might leave Hackney New College to join Priestley.[3]

While at Calne, Priestley had written five works that essentially unified his metaphysical groundings. He now was to do much the same for his theological base, with a series that again involved him in continuing controversy—and, this time, in violence and exile. The first of these, his *History of the Corruptions of Christianity,* set the tone in two volumes of 921 pages. Derivative, disorganized, wordy, and repetitive, detailed, exhaustive, and devastatingly argued, *Corruptions* and its defenses and extrapolations were to lead to eleven other publications (pamphlets and books amounting to more than four thousand pages) during Priestley's years in Birmingham and dominated his theological thinking for the remainder of his life.

A rough draft of *Corruptions* was complete by mid-April 1782, and although he had planned to keep it back "a few months" for revisions, Priestley sent it to press in early June; printing was nearly complete by mid-October.[4] Thankful that his own "more favourable education and situation in life" had not required the sacrifices that Lindsey had made, Priestley dedicated the work to his "Dear Friend," November 1782 (1:iv).[5] The preface (1:xi–xxiii) sets out the standard Socinian opinion that every change in belief from that of the early Jewish Christians had been a corruption of the true faith. Priestley aimed to trace each corruption to its source, with the arguments presented for its plausibility (1:xiv), using his favorite mode of exposition, the historical. He discussed only corruptions accepted in considerable parts of the Christian world, without intending offense and in the hope that persons with power in the Established church might be moved to amend its errors (1:xvi).[6]

3. Price to Priestley, 27 Jan. 1791, Price Papers, Bodleian Library, Oxford.

4. Priestley to Joshua Toulmin, to Joseph Bretland, and to Caleb Rotheram, from April through Oct. 1782; Priestley, *An History of the Corruptions of Christianity,* 2 vols. (Birmingham: Piercy and Jones, for J. Johnson, 1782).

5. Lindsey was a graduate of St. John's College, Cambridge, B.A. and fellow 1747, an incumbent of a valuable living until his resignation and adoption of Unitarianism in 1773. See Chapter 2.

6. He did not reference standard Socinian works in *Corruptions,* preferring to go to original authors, but his position mirrored most of their arguments. See, for example, Herbert J. McLachlan, *Socinianism in Seventeenth-Century England* (Oxford: Oxford University Press, 1951). His preference for historical exposition was described as early as his *Oratory and Criticism* (1777); see Schofield, *Enlightenment of Priestley,* 110, 139. As it is impossible to précis nearly a thousand pages in a few short ones, I have attempted to notice those parts eliciting the major responses.

He had originally designed the work as an appendage to his *Institutes of Natural and Revealed Religion* (1772–74) and intended there to use only respectable modern authorities: "What advantage do we derive from the labours of others, if we [cannot] . . . occasionally save ourselves some trouble?" In expanded form, however, he went generally to those original authors least liable to exception (1:xviii). The work is grounded in massive scholarship (thirty-seven editions of the principal authors quoted are listed), adumbrated by much of his previous writing, and repeated most elements in later works.

Essentially divided into two sections, the first related to Christ and the second (parts 2–12, with appendices) to the church, its services and personnel. Part 1 concerned corruptions of opinions on Christ, as they changed from the Jews' Messiah to Jewish Christians' *mere man*, to Gentile (learned and Platonic) Christians' proposing a preexistence for Jesus. Arius had responded to Platonic arguments about emanation, creation, and substance by providing a medium between the simple humanity of Christ and his absolute divinity, which nearly became the universal doctrine of the church until condemned at Nicaea.[7] A trinity, there asserted on liturgical and sacramental grounds, gradually developed into the now-orthodox version, reconciled in the sixth-century Athanasian Creed, of unknown origin, to the scandal of the heathen, "the most perplexed and absurd thing imposed upon the consciences of Christian . . . absolutely *incapable of being explained*," to be believed without understanding. Augustine attempted to illustrate the doctrine; the Schoolmen, with unequaled acuteness of speculation (the *Summa* of Aquinas filled Priestley with astonishment [119]) wasted their faculties devising explanations; disputes continue; but the Trinity had become the orthodox position (1:1–151).[8]

Many of these points were previously treated by Priestley, and each of them was expanded upon in concurrent papers in the *Theological Repository*. By 1769 he had read, in Nathaniel Lardner's *Letter on the Logos*, of learned Christians and their desire for a preexistent Christ. He argued with them as "Clemens" in "One Great End of the Life and Death of Christ" in the 1769 *Theological Repository*, and as "Liberius" in "Socinian Hypothesis Vindicated" in the 1771 volume of that journal. "Beryllus," "Josephus," and

---

7. This "medium" argument was condemned by Priestley, as "Josephus," in *Theological Repository* 4 (1784): 180–86.

8. "The Christian doctrine of the Trinity is, by general admission, unarticulated in the New Testament. . . . It emerged much later as a bitterly controversial development of theology requiring categories of thought and a terminology derived from Greek philosophy"; Cross, "Blessed Trinity," 231–40. The doctrine of the trinity was "hammered out . . . for more than three centuries"; Richardson, "Doctrine of the Trinity," 111.

"Pelagius" together in 1784 expanded upon the history of Arianism and the influence of philosophers.

The second section brought Priestley less trouble, though churchmen opponents did take umbrage. Most of the section was heavily dependant upon then-standard Protestant histories of the church, but with Unitarian bias and an occasional Priestleyan bite. He first took up the doctrine of atonement, against which he had written in his *Doctrine of Remission* (1761), denounced in the *Appeal to Serious and Candid Professors of Christianity* (1770) and the *Institutes of Natural and Revealed Religion* (1772–74), and enhanced as "Clemens" in the "Essay on the Great End of the Life and Death of Christ" in the *Theological Repository*. Scriptural allusions used to justify the doctrine contradicted the *"language of naked facts,"* which provided only the record of a man with extraordinary powers. The apostles could never have acted toward Jesus as they did, thinking him to be their "maker." Apostolic fathers and fathers of the church made little of atonement. "Some orthodox writers complain of the imperfect knowledge which the primitive Christian writers had of the Christian system in this respect" (152–280).[9]

Regarding the doctrines of grace, original sin, and predestination, Priestley had omitted reference to the sin of Adam in his *Catechism for Children* (1767), opposed notions of original sin, election, and reprobation in the popular *Appeal to Serious and Candid Professors of Christianity* (1770), as "Clemens" in the "Analogy to the Divine Dispensation" in the 1771 *Theological Repository* and in the *Institutes of Natural and Revealed Religion*, and preached against them in a 1779 sermon, the *Doctrine of Divine Influence*, part of which may have been written as early as 1757 (281–327). They were beliefs taken over from pagans, he argued, without scriptural justification, to ease the transition to Christianity (328–426). Ideas on the state of the dead began with the notion derived from Oriental philosophy of a soul distinct from the body.[10] There was no support from Scripture for the separation of body and soul. Powers of sensation and thought necessarily inhered in and belonged to the brain, just as electricity was a necessary property of glass and magnetism of the loadstone. The idea of purgatory was introduced by Augustine; Aquinas agreed and the doctrine was affirmed at Trent, but its nature was so uncertain that the "doctrine must have been discredited" were

9. Adolph Harnack, *History of Dogma* (1900; reprint, New York: Dover Publications, 1961) 3:315, agrees that the "West did not possess in antiquity a definite theory as to the atoning work of Christ."

10. Priestley here referred to his *Disquisitions* for a demonstration of the errors in this notion; see Chapter 4.

it not "for the profits which the popes, the priests, and the friars have made of it" (1:400–426).

Part 6 summarized Priestley's opinions on the Lord's Supper, about which he had written in 1768 in his *Free Address* on the Lord's Supper, with *Additions* (1770), in his *Considerations on Differences of Opinion* (1769), in his *Address on Giving the Lord's Supper to Children* (1773), and, of course, in the *Institutes of Natural and Revealed Religion*. An institution designed as a social festival to bond committed Christians every Lord's day had taken on the aspect of a sacrament. "Averroes, the great free thinker of his age, said that Judaism was the religion of children, and Mahometanism that of hogs, but he knew of no sect so foolish and absurd as the Christians, who adored what they ate" (2:1–65).

Priestley had also written previously on baptism—as "Liberius" on infant baptism in the 1771 *Theological Repository* and in the *Institutes of Natural and Revealed Religion*. It had come to have virtue as connected with notions of original sin. Dissenters as a group seemed to feel that the rite had some spiritual grace, but rational Dissenters considered it unimportant except as a formal acknowledgment of the profession of Christianity. This, the Lord's Supper, and the five other sacraments should be abandoned as undermining the godly disposition of mind and good works truly essential to salvation (2:97–106).

The conduct of public worship was another subject on which Priestley had previously written—in his *Free Address on Church Discipline* (1770), in "Communication of Religious Knowledge," in the *Institutes,* in the sermon *Constitution of a Christian Church* (1782), and in his *Forms of Prayer and other Offices* (1783). Forms were not really important, he argued, save when they replaced something more substantial. Latin was first used as generally understood and continued as giving priests authority and keeping the people ignorant. Other churches (Egyptian, Nestorian, Abyssinian) also used obsolete languages. The dress of priests and monks was originally that of the common people but became distinct by failing to change (2:107–41). Church discipline was also a repeated subject for Priestley's pen, as in *Considerations on Church-authority* (1769) and in the references for public worship. Its history showed a change from an emphasis on good conduct to a cover for every kind of immorality, as combination with civil power settled orthodoxy by the power of the state (2:143–23).

The role of ministers, and especially bishops, in the church was another subject Priestley had previously discussed, in his pamphlet on church discipline and his sermon on the constitution of a Christian church. In early days, he reminded his readers, the church was served by elders. How, then, did servants of the church come to be lords of it and of the world? Increased numbers of churches, the need for educated clergy, but especially the turning over of church discipline and general regulation of ecclesiastical matters to the supreme civil powers gave power, and wealth went with it, hand in hand. The greater clergy came to be entirely secular, attending councils of state, as they still do in England (2:233–85).

Appendix 1 to Parts 10 and 11 digressed to the subject of councils, which, Priestley argued, had assumed undue authority and been the principal supporters of corruption. There was never a true general council, in Priestley's view, and that of Trent was the least respectable of all (2:343–51).

Appendix 2 to Parts 10 and 11 discussed one of Priestley's obsessions, the authority of secular powers in matters of religion. The established religion of England was a "parliamentary religion, of a parliamentary God." Exclusive of the Articles of the Church of England, Dissenters chiefly objected to the authority by which they were enjoined, regarding it as the same as a tax imposed without the concurrence of Parliament. Every Dissenter ought to emulate the early Christians and separate himself from the Established church, whatever ridicule or persecution this might bring upon him (2:353–68).

Appendix 3 to the same parts considered the authority given to tradition and to Scripture. Priestley accepted the canonical books of the New Testament primarily on traditional grounds. The books were reasoned over, deliberated, and then accepted, before achieving the gloss of infallibility. The Council of Trent erred when it declared that the traditions of the church had the same authority as Scripture, and Dissenters must object to tradition when no grounds are found in Scripture and no sufficient rational authority exists.[11] They hold that the Bible alone is the religion of Protestants (2:369–84).[12]

11. This was a basis for Priestley's conviction that all Christian religious truth was that of the primitive church's reading of the Scriptures, a conviction somewhat surprising in a person believing in dialectical processes of achieving truth. The Church's contrary conviction was more adequately expressed as: "Revelation is progressive, and . . . all our additions and advances in truth and holiness represent a growth of humanity in the life of the Spirit." Richardson, "Doctrine of the Trinity."

12. He repeats that lack of total agreement is no challenge to the authority of the whole, with reference to "Paulinus" in *Theological Repository*, to the *Inst. of Natural and Revealed Religion* and to the preface (Observations) to his *Harmony of the Gospels*. William Paley's *Evidences of Christianity* (described in the *Dictionary of National Biography* as a compendium of the arguments produced by orthodox opponents of the eighteenth-century Deists) remarks in "Erroneous Opinions imputed to the Apostles" that the judgment of writers of the New Testament in interpreting passages of the Old or in receiving established interpretations was not necessarily connected with their veracity, such that a critical mistake might overthrow their historical credit. Bishop Burnet also sanctioned this view. Paley and Burnet were regarded as profoundly orthodox, but when Priestley said the same thing, he was called a wicked heretic.

The early history of Christian monasticism was fabulous and uncertain, according to Priestley, but examples existed in Judaism (Essenes) and among pagans (dervishes and fakirs). Some Christians used Scripture taken out of context to support austerity and celibacy. Except for the popes, no order of men increased in power and prerogatives like the monks—who are not mentioned in Scripture. Major supporters of papal power and of all the superstitions of Rome, the monks also contributed good and, until the Reformation, provided a retreat in time of war and the opportunity for research and writing, were principal repositories of learning with libraries and copiers, and were founders of schools and universities; but it was now to be hoped that their revenues would be turned to better uses (2:385–422).

Before it was abolished in England by Henry VIII, the Roman Church was in possession of a third of the landed property in the country. But the abuses of nonresidence and pluralities were not corrected in the Church of England, and some even increased. Inequality in income among clergy was shameful, for it had no relation to service or merit. "Without serious reformation of this and other crying abuses, the utter destruction of the present hierarchy must, in the natural course of events, be expected" (2:423–46).

Part 1 of the general conclusion is addressed to "unbelievers" and especially to Mr. Gibbon. The "system of Christianity" a priori seemed to Priestley little liable to corruption or abuse. There was nothing in it to lead to subtle speculation or encourage animosity; but abuses arose gradually by the operation of natural causes, in established and especially in heathen philosophical opinions. Abuses in the government of the church were the same as those of civil government, with worldly minded men always laying hold of opportunities to increase their power.[13]

13. Priestley, believing that Edward Gibbon had discredited Christianity in his *Decline and Fall of the Roman Empire* while pretending to befriend it, sent a copy of *Corruptions* to him, hoping to elicit a discussion. There was a short exchange of correspondence (Priestley to Gibbon, 11 Dec. 1782, 28 Jan., 3 Feb., 10 Feb., 25 Feb. 1783; Gibbon to Priestley, 28 Jan., 6 Feb., 22 Feb. 1783), with Gibbon declining any public discussion and Priestley denying that the correspondence could be kept confidential. He published it as appendix 4, 412–20 in vol. 1 of his *Discourses relating to the Evidences of Revealed Religion, delivered at Hackney in 1793, 1794* (London: J. Johnson, 1794). Gibbon resented *any* criticism and published two footnotes in the last volumes of *Decline and Fall* (1788) referring to Priestley's "scant creed" and recommending public attention to pages in *Corruptions* which, he thought, threatened the clergy and government. Dean Milman, "one of Gibbon's distinguished editors," declared that "there is something ludicrous if not offensive, in Gibbon's holding up to 'public animadversion' the opinions of any believer in Christianity." Quoted in Shelby T. McCloy, *Gibbon's Antagonism to Christianity* (London: Williams & Norgate, 1933), 190–91; while "J. B. B." [J. B. Bury], in "Edward Gibbon," *Encyclopedia Britannica*, 11th ed., 11:927–36, wrote of "the deep and settled grudge he has betrayed towards every form of Christian belief in all the writings of his maturity" (929C). Paul

Historians and philosophers were unable to account for the rise and establishment of Christianity! Gibbon admitted that the changes Christianity produced in opinions and conduct were astonishing, opposed by the civil powers and the learning, genius, and wit of the ages. Unlike the "elegant" mythologies of Greece and Rome that he liked so much, the Old Testament consisted primarily in histories, every tittle committed to writing at the time. Gibbon declared that Christianity had replaced older, discredited religions as another superstition for the vulgar, but Priestley responded that it was not the vulgar but philosophers for whom those religions were discredited, and that they did not reject but rather embraced and died for Christianity. Zeal and discipline were a result, not a cause, of Christianity and its spread. The facts of Christianity were attested by persons with the best opportunity of examining the evidence for even the most extraordinary events, evidence that we today would equally accept. Miracles were possible if there was a power enough in nature, and the creation of the universe and its laws showed that power to be available. Only low and abject minds thought argument respecting a future life uninteresting. Given the circumstances of early Christianity, the New Testament was most credible, and Gibbon's beliefs were more extraordinary than Priestley's. Gibbon should learn the gospel before writing against it (2:447–72).

Part 2 of the general conclusion was addressed to advocates of the present system and especially to Bishop Hurd.[14] Priestley wished that prelates would learn of the corruptions and try to rectify them. He has no personal Establishment ambition, just the hope that the powers of the world would cease meddling in the business of religion. Yet there were things to be achieved for others less rational then he, forced to subscribe to Articles they could not believe or painfully abandon preferment in the church. He had heard, during the past six months, of five instances of clergy becoming Unitarian and abandoning their prospects of advancement. The bishops' material circumstances

---

Turnbull, "Gibbon's Exchange with Joseph Priestley," *British Journal for Eighteenth-Century Studies* 14 (1991): 139–58, quarrels with interpretations of Gibbon as a nonbeliever, suggesting that he was primarily opposing enthusiasm in religion. Gibbon considered the value of an established religion to be independent of its intellectual soundness, and for anyone publicly to attack any part of it, on the basis of personal religious conviction, was in the highest degree "dangerous and irresponsible." Turnbull suggests, however, that "Gibbon's response to Priestley's attack, coming at the critical stage in crystallizing of a new political balance [the Fox-North coalition], can be read as a careful attempt to protect his diminished claims to political preferment" (148).

14. Richard Hurd (1720–1808), Bishop of Worcester and well connected politically, perhaps wisely declined to respond.

might well enable them to feel little for the unhappiness of the clergy under them, for it was difficult to place oneself in the place of another person, but "the *situation* produces wrong judgments and actions and therefore should lead to the removal of offence." It was sad, said Priestley, that men like Hurd, qualified to rank with Tillotson, Hoadley, and Clarke, would join their lessers in urging arguments so weak that even they didn't believe them. Hurd had acknowledged some reforms later than Queen Elizabeth's (the Enlightenment's achievement of religious toleration) and admitted some "quibbles and metaphysics" that pagan philosophers forgot to leave behind them when they were pressed into the church, but he failed to note that these were what he was defending. A progressive reformation of the partially reformed church probably awaited the fall of civil powers, which now supported the unnatural alliance of church and state (473–90). A final appendix summarized the evidence that primitive Christians believed in the simple humanity of Christ (2:491–95).

In January 1783 Lindsey reported that *Corruptions* was much approved in London, "by some excellent judges," such as Jebb and Kirwan. By summer, however, it was clear what the general reception of the work was to be, when a very critical review appeared in the *Monthly Review,* shortly to be followed by Samuel Horsley's *A Charge to the Clergy of the Archdeaconry of St Albans* (1783), which declared his intention "to destroy the writer's credit . . . by proof of his incompetency in every branch of literature connected with his present subject."[15] No doubt the appearance of second editions of Priestley's *Institutes of Natural and Revealed Religion, Disquisitions relating to Matter and Spirit,* and *Doctrine of Philosophical Necessity* increased the negative impact of his *History of the Corruptions of Christianity,* for all were published the same year. But the reaction to the *Corruptions* would have been extreme in any case, though the attack was generally limited to the first section, one-sixth of the whole, relating to the doctrine of the Trinity.

15. Lindsey to Turner, 21 Jan. 1783, W. 1.1:364; Priestley described Kirwan as "the best general scholar he ever met with and particularly able, also in theology." Reviewed by Samuel Badcock, "An History of the Corruptions of Christianity," *Monthly Review* 68 (1783): 515–26; 69 (1783): 89–105. The second part of the review was not harsh. It reiterated the preexistence of Christ from part 1, but mostly described the remainder of *Corruptions,* and if sometimes it described the provocative remarks as "breathing a rebellious spirit respecting civil establishments of religion" (104), it also referred to the ingenious and penetrating historian, his "sensible and judicious" observations (96), his pertinent and judicious reflections (100), and sensible remarks written with temper and decency (104). Priestley noted Horsley's pamphlet in a letter to Cappe, 20 Aug. 1783. *Corruptions* was burned by common hangman at Dordrecht in 1785 and the Hague Society for the Defence of the Christian Religion sponsored a prize contest for essays refuting the work.

Priestley's response to the negative review was, predictably, prompt and sharp. His *Reply to the Animadversions . . . in the Monthly Review* was dated July 21.[16] His answers to criticism were frequently barbed (in part because his critics were offensive), but here his reaction reveals a sense of betrayal. The *Monthly Review* had, unlike most contemporary journals, previously been generous. Later discovery that the reviewer was Samuel Badcock made things worse.[17] Badcock had been friendly from 1770. And Priestley was quite right: the censure was carping, failing to address seriously the general question of the section criticized, exhibiting only supposed defects without mentioning anything worthy of praise (vii), and, as he was to show, was mostly wrong. He was willing to discuss the work in a full and friendly matter, as he had done earlier with Richard Price (on *Materialism* and *Necessity*) and the Bishop of Waterford (on *Harmony of the Gospels*) (viii), but he was not now going to wait for the closure of the review to answer the charge that he supported Socinianism on the "specious footing" of antiquity (516), with perversion and misrepresentation (519).

Badcock, of course, had to respond and did so in a review of Priestley's *Reply to the Animadversions,* more than half the length of the *Reply.*[18] He disliked Priestley's not having noticed the second half of the first review, which had included some praise, but so far as the first half was concerned, he had no doubts as to the validity of the censures. Then this new review

16. Priestley, *Reply to the Animadversions on the History of the Corruptions of Christianity.* Note that this was published before the second part of the review and before the November discovery of the reviewer's identity.

17. Priestley's correspondence between November 1783 and November 1789 is studded with references to Badcock. It included a letter of Oct. 1789 to "Mr. Urban" (John Nichols) in the *Gentleman's Magazine* 59 (1789): 871, with an admiring letter of 1774 from Badcock to Priestley. Samuel Badcock (1747–88) had been a Dissenting minister at Barnstable, Devon (1769–78) until "his private character became at last so very exceptionable, that it was judged prudent of him to retire" (*Monthly Repository* 6 [1811]: 202). He was ordained and given a curacy in the Established church in 1787. He had contributed to the *Theological Repository* in 1770, visited Priestley at Calne in 1774, and corresponded with Priestley until 1778. He published a laudatory poem on Priestley in the May 1774 *Westminster Magazine* (republished in the *Monthly Repository* of 1819), wrote his "concurrence" with Priestley's theological sentiments, signing himself a "sincere and affectionate friend" in December 1774, acknowledged Priestley to be his "superior in every qualification" in a letter of July 1775, and favorably reviewed Priestley's *Additional Letters to a Philosophical Unbeliever* in 1782; see W. 19:533–38: "Of the Author's Intercourse with the late Mr. Badcock"; and "S.," Letter to "Mr. Urban," Hackney, Aug. 18; "Mr. Samuel Badcock, Strictures on his Behaviour to Dr. Priestley, &c.," *Gentleman's Magazine* 58 (1788): 781–84.

18. Samuel Badcock, "A Reply to the Animadversions on the History of the Corruptions of Christianity in the Monthly Review for June 1783 . . . , by Joseph Priestley," *Monthly Review* 69 (1783): 215–48.

essentially repeated, but in more detail, the previous arguments. These exchanges make clear that Priestley was, indeed, interpreting phrases to validate his claims about primitive Christians, but that Badcock was equally seeing everything in terms of a conservative orthodoxy. Badcock claimed to follow "direct evidence from writers of great credit and high antiquity," but these did not exist for the period when, according to Priestley, primitive Judeo-Christianity flourished. For this, Priestley, the historian, was obliged to make inferences that depended upon what Badcock's writers said of the common people. Badcock's response was revealing of the newly orthodox churchman: "For our part, we rather appeal to written records, than precarious tradition . . . notions of the vulgar herd of the people" (229). This attitude was even clearer in the next series of controversies raised over *Corruptions*, the continuing debate with Dr. (later Bishop) Samuel Horsley.[19]

The series began with *Letters to Dr. Horsley* (1783), continued with *Letters to Dr. Horsley, Part II* (1784), and *Letters to Dr. Horsley, Part III* (1786), and ended with a fourth letter to Horsley (as of 1788 Bishop of St. David's) included in *Defences of Unitarianism* for 1788 and 1789 (1790).[20] There were

19. Samuel Horsley (1733–1806) was the son of a man educated for the Dissenting ministry who later conformed. A Cambridge LL.B., Oxford B.C.L., D.C.L.; F.R.S. 1767, and secretary of the Royal Society until he withdrew after losing a bitter dispute with Sir Joseph Banks, he became Archdeacon of St. Albans in 1781, until his attack on Priestley, when Lord Chancellor Thurlow declared that those who defended the church ought to be supported by the church and presented him to a prebendal stall in the Church of Gloucester and, in 1788, made him Bishop of St. David's. See F. C. Mather, *High Church Prophet: Bishop Samuel Horsley (1733–1806) and the Caroline Tradition in the Later Georgian Church* (Oxford: Clarendon Press, 1992). In general Mather tries hard but cannot conceal that Horsley was arrogant, domineering, and headstrong, a self-satisfied snob about his university education, insolent and even malignant in controversy. "His conservative opinions usually sounded more extreme than they actually were because of the vehement language in which he chose to express them. . . . His hatred of the democracy which welled up around him in the closing decades of the eighteenth century can scarcely be denied" (248). Described by Overton and Relton as "the greatest figure in the Church since the death of Bishop Butler" (vii), Horsley was a good bishop in organizing his diocese, visitation of remote parishes, profuse hospitality, preparation for ordination, and his restoration of Rochester cathedral—i.e., in everything in which neither intense spirituality nor liberal reform of the Establishment was concerned.

20. Joseph Priestley, *Letters to Dr. Horsley, in Answer to his Animadversions on the History of the Corruptions of Christianity. With Additional Evidence that the Primitive Church was Unitarian* (Birmingham: J. Johnson, 1783); *Letters to Dr. Horsley, Part II. Containing Farther Evidence that the Primitive Church was Unitarian* (Birmingham: Pearson and Rollason, for J. Johnson, 1784); *Letters to Dr. Horsley. Part III. Containing an Answer to his Remarks on Letters, Part II. To which are added Strictures on Mr. Howe's Ninth Number of Observations on Books ancient and modern* (Birmingham: Pearson and Rollason, 1786); and *Defences of Unitarianism for the Years 1788 & 1789. Containing Letters to Dr. Horsley, Lord Bishop of St. David's, to the Rev. Mr. Barnard, the Rev. Dr. Knowles, and the Rev. Mr. Hawkins* (Birmingham: J. Johnson,

other publications in the same context. *Letters* (1783) included an appendix, "Remarks on the Article of the Monthly Review for September, 1783." The following year, there appeared *Remarks on the Monthly Review of the Letters to Dr. Horsley*. The same year, Priestley summarized his position in *A General View of the Arguments for the Unity of God; and against the Divinity and Pre-existence of Christ.*[21]

Finally, in 1786, there was the four-volume extrapolation of Part 1, "opinions concerning Christ," of *Corruptions: An History of Early Opinions concerning Jesus Christ*, published at Priestley's expense.[22] Begun as early as August 1784 and intended to make two volumes, by the time of its publication in the summer of 1786 it had grown to four. He promised friends to spare neither labor, expense, nor time in its completion.[23] Though it took less time than anticipated, when completed it contained more than fifteen hundred references and a thousand translated passages. Particularly addressed to "the learned," *Early Opinions* retraced the ground of Part 1, this time with detailed arguments from the original writers, with footnotes frequently giving the passages in the original languages.

Early among historical references to original writers, there appears, however, a reference to Priestley himself and his favorite monist argument against the preexistence of Christ:

> There is no more *reason* why a man should be supposed to have an immaterial principle within him, than that a dog, a plant, or a magnet, should have one. . . . There is just the same difficulty in imagining

---

n.d. [1790]). All four letters, with minor variations, were republished by Thomas Belsham as *Tracts in Controversy with Bishop Horsley, with Notes by the Editor, to which is Annexed, An Appendix, containing a Review of the Controversy, in Four Letters to the Bishops . . . never before Published* (London: London Unitarian Society, sold by J. Johnson and Co., and D. Eaton, 1815). I have consulted original editions of letters 1–3 and have read 4 in *Tracts*, 395–463.

21. Priestley, "Remarks on the Article of the Monthly Review for September, 1783 in Answer to the Reply to some Former Animadversions in that Work" in *Letters to Dr. Horsley* (1783); *Remarks on the Monthly Review of the Letters to Dr. Horsley; in which the Rev. Mr. Samuel Badcock, the writer of that Review, is called upon to Defend what he has Advanced in it* (Birmingham: J. Johnson, 1784); *W*. 28:125–42; *A General View of the Arguments for the Unity of God; and against the Divinity and Pre-existence of Christ, from Reason, from the Scriptures, and from History* (Birmingham: J. Johnson, 1783).

22. Joseph Priestley, *An History of Early Opinions concerning Jesus Christ, compiled from Original Writers; proving that the Christian Church was at first Unitarian* (Birmingham: for the author, 1786); Priestley to Theophilus Lindsey, 2 Nov. 1790. The whole impression was entirely his property.

23. Priestley to Joseph Bretland, to William Ashdowne, and to Caleb Rotheram late in 1784, and through most of 1785.

any connexion between the *visible matter*, of which they consist, and the *invisible powers*, of which they are possessed.... The organised brain of a man must be deemed to be the proper *seat*, and immediate *cause* of his sensation and thinking, as much as the inward structure of a magnet, whatever that be, is the cause of its power of attracting iron. The most inanimate parts of nature are possessed of *powers* or *properties*, between which and what we see and feel of them, we are not able to perceive any connexion whatever. There is just as much connexion between the principles of *sensation* and *thought* and the brain of a man, as ... between the principle of gravitation and the matter of which the earth and the sun are made; and whenever we shall be able to deduce the powers of a magnet from the other properties of iron, we may perhaps be able to deduce the powers of sensation and thought from the other properties of the brain.[24]

Two sections at the end of volume 4 list "names of the principal Persons mentioned" (120 of them), with their dates "corresponding to the Biographical Chart" facing page xxxii of volume 1, and cite "the editions [84] of the Ancient Writers" quoted in the work (350–64). Thomas Belsham was later to comment on Priestley's use of these writers:

> Dr. Priestley's argument for the unitarian doctrine ... is original and masterly ... but being new, it has been greatly misunderstood and misrepresented. . . . These important facts are established by Dr. Priestley upon the testimony of the primitive writers of the christian church ... of inadvertent concession, of incidental remark, of complaint, of caution, of affected candour, of apology, of inference.... To press the venerable fathers of the church ... to give evidence against themselves ... was an original and happy thought of the learned historian.[25]

24. Priestley, *Early Opinions*, 1:84–85. The reference is to Priestley's *Disquisitions on Matter and Spirit*, and the quoted statement is a more forceful repetition of that in his *Philosophical Necessity Illustrated*, 253–24. See Chapters 4 and 5.

25. Thomas Belsham, *A Vindication of Certain Passages in a Discourse, on the Death of Dr. Priestley, &c.; to which is annexed the Discourse on the Death of Dr. Priestley* (Boston: T. B. Wait & Co., 1809), 67–69, 71. This is, incidentally, much the same kind of argument that Priestley described in his *Lectures on History, and General Policy*, in which one infers, from laws, the state of society prior to the passage of the laws. See Chapter 12.

Not incidently, Horsley declined reading *Early Opinion,* on the grounds that it could contain nothing new to the argument and that he didn't want to increase its sales by noticing it.

There were four more theological publications of Priestley's Birmingham period, related to the dispute over the *Corruptions: Defences of Unitarianism for the Year 1786, Defences of Unitarianism for the Year 1787, Defences of Unitarianism for the Years 1788 and 1789,* and the *General History of the Christian Church to the Fall of the Western Empire.* Each of the *Defences* recapitulated some of the arguments with Badcock and Horsley, but each also contained some material that, in retrospect, promised dangers for the future.[26]

Each of them introduced questions relating to subscription to the Thirty-Nine Articles of the Church of England: "Letters to the Young Men" of 1786, to "Candidates for Orders" of 1787, and to "John Hawkins," with appendices 3 and 4, of 1788–89. Hawkins declared that the Articles should be accepted with a "latitude of interpretation" as "articles of peace" (109–10), but Priestley described them as contradictory and lacking sense, and suggested that subscription should not be made without personal assurance that each article was understood and accepted. This resulted in a repeat of the "Feather's Tavern" petition of 1772.[27] An unsuccessful Grace was introduced into the Senate House, Cambridge, in December 1787, signed by many bachelors and masters of art, asking that subscription be eliminated for advancement to the master's degree. The coming danger to Priestley was forecast in Spencer Madan's letter, answered by Priestley in *Defences,* 1787, where the rector of St. Philips, Birmingham, called upon the civil magistrates to come in aid of the Establishment (110–11).

---

26. See Chapter 12 for the discussion of Priestley's church history; Joseph Priestley, [*Defences of Unitarianism for the Year 1786, containing*] *Letters to Dr. Horne, Dean of Canterbury; to the Young Men, who are in a Course of Education for the Christian Ministry, at the Universities of Oxford and Cambridge; to Dr. Price; and to Mr. Parkhurst; on the Subject of the Person of Christ* (Birmingham: for the author, 1787); second printing (1788) adds heading here bracketed; *Defences of Unitarianism for the Year 1787, containing Letters to The Rev. Dr. Geddes, to The Rev. Dr. Price, Part II. And to The Candidates for Orders in the Two Universities, Part II. Relating to Mr. Howes's Appendix to his fourth Volume of Observations on Books, a Letter by an Under-Graduate of Oxford, Dr. Croft's Bampton Lectures, and several other Publications* (Birmingham: Pearson and Rollason, 1788), reviewed by William Enfield, "Defenses of Unitarianism for the Year 1787," *Monthly Review* 78 (1788): 457–59, chiefly stressing the errors of a Mr. Howe but concluding that inquiries were fruitless and people should retire from controversy. Priestley wrote to "Mr. Urban," 24 Dec. 1788; *Gentleman's Magazine* 59 (1789): 10–11, that he was writing no defense of Unitarianism that year, as nothing had been produced that appeared to require an answer. *Defences of Unitarianism for the Years 1788 and 1789.*

27. For the Feather's Tavern petition, see Schofield, *Enlightenment of Priestley,* 224.

The chief theological fight for Priestley, however, and that for which he was to be longest remembered in England, was the Priestley-Badcock-Horsley controversy over "opinions concerning Christ," in *Corruptions*. Priestley was not the only person to support his views in the immediate aftermath of publication. Newcome Cappe defended Priestley's Greek translations in the "finest piece of Greek criticism" Priestley had ever seen, for the *Monthly Review* (1783), as "O.B.Q." did for *Early Opinions* in the *Gentleman's Magazine* (1787). In 1785 William Godwin identified himself to Priestley as the author of an *English Review* article vindicating *Corruptions*, but showed restraint as that *Review* was friendly to the Establishment. Theophilus Lindsey wrote *Vindiciae Priestleianae: An Address to the Students of Oxford and Cambridge* (1788), defending Priestley's competence in religion. And in 1789, defending Priestley against Horsley's "Remarks upon Dr. Priestley's Second Letter," where "the Emeritus professor of Greek at Warrington," was attacked for finding the treatise *Parmenides* "unintelligible," "T.A.S." pointed out that Dr. John Burton (1696–1771), classical scholar and author of a Greek textbook, tutor and fellow of Corpus Christi, Oxford, had complained that "he found the whole work obscure and paradoxical, full of mysteries and enigmas, which he could not comprehend or expound."[28] The major burden, however had to be borne by Priestley, and against Horsley, as Badcock died in 1788.

Priestley had crossed swords with Samuel Horsley, somewhat inconclusively according to Priestley, in a letter included with his *Free Discussion* (1782) of materialism and necessity.[29] Given what he must have known about Horsley's temper and what was revealed in that *Charge to the Clergy of the Archdeaconry of St Albans*, it was scarcely wise to commence the first letter of *Letters* with a lecture on Greek and Hebrew grammar (7–8), but this was a controversy Priestley had entered, and was to continue, with enthusiasm. His correspondence between 1783 and 1789 related the progress of the

28. Priestley to Caleb Rotheram, 8 Aug. 1783; Priestley to Newcome Cappe, 20 Aug. 1783; William Godwin to Priestley, 1785, Bodleian Film-Godwin; "O. B. Q." to "Mr. Urban," *Gentleman's Magazine* 57 (1787): 53–55; "T. A. S." to "Mr. Urban," *Gentleman's Magazine* 59 (1789): 211. In 1820 a friendly "T. C. H." admitted in a letter to the editor that Priestley was guilty of hasty writing in *Early Opinions*, especially in translation, with examples from Greek and Latin. The writer noted that more correct translations would support Priestley's arguments even better. *Monthly Repository* 15 (1820): 335–36.

29. For the exchange over materialism and necessity, see Chapter 5. Horsley was to show his contempt for the "vulgar herd of the people" in a 1795 speech before the House of Lords: "the Mass of the People in every Country had nothing to do with the Laws but to obey them." Quoted in Albert Goodwin, *Friends of Liberty: The English Democratic Movement in the Age of the French Revolution* (Cambridge: Harvard University Press, 1979), 392–93.

dispute and his pleasure in it. He declared, in his fourth letter, which was never answered, that "Sparing nothing that the force of language could supply . . . [yet] all his arguments have not only been totally without *weight*, but in general destitute even of *plausibility*" (397), providing an example in Horsley's accusing him of dependence upon a book, by Zuicker, that he himself had never seen (417).[30]

Horsley suggested that Priestley's abilities in chemistry should not influence acceptance of his theology. Priestley responded by collecting information about Horsley's edition of the works of Sir Isaac Newton. He tried unsuccessfully to get an opinion from some mathematicians that he could quote on the merits of Horsley's *Prospectus*, "Commentary," and the *Works*.[31] He was finally obliged to say merely that although he could not speak of the merits of the "Commentary," "mathematicians of my acquaintance do not say that it does much credit to . . . [you or the nation], and that your Notes illustrate no real difficulty" (409–10).

The more than three thousand printed pages of Priestley's part of the controversy do not easily lend themselves to a summary. Fortunately, some events of the early nineteenth century make it easier by providing summaries, which themselves can be summarized. On Priestley's death in 1804, Belsham preached a funeral sermon in which he asserted, to the indignant denial of the church Establishment, that Priestley had won the controversy: *A Vindication of Certain Passages in a Discourse, on the Death of Dr. Priestley, &c.* (1808–9). In 1811 Belsham published his *Calm Inquiry into the Scripture Doctrine concerning the Person of Christ* (London, 1811), with an appendix in which he wrote of Horsley's failure to respond to a direct challenge from Priestley to continue the controversy: "To this animated challenge the right reverend adversary made no reply. The oracle was silent. The warfare was accomplished. The prize was won. And both the contending parties retired

---

30. Priestley to "Mr. Urban," 24 June 1789, *Gentleman's Magazine* 59 (1789): 488.

31. Lindsey was asked (Aug. to Nov. 1789) to make inquiries of Price, George Cadogan, and William Morgan. The remark on the "Commentary" is not surprising given Horsley's encouragement of Lord Monboddo in finding another philosophical basis for Newton's physics. See Chapter 5. Highly regarded as a mathematician in the eighteenth century he is not now so viewed. In 1785 he finished the edition of Sir Isaac Newton's works, projected in 1776 and begun in 1779. He had access to Newton's papers and found "a cartload" of unpublished religious manuscripts, but did not deem them fit to be published. Horsley intimated that Newton was "no Socinian," or not an anti-Trinitarian: "Sir Isaac Newton an Antitrinitarian," *Monthly Repository* 5 (n.s., 1831): 155. Those manuscripts demonstrated, as modern commentators agree, that he clearly was anti-Trinitarian. Herbert J. McLachlan, ed., *Sir Isaac Newton: Theological Manuscripts* (Liverpool: Liverpool University Press, 1950). Modern biographers and commentators have taken little notice of Horsley's *Newton*, though many note his comment on Newton's papers.

from the field equally well satisfied with the result of the conflict; Priestley with his VICTORY, and Dr. Horsley with his MITRE" (439). Horsley's son, Heneage, responded by republishing his father's *Tracts* (1812), with an intemperate appendix arguing his father's victory. Belsham answered with *The Claims of Dr. Priestley in the Controversy with Bishop Horsley restated and Vindicated,* which was essentially reprinted in the *Monthly Repository* in 1813, and with his edition of Priestley's *Tracts in Controversy with Bishop Horsley.*[32]

The first of the convenient summaries, then, is that of the series reprinted in the *Monthly Repository.* Claiming to dislike controversy and knowing that, in any event, it was useless to discuss theology with people who were prejudiced, dogmatic, and supercilious, Belsham answered to defend the reputation and victory of his deceased friend. He deplored the "despicable insult upon the memory and the sufferings of the venerable Priestley," that began Heneage's preface and continued with an effusive apology to Heneage's petulance. Belsham knew that Priestley was satisfied with his victory; he was sorry to hear that the bishop was not content with his mitre (175–76)!

Belsham went on to attack Horsley's arguments—his calling Origen a liar, his creating a spurious orthodox Jewish-Christian church of Jerusalem that survived in Aelia, his mistranslating Tertullian's *idiota* as idiots after deprecating Priestley's language skills, and his calling the *Epistle of Barnabas* apostolic. Belsham decried and refuted the sarcasm, abuse, and calumnies in Horsley's work and concluded: "if this *giant in controversy* may not, as the Quarterly Review asserts, be able to vanquish his mighty antagonist, he is fully competent to confute himself" (588).

The next "summary" was by Andrews Norton, premier American biblical scholar and lecturer within New England's developing Unitarian coterie, in an American journal, the *General Repository* for 1812–13. In itself, all of two hundred pages, it covered the documents of the controversy, including John Jamieson's *Vindication of the Doctrine of Scripture and of the Primitive Faith* (1795), written in response to Priestley's *Early Opinions.*[33] After

32. Thomas Belsham, "On the Controversy between Dr. Priestley and B Horsley; in Reply to the strictures of the Rev. H. Horsley, on the Calm Inquiry," *Monthly Repository* 8 (1813): 172–77, 294–97, 240–44, 383–88, 450–54, 583–88, 723–31.

33. [Andrews Norton], "An Account of the Controversy between Dr. Priestley and Dr. Horsley, the Monthly Reviewer, and Others," *General Repository and Review* 1 (1812): 26–58, 229–77; 2 (1812): 7–38, 257–88; 3 (1813): 13–42, 250–99. Published anonymously but identified by Wilbur, *History of Unitarianism,* 303n29, as having been written by Andrews Norton. Norton (1786–1853), conservative Unitarian and biblical scholar, graduated from Harvard, became a tutor, librarian, and lecturer on the Bible there. In 1819 he became Dexter Professor of Sacred Literature in Harvard Divinity School.

explaining the circumstances of the controversy, Norton proposed to give a general account of it, because of its importance and because the originals were not easily available in the United States. He followed with a brief survey of Priestley's position and of that of Badcock and Horsley (26–37). Norton described Priestley's style as perspicuous, his ideas as clear, definite, and well arranged. He composed rapidly and sometimes carelessly, but fewer errors were unlikely in a work of the same size (42). He described Horsley's manner as imposing, his learning as borrowed and incognizant of subjects he treated familiarly. He had little metaphysical acumen but was enormously skilled in the arts of controversy (40–41).

Norton then proceeded to consider the arguments of Badcock and Horsley. Their claim that the apostolic fathers believed in the divinity of Jesus was based on quotations that Priestley had declared were misunderstood ("A great part of the false criticism upon controverted passages . . . arise from real ignorance of the use of language" [48]), spurious, misdated, or manifestly interpolated. Norton added, partly on the authority of Michaelis and J. Semler, that Priestley's view prevailed more generally today (54). Horsley claimed the Nazarenes were orthodox believers. Horsley (and Jamieson) were quoted in direct error from authorities attempting to differentiate between them and the Ebionites, and Norton noted their misunderstandings of Epiphanius, observing that Huet had understood him as Priestley had done. Horsley even quoted an eighth-century Greek father on the orthodoxy of the apostolic Nazarenes (245), and persisted with an aberrant translation of Jerome.

It was in this connection that Horsley had created that spurious Jerusalem church of orthodox Jewish Christians that Belsham had earlier denied, as did Norton and the "modern authorities," Tillemont and Fleury. Horsley vigorously maintained, in the face of Priestley's opposition, that belief in the divinity of Christ was apostolic, citing the irrelevant *Epistle of St. Barnabas* as proof, and added, on the authority of Dr. Peter Allix, that the Jews had a notion of the Trinity. But Allix argued from the apocrypha, Philo, Chaldean paraphrases, and the cabbalists—none a convincing source. Horsley evaded Priestley's question of when the doctrine was disclosed and preached to the public, "in absence of those effects . . . so wonderful a doctrine would have produced." If these mysteries were kept from the common people, that would have included the disciples, and the difficulties of discovery, communication and preaching, argued by Priestley, "remain in full force" (229–77, 27–38).

Horsley challenged Priestley's translation of an Athanasian claim that the Trinity was taught slowly and cautiously for fear of offending Jewish zeal for the unity of God. Priestley replied that his translation had the support of that from the Latin, Beausobre, and passages of other church fathers; Norton added that these authorities were not contradicted despite Badcock's claim that Priestley's view was a gross and wicked misrepresentation. Jamieson added that, having the Scriptures of truth for ourselves, the opinions of the fathers were not the rule of our faith. Their belief that the apostles were cautious in divulging the divinity of Christ because of the prejudices of believing Jews did not mean that the primitive church was ignorant of that divinity or that the apostles never preached it (2:28n–29n, 30–35, 30n–34n).

Norton then turned to the arguments on the Unitarianism of the "ancient Gentile Church." Priestley claimed that the doctrine of the Trinity was introduced about the time of Justin Martyr and that a great majority of gentiles long remained Unitarian, using, as Belsham observed, implications by Trinitarian writers because Unitarian writings did not exist for this period. From a quotation by Justin (controverted by Badcock), Priestley inferred that the doctrine "was not thus generally prevalent, but on the contrary, a novel doctrine." His next "authority" was Tertullian's claim (rejected by Horsley with that gross mistranslation of the word "idiota" about which Belsham complained) that the common believers were shocked by the doctrine of the Trinity. Next Origen, Jerome, and Athanasius were cited; Priestley inferred "that the doctrine of Christ being any thing more than a man . . . was long considered as a more abstruse and refined principle, with which there was no occasion to trouble the common people," till after the time of Athanasius, or the council of Nice (2:237–88).

Priestley argued that the origin and form of the doctrine of the Trinity came from Platonic theology; that philosophic Christians conceived that Plato's *logos* was permanently personified in Christ, a willful conversion of an attribute of the Father. Horsley was incensed by this gross ignorance of Plato and the language of the fathers, but Norton noted that Horsley's "understanding" of Plato borrowed directly from the chief source of all his arguments, the *Defensio Fidei Nicaenae* (1685) of Bishop George Bull, who was also the source for Horsley's claim that Priestley has plagiarized Petavius and Huet.

Petavius, Huetius, Whitby, and Brucker "have to share with Dr. Priestley the disgrace of being patrons of that most absurd opinion which he has advanced, and are equally liable with him to the charge of 'total ignorance of the genuine principles' of the Platonic school, and 'gross misconstructions' of the language of the Fathers." This passage shows how little reliance was to be placed on Dr. Horsley's most confident assertions, and how unfounded were his most arrogant claims to superior learning (3:13–42). After listing a score of Priestley's errors, Norton concluded that few were of material importance, the whole number astonishingly small, and the charge of his carelessness, error, and misrepresentation wholly without foundation (3:290–91).

These summaries were, it is true, both by Unitarians, but any presumed bias on their part was hidden in a later mass of agreement with Priestley by late nineteenth- and early twentieth-century theologians and church historians.[34] One can at least say that on most specific items of the controversy, Priestley was more right than wrong, while Badcock and Horsley were most always wrong. Even F. C. Mather, Horsley's biographer, admits that "H. H. Jebb's view that he [Horsley] 'completely vanquished Priestley,' though widely accepted, will not withstand . . . the literature. . . . How far it is from the truth is clear from the fact that at the end of the debate Priestley could instance eleven serious historical points on which he claimed . . . to have received no satisfactory answer. . . . Priestley was right to claim that an important change in the Church's teaching regarding the person of Christ and the Trinity took place in the second and third centuries A.D. under platonic influences, though not in portraying it as a corruption."[35]

Examples of later agreement with Priestley are easily found. Almost all scholars accept the Unitarianism of early Jewish Christians. They accept that there was a complete break between Jewish Christians and gentiles after Hadrian closed Jerusalem to Jews. The identity of the Nazarenes and Ebionites is accepted by Harnack, who also confirms that there were so-called "Alogi," who agreed with the Ebionites. Lebreton and Zeiller agree, as do Bromiley, Clifton, and Rowley, while an anonymous "R. W." in 1847, and recently Philipp Vielhauer and Georg Strecker, argue, on different grounds, for their separation, though all agree that they were both Unitarian.[36] Priestley

---

34. I can hardly speak of Priestley's "correctness" in his *Corruptions* and *Early Opinions*, for the many and various professional theologians differ from one another, sometimes most bitterly. I can, however, assert that many later scholars adopted various of his positions. In the following discussions I have referred to, among others, Rudolf Bultmann, *Primitive Christianity in Its Contemporary Setting* (New York: Meridian, 1956); Henry Chadwick, *The Early Church* (New York: Dorset Press, 1967); Davies, *Early Christian Church;* J. G. Eichorn, "Biography of J. S. Semler," *General Repository and Review* 1 (1812): 58–72, 277–96; 2 (1812): 38–65, 213–40; Harnack, *History of Dogma;* Burnett Hillman Streeter, *The Primitive Church: Studied with Special Reference to the Origins of the Christian Ministry* (London: Macmillan, 1929); Johannes Weiss, *Earliest Christianity: A History of the Period A.D. 30–150,* 2 vols. (1937; Gloucester, Mass.: Peter Smith, 1970).

35. Mather, *High Church Prophet,* 58–59.

36. F. C. Conybeare, *History of New Testament Criticism* (New York: G. Putnam's Sons, 1910), 94, mentions that Priestley had early insisted on Jewish Christian Unitarianism. Chadwick, *Early Church,* 21; Streeter, *Primitive Church,* 42; Weiss, *Earliest Christianity,* 2:723; and Jules Lebreton and Jacques Zeiller, *The History of the Primitive Church* (London: Burns Oates &

was wrong that the group was monolithic in belief, but right when he wrote that they were more or less accepted in the growing church into the second century and persisted, in declining numbers, as late as the early fourth century.[37]

The influence of Greek (Hellenistic) thought on Christianity has been generally accepted, as in the classic *Influence of Greek Ideas on Christianity* (1889) by Eric Hatch, or in Bultmann, and Aall, although Fuller has recently presented a more conservative picture. That Justin Martyr was important to the development of logos Christianity is more or less confirmed by Harnack.[38]

By the mid-nineteenth century, even some clergy of the Established church were reading and accepting German criticism. One might wish that the Establishment had been equally indulgent toward Priestley's criticism, revealed in the work of these years in Birmingham, for in the area in which he hoped to be chiefly remembered, he is all but forgotten. There was some continued support of Priestley's rational Dissent. The *Monthly Repository, Christian Reformer,* and other Unitarian journals carried it on in England, but general acknowledgment of his ideas as his has never quite come.

Washbourne, 1944), 2:418–20, all refer to the post-Hadrian Jerusalem Church and the identity of Nazarene and Ebionites, as do S. G. F. Brandon, "Tübingen Vindicated," *Hibbert Journal* (1920): 41–47, and J. Munck, "Jewish Christianity in Post-Apostolic Times," *New Testament Studies* 6 (1960): 103–16. See also Harnack, *History of Dogma*, 1:42, 100, 152n, 287–317, and 3:19, 145; H. H. Rowley, *A Companion to the Bible*, 2d ed. (Edinburgh: T. & T. Clark, 1963), 503–4; "R. W.," "An Examination of the Arguments adduced by Dr. Priestley to Prove the Identity of the Nazarenes and Ebionites," *Christian Reformer* 4 (1837): 604–9, 651–58; Philipp Vielhauer and Georg Strecker, "Jewish-Christian Gospels," in *New Testament Apocrypha*, ed. Wilhelm Schneemelcher (London: James Clarke & Co.; Westminster: John Knox Press, 1991), 134–78, esp. 168.

37. By 1976 the existence and importance of Ebionites, so vehemently denied by Horsley and his Establishment churchmen, had become so much a commonplace that a journalistic popular biography, A. N. Wilson, *Paul: The Mind of the Apostle* (New York: W. W. Norton, 1976), assumed the fact as casually known: "as we know from the survival of that sect called the Ebionites, there were other Judaisms, other Christianities, and because they have been eliminated, or all but eliminated, we do not take account of them. . . . Before the eruption on the scene of Paul, it could be said that the Ebionites represented the mainstream Christian view. The Ebionites did not believe that Jesus was a divine being, or that he had been born of a virgin. . . . After the destruction of Jerusalem, most of the Ebionites or Nazarenes were destroyed also. Some, however, survived, into the Christian centuries, when they understandably fell foul of those Gentiles who were preaching a quite different message" (32n–33n).

38. Bultmann, *Primitive Christianity;* Anathon Aall, *The Hellenistic Elements in Christianity* (London: University of London Press, 1931); Reginald H. Fuller, *The New Testament in Current Study* (New York: Charles Scribner's Sons, 1962); Harnack, *History of Dogma*, 2:179–88, esp. 181–85, and 1:296; Streeter, *Primitive Church*, 17–20, 38, 41.

He had some immediate impact in the establishment of modern Unitarianism in England and the United States and in his personal influence on major figures in both places. The impact of his ideas, metaphysical and well as theological, on the young Samuel Taylor Coleridge is well documented.[39] The religion of the "Founding Fathers" of the United States was informed by the theology of Joseph Priestley. John Adams and Thomas Jefferson lightened their later years (1813–16) by a lengthy correspondence that included favorable remarks on Priestley's views of religion and extended comments on Priestley's writings.[40]

Two developments deflected attention from Priestley's theological writings. The first was a change in the nature of Unitarianism. Priestley's had been a militant reforming and missionary religion, and Thomas Belsham, till his death in 1829, and a few others publicly defended that form, in which they were aided, despite its idiosyncratic editing, by the publication of *The Theological and Miscellaneous Writings of Joseph Priestley.* But Priestley's militancy, necessarianism, and spiritual "materialism" were replaced during the nineteenth century by a transcendental theology. Ralph Waldo Emerson early read Priestley's *Lectures on History,* adopted a Priestley translation from Arian for his "Quotation" book, and read the *Doctrine of Heathen Philosophy Compared* for a Bowdoin prize essay on ethical philosophy, but he was impatient with doctrine and dogma, substituting free expression of emotion, and awareness of God in nature.[41]

William Ellery Channing acknowledged having derived much advantage from reading Priestley's works, but he also read Emerson. A romantic idealist and individualist unsuited to institutional building, he hoped that

39. Robert E. Schofield, "Joseph Priestley, Eighteenth-century British Neoplatonism, and S. T. Coleridge," in *Transformation and Tradition in the Sciences: Essays in Honor of I. Bernard Cohen,* ed. Everett Mendelsohn (Cambridge: Cambridge University Press, 1984).

40. See Daniel J. Boorstin, *The Lost World of Thomas Jefferson* (Boston: Beacon Press, 1960), 173–90. Jefferson declared, "I have read his [Priestley's] Corruptions of Christianity, and Early Opinions of Jesus, over and over again, and I rest on them, and on Middleton's writings as the basis of my own faith." See Henry Wilder Foote, *The Religion of Thomas Jefferson* (Boston: Beacon Press, 1947), and [John Adams and Thomas Jefferson], *Correspondence of John Adams and Thomas Jefferson, 1812–1826,* ed. Paul Wilstach (Indianapolis: Bobbs-Merrill, 1925), 77–79. Adams wrote comments, generally complimentary, in his copies of Priestley's writings, although he could never be a disciple of a man "absurd, inconsistent, credulous, and incomprehensible as Athanasius." See Zoltan Haraszti, *John Adams and the Prophets of Progress* (Cambridge: Harvard University Press, 1952), 282, 290; also [John Adams], *The Works of John Adams, Second President of the United States,* ed. Charles Francis Adams (1850–56; reprint, New York: Books for Libraries Press, 1969), 10:54–56, 66–69, 71–73, 82–86, 89–94, 227–28.

41. [Ralph Waldo Emerson], *The Journals and Miscellaneous Notebooks of Ralph Waldo Emerson* (Cambridge: Belknap Press of Harvard University Press, 1960), 254, 258, 350n, 378, 397.

his small-letter unitarianism might somehow be acceptable in society. As G. Adolf Koch wrote, nineteenth-century Unitarianism was to be achieved with the dignity and propriety becoming to a cultured upper class. Channing's English counterpart was James Martineau, who rejected the "rationalism" of Priestley's arguments in favor of an indeterminate, emotionally suggestive language. Despite (or maybe because of) the achievements of his sister, Martineau did not share Harriet's admiration of Priestley.[42]

On the hundredth anniversary (1896) of the founding of the First Unitarian Church of Philadelphia, which Priestley helped start, the celebration was marked by the presentation of a bust of Dr. Priestley and the publication of a series of lectures on the progress of Christian understanding. Curiously, the lecture by W. W. Fenn, "Biblical Authority During the Century," cites German contributions to biblical criticism while ignoring Priestley's critical activities, though Fenn does note the similarity of Priestley's argument, from *Corruptions,* against the Trinity with that of Baur. The same was true of John W. Chadwick's "Theology of the Century," which recognized that Priestley's answer to Paine's *Age of Reason* "had more intellectual force and scholarly ability" that that of Richard Watson, Bishop of Llandaff, but totally misunderstood Priestley's "materialism" and his "fatalism," and ridiculed his "hard-and-fast concept of the Bible as an authentic history of a supernatural revelation" and the "clumsy artifices by which he endeavored to save himself from the peculiar straits involved in this conception."[43]

Studies of Priestley's theology and religion are still confined almost entirely to analyses by Unitarian ministers or students: Alexander Gordon, Anne Holt, Herbert McLachlan, and, more recently, theological dissertations and essays by Americans, of which one of the best is that of John Ruskin Clark.[44] There are few ministers who seem able to overlook (or perhaps

42. [William Ellery Channing], *Memoirs of William Ellery Channing* (Boston: Wm. Crosby and H. Nichols, 1848), 1:100; G. Adolf Koch, *Religion of the American Enlightenment* (New York: Thomas Y. Crowell, 1968), 295; Martineau, "Life and Works of Priestley." Quote from Martineau in "Theology of the Century," in John W. Chadwick, *Sermons, Addresses, and Essays* (Philadelphia: by the Society, 1896), 92–93. Harriet Martineau hung a portrait of Priestley from her bookshelves. To illustrate economic theory she cited the story in a backwoods U.S. settlement and peopled it with characters modeled after the Priestley family. Harriet Martineau, *Illustrations of Political Economy,* vol. 8, "Briery Creek" (London: Charles Fox, 1834).

43. W. W. Fenn, "Biblical Authority During the Century," in W. W. Fenn, *Sermons, Addresses, and Essays* (Philadelphia: by the Society, 1896); Chadwick, "Theology of the Century," 52–84, 85–115. The present church building, at the northwest corner of Chestnut and Van Pelt, has a Priestley Memorial Chapel, a tablet and bust of Priestley, and some Priestleyana.

44. Lloyd W. Chapin, "The Theology of Joseph Priestley: A Study in Eighteenth-Century Apologetics," Th.D. diss., Union Theological Seminary, 1967; John Ruskin Clark, *Joseph Priestley: "A Comet in the System"* (Northumberland, Pa.: Friends of Joseph Priestley House,

enjoy) the genealogical fallacy of Priestley's historical and higher criticism and give him some credit for the direction taken by nineteenth- and early twentieth-century liberal theology. By the nineteenth century, many of the positions taken in the eighteenth century by Priestley had been adopted by Broad Church Anglicans: the lack of literal inspiration of Scripture, denial of the doctrines of atonement and eternal punishment, and even doubts about the divinity of Christ. Some Unitarians and Broad Churchmen went beyond Priestley in their denial of miracles. But there was little acknowledgement that Priestley had held these ideas![45]

When Thomas Hartwell Horne published his *Introduction to the Critical Study and Knowledge of the Holy Scriptures* (1818), he was given an honorary M.A. from King's College, Aberdeen, and a curacy and then rectorates in the Established church. A standard reference for scriptural study that went through a number of editions, Horne's *Critical Study* includes a vast number of quotations and almost verbatim transcriptions from Priestley, most not acknowledged. R. D. Hampden publicly contrasted traditional orthodoxy, a product of philosophical speculation and inference, with simple Christian belief; he became Regius Professor of Divinity at Oxford and Bishop of Hereford despite opposition from high churchmen. Werner Georg Kümmel's history of New Testament criticism cites a few non-German historical and philological critics prior to the nineteenth century and recognizes the influence of the English Deists, but fails to mention the work of English Dissenters, and no one has examined the debt that Priestley may himself have owed to contemporary German writers.[46]

By 1905 Priestley's arguments were part of generally accepted ideas among liberal philosopher-theologians, though Otto Pfleiderer assumes that

---

1994). Dr. Clark also graciously shared with me a copy of his "Joseph Priestley's Contribution to Unitarian Theology," in which he supposes that Priestley's theological views may have inspired the founding of the Meadville Theological School in Meadville, Pa. (37).

45. Dennis G. Wigmore-Beddoes, *Yesterday's Radicals: A Study of the Affinity Between Unitarianism and Broad Church Anglicanism in the Nineteenth Century* (Cambridge: James Clarke & Co. Ltd., 1971).

46. "The Rev. T. H. Horne's Obligations to Unitarian Authors," *Christian Repository* (1820): 57; R. D. Hampden, *The Scholastic Philosophy considered in its relation to Christian Theology* (Bampton Lecture, 1832); Werner Georg Kümmel, *The New Testament: The History of the Investigation of Its Problems* (Nashville: Abingdon Press, 1972), 13, 62. There is no reference to Priestley in the biographies of either of the two major figures leading the English Established church into adopting some of the liberal views in theology earlier held by Germans, English Deists, and Unitarians. See Arthur Westcott, *Life and Letters of Brooke Foss Westcott, sometime Bishop of Durham* (London: Macmillan, 1903); Arthur Fenton Hort, *Life and Letters of Fenton John Anthony Hort* (London: Macmillan, 1896).

questioning the nature of primitive Christianity began only with nineteenth-century "scientific theology," while Foakes Jackson's *History of Church History* typically has no reference to Priestley's work and ignores the work of eighteenth century Deists and Dissenters. There were some grudging admissions. F. C. Conybeare credited Priestley's denial of primitive Trinitarianism, but only because he accepted his rationalism. John Martin Creed granted that Jesus never claimed divinity, but not that Priestley had declared the same thing nearly a century and a half earlier. James Moffatt acknowledged that Priestley adopted the historical method of biblical analysis, but dismissed the amateurism of his work in favor of F. C. Baur, who came immediately after him.[47]

Priestley's Old Testament conservatism and his belief in miracles and prophecy constituted an embarrassment to nineteenth-century Unitarianism. His brand of Unitarianism was a grievance to churchmen, and any originality of Priestley's scholarship has long since been superseded. But in a long and distinguished career, Priestley wrote, compiled, and commented, in more than a dozen volumes and some fifteen thousand pages, on biblical criticism, the higher criticism, and the study of the ante-Nicene church fathers. All of this is next to forgotten, even in historical studies.[48]

47. Otto Pfleiderer, "The Christ of Primitive Christian Faith in the Light of Religio-Historical Criticism," *The Monist* 14 (1904): 323–54, 672–710; Foakes Jackson, *A History of Church History: Studies of Some Historians of the Christian Church* (Cambridge: W. Heffter & Sons, 1939); Conybeare, *History of New Testament Criticism*, 8, 94; John Martin Creed, *The Divinity of Jesus Christ: A Study in the History of Christian Doctrine Since Kant* (Cambridge: Cambridge University Press, 1938), 139; James Moffatt, *Approach to the New Testament* (London: Hodder and Stoughton, 1921), 117–18.

48. Note, for example, that apparently no reference was made to any of these in the periodical literature of theology in the course of thirty years; see the *Index to Religious Periodical Literature*, vol. 1 (1949–52)–vol. 15 (1981–82).

XII

EDUCATION, METAPHYSICS, HISTORY

One of the preface bits imported into the consolidated *Experiments and Observations* of 1790 was the semi-apology, from *Exp. & Obs. Nat. Phil. III* of 1786, about the time Priestley spent on the composition of the *History of the Corruptions of Christianity*, of the *Opinions concerning Christ*, and of the *Christian Church in general*. Priestley declared that the time he spent on any one of the six volumes of *Experiments and Observations* "is much more than I have given to three or four of those of which the other consist, and to all the controversial pieces that I have written in defence of them" (xxxiii). He did not say (and well he might not) that during the period from 1780 to 1790, while producing two volumes of *Experiments and Observations* and eight scientific papers of approximately 140 pages, he also composed, in addition to the cited eight volumes of theological histories and the some three hundred pages written in their defense, twenty religious pamphlets and thirty-eight contributions to the reopened *Theological Repository* (amounting to some eight hundred pages), five political pamphlets (more than two hundred pages), and two metaphysical pamphlets. In addition, during this period, he edited his *Lectures on History, and General Policy*, brought out new editions of his *Disquisitions, Philosophical Necessity*, and *Hartley's Theory*, and re-printed Anthony Collins's *Philosophical Inquiry concerning Human Liberty*.

It is perhaps true that crude page counts should not mean too much, particularly as much of the theology repeats the same scholarship. Still, more than five thousand pages representing Priestley's nonscientific work in Birmingham to 1791 has to be taken seriously, especially considering the clear evidence that Priestley had a major commitment to teaching as well as to theology. With the decrease in income on leaving Shelburne, Priestley contemplated taking pupils. On his arrival in Birmingham, he found that the education of children there was mostly conducted by persons associated with the Established church—"King Edward's Free Grammar School" and the Blue Coat charity school—though there was also a small "Protestant Dissenting Charity School" (a "School of Industry"). He consulted Dr. John Fothergill about the Quaker school at Ackworth, but by mid-September 1780 had given up any notion of establishing a school in Birmingham.[1] By December his acceptance of the invitation to be one of the ministers to New Meeting House obviated the financial necessity, but he took at least one special personal pupil, Samuel Vaughan Jr. (brother of Benjamin and William, two of his student boarders at Warrington Academy) to tutor in literary style, chemistry, and history.[2] He had, moreover, religious classes at New Meeting.

At Leeds he had established classes of religious instruction for young people and these he resumed at New Meeting. By March 1781 he had instituted two classes and had proposed three more, and started a religious library—soon to include a new edition (Birmingham, 1782) of his *Institutes of Natural and Revealed Religion*. He had 150 students "in a regular course of instruction" by July 1781, of whom eighty were between the ages of seventeen and thirty (W. 1.1:353). Theophilus Lindsey, describing a visit to Birmingham in September 1783, wrote that he saw near thirty young ladies (some of them married) being instructed in the principles of Christianity. "This was the third class that that had been before him that day; and this is his usual work every Sunday, added to his officiating to the whole congregation one part of it."[3]

In 1790 one of his classes sent him an unexpected gift of fifty guineas. He thanked them for their affectionate address, reminded them that knowledge was to be used in virtuous conduct, and accepted their gift (lest he insult

1. John Fothergill to Priestley, 24 Aug. 1780, in Anne Ogden Boyce, *Records of a Quaker Family: The Richardsons of Cleveland* (London: Samuel Harris & Co., 1889), 173–74; Elizabeth Belsham to Rev'd Mr. Belsham, 6 Sept. 1780, Wms.

2. Priestley to Samuel Vaughan Jr., 17 April, Samuel Vaughan Jr. to Priestley, 9 Sept. 1782, *SciAuto.,* 94, 97; Samuel Vaughan Jr. to brother Benjamin, 11 Jan. 1782, from his parents, 8 March, 3 April, and n.d., Library, Franklin Institute, Philadelphia.

3. Schofield, *Enlightenment of Priestley*, 170–72; Lindsey to William Turner, 1 Sept. 1782, W. 1.1:353n–354n.

them) as an expression of gratitude and good will. When he was forced to leave Birmingham by the riots of 1791, the New Meeting vestry reported that "the junior part of our Society, profiting by your advice and correspondence, are already assembled in regular classes . . . agreeable to the plan you established, so that your labours are still flourished among us, even in our present state of dispersion and persecution."[4]

The religious library instituted for New Meeting was independent of the Birmingham subscription library, which had been established in 1779. In 1782 Priestley restructured it to the form he had adopted in Leeds, giving it "that stability and method without which no institution can prosper." He "altered its original Plan, and put it on a more extensive scale, . . . amended and enlarged the Laws, and . . . paid a great Attention to its Welfare and growing interests" to the many and great obligations of the subscribers. By 1785 a collection of science books was added and the Birmingham Library was thriving; then the growing bigotry of the Birmingham Establishment incited a political/theological crisis with the library in 1787, but Priestley remained a subscriber, at least, until his banishment from Birmingham in 1791.[5]

Nor were religious classes at New Meeting the same thing as the New Meeting Sunday Schools to which Priestley made substantial contributions. Priestley had been criticized for his fears that state schools would enforce established religion over the protests of Dissenting parents.[6] He had moderated his stand by the mid-1780s, declaring in "Some Considerations on the State of the Poor in General" (prefixed to his edition of *An Account of a Society for Encouraging the Industrious Poor*), that it was "greatly to be wished that, by some public provision, all the poor should be taught to read and write." And, in lecture 38 ("Every thing worthy of Attention in History which contributes to make a Nation happy, populous, or secure") of his *Lectures on History, and General Policy,* he wrote, "Public instruction is an object in which the whole society is interested. It may therefore be proper that the government give some attention to it . . . it may be best for the state to do no more than appoint schools in every district. . . . As the arts of reading and writing are of particular importance to all persons, it

4. Priestley to his late class, 16 March 1790, *W.* 1.2:59–60; New Meeting vestry to Priestley, 5 Sept. 1791, *W.* 1.2:153.

5. Schofield, *Enlightenment of Priestley,* 164; Langford, *Birmingham Life,* 1:283–96.

6. Schofield, *Enlightenment of Priestley,* 205–6, 210–11. This was a general problem well into the nineteenth century. Not until the Education Act of 1870 established secular state schools was this conflict between Dissenting and Church of England interests evaded.

would seem that effectual provision ought to be made . . . that all should be instructed in them."[7]

Still, events in September 1786 should have demonstrated the validity of his early fears. In 1784 the Sunday School movement, which began in Gloucester in 1781, spread to Birmingham. These Sunday Schools were not religious in intent; they met on Sunday (a nonworking day), for the primary education of apprentices and the children of the poor. Supported by subscription (subscribers having the nomination of pupils), classes began at one o'clock and lasted until 5:30, with some pupils taken to church at 3:00 and returned to school, the remainder going to evening prayers at 6:00. A call for Birmingham subscribers was published in July 1784, money was raised, a committee of governors elected, teachers selected, schools opened, and by the fall of 1785 some fourteen hundred students had been admitted.

Early in March 1786 Dissenters requested that their children be permitted to attend "their own place of worship." Permission was granted and then, on 26 September, rescinded by majority vote of subscribers. Dissenters continued to contribute to these schools for a year, in hope of liberalization; then Radcliffe Scholefield's Old Meeting House established its own schools and, on 18 July 1787, New Meeting resolved to follow suit.[8] Priestley was appointed to the governing committee and on 27 January 1788 plans were set in motion. Subscriptions were opened "to every denomination of Christians"; children were allowed to attend any place of worship fixed upon by the subscribers recommending them. Schools were opened in March, with one male and one female teacher, and an enrollment of twenty-two boys and sixteen girls.

Minutes of the New Meeting Sunday School Committee report the successes of the schools and Priestley's participation.[9] He was involved in the

---

7. Joseph Priestley, "Some Considerations on the State of the Poor in General," prefixed to *An Account of a Society for Encouraging the Industrious Poor* (Birmingham: Pearson and Rollason, 1787); Joseph Priestley, *Lectures on History, and General Policy* . . . (Birmingham: J. Johnson, 1788), 276 (misprinted as 176). He later wrote that the French, after their Revolution, were wise in providing for a system of public instruction, in a letter to J. Gough, 23 Aug. 1793, W. 1.2:207–8.

8. Langford, *Birmingham Life*, 1:409–26; Thomas Walter Laqueur, *Religion and Respectability: Sunday Schools and Working-Class Culture, 1780–1850* (New Haven: Yale University Press, 1976), 70–71. These were quite different from the Protestant Dissenting Charity School, established by Old and New Meetings in 1761 and lasting till 1877.

9. MS, Transactions of the New Meeting Sunday School, Birmingham City Archives, Central Library, Birmingham. In 1817 there were three schools for girls with 160 to 190 pupils and ten schools for boys with 400 to 470 pupils; the schools then averaged about 600 pupils annually. By 1891 the New Meeting Sunday Schools possessed property in land, buildings, and fixtures valued at £1500.

planning, attended occasional committee meetings (they met during his religious classes, but Joseph Priestley Jr. acted as his surrogate), supplied books, recommended pupils, and preached a charity sermon for them. Thomas Wright Hill, later to achieve considerable reputation as an educator, founder of Hill Top, Bruce Castle, and Hazelwood Schools, and a founding member of the Royal Astronomical Society, was the first teacher chosen for a boy's school and credited this appointment as setting him upon the right course for his life.[10] "For about five years," he wrote, "I had great privileges in the pastoral services of Dr. Priestley and especially in his lectures to the younger members of his congregation, and in occasional conversations with him. This delightful period was closed by the Birmingham Riots." Teachers of New and Old Meeting Schools also formed a "Sunday Society" to continue the education of men after leaving the Sunday Schools. Open to former pupils of a basic Sunday School in town and providing instruction in natural and revealed religion, the Society also offered a class in mechanics, hydrostatics, electricity, pneumatics, and astronomy and another class, the "Cast Iron Philosophers," for workers in the foundries. The Society collected its own experimental apparatus, established a library, ran a weekly debating club, and gave free lectures to working men.[11]

Possibly Priestley's interest in Birmingham's Sunday Schools was reinforced by his disappointment at the adversities of his old schools.[12] Warrington Academy was transferred to Manchester in 1786 and Daventry Academy was moved back to Northampton, and entered its senescence in 1789, when Thomas Belsham became a Unitarian and resigned as senior tutor. The academies at Manchester and Northampton struggled on to their final amalgamation with others into London University in 1826, but for a

10. [Thomas Wright Hill], *Remains of the late Thomas Wright Hill, Esq., F.R.S.A., together with Notices of his Life, &c.* (London: Richard T. Benbow, 1859).

11. Charles A. Bennett, *History of Manual and Industrial Education up to 1870* (Peoria, Ill.: Charles A. Bennett Co., 1926), 301; John Money, "Joseph Priestley in Cultural Context: Philosophic Spectacle, Popular Belief, and Popular Politics in Eighteenth-Century Birmingham," *Enlightenment and Dissent* 7 (1988): 57–81, and 8 (1989): 74.

12. For Priestley's associations with Daventry and Warrington, see Schofield, *Enlightenment of Priestley*, chaps. 2, 4–6. Warrington struggled under bad financial management for years; Herbert J. McLachlan, "Warrington Academy," *Chetham Society: Remains* 107 (n.s., 1943): 15, declared that the treasurer never sent financial reports or balance sheets to the fund subscribers. Priestley had remained enough of a friend of John Aikin and of Warrington sufficient to recommend Gilbert Wakefield as classic tutor in 1779. See Lucy Aikin, *Memoir of John Aikin, M.D., with a Selection of his Miscellaneous Pieces, Biographical, Moral and Critical* (London: Baldwin, Cradock and Joy, 1823), 1:48. But he was especially sad at the fate of Daventry Academy. He wrote Lindsey, 18 Aug. 1790, that its situation had been uniquely favorable to study, the pupils being far removed from any company than their own.

time hopes of liberal Dissenters focused on a new academy, New College, Hackney. Priestley, who sent Andrew Kippis a plan for it, was hopeful that Hackney might rival Oxford and Cambridge in its quality of education, and according to Augustine Birrell, sometime Minister of Education in Campbell-Bannerman's Liberal cabinet of 1906, "As things were in England in 1793, Hackney College was a better *Studium Generale* than either Oxford or Cambridge at the same date."[13] Priestley's correspondence from 1786 and into 1791 is studded with references to academy failures, proposals for a London academy, for its tutors, and on its financial problems. He even preached an annual charity sermon, on the *"proper Objects of Education,"* for New College, Hackney, in April 1791.[14]

This sermon was a call to persons to become active in fulfilling the "general plan of Providence" for which there were always too few laborers (420), and to educate men "not for themselves only, but for their country and the world" (439). He hinted throughout at the great things portended by the imminent Christian Millennium and preached that the task of the Reformation was incomplete. The sermon also contained the usual digressions on the "corruptions of genuine Christianity" (428–32). Private institutions were better able than public ones (with their "unnatural *alliance of church and state*" [437]) for the task ahead, and Dissenters, who had been generous in the past, must continue to be so with their support. "It is *knowledge* that finally governs mankind, and *power,* though ever so refractory, must at length yield to it" (431). There must be free inquiry into matters of religion (431).

There was need, Priestley continued, for men regularly taught in theological and historical investigation, to explore "the curious and valuable remains of antiquity" (433) and the objects and uses of civil government. Given the political climate, Priestley was not as circumspect as he might have been, with his praise of the French Revolution and of France for "disclaiming all views of conquest" (435). He struck a particularly sensitive Establishment nerve in hoping that Hackney might produce a Hampden or Algernon Sidney, a William Penn, Franklin, or Washington (422)! And, given Edmund Burke's intemperate attack on Richard Price's sermon *On the Love of our*

13. Birrell quoted in J. W. Ashley Smith, *The Birth of Modern Education: The Contribution of the Dissenting Academies, 1660–1800* (London: Independent Press, Ltd., 1954; United Reformed Church in the United Kingdom, 1972), 176.

14. Priestley to Lindsey, to Richard Price, 23 Oct. 1786, 7 Jan., 4 Dec. 1787, 16 Feb. 1791, Price to Priestley, 27 Jan. 1791, Price Papers, Bodleian Library, Oxford; Priestley to Thomas Belsham, 17 Oct. 1790; Joseph Priestley, *The Proper Objects of Education in the present State of the World Represented in a Discourse delivered on Wednesday, April 27, 1791. At the Meeting-House in the Old-Jewry, London; to the Supporters of the New College at Hackney* (London: J. Johnson, 1791). I have used W. 15:420–40, 2d ed. of 1791.

Country, was it wise to close by recommending the example of the recently deceased Price?

With Priestley, as with all good teachers, a major element in his teaching had been his educational publications, and he continued that activity in Birmingham. In 1786 Benjamin Vaughan wrote to Shelburne (now the Marquis of Lansdowne), that he was going to propose that Priestley write a book on elementary general education. He had the general knowledge, wrote (on the whole) interestingly, and would be read throughout Europe. Priestley did not write a new book on the subject, though there were two new editions of his *Miscellaneous Observations relating to Education* and one of his *Lectures on Oratory and Criticism.* Joseph Bretland asked him to reprint the *Rudiments of English Grammar,* which Andrew Kippis also wanted available for use in his Academy at Hoxton. Property in the work was owned by several booksellers, but Joseph Johnson owned a share and Priestley wrote requesting that Bretland be permitted to print a new edition. That was done in 1786, with another printing of the new edition in 1789.[15]

In October 1782 Priestley wrote Caleb Rotheram that with the new editions of the *Disquisitions* and *Necessity* (1782), he had quite done with metaphysics. But in 1785 William Watson Jr. published *A Treatise on Time.* The preface thanked the "approbation of that eminent Philosopher Dr. Priestley (who thought it not unworthy of the public eye)." Its critical references to Reid and Beattie might well have been referenced to Priestley's *Examination* of the Common Sense Philosophers (1774) or his edition of Hartley (1775). Watson described them as "arbitrarily calling in aid the existence of a new original power to explain the perception of succession; we ought carefully to examine whether the knowledge we have that things succeed one another, may not be acquired by the ordinary operation of those powers by which we gain all other kind of information"—i.e., by experience gradually acquired.[16] Perhaps reading Watson *on Time* spurred Priestley, for by 1787 he informed Lindsey that he was "collecting facts concerning human nature . . . to illustrate and extend *Hartley's Theory,*" and he published a second edition of *Hartley's Theory of the Human Mind* in 1790.[17]

15. For Priestley's publications as a teacher, see Schofield, *Enlightenment of Priestley,* chaps. 4 and 5; B. Vaughan to Lansdowne, 8 Nov. 1786, copy, Library, APS; Priestley to Bretland, 14 Dec. 1782, 6 Jan. 1785, *Proceedings of the Massachusetts Historical Society 3* (2d ser., 1886): 15–16; 5 April 1785, 4 July 1786; Priestley to Joseph Johnson, 26 June 1783.

16. William Watson Jr., *A Treatise on Time* (London: J. Johnson, 1785).

17. There is a problem with this Priestley to Lindsey letter—the MS in Wms. has an endorsed date of "1790 after Dec. 23 say 26th"—but Rutt published it as "Birmingham, 1787," and the date of Priestley's address to the subscribers of the Birmingham Library mentioned in

Publication of a second edition of *Philosophical Necessity* may have reminded him that he had declared that Collins's *Philosophical Inquiry concerning Human Liberty* should be "reprinted, and more generally known and read." As no one had responded to this suggestion, he reprinted it himself.[18] Most of his preface is a recapitulation of his own *Philosophical Necessity* and of his "Pamphilus" papers in the revived *Theological Repository* 4 (1784). He reprinted Collins as the most concise, clear, and regular treatise on necessity, Hobbes not being systematical, Hartley's section too short, and Jonathan Edwards too diffuse (iii–v). For moral sentiment, Priestley recommended his own *Philosophical Necessity,* his *Free Discussion* with Price, and his *Letters* to Palmer. He did not always agree with Collins, particularly as some of his other writings had posed great difficulties for friends of Revelation, though he thought of him more as anticlerical than as an unbeliever (xi).

Collins's writings on the prophecies could never be properly answered so long as one continued to hold to the infallibility of judgment of Christ and the apostles (xi–xii). Collins's religious views were not significant to the value of his treatise on necessity, as it could be demonstrated that all necessarians (or Socinians, or materialists) were not unbelievers (xv). "If persons have strength of mind not to be frightened by *names,* and be capable of attending to *things* only, the strongest objections to the doctrine of necessity will not affect them. If they be unequal to this, they had better desist from the consideration of the subject. . . . Only let them cease to censure what they do not understand" (vii).

Priestley continued to write what can only be called historical-philosophical studies. He mentioned to Joseph Bretland in June 1782 that he had just printed "additional Letters to a Philosophical Unbeliever."[19] In the

---

the letter is 14 Aug. 1787, according to the appendix, in Rutt's reprinting of Part 2 of Priestley's *Appeal to the Public on the Riots in Birmingham,* 1792, and this is consistent with the political crisis at that library in that year.

18. Priestley, *Philosophical Necessity Illustrated,* xxvi–xxvii; Anthony Collins, *A Philosophical Inquiry concerning Human Liberty, Republished with a Preface by Joseph Priestley* (Birmingham: Thomas Pearson, for J. Johnson, 1790); I have used the modern reprinting, with an introduction by John Stephens. According to his letters to Lindsey, the preface was written in August and the last sheets printed in October; O'Higgins, *Anthony Collins.*

19. Priestley, *Additional Letters to a Philosophical Unbeliever, in Answer to Mr. William Hammon* (Birmingham: J. Johnson, 1787). I have used the edition bound into the second edition, 1787, of *Letters to a Philosophical Unbeliever. Part I.* According to W. 1.1:76, Wm. Hammon was a pseudonym for Matthew Turner, who taught Priestley his first lessons in chemistry at Warrington. Reviewed by Samuel Badcock, *Monthly Review* 68 (1783): 132–36. The review is mostly extracted quotation but begins: "This learned and ingenious Author . . . by a series of close but perspicuous arguments," and closes with the assessment that "It is reason speaking intelligibly, and in its clearness discovers its power."

first of the *Additional Letters*, Priestley declared that he had doubts that Hammon was quite what he claimed to be—for all the brave words about a readiness to "suffer *martyrdom* in the cause of atheism," there was no Hammon at the address given and no publisher's name was annexed to the challenge sent Priestley (242–43). Still, happy to have a professed atheist to answer, Priestley hoped that "as the world improves in wisdom," civil authorities would no more attempt to regulate modes of religion than they now did with modes of medicine or philosophy (230). "Let atheism triumph rather than religion by the help of force" (234). Weak Christians, by calling in the aid of magistrates, had got themselves masters who made use of them for their own purposes.

Priestley repeated arguments from design from his *Letters to a Philosophical Unbeliever,* part 1, but Hammon did not profess to believe that there was no design in the universe. Nor did he entirely reject the concept of an afterlife. He merely wanted to separate the designing principle from some supposed invisible supreme but hidden being. It was this pantheist implication to which Priestley responded. He found the notion of a universe causing itself manifestly absurd—an effect cannot cause itself—and certainly no less difficult in conception than an *"invisible first cause"* (256–61). And here Priestley repeated his monist "materialist" assertions about sensations and thought in the brain of man, as gravity in a stone and magnetism in a loadstone depending upon their respective substances (270–71).

Letter 4 treated the being of God, from Revelation. The existence of miracles disproved a self-creating universe operating according to its own internal logic. The morality of a deity permitting the existence of evil in the world was addressed in letter 5 and allowed Priestley an opportunity for one of his characteristic controversial bites. To Hammon's question, how could a deity allow a mortal to question his rights, titles, and even existence? Priestley responded, "You must have a high opinion of your own importance, and of the force of your writings, to imagine that a *miracle* is requisite to confute them" (287). The concluding "Miscellaneous Observations" addressed Hammon's misreading of Priestley's writings and ended: "As to what you are pleased to say I myself might have been, if I had not 'from my first initiation into science, being [been?] dedicated to what is called the immediate service of God,' it is a thing that cannot be known, except to my maker" (303).

Late in 1786 Priestley commenced a continuation of the *Letters;* by March 1787 copies were sent to Benjamin Vaughan, Thomas Belsham, and, in May 1790, to Charles James Fox. *Letters to a Philosophical Unbeliever. Part II* is more historical than philosophical, completing the series begun with *Letters.*

Part I and *Additional Letters,* dealing with proof of the existence of God from revealed religion, as part 1 dealt with natural religion.[20] The articles of religion that Priestley defended were "consonant to reason," and their proof rested on the same principles as those of all philosophical investigations (iii). He wished learned and candid Jews to consider that the divine mission of Christ was proved by arguments similar to those of Moses and therefore that their objections to Christianity must fail (v–vi). His arguments were particularly addressed to young people, as their minds "are not yet so much occupied, but that they might feel the full force of new truth" (x), as the present translation of the Scriptures was so "uncouth to an European ear" that the "noble simplicity and true sublimity of many parts of them" was missed unless met with early (xii).

His history of the promulgation of Christianity was derived from *Dr. Lardner's Jewish and Heathen Testimonies,* which he preferred to Edward Gibbon's account, which he had challenged (to no avail). Gibbon pretended to believe in Christianity but wrote as though it was mischievous as well as false (xvi–xx). Dr. Toulmin asserted the eternity of the human race but proved only a state of the earth previous to the Mosaic account of the creation, an opinion accepted by philosophical Christians and having little to do with the present race of man, whose account by Moses was probably very near the truth, as Moses was so near to their origin (xxi).

Priestley thought that belief in a future life must rest upon Revelation. No appearance in nature favored the opinion of an immaterial soul distinct from the body. "Whatever the powers of *perception* and *thought,* be in themselves, they evidently depend upon the organization of the brain" (2). "Whatever power it was that *established,* the same, no doubt, can *change,* the laws or nature, or suspend the operation of them" (8). The reality of miracle accounts in Scripture was evidenced by human testimony, justified by "indisputable facts" of the existence of the Jewish and Christian religions, which could not be or have been what they are without miracles (13). Natural religion was insufficient, as such things as the future life were not susceptible to observation. "Admitting the nature of man always to have been what we

20. Priestley to Benjamin Vaughan, 2 March 1787, Library, APS; to Lindsey, about the gift to Fox, 13 May 1790, Wms.; Joseph Priestley, *Letters to a Philosophical Unbeliever. Part II. Containing a State of the Evidence of revealed Religion, with Animadversions on the two last Chapters of the first Volume of Mr. Gibbon's History of the Decline and Fall of the Roman Empire* (Birmingham: Pearson and Rollason, for J. Johnson, 1787); reviewed by William Enfield, *Monthly Review* 78 (1788): 383–87: "Dr. Priestley has . . . on many occasions, appeared as a zealous advocate for Christianity; but never with greater credit and success, than in these Letters."

now observe it to be," the wisest method of originally informing man of the being, power, and nature of God was to assert them by extraordinary communications, which, as then written, became evidence for later generations, making modern miracles unnecessary (17–20).

Unbelievers were generally averse to reading the Scriptures, Priestley continued, many hoping that Christianity was untrue. Determining to pursue a course of action at all costs, they had no wish to inquire into evidence that might invite self-doubt (24–27). Speculative men, making new discoveries and thinking themselves wiser than the vulgar, rejected belief as superstitious and old-fashioned. But in their vanity, they could be the greatest of dupes, their singularity lost in the parochial company they kept. Old opinions were not necessarily false (31–32). In an extract the reviewer specially noted that "the very affectation of being free from vulgar prejudice, and of being wiser than the rest of mankind, must indispose them to the admission even of truth, if it should happen to be with the common people."[21]

Their history showed the Jews to be uniquely obstinate and intractable, the least likely to be imposed upon by fraudulent divine communication, and the nature of their religion showed that it could never have been derived from other peoples (41). The truth of Christianity was similar to, but easier than, that of the Jews, falling within the compass of authentic history, for the authenticity of the Gospels and Acts of Paul's letters, of the accounts of miracles was open to contemporaries to deny (56–62). Christianity spread faster than could be reasonably expected, given imperfect communications, the risk of acceptance, the unanticipated nature of the Messiah, and, by the second century, the start of its corruptions (68–75). "A more particular Account of the Nature of those Prejudices to which the Heathens were subject with Respect to Christianity" was painfully interesting, given Priestley's own reluctance to change his mind. When the mind was predisposed in favor of any opinion, a contrary one would not always be admitted on the authority of its evidence. Men may think there must be some fallacy in the new principle, though they cannot detect it. As "mere logicians," we may think argument sufficient, but customary beliefs, ease, reputation, and interest can be so strong that people will not listen to contrary reasoning. Nor was this unique to religion, as the cases of Galileo and Newton showed (89–91, 99).

History "written at the time" gave Jewish and Christian religions sound bases, while other religions depend upon tradition, heathen mythologies, and popish legends (100–102). Christian martyrs attested to the validity of

---

21. Quotation is from Enfield, review, *Monthly Review* 78 (1788): 384.

miracles they observed, while Christianity's enemies, such as Julian the Apostate, failed in their desire to discover impostures (104–10). There were no facts to examine in Mahomet's revelation of the Koran; his religion gained converts only under military power, and its most reputable parts were derived from the Christians and Jews. The books of the Hindus were old but not historical and were irrational in themselves (112–19). As ignorance and superstition went together, idolatry was linked to animism, fetishes, astrology, and divinations, not easily distinguishable from some moderns' fondness for fortune telling. Various gods were associated with the welfare of the state. Appropriate religions were, therefore, established by the state, and Christians, opposing or abstaining from ceremonies intended to appease the gods, were criminals. The wisest of Roman heathens really thought persecution of Christians promoted the welfare of the empire (122–48).

Although later princes suppressed them, it was possible to collect from fragments heathen arguments against Christianity (156–91). There was little debate over the history in the Old and New Testaments, but much over its interpretation. The miracles could have been acts of magicians and were too trivial for divinity; converts were few and of mean estate. The death of Christ was ignominious, but to respond by exalting him to a demi-God and then transform him into the one true God was worse. There were objections to doctrines, to glorification of the cross, the Mosaic account of the creation, contradictions in Scripture, disputes between followers. Many objections were wrong, others trivial, but modern unbelievers, such as Voltaire, Hume, and Gibbon, had repeated them all.

The last letter considered objections to Gibbon's *History of the Decline and Fall of the Roman Empire* not already discussed elsewhere. Priestley argued that Gibbon's work had made more unbelievers than anything recently published (199). Yet Gibbon misrepresented facts, ignored evidence that contradicted his insinuations, overlooked connections between secondary and primary causes, showed a careless indifference to the miracles of Moses and Joshua, and even made fun of the zeal and death of martyrs. Gibbon was, on the whole, undisturbed by these attacks on his *History,* though his attachment to the Established church seemed more social and political than theological. A recent biographer has declared: "I think it is not inaccurate to assert that toward religion in general Gibbon is sceptical; toward Christianity and Judaism, he is hostile; toward Paganism and Mohammedanism, he is indulgent."[22]

22. McCloy, *Gibbon's Antagonism to Christianity,* 47–48. Priestley's correspondence with Gibbon, related to his challenge, is reprinted in *W.* 27, appendix 7.

Priestley's major secular educational publishing project of the Birmingham years was to be that of his *Lectures on History*.[23] After they were first delivered, at Warrington Academy in the later 1760s, he belatedly planned their publication, but only the *Syllabus* was to be published at that time. Not until May 1779 was there again reference to the *Lectures,* when Priestley suggested to Shelburne that he complete them, but he then became differently employed, from mid-1779 to mid-1781, in his breakup with Shelburne, his move to Birmingham, and publication of *Exp. & Obs. Nat. Phil. II*. It appeared that he had abandoned the *Lectures.*

Possibly the critical reaction to the six volumes of historical studies in theology he published between 1782 and 1786 reminded him of the need for a text on how to do history. He had certainly felt a section, "Maxims of historical criticism," necessary for his 1783 defense of the *History of the Corruptions of Christianity*.[24] In March 1787 he was revising his *Lectures on History,* proposing only an elementary study. By July he had finished revisions; printing began in September, and the dedication, to Benjamin Vaughan, is dated 1 January 1788. Comparison of the *Syllabus of a Course of Lectures on the Study of History* (1765) and the *Lectures on History* (1788) shows occasional minor variations in the lectures at Warrington from those printed, but the material covered appears much the same. The *Lectures* lack the introductions to the history of England and its laws. Priestley explained that Robert Henry's *History of Great Britain* (1771–85), William Blackstone's *Commentaries on the Laws of England* (1765), and Francis Sullivan's *Historical Treatise on the Feudal Law and the Constitution and Laws of England* (1772) had made publication of lectures on these subjects unnecessary (vi).[25] He admitted that the *Lectures* were a "judicious selection" from books extant at the time they were composed, though he had since added material from Adam Smith's *Wealth of Nations* (1776), James Steuart's ("Stewart," afterward Denham,) *Principles of Political Oeconomy* (1767), John Blair's *Chronology and History of the World* (1782), and Joseph Towers's *Observations on Mr. Hume's History of England* (1778). As he had not originally intended to publish these lectures, he neglected to take notes of the books quoted (vii), but lectures 20–22 provided an extensive bibliography of historians.[26]

23. Priestley, *Lectures on History, and General Policy.*

24. Priestley, "Maxims of historical criticism," *Letters to Dr. Horsley in Answer to his Animadversions,* 135–40; Priestley to Vaughan, 2 March 1787, B. V46p, Library, APS.

25. The introductions were printed in *Essay on a Course of Liberal Education* (1765) (69–75 and 84–98) but were not included in the version of that *Essay* prefixed to the *Lectures.*

26. The decision to publish was made after the favorable response to the publication of the *Syllabus.* The index listed more than 180 names of persons whose works in history, biography,

The *Lectures* began with a discussion of the use of history—not only was it interesting and amusing (better than fiction), it anticipated experience, strengthened virtue, stimulated to great deeds, enabled us to understand human nature, and taught the truths of religion. All of these were of course commonplace to the historians of the century (e.g., Bolingbroke's "practical uses of history" in his *Letters on the Study and Use of History,* 1752) and were probably expounded by every teacher of the subject.[27] More important was his treatment of the sources of history. He explained the difference between direct and indirect sources and how to evaluate evidence, with a long digression derived from David Hartley containing a mathematical formula on the determination of the value of evidence from a series of witnesses (43). He stressed the superiority of records over material more liable to corruption through dishonesty and error—oral tradition and written accounts. He discussed the use of coins and medals, heraldry and place names, illustrating each with definite examples. In his lectures on indirect methods of ascertaining historical fact, he showed the possibility of learning from the style in which a document or book is written, while introducing an original observation on the value of a study of law: "As every new law is made to remove some inconvenience the state was subject to before the making of it . . . the law itself is a standing, and the most authentic, evidence we can require of the state of things previous to it" (76). Finally, the necessity for a close study of chronology introduced a discussion of methods of computing chronologies by astronomical records, though lecture 12 deludedly vindicated the use of Isaac Newton's *Chronology.*[28]

From sources, Priestley passed to a consideration of the general knowledge necessary to produce a good historian. This included, ideally, training in all the sciences, knowledge of human nature, philosophy, geography,

---

travel, law, chronicles, chronologies, etc., were referred to in the text. Most, from Agathias to Zosimus were historians and included French, Danish, Italian, and even South American and Indian accounts. Many of the names and summaries of works appear to have been derived from sources such as William Nicolson's ("Nicholson's") *English History Library* (1714), but taken together they represent a remarkable bibliography for what was to be an elementary text.

27. There is an admirable summary of the *Lectures* in Thomas Peardon, *Transition in English Historical Writing, 1760–1830* (New York: Columbia University Press 1933), 58–61, which provides the frame for my discussion. Priestley refers to Bolingbroke's work and extracts from it at least seven times, 6, 10, 66, 249, 253, 258, 260.

28. With the same ingenuity with which Newton adjusted the estimated sizes of air particles and their forces to confirm his theory of the speed of sound, he adjusted his chronology to confirm his conviction of the antiquity of the Hebrews and forced the remainder of his facts to fit; see Richard S. Westfall, *Never at Rest: A Biography of Isaac Newton* (Cambridge: Cambridge University Press, 1980), 805.

economics and statistics, and numistics. In lecture 15, "Of the Methods of estimating the Riches and Power of ancient and remote Nations," Priestley discussed how to determine the value of money at any time in the past—best done by "the price of mere *labour,* estimated by the wages given to persons of the lowest occupations. For these . . . in all ages and nations . . . [are] little more than a bare subsistence" (124). Part 4, "Directions for facilitating the study of history," consisted of sixteen lectures. These included a discussion of compendia and epitomes, chronological and genealogical tables (including Priestley's charts of biography and history), commonplace books, a series of précis of historians since Herodotus, and a lecture on terms of fortification.

Part 5, "Of the most important Objects of Attention to a Reader of History," encompassed more than half the volume. Among these "objects" were biography, politics, manufacturing and commerce, forms and problems of government and law, agriculture, the arts, colonies and colonization, money, luxury and manners, religion, population, war, and national finance. In lecture 34, "General Observations on Political Measures," Priestley observed that "in politics, as in every other branch of study, all just reasoning . . . is capable of being reduced to practice. A theory, or a general rule of conduct, can only be derived from the observation of a train of causes and effects in real life; and all acting is at random without regard to some theory" (254).

At least twice (275, 316) Priestley insisted on the importance of the "liberty of speaking and writing." He recommended enforced saving for the poor rather than any guarantee on sharing the common stock, lest improvidence and laziness be encouraged (279–81). "When great numbers of persons are supported by the revenues of a country, and are of course interested in the continuance of its burdens, the most upright ministers will find it difficult to afford it any relief" (506–7). Nations should not have "any large surplus of wealth at the disposal of their governors; as it would be sure to be squandered in some mischievous project" (517). Lecture 43 recommended prudence in the reform of old institutions: "no change of importance [should] be attempted in any long-established government, till the minds of the people be prepared for it . . . so as to have produced a general wish for a change" (319).[29]

---

29. Lecture 1, 13, had earlier declared that it was "extremely hazardous to introduce any material change into an established form of government. No human sagacity can foresee what inconvenience might arise from it." A note added in the U.S. edition of the *Lectures* (1803) asserted that this observation had been abundantly verified by the French Revolution, which was planned by men of great abilities, extensive reading and experience, yet had consequences so little foreseen that the system of 1803 was the very reverse of anything intended.

Lecture 47, "Of Laws," referred to John Howard, on prisons, and Cesare Beccaria's *Essay on Crime and Punishment* (English 1767), but surely this observation was mostly Priestley, and less than comforting to the innocent: "It is commonly said . . . that it is better that a hundred criminals should escape, than that one innocent person should suffer. But what the innocent daily suffer by the hundred criminals who escape should be taken into the account, as well as the chance of an innocent man suffering as a criminal. In this case he ought to consider his life as sacrificed to the security of the rest of his countrymen" (349).

Influenced by Adam Smith, Priestley declared that "money is only a convenience in making exchanges" (388). He suggested that "uniformity of weights and measures, as well as of coins, would greatly facilitate general commerce" (396). Persuaded by Pierre F. X. De Charlevoix, Francisco J. Clavijero ("Claviger"), and Cadwallader Colden, he denied the existence of the "noble savage." Society would never arrive at perfection "till the vices to which men are most prone be eradicated, or disguised, and the opposite virtues acquired, or counterfeited" (425). "The most interesting Periods in the History of Literature and the Arts" showed that "Saracens" had preserved, developed and transmitted sciences to the West, via Spain (264–65). Despite his dislike of "popery," Priestley credited the "exorbitant" power of the medieval popes and the "superstition of popish worship" for preventing total dissolution of the West upon the fall of Rome, preserving "the fine arts from being totally lost in the barbarism of Europe," contributing greatly to their revival and the revival of learning in the West (436–37).

By almost any measure, the *Lectures on History, and General Policy* is an extraordinary work, but it is, in many ways, a curious "history," particularly to modern readers. Half of the text is devoted to historiography—that is, the methodology of doing history; the remainder illustrates how eighteenth-century history lacked the historicism of the nineteenth, the engagement in a continuing process of development. Like Montesquieu, Priestley's history was a "static world of abstractions in spatial deployment instead of temporal succession." His concern was not the evolution of institutions through time but the illustration of timeless principles by reference to laws and institution of diverse times and places.[30] The whole "General Policy" part of the book was a series of citations of "social-history experiments" applied to

---

30. Sherman B. Barnes, "Historians in the Age of Enlightenment," in *Historiography Under the Impact of Rationalism and Revolution,* ed. Sherman B. Barnes and Alfred A. Skerpan (Kent: Kent State University Press, 1952), 13. See also Lois Whitney, *Primitivism and the Idea of Progress* (Baltimore: Johns Hopkins University Press, 1934), 174–83.

the understanding of modern social science phenomena; real history resembling, as Priestley said, "the experiments made by the air pump, the condensing engine, or electrical machine" exhibiting the operations of nature (5).

Few histories have approached their subject in such scope, but despite examples of bias and advocacy there is little indication that Priestley had any personal curiosity in the practice of the historian, except in theology.[31] Details of most political events were taken from Paul de Rapin's *L'Histoire d'Angleterre* (1724, English 1725–31). André Michel Rousseau believes that the *Lectures* were influenced by Voltaire, but references to him were only cautiously favorable. Other writers report Priestley's dependence on Montesquieu, Adam Smith, David Hartley, Ludwig Holberg, and Bolingbroke.[32]

There is no sign that Priestley did any research into purely secular history. He had started rewriting his *Lectures on History* while living in Calne as librarian/companion to Shelburne, when he is said to have catalogued the manuscripts of Shelburne's collection. None of these is specifically mentioned in lectures 30–31, which deal with English records and manuscripts, including those in "the Libraries and Museums of Noblemen and private Gentlemen" (234), and there is no indication that he consulted any of them. Wiltshire is extraordinarily rich in prehistoric remains; Calne is roughly twenty miles from Stonehenge and within ten miles of Avesbury circle. Neither of these, nor any other English monumental remains, is mentioned in the section on the historical value of "*visible monuments,* such as *pillars, edifices,* or mere *heaps of stones*" (48). James Keir and Jonathan Stokes became corresponding members of the Society of Antiquaries in Scotland, Josiah

31. He called Catherine Macaulay's work "very masterly history," while judging Hume's "idea of the characters of our princes of the Stewart family" too favorable (210). He criticized the dependence of the English Parliament on the court (294), and questioned the presence of bishops in the House of Lords; if the clergy were so represented, why not other classes of men, lawyers, physicians, Dissenters (337–38)? He opposed civil establishments of religion, especially when, as in Ireland, the church established was that of a small minority (450).

32. Andre Michel Rousseau, "L'Angleterres et Voltaire III," *Studies on Voltaire and the Eighteenth Century* 147 (1976): 844–46. See also John McLachlan, "Joseph Priestley and the Study of History," *Transactions of the Unitarian Historical Society* 19 (1987–90): 252–63; Herbert Weisinger, "The Middle Ages and Late Eighteenth-Century Historians," *Philological Quarterly* 27 (1948): 63–79; R. N. Stromberg, "History in the Eighteenth Century," *Journal of the History of Ideas* 12 (1951): 295–304; James Westfall Thompson, with J. Bernard Holm, *A History of Historical Writing* vol. 2, "The Eighteenth and Nineteenth Centuries" (New York: Macmillan, 1942); and A. W. Ward, "Historical and Political Writers. II: Bolingbroke," in *Cambridge History of English Literature,* ed. A. W. Ward and A. R. Waller, vol. 9 (Cambridge: Cambridge University Press, 1912), chap. 8; as well as Barnes, "Historians in the Age of Enlightenment," Peardon, *English Historical Writing,* and Whitney, *Primitivism and the Idea of Progress.*

Wedgwood of the Society of Antiquaries in London; Priestley never formally associated himself with the antiquaries. Roman remains were found just outside Daventry, where Priestley went to school; there were pottery finds at Needham Market. It is said that about 1785 (just two years before beginning the rewriting of the *Lectures*), "Dr. Priestley and other scientific men [of the Lunar Society?] were called to examine and label some early British and Roman Remains": "rings of silver, brass and iron; beads of blue ragstone, lead, clay and glass, 95 sticas of Northumbrian kings, 75 Roman coins," found by John Wilkinson in construction of his house at Castlehead, Lancaster.[33] None of these "finds" is mentioned in lecture 6, "Of Coins and Medals," or lecture 8, "Of the indirect Methods of collecting the Knowledge of past Events."

Whatever the degree of his personal involvement in doing secular history, his book was well received. It was favorably reviewed by a friend, William Enfield, who wrote, "the ingenious and indefatigable author has . . . judiciously provided the student with such preparatory information, as may serve to render the study of history pleasant, interesting, and useful . . . we make no scruple of recommending these Lectures to our readers, especially to young persons; who will find them of great use, not only to assist them in the study of history, but to awaken their attention to important objects, and lead them to a habit of reflection and inquiry" (8). The work was used in Dissenting academies, including Hackney, while Dr. John Symonds, Professor of Modern History at Cambridge from 1771, wrote:

> If I be liable to censure for having commended Dr. Priestley in my Essay, how shall I stand acquitted of a much more heinous charge . . . ? For ever since his *Lectures upon History* were published, I have constantly recommended them to the young students of our university as the best book in its kind which had fallen within my observation; and though I may dissent from the doctor in a few particulars . . . yet I should have deserved worse treatment than I received from the Apologists, if I had withholden my approbation of so judicious and useful a work."[34]

33. According to Edward Baines, *History of the County Palatine and Duchy of Lancaster* (London: Routledge and Sons, 1870), 2:46, 676, 686. There is no reference in Priestley's writings to this discovery.

34. Enfield, *Monthly Review* 80 (1789): 1–8; Symonds, "Observations upon . . . Revising the Present English Version of the . . . New Testament," prefixed by a "Short Reply to . . . a Pamphlet entitled: An Apology" (1794), quoted in *W.* 1.2:55n–56n.

In 1788 John Quincy Adams, while apprentice in a law office, read the *Lectures on History*, "a new publication of Dr. Priestley, whose literary powers may be truly called athletic . . . [a volume] which I take to be an excellent work." The *Lectures* were recommended for Rhode Island College (Brown) the same year. G. W. P. Washington read the *Lectures* as a student at the College of New Jersey (Princeton), Thomas Jefferson recommended it to Bishop James Madison as a text for William and Mary and for the library of his own University of Virginia. Juniors at Yale recited from Priestley's *Lectures on History* in the 1790s, and, circa 1803, the *Lectures on History* were in use by the junior class at Williams College. Ralph Waldo Emerson read the *Lectures on History* in 1821 and again in 1822, and a manual of history as late as 1882 found the value of Priestley's *Lectures* "still very considerable . . . may still be read with real profit."[35]

Hardly had this prescription for writing history been published when Priestley began writing a history of the Christian church.[36] In October 1788 he informed Lindsey he was working on it every day. From that date to its publication in January 1790, his correspondence is studded with references to the church history, which grew so rapidly that it was finally limited to two volumes, covering only the period to the end of the Western Roman Empire.[37] He scarcely followed his advice from the *Lectures*, doing no research save into previously published church histories and copying material from his own *Corruptions of Christianity, Early Opinions,* and the various *Letters to a Philosophical Unbeliever.* There is some attempt to follow a "natural" order of events, the historical mode of rhetoric he had favored since writing his *Lectures on Oratory and Criticism* (1777), but this was not

35. "The Diary of John Quincy Adams," 27 June, 18 July 1788, *Proceedings of the Massachusetts Historical Society* 16 (2d ser., 1902): 431, 441. Robert E. Schofield, "Joseph Priestley's American Education," in *Early Dickinsoniana: The Boyd Lee Spahr Lectures in Americana, 1957–1961* (Carlisle, Pa.: Library of Dickinson College, 1961); E. S. Morgan, *Gentle Puritan: A Life of Ezra Stiles, 1727–1795* (New Haven: Yale University Press, 1962), 389; Miller, *Brief Retrospect,* 3:338; [Emerson], *Journals,* 1:350n; C. K. Adams, *A Manual of Historical Literature* (New York: Harper & Bros., 1882), 193.

36. Joseph Priestley, *A General History of the Christian Church, to the fall of the Western Empire,* 2 vols. (Birmingham: sold by J. Johnson, 1790). There was a continuation of the church history, in four volumes, *from the Fall of the Western Empire to the Present Time* (Northumberland: for the author, 1802–3). Priestley observed to Lindsey, 2 Nov. 1790, Wms., that the first edition was all his property.

37. Priestley to Lindsey, 20 Oct. 1788 through 26 Jan. 1790; to Joshua Toulmin, 23 March, 12 May 1789; to Joseph Bretland, 7 May, 24 Oct. 1789; to Thomas Belsham, 18 Nov., 4 Dec. 1789, all in Wms., most in W. 1.2. Priestley to unknown, 17 July 1789, Birmingham Library; to Editor, 24 Dec. 1788, *Gentleman's Magazine* 59 (1789): 10–11.

a history of the ancient world, though some events of civil history were included to situate those of the church.

The dedication, dated 1 January 1790, to Samuel Shore, a longtime contributor to Priestley's various researches, repeated his opposition to the corrupting and tyrannical alliance between church and state. The preface declared that his studies of primitive Christianity having shown all ecclesiastical historians to be wrong, he determined to write a regular history of the Christian church on just principles, neither too long nor too concise and with events related to one another in their natural connection. In fact, most of his history is a replay of then-standard ecclesiastical histories, except that amid extensive selections from the "most respectable" of modern authorities and a liberal sprinkling of citations to ancient authorities, his obsessional themes were repeated.[38]

Volume 1 (538 pages) covered the progress of Christianity to its civil adoption by Constantine. Volume 2 (552 pages) considered ecclesiastical developments from Constantine to the end of the Western empire, dated at 475 A.D. Within the two, the standard account leaves room for emphasizing his compulsions—and the addition of an occasional provocative observation. The early spreading of the new religion, against all opposition, was miraculous (9–149).[39] The second edition (1803) added a reference to the silly inventions of miracle and prophecy introduced into biographies of Pythagoras and Apollonius Tyanaeus by the heathen philosophers Porphyry and Philostratus, attempting to counter the effect of the Christian story. Priestley contrasted their lack of supporting evidence with the accounts of the apostles, "written while numberless witnesses of them were living."[40] Though the Jews were perverse and obstinate, they remain God's "favoured people" and would return to greatness when they converted to Christianity (150–76).

Persecution under emperors before Constantine was fitful, but there were martyrs enough for detailed descriptions to titillate young readers—if, with two fat volumes, there were any. Priestley took nearly forty-five octavo

---

38. His modern sources particularly included Nathaniel Lardner's *Jewish and Heathen Testimonies* and *Credibility of the Gospel History*. The ancient authorities, in addition to the New Testament and the apostolic fathers (which he vetted), included the *Ecclesiastical History* of Eusebius, Josephus's *Antiquities of the Jews* and the *Jewish War*, Pliny the Younger's Letters, Justin Martyr, Origen, Athanasius, Socrates, Scholasticus, Cyril of Alexandria, Orosius, Theodoret (showing more good sense than any other writer in these early ages), Chrysostom, Jerome, and Augustine.

39. There followed a repetition of Priestley's arguments against Gibbon, in *Philosophical Unbeliever, Part II*, that no hypothesis other than truth and divine intervention could explain the growth of Christian belief.

40. For the second edition of the church history, I have used *W.* 8:208–11.

pages to describe only some of the martyrdoms. There he made a sly reference to Horsley's orthodox Jewish-Christian church of Aelia (210).

A sympathetic account of Gnosticism (211–19) allowed him to observe that it was less absurd than the later alliance of Christianity with Platonism. Priestley described the beginning of Trinitarianism, a corruption little better than heathenism. Rejected by Christians in general, the arguments were those of the overly learned, who did not attempt to impose them. Writings of ancient Unitarians had been lost, but Origen claimed, with citations to ten other writers, that violence against Unitarians was a development of the later church. So impressed was Priestley by Origen that he devoted nearly eight pages to outline his piety, genius, and application, an honor to Christianity and to human nature. Described as the most distinguished character and writer of his period (184–254 A.D.), unhappily too attached to heathen philosophy, he puzzled and silenced plain men with his ingenuity and eloquence.[41]

The account of Constantine's conversion is improbable and inconsistent. Priestley suspected that Constantine and Eusebius embroidered the sight of a parahelion into a superstitious vision of a cross on the sun (2:97–104). Under Constantine, Christians could celebrate freedom from persecution and even laws in their favor. By then a majority of imperial subjects thought well of Christianity, independent of civil power. But even before Constantine there had been controversies within the church. After him, freedom from external persecution inevitably brought schism. Priestley named, and partially identified, some thirteen "heretical" sects and subsects that disturbed the orthodox, before and after Constantine: Arian, Donatist, Eutychain, Gnostic, Manichaen, Marconite, Meletian, Millenarian, Montanist, Nestorian, Novatian, Pelagian, and Priscillian.[42] None of the measures to remove dissension had much success, proving the futility of government interference in religion and illustrating the mischief of attempting forcibly to establish a standard of orthodoxy. In fact, the growth of sects deterred the authority of bigots (379). With freedom of discussion, truth would prevail and uniformity be achieved without force (2:383).

The period was marred by internecine disputes. "It seems extraordinary that any christians who had suffered so much, and so lately, by persecution themselves should enter so warmly into the persecution of others. But this

41. The admiration of Origen shown here explains Priestley's indignation when Bishop Horsley attacked Origen's veracity. Chadwick, *Early Church*, 100–115, describes Origen's ideas, which suggests that there were many affinities between Priestley and Origen, despite their ultimate differences respecting the Trinity.

42. Eusebius so abused the Manichaeans that Priestley turned to Isaac de Beausobre's *Histoire de Manicheisme* and Lardner for that heresy.

has been the case from the time of Constantine to the present day" (2:80). Volume 2 featured problems caused by civil interference in matters of religion, in obstruction of free inquiry and in violence and injustice. Well meaning and deeply concerned with altercations and lack of union in the church, emperors tried to prevent the spread of mischief by raising and deposing bishops, calling councils and synods, and acting as moderators. Councils and synods were a cause of much mischief, their decrees logically contradictory, absurd, and meaningless. Winners at each council were insolent in their triumphs, presuming themselves omnipotent—until the next council. The heathen historian Marcellinus made merry with tales of continual dust rising on highways as troops of bishops galloped from one of these councils to another.

Strong bishops tried to establish Catholic policy. In the east there was John of Antioch, named Chrysostom for his eloquence, of great virtue but haughty and arbitrary. In the west it was Augustine ("Austin"), a great and good man and major oracle of that and future ages, but developer of absurd and shocking opinions that only his ingenuity was sufficient to supply. Only the principal writings of Augustine were mentioned in a short biographical sketch (2:495–96); Priestley thought his *City of God,* written to confute the heathen, one of the most valuable productions of Christian antiquity.

Volume 2 ended with an index to the whole, plus an addition citing more authorities for Priestley's claim that Trinitarianism was not taught with effect and clarity before the appearance of the Gospel of St. John. He lists Origen, Eusebius, and Chrysostom, who claimed that all New Testament writers prior to John were "children, who heard, but did not understand things" (570).[43]

With his history of the early church and its persistent attack on the use of civil authority in matters of religion, Priestley sealed his fate with the political and religious Establishment of late eighteenth-century England. But the growth of Dissent in general and the agreement with Priestley of liberal theological research of the early nineteenth century, coupled, perhaps, with some slight shame at the way he had been treated, led to the passage in 1813 of the "Unitarians Relief Bill," which was widely regarded as finally confirming, for Priestley, the victory in his controversy with the Established church.[44]

43. It also included a six-page (including a cancelland) table of the succession of emperors and of bishops of the greater sees: Rome, Jerusalem, Antioch, Alexandria, and Constantinople, to the fall of the Western Empire.

44. Without some objective modern appraisal of Priestley's work, it is difficult to judge its value, but Establishment church figures could not doubt its significance in 1813, nor could they doubt the persistence of dishonor associated with their exiling of Priestley in 1794. The "Act to relieve Persons who impugn the Doctrine of the Holy Trinity from certain Penalties," 53 Geo. III, c. 160, passed "without opposition or even debate." See Wilbur, *History of Unitarianism,* 340n64.

XIII

POLITICS AND THE BIRMINGHAM RIOTS

Whether that "victory" was one of or for Priestley is not entirely clear. That the "Unitarian" bill was passed on 14 July 1813, exactly twenty-two years from the date in 1791 when his home and chapel were destroyed in the Birmingham Church and King Riots, suggests that it was quite as much a belated apology for a political wrong as an acknowledgment of Priestley's achievement in theological opinion. Those riots were one of the rare occasions of persecution in modern England, when a man was ultimately driven into exile for expression of temporarily unacceptable opinions. The rarity was not so much one of riots in Birmingham. Riots were endemic throughout eighteenth-century England, and political capriciousness was one of Birmingham's characteristics.[1] In his *History of the Rebellion,* Clarendon described Birmingham as "of as great a fame for hearty, wilful, affected disloyalty to the King as any place in England."[2] But in 1714–15 there were Sacheverell riots, and New Meeting House was damaged to honor Tories and the high church. Between 1743 and 1759 there were riots in opposition to John Wesley and the Quakers. Then, following the four-day reactionary riots of 1791, Birmingham became a leader in liberal agitation for political

---

1. George Rudé, *Paris and London in the Eighteenth Century* (New York: Viking Press, 1971), describes in some detail the nature of rioting in eighteenth-century England.

2. Edward Hyde, Earl of Clarendon, *The History of the Rebellion and Civil Wars in England* (Oxford: Clarendon Press, 1717), vol. 2, pt. 1, 233.

reform.[3] The Church and King Riots of 1791 differed because of evidence that they were deliberately instigated against Priestley by Birmingham Establishment figures. The evidence now can only be circumstantial, but the circumstances are damning.

It is not as though Priestley had not been courting trouble for decades before his coming to Birmingham. He could not have helped being born a Dissenter, but his turning Arian at Daventry Academy and Unitarian at Leeds, without any concealment, was asking for persecution, as the Toleration Act of 1689 explicitly excluded non-Trinitarians, while the Act Against Blasphemy of 1698 held that declaring disbelief in the doctrine of the Trinity was punishable by imprisonment for life. Priestley had also been conspicuous in support of Dissenters' relief bills in 1772 and 1773 and written in favor of disestablishment of religion. Between 1773 and 1780 he had been active in support of the colonists in America. It would have been occasion for wonder if Establishment figures in Birmingham had not viewed his coming with great suspicion.

Initially they had little specific reason, but from the time Priestley settled in Birmingham, there was a persistent, deliberate attempt to inflame popular opinion against him. For all his later claims of enmity there between church Establishment and Dissent before his arrival, the cited instances appear to be little more than the social snobbery customary throughout England between clergy and Dissenting ministers. But gradually political events, combined with Priestley's activities, escalated both provocation and persecution.[4] Between 1781 and 1783, for example, Britain's defeat in the American Revolutionary War constituted an embarrassment for the Tory government and the church Establishment. This was compounded by the 1782 resignation of the North administration and its replacement by that of Rockingham and of Shelburne, with whom Priestley had so recently been associated.[5]

---

3. Conrad Gill, *History of Birmingham*, vol. 1, *Manor and Borough to 1865* (London: Oxford University Press, 1952), 200ff.; *The Priestley Memorial at Birmingham, August 1874* (Birmingham: Longman, Green, Reader, and Dyer, 1875), 151, quotes the *Manchester Guardian* for 3 Aug. 1874, noting "the revolution of local feeling which has made Birmingham more distinctly representative of Priestley's political views than any other place in the kingdom."

4. Bushrod, "Unitarianism in Birmingham," 3; the Birmingham clergy had been unfriendly and contemptuous toward Dissenting ministers even before Priestley's arrival. According to Priestley, *Appeal to the Public*, 4–5, clergy refused to ride or walk with Dissenting ministers at funerals. This was neither peculiar to Birmingham nor ephemeral; clergy declined to join Manchester's civic recognition of the death of the Quaker John Dalton in 1844 or the unveiling of the statue of Joseph Priestley in Birmingham in 1874. Herbert J. McLachlan, *Essays and Addresses* (Manchester: Manchester University Press, 1950), 69. Absence of the clergy at the Birmingham event is laughed about in the *Priestley Memorial*, 31, 34, 104–5.

5. See, for example, Bradley, *English Radicalism*, particularly 10–14, for the role the Establishment felt Dissenters had played in the American Revolution.

Priestley always insisted to friends on his disinterest in politics, declaring to Lindsey, in response to a letter late in 1788 (probably about the temporary insanity of King George III and the likelihood of a new ministry), "the subject that interests you all so much I seldom think of, though you oblige me . . . by informing me how things go on." He even dissociated himself explicitly from Shelburne (after 1784, Marquis of Lansdowne), ignoring his covert politicking in Shelburne's service.[6] Perhaps he was consciously avoiding trouble, as both he and his immediate family had happily settled into Birmingham, but he was a known associate of people who were identified with economic and political changes.

In 1782 he corresponded with Christopher Wyvill, chairman of the Yorkshire Association, and may have distributed copies of its circular letter advocating annual parliaments and equalization of representation in Commons.[7] The contest between the Whig oligarchy and the king and his friends, manifest in the administrations of Lord North, Chatham, Rockingham/Shelburne, and even of the younger Pitt, was becoming irrelevant to the real political situation of Britain. The change from agriculture to industry, from a rural to an urban society, was led by men without any stake in oligarchies or landed estates, middle-class men like Priestley's Lunar Society friends.[8] The mob cries encouraged during the 1791 riots included "No Philosophers" along with "Church and King," "No Popery," and "Damn the Presbyterians."

Lunar Society members were divided on the subject of the American Revolution, but they united in exerting influence for more immediate political ends. In 1783 Birmingham's merchants joined in a commercial committee to petition for laws favorable to their interests.[9] Priestley was not involved

6. He wrote Benjamin Vaughan, 2 March 1787, APS, that he took very little interest in political things. See Chapter 1, esp. n. 32, for an account of his political activities while with Shelburne.

7. Priestley to Wyvill, 14 Feb. 1782: "I am far from making myself a judge in political matters. . . . I think it right to have such pieces as this Address in the way of those who ought to read them," ZFW 7/2/28/2, North Riding Record Office, Yorkshire.

8. For the growing agitation by middle-class English entrepreneurs to win parliamentary representation, see Isaac Kramnick's intriguing article, "Republican Revisionism Revisited," *American Historical Review* 87 (1982): 629–64, esp. 636, 641–46. For a general account of Birmingham politics and its growing tensions during this period, see Money, *Experience and Identity*, esp. part 3, 158–243.

9. See Schofield, *Lunar Society*, 134–39, 351–54; Langford, *Birmingham Life*, 315–16, 318–19, 320–24. R. B. Rose, "The Priestley Riots of 1791," *Past and Present* 18 (1960): 70, suggests that churchmen and Dissenters worked together amicably in the commercial committee, but the membership does not appear to include persons committed to maintaining the Establishment and most were like the middle-class merchant and manufacturer members of Priestley's New Meeting.

in the activities of commercial committees, but he wrote against the poor laws and for principal manufacturers, when he edited, in 1787, the plans of a "society for encouraging the honest and industrious persons of both sexes and every age."[10] The bulk of *An Account of a Society for encouraging the Industrious Poor* consists of a table, with instructions for its use, for computing the amounts of payment required of laborers, at different ages, to generate a life annuity to replace poor law payments (18–31). The original intention of the promoters was simply that, but Priestley suggested to them that an account of the scheme would be of use (23), leading to his subtitle: "Some Considerations on the State of the Poor in General."

In this pamphlet Priestley made arguments frequently advanced against guaranteed payments to the unemployed poor: they lose any shame at being maintained by the public and any spirit of frugality and industry (4). "Men will always live without labour, or upon the labour of others, if they can" (6). The remedy was to return to the path of nature and providence, with every man responsible for himself and family, depending upon humane individuals for unforeseeable needs. But men should be given some reason for supposing that they could better their own condition—and the answer was to be found in schemes such as that proposed to Parliament by Francis Maseres and rejected in 1773, for funds into which laborers might deposit weekly sums for the purchase of annuities.[11] Priestley added that the poor should be required to contribute to such a fund—not a restriction of freedom, for no person who acquired property ever had the freedom to spend his money at will (13). He also favored a public provision for teaching the poor to read and write and the suppression of "supernumerary alehouses" (16).

Priestley was repeatedly to declare that his primary concern was theological, but his Establishment contemporaries could not always distinguish between his theology and his politics, and he did not much help in that problem. Before coming to Birmingham, while recovering from his illness,

10. Joseph Priestley, ed., *An Account of a Society for encouraging the Industrious Poor. With a Table for Their Use, To which are Prefixed, Some Considerations on the State of the Poor in General* (Birmingham: Pearson and Rollason, 1787), quotation from 12. There is no identification of the society and no real account of it. I don't know where Ronald E. Crook, *A Bibliography of Priestley, 1733–1804* (London: Library Association, 1966), item PS/278, found an author's ascription: ("By Joseph Priestley for the use of John Wilkinson, esquire / Iron works at Bradley"); my copy fails to list author or editor.

11. D. O. Thomas, "Francis Maseres, Richard Price, and the Industrious Poor," *Enlightenment and Dissent* 4 (1985): 65–82, discusses Maseres's "Proposal for establishing life-annuities in Parishes for the benefit of the Industrious Poor," twice published in newspapers in 1771, then in a pamphlet (London, 1772), before submission and rejection in Parliament. The "Proposal" was early submitted to Price, from whom Priestley could have learned of it.

he had responded to the Gordon Riots, taking advantage of the event to write against an establishment enforced by civil power. His *Free Address* was dated June 1780.[12] He was pleased that people were serious about religion, but their actions were not suitable to Christianity, which addressed the understanding and hearts of men, leaving judgment to God. "We are to shew our zeal and fortitude by *suffering* for our religion, not by fighting for it" (503). As petitioners, you differ from the rioters, Priestley wrote, but, like them, you appeal to civil authority, in imitation of that which is worst in the Church of Rome. He urged his readers to be practical; Protestants could be abused in Papist countries. "We make the *Papists* our enemies by becoming theirs" (507).

Papists were not as they had been in the days of the Stuarts. They could escape penalties by taking civil oaths, but did not do so as they did not believe in the dispensing power of the pope. They sent their children abroad for education, for English schools and universities were not open to them, as they ought to be. Remove the restrictions they were under, and they would be as attached to England and its government as any other subjects. Priestley's religious principles were as far from those of Rome as anyone's, but "I stand in need of liberty myself, and I wish that every creature of God may enjoy it equally with myself" (516).

Hardly had he arrived in Birmingham than he affirmed his Unitarianism from the pulpit of New Meeting in his inaugural sermon. Between 1781 and 1790 a Unitarian movement was clearly growing in Britain. The publication, from 1782, of Priestley's *History of Corruptions,* its defenses, the *History of Early Opinions* of 1786, the various *Defences of Unitarianism,* and the *History of the Christian Church* (1790), all made matters worse. Not only did Priestley affirm theological positions contrary to those of the Established church, he pointed to its organizational inadequacies—contradictions in subscription to its Articles, inequalities in revenues, pluralities and absentees—and suggested that their reformation might need to wait for the fall of the civil powers that supported them. And he had the indecency to reply

---

12. [Priestley], "A Lover of Peace and Truth," *A Free Address to those who have Petitioned for the Repeal of the Late Act of Parliament in Favour of Roman Catholics* (London: J. Johnson, 1780); I have used *W.* 22:499–516. Priestley had favored toleration for Roman Catholics as early as 1768 and in 1789 agreed with Lindsey and the Standing Committee of Dissenters in England and Wales in supporting Catholic petitions for relief from the penal code. He noted that the ministry would be obliged to pass the "Catholic Bill," which was indeed passed without division in Commons and in Lords with minor amendment on 6 April 1791. His support and that of William Russell for the Catholic Relief Bill may explain the "no Popery" cries of the Birmingham rioters.

with sarcasm and contempt to scurrilous attacks made on him by admired church figures. One can easily imagine a conference in some bishop's palace and a paraphrase of Henry II's supposed angry question respecting Thomas à Becket: Will no one free us of this pestilential Priestley?[13]

The penultimate indignity, apparently, was Priestley's connections with attempts to repeal the Test and Corporation Acts, attempts that he defined as religious and his opponents as political. The social and political system of eighteenth-century England was based on a network of oligarchies, of which the church was a part and Dissent was not. Those Acts protected the privileged positions of those within the system, against the outsiders demanding entry. The Acts were frequently ignored. Dissenters held offices by "occasional conformity" or "with hazard" and were rarely persecuted, but both sides of the fight acted as though they were in full operation and the mere fact that the Acts existed suggested a prejudice and perpetuated it.[14]

In 1787 Dissenters once again moved for a repeal of the badges of their inferiority and expected the support of Pitt. In the debates of 28 March 1787, Pitt not only did not support Dissent, he openly opposed it, and the motion lost by 176 to 98. Priestley was keenly aware of the labors of Horsley and the bishops to defeat the motion and of their delight at its failure.[15] Although there is no direct evidence that Priestley was directly active in this agitation for religious and political reform, his New Meeting congregation, and especially William Russell, its chief vestryman and friend of Priestley, certainly were. The efforts of the younger Pitt in 1785 to abolish some rotten boroughs and add country members to Parliament may have contributed to Priestley's mistaken belief that Pitt was sympathetic to the cause of liberal reform.[16] He expressed his disappointment in a published letter to Pitt, dated 31 March 1787.[17]

13. Priestley noted this analogy in his *Appeal to the Public*, 58n*.

14. Richard W. Davis, *Dissent in Politics, 1780–1830: The Political Life of William Smith, M.P.* (London: Epworth Press, 1971). Essentially a conservative appraisal of a reforming Unitarian politician, this work discusses the Establishment position regarding repeal of the Test and Corporation Acts (42–50, 62).

15. Priestley to Lindsey, March 1787, on Horsley publishing on the Test Act; and of his disappointment at the failure of the motion and of the happiness of the bishops and Dr. Horsley.

16. Davis, *Dissent in Politics*, discusses the younger Pitt's one move toward reform, pointing out that London's middling and smaller merchants, manufacturers, and tradesmen supported reform, while the larger merchants and financiers tended to support the status quo (21–23).

17. Joseph Priestley, *A Letter to the Right Honourable William Pitt, First Lord of the Treasury, and Chancellor of the Exchequer; on the Subjects of Toleration and Church Establishments; Occasioned by his Speech against the Repeal of the Test and Corporation Acts, on Wednesday the*

Priestley's *Letter to William Pitt* takes the position, based on his having heard Pitt's speech against repeal, that the politician was ignorant of the real circumstances of the case. Having been educated by biased clergyman, and wishing to recommend himself to the majority of the people, he had taken a position not justified by right or reason. Why take advice from bishops, always the most jealous of men in protection of their prerogatives? There was no inseparable connection between the political constitution of the nation and an Established church. "If you must have a *state religion*," Priestley wrote, "let it be rational and intelligible." Redress the requirements for subscription at the universities—an absurdity peculiar to England and not successful in preventing learning among Dissenters, whose schools were more liberal and more inclusive of subjects. Subscription should be limited to candidates for orders in the Church of England and administered on entering them.[18] Bishops should not hold seats in the House of Lords (31). Collection of tithes from Dissenters was tyrannical, unnecessary, and disgraceful. The Establishment in Ireland was an abuse, contradicting the arguments for establishments as the religion of the majority (36).

What danger had resulted from Dissenter Peers or M.P.s, or from those who, by occasional conformity, now acted as J.P.s, mayors, aldermen, excisemen (11)? If some Dissenters were more enemies than others to ecclesiastical establishments (and Priestley admitted being one of them), then discriminate against these and not against all Dissenters. Give Dissent those things that would not affect the Establishment; make them secure in their professions and religion. Dissenters did not propose changes by force but by persuasion. Free discussion would, in time, produce a rational and permanent uniformity (26). His only interest lay in the reputation and flourishing state of the country; Priestley did not seek emoluments and declared (in 1787!) that he had done nothing for which he apprehended he had anything to fear (41). Experience had shown Dissenters not to expect gratitude from statesmen or courts, he went on; they might well withhold support from those who oppose measures they favor (45).

28th of March 1787 (London: J. Johnson and J. Debrett, 1787), 2d ed. 1787. Lindsey and Priestley sat for thirteen hours listening to the debate in the House of Commons; see McLachlan, "More Letters of Theophilus Lindsey," 370.

18. Priestley's *Letter to Pitt* was clearly the inspiration for the Grace, advanced by William Frend and introduced to the Senate House, Cambridge, in Dec. 1787, for relieving M.A. candidates of their obligation to subscribe to the Thirty-Nine Articles of the Church on taking their degrees. Priestley wrote to Lindsey, 29 Sept. 1788, about Frend's subsequent troubles at Cambridge: "I fear he is deficient in prudence"; and to Frend, 12 Aug. 1790, that Cambridge should not be limited to adherents of the Church of England.

Birmingham's Establishment reacted promptly, with its first overt attempt to silence Priestley. There had already been one episode in the Birmingham war of church versus Dissent in September 1786, when the Rev. Charles Curtis carried the resolution leading to the bifurcation of Birmingham's Sunday School, but that was not specifically directed toward Priestley.[19] This time, although it was later denied, Priestley was the direct object of blatant censorship. In August 1787 Mr. Charles Cooke presented a proposition to the subscribers of the Birmingham Library to cease purchase of "so many books on religious disputes" and gave notice that he intended to resolve the exclusion of all books on controversial divinity. Priestley responded that he had remodeled the library, upon his arrival in 1780, after the form of that in Leeds, which gave selection of books to a committee annually elected by subscribers. If the latter were unsatisfied by the selection, they could change the committee. The "many books" of which Cooke complained amounted in cost to about £5 out of a total of £700 to £800. He could, as Cooke declared, have given his books to the library and had not done so, lest he be thought to be obtruding them. He had in fact attempted to prevent the purchase of his books until the library bought (with his approval) those written against him. It now appeared that the clergy, wanting to exclude Priestley's books, had "in all decency" to reject all controversy. The motion and Priestley's answer excited a pamphlet war until, on 12 December 1787, the motion appears to have lost by a two-thirds vote.[20] Birmingham's Establishment had lost its first battle with Priestley.

Early in 1788 a rare instance of cooperation between the Anglican Church and the Dissenters occurred in their mutual opposition to the slave trade. But a dinner held later that year to celebrate the centenary of the landing in England of William of Orange restored the status quo. "None of the clergy of the town would attend, because we refused to drink *the Church and Constitution.*" During 1788 members of New Meeting returned to the fray when, in correspondence with the Dissenting Committee in London, they began organizing to bring up yet again a bill for repeal of the Test and Corporation Acts.[21] Early the following year, delegates from all of Birmingham's

19. The Rev. Edward Burn later tried to deny that permission for Dissenters to send their children to their meeting houses had ever been rescinded and was bluntly set right. Joseph Priestley, *An Appeal to the Public on the Subject of the Riots in Birmingham, Part II. To which is added, A Letter from Works Russell, Esq. to the Author* (London: J. Johnson, 1792); I have used the version in *W.* 19:434–508, appendices 17–22.

20. Langford, *Birmingham Life*, 288–91; Priestley, *Appeal, Part II*, appendix 25, 583–89. Langford thought the motion carried, but Priestley reported its loss to Lindsey.

21. Bushrod, "Unitarianism in Birmingham," 130.

Dissenting congregations, led by Russell, met to choose delegates to join the London Committee, and on 8 May 1789 the matter was raised in the House of Commons. Raised, and again defeated, but in a reduced House the majority had shrunk to twenty—122 nays to 102 yeas. Pitt had again spoken against the measure, and Fox in its favor. Priestley was delighted, writing to Lindsey that Fox was bound to regain popularity with Dissenters and Pitt to lose, while a repeal bill was bound to win on the next attempt.

Dissenters began promptly to prepare for that next attempt. Delegates from Dissenting congregations met in Wiltshire in September 1789 to plan a united approach. Dr. John Aikin, son of Priestley's old friend of Warrington days, wrote a pamphlet comparing, and distinguishing between, the constitution of the state and that of the Church of England, to which Priestley added remarks on some letters addressed to the delegates by an anonymous Church of England clergyman opposing repeal.[22] The letters must be those of some clergyman totally ignorant of Dissent and Dissenters, Priestley wrote, and without respect for the principles and consciences of others. Repeal did not require selection of Dissenters, merely their eligibility (19–20). As a minority, any "sectaries" selected would have too little influence to be dangerous to the state, whose civil constitution they support while disapproving of the ecclesiastical part. Is an establishment, he asked, not required in many other countries (specifically the United States), worth guarding at so great expense of justice and humanity (32–36)? In Ireland the church required the aid of Dissenters against the Catholic majority, as in the past it had required its aid against King James II. The church wrongly feared the Toleration Act and the easing of the burden on Dissenting ministers, as it now feared repeal. Must Dissenters launch a major inquiry into the doubtful uses of an establishment (42)?

In October 1789 a committee of the seven congregations of the three denominations of Protestant Dissenters in Birmingham, with William Russell as chairman, met to support repeal of the Test and Corporation Acts. In November, at the committee's request, Priestley observed the anniversary of the Gun Powder Plot with a sermon on repeal.[23] Though we must acquiesce

22. John Aikin, M.D., *The Spirit of the Constitution and that of the Church of England, compared. To which are Added by another hand* [Joseph Priestley], *Remarks on Two Letters, addressed to the Delegates of the Several Congregations of Protestant Dissenters, Who met at Devizes, September 14, 1789* (London: J. Johnson, 1790); Priestley, *Remarks*, 15–42.

23. Joseph Priestley, *The Conduct to be Observed by Dissenters, in Order to Procure the Repeal of the Corporation and Test Acts, recommended in a Sermon* [on 1 Cor. 7:21], *preached before the Congregations of the Old and New Meetings, at Birmingham, November 5, 1789. Printed at the Request of the Committees of the Seven Congregations of the Three Denominations*

in the condition in which God has placed us, it was still a Christian's duty to improve one's circumstances if possible. Attempts to repeal the Corporation and Test Acts had twice been repelled, but by decreasing amounts. We must try again, for "It is injurious and unjust to exclude from office loyal supporters of government." The Test Act was directed toward Roman Catholics, not Dissenters; its repeal was an imaginary danger to the Established church. If repeal was a violation of the constitution, so has been every change in law, from King Henry VIII to the Hanoverians. This called for patience, perseverance, and a peaceable representation to Parliament. Make common cause with the three denominations in London, agreeing on Christians before Protestants and Protestants before Dissenters. Solicit justice for ourselves, Priestley urged, not forgetting the rights of others, e.g., poor Negroes, and pray for the French as they claimed a free and equal government.

Delegates of the three denominations of Dissenters in Midlands met at Leicester on 12 January 1790, electing William Russell treasurer and secretary for the district, to plan agitation for repeal. Country Dissenters were dissatisfied with the London Committee's strategy, but Priestley was not discouraged, though the proposal might not be successful this session or perhaps not this reign. Birmingham clergy responded by organizing opposition: Priestley suspected they would do something violent, but instead they commenced a public campaign against Priestley. Edward Burn, a local clergyman, began it with the publication of critical letters in 1789—which, of course, Priestley answered in a series of letters dated 17 February 1790.[24] In the preface to his *Letters to Burn*, Priestley declared his disinclination for controversy with persons in the same community, but in this case Burn was the aggressor.[25] He denied any particular hostility toward Establishment clergy. Burn apparently

---

of Protestant Dissenters, in Birmingham (Birmingham: J. Johnson, 1789); I have used W. 15:387–404, from the second edition of 1789.

24. Joseph Priestley, *Letters to the Rev. Edward Burn, of St. Mary's Chapel, Birmingham, in Answer to his, on the Infallibility of the Apostolic Testimony, concerning the Person of Christ* (Birmingham: J. Thompson, 1790); I have used W. 19:305–44. Burn's *Letters* and his subsequent *Vindication* were published in Birmingham and London; the former had at least three editions.

25. Burn, a Methodist evangelist, was quoted in 1820 as having said to a touring American minister: "He had always entertained the highest esteem and respect for the character and talents of Dr. Priestley, and was on the footing of intimacy with him." He thought Priestley had handled him much too roughly in their controversy, though admittedly there "were many things in his pieces which only youth could excuse." He publicly apologized at the 1825 annual dinner of the low Baliff of Birmingham for the asperities of feelings and expressions he had used in his controversy with Priestley. "Critical Notices. The Miscellaneous Writings of F. W. Greenwood, D.D. . . . ," *Christian Reformer* 3 (n.s., 1847): 170–72, 171; also *Monthly Repository* 20 (1825): 753.

knew nothing of Priestley, supposing him an enemy of Revelation, whereas his acquaintance with and love of Scripture was apparent in all his writing (308–9). The real issue, Priestley wrote, was the violent opposition of the high church party to repeal of the Corporation and Test Acts, with its penal statutes, which might still be executed at will.

Priestley denied having questioned apostolic testimony and professed shock that a Christian minister could advance such unfounded charges. He repeated his arguments from *Corruptions, Early Opinions,* and the *Letters to Horsley* (315–26) and declined to join with those who had no scruples about misrepresentation or abuse to advance a cause, however good the cause might be.

But it was the infelicitous phrase with which Priestley hailed the warmth of Establishment arguments, ripped from context and sent to all the bishops and members of Commons the day before the debate, which contributed to the defeat of the repeal motion of 1790: "If their system be not well-founded, they are only accelerating its destruction . . . they are assisting me in the proper disposal of those grains of gunpowder, which have been some time accumulating . . . and which will certainly blow it up at length; and perhaps as suddenly, as unexpectedly and as completely, as the overthrow of the late arbitrary government of France" (311). Charles James Fox brought forward the motion to repeal on 2 March 1790, to a full House of Commons. Again the administration (Pitt) spoke against it, "Gun-powder Joe" was quoted, and Burke declaimed on the danger to the church represented by such men as Richard Price and Priestley. The motion lost: 294 against, 105 for repeal.

Probably the motion would have lost even without Priestley's unwise remarks.[26] The Birmingham Establishment had already made arrangements prior to the vote to ring bells and illuminate buildings. "We apprehend the mob will be instigated to do mischief." In the event, the high church party in Birmingham was restrained, bells were rung but only for a time, and there was no illumination. But later that month, Burn threatened to charge Priestley before the Spiritual Court (holding nominal jurisdiction till the reign of Queen Victoria) and that threat was not dropped before April. Of course, neither the defeat in Commons nor the published attacks of Birmingham's Establishment silenced Priestley.

---

26. He responded the same day as their distribution with a broadside to the bishops and M.P.s, and followed this with a letter of 4 March 1790 to the same persons, also published in the *St. James Chronicle,* pointing to the distortion of intent and to his advice that Dissenters acquiesce in their disabilities "till it please God . . . to open the eyes and enlarge the minds of our countrymen," W., appendix 8, 539–40.

On 4 March he began a series of thirty-two open letters, continued through five parts to 7 June, to the inhabitants of Birmingham, answering attacks by the Rev. Spencer Madan. Madan had started a deliberate offensive against Unitarians in general and Priestley in particular, as their chief spokesman, charging him and them with being enemies of church and state by their attempt to gain repeal of the Test and Corporation Acts. After Priestley had the gracelessness to defend himself, the assault continued in "most violent and menacing letters."[27]

Madan's fears of the meetings of Dissenters were groundless, Priestley insisted. They were merely the actions of Englishmen bringing their grievances to public attention (139–44). Madan seemed to be ignorant of the facts of the English Civil War, which was begun by Episcopalians. Presbyterians were not anti-monarchy; the king had been killed by Independents. Jacobite clergy retained a deep-rooted attachment to Catholic Stuarts, while Dissenters were loyal to Protestant Hanover (144–52).

The Test Act was stupid and its legal requirement of "occasional conformity" was a prostitution of a sacred ordinance (159–68). No test was needed in Scotland or Ireland, where it was repealed. Repeal would be proposed for England, fifty times if necessary, until reason, justice and sound policy succeeded (169–76). The 1689 Act of Toleration was a decision of the state, not of the church, which was not and is not tolerant. Madan's "great constitutional cause" of a religious Establishment was a cause for the clergy only. The general population did not share it and neither Scripture nor common sense supported it. There was no "axiomatic" need for a national church, as America had shown (183–206). If the Establishment was to be the church of the majority, why was Ireland, where most were Roman Catholic, burdened? And why were the inhabitants of Birmingham, where more people attended the fourteen chapels for Dissenters and Methodists than the five Establishment churches, taxed with tithes to support a minority?

The Articles of the church were contradictory and joined Calvinistic statements to popish ones. Article 36 was even belied by acts of Parliament,

---

27. Joseph Priestley, *Familiar Letters, addressed to the Inhabitants of Birmingham, in Refutation of several Charges, advanced against the Dissenters, by the Rev. Mr. Madan, Rector of St. Philip's, in his Sermon, entitled "The principal Claims of the Dissenters considered."* Preached at St. Philip's Church, on Sunday, February 14, 1790. Part I (II, III, IV, V) (Birmingham: J. Thompson, 1790). I have used W. 19:135–304, from the second printing of the collected edition. Madan's sermon was published as well as his later attacks. Priestley was later to think that Madan, like Horsley, had been rewarded for his attack with a bishopric, but was misinformed. See Priestley to William Russell, 25 April 1792, W. 1.2:182n; the Spencer Madan made Bishop of Bristol was the father of Madan in Birmingham.

which the church was bound by the oath of supremacy to accept (230–44, appendices 3–4). Priestley would not query the veracity of any clergyman who said he believed the Articles, but the majority did not. Neither Dissent in general nor Unitarianism in particular was dangerous to the state. The church merely feared a loss in its income. The church was in fact in danger only from from its internal defects: unqualified persons in the clergy, many by purchase; inequality in income, pluralities and nonresidency, and sub-servience to the Crown.[28]

Why was the person who was wantonly attacked always charged with love of controversy, when he was only defending himself and his writings? The publications of Burns and Madan were offensive and controversial, while Horsley's *Review of the Case of the Protestant Dissenters* lacked charity and candor, was contradictory, inconsistent, weak, and sophistical, full of mis-representations and lies (224–30).

Priestley had not suggested the late application to Parliament and had lit-tle to do in promoting what his extreme unpopularity would have harmed. "Theodosius" lied when he said that Silas Deane confessed on his deathbed that Priestley had made him an atheist. A letter from Edward Bancroft denied that tale, while another from Matthew Dexter, a Baptist minister, stated that he was present at Deane's death and no one of Theodosius's description was present.[29] The series closed by thanking Burn and Madan. Though they had made unjust and railing accusations against persons who had done them no harm, they had provided the opportunity for an open discussion of differ-ences, which should lead to good community understanding.

While he was writing his *Familiar Letters,* Priestley was also attempting to deal with another example of Establishment prejudice and censorship. On 25 April he wrote to Sir Joseph Banks protesting the rejection by the Royal Society of the candidacy of Thomas Cooper, whose nomination certificate had been signed by Adair Crawford, Priestley, James Watt, and William Wat-son. Cooper was distinguished for his knowledge, abilities and activities, and his rejection was an affront to himself and unworthy of the Society. Banks

28. These direct attacks on the practices of the Established church—inequality of clergy income, inequity of tithes, and bishops in the House of Lords—began as early as 1773 and Priestley's *Letter of Advice . . . to Dissenters,* but their range and frequency had increased with *Corruptions* (1782), the *Letter to Pitt* (1787), "Remarks on Two Letters" (1790), and here.

29. See 290–300 and appendix 5. Priestley sent a notice to "Mr. Urban," 13 May 1790, *Gen-tleman's Magazine* 60 (1790): 384, asking for the insertion of Bancroft's letter totally refuting "Theodosius." "Theodosius" was tentatively identified as a Rev. Dr. Withers, but when Lindsey proposed that he be prosecuted for libel, Dr. Wither was already in Newgate, serving time for libeling Mrs. Fitzherbert; he died in prison on 24 July 1790.

responded, admitting that he had voted against Cooper, having no token of his scientific merit brought before the Society. No affront to Priestley was intended, he said, and no religious prejudice, but reasons independent of religion fully justified the Society's decision. Banks's answer was equivocal and Priestley knew it. Scientific merit was not required in more than one in ten of the Society's fellows, while Cooper's published *Essays* gave proof of mental ability and knowledge of chemistry.[30] The rejection was no doubt organized by Banks, very much a dictatorial president of the Royal Society, as Cooper was known to be a political radical.[31] Banks regarded his position as that of a privy councilor whose duties were more to promote the state than to encourage science. Cooper's entrepreneurial activities with chlorine bleaching were less important than his views of political reform and his approval of the French Revolution.

The assumed relationship between the French Revolution, agitation for political reform, and repeal of the Test and Corporation Acts was to poison English politics for several decades and provide the final reason for silencing Priestley.[32] Fox declared in Parliament that the Dissenters' motion to repeal had no relation to the situation in France, but adverse propaganda, avidly sponsored by the Pitt administration, drew parallels between the movements. There is little indication that repeal would have been granted independent of French upheavals, but the French Revolution certainly hardened Establishment hostility and political exigencies spread it.

The administration of William Pitt had come to power in 1784 without the backing of a majority in Commons. The election of that year, which gained him a majority, had been obtained with the active support of the

---

30. Priestley to Sir Joseph Banks, 25 April, 27 April 1790, Dibner Library, Smithsonian Institution Libraries; Banks to Priestley, 26 April 1790, draft, Banks Correspondence 2.9, Kew Gardens, Library. Banks's letter has on its verso a list of the voters and the way they voted. For an account of Banks's arrogance in dictating votes for fellows, see "A Correspondent" [Olinthus Gregory], "A Review of some leading Points in the Official Character and Proceedings of the late President of the Royal Society," *Philosophical Magazine* 56 (1820): 161–74, 241–57.

31. The application for Cooper was renewed in 1791 and again rejected. John Reeves, agent-provocateur for Pitt's Home Office in archreactionary activities against political and religious reformers and devoid of "scientific merit," was elected fellow of the Society the year that Cooper was rejected. Frida Knight, *Strange Case of Thomas Walker* (London: Lawrence & Wishart, 1957), 153–56, provides evidence that by 1794 Banks was closely associated with Reeves. John Gascoigne, "The Royal Society and the Emergence of Science as an Instrument of State Policy," *British Journal for the History of Science* 32 (1999): 171–84, argues the government role that Banks felt that he filled.

32. For a detailed treatment of this issue, see Goodwin, *Friends of Liberty;* also Davis, *Dissent in Politics,* 59–62.

king and his friends, but the king's intermittent madness from 1780 cast doubt on the continued effectiveness of his support. The threat of an apparently Whig-dominated Prince of Wales during the regency crisis of 1789–90 emphasized just how uncertain Pitt's administration might be. Then, with the invaluable help of Edmund Burke, a solution was found in "dangers to state and church" represented by Dissenters and other reformers emulating the French.

The initial reaction of most of the English to the French Revolution appears to have been one of satisfaction that the French were now to have the blessings of the English constitution. Certainly the majority of Priestley's Lunar Society friends were initially in favor. Mary Anne Schimmelpenninck (née Galton) described a Lunar Society meeting at the Galtons' in October 1788, when members crowded around Matthew Robinson Boulton to report on political discontent in France. She later wrote, "I have seen the reception of the news of the victory of Waterloo, and of the carrying of the Reform Bill, but I never saw joy comparable in its vivid intensity and universality to that occasioned by the early promise of the French Revolution. . . . Even with my father's scientific friends, politics became all-absorbing."[33]

Priestley and his Dissenter friends were ecstatic, seeing, in the religious toleration of a French constitutional monarchy, a pattern for themselves and (for Priestley at least) a harbinger of the millenarian restoration. Priestley's son, William, and brother-in law, William Wilkinson, were in France during July and August 1789 and described the "great scene. . . . There is indeed a glorious prospect for mankind before us. . . . [W]hen civil tyranny is all at an end, that of the church will soon be disposed of." He sent congratulations "on the glorious effulgence of liberty in France" to Richard Price, as a share of credit was his.[34]

Most of this enthusiasm for the Revolution came before the national convention and the Reign of Terror, but even after some instances of violence become known, most of the liberal reformers remained steadfast until the execution of Louis XVI and the war with France. William Smith, the Unitarian M.P., for example, excused "the excesses" because of the oppressive regime that preceded them, and expressed his conviction that the French

33. The vice-chancellor of Cambridge even issued a proclamation acclaiming the capture of the Bastille. See Ford K. Brown, *Life of William Godwin* (London: J. M. Dent, 1926), 34. See Eric Robinson, "The English 'Philosophes' and the French Revolution," *History Today* (1956): 116–21, and "An English Jacobin; James Watt, Junior, 1769–1848," *Cambridge Historical Journal* 3 (1960): 349–55; see also Schofield, *Lunar Society,* 244, 358–59, 370.

34. Priestley to Adam Walker, 21 Oct. 1789; to Richard Price, 29 Oct. 1790, Price Papers, Bodleian Library, Oxford; also Priestley to Lindsey, 22 July, 14 Aug, 21 Sept. 1789.

approved and that it was none of England's business.[35] But as news came from France, Priestley was concerned that the court in England would rally against the Revolution. His fears were soon realized in the opposition of the court and Pitt's administration, strongly supported, if not guided, by the self-fulfilling prophecies of Edmund Burke's *Reflections on the Revolution in France,* dated November 1790.[36]

There have been a number of attempts to explain what seemed to many persons (including Joseph Priestley) to be Burke's about-face, given his famous speeches of 1775 on conciliation with the American colonies. It seems clear, however, that this "Knight Errant of Feudality" had always been conservative. His famous *Reflections* was but another example of his romantic reaction against the rationalism of the Enlightenment, exhibited as early as 1756 and his *Philosophical Enquiry into the Origin of our Ideas of the Sublime and Beautiful. Reflections* is an overwrought expression of sympathy for the French nobility (and especially for the queen), without knowledge of French government or the unhappiness of the majority of Frenchmen, but it went through eleven editions within a year and is said to have reversed the attitude of the English toward the Revolution.[37]

There was, at first, a flood of responses to Burke's *Reflections,* ranging from the anonymous and angry *Reply of the Swinish Multitude to Mr. Burke* (picking up on one of Burke's less happy phrases) to Sir James Mackintosh's reasoned *Vindiciae Gallicae.* It provided the occasion for the first part of Tom Paine's *Rights of Man,* and of course Priestley also came to the defense of his friend, Richard Price, whose *Discourse on the Love of our Country*

---

35. Davis, *Dissent in Politics,* 65.

36. Louis Gottschalk, "Reflections on Burke's *Reflections on the French Revolution,*" *Proceedings of the American Philosophical Society* 100 (1956): 429: "Burke is not without responsibility for the misfortune he had foreseen . . . to an extent that no one can estimate accurately but that must have been considerable." One can, at least, argue that without the external enemies that Burke sanctioned, if not created, the French Revolution would have been quite different.

37. The phrase "Knight Errant" was quoted in Henry Yorke's *Spirit of John Locke on Civil Government* (1794) by Kramnick, "Republican Revisionism Revisited," 655. The bias of Burke's *Reflections* is spelled out in Iain Hampsher-Monk's review of *The Writings and Speeches of of Edmund Burke . . . .,* vol. 8, *The French Revolution 1790–1794 . . . ,*" *History of Political Thought* 12 (1991): 179–83. Goodwin's *Friends of Liberty,* 99–135, assesses the impact of Burke's *Reflections.* Two-thirds of James T. Boulton, *The Language of Politics in the Age of Wilkes and Burke* (London: Routledge & Kegan Paul, 1963), is devoted to Burke's *Reflections* and its answerers. It neglects Priestley's, though it quotes from it and cites one contemporary as saying Priestley was "by many degrees the ablest and most masterly of [Burke's] antagonists" (61). Richard Watson, Bishop of Landaff, wrote to Thomas Percival, 11 May 1791: "I have read both Dr. Priestley's and Mr. Paine's answers to Mr. Burke; and admire them both." Percival, *W.,* 1:clxix.

(1789) was ostensibly the inspiration for Burke's violent attack on the Enlightenment, radical political theory, and the French Revolution.[38]

Priestley had thought of Burke as an old friend. They had been acquainted since 1769, even dining together in Burke's London rooms. Burke subscribed to the *History of Optics* in 1772. Priestley heard Burke speak in the House of Commons on 3 April 1773, supporting the bill allowing Dissenters freedom from subscription, and in January 1774 Burke procured admission for Priestley to the Privy Council in which Wedderburn attacked Franklin. Both had supported the American Revolution. They were thrown together during Priestley's years with Shelburne, and when Priestley went to Birmingham, Burke visited him there, later describing Priestley as the most happy of men and the most to be envied! Subsequently, Priestley wrote for some "covers" that Burke had promised and provided some chemical information, "as you seemed to give some attention to the object of my experiments." The intimacy lasted till 1783 and Burke's participation in the Fox-North coalition. He encouraged the Prince of Wales to permit dedication to him of the methodized *Experiments and Observations:* "He is of considerable estimation in the learned world and a leader of weight & consequence among the Dissenters."[39] As late as 1789 Burke advised Fox that "Priestley is a very considerable leader among a set of men powerful . . . in elections, and I am quite sure that the good or ill humor of these men will be sensibly felt at the general election."

Priestley's *Letters to Burke,* written within two months of the appearance of *Reflections,* mourned the end of that friendship and mutual respect. He was sorry that Burke could no longer be classed among the friends of the *"cause of liberty, civil* or *religious."* He had heard Burke plead the cause of American liberty with singular satisfaction (39), but now he found him on the side of bigoted clergy, classing the enemies of establishments as *"cheats and hypocrites."*

Burke's intemperate publication, unrestrained by any regard to decency, was unworthy of him (46, 48), but the issue was not an individual's conduct

---

38. Joseph Priestley, *Letters to the Right Honourable Edmund Burke, occasioned by his Reflections on the Revolution in France, &c.* (Birmingham: J. Johnson, 1791), dated 1 Jan. 1791. I have used the second edition, 1791.

39. Priestley reported on his intimacy with Burke in a letter to the editor of the *Monthly Magazine,* dated 1 Feb. 1804 (just days before his death, and printed as appendix 24 in *W.* 25: 391–98). The phrase "happiest of men" is quoted in a letter, Lindsey to Turner, 1 Sept. 1783, *W.* 1.1:253–54. Priestley to Edmund Burke, 11 Dec. 1782, *SciAuto.,* 102; Burke to Fox, 9 Sept. 1789; Burke to J. W. Payne, secretary to the Prince of Wales, 24, 28 Sept., 1 Oct. 1789, in [Edmund Burke], *Correspondence of Edmund Burke,* ed. Alfred Cobban and Robert A. Smith (Cambridge: Cambridge University Press, 1967), 6:14–15, 22–24, 27–28.

but the wisdom of connecting religion with the business of the state. The real question was whether the French were justified in changing an arbitrary form of government for another. Burke had misrepresented his sources. "His *new* principles are the *old* ones of *passive obedience* and *non-resistance*," with no way of changing past governance.

If one conceded that government exists for the good of the people, then surely the French had both the right and the obligation to change theirs if it did not work—and their neighbors had no business in the affair. It was wrongly predicted that the Americans would run into confusion; why should the French not emulate them, especially "as they have no enemies to contend with and interrupt their proceedings" (9). Perhaps the National Assembly had acted injudiciously on occasion, but the nation obviously approved of it, and its composition was more truly representative than the English House of Commons.

Somers, Hoadley, Locke and others had explained the first principles of government. Kings were servants of the people, and no pompous words, superstitious respect, or pride in idolatry of a fellow creature could change that. The French queen probably deserved impolite treatment, if she was intriguing against the liberties of the people (18).[40] The facts of the case in England were that the people in 1688 chose a king and a line of succession for future kings, establishing a precedent that would keep princes within bounds. The acts of Queen Anne's Parliament showed that Burke's contrary assertion amounted to high treason (37).[41]

Priestley denounced Burke also for his treatment of Price, who was well known for his patriotism, benevolence and public spirit, wisdom and virtue. The clergy annually used the pulpit on 30 January to defend arbitrary power. How was Price worse for using his to preach in favor of liberty? Apparently Burke would support any establishment of any religion so long as it was not a conventicle. Governments were human contrivances and had nothing to do with the worship of God. To intrude civil power into religion, as England had done, with the church in the power of king and Parliament, was the greatest absurdity in the world. The church's concern was for its revenues, which, by the British constitution, were never independent of state authority.

---

40. Burke's emotional reaction to the humiliation (as it was then) of Marie Antoinette prompted Tom Paine's famous riposte, in *Rights of Man,* that Burke pitied the plumage but forgot the dying bird.

41. This was the ground for Lord Stanhope's scheme to impeach Burke for high treason; see Priestley to Lindsey, 26 Nov. 1790, where he also noted the attempts of aristocrats to subvert the French government.

Religion, moreover, was not the source of all social good: it neither fed nor clothed the people. Dissenting ministers and Methodist leaders were more respected by their congregations than the Anglican clergy by theirs. Experience had shown, Priestley argued, that ministers were more responsible, and more productive of science and works of erudition, when dependent upon their congregations for their places and income (103).

After twice making no opposition to the application by Dissenters for admission to places of trust and profit in the government, Burke now, unexpectedly, opposed with peculiar warmth and fierceness even a simple discussion of anything relating to religion.[42] The real danger to the church lay not in repeal of the Test Acts but in the growth of public debt. An insupportable burden of debt would lead to a necessary reformation of the civil government, to be followed by that of the church: bishops losing their seats in Parliament; abandonment of spiritual courts, tithes, and subscription to the Thirty-Nine Articles; repeal of the Test laws, and the opening of the universities to Dissenters. And these reforms would make the church stronger.

The French nation and the liberal, rational, and virtuous part of the world were to be congratulated on the prospect of civil and religious liberty opened by the French Revolution. The French and American Revolutions made a wonderful and important era in the history of mankind, a change from debasing servitude to exalted freedom. They held out the promise of a government calculated for the general good, leaving men the enjoyment of as many of their natural rights as possible and not interfering with matters of religion any more than with philosophy or medicine (145). The empire of reason would be the reign of universal peace and good will (150).

The mention of natural rights emphasizes the basic cultural difference between the Priestleys of the eighteenth century and the Burkes of the approaching nineteenth. Sprinkled through the *Letters to Burke* are phrases that Burke would strongly reject, representing the reaction of incipient Romanticism to the Enlightenment. "What is *metaphysically* true is *strictly* and *properly* true; in what sense can it be false?" "Laws are made by men and may be changed by them" (33). "The folly of one age ought to be removed by the wisdom of a subsequent one" (118).

The *Letters* were Priestley's strongest public criticism to date of the British constitution, though he actually softened parts of *Letters* on Lindsey's advice, deleting one letter entirely and also removing a leaf where he had

---

42. McCalman, "New Jerusalems," declares: "Burke, of course, had been connecting Dissenting politics with subversion long before the Price sermon; his fears for his house and family during the Gordon Riots probably account for much of his later anti-Dissenting rabidity" (314).

(correctly) claimed that the Pitt administration was unfavorable to the French Revolution.[43] Given Burke's notorious temper and touchiness, there would be no hope for a reconciliation after publication of the *Letters,* and in fact Burke was furious and denounced Priestley and his friends in the House of Commons.[44] There was also no hope that Priestley would ever gain favor with Pitt or his friends, though they should have been grateful to him for providing a focus for the turmoil they were creating.

During the period from 1788 to 1792 the Pitt administration controlled at least ten morning newspapers and planted most news accounts of political activities. Burke's *Reflections* and his subsequent speeches would not have had their influence had William Pitt not supplied the evidence upon which Burke's arguments depended. Seeing to it that the country seemed to be in peril, Pitt's newspapers referred darkly to certain seditious activities that they could not at the time specify, hinting at ominous information that could not be revealed. There was no evidence and hence nothing which could be proved or disproved by opposition newspapers. And, for the public unreached by newspapers, there were the vicious cartoons, especially those of James Gillray, also in the pay of Pitt's Treasury secretary, displayed in shop windows, clubs, workshops, and alehouses.[45] In the long run, Pitt and Burke

43. Sometime during 1791 there was published anonymously a pamphlet entitled *A Political Dialogue on the General Principles of Government* (London, 1791), which is more critical. It has been assumed that this was written by Priestley, as it begins with a reference to his anonymous "dialogue form," *Present State of Liberty in Great Britain* (1769), and it is included in the catalogue of books written by Priestley appended by Thomas Cooper to the first edition of *Memoirs of Dr. Joseph Priestley, to the Year 1795 . . . With a Continuation . . . by his son . . . and Observations on his Writings, by Thomas Cooper* (London: J. Johnson, 1807), catalogue, iii, item 21; and it may be "my Political Tract," mentioned in a 1791 letter to Theophilus Lindsey. I do not believe this is by Priestley. The style is too direct, the role of protagonists of the 1769 dialogue are reversed, and the criticisms of the English constitution fail to mention Priestley's major political concern—the Established church. Priestley does not refer to the pamphlet in any of his writings, including the U.S. edition of his *Lectures on History, and General Policy,* with its additional lecture (42), where the reference would be appropriate in his criticism of the English constitution. Crook, *Bibliography of Priestley,* had not seen a copy, and I have consulted W. 25:81–108.

44. Priestley to Lindsey, 23 Dec. 1790: "I cannot read Burke anymore." Lucyle Werkmeister, *The London Press, 1772–1792* (Lincoln: University of Nebraska Press, 1963), 9, 16–18, and elsewhere, suggests that Burke's behavior respecting the Foxite Whigs had partially to do with their failure to support him in the Hastings Trial as he thought himself entitled to be. Vanity, hurt *amour propre,* pomposity, and an inordinate (for a politician) dread of ridicule made him unduly excitable and an easy victim of Pitt's allurements.

45. Most of the information on newspapers is derived, to an occasional paraphrase, from Werkmeister's *London Press,* esp. 344. Carl B. Cone, *English Jacobins: Reformers in Late Eighteenth-Century England* (New York: Charles Scribner's Sons, 1968), 201–2, doubts that Pitt deliberately stirred up fears of "Jacobins" to further his political ambitions. William Thomas

Fig. 4 Gillray anti-Priestley cartoon, c. 1791

encouraged those "enemies to contend with" whom Priestley had noted lacking in the French Revolution. In the shorter run, they inadvertently encouraged Birmingham rioters.

For Birmingham, the home of the great heresiarch, embraced the picture of danger and impending violence. As early as mid-December 1789 its magistrates arranged with the War Office for dragoons to be available should the Dissenters riot when the Establishment celebrated the 1790 defeat of the Repeal bill, a fear mirrored in Spencer Madan's sermon of 14 February and his letters. The event passed without incident and the dragoons were freed for other duties, but Establishment tempers were not eased by Priestley's *Familiar Letters* or his *Letters to Burke*. In June 1791 Priestley attempted to enlist Boulton and Watt in a Warwickshire Constitutional Society. They declined—it was imprudent "during the present effervescence in other countries" to risk overturning all good government—and the Society apparently did not prosper.[46] However, on 11 July a group calling themselves "the

Laprade, *England and the French Revolution, 1789–1797* (Baltimore: Johns Hopkins University Press, 1909), 184–86, convincingly argued otherwise.

46. Priestley to Watt, 27 June; Watt to Priestley, draft, 8 July 1791, Priestley Misc. Doc. 3, JWP C1/18; JWP C1/20, Birmingham City Archives. Eric Robinson, "New Light on the Priestley Riots," *Historical Journal* 3 (1960): 73–75, reports that the answer was signed by both

Friends of Freedom" advertised in Aris's *Birmingham Gazette* that a dinner would be held at Thomas Dadley's Hotel, Temple Row, on 14 July 1791 to commemorate the second anniversary of the fall of the Bastille. That notice was immediately followed by another, warning that a list of the persons attending the dinner would be published the next day. Also on the 11th, anonymous and inflammatory handbills, one ultrarevolutionary and the other reactionary, were distributed throughout the town. By 12 July there were rumors that a riot was to be expected on the 14th, but Dadley protested a move to cancel the dinner and it was held as scheduled.

The dinner commenced at about three o'clock, attended by eighty-one persons and chaired by James Keir. The diners were verbally harassed as they assembled, but the hecklers dispersed—to return between seven and eight, when the celebrants had long since scattered in peace. The crowd grew in number and milled about, frustrated and uncertain until about 9:30 and a suggestion that they go on to the "meetings." The crowd now became a mob; New Meeting House was destroyed, Old Meeting partially demolished; and then Priestley's house was struck.

Priestley was not there, nor had he attended the dinner, yielding to the requests of friends that he stay away. When news reached him that a mob was coming, he was persuaded to leave his house and seek refuge with the Russells. Catherine Russell later described Priestley's behavior: "The extreme agitation of our minds did not prevent us from admiring the divine appearance of the excellent Dr. Priestley. No human being could, in my opinion, appear in any trial more like divine, or shew a nearer resemblance to our Saviour, than he did then. . . . Countenance expressing the highest devotion, turned as it were from this scene [the destruction of his home] and fixed with pure and calm resignation."[47] News reached him that the mob had sworn to kill him, and he and his family, at some hazard, went on to Heath and safety with his daughter and son-in-law, Mr. and Mrs. William Finch. That soon became inconvenient, and he continued on to London, reaching refuge with the Vaughan family.

Boulton and Watt. Priestley mentions the abortive attempt to form a constitutional society in Warwickshire in his *Appeal to the Public*, 24–25. The apparent failure of that society perhaps explains Priestley's indignant (and less than candid) letter of 7 March 1793 to the editor of the *Morning Chronicle* denying Burke's claim that he was, or had ever been, a member of any political society, or signed any paper originating with one. *W.* 15:499–501.

47. [Catherine Russell], "Journal relating to the Birmingham riots, by a young lady of one of the persecuted families," dated 14 July 1791, *The Christian Reformer* 2 (1835): 293–304, 295–97.

The riots were now well begun and would continue for two and a half days. By the time they had been quelled, twenty-seven houses and four Meeting Houses had been destroyed. This is the skeleton of the story. Now, more than two centuries later, that story can be fleshed out only by reference to eyewitness accounts, hearsay, and thirty-six affidavits collected by William Russell—most of them from an anti-Establishment position. Nonetheless, there is enough agreement in accounts from different sources for modern assessments to concede that the riots were probably prompted and later directed by local Establishment figures—specifically by three local magistrates: Dr. Benjamin Spencer, vicar of Aston, Joseph Carles of Handsworth, a J.P. of Staffordshire and Warwickshire, and John Brooke, undersheriff of Warwickshire.[48]

The fuller account declares that warnings of an expected riot were widespread two days before it began. Spencer and Carles were among the crowd harassing diners on their way into the hotel. Dadley located the magistrates drinking at the Swan Inn and thrice begged them to intervene as the crowd gathered after the dinner. They finally returned to the hotel, but made no attempt to disperse the mob until Carles (or Brooke, whose house next to the hotel was endangered) directed them to the New Meeting, promising protection so long as they did not attack private property. The key to the fire engine hut was missing until found in the possession of the Rev. Mr. Curtis, too late for the engine to be used at the New Meeting fire.[49]

48. The best general account of the Birmingham Riots is probably that of Rose, "Priestley Riots of 1791." The best local assessment that of Dennis Martineau, "Playing Detective: The Priestley Riots of 1791," *Birmingham Historian* 12 & 13 (1997): 11–18. Each concludes that responsibility, if any, lay with local Establishment figures, who were later dismayed to learn that the national government disapproved but would cover up for them. Eugene Charlton Black, *The Associations: British Extraparliamentary Political Organization, 1769–1793* (Cambridge: Harvard University Press, 1963), writes that papers in the Public Record Office (HO 42/19 and TS 11/923/ 3304) seem to dispose of any notion that the magistracy was not involved (234). See also R. E. S. Maddison and Francis R. Maddison, "Joseph Priestley and the Birmingham Riots," *Notes and Records of the Royal Society of London* 12 (1957): 98–113; Arthur Sheps, "Public Perception of Joseph Priestley, the Birmingham Dissenters, and the Church-and-King Riots of 1791," *Eighteenth Century* 13 (1989): 46–64; and Goodwin, *Friends of Liberty,* 181.

49. There are a number of contemporary accounts of the riots, among them John Ryland, "Recollections of Dr. Priestley," and S[amuel] K[enrick] to a friend, 21 July 1791, in John Creasey, "The Birmingham Riots of 1791," *Transactions of the Unitarian Historical Society* 4 (1927–30): 417–29, and 13 (1963–66): 111–17, 113–17; [Mrs. W. Byng Kenrick], ed., *Chronicles of a Nonconformist Family: The Kenricks of Wynne Hall, Exeter and Birmingham* (Birmingham: Cornish Brothers, 1932), 58–59; [Russell], "Journal relating to the Birmingham riots"; William Hutton, *The Life of William Hutton, F.A.S.S., including a Particular Account of the Riots at Birmingham in 1791* (London: Baldwin, Cradock, and Joy, 1816), esp. 151–213, written in August 1791. Hutton, who was not a Unitarian but suffered because he was commissioner of

Fig. 5   Lithograph print of the ruins of Priestley's Birmingham home after the riots

Thomas Wright Hill, Thomas Clark, and a small body of fellow pupils in Priestley's religious classes offered to defend Fair Hill against the rioters but Priestley declined, thinking it wrong to oppose violence caused by religious bias. Hill and Clark moved some of the contents to an adjoining field, barred the doors and closed the shutters, but the mob broke in; Spencer witnessed the proceedings and did not protest. Hill seized one of the mob and took him to the jail, but the keeper released the rioter, declaring that he "had orders to take in no prisoners that night." One of the magistrates (Spencer or Carles) released a looter captured at the Rylands on 15 July. Hill's fiancée heard one of the magistrates (Spencer) say to Mrs. Anderton, the morning after the riots began, "We'n gin it 'em." She never doubted that the high church gentry, including the magistrates (some, if not all) instigated the riots.[50]

the Court of Requests, particularly blamed "a hungry attorney" (Carles) and "a leading justice" (Brooke) and delighted in claims that both were bankrupt in later years (63n).

    50. Eliezer Edwards, *Sir Rowland Hill, K.C.B.: A Biographical and Historical Sketch, with records of the Family to which He belonged* (London: Frederick Warne and Co., 1879), 19–20;

Fig. 6   Lithograph print of New Meeting Chapel in ruins after riots of 1791

By early Friday the 15th, there were extensive reports of a list of the houses to be destroyed. The riot act was not read. The magistrates rejected the volunteered aid of an army recruiting party, then in Birmingham, with the words, "We have our plans, We have our own plans." The mob was tripartite: local apprentices and laborers for fun, transient looters, and a disciplined nucleus of rioters, consisting of a group of thirty men "kept sober for night work." Samuel Garbett, a churchman, reporting on the riots to Lord Lansdowne on 26 July 1791, cited indications that the rioters were led by "a decent man" and subject to some kind of discipline. Some part, clearly not rabble, hunted refugees on horseback and one of these declared, in Catherine Russell's hearing: "I know there's a d— —d Presbyterian hereabouts, we'll have him before morning." The magistrates declined sending for troops on

[Hill], *Remains of Hill,* 116; Obituary of Thomas Clark dated 25 Oct. notes that Priestley gave Clark several volumes of his works, inscribed with thanks for his services at the riots (*Christian Reformer* [1847]: 759–60).

the 14th, while the meeting houses were destroyed. George Humphreys, whose house was destroyed on the 16th, went to Dr. Spencer at the house of Mr. Anderton on the 15th to ask if troops had been sent for and found they had not. The magistrates waited until late that afternoon to send a request for troops to the Home Office in London, forestalling private appeals by Russell and by Garbett.[51] When the troops arrived from Nottingham on Sunday afternoon, 17 July, the mob just melted away.

On 27 July the government issued a proclamation in the king's name, offering a £100 reward for detection and conviction of persons who had engaged in the riots. A solicitor of the treasury in Pitt's administration as well as the Foxite M.P. William Smith, acting for the Committee of the Deputies and Delegates of the Dissenters in London, were sent to Birmingham to see that the matter was brought to trial. The trial, held at the Warwick Assizes in August, was a travesty.[52] Samuel Whitbread, another "Old Whig" M.P., therefore asked the Commons, in May 1792, for a government inquiry into the riots. The request was based on "thirty-six affidavits, taken before a commissioner of the court of King's-bench for taking affidavits, all agreeing in substance, and all charging upon the magistrates a gross neglect of duty; and some carrying their charges to a much greater extent." These were affidavits obtained by Russell, at the suggestion of Smith and on the advice of the Treasury solicitor, for submission at the abortive trial of the rioters. Whitbread and Smith read extracts from them and, as was to be expected, these included extreme and perhaps exaggerated impressions of the magistrates' behavior.

Carles was quoted assuring the mob that "the justices would protect them in every thing that was right. . . . 'Do not do any other mischief than pulling down the meetings, and I will stand your friend, as far as lies in my power.' Members of the mob cried 'to the New Meeting, justice Carles will protect us.' On Sunday the 17th, he cried 'Church and King for ever. . . . Don't leave them Presbyterian dogs a place standing.' Dr. Spencer called several of the

---

51. "Letters, Copies of Letters and other Papers chiefly Correspondence . . . from Samuel Garbett to the Earl of Shelburne," photostatic reproductions, Birmingham Reference Library, iii, #56, 23 July; #58 in copy of letter to the Dean of Christ Church, Oxford; #65, 31 July; #67, 26 July; #68, 31 Aug.; #69, 5 Aug., all 1791.

52. By act of Parliament, 1 George I, the Riot Act of 1716, it was a duty of the magistrates to have rioters apprehended and brought to trial within twelve months of their offense. In this case, the trial was supererogatory. *A Full and Accurate Report of the Trials of the Birmingham Rioters, at the late Assizes for the Country of Warwick; containing Sir Richard Perryn's Charge to the Grand Jury, the Speeches of Counsel, at length, and the Whole of the Evidence* (London: J. Walter, T. Longman, W. Richardson, and all other Booksellers, 1791). The jurors were selected by Brooke, and only twelve persons were arraigned. Five were found not guilty and two acquitted on the most frivolous of grounds, one excused on account of his age, and four were convicted, of whom one was pardoned by the king and three, notorious criminals all, were executed.

mob to him and made them huzza and join with him in the shout of 'Church and King' saying 'you have done very well what you have done.' Brooke said 'My lads, you see your power; my boys, you see that if any attempt is made against the government of this country, you have it in your power to quash it, You have done enough, now go home.'"

Many of these remarks might be read as those of despairing magistrates attempting to minimize a political crisis beyond their control. Instead of taking that line, Pitt's ministers moved to balk the inquiry—which suggests that the zeal of the Birmingham magistrates was at least suspect. The attorney general protested that the affidavits were not in proper form and that the substance ought to have been taken in the shape of information. Smith replied that the solicitor to the Treasury had advised the concerned persons to adopt the method now complained of. Dundas protested that the government had not been remiss—which was not at issue. A petition to the king sent from Birmingham, thanking him for sending troops, was cited to show that there were no grievances to remedy. After specious arguments against the motion sufficient to inform the House that the government opposed, the House divided, with 46 votes for and 189 against.[53]

Priestley intended to return to Birmingham. Indeed, he planned to deliver a sermon from the ruins of New Meeting on the text "Father, forgive them, for they know not what they do." It would have been a dramatic performance—and probably a deadly one as well, given the sentiments rife in Birmingham at the time. His friends united in discouraging such imprudence and their wisdom prevailed, though Samuel Galton declared that he would meet him "happy in an occasion to avow the most explicit attachment to a person whose friendship does me the greatest honor." Watt wrote that Priestley had a duty "to your family, to your friends, & to humanity in general . . . not to risk a life so valuable to them all."[54] At the age of fifty-eight Priestley had been driven from his home, house, laboratory, manuscripts destroyed and library dispersed, exiled first to London/Hackney and eventually to the United States.

53. "Debate on Mr. Whitbread's Motion respecting the Riots at Birmingham," 21 May 1792, *Parliamentary History of England,* ed. J. Wright (London: T. C. Hansard, for Longman, Hurst, Rees, Orme & Brown, 1817), 29:1431–63. The affidavits are preserved in the Public Record Office, London, HO 42/19. Davis, *Dissent in Politics,* 81; Draft petition n.d., JWP/W/13/3, Birmingham City Archives.

54. See Samuel Garbett to Lansdowne, 23 July 1791, extract of Priestley letter, Garbett-Shelburne Papers, 3:65. See also Priestley to John Wilkinson, 8 Sept. 1791, containing a copy of Galton's letter, Warr.; Schofield, *Lunar Society,* 361; Priestley to the New Meeting congregation, 8 Oct. 1791; James Watt to Priestley, 21 Oct. 1791, draft, JWP W/13/5, Birmingham City Archives, Reference Library.

PART III

CLAPTON/HACKNEY
(1791–1794)
AND
NORTHUMBERLAND, PENNSYLVANIA
(1794–1804)

XIV

POLITICS, SCIENCE, EDUCATION, RELIGION

Once free of the rioters, Priestley was still unsettled. He couldn't remain at Heath, though his wife had to be there for the birth of her first grandchild. He stayed for a time with the Vaughan family, Samuel Salte, and Joseph Johnson, his London publisher, but was reluctant to tarry with anybody lest he attract rioters. He wrote to friends, briefly reporting events and letting them know he was safe, and they in turn sent him their condolences. By 7 October he had settled on a house in Clapton, just north of Hackney, about two miles northeast of London, a five-minute walk to Gravel-Pit Meeting and a few hundred yards west of New College.[1]

He seems to have become reasonably happy at Clapton/Hackney. He felt uneasy venturing far as malignity increased against everything liberal, but he had a group of friendly and intelligent persons with whom to interact— those known on previous visits to London: Joseph Johnson, Lindsey, Mary Wollstonecraft, John Paradise, and the Vaughans—and new ones, such as George Dyer and Samuel Rogers, essayist and poet, in whose home he spent a night before leaving for America. He read William Godwin's *Enquiry*

---

1. Mike Gray, "Joseph Priestley in Hackney," *Enlightenment and Dissent* 2 (1983): 107–10, has identified the site of the house as that now occupied by 111–115 Lower Clapton Road, south of the junction with Clapton Passage. According to William P. Griffith, "Priestley in London," *Notes and Records of the Royal Society of London* 38 (1983): 16n47, a photograph of the house as it appeared in 1880 is preserved in the Hackney Archives.

concerning Political Justice, stating his "opinion that the book contains a great quantity of original thinking, and will be uncommonly useful."[2] He even visited Tom Paine at the house of Thomas C. Rickman and met Horne Tooke while dining with Romney and Samuel Rogers at Tuffins Coffeehouse.

Before he could begin to settle in at Clapton/Hackney, Priestley had unfinished business related to Birmingham. First, he needed to set the story straight respecting the riots with people at large and, a belated second, to arrange for his compensation for damages according to statutes. On 19 July 1791 Priestley wrote a letter to "My late townsmen and Neighbours," sent to the editor of the *Morning Chronicle* along with another by William Russell. The same month he and Keir signed a letter sent to the printer of the *Birmingham and Stafford Chronicle,* and in August Priestley sent a letter to the printer of the *Birmingham Gazette,* complaining that his private letters had been taken and circulated, with a warning that this was theft.[3]

The letter to his townsmen was a short self-exculpation. He had lived peacefully in Birmingham for eleven years. The people's bigoted superiors had led them to the destruction of "the most truly valuable and useful apparatus of philosophical instruments . . . ever possessed . . . a library corresponding to that apparatus . . . destroyed *manuscripts,* which have been the result of the laborious study of many years" (4). This had been done "to one who neither did nor imagined harm to you. I know nothing of inflammatory hand-bills, did not attend the dinner (an innocent expression of joy in the emancipation from tyranny of a neighbouring nation). Your conduct has dealt your cause a greater blow . . . than I and all my friends have ever aimed at it" (5).

As early as August 1791 Priestley began the composition of *An Appeal to the Public on the Subject of the Riots in Birmingham.* Copies of the *Appeal* were sent in sheets to his friends—chiefly Lindsey and Russell in London and Galton, Keir, Wedgwood, and Withering, of the Lunar Society, for criticism.

---

2. M. Ray Adams, *Studies in the Literary Background of English Radicalism* (Lancaster: Franklin and Marshall College Studies, No. 5., 1957), 36. See P. W. Clayden, *Early Life of Samuel Rogers* (Boston: Roberts Brothers, 1888), 182, 214, 229. On Godwin, see Martin Fitzpatrick, "William Godwin and the Rational Dissenters," *Price-Priestley Newsletter* 3 (1979): 11–13; Fitzpatrick even suggests that some revisions in the *Enquiry* may be owing to Priestley suggestions.

3. The first three letters were printed together as *Dr. Priestley's Letter to the Inhabitants of Birmingham, Mr. Keir's Vindication of the Revolution Dinner, and Mr. Russell's Account of Proceedings relating to it, with the Toasts, &c.* (London: J. Johnson, 1791) and included as appendices in Priestley's *Appeal to the Public, on the Subject of the Riots in Birmingham.* See Priestley to the Birmingham Gazette, Aug. 1791, W. 1.2:132.

His Dissenter friends in London made some suggestions but urged him on. His friends in the Lunar Society recommended suspension of its publication or some alteration of some of the passages. Keir, for example, wrote to Priestley on 18 November to dissuade him from publishing the *Appeal* in its proposed form, stating that it would "irritate his professed enemies, and furnish them with a new source of abuse"; he feared that "government would become more remiss in prosecuting the magistrates and in protecting the dissenters in future if they should meet with any passage that should give them offence." Priestley "cancelled eleven leaves" in an attempt to meet these criticisms, but continued with the publication, as Dissenter friends from London approved and he had formally announced his intention to publish such an appeal.[4]

His *Appeal to the Public,* dedicated "To the People of England" and signed 1 November 1791, was published that year.[5] It is not conciliatory, accusing his townsmen and others of violating the principles of English government (v–xv). The preface declares that his enemies were incapable of being satisfied; to them, his facts were falsehoods, his indignation insolence, and his Christian meekness hypocrisy. He appealed to his countrymen in general against the high church party, whose violation of the law was as bad as anything in the French Revolution. He had pointed out deficiencies in the constitution out of a love of his country and now trusted that this illustration of bigotry would show the evils of a civil establishment of religion.

By the time of publication Priestley had received twenty-two condolences (including seven from France), but from England, revealingly, only one (from the Derby Philosophical Society) that was not from Dissenters.[6]

4. Priestley to William Russell, Lindsey, Bretland; to John Wilkinson, 23 Nov. 1791, Warr.; to Josiah Wedgwood, 22 Nov. 1791, Bolton, #68. Wedgwood responded with some six pages of detailed critique, 30 Nov. 1791, John Rylands University Library of Manchester, which, when compared with the text of the first and second editions of the *Appeal,* show that some variations were made before publication. Priestley to William Withering, 2 Dec. 1791, Bolton, #69. James Keir to Priestley, 18 Nov. 1791, Priestley to James Keir, 12 Jan. 1792, in Moillet, *James Keir,* 123–25, 127–28; Bolton, #119n1, 72.

5. Priestley, *Appeal on to the Public, on the Subject of the Riots in Birmingham, to which are added, Strictures on a Pamphlet intitled "Thoughts on the late Riot in Birmingham"* (Birmingham: J. Johnson, 1791).

6. In this instance, at least, Priestley's *Appeal* was wrong by the second edition. The Rev. Thomas Edwards, fellow of Jesus College, Cambridge, and an Establishment clergyman, expressed his dismay at the bigotry of the Church-and-King riots in his *Discourse on the Limits and Importance of Free Enquiry in Matters of Religion* (Cambridge, 1792). There was also an "Address not yet signed, from the Bishops and Clergy of the Church of England to the Rev. Dr. Priestley," compiled anonymously. See also *An Appendix to the Account of the Birmingham Riots; containing Interesting Papers omitted in that Work, or since Published. With the Damages*

He had declined invitations to go to France, believing his duty lay in employing his remaining years to the most advantage to his own country. He challenged those who asserted his presence at the fateful dinner, his introduction of controversy into Birmingham, to bring him to court; there would be a higher court before which they must finally appear.

Much of the *Appeal* repeated at length what Priestley had already written (at length) in his *Letter to Pitt* (1787), *Conduct by Dissenters* sermon (1789), preface to his *Letter to Burn* (1790), *Familiar Letters to . . . Birmingham* (1790), *Remarks on Two Letters* (1790), and the *Letters to Burke* (1791)— e.g., the bigotry of Birmingham clergy (with examples) contrasted to his previous friendships with clergymen, his denial of significant involvement in appeals for repeal of the Test and Corporation Acts, and the innocence of celebrating the French Revolution.

He described the riots, emphasizing their organized character and their basic lack of any real connection with the famous dinner. The issue was religion, not politics. But why, he asked, should Dissenters not take an interest in politics? When the government was friendly to Dissent, its rulers were glad to avail themselves of their pens and swords; why now the violent objections? The high church party had, it was true, never been tolerant. "There is a kind of ignorance that is highly criminal, arising . . . from a secret malignity of temper which conceals itself under the notion of zeal for religion" (96).

A good police system, Priestley wrote, could have put down both the Gordon and the Birmingham riots, without need for a standing army or voluntary associations for self-defense. The difference between the severe retribution suffered by the Gordon rioters and the mildness toward those of Birmingham was striking, while nothing could compensate for his personal loss of laboratory apparatus, library, and manuscripts.[7] Attempts to suppress expression of man's sentiments, he warned, inevitably backfired. At the worst

---

claimed by, and Allowed to, the Sufferers (no publisher, n.d., 1792/3?), while Rev. Samuel Parr wrote in defense of Priestley in his *Letter from Irenopolis* (Birmingham, 1792) and *A Sequel to the Printed Paper* (London, 1792), in William Field, *Memoirs of the Life, Writings, and Opinions of the Rev. Samuel Parr . . .* (London: Henry Colburn, 1828). Samuel Parr is quoted as saying of Priestley: "He has done more to promote human learning than any man in Europe."

7. He listed the losses of manuscripts, for which no reparation could be made: his *Diaries* from 1752; several *Commonplace Books* with notes of reading; a *Register* of philosophical experiments; his *Sermons, Prayers,* &c.; *Notes* and a *Paraphrase of the New Testament;* a *New Translation* of *Psalms, Proverbs, Ecclesiastes; Letters to Members of New Jerusalem Church* (subsequently published from a copy); his *Memoirs; letters* from friends and learned foreigners; biographical account of persons in his *Chart of Biography; Illustrations of Hartley's Doctrine of Associations of Ideas* and *farther Observations on the Human Mind; Lectures on the Constitution and Laws of England* and on the *History of England;* his *Will, Receipts,* and *Accounts.*

suppression could, as in France, lead to revolution, at best to emigration, which weakened the country, as with the Moriscos of Spain, the Protestants of France at the revocation of the Edict of Nantes, and the Puritans of England. Half the wealth of the nation, he claimed, had been the work of Dissenters, and this was threatened by the intolerance of the Church of England. The church's behavior at Birmingham had, in the eyes of all Europe, covered the country with shame.

Inevitably, the *Appeal* elicited a number of critical responses. To that by the Rev. Edward Burn of Birmingham Priestley just as inevitably replied in his *Appeal to the Public, Part II*.[8] The truth of the facts asserted in part 1, being incontrovertible and attested by affidavits reported in Mr. Debrett's *Parliamentary Register,* it should have been unnecessary to write more, Priestley said, but the Birmingham clergy had selected Mr. Burn to deny facts and repeat their censures of Dissent. It behooved them to produce contrary evidence. This "Age of Revolutions" should teach the high church party moderation, not insolence (437).

Priestley added, in appendix 17, a condolence sent by the "Deputies and Delegates of the Dissenters in England" in answer to the sneers in the *Gentleman's Magazine* that Dissenters in general, and especially their delegates in London, had failed to sympathize. A copy of that condolence was sent to the editor of the *Gentleman's,* where it was neither printed nor acknowledged. The rest of part 2 primarily reasserted, with more specifics, the accusations of the *Appeal.* Priestley neatly turned the infamous "Gunpowder Joe" metaphor back upon the Birmingham clergy—it was they who had employed violence (467). He catalogued events since the riots: invention of new falsehoods against Dissent, proceedings of the abortive trial, refusal of Commons to inquire into the riots' causes, and failure to return adequate recompense for losses—all confirmed the religious prejudices and biases of the high church party.

During the riots an advertisement had appeared in Birmingham papers and been posted on broadsides, reading in part: "the great losses which are sustained by *your burning* and *destroying* of the houses of so many individuals, will eventually fall upon the *county at large* . . . the whole of which . . . will be charged upon the respective parishes and paid out of the rates."[9]

8. Priestley, *An Appeal to the Public on the Subject of the Riots in Birmingham. Part II. To which is added, a Letter from W. Russell, Esq. to the Author* (London: J. Johnson, 1792), but with preface signed 1 Jan. 1793. I have used the version in *W.* 19:434–600, including 32 appendices.

9. Reprinted in appendix 8 of *Appeal to the Public,* 144–45. The Act of 1716, which established the responses required of magistrates at a riot, included also the civil remedy against the Hundred for restitution due to persons whose property was damaged.

Nevertheless, the efforts of the sufferers to obtain their damages dragged on and on. In Birmingham, property to the value of £50,000 was destroyed, of which £26,961 2s. 3d. was finally paid by a rate on the "Hundred," in which Birmingham was included. The committee that acted for the Hundred of Hemlingford respecting damages included the justices who incited the riots. George Hardinge, attorney general for the queen from 1789, with a reputation for professional eloquence before juries, was employed at Warwick in April 1792 as counsel for the Hundred against the claimants. He employed his abilities to abuse Priestley, who attended the assize against the advice of friends. Samuel Garbett wrote to Lord Lansdowne (Shelburne) that as much as £7,000 "were expended by Country Gentlemen to prevent the Sufferers obtaining reasonable Compensation for their Losses, and to defend the Rioters."[10]

Priestley began to catalogue his losses for the assizes in August 1791, and by late February 1792 had a formal schedule of some sixty-five pages, listing damages to his house, household goods, books, manuscripts, and scientific instruments. He had engaged nine surveyors, appraisers, booksellers, and instrument makers in acquiring valuations, and in March 1792 asked his attorney, John Lee, to interview people, particularly members of the Lunar Society, to confirm the amounts. Some of his private papers, including unfinished manuscripts, were handed to the Rev. Charles Curtis, who sent them to Dundas, the home secretary; they were never returned. In January 1792 George Humphrey, owner of the Birmingham house, demanded payment of expenses in the survey of the house and furnishings and attempted to hold him to his lease. Priestley eventually paid £1,000 to free himself from expenses due to damage to the house.[11]

Unfortunately, although the valuations are clear enough, there are appended corrections and additions to the summations which are themselves unclear, and these have given rise to a variety of reports as to Priestley's total losses.[12] The formal schedule of estimates claims a total of £4,083 10s 3d, with

10. Thomas Payne, bookseller, to William Hutton, 14 April 1792, L. Add. 506, Birmingham University Library; Samuel Garbett to Lord Lansdowne (Shelburne), 7 Nov. 1792 and 30 April 1793, photostatic reproductions, Birmingham Reference Library, Garbett-Shelburne Papers, 4:125, 161. Samuel Horsley's letter to Hardinge, 7 June 1792, indicates Hardinge's attitude toward Priestley; see John Nichols, *Illustrations of the Literary History of the Eighteenth Century* (London, 1817–18), 3:150–51.

11. "Plaintiff's Schedule and Inventory," 21 Feb. 1792, MS 174683, Birmingham City Archives, Reference Library; Priestley to John Lee, 13 March 1792, Reference Library, Birmingham; Bolton, #74. For Curtis, see *W.* 1.2:132n†; on George Humphrey, see *Appeal to the Public II*, 495.

12. There are 32 pages listing clothes, furniture, and personal possessions; 12 pages for books, including some 350 titles, many of more than one volume and 75 of them on science, and

£432 15s 6d for books, £420 15s for manuscripts, and £605 2s for apparatus, etc. The jury allowed next to nothing for books, apparatus, or manuscripts and drastically reduced the amounts allowed for damage to the house. Its final award was only £2,996 10s, of which £493 12s was for costs of his claim. Priestley estimated his total losses to be £3,066 13s 6d. Yet there was a "Little Riot" in 1793, caused by a reluctance to pay for the damage done in 1791. As late as June 1793 Priestley had not yet received his compensation, but he finally received £3,098 6d, which included £101 10s 6d interest.[13]

John Wilkinson assured Priestley that he would make good any losses that money could repair, though he gave his opinion that Priestley should emigrate. He also gave Priestley £500 and sent £5,000 to Benjamin Vaughan to invest in French funds on Priestley's behalf. Friends in Norwich sent a contribution as early as July 1791. Old and New Meetings, Birmingham, together offered to contribute £500 to help Priestley, which he refused, writing that "generous friends of liberty in other parts of the country . . . and some of them members of the establishment, have already indemnified me for my pecuniary losses." In October 1791 Priestley sold his investment in English funds ("You will not wonder that I do not chuse to have my property in the English Funds") and had John Vaughan purchase American funds with the proceeds.[14]

---

14 pages of scientific instruments, etc. Douglas McKie, "Priestley's Laboratory and Library and Other of his Effects," *Notes and Records of the Royal Society of London* 12 (1956): 114–36; and Eric Robinson, "Priestley's Library of Scientific Books: A New List," *Studies in History and Philosophy of Science* 1 (1970): 145–60, concern themselves with the scientific apparatus and books for which Priestley presented his claim for damages. Gibbs, *Joseph Priestley*, 212; Bolton, #116–17; Hutton, *Life of William Hutton*, 219; and Maddison and Maddison, "Priestley and the Riots," all give values, which seem to conflict. The values in Gibbs appear to agree best with the formal schedule, while the figures given in Priestley, *Appeal to the Public, Part II*, 493–95, which are to the amounts reduced at the trial with additions of amounts not previously included and expenses of removing, etc., differ from the original schedule and within themselves. *Appendix to the Account*, 36, reports £4,112 16s 9d damages, £3,628 8s 9d claimed in court, and £2,502 18s 0d allowed, which disagree slightly with the amounts reported by Priestley.

13. Priestley to William Russell, 31 Jan., 6 Feb. 1792, 17 June 1793, Russell Papers, Add. MSS 44992, British Library; W. 1.2:202–3. The receipt for the sum received of Thomas Lee, dated 5 (?) Sept. 1793, is in the Library of Congress, Washington, D.C.

14. Priestley to Josiah Wedgwood, c. 31 July 1791, regarding Wilkinson's promise, Cambridge Free Library, Bolton, #64. By April 1793 Priestley had concluded that money in French funds was essentially lost. As late as 1798 he was still attempting to recover some part of that investment. Priestley to Lewis Hayward, 27 July 1791, Bodleian Library, Oxford. James West and Philip Martineau raised nearly £700 by subscription, West to Martineau, 4 June, Martineau to Priestley, 30 July 1792, Harris Manchester College, Bodleian Library, Oxford. Priestley to the congregations of Old and New Meetings, 22 Nov. 1792; to John Vaughan, 22 Oct., 15 Nov., 7 Dec. 1791, B.P931.2,3 Library, APS.

When he obtained his compensation, he transferred £900 to George Humphrey in Birmingham and £2,000 to John Vaughan to settle on his sons William and Henry. The riots having effected something of a reconciliation with his relatives, he set up an annual payment of £15 for his sister, Mrs. Crouch.[15] By June 1793 he had arranged to have the annuity from Shelburne conveyed through William Vaughan. Before he left for the United States, Priestley settled with Galton and Boulton to be trustees for an annuity fund to support his daughter, Sally Priestley Finch, and her children.

Priestley went into his home at Clapton in September 1791 and started reconstructing his laboratory and library. The house was, he told Wilkinson, in need of repair and larger than he ought to have, were it not for need of library and laboratory, "but without room for these things . . . I am useless." He wrote to friends of the Lunar Society that he was uncertain that he could establish a laboratory again, but in fact he succeeded far beyond what he thought possible. Sir Joseph Banks responded to a request for help in restoring the laboratory with a gift of some chemicals. Galton and Withering sent money, Keir sent chemicals, Watt sent (for himself and Boulton) a copying press, a digester, and some tubing, and promised a chemical lamp and some minerals; Josiah and Thomas Wedgwood sent money and apparatus.[16] Friends had managed to save some of his books and papers, though shocking havoc had been made of them.[17]

He was unable, at first, to settle down to productive work and in this regard the Lunar Society encouraged him to continue his scientific studies,

---

15. Priestley to Mrs. Crouch, 29 Dec. 1791, 31 Dec. 1792, Yates's *Priestleyana*, Royal Society of London; Bolton, #70, 79. First he assured her that he was safe and that she could expect the gift "as long as I live," then he reiterated the gift and exchanged some little family news. See also Schofield, *Lunar Society,* 372.

16. Priestley to Keir, 22 July, 29 July 1791, in Moillet, *James Keir,* 119; Bolton, #60, 62; Priestley to Watt, 2 Nov. 1791, 16 March 1792, 14 Nov. 1793, JWP W/13/1, 2; JWP 4/66/33 Birmingham City Archives, Reference Library; Priestley to Wedgwood, 26 July 1791, Fay-Priestley Collection, Dickinson College, Carlisle, Pa.; Bolton, #61; and to Thomas Wedgwood, 5 May 1792, Bolton, #76; Priestley to Sir Joseph Banks, 10 Jan. 1792, Burndy Library, Smithsonian Institution Libraries; Bolton, #71, *SciAuto.,* 143: on the verso of the letter, Banks wrote a memo listing the chemicals he had offered to send. Priestley to Keir, 12 Jan. 1792, Bolton, #72.

17. Priestley to John Wilkinson, 23 Nov. 1791, Warr.; to Judith Mansell, 22 Dec. 1791, APS (he asked Mansell to send any fragments of apparatus saved, but not furniture, "unless in good condition, as it hurts my wife not a little to see such things in the state in which they have generally come to her hands"); Priestley to William Russell, 6 Feb. 1792, Russell Papers, Add. MSS 44992, British Library. Lindsey declared that some 2,000 volumes of Priestley's 3,300-plus-volume library had been saved (but many in poor condition and incomplete sets) and a number of the manuscripts, including his exposition of the New Testament, his Memoirs, and a register of his experiments. See McLachlan, "More Letters of Theophilus Lindsey," 376.

while Priestley consistently and publicly praised the work of his Lunar Society friends. On 2 September 1791 Wedgwood wrote Priestley for his opinion on refractory clays for furnaces, which Lavoisier and Sequin had requested in August. Priestley responded that he knew of no refractory better than magnesia, of his plan of experiments on heat using Wedgwood's "thermometer," and with a request for apparatus. Garbett wrote Lord Lansdowne that Priestley had intended to attend a Lunar Society meeting on 12 September at Galton's, so Watt came armed, and Boulton did not attend. Neither did Priestley, who complained that his friends had not supported him. By mid-October 1791 Priestley had adopted the role of science advisor to Tom Wedgwood, encouraging him to continue experiments, "a business reserved for you," on properties of heat and light and their connections—these experiments, carried on with the assistance of John Leslie, were to lead to photochemical studies with silver nitrate.[18]

He began a correspondence with William Withering in November 1791 that continued through October 1793, thanking him for a donation toward his laboratory, expressing his wish to fill out his riot-damaged copy of Withering's botany, lamenting the loss of the Lunar Society and the coldness of London philosophical "friends" (he never went near the Royal Society). He noted his disapproval of the conduct of the French and his intention to follow his sons to American, and reported the resumption of his experiments on phlogiston and water. "I think, with you, that their *carbon* or *hydrogene* will prove to be nothing more than another name for *phlogiston*," he wrote, adding, "Air seems produceable from pure water, by means of heat, without limit." Priestley's only surviving letter to Lavoisier, to introduce David Jones, his successor at New Meeting and formerly lecturer in chemistry at Hackney, also announced the refitting of his laboratory and continued opposition to the new chemistry.[19]

18. Wedgwood to Priestley, draft, 2 Sept.; Priestley to Wedgwood, 7 Sept. 1791, John Rylands University Library of Manchester; Bolton, #65, *SciAuto.*, 142; Garbett to Lansdowne, 24 Sept. 1791, photostatic reproductions, Birmingham Reference Library, Garbett-Shelburne Papers, vol. 3; Priestley to Thomas Wedgwood, 18 Oct. 1791, 25 Feb., 13 March, 5 May 1792, Fay-Priestley Collection, Dickinson College Library, Carlisle, Pa.; Bolton, #66, 73, 75, 76; Schofield, *Lunar Society*, 422–23. His science publications and correspondence continued to recommend the work of his friends: the *Heads of Lectures on a Course of Experimental Philosophy* referred to Wedgwood's "thermometer" and to Watt's steam engine, while as late as 26 March 1794 he wrote that Benjamin Flower's *Intelligencer* wrongly credited Priestley for a method of gilding which was rightly owing to Boulton.

19. Priestley to William Withering, 5 Nov. 1791, 2 Oct. 1792, 15 April, 22 Oct. 1793, Library, Yale Medical School, Bolton, #67; Reference Library, Birmingham; Bolton, #78, 80, *SciAuto.*, 145, 146; Bolton, #82. He also referred to Withering's account of "tough glass" and analysis of

That opposition was reiterated in a pamphlet, *Experiments on the Generation of Air from Water*.[20] Its dedication, dated 16 November 1793, was to his fellow members of the Lunar Society: Boulton, Galton, R. A. Johnson, Keir, Watt, and Withering. In one of the few contemporary public references to the Society, Priestley regretted his loss of its fellowship. Neither religion nor politics had ever been the subject of the Society's conversations, he wrote. There were more important objects in this world than the political, philosophy being one. Religion was another, and although he had never approached the members as a minister, and differed from all in religious persuasion, he now prayed that they had the protection and blessings of God.

The Society had encouraged Priestley's work in natural philosophy, which had been interrupted for more than two years. Now resumed with its assistance, he dedicated to it the first fruits in pamphlet form, as he had concluded that any communication from him to the Royal Society would be unacceptable (viii). He included his late *Philosophical Transactions* paper, wishing all his philosophical papers not in the condensed three-volume *Experiments and Observations* (1790) or the *History of Electricity* to have this independent form.

He believed he could explain the experiments of the French within the doctrine of phlogiston and doubted that they could explain his by their system. The reprinted paper (11–22), added the note that experiments by Fourcroy, Vauquelin, and Seguin on the combustion of the two airs ended with more phlogisticated air than was in the combined airs at the beginning. The new material (23–39) started a bewildering series of experiments on the heating of water, which would be repeated for the rest of his life. He had begun pneumatic studies with a concern for two problems: the constitutional difference between vapor of water and other fluids and air, and the origin of the atmosphere. These new experiments, he believed, shed light on both.

By repeatedly heating, or even distilling, water, he produced air, which led him to believe that "the whole of any quantity of water is convertible into air by means of heat or some principle of repulsion acquired in the act of converting it into vapour" (36). Water, therefore, was the proper basis of every

---

Lisbon mineral water; see Schofield, *Lunar Society*, 391–92. The Royal Society never expressed regret at the destruction of Priestley's laboratory, his emigration, or the occasion of his death. Priestley to Lavoisier, 2 June 1792, Bolton, #77; *SciAuto.*, 144.

20. Joseph Priestley, *Experiments on the Generation of Air from Water; to which are prefixed, Experiments relating to the Decomposition of Dephlogisticated and Inflammable Air, from the Philosophical Transactions Vol. LXXXI, p. 213* (London: J. Johnson, 1793), dedication reprinted in *W.* 1.2:210–11. The *Philosophical Transactions* paper of 1791 is discussed in Chapter 9.

kind of air. Together, the reprinted paper and the text of the pamphlet itself began the pattern of anticlimax that he repeated for the rest of his life. The experiments, on the whole, were true enough, but the results were open to more than one interpretation, and the one that he chose was, to modern eyes (and even to most of his contemporaries), the wrong one.[21]

A final comment in the paper came close to explaining those different interpretations: "The advances we are continually making in the analysis of natural substances into the *elements* of which they consist, bring us but one step nearer to their constitutional differences; since as much depends upon the *mode of arrangement,* concerning which we know nothing at all, as upon the elements themselves" (38). This was clearly a derivation from Priestley's earliest natural philosophy concerns, with their corpuscular overtones, but it also seems to approach nineteenth-century structural chemistry—until he went on to illustrate that nitrous acid, nitrous air, fixed air, phlogisticated air, alkaline air, and probably all the other kinds of air were composed of phlogiston and dephlogisticated air.

The pamphlet was attacked in the *Gentleman's Magazine,* which had a particular aversion to Priestley's political, religious, *and* scientific views. Curiously, Robert Harrington, author of "A New Year's Gift to Dr. Priestley," was a phlogistonist, but he appeared to have believed that phlogiston was material fire when united with other bodies, and he liberally castigated all "modern philosophers" who failed to agree with him.[22] He praised Priestley's experiments, but claimed that they could only be explained upon "my system of air," not by his "absurd reasonings." What that "system" might have been is hard to perceive, though it appeared that water entered the composition of almost all common bodies, that airs consisted of fire, water, and

---

21. On 24–26n*, there is a reprinted extract of his 24 Nov. 1787 (misprinted as 21) letter to Jan Ingenhousz, disclaiming any desire to detract from him, though "the merit of all philosophical discoveries is in my opinion greatly overrated." For the problematical interpretations in the reprinted paper, see Chapter 9. The repeated appearance of air on heating water can only be explained as a mistake in manipulation, but it should be pointed out that Jean-Servais Stas (1813–91) found it next to impossible, without extreme precautions and heating over a period of days, to obtain water without occluded air.

22. See Alan Ruston, "Joseph Priestley and the Gentleman's Magazine," *Transactions of the Unitarian Historical Society* 18 (1983–86): 9–13; Robert Harrington, "A New Year's Gift to Dr. Priestley, on the Subject of the Generation of Air from Water," *Gentleman's Magazine* 64 (1794): 36–40, 133–38. Harrington is described, in the *Dictionary of National Biography,* as "an eccentric writer on natural philosophy," with an "uncouth style and desultory reasoning." Between 1781 and 1819 he variously attacked Priestley, Lavoisier, Henry Cavendish, William Herschel, Richard Kirwan, Humphry Davy, John Leslie, Count Rumford, and John Dalton, among others.

acids, which in turn contained water and earth, and that chemical processes could be explained by use of "the doctrine of chemical attractions" as displayed in "the table of elective attractions which has been handed down to us undisputed."

It is, perhaps, not surprising that "modern aërial chemists" did not take Harrington seriously, though it is likely that Priestley, concerned as he was with family problems and the logistics of approaching emigration, never saw the article. That at least would explain his failure to respond to Harrington's repeated accusations of plagiarism. This, however, was not the explanation given by "Cambriensis" in a note for the May issue of the *Gentleman's Magazine*. Priestley, he asserted, was so chagrined at the justice of Harrington's assault that the evening before the March issue of the magazine, possibly continuing the attack, was due to appear, he fled to board ship, though it was unlikely to sail soon. In June Joshua Toulmin replied that "Cambriensis" should verify his facts before "obtruding invention and falsehood on the Public."[23] Priestley had appeared up until Sunday, 6 April, attending public worship that day at Essex Street Chapel. He did not go to Gravesend till Monday morning or go on board before Tuesday, 8 April—a full week after the appearance of the March issue of *Gentleman's Magazine*.

The most significant scientific action of Priestley's Clapton/Hackney period was probably the series of lectures he delivered at Hackney New College. Almost by accident, early in 1792, he returned to his great strength in teaching by offering his assistance to the college, lecturing there in history and natural philosophy. For his Saturday lectures, Priestley prepared and published his *Heads of Lectures on a Course of Experimental Philosophy*, to save the students the trouble of transcribing them.[24] Whatever the value of the lectures themselves (only an outline of any branch of science, with experimental illustrations), they have the merit of presenting the only general account of experimental philosophy that Priestley ever wrote. Unfortunately,

23. "Cambriensis," "Other Reasons assigned for a certain Reverend Philosopher's leaving this Country," and Joshua Toulmin, note to "Mr. Urban," *Gentleman's Magazine* 64 (1794): 428–30, 495. Priestley generally reacted strongly to charges of plagiarism; see, e.g., his *Philosophical Empiricism* (1776). It is hard to believe he would have failed to answer had he seen the accusation or not been preoccupied.

24. Priestley, *Heads of Lectures on Experimental Philosophy, particularly including Chemistry, delivered at the New College in Hackney* (London: J. Johnson, 1794) was reviewed [by John Leslie] in *Monthly Review* 16 (1795): 271–76, as "a neat abstract of present chemical knowledge, notwithstanding the incorrect theory which sometimes obscures them." Leslie then listed fifteen passages where he disagreed with "this able experimenter," and concluded that the work chiefly suffered by too closely following the beaten road, but might be recommended as an "agreeable introduction to the perusal of larger systems."

that merit is moot. The introductions to his scientific books and papers and occasional remarks in them are more revealing of his philosophical attitudes. On the whole, the work validates the judgment of his reviewer, John Leslie, that the work was dependent on commonly received (and old-fashioned) opinions and permeated with notions of phlogiston. The exceptions were in the lectures on the nature of matter (which he had previously better discussed elsewhere) and on electricity.

The dedication reminded the students of New College, Hackney, that they were responsible for the reputation of the school and of themselves. It was a necessary reminder. Operation of the school was left in the hands of a committee, making disciplining the students difficult—this at a time of revolutionary ferment. The students objected passionately to the "tyranny" of their instructors; they entertained Tom Paine at a republican supper at the college and called *Ça ira* instead of "God save the King" at a theater. Burke described Hackney New College as a "hot bed of sedition," and it cannot have helped public perception of the college that Priestley and Price were connected with it.[25] Priestley attempted to dampen the fervor of the students and direct it into virtuous, useful, and peaceful channels. Understandable vanity may lead to feelings of superiority, he told them, but you have much to learn. Genius and virtue were not confined to scholars. They should show by conversation and conduct that they were friends of peace and good order and would work to preserve the form of government approved by the generality of their countrymen (xx).

If the record of some of those students is any measure, Priestley achieved what every dedicated teacher hopes to realize. Among those who can be identified were his son, Harry, and William Hazlitt, and, more significantly, his hearers included Arthur Aikin, Francis Baily, John Bostock, and Richard Knight (probably by private tuition).[26] Priestley also suggested the

25. Herbert J. McLachlan, "The Old Hackney College 1786–1796," *Transactions of the Unitarian Historical Society* 3 (1923–26): 185–205; H. W. Stephenson, "Hackney College and William Hazlitt," *Transactions of the Unitarian Historical Society* 3 (1923–26): 185–205; 4 (1927–30): 219–47, 376–411. For Burke, see *W.* 25:386n. Priestley feared for the continued existence of the college as early as June 1793. The school closed in 1796 and the building was demolished in 1802.

26. Hazlitt became one of England's foremost essayists. Aikin lectured on chemistry at Guy's Hospital for thirty-two years, was a founder of the Chemistry Society (and its first treasurer and second president), a founder of the Geological Society, honorary secretary of the Institution of Civil Engineers, fellow of the Linnean Society, and author of popular science works. Baily was a founder of the Royal Astronomical Society, and twice president of its predecessor, the Astronomical Society, known for his vivid description of "Baily's beads" and his star

establishment of a Hackney Literary and Philosophical Society, numbering nearly thirty members by 1794. It vanished when Priestley emigrated.[27]

Lecture 1 (1–9) introduced the subject of natural philosophy—an investigation of the wisdom of God in the works and laws of nature. Knowledge of natural laws was the source of all the powers of man, said Priestley, and the text emphasized practical uses throughout. The properties of natural substances and their changes could only be learned by experiment or observation.

> Of the circumstances which occasion a change in the properties of bodies, some are the addition of what are properly called *substances,* or things that are the objects of our senses, being *visible, tangible,* or having *weight,* &c. . . . But other changes are occasioned either by a change of texture in the substance itself, or the addition of some thing that is not the object of our senses. Thus, a piece of steel becomes a magnet by the touch of another magnet. . . . Such also, in the opinion of some is the difference between hot and cold substances.
>
> Till the nature of the cause be ascertained, it is convenient to make use of the term *principle,* as including both of the above-mentioned causes of the change of properties in bodies. Thus, whatever be the real cause of *gravity,* or of *inflammability,* whether, with Newton, we suppose gravity to be occasioned by a fluid pervading the whole universe, which he termed *aether,* and whether inflammability be caused by the presence of a real substance called phlogiston or not. (4–5)

---

catalogues. His "taste for and knowledge of electricity and chemistry were probably acquired from Dr. Priestley, with whom, at the age of seventeen, he became intimately acquainted, and of whom he always continued a warm admirer." Francis Baily, *Journal of a Tour in Unsettled Parts of North America in 1796 & 1797, with a Memoir of the Author* (London: Baily Brothers, 1856), 3. Bostock became a medical chemist, lecturer at Guy's Hospital, president of the Geological Society, fellow and vice president of the Royal Society. He wrote Benjamin Rush, "I . . . spent some time in an academy in the neighbourhood of London, where I had the peculiar happiness to be the pupil of Dr. Priestley in Chemistry and natural philosophy" (4 June 1805, Rush ms, ser. 25, No. 71, Library Company of Philadelphia). Knight was a founding member of the British Mineralogical Society, Geological Society, and Royal Institution, proprietor of a supply house for chemicals and science apparatus; see Leslie B. Hunt and Peta D. Buchanan, "Richard Knight (1768–1844): A Forgotten Chemist and Apparatus Designer," *Ambix* 31 (1984): 57–67.

27. John Aikin to John Haygarth, March 1794, in Aikin, *Memoir of John Aikin,* 96. This is probably the "friendly and innocent club" at Hackney that his critics considered Jacobin, mentioned by Priestley in his 1794 Fast Day sermon (xiii).

Changes made by the addition of substances were called chemical. The properties of similar compounds (e.g., metals!) were similar, but properties could not be deduced from component parts.

Substances could be "ordered" by kingdoms, by the elements entering their composition, or by the form in which they were found. Given his mechanistic predilections, Priestley naturally preferred the latter, but he did list "the elements which compose all natural substances: *dephlogisticated air,* or the *acidifying principle; phlogiston,* or the *alkaline principle;* different earths, the principles of *heat, light,* and *electricity;* and the principles not yet proved to be substances: *attraction, repulsion,* and *magnetism*—which enable us to explain all appearances that have yet occurred to us."[28]

Priestley then reiterated his skepticism of man's knowledge of substance, adding, "we cannot speak of the properties of substances, such as *hard, round, coloured, &c., &c., &c.* . . . without saying that they inhere in, or belong to, some *thing,* substance, or substratum" (9–10). All substances had the properties of extension and infinite divisibility (denied by Leslie as a geometrical abstract, but a difficulty removed by the *componibility* of the ingenious Boscovich, 272), and added the powers of *attraction* and *repulsion,* their due balance being responsible for retaining component parts in their places. "If, by any means, the particles of a substance be removed beyond their sphere of mutual attraction, they repel one another" (12). He denied that *vis inertia* and impenetrability were properties, the former being an effect requiring a cause and the latter produced by a power of repulsion acting at a real distance from the body's surface. The causes of attractions—gravitational, cohesion, and short-range chemical affinities—were unknown.

A discussion of the physical state of substances followed. The treatment was consistently phlogistic, emphasizing methods of composition and decomposition. Differentiation was primarily by physical characteristics, beginning with the "aeriform," which were true substances, possessing weight and differing primarily in color, solubility, and comparative weight (15–40). He also discussed eudiometry, and although Priestley had not achieved a sense of compound in the Lavoisian sense, he didn't make the mistake that Leslie did (272) in assuming that nitrous acid was variable in the proportions of its ingredients. He mentioned at least three types of inflammable air—from

28. Priestley, *Heads of Lectures on Experimental Philosophy,* 9. Note that he temporarily accepted Lavoisier's designation of dephlogisticated air as the acidifying agent, retained phlogiston, now as an alkaline principle, and accepted substances of heat, light, and electricity. He had previously argued against most of these positions and would, typically, argue against any one of them in subsequent years.

acids, combustibles, and animal or vegetable—and he even distinguished them from one another by weight, but made no suggestion that these were different airs. Leslie denied the evidence of kinetic motion of gaseous particles that Priestley described: passage through a bladder (25 vs. 272) and diffusion through one another (39 vs. 273).

He next treated the liquids: water (cannot be converted into an earth, but the compositional theory "does not satisfy me"), the acids (distinguished from alkalies by testing on vegetable colors and from one another by their actions, particularly on metals), alkalies and liquid inflammables and oils. There is here a side reference to efflorescence and deliquescence.

Then came the solids (76–127): argillaceous, metallic, and the solid combustibles excepting diamonds, which are different. All could become fluid and most vaporous by heat. They are called earths or stones, except for the salts, and differ by texture and whether they are metallizable. The brief descriptions of the metals appear to have been lifted from standard texts.

The next lecture, on phlogiston and the composition of water, repeated Priestley's usual arguments against French chemistry; the only addition being the suggestion that water becomes atmospheric air with heat and therefore contains elements of dephlogisticated and phlogisticated airs. The lectures (135–48) on heat and animal heat referred to the dispute over heat's substantiality, cited its transference from one body to another, and defined heat capacity, latent heats of fusion and vaporization, and (following Adair Crawford) gave a curious estimate of absolute zero and of the origin of animal heat, the conversion of latent heat of respired air to sensible. Priestley derived his lecture on light from Newton, with its confusion over materiality vs. undulation of aetherial fluid, its suggestions that colors in prismatic spectra are divided like a musical chord, and that light particles have different sides. Leslie objected to this, as he did to Priestley's explanation of phosphorescence.

Finally, the lectures (155–80) on magnetism and electricity were rudimentary but reasonably good, as might be expected from the author of a *History of Electricity*. Priestley now conceded a fluid theory of electricity and was open to argument that there might be two fluids. A major new ingredient in his treatment, however, came "in a *series of propositions,* drawn up by an intelligent friend" (probably Volta and his *Philosophical Transactions* paper of 1793), where Priestley described the experiments of Galvani and Volta on animal electricity (165–69) and showed how contemporary his science information was.

The disruption of his laboratory, or even of his library, did not prevent Priestley's continuation of his primary mission, that of preacher and theologian. His new role as religious martyr opened a range of pulpits to him. In early October he preached for the first time since the riots, for a congrega-tion of Calvinistic Baptists at Amersham, near Missenden (Bucks), and was invited to preach at two other places, including an Independent congregation at Beaconsfield, near Burke's residence. As late as July 1793 he was invited to preach, while recovering from illness, at Wooton, Gloucester. In October 1791 he wrote the congregation at New Meeting, resigning his post, hinting that Mary Priestley did not wish to return to Birmingham. Meanwhile he was hoping for an invitation to succeed Richard Price at Gravel Pit Meeting, Hackney, though he had heard that about a third of the congregation was opposed out of fear.[29] Finally, on 7 November, he received an invitation to become morning preacher there, at a salary of 150 guineas. He accepted the invitation by the 12th, expressing, however, a little disquiet that an afternoon preacher with Arian instead of Socinian sentiments was deliberately to be selected to assist him.

He preached his first sermon there on 4 December and its publication began a spate of published sermons that continued until the last sermon Priestley preached before leaving for America. *A Particular Attention to the Instruction of the Youth* (1791) began with a preface (iii–x, plus four pages tipped in) describing his Sunday religious classes at Birmingham: he taught children age five to twelve before morning service, twelve to eighteen be-tween services, and sixteen to thirty after evening service.[30] The Scriptures were the source of all religious teaching, but he added his own publications: the catechisms, *Institutes,* and *History of Corruptions,* plus maps, contests, and essays, for what was the most satisfactory part of his ministry. A letter and resolution from the Birmingham congregation affirmed the value of these efforts.

The text began with repetition of material from his earliest essay on church discipline (1770), his first sermon at Birmingham (1780), and that on the proper constitution of a Christian church (1782). He outlined to the Hackney congregation his understanding of his particular (as opposed to "ordinary and well-known") duties. He commented on and read the Scriptures, going through the whole of the New Testament in the form of a temporal harmony. He reminded hearers of why they were Christians, why Protestants, and why

29. Alan Ruston, "Joseph Priestley at the Gravel Pit Chapel, Hackney: The Collier MS.," *Enlightenment and Dissent* 2 (1983): 111–19. The building was on Ram Place, south of Morn-ing Lane, site now of factory units. In 1983 application was made for a plaque identifying the site with Priestley; see Gray, "Priestley in Hackney," 109.

30. Joseph Priestley, *A Particular Attention to the Instruction of the Young recommended, in A Discourse* [on 2 Cor. 8:9], *delivered at the Gravel-Pit Meeting, in Hackney, December 4, 1791, on entering on the Office of Pastor to the Congregation of Protestant Dissenters, assembling in that Place* (London: J. Johnson, 1791).

Protestant Dissenters. "I shall never fail to lay greater stress upon Christianity itself, in any form, than upon my own peculiar ideas concerning it" (33). And, following the example of their beloved Dr. Price, he emphasized that the greatest duty of a Christian was obedience to God's commands, fulfilling his love for mankind.

An advertisement in *The Instruction of Youth* announced publication of the sermon he had intended to preach in the ruins of New Meeting, Birmingham. Violence against him there not abating, *The Duty of Forgiveness of Injuries* was instead delivered by Mr. Coates, minister of Old Meeting, and printed at the request of both Old and New Meeting congregations.[31] Its publication did not ease resentment in Birmingham or of the Establishment in general. A preface abstained from comment on the riots themselves, leaving that to his *Appeal*. Nor did he encourage expressions of resentment toward the rioters, but he did note that "neither common candor nor Christian benevolence requires that we turn our eyes from injustice and villainy."

The text expanded on the theme "Father, forgive them, for they know not what they do," and was applied in particular to the authors and abettors of the riots. The ignorant rioters had followed orders, their instigators were also ignorant—of the true nature of religion, of Dissent, and "of *human nature* and *history.*" Forgiveness was proper in emulation of Christ and as a display of dignity and greatness of mind. It was also reasonable as well as magnanimous, for the riots had shown the strength of Dissenters' religious principles, and their generosity of spirit would impress their enemies.

Early in 1792 Priestley published the first of his *Letters to a Young Man* in answer to Gilbert Wakefield's *Short Enquiry into the Expediency and Propriety of Public or Social Worship* (1791, 1792) and Edward Evanson's *Arguments against and for the Sabbatical Observance of Sunday* (1792).[32] Wakefield, an idiosyncratic convert to Unitarianism from the Established church, never formally associated himself with any Dissenting body and retained an aesthetic

31. Joseph Priestley, *The Duty of Forgiveness of Injuries: A Discourse* [on Luke 23:34], *intended to be delivered soon after the Riots in Birmingham* (Birmingham: J. Johnson, 1791). I have used the version in *W.* 15:475–93.

32. Priestley, *Letters to a Young Man, occasioned by Mr. Wakefield's Essay on Public Worship; to which is added, a Reply to Mr. Evanson's Objections to the Observation of the Lord's Day* (London: J. Johnson, 1792). I have used the version in *W.* 20:303–51, but note here one of the problems in using the Rutt edition. Rutt uses, without explanation, any edition that he has at hand—in this instance a second edition of 1793, with Part 1 added to the title and notes added from revised editions of Wakefield and Wakefield's *Strictures* on Priestley's first edition, though the published text is still dated 24 March 1792.

distaste for Dissenting worship. He admitted that his system was inconsistent and without authority from the Gospels, but the lengthy prayers and lack of liturgy of Dissenting chapels disturbed him almost as much as the unsophisticated and undereducated nature of Dissenting ministers.

Priestley replied that Wakefield's plan, to be used until individuals had disciplined themselves enough to conform to the spirit of Christianity without display, was not unlike that used in many Unitarian chapels.[33] He added that Dissenting ministers might be undereducated in the classic languages, but they compensated for their lack of social and intellectual polish by their much greater knowledge of Scripture than the average Establishment clergyman (309). Priestley also indignantly rejected Wakefield's description of Price as "no true friend of religious liberty." Price had opposed Wakefield's appointment as tutor at Hackney because he failed to attend religious services. Wakefield's personal beliefs were not attacked, but he had no claims on institutions that differed with him. Everyone must bear with the consequences of following their convictions.

There were valid grounds against any prayers to an omnipotent, benevolent being, but if any prayers were reasonable, there were no plausible objections to communal ones. "An institution recommended by the observance of all ages and all nations, and especially by all Christians . . . will probably be found to have serious uses, and certainly should not be abandoned till after deliberate examination" (330). Before his reply to Evanson, Priestley inserted his paper, as "Hermas," from the *Theological Repository* (1788), answering Evanson's "Ebulus," who had objected to a weekly day of rest. Priestley thought "Hermas" had proved otherwise but, ignoring Evanson's peevish and even perverse new objections, he provided new and relevant arguments. To prove any procedure among Christians in the immediate postapostolic period was difficult, but universal practice among all discordant sects in the later period suggested coherence from the beginning. He agreed with Evanson that civil governors ought not interfere with religious practice and that necessary work ought to be done even on the Sabbath, while social and cheerful entertainment was consistent with the day's sanctity.

His next religious publication, dated 21 January 1793, was addressed to the *Philosophers and Politicians of France*, as an honorary citizen and potential

---

33. Recall Priestley's *Letter to a Layman* (1774) on Lindsey's reformed worship at Essex Street Chapel (see Chapter 2). He added that the only lengthy prayer he had ever recommended, filling thirteen pages in his *Forms of Prayer and Other Offices* (1783), was that of an Establishment clergyman, Bishop Hoadley.

member of the conventional assembly of France.[34] Priestley chided the French for "incautiously" deriding religion. Comparing religion to chemistry, he wrote that the latter had not been discarded though it was once overloaded with false ideas. Neither ought we to discard religion, of infinite magnitude compared to chemistry, now that superstition and priestcraft were exploded. What followed was mainly a reprinting of the arguments in *Letters to a Philosophical Unbeliever* and *Institutes of Natural and Revealed Religion*. A significant addition advised politicians to relieve the civil government (whose proper concern was the security of a man's person and property) of all concern about religion.

The outbreak of war with France in February 1793 prompted a king's proclamation of a general fast day, as an act of public humiliation and prayer. Many Dissenting congregations disapproved of such "days" appointed by civil governors, but the whole nation could agree to voice its resignation to the wisdom and will of God, and in that spirit Priestley preached his *Fast Day Sermon* of 1793.[35] He could not concur with government in praying for success in a war that he thought neither just nor necessary, any more than he could have supported the English war in America. He prayed that war would end in firmer establishment of the liberties and happiness of every nation.

It appeared, Priestley continued, that an *Index Expurgatorius* had been created for the *Constitution of England*, but Mr. Burke had neither the ability to support nor the virtue to retract his charge that Priestley was hostile to the constitution, and Priestley appended a copy of his "Letter to the Editor of the Morning Chronicle," 7 March 1973 (sent also, 12 March 1793, to "Mr. Urban" of the *Gentleman's Magazine* 63 [1793]), denying Burke's charge and asserting that he (Priestley) was a better friend to the true principles of the constitution than that pensioner of the government. "If any mischief is to be apprehended to this country from political writings, it has been wholly occasioned by his own." It was neither treason nor sedition to argue that there might be, for some nations other than England, better forms of government than those now in existence.

Avoiding praising or blaming the administration for bringing the nation to this pass, Priestley declared that "we are ready to join our brethren, of whatever denomination, in contrition and prayer." If there had to be a war,

---

34. Joseph Priestley, *Letters addressed to the Philosophers and Politicians of France, on the Subject of Religion* (London: J. Johnson, 1793). I have used the Philadelphia edition (1794).

35. Joseph Priestley, *A Sermon* [on Psalm 46:1] *Preached at the Gravel-Pit Meeting in Hackney, April 19, 1793. Being the Day appointed for a General Fast* (London: J. Johnson, 1793). I have used W. 15:494–518.

let it be a war fought by Christians, free of the spirit of revenge, exultation in the calamities of one's enemies, or delight in war itself. This war being about principles of government, including the role of civil government in the business of religion, Priestley hoped that it would lead to a discussion of them, for "all discussion leads to knowledge, and all real knowledge, to improvement" (512). Events now suggested what prophecy had foretold, the coming happy state of the world.

Part 2 of Priestley's *Letters to a Young Man* was dated August 1793 and was directed entirely to Edward Evanson's *Dissonance of the four . . . Evangelists* (1792).[36] Another convert to Unitarianism from the established clergy, Evanson focused on prophecy, the only "lasting supernatural evidence," while the authority and credibility of Christian histories must be established before miracles can be admitted. Priestley, who was especially fond of miracles as guarantors of divine missions, attempted to treat seriously and without prejudice Evanson's arguments, though they were tainted by levity. The result mirrored that combination of critical insight, credulity, and conservatism he exhibited as "Liberius" in the *Theological Repository* of 1770 and 1771 and reprinted in his Greek and English *Harmonies* of 1777 and 1780.

Evanson confounded the authenticity of the Gospels with the credibility of their facts, but the base of our faith was independent of the authenticity of any of the books in gospel history. "The books called *the Gospels* were not the *cause,* but the *effect,* of the belief of Christianity in the first ages." Christians received the books because they knew the contents were true.

Evanson particularly objected to Matthew, Mark, John, and the Epistle to the Romans, though he also criticized some other books, and compared them all to Luke, which he accepted without subjecting it to his hypercritical analysis. Priestley pointed out that the authenticity of Luke rested on the same foundation as that of the others. All were read as authentic from very early, while forgery as late as the second century would be almost impossible because of the peculiarity of context and style. Matthew and Mark were as likely sources for Luke as the reverse. Evanson explained questionable events in Luke as interpolations but would not accept the same explanation for other books. Although Evanson had more objections to Matthew than to Mark and John and was cursory in writing against the Epistles (mainly because none contained prophecies), Priestley defended them all. A canonical

36. Joseph Priestley, *Letters to a Young Man, Part II. Occasioned by Mr. Evanson's Treatise on the Dissonance of the Four Generally Received Evangelists* (London: J. Johnson, 1793). In his correspondence with Lindsey about these *Letters,* Priestley said the appendix was an attempt to deal with Mr. Dodson's approval of some of Evanson's arguments.

book of the New Testament was "nothing more than a book written by an apostle, or other person of their age, qualified to transmit an account of the promulgation of Christianity to posterity, and deserving the attention of all Christians" (140).

There was another fast day appointed for 28 February 1794, and Priestley gave another fast-day sermon. *The Present State of Europe compared with Antient Prophecies,* had, however, a very different message from that of 1793.[37] It began with a lengthy preface explaining his decision to leave England. Many people had expected (and some wished) that he would leave after the riots, but he could not, he said, have been as useful elsewhere and had no personal guilt regarding that violence. Having fixed himself, at considerable expense, at Clapton and taken a worthy new post, he could accept the continued obloquy to which he was subjected: the abuse of clergy, Burke's inveighing against him "in a place where he knows I cannot reply to him," attacks in "treasury" newspapers and other popular publications (xiii). His sons, however, had found themselves unable to find any provision in this country, and, having witnessed the treatment of their father at the assizes, had resolved to go to America. Priestley decided to follow. "I see no occasion to expose myself to danger without any prospect of doing good, or to continue any longer in a country in which I am so unjustly become the object of general dislike." He would go where he would be better received and still be useful. He left in sorrow and hoped the time would come when he could return to visit friends and even be buried in the land that gave him birth.

After this reasonable preface, the text of the sermon comes as a surprise to most modern readers. This second call by our rulers to humble ourselves, Priestley wrote, was a special opportunity for repentance on account of the portents in the language of prophecy foretelling the day of final judgment. Priestley had searched the Old and New Testaments, and particularly Daniel and Revelation, for signs of the approaching millennial event and strongly suspected that he had found them. The French Revolution had accomplished part of Revelation, and soon the destruction of papal power would follow, as would the destruction of the Turkish empire and the restoration of the Jews to their own country. No man could know when, but "For our own sakes . . . for the sake of our friends, of our country, and of every thing that

---

37. Joseph Priestley, *The Present State of Europe compared with Antient Prophecies; A Sermon* [on Matt. 3:2], *preached at the Gravel Pit Meeting in Hackney, February 28, 1794, being the Day appointed for a General Fast. With a Preface, containing the Reasons for the Author's leaving England* (London: J. Johnson, 1794). Portions of this sermon were included in an anthology, *Wonderful Prophecies, being a Dissertation on the Existence, Nature and Extent of the Prophetic Powers in the Human Mind* (London, 1795).

is dear to us in it, let us attend to the admonition of my text: 'to repent, for the kingdom of heaven is at hand.'"

In March 1794 Priestley's *Discourses on the Evidences of Revealed Religion* was published, dedicated to Thomas Belsham, resident tutor at Hackney, as someone to whose coincident views he was leaving his congregation and classes.[38] The preface cited Priestley's *Institutes, History of the Church, Letters* to *Philosophical Unbelievers,* to *Philosophers and Politicians,* to the *Jews,* and conclusion of his *History of Corruptions* as containing the message he repeated here. However, considering the present state of Europe and its portents, he felt that a demonstration was especially called for that Christianity was not a *"cunningly devised fable"* but was built on the same evidence of fact as any other ancient episode of history. As a record of twelve sermons delivered at Hackney, it was also a demonstration that he did not regularly indulge in politics or heresy.

The twelve sermons ranged in subject from the general importance of religion to the caution against conceit of the intellect (save that reason supports revelation in belief of miracles). Ten of them argued the validity and importance of miracles. Miracles, as clear proofs of actual deviations from the natural order, proved the existence of God in a shorter and more satisfactory manner than observance of the uninterrupted course of nature (345). Sufficient evidence for miracles was supplied in accounts written at the time and with all the marks of authenticity of any modern journal (58). The approach of the day of judgment upon persecutors of the Jews behooved us to look to our own sentiments and conduct, respecting persecution, whether of Jews or Christians (241). The greatest miracle was the impotence of the authorities to prevent the spread of Christianity (299). "No other facts in the whole compass of history . . . underwent a thousandth part of the investigation that . . . these [of the Resurrection] must have done . . . when the investigation was most easy." Yet no marks of imposture were discovered (331). Revelation also taught the placability of God to the penitent, rejecting salvation by righteousness not our own (385)—and thus we are brought full circle back to Priestley's first theological publication, his *Doctrine of Remission* of 1761.

38. Priestley, *Discourses on the Evidences of Revealed Religion, "as delivered at Hackney in 1793, 1794,"* 2d ed. (London: J. Johnson, 1794). Includes twelve discourses, 1, 3, and 5 reprinted by the Unitarian Society in 1799 and again as *Tracts III. Second Series,* in 1805. Discourse 11 is a reprint of *The Evidence of the Resurrection of Jesus considered . . .* (Birmingham: J. Johnson, 1790). Discourse 12 is a reprint of *A View of Revealed Religion; a Sermon preached at the Ordination of the Rev. William Field of Warwick, July 12, 1790 . . .* (Birmingham: J. Johnson, 1790). Appendices include "Address to the Jews," explanation of the occasion and reception of Discourse 11, and a copy of correspondence with Gibbon.

Priestley's last sermon in England, *The Use of Christianity, especially in Difficult Times*, was delivered on 30 March 1794, a week before he and Mary Priestley left for America.[39] It opened with expressions of gratitude toward the groups that had supported him in the past and of his hopes that the strangers crowding into Gravel Pit Meeting might be a symptom of diminishing prejudice. The text prayed that God would direct the congregation in the spirit and duties of Christian societies—preparation for their future happiness as citizens of heaven. As his personal experiences at Birmingham, and now at Hackney, had demonstrated, even the most endearing and important connections on earth are slight and transient.

The present situation of Dissenters was conducive to the exercise of the Christian principles of patience, fortitude, meekness, and forgiveness of injuries. Conscious of our integrity, we should "look down upon our enemies" (75) with compassion, for they acted a part assigned them by the Supreme Ruler of the Universe, and good would finally result from present evil. One personal recompense, he added, had been the seasonable and generous reception given him. He hoped to find a similar sphere of usefulness and happiness in America. Calamitous times were coming and Christian principles would be needed to teach people how to act—and how to suffer. "Let the strangers here now," he concluded, "hoping to find occasion for harm, depart disappointed."

An appendix dated 21 February assured the congregation at Gravel Pit Meeting that, in leaving, Priestley intended no complaint against them; the congregation accepted on 16 March the propriety of his retiring when he had little prospect of comfort and safety. Forty-one members of his religious classes signed their expression of gratitude for his teaching, the Unitarian Society regretted his departure, and the united congregations of Old and New Meetings, Birmingham, bid him an affectionate farewell. Priestley and his family left London for Gravesend on Monday, 7 April 1794, to board ship. Leaving Sally Priestley Finch behind (her husband would not agree to emigrate), they sailed, but were still in sight of England within an hour of Deal on the 9th, dropped anchor off Falmouth on the 11th to wait out a storm, and then were off for America.

---

39. Priestley, *The Use of Christianity, especially in Difficult Times; a Sermon* [on Acts 20:32] *delivered at the Gravel Pit Meeting in Hackney, March 30, 1794, being the Author's Farewell Discourse to his Congregation* (London: J. Johnson, 1794), second edition, 1794; my copy bound, as pages 66–100, in the fourth edition, 1794, of *The Present State of Europe*. Sections from this sermon were quoted in H. W. Crosskey's sermon at the Church of the Messiah (formerly New Meeting), 2 Aug. 1874, and printed in the *Priestley Memorial*, 55–56.

XV

Emigration to the United States, Politics, and Education

There is no question that Priestley was concerned over the future of his sons. Much of his correspondence between 1787 and 1794 expressed worry over the problems of finding positions for Joseph Jr. (Jos) and William; Henry, age seventeen in 1794, was still too young to worry about. In 1787 John and William Wilkinson had quarreled and by July 1790 had finally separated their interests, dimming Priestley's expectations that his sons would find secure posts in the iron trade with their uncles. Jos had been working for his uncle, John, but that fell apart when he wanted to marry and John would not increase his responsibilities or income. Jos had liked the iron business, but jealousy of John Wilkinson by other iron masters precluded his finding another situation in that field.

Jos and James Watt Jr. made tentative plans to go into business together, but Watt Sr. stopped that. He wanted his son to gain experience in an established firm. Joseph Johnson was approached for a partnership for Jos in bookselling; then Jos bought into a mercantile business with a Mr. Ashworth in Manchester. Priestley suggested, without success, that William take Jos's place with John Wilkinson, but there was no future for him there. William, though too high-spirited and hot-tempered for trade, was to apprentice with William Russell, with a view to becoming his business agent in the United States.[1]

1. Priestley and Jos to John Wilkinson, late 1790, early 1791, Warr.; Priestley to Josiah Wedgwood, 16 Feb. 1791, Bolton, #57; to James Watt, n.d. [late 1790], 6 Jan., 2 Feb. 1791, JWP W/13/7, 8, 11; Doc. 3/11, 12, 13, Birmingham City Archives, Reference Library.

After the riots, even these makeshift arrangements fell apart. Ashworth panicked and wanted out of his arrangement with Jos, and Russell was now in no position to take on an apprentice. By February 1793 the sons were preparing to go to France or America and Mary Priestley was ready to follow. As early as September 1791 Priestley had considered going to France, possibly in the neighborhood of Dijon, while he had been offered a furnished house near Paris, and a society at Toulouse invited him to the south of France, where a vacant monastery could be put at his disposal.[2] William, visiting Paris with his uncle William, was presented to the National Assembly on 8 June 1792 as a representative of his father and given French citizenship. By a decree of 26 August 1792 the National Assembly named Joseph Priestley a citizen of France and in September he was elected to the National Convention by three different departments.[3]

The declaration of war in February 1793 made a move to France untenable.[4] Priestley wrote to John Adams, then vice president of the United States, advising him that his sons were shortly to arrive in America and that he was likely soon to follow.[5] Adams had known and admired Priestley since his days as U.S. envoy to Britain (1785–88), and he replied with welcome for the sons and the "great personal pleasure" he would have in seeing Priestley in Boston. William left France for America and Joseph Jr., Henry, and Thomas Cooper sailed from England in late August. Mary Priestley was now determined on the journey to America—more ready than her husband. As early as August 1791 she had written Mrs. Barbauld, "I do not think that

2. Priestley to John Wilkinson, answered 24 Sept. 1791, Warr. Gibbs, *Joseph Priestley*, 211. Up to 6 Feb. 1793 he had inclined toward France so that he and Mary might be near their daughter and son, William, but changing circumstances made him lean toward Boston in America. Priestley to John Vaughan, Priestley Papers B. 931, Library, APS.

3. François de Neufchâteau to Priestley, 10 Sept. 1792, and Priestley's answer to "Members of the National Assembly," 13 Sept., Edgar Fahs Smith Library, University of Pennsylvania, Philadelphia. He accepted citizenship but declined a position in the Convention, being unable to speak French. Priestley to M. Rabaud, 21 Sept. 1792, Library, Pennsylvania State University, University Park, Pa., *W.* 1.2:190–91. See also [J.-Brissot de Warville], *Mémoires* (Paris: Alphonse Picard & Fils, 1911), 1:372n1; Priestley to John Hurlford Stone lamented recent violence in France and especially violence done to his old friend, LaRochefoucauld, 17 June 1792, APS; Priestley to William Priestley, 25 June 1792, cautioned him to attend to business (including obtaining interest on the investment in French funds) and not be led astray by the attention paid him, Bibliotheque Municipale, Nantes; *Notes and Queries* XI (3d ser., 1867): 186.

4. An Aliens Bill of March 1793 forbade correspondence between England and France and prevented persons from going to or from France without government approval.

5. Adams met Priestley and heard him preach at Essex Street Chapel in 1786; see his diary, [Adams], *Works*, 3:396–97; Priestley to John Adams, 23 Feb. 1793, John Adams to Priestley, 12 May 1793, Adams Papers, Reel 376, 116, Massachusetts Historical Society, Boston.

God can require it of us, as a duty, after they have smote one cheek, to turn the other. I am for trying a fresh soil."[6] But Priestley was reluctant. Part of the problem may have been Mary Priestley's health—she had suffered consumptive symptoms since 1790 and neither the trip nor resettlement would be easy for her. But there were other difficulties. Priestley did not really want to leave England. He estimated he would lose an income of more than £300 by leaving, he had a useful position and work to do in a familiar and loved setting, and he was, after all, sixty-one years old—not a good age at which to be starting fresh in a distant land. When he decided that he must leave, there was more involved than the uncertain future of his sons; there were increasing signs of threats to his personal safety and freedom of action.[7]

For the campaign against Dissent and liberal reform, begun with the Birmingham Riots of 1791, had continued and intensified. Although the professed object of repression was radical political reformers, Priestley was always convinced that the real plot, starting with the riots, originated in the court and was not political but religious.[8] Nor was he alone in this belief or in expressing it. In 1794 Coleridge, still in his liberal period, believed that the Birmingham Riots were encouraged by the clergy: "Priestley . . . from his loved native land / Statesmen blood-stained and priests idolatrous / By dark lies maddening the blind multitude / Drove with vain hate." So also did Wordsworth, who, in his "Letter to the Bishop of Llandaff," wrote, "Left to the quiet exercise of their own judgment, do you think that the people would have thought it necessary to set fire to the house of the philosophic Priestley, and to hunt down his life like that of a traitor or a parricide?"[9]

6. Priestley to John Wilkinson, 19 March, 6 April 1793, Warr.; William arrived in Philadelphia the summer of 1793, Priestley to Lindsey, July, Aug., and Sept. 1793; Mary Priestley to Anna Laetitia Barbauld, 26 Aug. 1791, *W.* 1.2:365–67.

7. On Mary Priestley's illness, see Priestley to Lindsey, 13, 21 June 1790, Wms.; Priestley to John Wilkinson, 6 June 1793, and again soon after landing in the United States, 24 July 1794, Warr.; and to William Russell, 17 Dec. 1795, *W.* 1.2:329–30. Priestley wrote Wilkinson, 20 Jan. 1793, that he was determined not to leave at present; in Sept., that friends were urging him to go as soon as possible, and as late as 7 Feb. 1794, he told him he was leaving with regret, Warr. His letters from the United States reiterate his enjoyment of America but also tell of his greater pleasure with his activities in England, his missing his friends, and his longing to return before his death; see Priestley to Radcliffe Scholefield, c. Oct. 1794, New York Historical Society; to Thomas Belsham ("I shall always feel a stranger") 3 Aug. 1795 and 16 April 1799.

8. Priestley defined his campaigns for repeal of the Test and Corporation Acts and disestablishment of the church as religious; the Establishment naturally regarded them as political.

9. [Samuel Taylor Coleridge], "Religious Musings," in *Poems of Samuel Taylor Coleridge* (London: Oxford University Press, 1912), 123, lines 371–76. Wordsworth quoted by Leslie Chard, *Dissenting Republican: Wordsworth's Early Life and Thought in Their Political Context* (The Hague: Mounton, 1972), 115.

Some members of the University of Cambridge (including William Frend and some twelve others) presented Priestley with an inscribed silver inkstand on the eve of his departure, lamenting the ingratitude of their country.

But Priestley and his friends were only partially right. Although court and administration rather clearly approved, there is no evidence that either had any role in planning or conducting the riots. King George III's letter— "I cannot but feel better pleased that Priestley is the sufferer for the doctrines he and his party have instilled, and that people see them in their true light"—was written to Henry Dundas, commending the home secretary for the measures taken to suppress the rioters. There was, nevertheless, a strong element of anti-Dissent in the "White Terror" activities of the court and administration during the decades immediately following the French Revolution. George III's rigid championship of the church of which he was head was proverbial. Dundas, in an early hearing with William Russell, "expressed a great dislike of the Dissenters in general," and Pitt considered an amendment to the Toleration Act that would have severely limited the freedom of Dissenting preachers and teachers.

Though John Reeves, leading provocateur in the forming of Tory associations and *ex officio* advisor to the Home Office, denied that the associations were anti-Dissent, the deputies and delegates of the Dissenters in London were not convinced by his denial. A manifesto of his "Society for Preserving Liberty and Property against Republicans and Levellers" denounced Dissenters, claiming that they had brought on the American Revolution.[10] Considering the amount and skill of the propaganda launched against them, it is remarkable that Dissenters suffered as little as they did. But the persecutions remained local and were countered by action of the London Dissenting deputies and, surprisingly, with the sometime aid of Pitt's administration. A notable example was the grant of £2,000 from the "King's Purse," when trustees of New Meeting were unable to produce evidence of registration as a meeting house and were therefore denied compensation for destruction in the riots of 1791.[11]

10. [King George III], *The Later Correspondence of King George III*, ed. Arthur Aspinall (Cambridge: Cambridge University Press, 1962), 1:551; Rose, "Priestley Riots of 1791," 77; Priestley to Theophilus Lindsey, 30 Aug. 1791; John Reeves, in a letter to the chairman of the Deputies, 18 Dec. 1792; reply by Edward Jeffries, chairman, and approved by the General Meeting of that day, 21 Dec., in Davis, *Dissent in Politics*, 70n2.

11. Davis, *Dissent in Politics*, 78. Davis contends that Pitt's administration was friendlier to Dissenting interests than I can find evidence for. Bushrod, "Unitarianism in Birmingham," 3; Henry R. Winkler, "The Pamphlet Campaign Against Political Reform in Great Britain, 1790–1795," *The Historian* 15 (1952): 23–40.

Until the outbreak of war, Pitt could not be secure in his majority; Dissenters could powerfully affect votes, and the riots had united Dissenters as never before and made of them, for a time, a formidable political party. That union was interrupted during the long war years, was frequently ineffective locally, and was often ignored by orthodox Dissenters when it was Unitarians who were persecuted. Anna Laetitia Barbauld (neé Aikin and herself an Arian) wrote deriding the timid and cautious who failed to support Priestley when his house was burned down during the riots, and those who, "With low obeisance, and with servile phrase / File behind file, advance, with supple knee, / And lay their necks beneath the foot of power."[12] But the Pitt ministry early commenced a deliberate policy of repression against reformers. In May 1792 a royal proclamation was issued against seditious meetings and political "libels." Neither Pitt, Dundas, Lord Portland (home secretary 1794–1801), Sir John Scott (attorney general), nor Sir John Mitford (solicitor general) was noted for liberality or capable of making fine distinctions. There evolved a network of reactionary organizations, employing a cadre of spies, informers, and agent provocateurs to attack any differences of opinion than their own. Minor reformers (e.g., Thomas Muir, Joseph Gerrald) and ministers of Dissenting (frequently Unitarian) congregations (e.g., Thomas Fyshe Palmer, William Winterbotham) were arrested, tried, and convicted on the flimsiest of grounds. Pitt even supported the sentences of the Scottish court headed by Lord Braxfield, the "Judge Jeffreys of Scotland," on the transportation of Palmer and Muir, in a shoddy speech before the House of Commons, 10 March 1794.[13]

Booksellers like James Belcher of Birmingham and Joseph Johnson of London were convicted for selling the works of Thomas Paine. Benjamin Flower, editor of the *Cambridge Intelligencer,* Thomas Evans, Unitarian minister in Carmarthenshire, Jeremiah Joyce, tutor to the sons of Lord Stanhope, James Montgomery, Moravian editor of the *Sheffield Iris,* and Gilbert Wakefield were imprisoned on suspicion of treason or for seditious libel. Such was the political atmosphere that many persons besides the Priestley sons chose to leave England for America.

12. Grace A. Ellis, *A Memoir of Mrs. Anna Laetitia Barbauld, with many of her Letters* (Boston: James R. Osgood and Co., 1874), 1:230.

13. See, for example, B. Mardon, "Memoirs of the Rev. Thomas Fyshe Palmer," *Christian Reformer* 4 (1837): 275–81, 337–42; and L. Baker Short, "Thomas Fyshe Palmer: From Eton to Botany Bay," *Transactions of the Unitarian Historical Society* 13 (1963–66): 37–68. Philip A. Brown, *The French Revolution in English History* (1918; reprint, London: George Allen & Unwin, 1923), 33, claims that Robert Burns's "Scots wha hae wi' Wallace bled," was inspired by the conviction and transportation of Thomas Muir.

It has been estimated that some ten thousand persons emigrated to the United States in 1794, and more followed in subsequent years. Many were English and known to Priestley; these included William Christie (Unitarian minister), Thomas Cooper (Manchester entrepreneur), Joseph Gales (newspaper editor in Sheffield), Thomas Henry Jr. (son of the Manchester chemical manufacturer), George Humphreys and William Russell (Birmingham merchants), Henry Toulmin (Unitarian minister), and Benjamin Vaughan (M.P. for Calne). The ship taken by the young Priestleys was crowded with passengers, as was every other ship sailing for America, for, as Priestley wrote George Thatcher in the United States, it seemed the wish of the court and country in general to drive all liberal thinkers out of it.[14]

Priestley's "martyrdom" at Birmingham and his trenchant pen seemed at first to lend him some immunity from government persecution. The flood of letters, published as appendices to his *Appeal,* provided cautionary evidence of public support. Letters of condolence from the Académie des Sciences, French Chemists, and the Hollandsche Maatschappij der Wetenschappen suggested that European intellectual opinion condemned England.[15] This support was somewhat offset by condolences of the Jacobin "Friends of the Constitution," English Constitutional and Revolution Societies, Christopher Wyvill, and the Society of United Irishmen. Meanwhile, false rumors were rife.

The Marquis of Buckingham wrote to Lord Grenville in July 1791 that a Birmingham coachman vouched for the treasonable toast at the dinner

14. For the estimate, see Jenny Graham, "Revolutionary in Exile: The Emigration of Joseph Priestley to America, 1794–1804," *Transactions of the American Philosophical Society* 85 (1995): part 2, 1; Michael R. Watts, *The Expansion of Evangelical Nonconformity,* vol. 2 of *The Dissenters* (Oxford: Clarendon Press, 1995), 354–55; Goodwin, *Friends of Liberty,* 307–58; [Kenrick], *Chronicles of a Nonconformist Family,* 79. For the crowded ships, see Priestley to John Wilkinson, 19 Aug. 1793, Warr.; Priestley to George Thatcher, 21 Aug. 1793, Houghton Library, Harvard University; *Proceedings of the Massachusetts Historical Society* 3 (2d ser., 1886–87): 16.

15. M.J.A.N. C de Condorcet, for the Academy of Sciences, to Priestley, 30 July 1791, MS Copy, Bodleian Library, Oxford; *W.* 1.2:127–29; Chemists of Paris to Priestley, MS Draft, c. July 1791, Burndy Library, Smithsonian Institution Libraries, Washington, D.C.; *SciAuto.,* 140. Kurt Loewenfeld, "Contributions to the History of Science," *Memoirs of the Manchester Literary and Philosophical Society* 57 (1912–13): 46, claims that corrections to the latter are in the hand of Lavoisier. Martinus van Marum, draft, 20 June 1792, Archives, Koninklijke Hollandsche Maatschappij der Wetenschappen, Haarlem; "Friends of the Constitution" to Priestley, c. Aug. 1791, *W.* 1.2:130–32; English Constitutional and Revolution Societies to Priestley, 16 Aug. 1791, *W.* 1.2:142–44, answered in *W.* 1.2:145–46; Christopher Wyvill to Priestley, 7, 13 March 1793, ZFW Y/2/84/5, 8 North Riding Record Office, Yorks; Society of United Irishmen to Priestley, with the prediction that Priestley's forced emigration would be the characteristic example of the times, 28 March 1794, *W.* 1.2:218–22.

and that pamphlets found in Priestley's house (amounting to thousands in number) ready for distribution had done more to inflame the mob than any other circumstance. James B. Burgess, undersecretary for foreign affairs, wrote Lord Auckland, serving as ambassador extraordinary at The Hague, on 4 September 1792, reporting news brought by a messenger from Paris: "Tom Paine is at Paris, and has just been appointed to some post in the executive government. Dr. Priestley is also there, and is looked upon as the great adviser to the present ministers, being consulted by them on all occasions." John Wilkinson was suspected of sedition in 1792, partly because he was Priestley's brother-in-law but also because he paid his workers in trade tokens ("Assignats"), accepted by the tradesmen in the neighborhood who were said to use them for proselytizing Presbyterianism and Paine's *Rights of Man.* Finally, Priestley was included in a Home Office list of 28 July 1792 of "Disaffected and seditious Persons."[16]

The conviction of Winterbotham for a sermon preached in commemoration of the landing of William of Orange was a blow to liberal Dissenters who had frequently preached such sermons, and Lindsey, Priestley, and others sent him financial assistance. But it was the sentence passed on Thomas Fyshe Palmer in September 1793 that most frightened Priestley's friends. Palmer had left the Anglican clergy to become a Unitarian minister under Priestley's influence, had written articles for the *Theological Repository,* and was convicted on the testimony of suborned informers. It was after the sentence passed on Palmer that Priestley's friends urged him to leave England "lest he should fall a victim to the same malevolent tyranny."[17]

By 28 February 1794 Priestley had begun to pack. To safeguard his investment in the French funds, he had written the American ambassador in September 1793 of his intention to become a citizen of the United States, in the expectation that word would be passed to Paris.[18] In March he wrote

16. Marquis of Buckingham to Lord Grenville, 19 July 1791, Grenville Papers, *Her Majesty's Historical Manuscript Commission Report* 14th, Appendix 5, Part 2, 133–34; James B. Burgess to Lord Auckland, 4 Sept. 1792, [Lord William Auckland], *Journals and Correspondence of Ld. Auckland* (London: Richard Bentley, 1860–62), 2:437–38; Raymond V. Holt, *Unitarian Contributions to Social Progress in England* (London: George Allen & Unwin, 1938), 63–64. Public Record Office MS HO 42.21, cited in Trevor H. Levere, "Dr. Thomas Beddoes at Oxford," *Ambix* 28 (1981): 61–67.

17. Samuel Rogers quoted in Clayden, *Early Life of Samuel Rogers,* 251–52. Priestley had written to John Wilkinson, 2 Dec. 1793, Warr., that Winterbotham's case showed that no man was safe, however innocent. In Dec. 1795 and Aug. 1796, Priestley joined Lindsey in an annual subscription for Palmer, Muir, and Winterbotham.

18. The French funds were never to be of any use to him. In April 1794 Thomas Cooper was consulting Wilkinson about Priestley's investment in the French funds and Priestley complained,

to Lord Auckland of his proposed sailing.[19] He made it clear that he was not fleeing persecution and requested a letter from the English government that would serve as protection against piracy. The request was granted and the Priestley family was on its way on 7 April. Five weeks later, while the Priestleys were on the high seas, Pitt's government began making arrests, starting with Thomas Hardy and continuing to John Thelwall, Jeremiah Joyce, Horne Tooke, Thomas Holcroft, and others, for a total of twelve reformers. *Habeas corpus* was temporarily suspended the third week in May and one may easily conjecture that Joseph Priestley might have been one of the number tried for high treason in the infamous, abortive trials that lasted from mid-October through mid-December 1794. But Priestley was, by then, safely in the United States.[20]

He sailed on 8 April in the ship *Sansom*, and spent the eight weeks and a day of the voyage, when not seasick, in reading, writing sermons, preaching, and, following the example of Franklin, making experiments and observations on the sea.[21] On the evening of 4 June, while the ship waited off Sandy-Hook for a pilot, the Priestleys were met by Joseph Jr., privately rowed to Old Battery, New York, and taken to a lodging house.[22] The next

---

14 June, that the funds were not productive, Warr. In July 1794 Priestley twice wrote to Dallende Swan & Co., Paris, about those funds, sending a power of attorney, 8, 10 July 1794; APS and John Vaughan wrote them with a certificate of Priestley's residence in the United States, a copy of his holdings in the French funds, and a plea that the French government have some sympathy for their honorary citizen, 10 July 1794, APS. Priestley wrote Vaughan on 31 Aug. 1795, APS, and Citizen Perigaux, 12 April 1801, Bolton, #93, about trying to get at least some interest from the French funds and French confusion about ownership. As late as 1821 Joseph Jr. was still attempting to settle the family claim on the French, of 55,000 francs. He was informed that it would be settled by commissioners, at one-quarter of initial value, on which they would allow only 3 percent interest—which would only repay the cost of recovering it; see his letters to his son, Joseph Rayner Priestley, Dickinson College Library, Carlisle, Pa.

19. Priestley to John Wilkinson, c. Sept. 1793, Warr.; to William Eden, Lord Aukland, 25 March 1794, Add. MSS 34, 452 fol. 392, British Library, London. He never, in fact, did become a citizen of the United States.

20. He wrote Lindsey, 5 July 1794, Wms. (omitted by Rutt), that he suspected he would have joined his friends in trouble had he remained. He was anxious for news in Jan. 1795, having just heard of Tooke's trial.

21. In addition to Priestley's report to Lindsey, Mary Priestley reported on the voyage, in one of her few extant letters, to Thomas Belsham, 15 June 1794, *W.* 1.2:235–38, with some details—of icebergs, water spouts, and great gusts of wind, which Priestley failed to mention.

22. Priestley's decade in the United States has probably been treated more thoroughly than any other period of his life. See, for example, William Bakewell, "Some Particulars of Dr. Priestley's Residence at Northumberland, America," *Monthly Repository* 1 (1806): 393–97, 504–8, 564–67, 622–25; Edgar F. Smith, *Priestley in America, 1794–1804* (Philadelphia: Blakiston's Son & Co., 1920); Detlev W. Bronk, "Joseph Priestley and the Early History of the American

morning they were visited by Governor Clinton, the Bishop of New York, principal merchants, and deputations of corporate bodies and societies. The *American Daily Advertiser* (New York) welcomed Priestley in an editorial, glorying that "The United States of America, the land of freedom and independence, has become the asylum of the greatest characters of the present age, who have been persecuted in Europe, merely because they have defended the rights of the enslaved nations," and went on to declare that "England will one day regret her ungrateful treatment to this venerable and illustrious man . . . his arrival in this City calls upon us to testify our respect and esteem for a man whose whole life has been devoted to the sacred duty of diffusing knowledge and happiness among nations."

There were welcoming addresses from the Democratic Society of the City of New York on 7 June, from the Tammany Society on 11 June, from the Associated Teachers in the City of New York, the Medical Society of the State of New York, and a rather inflammatory address from "The Republican Natives of Great Britain and Ireland resident in the city of New York." These may be seen as much an attempt to gain Priestley's support for their causes as congratulations on his arrival. Priestley, avoiding any explicit endorsement of their opinions, responded that he rejoiced in his asylum in the United States but bore no ill will toward England, despite his treatment, and hoped a perpetual friendship might exist between the countries.[23]

The Priestleys were delighted with New York. They were taken to see Revolutionary battle lines and heroes and visited and dined with Governor Clinton several times. But they were eager to get to the home prepared by their sons and left New York for Philadelphia on 18 June 1794, stopping at Princeton to view the college on their way. The Philadelphia *General Advertiser* declared on 21 June 1794: "Last Thursday evening arrived in town from New York, the justly celebrated philosopher, Dr. Joseph Priestley," and

---

Philosophical Society," *Proceedings of the American Philosophical Society* 86 (1942): 103–7; Joseph Samuel Hepburn, "The Pennsylvania Associations of Joseph Priestley," *Journal of the Franklin Institute* 244 (1947): 63–72, 95–107; Schofield, "Priestley's American Education"; Caroline Robbins, "Honest Heretic: Joseph Priestley in America, 1794–1804," *Proceedings of the American Philosophical Society* 11 (1962): 60–76; Colin Bonwick, "Joseph Priestley, Emigrant and Jeffersonian," *Enlightenment and Dissent* 2 (1983): 3–22; Peter M. Lukehart, ed., *Joseph Priestley in America 1794–1804* (Carlisle, Pa.: Trout Gallery, Dickinson College, 1994). Most recently, Jenny Graham's "Revolutionary in Exile" concerns particularly Priestley's politics; she has made most effective use of his correspondence, especially with the originals in Dr. Williams's Library, for Rutt seems to have omitted most references to politics in his edition of the letters (*W.* 1.2).

23. Copies of the addresses and Priestley's responses are printed in *W.* 1.2:241–55.

republished the addresses he had received in New York and his replies. David Rittenhouse, president of the American Philosophical Society, sent a welcoming message for himself and colleagues, and again there was a flood of greetings, though none, regrettably, from his old friend Benjamin Franklin, who had died four years earlier.[24]

The enthusiasm of these greetings was, for many reasons, no surprise. Long before he decided to leave England, Priestley was known in the United States for his friendship with Benjamin Franklin, his record of support for the colonists in their struggle for independence, and his published writings. The United States was, in fact, probably the only country in the Western world that knew him more for his nonscientific work than for his science. Before he arrived, at least twelve editions of some seven different works by Priestley had been published in America, none of them scientific: his criticism of Blackstone's *Commentaries* on English law, printed in four editions; his *Address to Protestant Dissenters* supporting the colonists, printed in Boston, Philadelphia, and Wilmington; his *Letter to Burke,* reprinted in New York the year it appeared in England. There were also U.S. editions of the *Description* of the chart of history and of three of his less extreme theological works.

And this pattern continued. Some twenty of his works would be reprinted during the decade of Priestley's residence in the United States. Between 1794 and 1804 he was also to publish more than twenty-five new pamphlets or books (some in several volumes). Three of these were political, three scientific; the remainder were educational, religious, and theological. Of course, his scientific and metaphysical work was known. Copies printed in England were shipped to persons and institutions in the United States, but Americans were content to receive indirectly works printed in many editions, translated, quoted, and abstracted in Great Britain and Europe. Science was still a luxury even to American intellectuals, while politics and theology were obsessions to almost everyone in the country.[25] And there

24. Henry Wansey, *The Journal of an Excursion to the United States of North America in the Summer of 1794* (New York: Johnson Reprint Corporation, 1969), 86–92. [David English], "A Brief Description of Joseph Priestley in a letter of David English to Charles D. Green, Princeton June 20, 1794," *Journal of the Presbyterian Historical Society* 38 (1960): 124–27. Rittenhouse's welcome was drafted by a committee of the Society and was to be personally presented at the Society's hall, 21 June: from the Society's minutes by Bronk, "Priestley and the American Philosophical Society," 106. For the welcome and Priestley's response, 20, 21 June 1794, W. 1.2: 261–63. Priestley wrote Wilkinson on 27 June 1794 that his reception in Philadelphia was as flattering as that in New York, Warr.

25. The bibliography of Priestley's works printed in America is incomplete, while the availability of works through imported gifts and purchases is unknowable. Franklin, Lindsey,

were many personal contacts who spoke of his political and theological ideas and alerted people of his intention to escape the bigotry and persecution he had experienced in England.[26]

The address from "The Republican Natives of Great Britain and Ireland resident in the city of New York" hoped that Priestley was "now completely removed from the effects of every species of intolerance," but if he believed that, he was soon proved wrong. He had been warned. James Freeman of Boston had written Theophilus Lindsey in June 1793:

> Bigotry is not yet extinct among us. . . . I mention it freely because it gives me an opportunity of observing . . . that the people in America are much less liberal than is generally imagined. . . . there are men who are disposed to persecute . . . as far as they can, with uncharitable censures. . . . [Liberal Dissenters of England migrating to this country] will hope to find us as little subject to the dominion of prejudice as we are to the tyranny of arbitrary laws. But they will soon be convinced that ignorance and bigotry are not confined to England.[27]

Priestley was soon to discover for himself the truth of Freeman's warning, though he attempted to be circumspect. At the end of a set of thirteen religious discourses delivered in Philadelphia in 1794, he added another about which he warned his hearers in a "Conclusion," printed separately with *Unitarianism explained and defended*.[28] Except for the slight reference to monism in Discourse 8, there had been nothing in the *Discourses* to which a reasonable sectarian might take offense. In this added discourse, Priestley hoped to lessen the horror that many had conceived of Unitarians, who in fact agreed with all other Christians "with respect to every thing that is really fundamental"

Priestley himself, and the Rev. William Hazlitt (father of the essayist and sometime visitor to the United States) all sent copies of various works.

26. In addition to John Adams, Priestley to the Rev. Dr. James Abercrombie, Philadelphia, 21 Aug. 1793, Bolton, #81; to Mr. J. Gough, at Savannah, 25 Aug. 1793, W. 1.2:207–8. T. Brand Hollis and J. C. Lettsom informed Joseph Willard at Harvard of Priestley's misfortunes, while Priestley wrote him, April 1793, introducing Harry Toulmin and intimating his intention of coming to America, 4 Nov. 1791, 12 March 1792, 10 April 1793, *Proceedings of the Massachusetts Historical Society* 43 (1910): 634–36, 637–39, 639–40.

27. Freeman to Lindsey, 16 June 1793, Wms.

28. Joseph Priestley, *Unitarianism explained and defended, in a Discourse delivered in the Church of the Universalists at Philadelphia* (Philadelphia: John Thompson, 1796); I have used W. 16:195–96 (the "Conclusion"), 472–89.

(195). Ostensibly a religious discourse, there are political overtones and consequences to *Unitarianism explained.*

Although he wished that a place of public Unitarian worship might be established—a *"city that is set on a hill, that cannot be hid,"* with services open to all—he recommended the forms of the primitive church, without a minister, as described in his 1782 sermon on the *Constitution of the Christian Church* and supplied with his 1783 *Forms of Prayer and Other Offices.* Being excluded from almost every pulpit in the country, Priestley was reminded of Paul at Athens, who also was mistakenly accused of propagating a mischievous doctrine. Like Paul, Priestley preached only Jesus and the Resurrection. Some religious truths, of secondary but considerable importance, needed stating, however (and Priestley recommended the reading of his *Familiar Illustration* [1772], *History of Corruptions,* and *of Early Opinions*). One corruption, that of atonement, had been condemned by the "founder of this colony, William Penn," while neither original sin nor predestination was an essential part of the Christian religion.

Following this discourse, twenty young men organized the "First Society of Unitarian Christians." Priestley gave his assistance in the organization of the Society and became one of its members, but declined to become its minister, declaring that Americans should choose their leaders from among themselves. Services were then conducted, as Priestley had advised, by members of the Society in their homes.[29] Priestley congratulated the Society in an address early in 1797, and gave them additional Sunday lectures on Unitarianism from time to time. His *Address to the Unitarian Congregation* advised them to avoid taking an active part in the political affairs of this country in which they had found asylum. He urged his listeners to show that there was no danger to any state from the liberty Unitarianism enjoyed there by their peaceful behavior, meekness, and candor toward those who differed from them.[30] Let the orthodox prove their superior holiness by ostentatious effects and austerities.

29. The original constitution and rules of discipline are dated 8 Aug. 1796. Members included John Vaughan, Ralph Eddowes (a former student at Warrington), and James Taylor. In 1807 William Christie presided over the congregation, but not till 1813 did they erect a meeting house, the first erected for the sole purpose of Unitarian worship, Archive, First Unitarian Church of Philadelphia, unidentified newspaper clipping about its centenary, 1876, also brochure of the First Unitarian Church of Philadelphia, n.d., has organization document, dated 12 June 1796.

30. Priestley, *An Address to the Unitarian Congregation at Philadelphia, delivered on Sunday, March 5th, 1797* (Philadelphia: Joseph Gales, 1797); I have used W. 16:490–99.

Neither his caution here on religion nor his explicit disavowal of interest in politics protected him, however, and this was not entirely Priestley's fault. The addresses he had received in New York and his conciliatory responses roused the fury of William Cobbett, then temporarily expatriate from England and not yet into the reactionary conservatism on which his fame was built. Writing under the name of Peter Porcupine, Cobbett's first diatribe, *Observations on the Emigration of Dr. Joseph Priestley* (1795), crudely overemphasized Priestley's faults, denounced his disloyalty to king and church, belittled his writing style, and attacked his reputation as a scientist with (in the third edition) references to the charges by Harrington and "Cambriensis."[31] This first attack was followed by a veritable campaign, and as tensions heightened between the United States and France, Porcupine was joined by other Anglophile and Francophobe writers.

Yet Priestley was not wholly blameless. Of course, his emigration was in itself a political statement, as was the colony he hoped to establish in north-central Pennsylvania. For the Priestleys did not intend to settle in aristocratic Philadelphia; by mid-July they were on their way to the rural isolation of Northumberland. They were not, however, going permanently into a cultural wilderness. Soon there was to be settled in the area a community of like-minded Englishmen, politically and theological liberal, escaping from persecution in England, for which Priestley was to be pastor and schoolmaster. This was the justification for the land-speculation venture of Thomas Cooper, Joseph Priestley Jr., William Russell, and others, optioning land between the west and northeast branches of the Susquehanna River near Loyalsock Creek, about fifty miles from Northumberland near what is now Williamsport, Pennsylvania. There is no indication that Priestley was personally involved in the speculations, but he *was* concerned in planning the settlement and found consolation for his emigration in the prospect of service there. The prospective settlement was given up by mid-September 1794.

31. See Lyman C. Newell, "Peter Porcupine's Persecution of Priestley," *Journal of Chemical Education* 10 (1933): 151–59; and William Reitzel, "William Cobbett and Philadelphia Journalism: 1794–1800," *Pennsylvania Magazine of History and Biography* 5 (1935): 223–44. Cobbett was an outspoken supporter of Federalist causes in a number of pamphlets and in a Philadelphia and, later, a New York newspaper. The *Philadelphia General Advertiser* for 1 Aug. 1794 denounced Porcupine's *Observations* as unfit for publication in the United States. After losing a trial for libel, Cobbett fled the United States and returned to England in 1800. The edition of *Porcupine's Works* republished in London in 1801 was dedicated to George Reeves and subscribed to by George, Prince of Wales, Pitt's secretary, and other notorious Tories. Cobbett soon shed his Tory sentiments and achieved a notable reputation as a reactionary reformer. For a favorable study of Cobbett, see G. D. H. Cole, *The Life of William Cobbett* (New York: Harcourt, Brace, 1924). For the Harrington/"Cambriensis" episode, see Chapter 14.

The land leased by the speculators was not as described, while experience indicated that colonizing the frontier was not a task for urban Englishmen.[32] And although the venturers could not be aware of it, the pressure on liberal reformers to emigrate was soon to be substantially lessened with the December 1794 acquittal at the treason trials of Thelwall, Horne Tooke, and others.[33] Failure of the settlement scheme did not lessen Priestley's own commitment to the purposes behind the ideal, and though he did not mourn the failure of the colony, he attempted to salvage the church and, especially, the school. As early as 1793 he had written to John Wilkinson of a college possibly to be established in backwoods America, with his library and Lindsey's, plus his scientific apparatus to go to it. In January 1794 he heard that some "principal gentlemen of New York" were urging him to settle there and "undertake some department of their college," but he was then still committed to his liberal settlement. When that failed, and even though he was invited to teach at the University of Pennsylvania, he transferred his plans to the creation of a college in Northumberland.

By September 1794 he had written Benjamin Rush about his hopes and plans for the college, and he continued writing Rush until May 1795, thanking him for the pains he had taken in its establishment. He wrote John Vaughan on 4 January 1795, reminding him of the business of the proposed college. Harry Toulmin, then president of Transylvania University in Lexington, Kentucky, might join, and other tutors come from England. On 11 August the college was still on his mind, though nothing could be done till the buildings were erected the next year. He informed Withering in October that building for the college was to start the next spring and that he was to

32. Accounts of the speculation are confused, especially when mixed into the story of the "utopia," called pantisocracy, feverishly envisioned by Southey, Coleridge, and others. See, for example, Mary Cathryne Park, "Joseph Priestley and the Problem of Pantisocracy," *Proceedings of the Delaware County Institute of Science* 11 (1947): 1–60. Maurice W. Kelley, "Thomas Cooper and Pantisocracy," *Modern Language Notes* (April 1930): 218–20, refers to a *Plan de Vente de Trois Cent Mille Acres de Terres Situées dans les Comtés de Northumberland et de Huntingdon dans L'Etat de Pennsylvanie . . . par une Societé de Citoyens des Etats-Unis de L'Amerique* (Philadelphia, 1794) as outlining the project. Clarke Garrett, "Which Cooper? The Site of Coleridge's Utopia on the Susquehanna," *John and Mary's Journal* 5 (1979): 17–28, agrees that the Pantisocrats read Cooper's *Some Information Concerning America* (London, 1794), and were at the time desirous of joining Priestley, but argues against Pantisocracy being sited on the land held by the Priestley/Cooper consortium.

33. Priestley described the failure of the scheme to Lindsey and to John Vaughan, 17 Sept. 1794, APS; repeated in William Vaughan to John Wilkinson, 25 Oct., Warr.; and discussed in Joseph Priestley Jr. to James Watt Jr., 20 Nov. 1794, Birmingham City Archives, Reference Library. Priestley wrote William Russell that people not prepared to labor regret leaving England, 25 June 1794, Russell Papers, Add. MSS 44992, British Library.

be president. Almost everything but natural history he could, *pro tempore* and in some measure, teach himself. When the common hall was erected, he would make use of it as a chapel, as the bigotry of the place was such that pulpits were all shut to him.[34]

He won the support of several of the principal landowners in the vicinity who subscribed money and land for the purpose. Priestley drew up a plan for a course of study and rules for internal management but declined to be its president after all, proposing instead that he would give such lectures as he was qualified for, *gratis,* and would give the institution use of his library and apparatus, quite rightly believing his library superior to the academic libraries of most of the colleges of the country. There were, inevitably, delays, but a committee of the "Academy" was organized and met in September 1797, resolving to rent a building for classes to commence in April 1798 and to appeal for state support in raising a building.[35] Then some contributors defaulted on their pledges and the legislature refused to act. The scheme failed because of a financial panic in 1797, and perhaps also because of political changes.

For moving from urban and mercantile Philadelphia to rural Pennsylvania had placed Priestley in a different political environment, and he soon allied himself with the interests of the small landowners.[36] He had assured John Vaughan within days of his arrival in the United States that he intended to avoid any discussion of politics, only to praise, in the next breath, the advantages of political debates and associations. On his arrival in New York City he dined with the Osgoods, late envoy to Great Britain, where he met Citizen Genet and, with the Bishop of New York, enjoyed conversation after dinner, "especially on political subjects." An early letter to Lindsey claimed that he was avoiding party politics and exercising caution in replies to addresses, but Porcupine found in those replies fuel for his attack. Priestley wrote John Adams that he had "made it a rule to take no part whatever in

34. Priestley to John Wilkinson, 18 Feb., 16 May 1793, 9 Jan. 1794, Warr.; to Benjamin Rush, 14 Sept., 28 Oct., 3, 11 Nov. 1794, 22 May 1795, Bolton, #83, 84, 86, 87, though all the support Rush gave was canceling payment on land Priestley had bought from him in lieu of a subscription to the college. John Vaughan, 4 Jan., 11 Aug. 1795, Vaughan Papers BV 492, Priestley Papers B 931, APS; Priestley to William Withering, 27 Oct. 1795, Library, APS.

35. Priestley to Lindsey, 14 Sept. 1797, 3 May 1799. The best account of Northumberland Academy is that of Hepburn, "Pennsylvania Associations," part 2, 95–103. See also Schofield, "Priestley's American Education." For the sizes of American academic libraries in the period, see Theodore Horberger, *Scientific Thought in the American Colleges, 1638–1800* (Austin: University of Texas Press, 1945).

36. By August 1794 he was deploring the existence of excise taxes and sympathizing with the natives in the Whiskey Rebellion. Priestley to John Vaughan, 4, 25 Aug. 1794, APS.

the politics of a country in which I am a stranger, and in which I only wish to live undisturbed as such," but many of his actions were political.[37]

Early in July 1794 he was flattered by an invitation to join Thomas McKean, then Chief Justice of Pennsylvania, on a visit to President George Washington, and he bragged to Lindsey in February 1796 of a two-hour visit with Washington and Adams, where he took tea: "every thing here is the reverse of what it is with you."[38] He visited Washington again in May 1796 in the company of William Russell, and in March 1797 he wrote Belsham that he had paid his respects with a visit to the former president, who had invited him to Mount Vernon. By that time politics had polarized the country between a Federalist Party headed by Alexander Hamilton, representing conservative, pro-British industrial and mercantile interests who favored a strong centralized government, and the anti-Federalists (or Democrats), headed by Thomas Jefferson, who favored agrarianism, small businessmen, limited federal government, and were pro-French. Though he continued to deny his interest in politics, Priestley had already committed himself to favor the anti-Federalists.

In mid-February 1797 he preached a sermon/discourse, *The Case of Poor Emigrants, recommended,* in answer to the growing xenophobia of the Federalists.[39] As an emigrant himself, he commended poor emigrants to the favorable notice and charitable assistance of the public, as a "natural" but not a "legal" claim (*pace* the poor laws of England) on the God-given superfluity of others. He proposed a public institution, administered by persons of discretion, from which temporary relief might be given, perhaps as a loan returnable to the institution in time.

Emigrants were, in general, he said, of the more industrious class, the indolent, weak, sickly, and timid staying home. But information about their

37. [Henry Wansey], "Henry Wansey and His American Journal, 1794," ed. D. J. Jeremy, *Memoir of the American Philosophical Society* 82 (1970): 127; Priestley to John Vaughan, 8 June 1794, APS; to Theophilus Lindsey, 15 June 1794, Wms.; to John Adams, 13 Nov. 1794, Adams Papers, Reel 378, Massachusetts Historical Society.

38. George Washington to Chief Justice McKean, 9 July 1794, Historical Society of Pennsylvania; Priestley to Benjamin Vaughan, 30 July 1794, Warr.

39. Early in 1795 Priestley had written to Adams that he had no intention of becoming naturalized, but he lamented that Congress was discouraging democratically minded immigrants [Jan. 1795], Adams Papers Reel 379, Massachusetts Historical Society. Joseph Priestley, *The Case of Poor Emigrants, recommended in a Discourse, delivered at the University Hall in Philadelphia, on Sunday, February 19, 1797* (Philadelphia: John Gales, 1797); I have used W. 16:500–511. Adams wrote Pickering in 1798: "we have had too many French philosophers already, and I really begin to think, or rather suspect, that learned academies, not under the immediate inspection and control of government, have disorganized the world, and are incompatible with social order." [Adams], *Works,* 8:596.

new country was hard come by, and many needed advice more than money. He paid special attention to emigrants from the oppressed states of Europe, and those from Great Britain and Ireland who were unable to bear encroachments on their liberty. Some of these brought enriching capital that helped assist others who were distressed.

Your ancestors, if not yourselves, were driven from Europe, and you should now feel for those who follow, Priestley urged his hearers. "Receive then, with open arms, those who, at a distance, were praying for your success, and in various ways . . . contributing to it, and for which they now suffer; for the crime of wishing well to the liberty and independence of *America* will never be forgiven by the *Court of Great Britain*" (507). Emigrants from France who opposed changes in their government might have been wrong, but they had acted on principle and should find kindness here. Nor was there reason to fear the extremes of either right or left, as each was but a small minority in the great body of enlightened people. "Where there is perfect liberty of speaking and writing, no principles can be dangerous." Truth would prevail in the end. A private society for emigrants, without distinction of country, religion, or political principles had already been established and been successful.

John Adams, a moderate Federalist, became president in March 1797 and Priestley, as a supposed friend of France, was increasingly an object of abuse by the Federalist press. Adams had never doubted that the French Revolution would be a disaster, and he challenged Priestley's hopes, based on Revelation and the prophecies. Nonetheless, the two remained more or less friendly. Priestley even requested Adams's help, shortly after his inauguration, for aid in arranging for travel to France.[40] Then, in February 1798, Priestley's "Maxims of Political Arithmetic," was published in the Philadelphia newspaper the *Aurora*. Adams despised and feared the *Aurora*, considering it an implacable and unenlightened enemy, capable of doing him much harm. He correctly regarded Priestley's "Maxims" as an attack on his government and, incorrectly, as petty revenge for his refusal to grant Thomas Cooper, on

---

40. Adams wrote to Priestley as early as 27 Feb. 1793, in a letter passed to Shelburne: "I think that all the ages and nations of the world never furnished so strong an argument against a pure republic as the French have done," and discussed Priestley's emigration to the United States, Marquis of Lansdowne Papers, *Historical Manuscripts Commission Reports* 88, No. 2, 252. See also Adams to Jefferson, 15 Aug. 1823, [Adams], *Works*, 10:408–10. Early in 1797 Priestley proposed resettling in France to realize some income from his French funds for the support of his daughter after William Finch declared bankruptcy. See Priestley to John Adams, (March–April 1797), Adams Papers, Reel 383, Massachusetts Historical Society. This proposal discredits his later (1799) denial of any intent to leave the United States.

Priestley's recommendation, a federal position. Why Priestley chose to publish a political piece at this time is unclear, but it represented his long-held opinions on the rashness of Hamilton's economic policies. It also mirrored the policies of Adam's political adversaries, the Jeffersonian anti-Federalists.[41]

"Maxims of Political Arithmetic" began with the recommendation that the country should do what it did best—raise in the greatest quantity and perfection productions that feed, clothe, and habituate its inhabitants, exchanging any surplus for articles that other countries best supplied. Money spent for ambassadors to foreign and distant countries with which the United States had little or no intercourse, and for a navy to protect shipping, made the carrying trade prohibitively expensive. All other nations, regardless of politics, wanted to trade with the United States, which should not risk its advantage by one-sided treaties. Duties on imports and bounties on exports were equally unnecessary; particularly impolitic was the duty on importation of books. Capital was better spent in sending men of science to purchase works of literature and philosophic instruments, which the country's universities and colleges disgracefully lacked, or on the roads, bridges, and canals that contributed more to laborers than did seamen or soldiers.

Publication, in the spring of 1798, of the XYZ correspondence raised a spirit of extreme nationalism among the Federalists, resulting in the four acts known as the Alien and Sedition Acts, passed by Congress in June and July and directed particularly against anti-Federalist Francophiles, including Thomas Cooper and Joseph Priestley. Priestley was bitter about the acts, for he was aware that Timothy Pickering, Adams's secretary of state, wanted to evict him. He wrote to George Thatcher, then a member of Congress, on 26 July 1798, "I find I am at the mercy of one man, who, if he pleases, may, even without giving me a hearing, or a minute's warning, either confine me, or send me out of the country."[42] His correspondence with Thatcher, starting as

41. [Priestley], "A Quaker in Politics," "Maxims of Political Arithmetic, applied to the Case of the United States of America," *Aurora* 26 and 27 (Feb. 1798), reprinted in *Letters to the Inhabitants of Northumberland* (1799), which I have used in *W.* 25:175–82. Graham believes these essays originated in discussions with Jefferson late in 1797; see Graham, "Revolutionary in Exile," 103n278. Adams claimed to have "great complaints against him for personal injuries and persecution" but prayed that Priestley might "be pardoned" for them and declared that he should have liked to correspond with him had he lived. [Adams], *Works*, 10:83

42. For a detailed account of this episode, see James Morton Smith, *Freedom's Fetters: The Alien and Sedition Laws and American Civil Liberties* (Ithaca: Cornell University Press, 1966). Many years later Adams rather ingenuously disclaimed responsibility for the Alien and Sedition Laws; see [Adams], *Works*, 10:42. The exaggerations, violence, and coarseness of the attacks on Priestley between 1794 and 1804 can only be justified as typical of attacks on all persons from *both* sides of the political spectrum; for examples, see Charles Warren, *Jacobin and Junto, or,*

early as 1793, began and continued over a shared interest in millenarianism and Unitarian theology, but added politics when Thatcher came to Philadelphia as a congressman for Massachusetts. Though a determined Federalist, he was Priestley's major political correspondent in the United States and may have shared some of Priestley's ideas with colleagues, including Priestley's description of France, late in 1798, as "that abominable nation."[43]

Pickering wrote Adams that Priestley had attended a "*democratic* assembly on the 4th of July at Northumberland" and demonstrated a "want of decency," in getting an anti-Federalist address by Thomas Cooper printed and distributed. Adams rejected any suggestion that he be deported: "I do not think it wise to execute the alien law against poor Priestley. . . . He is as weak as water, as unstable as Reuban, or the wind. His influence is not an atom in the world." Yet in 1813 Adams described Priestley as "a great and extraordinary man, whom I sincerely loved, esteemed, and respected . . . a phenomenon; a comet in the system, like Voltaire, Bolingbroke, and Hume . . . this great, this learned, indefatigable, most excellent and extraordinary man."[44]

The situation was made much worse for Priestley by Cobbett's reprinting, in the 20 August 1798 issue of his *Gazette*, of a set of seditious and malicious letters by Hurford Stone in Paris to Priestley and Benjamin Vaughan that had been captured by the British and published in London. Priestley promptly disclaimed responsibility for what was written to him, but the damage was done. Priestley was declared a "French agent" corresponding with "their other spies in this country," called the "eldest son of Disorder" who would want "to reform the Government of Heaven should he ever get there," a "journeyman of discontent and sedition," and director of Jacobin

---

Early American Politics as Viewed in the Diary of Dr. Nathaniel Ames, 1758–1822 (Cambridge: Harvard University Press, 1931).

43. Priestley to George Thatcher, 26 July 1798, Boston Public Library; *Proceedings of the Massachusetts Historical Society* 3 (2d ser., 1886): 23–24. Most of Priestley's extensive correspondence with Thatcher is preserved in the Massachusetts Historical Society and was printed in the *Proceedings*, 21 Aug. 1793; 1, 10 March, 19 April, 10, 31 May, 28 June, 5, 26 July, 20 Dec. 1798, 10, 17, 24 Jan., 14 Feb., 1 March, 12 Dec. 1799; 9, 23 Jan., 20 Feb., 6, 20 March, 23 April, 10 May, 8 Aug. 1800: 3 (2d ser., 1886): 16–34, 36–39. Spelling of the name was changed to Thacher early in the nineteenth century.

44. Timothy Pickering to John Adams, 1 Aug. 1799, Pickering Papers 11:524, Massachusetts Historical Society. The information came from Charles Hall, the man appointed to the position for which Priestley had recommended Cooper. John Adams to Timothy Pickering, 13 Aug. 1799, [Adams], *Works*, 9:5–6, 13–14. Wilstach, *Adams and Jefferson Correspondence*, 68–69, 71. Adams despised Pickering, whom he soon dismissed for excessive anti-French agitation and for political maneuverings; he described him to Jefferson as a rogue whom he should like to have whipped till the blood came. Wilstach, ibid., 155–56.

interests in the western country.[45] Though some of his friends thought he should stay quiet, Priestley was finally brought publicly to defend himself among his immediate neighbors (probably with memories of the actions of his Birmingham neighbors in mind) with his *Letters to the Inhabitants of Northumberland.*

In the preface to the second edition (1801), Priestley claimed the first edition had had good effect, as even more zealous Federalists now had a more favorable opinion than they had. With the change of general sentiments since that edition, freedom of speech and press had been revived, the fiction of a standing army needed to repel invasion conceded. The Alien and Sedition Acts had been acknowledged unconstitutional, and Judge Chase's doctrine of constructive treason censured.[46]

He had not become naturalized so as to keep free from suspicion, but that had left him open as an alien. He was proud of England and wished her well, but with house, garden, library, and laboratory in place, how could any suppose him, at his age, anxious to move? And those material circumstances certainly furnished no motive for faction. True, like Wilberforce and General Washington, he was an honorary citizen of France, but this did not mean he was an enemy to America, whose principles of general liberty were the inspiration for those of France, which once gave material assistance to the American colonists in their battle for independence.

Federalists asserted that Priestley and his friends were democrats, but that was no crime; indeed every man *not* a democrat was an enemy to that constitution which the Federalists apparently wished to change. Democracy was not a state of anarchy and mob rule. Priestley condemned the atrocities of Robespierre as much as any one. He had as much right to have opinions

---

45. Stone praised the successes of French armies and anticipated their invasion of England. Priestley to Cobbett, 4 Sept. 1798, *W.* 1.2:406–7; Charles Nisbet to Charles Wallace, 25 Oct. 1798, Nisbet Correspondence, Manuscript Division, New York Public Library. Nisbet, president of Dickinson College, had been critical of Priestley since his arrival in the United States, partly out of fear that his friendship for Benjamin Rush would divert the latter's support from Dickinson to a proposed college for Priestley in Northumberland. See his letter to the Earl of Buchan, 15 Oct. 1794, Dickinson College Library, Carlisle, Pa. Nicholas Ridgely, chancellor of Delaware, to Sec. Appleton, 21 Dec. 1799, Gratz Collection, Case 3, box 32, Historical Society of Pennsylvania; Letter by "A Federal Republican" published in the *Philadelphia Gazette,* 12 March 1800.

46. Joseph Priestley, *Letters to the Inhabitants of Northumberland and its Neighbourhood, on Subjects interesting to the Author, and to Them* (Northumberland: Andrew Kennedy, 1799); 2d edition, *with Additions, to which is added a Letter to a Friend in Paris, relating to Mr. Liancourt's Travels in the North American States* (Philadelphia: John Conrad, 1801). I have used *W.* 25:109–87, from the second edition. There is no preface in the first edition.

respecting the government of the country in which he lived as did Peter Porcupine, who was also an alien. Indeed, as politics was the universal topic of conversation and newspapers, how could one avoid forming an opinion? Given his *First Principles of Government,* his *Lectures on History,* his experiences with Lord Shelburne and acquaintance with leading politicians from all parts of Europe, his extensive reading of political publications (e.g., Adam Smith), he thought that the opinions of "this old man" should have some value. Adams had quoted one of his political statements, as had Benjamin Franklin.

He had had little time for attention to the peculiar politics of this country, what with his publications and experiments. He had sided with the Democrats against the Federalists, who appeared friendly to monarchy and the English Establishment, but he had not imposed those sentiments on others. He did write "Maxims" for the *Aurora* and contributed $1 toward the printing of Cooper's *Essays,* but he promised an equal donation for printing a comprehensive, dispassionate view of the Federalist position—if such could be found. He was not a patron of Cooper's work, he continued, though he generally approved it. Yes, he had attended 4th of July celebrations at which democratic toasts were drunk, and had responded to the scurrilous attacks of Porcupine in a letter published in several newspapers.

But he was not responsible for what people wrote to him (though the letters of Mr. Stone had given him some pleasure). He believed that a revolution was needed in England to reform abuses (limit power of the throne, give representation to the respectable class of citizens), but hoped it might be achieved peaceably and without the intervention of a foreign power. All friends of liberty were shocked at the enormities in France, but even Mr. Robson ("who makes me a coconspirator against all religions and governments of Europe") admitted the gross inequities in France before the Revolution. Other European kingdoms were almost as bad as the French, and every person friendly to liberty and humanity wished for emancipation there.

Cobbett's abuse revealed low education, character, and manners. Though it was symbolic of what he had endured for more than twenty years, rarely had Priestley's English antagonists been so low. Cobbett's erroneous, contradictory, illogical assertions came from a man Priestley had never met and to whose invectives he had never replied. President Adams would attest that Priestley was neither Deist nor atheist; Unitarians acknowledged the Scriptures—they just interpreted them differently.

He esteemed Adams and honored his integrity, even his prejudices. He wished, therefore, that Adams had prevented misrepresentation of the exchange of letters recommending Cooper for a government position.[47] Happily, Priestley had retained copies of the letters and could correct the claims of the editor. Free discussion of political subjects was not an attack on government, nor was criticism of government an attack on the country. Opinions should be perfectly free, because they could do no harm, while overt acts should be watched with care. Let everything be open to free discussion, let truth and error have equal advantage, and truth would in due time be universally accepted.

The ninth letter acknowledged the virtues of the U.S. Constitution—the best ever devised by man—but Priestley suggested some improvements, "as no work of man is perfect": "(1) Limitation of terms, especially of the presidency lest great power be amassed by repeated running. 2) Veto power, such as that of the Senate over the House of Representatives, should not be absolute. 3) There should be provision made to guard against violations of the Constitution. Perhaps a special court of deputies from all states, to be convened by the legislature of any separate state. 4) Eliminate the oath of allegiance. Require satisfying time of residency before admission to offices of trust."

Priestley had come to the country chiefly in admiration of its Constitution, but that had now been infringed by the Congress, which had made laws on subjects expressly forbidden to them respecting treaties of commerce, powers of making peace and war, and restrictions on freedom of speech and the press. The aliens and naturalization laws passed since Priestley's arrival were "particularly unwise."

The Treat of Amity with England represented a mistake in foreign policy. It should not have been entered without the knowledge of the French, who had materially assisted the Americans' independence. The United States was ideally situated to derive advantage from all nations, receiving injury from none. All intercourse with foreign nations should be commercial, and they could undertake the shipping. There followed a reprinting of the "Maxims of Political Arithmetic" and a "Letter to a Friend in France" refuting a series of untruths by Liancourt in his *Travels,* untruths which could easily have been corrected by simple enquiry.

Publication of the *Letters* apparently did Priestley good in his immediate neighborhood and impressed some of the readers in the wider world. Graham describes them as "a testimony of political extremism," of "unswerving, naive, even ruthless idealism," but this is excessive. Priestley sent a copy

---

47. Priestley to John Adams, 11 Aug. 1797, Adams Papers, Reel 385, Massachusetts Historical Society; printed in Cobbett's *Rush-Light* (30 April 1800), dated 12 August.

to his anti-Federalist New York friend, Robert R. Livingston, who arranged for republication in Albany; Jefferson distributed a dozen sets in Virginia; and one of his favorite Philadelphia conversationalists, the violent Federalist John Andrews, informed Priestley that he "had done them [the Federalists] more mischief than any other man."[48]

By the time the second edition of the *Letters* was published there had been a change of administration and Jefferson was the new president. A few days after his inauguration, Jefferson wrote a long letter to Priestley, condemning "the bigotry and reaction of the barbarians" and praising him as "the great apostle of science and honesty." "It is with heartfelt satisfaction that, in the first moments of my public action, I can hail you with welcome to our land, tender to you the homage of its respect and esteem, cover you under the protection of those laws which were made for the wise and good like you, and disdain the legitimacy of that libel on legislation, which, under the form of a law, was for some time placed among them."[49]

In 1799 Thomas McKean, an anti-Federalist, had been elected governor of Pennsylvania, and the parallel change in 1800 on the federal level opened the possibility of state help for the moribund Northumberland Academy. By this time Priestley had gathered in his home a class of fourteen young men, to whom he lectured regularly on theology and philosophy, but this was not the school he had envisioned. The Pennsylvania General Assembly was petitioned and an "Act in aid of the Northumberland Academy in the town and county of Northumberland" was approved in January 1804. Priestley's library was cited as an academy asset and an unfinished building and debts already contracted were mentioned. The act provided that $2,000 in state taxes due from the county be granted to the trustees of the academy. And once Priestley or his appointees had certified that he had a library of not less than two thousand volumes, approved by the trustees of the academy and ready to be donated to the academy, the governor was to appoint two

48. Priestley told Thatcher, 9 Jan. 1800, "in consequence of the candid account of my principles and conduct, I shall have no occasion to trouble the public with anything farther on the subject." Graham, "Revolutionary in Exile," 137. Priestley to Robert R. Livingston, 17 April 1800, Historical Society of Pennsylvania; Thomas Jefferson to Priestley, 18 Jan. 1800, Jefferson Papers, Library of Congress; [Thomas Jefferson], *Works of Thomas Jefferson*, ed. P. L. Ford (New York: G. Putnam's Sons, 1904–5), 9:96; Priestley to Jefferson, 30 Jan. 1800, Jefferson Papers, Library of Congress; to Lindsey, 29 May 1800, n.d (received 16 March 1801), *W.* 1.2:434–57.

49. Jefferson to Priestley, 21 March 1801, [Jefferson], *Works*, 8:22. Early in 1802 a Jeffersonian, George Logan, consulted Priestley about Jefferson's message to Congress and got the usual disingenuous declaration of no interest in politics, followed by some suggestions, including a request that duty on books and scientific instruments be taken off; Priestley to Logan, 18 Jan. 1802, Logan Papers V.36, Historical Society of Pennsylvania.

disinterested appraisers to value the library. The state would match its value up to $3,000. The act was approved by Governor McKean, but it came too late to do any good.[50] Priestley's contributions to American education were to be on a less public scene.

Priestley had seen a good deal of Jefferson since his visit to Philadelphia in 1797 and they seem to have commenced a correspondence, chiefly centered on politics and theology. But in Jefferson's letter to Priestley acknowledging receipt of Priestley's *Maxims* and *Letters to Northumberland*, he asked, at the request of "the ablest and brightest characters of the state," for a plan for a college to be established in Virginia. It was even suggested that Priestley might, on moving from Northumberland to Virginia, become a professor in it, but Priestley declined; he was too old and ill to contemplate moving. Though he had had more to do with places of education than most men in Europe, he hesitated to offer advice in this sphere. He would, however, send hints as they occurred to him and could recommend some tutors from England. On 8 May 1800 Priestley finally responded with "Hints concerning Public Education."[51]

These "Hints" mostly echoed what he had written in his Warrington pamphlet *Essay on a Course of Liberal Education for Civil and Active Life* (1765), with more detail, perhaps, in the way of explicit recommendations for Jefferson's College of Virginia. Specifically, schools for the education of youth involved teaching, feeding, and governing, and each of these require different qualifications.

---

50. After Priestley's death, an Act of 28 March 1808 "for the relief of the trustees of the Northumberland Academy" revealed that they had received only $430 of the absolute grant of $2,000 and none of the conditional grant of $3,000 "owing to the impossibility of complying with the conditions thereto annexed." The trustees had borrowed money to finish half of the building, and the act provided that the treasurer of Northumberland county was to pay the trustees $2,000 out of loan office money, provided they released claim to the money previously granted. The academy opened for instruction in May 1813 under the leadership of an Isaac Grier, and early histories of Northumberland County contain brief references to it. There were numerous suits for debts against trustees of the academy, including two, in 1824, served on Joseph Raynor Priestley, Priestley's grandson, who appears to have held title to the land from 1856 until his death in 1863. There is some indication that a Northumberland Academy was in operation in 1827, but by 24 August 1831 ground and building were seized in a friendly action for recovery of debt owed John Vaughan, and a notation in the *Report of the Superintendent of Common School of Pennsylvania* of 2 June 1862 declared "Not in operation for years," while an act of the Assembly of 5 April that year provided that any property of the academy should be turned over to the borough for use of the school district of Northumberland.

51. Jefferson to Priestley, 18, 27 Jan. 1800, Jefferson Papers, Library of Congress; [Jefferson], *Works*, 9:96, 102–5; Priestley to Jefferson, 30 Jan. 1800, 8 May 1800, Jefferson Papers, Library of Congress.

Two or three medical schools should be sufficient for the whole United States for some years, but respecting these Priestley did not pretend sufficient knowledge to give any opinion. Places of liberal education should be more numerous and provide lectures in ancient languages, *belles lettres* (including universal grammar, oratory, criticism, and bibliography); mathematics, natural history, experimental philosophy, chemistry (including theory of agriculture), anatomy and medicine, geography and history, law, and general policy, metaphysics, morals, and theology.

There should be a division of courses between those intended for professional men and those for gentlemen. Several professors would be needed in the first category, especially for medicine, though someone in the medical faculty should be prepared to lecture generally for those getting a liberal education. One professor should be sufficient for lessons qualifying persons to begin preaching. "To acquire more knowledge, as that of the scriptures, ecclesiastical history, etc. must be the business of their future lives." Every liberally educated person needed a general knowledge of metaphysics and the theory of morals, and religion and popular lectures of this kind should be provided. One professor for ancient languages was sufficient and no provision was needed for modern languages, "for tho' the knowledge of them, as well as skill in fencing, dancing and riding, is proper for gentlemen, instruction in them may be procured on reasonable terms without burdening the funds of the seminary with them."

Different teachers would be required for abstract mathematics and natural philosophy; one was enough for the former but the latter must be subdivided: one for natural history, another for experimental philosophy in general, a third for chemistry. Botany, mineralogy, and other kinds of natural history were sufficiently distinct to admit of different teachers, but general knowledge of each and directions for acquiring more extensive knowledge was enough for any place of education. A large and well chosen library would be useful. "Not that the students should be encouraged to read books while they are under tuition, but an opportunity of seeing books, and looking into them, will give them a better idea of the value of them." A large collection of books would also be useful to the lecturer in bibliography and would recommend the seminary to professors and make it a desirable place of residence for gentlemen of a studious turn.

Fixed salaries would be necessary to engage able professors, but they should not be much more than bare subsistence, to encourage exertion and obtain fees of students. Priestley advised Jefferson to select younger men as professors, for they want to acquire reputations, while persons of advanced years and established reputation would be less active and less willing to accommodate themselves to "the increasing light of the age." Younger men would also be more expert at teaching, having lately learned the minutiae necessary to teachers, which had generally been forgotten by advanced scholars. Do not have recourse to foreign countries for professors unless necessary, he urged Jefferson, for they expected too much deference and made natives jealous.

Although the initial distribution of courses among a limited professorial staff at the University of Virginia bears some resemblance to this plan, so many years had elapsed between Priestley's "Hints" and the establishment of the university in 1819—years during which Jefferson had queried many other persons, including Priestley's friend, Thomas Cooper—that one cannot claim those hints materially affected it. There is, however, other evidence of the influence of Priestley's educational ideas on Jefferson and on the United States. Jefferson corresponded with the Rev. James Madison, president of William and Mary College, during the 1800s and sent him copies of Priestley's work and correspondence.[52] Madison wrote, "He stands certainly in the first grade of Philosophers, physical or moral." In 1814 Jefferson recommended a course of reading for the law. Most of the works on English history and biography were those recommended in Priestley's *Lectures on History* and *Description of a Chart of Biography*. In 1825 Jefferson suggested authors and methods for the teaching of history to a member of the University of Virginia's faculty. He might as well have sent the *Lectures on History*, for the authors recommended, the order followed, the reasons given, and almost the language used can be found in Priestley's book. The historical and biographical charts, the *Lectures on History*, and the *Course of Liberal Education* were reprinted in the United States. The *Lectures on History* had been recommended to the president of Rhode Island College as early as 1788, were used at Yale between 1790 and 1800, and were read at Princeton in 1797.[53] However anticlimactic or repetitious his "new" work in science and theology might have been, in politics and education Priestley had achieved his wish, to still be useful in exile.

Priestley was so grateful to Jefferson that he dedicated his *General History of the Christian Church* to him. "Tho' I am arrived at the usual term

52. Madison to Jefferson, 17 Jan., 1 Feb. 1800, "Letters of Rev. James Madison, President of William and Mary College, to Thomas Jefferson," *William and Mary College Quarterly* 5 (2d ser., 1925): 145–51. See also R. J. Honeywell, *The Educational Work of Thomas Jefferson* (Cambridge: Harvard University Press, 1931), 121, 172–73.

53. Lewis Franklin Snow, *The College Curriculum in the United States* (New York: Columbia University Teachers College, 1907), 91; and "Letters of G. W. Custis to George Washington, 1797–1798," *Virginia Magazine of History* 20 (1912): 299–302.

of human life, it is now only that I can say I see nothing to fear from the hand of power, the government under which I live being for the first time truly favourable to me."[54] Resigned at last to his home in exile, Priestley left it a final present. The Philadelphia edition of his *Lectures on History, and General Policy* (1803) contained an additional lecture, "Of the Constitution of the United States of America." It repeated some of the suggestions proposed in Letters 9–12 of *Letters* (1801) but added: "Nothing that is human can ever be absolutely perfect; but in this constitution every evil incident to society is, to appearance, as well guarded against as human wisdom could devise; and the experience of more than fourteen years has discovered but few things that seem to want amendment."[55]

This commitment to political liberalism had provided the excuse for Priestley's exile, and this has, to some degree, remained an excuse for the neglect he has received from historians until lately. There has always been a small coterie of scholars who regarded him sympathetically, starting with his own liberal contemporaries. Christopher Wyvill praised his political ideas as late as 1822, and in 1853 Richard Cobden, writing to Joseph Parkes, Priestley's grandson-in-law, invoked the name of Joseph Priestley against historians who were attacking the Whigs, among them Fox, Lansdowne, and others who had supported the French Revolution and opposed the war with France.[56] At the same time, radical historians found Priestley's ideals too conservative. In the United States, more tolerant of Priestley's politics and gratified by his immigration, there have long been a number of papers and books on Priestley, English Dissent, and politics. The most recent contribution to this scholarship is Jenny Graham's 1995 paper in the *Transactions of the American Philosophical Society*. And more recent British scholarship, especially in the "red brick" universities, has sympathized with Priestley's anti-Establishment position. The founding, at the University College of Wales, of the *Price-Priestley Newsletter* (1977–80), which became *Enlightenment and Dissent* (founded 1982) epitomized this change, but the latter title suggested another hindrance to Priestley research. Nineteenth-century Romanticism indignantly rejected the Enlightenment, and as Frederic Harrison, Britain's apostle of Positivism, has pointed out, Priestley was the embodiment of the English Enlightenment, as Dissenters had been its chief supporters. With the fading of romantic idealism, the way has been opened for a more nuanced picture of Priestley.

54. Priestley, *General History of the Christian Church*, vi.
55. Priestley, *Lectures on History, and General Policy*, lecture 43. I have used W. 24:250–60; the quotation is from p. 256.
56. Cobden to Joseph Parkes, 8 Feb. 1853, Parkes Papers, Birmingham Reference Library.

XVI

SCIENCE

The Priestleys left Philadelphia about the middle of July 1794 for the 130-mile journey to Northumberland, a town of fewer than one hundred houses (which appealed to Mary Priestley's justly acquired fear of cities) sited within the forks of the Susquehanna River.[1] The wagon trip took five days over bad roads, but by 14 September Priestley could write to Lindsey that he was delighted with the place. In fact, he was not at all sure that he would stay there, for it was isolated and communication was difficult.[2] He desperately missed regular discourse with friends and interaction with his congregation and students. John Adams had invited him to settle in Boston, but that would not have solved the problem. It was his English friends, congregation, and students that he was to long for the rest of his life, for as he wrote Lindsey on 12 July 1795, "I shall never feel otherwise than an Englishman. Here I feel and always shall, as a stranger." He found the social isolation of Northumberland hard to bear, out of touch with the interesting things going on in

---

1. By 1800 the population of Northumberland had grown to more than 2,700, but Mary had by then been dead for nearly four years. For information about Northumberland, see, for example, Lukehart, *Priestley in America;* Herbert C. Bell, ed. "Northumberland," from *History of Northumberland County, Pennsylvania* (1891), reprinted in *Proceedings and Addresses, The Northumberland County Historical Society* 32 (1994): 35–59.

2. Priestley wrote to John Adams in Nov. 1794, and again in Jan. 1795, responding to the latter's offer of help respecting the post office at Northumberland, to aid in communications, 29 Nov. 1794, [Jan. 1795], Adams Papers, Reel 378, 379, Massachusetts Historical Society.

the world, with no immediate access to English newspapers, while those in America contained only brief extracts on world affairs.

He attempted a substitute through correspondence, writing some three hundred letters during his last decade. Nearly half of these were to Theophilus Lindsey and Thomas Belsham in England, numbered so that he, and they, could keep track and maintain a dialogue despite the six to eight months required to complete an exchange.[3] He might have found solace in preaching and teaching in Philadelphia but was disturbed at the expense of living there, where, he wrote John Wilkinson, costs were five times those in Northumberland. He had some thoughts of settling in Germantown, which was cheaper than Philadelphia and lacked the problems of transport and communication of Northumberland. But Mary Priestley, who was sick again, resisted. She wanted to be near her sons, dreaded the tumult of the city, and very much liked the country retreat. By the end of July Priestley was resigned to staying in Northumberland until the projected settlement was established.[4] When that establishment was given up, he hoped (in vain) to gather around him some friends, such as Benjamin Vaughan and the Russells, who disappointed him by preferring more cultivated areas.[5]

Having moved family, baggage, library, and laboratory, and at Mary Priestley's decided preference, Priestley determined to settle in Northumberland.[6] The town was laid out as an English village centered on a green and

3. He ceased writing his *Memoirs* in March 1795, so even that scant summarizing of his activities is lost to us, and the *Continuation* by Joseph Jr. is of little help. The letters are therefore our major source of information about his life in the United States. Those to his clerical circle are preserved in Wms. and printed in W. 1.2, though Graham, who used the originals in "Revolutionary in Exile," has shown how very much, particularly the political, was omitted by Rutt. I have cited the sources of all others used here. Most of the letters he received were destroyed, at his death, by Joseph Jr., preserving the privacy of the writers and maddening historians and biographers.

4. Priestley to John Wilkinson, 27 June, 24 July 1794, to Benjamin Vaughan, 30 July 1794, Warr.; to John Vaughan, 21 July, 4 Aug. 1794, Historical Society of Pennsylvania, APS. Mary Priestley wrote about how happy and busy she was, of her liking for America and Americans, and her delight that Priestley liked it as well, though she was to complain of the difficulty of finding and keeping servants to [unidentified], 12 Aug. 1794, Anne Holt, *A Life of Joseph Priestley* (London: Oxford University Press, 1931), 188; Priestley to William Vaughan, 26 Aug. 1794: Warr. Priestley's friends were unhappy about the isolation. Lindsey wrote Mrs. Cappe: "Anybody but Dr. P with his pittance, ought to live there. But he would be buried; nobody to teach; no means of continuing his philosophical pursuits," Catherine Cappe, *Memoirs*, 264–65.

5. Priestley to Lindsey, 9 Nov., 6 Dec. 1795; to William Vaughan, 1 Nov. 1796, Bolton, #90. Vaughan settled in Maine; the Russells, after a time in Connecticut, returned to England.

6. On 5 June 1794 Priestley made a formal declaration to Charles Tillinghast, of New York Customs, of articles brought into the United States solely intended for the use of himself and family and not intended for sale, Division of Public Records, Pennsylvania Historical and

was described, in 1794–95, as delightful, with an excellent supply of every-thing necessary in the neighborhood. There was a Quaker and a Wesleyan meeting house, a brewery, two potteries, a potash manufacturer, a clock maker, a printing office with a weekly newspaper, and a number of stores.[7] Priestley purchased a lot from a Mr. Wallis of Sunbury and, for one hundred pounds, four lots from Reuban Haines, Philadelphia land speculator, who had taken up and developed the town from 1774. On those lots, overlook-ing the Susquehanna River, Priestley began to build a house on a plan by Mary Priestley. It was to be a substantial wood-framed Federalist structure of two and one-half stories and was not completed until 1798.[8]

While their house was building, the Priestleys lived with Jos until they bought a small house. In both situations Priestley had poor access to his books and apparatus. As late as December 1794 his books were still scattered and his apparatus unpacked. Although he complained about the difficulties of transportation and communication, most visitors reported that he looked cheerful, had left off his wig, and found satisfaction and entertainment in hav-ing a printing press close by. He was easy of access, and hoping for an increase

---

Museum Commission, Harrisburg; *The Collector* 16 (1903): 63. The articles listed were eleven casks, fifty-six cases, seven crates, six bedsteads, one chest, one bundle of matting, six bundles of boards, two headboards, one clock case, one bale, one box, six trunks and one portmanteau containing books, wearing apparel; philosophical, chemical, and electrical apparatus; household furniture, three boxes, two hampers, two beds and bedding.

7. The description is that of Wm. Davy in [W. Davy], "Mr. Davy's Diary 1794," ed. Normal B. Wilkinson, *Pennsylvania History* 20 (1953): 258–60, who lists prices for various articles: food, sheep, cattle, horses, wood, whiskey at Northumberland, 274–75. Davy visited the United States and especially Pennsylvania in 1794–95, scouting the land as a settlement for English fam-ilies. Davy and family were escorted on a journey into the interior of Pennsylvania by Joseph Priestley Jr. His only known land venture was a half-interest in a two-hundred-acre farm near Northumberland, purchased, with Dr. Joseph Priestley, for £300. He and his wife, Susannah, sold their interest to Joseph Priestley Jr. in August 1795, for £200 "lawful money of Pennsylva-nia," but he remained in the United States as a substantial merchant until returning to England in 1817 as U.S. Consul at Hull.

8. He told Benjamin Rush, 28 Oct. 1794, Bolton, #84, that the proposed house was too large for the family, but the space was needed for his library and laboratory, and acknowledged to John Wilkinson that the house was disproportionate to his income, given that his money in the French funds had become unproductive, 30 Nov. 1797, Warr. Still standing, the house has become a museum administered by the Pennsylvania Historical and Museum Commission and is at the time of this writing still in the process of being completely restored to the plans Mary Priestley had intended for it. It has been designated a National Historic Landmark by the National Park Service and a National Historic Chemical Landmark by the American Chemical Society; it is listed in the National Register of Historic Places. The best description of the house is that of William N. Richardson, "The Current Interpretation of the Joseph Priestley House," in Lukehart, *Priestley in America*, 20–28, and "Joseph Priestley's American Home," *Proceedings and Addresses, The Northumberland County Historical Society* 32 (1994): 60–70.

Fig. 7   Priestley's House in Northumberland, Pennsylvania.

in population, so that he might establish a meetinghouse and school, in which he "would happily engage . . . without any Prospect of Fees or pecuniary Reward."⁹

In the closing months of 1795 Harry Priestley sickened and died, probably of malaria. He was buried in the Society of Friends cemetery at Northumberland, the funeral conducted by Priestley himself. Nine months later, Mary Priestley died. She had been ill intermittently at least since 1792, periodically spitting blood; the move to the United States, while easing her mind, increased the stress on her body, and she never quite recovered from Harry's death. Priestley wrote John Wilkinson to inform him of her death. "It has been a happy union to me for more than 34 years, in which I have had no care about anything, so that, without any anxiety, I have been able to give all my time to my own pursuits. I always said I was only a lodger in her house." In January he wrote that he would never recover his state of mind after her

9. Priestley to Lindsey, 20 Dec. 1794, Wms.; [Davy], "Mr. Davy's Diary," 140, 258, 268–69; Bakewell, "Dr. Priestley's Residence at Northumberland." The Duc de la Rochefoucauld-Liancourt had a very different report on the Priestley's situation; see *Travels through the United States of North America* (London: R. Phillips, 1799), 2:73–76; Priestley responded with some asperity in his *Letters to the Inhabitants of Northumberland.*

death. "I feel quite unhinged and incapable of the exertions I used to make. Having been always very domestic, reading and writing with my wife sitting near me, and often reading to her, I miss her everywhere."[10] Priestley now had nothing seriously to occupy himself but letter writing and his work.

The expenses involved in building so large a house, along with repairs on a temporary residence and purchases of land for his sons' farms, left Priestley overextended. Between the time of his landing and late 1795, there was a major inflation, and the building cost considerably more than he had expected. The money he and Wilkinson had quixotically invested in French funds was bringing no return, and his letters to Wilkinson, but especially to John Vaughan (who had all of Priestley's investment money in the United States and his power of attorney), dwelled continually on finances. There were financial woes in Philadelphia in 1797, as well, and Vaughan was bankrupt in 1799. John and Charles Vaughan had given Priestley a bond for his money, with land as security, but unimproved land could not be sold and yielded no revenue. By February 1799 Priestley had sold his small house to a Mr. DeGrunchy and moved into the big house with his son Jos and family. That gave him some slack, but he was still in some distress. In June 1800 Priestley informed Wilkinson that John Vaughan's business had failed. Vaughan's assignees were prevailed upon to make Priestley an annual allowance of $500 for five years, but Priestley wrote, "I cannot want anything long and I have much to be thankful for."[11]

As Wilkinson's investments for Priestley's benefit were not yielding any interest, he had allowed him to draw £200 a year, but this was meant primarily

10. Harry died at on 11 Dec. 1795 at age eighteen; Priestley to Lindsey, 17 Dec. 1795. Mary died on 17 Sept. 1796, Priestley to John Wilkinson, 19 Sept. 1796, 25 Jan. 1797, Warr. Priestley wrote to Lindsey on 19 Sept. 1796, "For activity in contriving and executing every thing usually done by women, and some things by men, I do not think she ever had a superior, or in generosity and disinterestedness; always caring for others and never for herself. My loss is proportionably greater, though I am thankful that she had been preserved so long." He wrote to Judith Mansell on 27 Jan. 1797, APS, "I shall never entirely recover it. Having always been very domestic, I feel quite unhinged, and incapable of the exertion I have been used to make. . . . I should feel more than you will conceive to leave the place where she and Harry are buried." Herbert J. McLachlan has a tribute; "Mary Priestley: A Woman of Character," in *Motion Toward Perfection: The Achievement of Joseph Priestley*, ed. A. Truman Schwartz and John G. McEvoy (Boston: Skinner House Books, 1990).

11. Priestley to Benjamin Rush, 28 Oct. 1794, Bolton, #84; to Lindsey, 17 May, 12 Aug. 1795 (omitted in W. 1.2:314–15). He had bought three hundred acres at thirty shillings per acre, besides the eleven acres for his house. Priestley was constantly writing poor John Vaughan about funds for his building—sometimes three times a week. See Priestley to Vaughan, 16, 25, 30 Aug., 17 Sept. 13, 17 Oct. (Bolton, #88), 17 Nov., 10, 12, 16 Dec. 1794, APS. The power of attorney, for his American funds, is dated 17 Feb. 1795 and distress at Vaughan's financial failure is expressed in a letter of 21 March 1799, APS. Priestley to Lindsey, 14 Feb. 1799 (omitted in W. 1.2:414–15); Priestley to John Wilkinson, June 1800, Warr.

as continued support for his sister Mary. In October 1796 Priestley wrote George Dyer about how happy he was in his peaceful retirement, how great the country was, and how he could not contemplate leaving the place where his son and wife were buried. But in November he got an accounting from Wilkinson showing that he owed $56,219, plus the £200 he had recently drawn. Priestley panicked, for he had believed the money was a gift and had no means by which to repay that sum. Having shown his whip hand, Wilkinson relented and apparently reassured Priestley about the debt. That, however, still left major financial problems. With Wilkinson withholding his allowance and Sally Priestley Finch in need, Priestley actually considered relocating to France to try to take advantage of the money tied up in French funds.[12] Priestley told Wilkinson in November 1797 that his philosophical friends had in general dropped their subscriptions, but his religious friends had not forgotten him. He was receiving occasional monetary gifts and bequests from England, usually via Lindsey. William Heberden had sent a benefaction as had Mr. Salte, and Elizabeth Rayner and the Duke of Grafton together contributed a sum of £90 a year. Finally, in 1800, Priestley was freed of his financial problems by a bequest of £2,000 left him when Mrs. Rayner died.[13]

In August 1794, seeking to justify sequestering himself in backwoods Pennsylvania, Priestley declared that he could promote science better by experimenting than by lecturing, though he had told Benjamin Vaughan in July that he could not fix a place of residence or have easy access to his library or apparatus until the next spring. He assured John Wilkinson that everything needed for his experiments except glassware could be obtained in Northumberland, and in late June he had written to the London glassmaker, Samuel Parker, about some laboratory apparatus he wanted sent to him.[14] Then, in

12. Not until 15 March 1798 could Priestley inform Wilkinson that the French Directory had agreed to allow him about £50 a year, a grossly inadequate return on the investment, Warr. Priestley to George Dyer, 4 Oct. 1796, W. 1.2:355–57; to John Wilkinson, 25 Jan. 1797, Warr. See Chapter 15, n. 37. In something of a justification for Wilkinson, he had just suffered an unexpected legal and financial setback in his quarrel with his brother William. He seems also to have relented with respect to the yearly allowance, for Priestley was again drawing £200 on Wilkinson by 14 June 1799, which Priestley acknowledged on 14 June 1800 as "given to promote useful science and useful knowledge in general," Warr.

13. Priestley to Lindsey, 29 May 1797, acknowledges £44 from the "Duke" of Grafton; 18 June, 4 Nov. 1797, 16 Nov. 1797, 16 Oct. 1800, gifts and the bequest from Mrs. Rayner; Priestley to John Wilkinson, 30 Nov. 1797, Warr.

14. Priestley to Benjamin Vaughan, 30 July 1794, to John Wilkinson, 24 July 1794, Warr.; to Samuel Parker, 27 June 1794, SciAuto., 147. He wrote Parker again on 20 Jan. 1795, SciAuto., 150, about replacing some glass apparatus damaged in transport, and as late as August 1800 the Parkers were still sending him glassware. Priestley to William Parker, 13 Aug. 1800, MSS Collections, New York Public Library.

November 1794, he was elected professor of chymistry by the trustees of the University of Pennsylvania.

On 14 September 1794 Priestley had written Benjamin Rush, who had suggested the appointment, that the post had some attractions, but there were insuperable difficulties to accepting such an invitation: he was not prepared to lecture at length on chemistry, his apparatus and library were still unpacked, and winter made experimenting difficult—perhaps next year? On 3 November he wrote Rush that he would not be a candidate for the position but that, if offered, he would do his best to discharge its duties. Now, on 11 November, faced with the appointment, he wrote Rush and Lindsey that he was declining the honor. He could not contemplate moving his library and apparatus, or leaving his family alone four months of every year. The trustees acknowledged his refusal on 3 March 1795.[15]

Still, Priestley resolved to visit Philadelphia annually, just as he had visited London from Birmingham, with the American Philosophical Society substituting for the Royal Society. There were also visits to a Chemical Society of Philadelphia, of which Priestley was a member as were Robert Hare and James Woodhouse, who filled the empty post at the University of Pennsylvania and with whom Priestley performed some experiments.[16] He also acquired, in the persons of Benjamin Smith Barton, Benjamin Rush, George Thatcher, and John Vaughan, persons who would perform minor chores there for him in his absence.

Barton became Priestley's major American correspondent on matters of science. Priestley read Barton's papers on botany, natural history, ethnology, and etymology. He lent him his rare copy of the *Vocabularia Comparativa* by Peter Simon Pallas. Barton defended Priestley's dignity against encroaching upstarts and ran occasional errands for him in Philadelphia. Rush was also a helpful correspondent but was more interested in theology, land speculation, and the plans of a college than in details of Priestley's experiments.[17]

15. Hepburn, "Pennsylvania Associations," 68–69; Minutes of the Trustees of the University of Pennsylvania, 11 Nov. 1794; 3 March 1795, letter of chairman, Thomas McKean, 12 Nov. 1794, formal election of Priestley to take the place of the deceased John Carson, then noting his refusal; Wyndham Miles, "Benjamin Rush, Chemist," *Chymia* 4 (1953): 37–77, 68–70; Priestley to Lindsey, 12 Nov. 1794: Wms.; to Benjamin Rush, 14 Sept.; 3, 11 Nov. 1794. See note 17 below.

16. The Chemical Society of Philadelphia was active from 1792 but disbanded sometime between 1805 and 1810; see Wyndham Miles, "Early American Chemical Societies," *Chymia* 3 (1950): 95–113. Edgar Fahs Smith, "Early Science in Philadelphia," *Pennsylvania Magazine of History and Biography* 51 (1927): 15–26.

17. Priestley to Barton, 20 July, 8 Oct. 1796; 15 July, 8, 16 Aug. 1798; 25 June 1799; 27 Nov. 1800; 7 July 1801; 18 May, 12 July 1803, Historical Society of Pennsylvania; Priestley to Benjamin Rush, 14 Sept., 28 Oct., 3, 11 Nov. 1794; 22 May 1795, 8 Aug. 1799; 7 May 1801; 27 Jan., 5 Aug. 1802, Bolton, #83–87, 92, 94–96; 6 Jan. 1800, Rush MSS, ibid.; 4 May 1801, Courtney R.

Clearly, in light of the invitation from the University of Pennsylvania, knowledgeable persons in the United States were aware of Priestley's scientific work and had formed opinions about it. Samuel Vaughan, writing from Philadelphia as early as 1786, spoke of "his rapid, valuable, original discoveries and researches into works of nature. . . . Many here wish he would drop his theological pursuits and stick to philosophical." Samuel Latham Mitchill, professor of chemistry at Columbia College, New York City, wrote in late 1793 of "a man whose successful labours in advancing . . . [chemistry] recommend him to the admiration and love of posterity; I mean Joseph Priestley and I write this paragraph to inform you there is a prospect of his becoming a citizen of the United States, as I learn by a letter from him. . . . The people of this country, the asylum of persecuted virtue, will receive him with open arms."[18]

Having rejected the opportunity of science lecturing in Philadelphia, Priestley would henceforth support chemistry as he had done in the past—by experiments, publications, and correspondence. His books and instruments were still in a room in his son's house in May 1795, and he could do little in the way of experiments, though he had readied his apparatus enough to confirm that the air at Northumberland was not sensibly different from that of England. By July he wrote, "I make some experiments every day, and shall soon draw up a paper for the Philosophical Society at Philadelphia," and in December he entrusted the copy of a paper intended for that Society to the keeping of Dr. Young, en route for Europe, to be delivered to his Lunar Society friends—especially Mr. Galton. "I have much more to do in my laboratory, but am under a necessity of shutting up for the winter, as the frost will make it impossible to keep my water fit for use without such provision as I cannot make until I get my own laboratory prepared on purpose." In October 1796 he wrote Barton that he had completed the arrangement of his new laboratory but could not do much till he lived in the house connected.[19]

Hall, *A Scientist in the Early Republic: Samuel Latham Mitchill, 1764–1831* (New York: Columbia University Press, 1934), 55n. Some of the land involved in the speculations of Priestley Jr. was optioned from Rush.

18. Samuel Vaughan to Richard Price, Price Letters, *Proceedings of the Massachusetts Historical Society* 17 (2d ser., 1903): 354–56; preface to Samuel Latham Mitchill, *The Nomenclature of the New Chemistry* (New York, 1794), in Denis I. Duveen and Herbert S. Klickstein, "The Introduction of Lavoisier's Chemical Nomenclature into America," *Isis* 45 (1954): 287n19. Although he was one of the first Americans to adopt and explain (with modifications) the new chemistry of Lavoisier, he was willing to listen to Priestley's arguments and was to give them space in the *New York Medical Repository*, the first medical journal in the United States, of which he was founder and chief editor between 1797 and 1824. On Mitchill in general, see Hall, *Scientist in the Early Republic*.

19. Priestley to Lindsey, 17 May 1795; to Benjamin Rush, 22 May 1795; to Lindsey, 12 July, 6 December 1795; to Benjamin Smith Barton, 8 Oct. 1796.

He communicated his ideas and descriptions of experiments to Lunar Society members and they answered. A letter to Josiah Wedgwood recommended Barton as a customer for apparatus and mentioned his rejection of the professorship at the University of Pennsylvania, the failure of the settlement scheme, his hopes for a college at Northumberland, and his resumption of experiments on the generation of air from water. Another letter discussed Withering's work on a new edition of his *Botanical Arrangement,* an apparatus for generating air invented by Watt, a letter from Galton, and his own phlogiston experiments, though he could not as yet do much until his own house and laboratory were built. Members of the Society continued to support his research and, Priestley believed, accepted phlogiston as late as 1803. Samuel Galton Jr.'s records show a subscription of eighty guineas for four years' support of Priestley's laboratory in 1798 and a further subscription as late as 1803, while Watt sent his "apparatus," a furnace and supply of Cornish clay, as a gift in 1801.[20]

And, of course, he communicated news of his experiments to non–Lunar Society friends in the United States and Britain. He wrote to Lindsey, Rush, and Barton, and also to Thatcher (who was hardly interested) and Robert R. Livingston, and renewed a correspondence with B. Lynde Oliver. Writing to people in England about his experiments, he also begged for information to reduce his philosophical isolation. To Humphry Davy, shortly to become the foremost English chemist, he expressed admiration for Davy's recent publications, hoped that he might be sent philosophical news, and called attention to his own publications. To Richard Price's nephew, William Morgan, he wrote in 1802 about galvanic experiments and of his pleasure that people were finally paying some attention to his articles. He had been in correspondence with Kirwan up to October 1796, but had heard he was dead. The Royal Society of Dublin sent him the five volumes of their transactions, but Sir Joseph Banks said the Royal Society of London could not complete his set of *Transactions,* broken by the riots. And, at his request, his Philadelphia publisher, Thomas Dobson, sent copies of his works published in America to van Marum in Holland.[21]

20. Priestley to Josiah Wedgwood, 17 March 1795, Gratz Collection, Historical Society of Pennsylvania; Priestley to Withering, 27 Oct. 1795, APS; Schofield. *Lunar Society,* 364–65.

21. Priestley to B. Lynde Oliver, 3 April, 8 Aug. 1800, *Proceedings of the Massachusetts Historical Society* 3 (2d ser., 1886): 34–35, 37–39; to Humphry Davy, 31 Oct. 1801, in [Humphry Davy], *Fragmentary Remains, Literary and Scientific, of Sir Humphry Davy,* ed. John Davy (London: J. Churchill, 1858), 51; *SciAuto.,* 172. Davy had friendly ties with members of the Lunar Society and with Joseph Priestley Jr. Priestley to William Morgan, 23 Oct. 1802, W. 1.2:495–97; Priestley to Sir Joseph Banks, 14 March 1802, Add. MSS 8099.194, British Library;

Priestley's official connection with science in the United States was with the American Philosophical Society. His response to the Society's welcome acknowledged his membership in that group as early as 1785.[22] He attended Society meetings when visiting Philadelphia—three times in 1796, twice in 1797, three times in 1801, and once in 1803. Unlike his situation in London with the Royal Society, he was respected by fellow members of the American Philosophical Society. He was considered for president of the Society on the death of David Rittenhouse in 1796, but declined in favor of Jefferson. On 3 February 1797 he was elected "orator" for the meeting of the last of December, but declined the election on 10 February, when the committee waited upon him. In March 1803 the Society gave a testimonial dinner for Priestley, and on his death in 1804 a formal eulogium recognizing his contributions was ordered, to be delivered by Barton. It was delivered in the First Presbyterian Church on 3 January 1805, preceded by a procession from the Society's hall.[23] The Society has since become a repository for some of Priestley's correspondence and various mementoes, e.g., a plaster profile and medallion, a profile in black leather, and an oil portrait.

Priestley published more scientific items during his decade in the United States than during all his years in England: some forty-five papers, not counting reprintings, and four pamphlets, not counting subsequent editions, but in general his science was now anticlimactic. Few of his papers contributed anything significantly new to the field of chemistry; most were committed to combatting the new chemistry. In May 1797 he wrote Lindsey, "Tho' all the world is at present against me, I see no reason to dispair of the old system,

---

summarized in Sir Joseph Banks, *The Banks Letters*, No. 9. Thomas Dobson to Martinus van Marum, 26 April 1799, Archives, Koninklijke Hollandsche Maatschappij der Wetenschappen.

22. Rittenhouse's welcome and Priestley's response were noted in the Society's minutes for 20 June and 18 July 1794. Priestley's "Phlogiston and the Seeming Conversion of Water into Air" was read to the American Philosophical Society in 1784, and one year later he was elected to membership in the Society as one of "28 new members" chosen in January of that year. For Priestley's relations with the American Philosophical Society, see Bronk, "Priestley and the American Philosophical Society." Note that Priestley was, by the time he left England, also a member of the American Academy of Arts and Sciences, Boston.

23. Priestley to Benjamin Smith Barton, 8 Oct. 1796, Historical Society of Pennsylvania; *SciAuto.*, 155. Printed Invitation to American Philosophical Society testimonial dinner for Joseph Priestley, March 1803, Bolton, #161; *SciAuto.*, 175. Priestley sent the Society a formal acceptance of the invitation on 2 March 1803, Archives, APS, *SciAuto.*, 176. Announcement of Priestley Memorial Service, 29 Dec. 1804, Archives, APS; *SciAuto.*, 180. Barton's Eulogy was ordered to be printed in the Society's *Transactions* on 18 Jan. 1805, but the order was withdrawn on 20 Nov. 1812 at Barton's request, so the eulogy could be enlarged and published separately— it has never appeared.

and yet, if I should see reason to change my opinion, I think I should rather feel a pride in making the most public acknowledgement of it." In June he wrote, "I am well aware that at present my character as a philosopher is under a cloud, but depend upon it, in a reasonable time, every thing will be cleared up, and then I hope my character as a *theologian* will gain in consequence . . . it is in this light chiefly that I regard it." And in April 1800 he wrote, "I was never more busy or more successful . . . [with his experiments] when I was in England; and I am very thankful to Providence for the means and the leisure for these pursuits."

The pattern can be seen in the first eight items printed. The earliest were the two papers presented to the American Philosophical Society on the evenings of 5 and 19 February 1796, his first appearances in the Society in person: "Experiments and Observations relating to the Analysis of Atmospherical Air" and "Further Experiments relating to the Generation of Air from Water," along with an appendix read 23 November 1798.[24] These were followed by the pamphlet *Considerations on the Doctrine of Phlogiston and the Decomposition of Water.* And, when this was answered by Pierre Adet and John Maclean, Priestley replied with *Observations on the Doctrine of Phlogiston, and the Decomposition of Water, Part II.*[25]

Being concerned that publications in the United States would not be read abroad, he sent a summary of his latest ideas to be published in the *Monthly Magazine,* which was owned by his friend Richard Phillips and edited by John Aikin, son of his Warrington colleague. He was also, and always, concerned about prompt announcement of his discoveries. On 8 August 1798 he informed Benjamin Smith Barton that the Philosophical Society's *Transactions* being published so infrequently, he was going to send accounts of his work to Samuel Latham Mitchill's *New York Medical Repository.* He had written Mitchill in June of his pleasure that the *Medical Repository* was open

24. Joseph Priestley, "Experiments and Observations relating to the Analysis of Atmospherical Air," "Further Experiments relating to the Generation of Air from Water," "An Appendix to the two Articles in this Volume," *Transactions of the American Philosophical Society* 4 (1799): 1–11, 11–20, 382–86.

25. Joseph Priestley, *Considerations on the Doctrine of Phlogiston and the Decomposition of Water* (Philadelphia: Thomas Dobson, 1796). This was answered by John Maclean's *Two Lectures on Combustion: Supplementary to a Course of Lectures on Chemistry. Read at Nassau-Hall. Containing An Examination of Dr. Priestley's Considerations on the Doctrine of Phlogiston, and the Decomposition of Water* (Philadelphia, 1797), and Priestley responded with his *Observations on the Doctrine of Phlogiston, and the Decomposition of Water, Part II* (Philadelphia: Thomas Dobson, 1797). The first pamphlet was reprinted, along with Maclean's answer, as *Considerations on the Doctrine of Phlogiston . . . And Two Lectures on Combustion . . .*, ed. William Foster (Princeton: Princeton University Press, 1929).

to general philosophy and chemistry, in a letter later published as "A Second Letter from Dr. Priestley to Dr. Mitchill."[26]

A major problem in Priestley's controversy over the new chemistry was his persistent and erroneous conviction that he could invalidate the new system by disproving experiments of the antiphlogistonists. One of the reasons he was wrong was that they ignored his experiments. The preface of *Considerations* illustrated the point by its letter to Berthollet, LaPlace, Monges, Morveau, Fourcroy, and Hasenfratz, "the surviving answerers of Mr. Kirwan," dated 15 June 1796 and requesting attention to his objections to the new theory. He esteemed the opinions of all those who had adopted their hypothesis, but "you would not, I am persuaded, have your reign to resemble that of *Robespierre*," rather preferring to persuade than to silence by power. And it was not just the French who ignored Priestley's experiments. John Maclean, professor of natural philosophy at the College of New Jersey (Princeton) performed no experiments but repeated what the French had written: "Whatever is asserted by any antiphlogistonist he never hesitates to admit; but he makes no difficulty of disregarding any thing I assert to the contrary." Most modern historians of chemistry also ignore Priestley's arguments and imitate Maclean.[27]

They ignore him because he was "wrong," because a few errors were insufficient to overturn an otherwise successful system, and because explanations were later (sometimes much later) found for Priestley's objections. The first class of these were Priestley's personal errors of manipulation or interpretation, though these were frequently shared by his opponents: the difficulty of freeing water of its occluded air, the quantitative errors in measuring mercury in the reduction of mercuric oxide, and long confinement of gases over water or in bladders, though he wrote that "any kind of air, confined by water, whose surface is exposed to common air, will be wholly absorbed by it," though it might be supposed that the water was fully saturated with air (APS 1799, appendix 382).

26. An "Interesting Chemical Letter from Dr. Priestley," *Monthly Magazine* 5 (1798): 159–60; Priestley to Samuel L. Mitchill, 14 June 1798, Edgar Fahs Smith Library, University of Pennsylvania, printed as "A Second Letter from Dr. Priestley to Dr. Mitchill," *New York Medical Repository* 2 (1799): 48–49; 3d ed. (1805): 45–47; letter no. 1 had been a skeptical response to Mitchill's attempt to arbitrate between phlogistonists and anti-phlogistonists: see "A Letter to Dr. Mitchill, in reply to the preceding," *New York Medical Repository* 1 (1797; 2d ed., 1800): 511–12. See also Priestley to Samuel L. Mitchill, 16 July 1801, Historical Society of Pennsylvania; *SciAuto.*, 170, for his pleasure in having prompt publication in the *Repository*.

27. The *Monthly Magazine* letter also requested attention to his experiments. Priestley, *Observations II*, 27. Partington, *History of Chemistry*, 3:272, for example, notes Maclean's criticism of Priestley without noting Maclean's major errors and Priestley's quite correct responses.

Then there were the substantive errors of interpretation that the opponents ignored because they could not answer: (1) the persistent confusion of inflammable airs, not to be solved until the work of William Cruickshank in 1801; (2) the problem of reaction energies represented in the incidental production of acid in composition-of-water experiments, where Priestley correctly noted that French experiments confirmed his own (the large-scale water-production experiments not admitting "of so much accuracy as the conclusion requires; and there is too much of correction, allowance, and computation, in deducing the result"; (3) the belief of antiphlogistonists that the only source of inflammable air (H_2) as, for example, in the solution of metals in acids, was the decomposition of water. There being no residual oxygen, Priestley (also erroneously) concluded that the inflammable air came from the metals.

Priestley had also a disconcerting instinct for weaknesses in French arguments. There were the disingenuous comments about the "universally allowed" materiality of light and heat, though no one had been able to weigh them and they passed easily through glass—so too, perhaps, could phlogiston. He had a knack for selecting substances with many varying properties, especially considering that no one was yet acquainted with the confusion represented by the "— —ous" and "— —ic" varieties of compounds. He had long emphasized the various nitrogen compounds and toyed with organic substances; now he chose to stress experiments with iron, subject to varying amounts of carbon in available samples, to the ferrous and ferric complications, and also a ferrosopheric oxide (finery cinder, Fe_3O_4), which he had used to confuse interpretation as early as the *Philosophical Transactions* papers of 1785 and 1786.

Many antiphlogistonists supposed that all metallic calces were oxides. This led to confusion over Priestley's experiments with zinc, with its oxide, hydroxide, carbonate, and sulphate, but more particularly to Maclean's supposition that finery cinder was the same as ferrous sulphate, though Priestley correctly pointed out that reduction of finery cinder by H_2 produced more water than reduction of $FeSO_4$ by heat to ferric oxide (Fe_2O_3) and subsequent reduction by hydrogen. Maclean, Adet, and Monnet also supposed turbith mineral ($HgSO_4$) to be some kind of oxide, reducible by heat, ignoring Priestley's disclaimer.

The pattern continued in nine short papers written during 1798 and 1799 and appearing first in the *New York Medical Repository*.[28] Averaging between

28. (1) "On Red Precipitate of Mercury as favourable to the Doctrine of Phlogiston," 20 July 1798, *New York Medical Repository* 2 (1799): 163–65 (3d ed. 1805, 152–55); (2) "Objections

three and four pages, most simply rehearsed arguments from earlier work. There were some new observations: a citation to new work by James Watt and Thomas Beddoes on the medicinal use of factitious airs; finery cinder may contain oxygen, but an "entire new system of chemistry cannot be admitted on mere possibilities" (3:264); the "azote" produced when copper dissolved in volatile alkali; new complications of sulphur and oxygen compounds: sulphuric acid, sulphur dioxide and trioxide.

Some of these papers were responses to the antiphlogistonist arguments elicited by his late papers and particularly those of his friend James Woodhouse. Woodhouse's "Answer to Dr. Joseph Priestley on the Doctrine of Phlogiston" admitted that the French were wrong in their assumption that "turbith mineral" was a "pure oxyd of mercury" and in their denial that it contained "one particle of sulphuric acid." Priestley's experiments had demonstrated the presence of sulphur. Woodhouse continued to answer Priestley's experiments with his own, but he employed quantitative arguments that Priestley could not, or would not, answer.[29] Priestley could, however, pose some tricky quantitative problems of his own. In the reduction of mercuric oxide by inflammable air, an inadequate amount of water was

---

to the Antiphlogistic Doctrine of Water," 23 Aug. 1798, *New York Medical Repository* 2 (1799): 166–67 (3d ed. 1805, 155–57), essentially repeated in "A Letter to the Editor," 22 August 1798, *Monthly Magazine* 6 (1798): 237–38; (3) "Experiments relating to the Calces of Metals, communicated in a fifth Letter to Dr. Mitchill," 11 Oct. 1798, *New York Medical Repository* 2 (1799): 263–68, substantially repeated in "A Letter to the Editor," *Monthly Magazine* 7 (1799): 261–64; (4) "Of some Experiments made with Ivory Black and also with Diamonds," 11 Oct. 1798, *New York Medical Repository* 2 (1799): 269–71, repeated in *Monthly Magazine* 7 (1799): 353–54; (5) "On the Phlogistic Theory," 17 Jan. 1799, *New York Medical Repository* 2 (1799): 383–87, substantially repeated in "A Letter to the Editor," 17 Jan. 1799, *Monthly Magazine* 7 (1799): 354–56; (6) "On the same Subject," 1 Feb. 1799, *New York Medical Repository* 2 (1799): 388–89; (7) "Dr. Priestley's Reply to his Antiphlogistian Opponents, No. 1" 18 July 1799, *New York Medical Repository* 3 (1800): 116–21; (8) "Dr. Priestley's Reply to his Antiphlogistian Opponents, No. 2," 24 July 1799, *New York Medical Repository* 3 (1800): 121–24; (9) "Dr. Priestley's Reply to his Antiphlogistian Opponents, No. 3," 26 July 1799, *New York Medical Repository* 3 (1800): 124–27.

29. Turbith mineral can be partially reduced by heat above 400 degrees, but this produces mercurous sulfate along with some Hg. Woodhouse's answer was originally in *Transactions of the American Philosophical Society* 4 (1799): 452ff.; it is summarized with commentary by John J. Beer, *Journal of Chemical Education* 53 (1976): 414–18. Priestley was offended by Maclean's neglecting to treat him with the civility he thought he deserved ("Letter to Mitchill," 512). Woodhouse, answering Priestley's *Considerations* respectfully but vigorously, acknowledged obligations to Priestley "for his polite attention in shewing me a variety of experiments in . . . Northumberland, and for the instruction derived from reading his very valuable dissertations, on different kinds of air. . . . I do not agree with the Doctor . . . yet I conceive his entrance on . . . Pneumatic chemistry, will ever be considered, as marking an aera in the science."

produced and the remaining air detonated. He correctly insisted that fixed air weighed between three and four times as much as carbon and thought that this disproved its proposed composition (8). John Wilkinson's experience was cited to support the claim that, in reduction, finery cinder lost about one-third of its weight, casting doubts as to its designation as a calx. Priestley challenged both Woodhouse's designation of heavy inflammable air as "carbonated hydrogen gas" and his supposition that a new inflammable air was made by decomposition of water as steam is passed over hot carbon.

There followed, perhaps more respectably, a series of papers for the American Philosophical Society.[30] These papers illustrate how much his work in the United States had repeated that in England. The first (read 20 December 1799) and the last (read 18 August 1800) described the results of heating airs in tubes of iron, copper, silver, or gold; passing vapors of nitric or hydrochloric acids over the metals, sulphur, and carbon. The results were admittedly and correctly reported as "experiments less worthy of publication" than those in the *Philosophical Transaction* papers of 1789. The second paper took up observations on the transmission of gases through bladders and earthen vessels first reported as early as 1781 and emphasized in his *Philosophical Transactions* paper of 1783. He now explicitly recognized that when any kind of air in an earthen vessel was inverted in a glass jar filled with a different air, both airs would, in time, be found mixed; and the same two-way transmission also occurred with bladders. As he could "not ascertain the cause" (15), he cannot quite be credited as recognizing gaseous diffusion.

The next paper is a frustration for anyone who reads it, for it reveals that Priestley's skills in analyzing arguments was not matched by an ability to synthesize arguments of his own. In examining the absorption of air by water, a continuation of work reported in his first paper for the American

---

30. (1) "Experiments on the Transmission of Acids, and other Liquors, in the form of Vapour, over Several Substances in a hot earth tube," read 20 Dec. 1799; (2) "Experiments relating to the Change of Place in different kinds of Air through several interposing Substances," read 20 Dec. 1799; (3) "Experiments relating to the Absorption of Air by Water"; (4) "Miscellaneous Experiments relating to the Doctrine of Phlogiston"; (5) "Experiments on the Production of Air by the Freezing of Water," read 18 April 1800 (substantially the same as that in *New York Medical Repository* 4 [1801]: 17–21, with a preliminary note: "Air produced, without Limitation, from Water by Freezing," *New York Medical Repository* 3 [1800]: 422–23, repeated in *Journal of Natural Philosophy, Science and the Arts* 4 [1801]: 193–96); and (6) "Experiments on Air exposed to Heat in Metallic Tubes," read 15 Aug. 1800, *Transactions of the American Philosophical Society* 5 (1802): 1–13, 14–20, 21–27, 28–35, 36–41; 42–50. These papers also are said to appear in a prepublication pamphlet entitled *Six Chemical Essays*, presumably published in Philadelphia in 1800, but I have been unable to locate any copy or bibliographic reference to a copy.

Philosophical Society, he failed to connect his results with those of the paper just printed. He wrote that the whole of any quantity of any kind of air "would be wholly absorbed, though a large surface of the water in which the vessels containing them were placed was exposed to the common atmosphere, and therefore had an opportunity of saturating itself with air, and of a purer kind than several of those that were in the jars" (22–23). Now, the vessels filled with air were not emptied in this "absorption"; that remaining, in time, when subjected to the nitrous air test simply proved to be dephlogisticated rather than that which had originally filled them. Priestley had known at least as early as 1786 that water was not a barrier to the exchange of airs between the atmosphere and air inside an inverted container, but he failed to connect this observation with the transmission of air through bladders or earthenware tubes, and he did not recognize that his nitrous-air test had systematically depleted the residual air, leaving only the dephlogisticated.[31]

The experiments reported in the fourth paper were primarily repetitions of previous ones supporting the doctrine of phlogiston. The fifth paper, read 18 April 1800, was a continuation of Priestley's pamphlet of 1793 on the generation of air from water, and of his second paper, of 1799, for the American Philosophical Society. Somehow he continually produced air from the same parcel of water, by heating or freezing. These are, perhaps, the "precious" experiments, "without reference to their value," of which Edgar F. Smith wrote, for no one seems to have found an explanation for them except to suggest a common failure in experimental technique in insufficiently clearing his containers of adhesing air.[32]

Much of Priestley's allotment of natural philosophy time in late 1799 and early 1800 was devoted to the preparation of the pamphlet that he expected would be his last word on the new chemistry. His journal papers during that period were, therefore, of an eccentric nature. Samuel L. Mitchill, attempting to moderate between the old and new chemistries and further his career as a physician, conceived that nitric acid was a cause of contagious fevers and that its base, which the French had named "Azote," should rather be called "Septon," from the Greek root "Se-" as in sepsis. He printed an extract from a Priestley letter of 24 July 1799 congratulating him on his discovery, and

31. The basic problem, and one shared by his contemporaries, was his belief in a static rather than a kinetic view of gases. He had observed permeability of bladders as early as 1772. For the diffusion through water and bladders, see Chapter 9.

32. Smith, *Priestley in America*, 62. The difficulties in obtaining absolutely pure water have plagued chemists as varied as Jean-Servais Stas and Edward Morley, particularly in the removal of dissolved air, but no one but Priestley ever experienced the continued production of air in his experiments.

another of 30 January 1800 that cited a letter from James Watt on the medical uses of factitious airs, particularly including "dephlogisticated nitrous air" (nitrous oxide, laughing gas), and announced his forthcoming work establishing the doctrine of phlogiston. Early the next year Mitchill published a summary of Priestley experiments to confirm a discovery of Christoph Girtanner that azote was a compound of hydrogen and oxygen—these particularly emphasized Priestley's acidulated composition of water.[33]

Early in 1800 (dedication to Samuel Galton and preface dated 1 February 1800), Priestley published *The Doctrine of Phlogiston established*.[34] This was to be his final support of the doctrine, in which he republished "all that I think of importance" (v–vi) to demonstrate the existence of phlogiston and refute the composition of water. Roughly one-third of its ninety pages is an almost verbatim transcription of the *Considerations* of 1796, the *Observations* of 1797, or occasional paragraphs from the *Experiments and Observations*. Priestley noted that most chemists had abandoned phlogiston; it had no supporters in the United States, few in England (he thought surviving members of the Lunar Society still believed) and none of those still writing, fewer yet in France, and only Crell, Gmelin, Mayer, and Westrumb in Germany. He sounded positive but again maintained, to the French chemists he had earlier addressed in *Considerations,* his readiness to accept the new system if he saw reason to do so, adding that he trusted "that your political revolution will be more stable than this chemical one" (xiii).

He repeated his insistence that metals were compounds containing phlogiston. It was easy on phlogistic grounds to account for release of inflammable air from a solution in which one metal was replaced by another. When iron was heated in nitrous air, phlogisticated air was produced, which showed

33. "Priestley's Sentiments on the Doctrine of Septon," quoted in a letter of 24 July 1799, *New York Medical Repository* 3 (1800): 307. Joseph Priestley, "Singular Effects of Gaseous Oxyd of Septon (dephlogisticated Nitrous Air)," 30 Jan. 1800, *New York Medical Repository* 3 (1800): 305, repeated in *Monthly Magazine* 9 (1800): 409; see also Hall, *Samuel Latham Mitchill*, 55. "Experiments tending to show that Azote is a Compound of Hydrogen and Oxygen," *New York Medical Repository* 4 (1801): 192–94.

34. Joseph Priestley, *The Doctrine of Phlogiston established and that of the Composition of Water refuted* (Northumberland: for the author, 1800), 2d ed., with additions (Northumberland: Byrne; Philadelphia, 1803). There was an English printing of second edition, with the addition of *Observations on the Conversion of Iron into Steel, in a Letter to Mr. Nicolson* (from the *Journal of Natural Philosophy, Chemistry, and the Arts* 2 [n.s., 1802]: 233–34) (London: J. Johnson, 1803). According to a letter to Lindsey, 6 March 1800, Wms. (passage omitted in *W.*), Priestley sent copies to Thomas Beddoes, Humphry Davy, Samuel Galton, William Heberden, James Holborn, Richard Kirwan, William Morgan, Samuel Parker, Bishop Watson, Thomas Wedgwood (Josiah had died in 1795, Withering in 1799), John Wilkinson, and the Royal Society of London.

that iron was not a simple substance and, by analogy, that neither were other metals. He returned to the problem of finery cinder, again revealing the difficulties of multiple iron oxides but also illustrating a problem of nomenclature (which Priestley made still worse by intermittently using the new system), when phlogisticated air may mean any air with the oxygen removed, but here, in the case of dephlogisticated marine acid, meant without hydrogen. Again there was the confusion of multiple inflammables, and again the calces that are not oxides. Though the antiphlogistonists argued that all inflammable air came from the decomposition of water and that there must be water either in finery cinder or charcoal, Priestley's experiments showed that there was none in either. When Priestley examined the calces of zinc, he again exploited the multiplicity of inflammables, but may also have exhibited a failure in experimental technique when he argued that he obtained a calx with no increase in weight of the zinc! Did he lose some zinc by sublimation?

Section 5 ran into the problem of multiple oxides of sulphur, phosphorus, and nitrogen. (There are six oxides of sulphur, four of phosphorus, five of nitrogen, and six acid forms of phosphorus.) Priestley wrote of sulphur produced from water impregnated with vitriolic acid air (sulphur dioxide) as sulphuric acid and phlogiston "made to form a different mode of combination by the heat in a tube hermetically sealed" (30). Section 6, on calces of mercury, posed again the possibility that phlogiston passed through glass as did matters of heat and light. Heat and inflammable air equally reducing mercuric oxide, heat delivered the same principle through glass that inflammable air (phlogiston) added directly. Mercuric oxide combined with inflammable air sometimes produced an explosion, sometimes not. He explained different experimental results by pointing out that "the same substances in different combinations and in different states, have different properties" (35), referring to chemical affinities, which Lavoisier had explicitly avoided.[35] And sometimes the "same" substances were not the same—i.e., light (hydrogen) and heavy (carbon monoxide) inflammable airs.

He then returned to the pesky decomposition (and recomposition) of water and the persistence of acidity. He demanded (50) that the French find a substance to combine with their hydrogen in water, releasing the oxygen— something that Humphry Davy was to do with dephlogisticated marine acid (Cl): $2Cl_2 + 2H_2O = 4HCl + O_2$. Again there was the confusion over different inflammables, with Priestley recognizing a heavy inflammable air but not

---

35. Sometimes $HgO + heat + H_2 = Hg + O + H_2$, which would explode; other times $2HgO + heat = 2Hg + O_2$, which, in an atmosphere of H_2 might combine into water without exploding. See Lavoisier, *Elements of Chemistry*, xxi.

distinguishing any difference in behavior and again insisting that "substances possessed of very different properties may be composed of the same elements, in different proportions, and different modes of combination" (55). In Sections 10–11 he presented some evidence of contemporary experimental problems, where the carbon dioxide normally found in atmospheric air, organic dust, and the hydroxides and carbonates of substances like lead and tin kept too long in laboratory air seemed to have confused Priestley's results. There was one prescient remark—that "inflammable air holding the carbon in solution would be of the heavy, and not of the lighter and purer kind" (63). Priestley did not understand why Berthollet and Fourcroy had challenged the validity of the "nitrous air test," though he himself had experienced the different proportions with which NO can combine with oxygen because of impurities of other oxides of nitrogen. One objection to the different values he obtained from the nitrous air test employed over different times was answered, Priestley says in a footnote (69n–70n), by the change of place of airs through earthenware vessels or bladders, "the cause of which I have not even a conjecture."

In the conclusion (76–78), Priestley declared that the new theory could be established only when (1) a due proportion of oxygen was produced whenever inflammable air was obtained (addressing the antiphlogistonist claim that water is the only source for hydrogen); and (2) water is produced without acidity. He added that recent experiments by Humphry Davy and Count Rumford had demonstrated that calorique was not a substance.

An appendix (79–90) addressed four problems: (1) Mitchill's failed attempt to reconcile the old and new systems of chemistry; (2) Jan Ingenhousz's dissatisfaction with Priestley's claims to the discovery of photosynthesis. Priestley repeated a note from the 1793 *Philosophical Transactions* paper on air from water and published a letter from Ingenhousz. Air was not emitted from animal skin, nor could plants give out air in the dark. He agreed that Ingenhousz certainly published about air from leaves in sunlight before Priestley published about air from whole plants. But having pointed out to many persons, including Ingenhousz, that "green matter" evolved air in sunlight, that was equivalent, when green matter was shown to be plant, to saying that, by natural analogy, plants as a whole did so. To deny that green matter was a proper plant (arising from seed as do other plants), as Ingenhousz was inclined to do (by saying that water or some substance in the water was changed, by equivocal generation, into vegetation), was to lose most of the merit of the discovery; (3) Priestley challenged Lavoisier's claim that he had discovered dephlogisticated air, an air "discovered almost at the same time by Mr. Priestley, Mr. Scheele, and myself." He had told Lavoisier in 1774 about the air in which a candle burned better than in common air. Lavoisier's work on dephlogisticated air followed that announcement. Mr. Scheele's discovery was certainly made independent of mine, "tho I believe [incorrectly] not made quite so early" (88); and (4) Mr. Davy's claim that water was decomposed in the growth of plants and his hasty introduction of new terms into chemistry. Priestley had derived a high opinion of Humphry Davy's essays (89–90) published in Dr. Beddoe's *Contributions to Physical and Medical Knowledge* (1799), but his nitrogen was likely to last no longer than the French hydrogen; the term "phlogisticated air" was better, as describing the air rendered unfit for respiration or combustion.

Phlogiston Established was intended to be Priestley's last word on the new chemistry, but he felt compelled to correct misstatements in an otherwise "candid and impartial review" of that work, in a letter to the editors of the *Medical Repository.* Nor could he resist adding a paper with what he felt were additional supporting experiments on manganese in inflammable air.[36] As manganese possesses five oxides and Priestley was unclear whether he used light or heavy inflammable air, his experiments contributed nothing new, but he was now free to indulge in some random experiments, exploiting his talent for observation without prior commitments.

In some observations on hearing, Priestley provided an almost clinical description of his affliction with monaural diplacusis. In a published letter of 4 May 1801 to Benjamin Rush, he naïvely admired and was convinced by the "judicious" arguments of Noah Webster's *Brief History of Epidemic and Pestilential Diseases* (1799) that these disorders were owed to an atmosphere vitiated by earthquakes, meteors, comets, and volcanoes; and he offered as collaboration the account of illness produced on the island of Santorin by the sudden appearance of a volcano exuding effluvia (probably hydrogen sulphide). He believed that Mitchill's proposal of alkaline remedies for these diseases was supported by Webster's arguments, but could not understand how Webster's belief in Revelation and a supreme intelligence was consistent with his support of equivocal generation. In a postscript, Priestley thanked Rush for saving his life by bloodletting, which he had opposed!

In "Some Thoughts concerning Dreams," Priestley used dreams in support of David Hartley's vibratory theory of how the brain receives and retains ideas. A set of ideas might appear to disappear because the relevant

---

36. Joseph Priestley, "To the Editor of the Medical Repository," correcting a review, 6 July 1800, and "Experiments on heating Manganese in Inflammable Air," *New York Medical Repository* 4 (1801): 103, 135–37.

region of the brain was out of reach of ordinary excitement, but the ideas might be revived in particular circumstances, as in dreams, delirium, and intoxication. Priestley was not satisfied with this conjecture on the circumstances involved in the brain's dream-revival of ideas, but he wished to draw the attention of anatomists and physiologists to the subject.

In July 1801, in "Miscellaneous Observations relating to the Doctrine of Air," Priestley asked again what constituted any permanent air. The element of heat, "if there be any such substance," entered the composition of all "aëriform substances," and water was the basis of the weight of different airs, but what made them permanent? A "knowledge of the *elements* which enter into the composition of natural substances, is but a small part of what it is desirable to investigate with respect to them, the principle, and the mode of their *combination:* as how it is that they become hard or soft, elastic or non-elastic, solid or fluid, &c. &c. &c. is quite another subject, of which we have, as yet, very little knowledge, or rather none at all" (266). Priestley was now sure that dephlogisticated air entered the composition of azote, and he explained that in some previous experiments the dephlogisticated air came from the atmosphere through the water in which the process was made. Noting that inflammable air confined for several months by water had been contaminated in that way, he was on the point of a significant technical observation—only to confuse the issue with the suggestion that the inflammable air might, in the course of time, be "converted" into phlogisticated air.[37]

This happy, unobsessed miscellany was interrupted with the discovery of the electrolysis of water and the identification of carbon monoxide. Each of these discoveries had reference to the new chemistry. To each Priestley felt

37. Joseph Priestley, "Some Observations relating to the Sense of Hearing," 8 May 1800, and "Remarks on the Work entitled 'A Brief History of Epidemic and Pestilential Diseases,'" 4 May 1801, *New York Medical Repository* 4 (1801): 247–48, and 5 (1802): 32–36. The first explicit description of diplacusis seems to be that of Carl Stumpf in *Tonpsychologie* (1883). The curious work by Webster is discussed in George Rosen, "Noah Webster: Historical Epidemiologist," *Journal of the History of Medicine and Allied Sciences* 20 (1965): 97–114. A product of American rational enlightenment, besides its value as a source of historical information, the work included suggestions for sanitary reform; it otherwise represents a layman's faulty generalization for all its insistence, which appealed to Priestley, that theories were of little use while facts were of infinite importance. "Some Thoughts concerning Dreams," *New York Medical Repository* 5 (1802): 125–29. The original reference is, of course, to his edition of Hartley's *Observations.* The article refers to Benjamin Rush's *Life of Mr. Drinker,* and he acknowledged to Benjamin Rush, 7 May 1801, that "the most important part is what I borrowed from you." "Miscellaneous Observations relating to the Doctrine of Air," 30 July 1801, *New York Medical Repository* 5 (1802): 264–67.

compelled to respond, and in each case he had some characteristic idiosyncratic observations. Naturally, neither discovery proved to him the merit of the new chemistry. His "Observations" on the voltaic pile were, in fact, not on Volta's pile but on the electrolysis experiments of Anthony Carlisle and William Nicholson and those of Humphry Davy immediately following, all published in Nicholson's *Journal* in 1800. A Mr. Weatherby Phipson of Birmingham had sent Priestley a fine apparatus for voltaic experiments, which he used in repeating those respecting the composition of water.

He achieved some of the same results: the hydrogen released at one pole may be in the proportion to oxygen required by the composition hypothesis, but Priestley thought it came from air held in solution in the water, for its production ceased if access to the atmosphere was cut off (Davy's observations agreed) and the oxygen obtained at the other pole was deficient in the quantity and quality required. Moreover, the wire at that pole was rapidly decomposed and there was scarcely any acidity from the oxygen proportional to hydrogen produced. Having observed the "secondary action" rather than the primary in almost all his experiments, he was led to suppose that positive electricity was the principle of oxygen and negative that of phlogiston.[38]

It was, of course, possible for Americans to read about Galvanism and electrolysis in magazines from abroad—the *Philosophical Transactions,* Nicholson's *Journal,* the *Philosophical Magazine,* or even the *Monthly Magazine,* but Priestley's account serves as an indication of his significance to American science. His interpretation of phenomena might have been unique, but his work brought reference to, and a sense of participation in, the most recent scientific developments. This situation becomes even clearer respecting William Cruickshank's 1801 identification of the heavy inflammable air as a separate species of air. One of Priestley's persistent attacks on the new chemistry involved the reduction of finery cinder by carbon, with the production of inflammable air though no water was decomposed (a Lavoisian prerequisite). The attacks had been ignored by the antiphlogistonists because they could not answer them. Now Cruickshank had "solved" the problem

38. Priestley, "Observations and Experiments relating to the Pile of Volta," 16 and 29 Sept. 1801, *New York Medical Repository* 5 (1802): 153–59, substantially repeated in *Journal of Natural Philosophy, Chemistry, and the Arts* 1 (n.s., 1802): 198–204. See Priestley to Lindsey, 2 Oct. 1801, *SciAuto.,* 171, to Samuel L. Mitchill, 5 Jan. 1802, copy, Edgar Fahs Smith Library, University of Pennsylvania; *SciAuto.,* 173. He had included some minor information on Galvanism in his *Heads of Lectures* (1794) and 3 April 1800 letter to B. Lynde Oliver. Johann Ritter also supposed electricity and phlogiston to be the same, and suggested that water minus electricity/phlogiston was oxygen, water plus electricity/phlogiston, hydrogen.

by identifying a new inflammable air, the "gaseous oxide of carbone" (carbon monoxide), inciting Priestley to write a spate of four papers answering Cruickshank, each with a reprinting in Nicholson's *Journal of Natural Philosophy*, and with a partial summary of the whole in the *Monthly Magazine*.[39]

The first reply to Cruickshank was somewhat disorganized, perhaps reflecting Priestley's haste in responding. There was not, however, any loss of energy in argument. He pointed out that antiphlogistonists had insisted that all inflammable air was derived from water; now Cruickshank denied that water was necessary. The inflammable air came from the partial decomposition of carbon dioxide (formed from the oxygen in finery cinder and the carbon) in contact with hot finery. But, Priestley argued, the decomposition of heavy inflammable air produced carbon dioxide, not the other way around. Cruickshank had found carbon dioxide where it could not be formed and found it decomposed by substances without the power to do so.

In his follow-up letter, Priestley noted his surprise that chemists in Paris boasted of Cruickshank's findings, which abandoned an essential part of the new chemistry, that water was essential to the formation of inflammable air—and he quoted from Lavoisier's *Elements* to that point. If French chemists could not better defend their system, let them abandon it. In his "Remarks" on Cruickshank, Priestley responded to an answer by the latter. The heavy inflammable airs, produced in a number of different processes, were similar only in their releasing carbon dioxide when decomposed in oxygen. Cruickshank chose to call one of these "gaseous oxyd of carbon," while others were to be called hydrocarbons. Now, the first air was certainly

39. (1) Priestley, "A Reply to Mr. Cruickshank's Observations in Defence of the New System of Chemistry, in the fifth volume of Mr. Nicholson's Journal 1, &c.," 21 Nov. 1801, *New York Medical Repository* 5 (1802): 390–92, substantially the same as *Journal of Natural Philosophy, Science and the Arts* 1 (n.s., 1802): 181–84; (2) "Additional Remarks on the Same," *New York Medical Repository* 5 (1802): 393, repeated as "On the Theory of Chemistry," 20 Feb. 1802, *Journal of Natural Philosophy, Chemistry, and the Arts* 2 (n.s., 1802): 69–70; (3) "Remarks on Mr. Cruickshank's Experiments upon Finery Cinder and Charcoal," 12 April 1802, *New York Medical Repository* 6 (1803): 24–26, repeated as "On Air from Finery cinder and Charcoal with other Remarks on the Experiments and Observations of Mr. Cruickshank," *Journal of Natural Philosophy, Chemistry, and the Arts* 3 (n.s., 1803): 52–54, all summarized in "A Letter to the Editor," *Monthly Magazine* 14 (1802): 2–3; (4) "Additional Remarks on Mr. Cruickshank's Experiments on Finery Cinder and Charcoal," 15 Nov. 1802, *New York Medical Repository* 6 (1803): 271–73, essentially repeated in "Answer to the Observations of Mr. William Cruickshank upon the Doctrine of Phlogiston," *Journal of Natural Philosophy, Chemistry, and the Arts* 3 (n.s., 1803): 65–69; with another paper really addressing some of the same problems: "Observations on the Conversion of Iron into Steel," *New York Medical Repository* 6 (1803): 158–59, repeated 22 May 1802, *Journal of Natural Philosophy, Chemistry, and the Arts* 2 (n.s., 1802): 233–34.

inflammable, but other oxyds were not, being already saturated with oxygen. Cruickshank had thus abandoned another of the new chemistry's fundamental principles. "Additional Remarks" essentially summarized the three earlier papers.

An additional paper, on the conversion of iron to steel, really addressed another aspect of the same issue. What happened when iron was heated with carbon? The received opinion was that iron imbibed carbon, increasing in weight and changing color. But iron became steel by imbibing finery cinder. The change in color came from thin films of oxide on the surface of steel objects. The whole set of arguments appeared to center on the complicated processes involving iron and its included carbon reacting variously with carbon, carbon monoxide, and carbon dioxide, producing the various kinds of iron—pure, cast, wrought, and steel—and the various oxides: ferric, ferrous, and ferrosoferric. But in fact the issue of the controversy was a feature of the antiphlogistic chemistry against which Priestley was to tilt in vain.

Cruickshank's experiments, his responses to Priestley, and the approval of antiphlogistic chemists all demonstrated that the new chemistry did not depend upon every inference from Lavoisier's initial proposals. Priestley notwithstanding, the new chemistry was not an assembly of experimental results but of explanations based on assumptions about the nature of chemical processes. These assumptions were limited in scope and would eventually have to include some elements that Priestley insisted upon, but that was irrelevant at this stage in the development of the science. Perhaps Priestley came finally to realize that attacks on individual experiments were futile, or perhaps he was merely tired. For he was sixty-eight years old when he wrote these papers and he had no coherent system to substitute for the one he felt was inadequate. In any event, he returned to the miscellaneous experiments on which he could have fun.

The result was two papers read to the American Philosophical Society late in 1803; the last one fewer than three months before his death and not to be published for five years after it.[40] The slighter second paper, addressed to Caspar Wistar, referred to his visit at Northumberland and explained an observation of an apparent conversion of common salt into nitre. Having used and reused a portion of salt to mix with snow in a series of experiments on the production of air from freezing water, Priestley decided to use that

---

40. Priestley, "Observations and Experiments relating to Equivocal, or Spontaneous Generation," read 18 Nov. 1803; "Observations on the Discovery of Nitre, in common Salt, which had been frequently mixed with Snow," read 2 Dec. 1803, in a letter to Caspar Wistar, *Transactions of the American Philosophical Society* 6 (1809): 119–29, 129–32.

salt for making marine acid. To his surprise, on combining it with dilute sulphuric acid, he obtained the red fumes of nitrous acid vapor. This must, he concluded, be the result of the snow having dissolved nitrous air formed in the atmosphere by electrical phenomena such as aurora borealis, falling stars, and lightning.

The first and more important paper, on spontaneous generation, was in the first instance incited by Erasmus Darwin's *Temple of Nature* (1803), but it harkened back at least to 1780 and the first of Priestley's *Letters to a Philosophical Believer,* with its concern for design and causality. Darwin was but one of the persons who maintained that living bodies could arise from brute matter without the interposition of creative power. But he had used Priestley's "green matter" as an example of such spontaneous generation, supported by observations of Jan Ingenhousz and Christoph Girtanner. Priestley objected, offering new experiments to show that water deprived of access to the atmosphere failed to develop green matter. These experiments supported the supposition of microscopic seeds floating in the atmosphere, insinuating themselves through the smallest apertures into the water. Darwin's experiments, involving boiling broth, were not described sufficiently to allow verification, while everyone knew that boiling water failed to destroy some insects, their eggs, or embryos.

The division of living things into simple or complete, imperfect or perfect, ignored the observation that microscopic vegetables and animals were as complete and exquisite in structure as the larger, and as well adapted to their places in the design of nature. Though their minuteness eluded any search for the seeds or "germs" by which they propagated or the manner of their conveyance, one must not base an argument of their nonexistence on ignorance. Darwin suggested that spontaneous vitality was the beginning of a perpetual development by reproduction to larger and more complicated beings over uncounted age, but there was no evidence, Priestley maintained, for a change in the nature of plants or animals, which had remained as described in Homer and the Book of Job.

Darwin evaded the charge of atheism by suggesting that the Supreme Author of all things was the Cause of all Causes, and therefore the cause of the process of equivocal generation, but Priestley pointed out that causes in nature had regular connections, and changes contrary to the observed analogy of nature were miracles. Advocates of spontaneous generation denied the existence of miracles. Changes were, to them, events without a cause— atheism indeed. That organic particles might have powers of attraction merely pushed causation to another level, for powers of attraction, as in electricity or magnetism, still carried marks of design and therefore the necessity of a designing cause.

This reaction to Erasmus Darwin was not Priestley's first connection with him, nor were the earlier connections all negative. Darwin had been a member (mostly in absentia) of the Lunar Society during Priestley's tenure. His most famous work, a lengthy poem called *The Botanic Garden* (1789, 1791) had included references to Priestley's work, and his medical treatise, *The Zoonomia* (1796–97), contained some almost gratuitous compliments to "the great Dr. Priestley" and his work in optics and chemistry. Priestley wrote Lindsey on 3 December 1796 that he admired the *Zoonomia*, which could lead him to a study of medicine. There were also references to Priestley in Darwin's agricultural study, *Phytologia* (1800), which linked him again to the Lunar Society's practical concerns.[41]

The major *Phytologia* references were to Priestley's work on respiration and the "photosynthesis" discovery, but Darwin also made a curious comment: "Dr. Priestley gave to a cow for some time a strong infusion of hay in large quantity for her drink, and found, that she produced during this treatment above double the quantity of milk." There is a quotation from a 1797 letter from Priestley to Sir John Sinclair, president of the Board of Agriculture in London, on a Joseph Cooper's experiments with seed selection. The experiment with the cow is also described in volume 2 of the *Zoonomia* and probably predates 1791, while the letter to Sinclair is reprinted from the *Communications* to the Board of Agriculture.[42]

With his sons all involved in farming, it was inevitable that Priestley would discover an interest in that subject, as he would also in that of house construction. In a letter to Benjamin Vaughan he described the kiln drying of boards: "A house constructed with such boards I prefer to one of brick or stone." Late in 1798 he sent Joseph Jr. to Sinclair with a letter requesting that he be assisted in learning "everything new and important relating to agriculture. . . . My pursuits have but little connexion with yours. I admire, however, the zeal and intelligence with which you apply to them, and rejoice in your success." In 1799, in a postscript to his "Second Letter to Dr.

41. See Schofield, *Lunar Society*, 90, 204, 207, 397–98, 401, 404, 404n.

42. On 11 Sept. 1796 Priestley wrote to Lindsey: "I had, lately, a letter from Sir John Sinclair, who says he hopes soon to see me in England and renew his acquaintance with me. Now I do not remember ever to have known him." Priestley answered Sinclair, 29 April 1797, printed in *Communications* to the Board of Agriculture, vol. 1, part 3: "though not employed in agriculture . . . and not able to supply you with anything out of my own stores" with a description of the agricultural experiments of a Mr. Joseph Cooper on the improvement of crops through careful selection of seeds.

Mitchill," Priestley inquired about a solution of gypsum as nutrition for growing clover. According to Thomas Twining, Priestley asked him about cashmere goats as well as other natural and cultural aspects of India and mentioned that he had once visited Bakewell and inquired about his breeding experiments.[43]

Priestley did not require a personal interest in practical matters in order to become involved. At Northumberland, as at Birmingham in the company of the Lunar Society, Priestley addressed technological problems. In 1796 B. F. Young, a Northumberland physician, wrote to his friend Charles P. Williamson about a sample of sulphur recovered from a mound surrounding the sulphur springs at Clifton Springs, New York. He reported that Priestley was impressed with the importance of the discovery and declared it "equal to a gold or silver mine." By early 1800 Priestley was in correspondence with Williamson himself, sending a diary of weather temperatures from 1 September 1799 to 1 January 1800, by Fahrenheit's thermometer, to add to his "account of the climate in different parts of this continent."[44]

In April 1799 Robert R. Livingston wrote to Priestley about a steam engine design that appears to have used mercury as a piston seal. Priestley responded in a letter of 17 April 1800 that chiefly concerned the reprinting of his *Letters to Northumberland* but included information about his experiments and doubts about the use of mercury in a heated situation, and encouraged further correspondence. Livingston answered with a long and confusing letter about steam engine design and support for Priestley's defense of phlogiston. He also sent Priestley the notice of his patent application for a paper-manufacturing process, and Priestley congratulated him on his discovery of a new material for making paper.[45]

43. Priestley to Benjamin Vaughan, 19 April 1798, Bolton, #91; to Sinclair, in [Sir John Sinclair], *The Correspondence of the Right Honourable Sir John Sinclair, Bart* (London: Henry Colburn and Richard Bentley, 1831), 416–20. Thomas Twining, *Travels in America 100 Years Ago, being Notes and Reminiscences* (New York: Harper & Brothers, 1893), 48–49.

44. B. F. Young to Charles Williamson, 7 July 1796, quoted in Helen I. Cowan, *Charles Williamson: Genesee Promoter—Friend of Anglo-American Rapprochement* (Rochester, N.Y.: Rochester Historical Society, 1941), 155–56; Priestley to Charles Williamson, 15 Jan. 1800, Houghton Library, Harvard University.

45. Livingston to Priestley, April 1799, Division of Public Records, Pennsylvania Historical Commission, Harrisburg; Priestley to Livingston, 16 April 1799, Historical Society of Pennsylvania; Livingston to Priestley, 8 Aug. 1799, MS Draft, Robert R. Livingston Papers, New York Public Library; Priestley to Livingston, 24 Oct. 1799, Charles Roberts Autograph Collection, Haverford College Library. Livingston needed an engine for his steamboat on the Hudson and was unable to obtain one from Boulton & Watt owing to British laws. His patent on paper from a riverweed was granted in Oct. 1799 but never proved commercial. See George Dangerfield, *Chancellor Robert R. Livingston of New York, 1746–1813* (New York: Harcourt, Brace, 1960).

Different circumstances and companions had produced a new set of practical interests. Unfortunately, the same could not be said of most of his natural philosophy concerns. He had brought with him an obsession respecting the new chemistry and, equally unfortunately, he had also brought most of the experimental details that he was to repeat during this last decade of his life. Only the identification of carbon monoxide had any relationship to the experiments of Priestley's American years, and that must inevitably have occurred, for the existence of light and heavy inflammable airs was well known and cried out for explanation. European and English chemistry had left him behind, save as a curious historical figure.

The situation in the United States was slightly different, for there Priestley had become something of a cultural hero, and chemistry, for its practical and especially its medical uses, was avidly pursued. Few American chemists followed his theoretical lead, but contemporaries acknowledged that "The arrival of Dr. Priestley gave a spring to the study of chemistry on that side of the Atlantic" and his experiments and publications "contributed to excite a spirit of inquiry and to improve the public taste for chemical philosophy." Some of his chemical apparatus was given to Dickinson College and treasured there, while other parts were for a time displayed at the Smithsonian Institution in Washington, D.C. The centennial of the discovery of oxygen was celebrated in the United States by a meeting in Northumberland, at which a proposal for the formation of a national chemical society was made. The American Chemical Society is thus historically tied to Priestley.[46]

46. John J. Beer, "The Chemistry of the Founding Fathers," *Journal of Chemical Education* 53 (1976): 405–8. Quotation of Samuel Miller, Presbyterian minister and professor at Princeton and no follower of Priestley in theology, in Miller, *Brief Retrospect*, 263–64. Note that Aaron J. Ihde somewhat disagrees, saying that "Priestley's influence on American chemistry was not profound," "European Tradition in Nineteenth-Century American Chemistry," *Journal of Chemical Education* 53 (1976): 741. See also Hepburn, "Pennsylvania Associations." A slight report of archaeological discoveries at Priestley's Northumberland laboratory was reported in the "Science Notebook" of the *Washington Post*, 25 Aug. 1986, and in the *Minneapolis Star-Tribune*, 27 Aug. 1986, and a commemorative stamp bearing the likeness of Priestley by Gilbert Stuart was issued by the United States Postal Service on 13 April 1974, in celebration of his discovery of "oxygen." Statues of Priestley at the Oxford University Museum, Birmingham, and Leeds also celebrate the discovery of oxygen.

XVII

RELIGION, DEATH

As in politics and science, so in theology, Priestley's reputation preceded him to the United States. As early as 1776 Lindsey was sending copies of Priestley's works to the library of Harvard College. Joseph Willard, the president of Harvard, corresponded with Priestley and Richard Price in 1786, when Price described Priestley's wonderful abilities and ardor as philosopher and divine: "In Philosophy and Politics he and I are perfectly agree'd, but in Metaphysics and Theology we differ much." In 1790 Price and Priestley joined in a request that Harvard grant Joshua Toulmin a doctorate. By that time the Rev. William Hazlitt had made a brief visit to America, where he preached, published some Priestley tracts, and distributed Priestley publications, including the *Appeal to Serious and Candid Professors of Christianity*, before returning to England.[1] Not all of these previews were favorable. In 1786 a Moravian missionary with a congregation in New York wrote his friend Benjamin Latrobe: "By this you will see that we grow a little and our kind & precious Savr. owns us in this Babylon where Mr. P——s

1. On the gifts to Harvard Library, see Conrad Wright, *The Beginnings of Unitarianism in America* (Boston: Beacon Press, 1955), 393. Willard to Price and Price to Willard, 6 April 1786, 24 July 1786, "Price Letters," *Proceedings of the Massachusetts Historical Society* 17 (1903): 338–39, and 23 (1909–10): 624–25; Price to Priestley, 29 Aug. 1790, Price Papers, Bodleian Library, Oxford; "The Hazlitt Papers," *Christian Reformer* 5 (1838): 505–12, 697–705, 756–64, and 6 (1839): 15–24, 373–74.

Doctrine & Books is embraced with greediness & Multiplies amazingly."
Ezra Stiles, at Yale, was sent a copy of Priestley's *Appeal* as early as 1772
and knew his *Corruptions* by 1782, thinking him an "Unhappy Divine" for
denying the doctrine of atonement.[2]

Some American ministers, chiefly James Freeman of Boston and William
Bentley of Salem, Massachusetts, read and even encouraged American publication of Priestley's theological works. Bentley's diary shows that he was
reading Priestley as early as 1789 and preaching his views in 1791. Freeman
corresponded with Lindsey at least as early as 1793, referring to Priestley's
Letters to the Philosophers and Politicians of France, then being reprinted
in Boston. Priestley wrote Freeman in June 1794 of his arrival in the United
States, and in 1800 of the bigotry in his neighborhood, of a small society of
Unitarians in Northumberland, and asked how Unitarianism was received
in Freeman's congregation.[3] A Unitarian society was formed in Portland,
Maine, in 1792, by Thomas Oxnard, who was prompted to read Lindsey and
Priestley by James Freeman. One of Oxnard's hearers was George Thatcher,
Priestley's friend and correspondent when he came to Philadelphia. And in
1790 Alexander Sparkes wrote from Quebec, thanking Priestley for a copy
of his *Church History* and praising his other writings.[4]

Yet Priestley lamented that he had not been invited to preach on his
arrival in the United States, for all the enthusiasm of his welcome. There
were attacks on Unitarianism from New York and Philadelphia pulpits and
he failed to establish a church in Northumberland. Nevertheless, he was convinced that New York and Philadelphia were open to Unitarianism.[5] He
wrote Lindsey in August 1794 that he sometimes preached in local Presbyterian meetings but made a point of "saying nothing to offend them. This,

2. James Birkby to Benjamin Latrobe, 28 Oct. 1786, Packet A, box A.3, Moravian House,
London. I owe this reference to Dr. Darwin Stapleton, archivist, Rockefeller Foundation.
[Stiles], *Literary Diary,* 1:225, 3:101.

3. Freeman oversaw the Boston edition of Priestley's *Discourses on the Evidence of
Revealed Religion* (Boston: Wm. Spotswood, 1795). He sent Bentley a copy of Priestley's hymn
and psalm book, received when William Priestley was welcomed by Freeman and Bentley on his
visit to Massachusetts in 1794–95; see "Correspondence of Dr. William Bentley," *New-England
Historical & Genealogical Register* 27 (1873): 352, 356–57; Priestley to Freeman, June 1794,
Wms.; to Freeman, 6 March 1800, *Proceedings of the Massachusetts Historical Society* 3 (2d ser.,
1886): 33–34.

4. Wilbur, *History of Unitarianism,* 393–94; Vincent Brown Silliman, "An Early Unitarian
Society in Portland, Maine," *Transactions of the Unitarian Historical Society* (U.S.) 2 (1931):
31–34; Alexander Sparkes to Priestley, 18 Oct. 1790, *W.* 1.2:91–92.

5. [Wansey], *Journal,* 86. Priestley to Lindsey, 15, 24 June, 5 July, 14 Sept., 12 Nov., 20 Dec.
1794, Wms.

however, tends to abate prejudice and will prepare the way. . . . They all know my opinions and in general do not seem to be much shocked at them." In October he preached to troops assembled to put down the Whiskey Rebellion and was well attended. He was invited by judges of the Pennsylvania Supreme Court to preach for them when on their circuit. They were pleased and invited him to dine with them, though the clerk of the Presbyterian church where the service was held refused to officiate. And he held Sunday services at his son's house and then in his own, which people other than family attended.[6]

While at sea, Priestley had composed "Observations on the Cause of the present Prevalence of Infidelity," and these were prefixed to the Philadelphia edition (1794) of his *Letters addressed to the Philosophers and Politicians of France.*[7] He stated in the preface the hope that his defense of common principles compensated for offending the generality of Americans by his opposition to the corruptions of Christianity. The truth of Revelation was not revealed in number and quantity, which could not be denied, but in a form differently interpreted by persons not predisposed to believe. Men chiefly based their opinions on those of others and many followed men such as Hume, Voltaire, Rousseau, and Franklin. But these writers were ignorant of religion and hadn't the curiosity to read the Scriptures, though this most ancient of literatures should invite liberal study, even in the absence of the historical truths and superior morality contained therein. Some unbelievers feared their disappointment, should religion prove false, others the retribution to come should it be true. Still others were dismayed by the behavior of some believers, while Deists, in their presumption, argued inconsistency with natural law.

It was noted in October 1774 that Priestley, "having a Printing Press close by him . . . is now printing a Sequel to his Letters to French Philosophers & an answer to Paine's Age of Reason (a Book much read in this Country)."

6. Jasper Yeates wrote Sarah Yeates from Sunbury, 12 Oct. 1798, that he had heard Priestley preach and dined with him at Northumberland, Gratz Collection, Case 16, box 17, Historical Society of Pennsylvania. Priestley to Lindsey, 14 Aug. 1794, Dickinson College Library, Carlisle, Pa.; [Davy], "Mr. Davy's Diary," 267–68; [Kenrick], *Chronicles of a Nonconformist Family,* 102–5; Priestley to Radcliffe Scholefield, c. Oct. 1794, Misc. MSS, New York Historical Society. A Unitarian Fellowship, organized by Priestley in his home, continued after his death more or less continuously to 1964, is represented in the Joseph Priestley Memorial Chapel, Northumberland, maintained as a perpetual memorial by the American Unitarian Association. See the *Unitarian/Universalist World,* 15 Oct. 1977, 9, discussing attempts to maintain the chapel.

7. Priestley, *Observations relating to the Causes of the General Prevalence of Infidelity,* prefixed to the American edition of *Letters addressed to the Philosophers and Politicians of France, on the Subject of Religion* (Philadelphia: Thomas Dobson, 1794).

He also printed there an enlarged edition of the *Observations on Infidelity*, and a third edition (nearly double again in size) was printed in Philadelphia in 1797.[8] The large additions to the third edition were a result of his reading Voltaire's *Letters* and the Comte de Volney's *Ruins, or the Revolutions of Empires*, each filled with "confident and ill-founded assertions, gross mistakes, or misrepresentations."

The new edition of *Observations* contained a preface (lacking in the first edition), noting that there was less infidelity in the United States, where no corrupt established system existed. The new sections referred to Hartley, Paine's *Age of Reason* (which Priestley thought contained more palpable mistakes of notorious facts and inconclusive reasoning than any other book), repeated the assertion that religions existed prior to priestcraft, and reminded readers of non–Judeo-Christian references to the Scriptures and to Jesus.

Priestley quoted freely from the letters of Voltaire and d'Alembert, giving the original French in footnotes. Unable to understand differential equations and rational mechanics, he included d'Alembert in condemning these authors for their failure to make real advances in useful knowledge. He worried that (his) monism seemed to cast doubt on the existence of the soul. True understanding required revelation to supplement logic! Voltaire's writing was lively and entertaining but filled with conceit, jealousy, malignity, and whining. The writers confounded popery with Christianity (46–75).

Another section examined the writing of Volney and Charles François Dupuis's *Origin of all Religions*.[9] Priestley poked fun at their fanciful etymologies, capricious imaginations, and failure to appreciate the difference between polytheism and monotheism. Moses' account of the primitive state of man, though a fable, was (in Priestley's view) certainly more probable

8. The Northumberland press was that of Andrew Kennedy, who published the *Sunbury and Northumberland Gazette;* [Davy], "Mr. Davy's Diary," 268–69; Priestley, *Observation on the Increase of Infidelity, to which are added, Animadversions on the writings of several Modern Unbelievers, and especially the Ruins of Mr. Volney* (Philadelphia: Thomas Dobson, 1797); I have used W. 17:1–110, appendices 1–3, 520–27.

9. Constantin François de Chasseboef, Comte de Volney, *Les Ruines; ou Méditation sur les Révolutions des Empires* (of 1791) made use of C. F. Dupuis's urging, before Strauss, that Jesus was no more a historical personage than the savior gods Adonis, Attis, and Osiris. Their works are described in George Wells, "Stages of New Testament Criticism," *Journal of the History of Ideas* 30 (1969): 147–60. Volney and Dupuis found parallels between pre-Christian and Christian lore that were a source of embarrassment to Christian writers. Curiously, the Moravian architect and builder Benjamin Henry Latrobe found Volney's response to Priestley an "elegant little thing" and a devastating answer. Apparently Latrobe found Priestley's Unitarianism far worse than Volney's paganism; see [Benjamin Henry Latrobe], *The Virginia Journals of Benjamin Henry Latrobe, 1795–1798,* ed. Edward C. Carter II (New Haven: Yale University Press, 1977), 2:381–84.

than that of M. Volney (99). Appendices 2 and 3 (522–27) also addressed the arguments of Volney, Dupuis (whose speculations on the age of the earth disagreed with Newton's), and Nicolas Fréret, whose apparent learned criticisms "contain nothing of the least importance with respect to which the facts he alleges are not greatly misrepresented and false conclusions drawn from them" (527). Volney objected to Priestley's attack, and Priestley responded with *Letters to M. Volney*, dated 22 March 1797.[10] If Volney disliked religious controversy, he shouldn't provoke it. His work revealed ignorance and inattention. Priestley summarized the *Observations* and challenged Volney to justify conflating the God of Moses with pagan gods.

That sequel to the *Letters to the Philosophers of France* was printed at Northumberland as *A Continuation of the Letters to the Philosophers and Politicians of France, on the Subject of Religion; and of the Letters to a Philosophical Unbeliever; in Answer to Mr. Paine's Age of Reason.*[11] A preface to the essays noted that prejudice against religion had begun to wear off but that infidelity continued, as one could see in Paine's superficial, frivolous, and ignorant *Age of Reason*. France's National Assembly, under Robespierre's leadership, had formally recognized the existence of God and recommended worship. This declaration differed greatly from the view exhibited when Priestley visited France in 1774 but was Deistic, not Christian, and thus failed seriously to address its moral purposes.[12] Only Christian revelation ensured belief in a future state; and only Unitarianism, free from corruptions and the abuses of civil power, showed a Christianity favorable to liberty and equality.

To a Philosophical Unbeliever III (128–69) is the part of *Continuation* that addressed Paine. Distinguished and important in politics, vigorous of mind and strong of expression, Paine impressed readers with his *Age of Reason*, but he lacked his earlier mastery of his subject. Deism was not a sufficient

10. Joseph Priestley, *Letters to M. Volney, occasioned by a Work of his entitled Ruins, and by his Letter to the Author* (Philadelphia: Thomas Dobson, 1797); I have used W. 27:111–28. Volney's only reply regarding Priestley's pamphlet addressed to him was that "he would not read the pamphlet." Smith, *Priestley in America*, 95.

11. Joseph Priestley, *A Continuation of the Letters to the Philosophers and Politicians of France . . .* (Northumberland: Andrew Kennedy, 1794); I have used W. 21:109–27, 128–69. There was apparently also a printing of this as *An Answer to Mr. Paine's Age of Reason, being a Continuation of Letters to the Philosophers and Politicians of France . . . and of the Letters to a Philosophical Unbeliever* (Northumberland: Andrew Kennedy, 1794), which was reprinted, with a preface by Theophilus Lindsey (London: J. Johnson, 1795).

12. A Rutt footnote complains that Priestley says nothing here condemning Robespierre. As the "Reign of Terror" had not seriously begun before June, it is quite possible that Priestley knew nothing of it or of Robespierre's death in July when writing this passage in October. Rutt was a devoted admirer, but neither a historian nor a scholar.

guide for morality. The second letter (134–38) criticized Paine's attack on miracles and his insistence that revelation was possible only firsthand. That would mean that nothing not personally experienced could be believed. His quibble about the mistranslation of ideas from one language to another applied as well to the histories and literature of ancient Greece and Rome. Paine's work only illustrated his ignorance and inconsistency. The corruption of power in national institutional churches was not true Christianity. Our accounts of Jesus *are* secondhand, Priestley argued, but so are those of Socrates. There was no evidence that Jesus was a political revolutionary. Paine's account of the antiquity of Christianity was worthless, as the books of the New Testament existed prior to that of the church Paine credited for their composition.

Paine loaded the Christian system with absurdities long discarded by intelligent Christians. His definition of prophecy eliminated any serious discussion of its evidential value. Some contemporary commentators viewed biblical prophecies as merely interpretive, but Priestley believed that prophecy predicts events. Acknowledging the vices displayed in the Bible, Priestley countered them with the piety, benevolence, dignity, and divine authority also illustrated there.

He wrote John Vaughan in May 1795 of his design to spend about two months every year in Philadelphia, but only if he could appear as a minister of the gospel. "I will not make any considerable stay in your city, and be reduced to a disgraceful silence by the bigotry and jealousy of the preachers." Vaughan found that the Universalist Church, needing money to complete their building, had offered its use to any sect of Christians who would help.[13] Priestley's friends provided for its completion and there, in February 1796, Priestley delivered the first of a series of thirteen discourses on the evidence of Revelation. The discourses attracted much purely curious attention, but they were also admired by his friends. George Thatcher wrote Freeman that Priestley had given "universal satisfaction" to a crowded audience. "Every tongue was engaged in speaking his praise." Rush wrote Griffith Evans that Priestley preached to "crowded and respectable audiences. His

13. Priestley to Vaughan, 6 May 1795, APS; 25 July 1795, Houghton Library, Harvard University. He rented rooms in one of a row of small houses on High Street, between Sixth and Seventh Streets, in which to stay while delivering his discourses. See Smith, "Early Science in Philadelphia," 25. The First Universalist Church in Philadelphia, on Lombard Street between Fourth and Fifth Streets, was being built in 1794. It is the only structure in which Priestley preached that is still standing. In 1890 the Universalists sold the building to a Jewish Congregation called B'nai Jacob and today it houses the Jewish Congregation Kersher Israel. See the *Unitarian/Universalist World* 7 (15 March 1976): 1–2.

Fig. 8 Universalist Church, Philadelphia, in which Priestley preached in 1795, now owned by the Jewish congregation, Kersher Israel. This is the only building still standing in which Priestley preached.

sermons (one excepted) were very popular. The unpopular one gave offence only by detailing the vices of Heathens in too gross language." Writing John Dickinson that Priestley desired a meeting, Rush repeated his opinion of the *Discourses,* adding, "I have never met with so much knowledge, accompanied with so much simplicity of manners. You will be charmed with him."[14]

On 13 March 1796 John Adams wrote his wife, "I am going to hear Dr. Priestley. His discourses are learned, ingeneous, and useful. They will be printed, and, he says, dedicated to me. . . . It will get me the character of a heretic I fear. I presume, however, that dedicating a book to a man will not imply that he approves every thing in it." Published in May 1796, the dedication declared that Adams had expressed a wish for publication, while the

14. Thatcher to Freeman, 14 Feb. 1796, *Proceedings of the Massachusetts Historical Society* 3 (2d ser., 1886): 39–40. Rush to Griffith Evans, 4 March 1796, *Pennsylvania Magazine* 6 (1882): 113. Rush to John Dickinson, 5 April, 1796, Rush Papers, Historical Society of Pennsylvania, printed in "Four Letters addressed to John Dickinson," *Pennsylvania Magazine* 29 (1905): 226–27.

preface claimed that friends had requested Priestley's preaching.[15] The preface admitted that there would be some repetition of the London *Discourses*, and in fact these and succeeding discourses and writing illustrate that Priestley's American theology was, like his science, anticlimactic. Only when he dealt with popular new unbelievers or details of comparative religions had he much to add that differed from previous publications.

Discourses 1 and 2, on the importance of religion in general and of revealed religion in particular, might be substituted for sections in the London *Discourses*, but also for the 1794 *Continuation* of letters to France and to the philosophical unbeliever. Discourses 3 and 4 (56–113), and specifically the latter, contained the material Rush described as relating the vices of heathens in too gross language. Taking particular notice of Voltaire's praise of the beauty and moral innocence of heathen religions, Priestley described heathen practices in all their "ignorance and depravity."

Discourses 5 and 6 (114–75) systematically contrasted the baseness of 3 and 4 with edifying examples from the Old Testament. Attacking Voltaire's description of the Jews as ignorant, superstitious, avaricious, and barbarous, Priestley quoted from the Old Testament to show that they excelled in morality, the arts of war and of literature, while construction of the tabernacle and temple showed them the equal of other countries in the ingenious arts and knowledge of real science. Discourses 7 and 8 (176–236) ransacked Brucker's *History of Philosophy*, abridged by Enfield, to address the suggestion that the practices of 3 and 4 were those of the vulgar, not of the more intelligent. Priestley referred to the proposals of Plato, Aristotle, Strato, Democritus, Epicurus, Zeno, the Stoics, Seneca, the Gnostics, Plotinus, and Oriental philosophers. Most of them failed to condemn and some even conformed and recommended the superstitious, horrid, and abominable practices of heathens. "Are not their minds . . . darkened, who can prefer the absurd conceits of these philosophers, to the rational doctrines of revelation?" (189).

Discourses 9–11 (237–355) discussed the evidence for the Mosaic and Christian religions. Priestley frequently repeated material from the London *Discourses* on the evidentiary value of miracles, with added specifications on their identification. The miracles described in both the Old and New

---

15. [Adams], *Works*, 1:488; Priestley, *Discourses relating to the Evidences of Revealed Religion, delivered in the Church of the Universalists, at Philadelphia, 1796* (Philadelphia: John Thompson, 1796). Perhaps the substantial aid to the building of the church justifies a claim that friends requested the *Discourses*. Reprinted as *Discourses . . . , Vol. II. Being the first delivered at Philadelphia in 1796* (London: J. Johnson, 1796).

Testaments satisfied these criteria. We cannot doubt, for example, that Christ's Resurrection was thoroughly investigated in attempts to disprove it. Examination of the Pentateuch and of the prophets showed that they were written by the persons named as the authors, and were written coeval with the events and received as such. Priestley gave similar evidence for the books of the New Testament.

Genuine prophecy was exclusively the province of the Supreme Being and had the effect of a miracle (313–14). Except for the obscurity of Daniel, declarations from God were clear and open, unlike enigmatic false oracles— yet Priestley's ultimate criteria for true prophecy was circular: if a prediction went unfulfilled, it was clearly not from God. Jesus was truly the Christ; his behavior was inconsistent with imposture. Conscious of a divine mission, he challenged the great and the commonality with religious preaching that should have been derided but instead earned respect, reverence, or apprehension. *Discourses* ends with a mini-sermon, reflecting the London *Discourses* and Discourses 1 and 2, on the value of religion in general and of revelation in particular. Priestley recommended daily study of Scripture—Newton, after all, devoted his last forty-odd years to theology (424).

The discourse on Unitarianism, separately added to these of 1794 and published as *Unitarianism explained and defended,* closed with Priestley's concurrence with the Universalists. The doctrine of eternal torment was indefensible. Priestley cited Hartley's *Observations* in support of this view, which was at least implied in his own *Philosophical Necessity,* but his final conversion to Universalism may well have been a consequence of a son's misbehavior (William couldn't adjust to life as an ordinary farmer) and a father's hope that he would eventually achieve salvation.

During his visit to Philadelphia in 1797, Priestley gave another series of discourses. The English ambassador, Mr. Lister, attended his first discourse and Priestley dined with him the following day. John Adams attended only the first, which rather disappointed Priestley, as did Adams's failure to subscribe to his *Church History.* Adams, he explained, was unhappy that Priestley did not share his dislike of the French. Printed by 28 March 1797, the seven discourses and two appendices filled 474 octavo pages.[16] The preface acknowledged that the set continued the London (1794) and Philadelphia (1796) *Discourses* and admitted that there was repetition, but added, "What

16. Smith, *Priestley in America,* 94, 101–2. Priestley, *Discourses relating to the Evidences of Revealed Religion, delivered in Philadelphia.* Vol. 2. (Philadelphia: Thomas Dobson, 1797). Reprinted as *Discourses . . . Vol. III, Being the second delivered at Philadelphia in 1797* (London: J. Johnson, 1799).

the Divine Being did not think too much to teach, and repeat . . . we cannot think too much . . . to learn and give repeated attention to" (5).

Discourses II show that Priestley had taken his own advice about intensive study of the Scriptures, as the text consisted largely of biblical quotations meant to illustrate the topics of the 1796 *Discourses.* Roughly two-thirds of the first discourse consisted of quotations from Psalms, Proverbs, the Gospels, and the Epistles relating to the morality of Revelation. The second expanded, by copious quotations from the Gospels, the 1796 *Discourses,* demonstrating the character of Jesus and manifesting his divine mission compared with attitudes of later false prophets.

Discourse 3 reviewed, with appropriate quotations from the parables and the Sermon on the Mount, the New Testament doctrine of morals, extending discourses 1 and 2, and the mini-sermon of discourse 13 of the 1796 *Discourses.*

Discourse 5 (243–380) departed from the loving recapitulation of scriptural passages to dwell on contrasting quotations from George Sale's translation of the Koran. A man of considerable ability, Mahomet had a serious, devotional turn of mind and was initially of temperate behavior, but it was easy to reveal his pretensions and the fraudulency of his system. The Koran was filled with improbable stories, many seemingly borrowed from Scripture (Priestley's text quoted fourteen pages of the Koran derived from the Old Testament and ten from the New) altered to fit a new dispensation. No public miracles supported Mahomet's "divine mission," although, as the Koran showed, skeptics repeatedly called for them. The Koran displayed no signs of divine inspiration, disseminated a perfunctory morality, and described a paradise of the grossest sensual pleasures and a literally burning hell. Far from an improvement on Christianity, everything really valuable in Mahomet's system was derived from it. His religion was, like Cromwell's, swallowed up by ambition (243–380).

Discourses 6 and 7 illustrated again Priestley's conservatism in his attempts to defend the authenticity of the Book of Daniel. Daniel's "predictions" were in such exact agreement with events to the reign of Antiochus Epiphanes that unbelievers had denied their antiquity. Priestley failed to address the indications that had led commentators to date its writing to a period between 167 and 165 B.C., and argued instead the book's acceptance by Jews and its inclusion in the Old Testament canon. The importance of Daniel, to Priestley's mind, was its "predictions" of recent events. As its language was enigmatic, he could relate predicted events to times long after those of Antiochus, especially to Rome and the papacy, with supporting passages from the equally enigmatic language of the Revelation of St. John.

Priestley was not alone in his fixation on the predicted coming of the kingdom of heaven. His correspondence with George Thatcher on theological matters was largely about millenarianism, and Belsham was sympathetic, but other friends were concerned. When Priestley confessed in August 1797 that he gave more attention every day to prophecy, Lindsey cautioned him. Priestley responded, in November, "You need not fear my publishing any thing upon this subject before I get more light than I yet have." But he was also defensive. "As to my speculations about the Millennium, and the present condition of Christ, &c., surely they are innocent. To myself they are something more than amusing; and that they should *offend* any body really surprises me."[17] Given his age and the deaths of his wife and favorite son, it was very tempting for him to hope that the second coming was at hand.

For persons unable or unwilling to obtain copies of his *Discourses,* but also in order to give the "whole compass of the argumentation," Priestley published *An Outline of the Evidences of Revealed Religion.*[18] Inconsistencies in some accounts and doubts as to the authenticity of parts of some books of Scripture were irrelevant, for it was the whole of Revelation that was important. He summarized the arguments from the tripartite *Letters to a Philosophical Unbeliever,* the bipartite *Letters to the Philosophers and Politicians of France, Observations on the Increases of Infidelity,* and the three volumes of *Discourses on the Evidences of Revealed Religion*—especially the discourse of the London/Hackney set on the resurrection of Jesus. He repeated an earlier discussion of the nature of evidence in general, then continued to the historical and miraculous evidences for Revelation.

Priestley next responded to the fondness of some philosophers and philosophes for "philosophical" Hinduism. Edmund Burke, for example, thought Hindu piety admirable and praised it during the trial of Warren Hastings. Priestley had written on Eastern religions in his *Matter and Spirit* in 1777 and continued an interest in the subject as "Scrutator" in the *Theological Repository* for 1788. In 1793 he interviewed Thomas Twining on natural and cultural aspects of life in India and as early as May 1797 began

17. Priestley to Lindsey, 16 June 1798; see also his letters to Lindsey, 12 Nov., 20 Dec. 1794, 12 Aug. 1795, 27 Aug., 16 Nov. 1797, Wms. [George Thatcher], "Letters to George Thatcher," *Proceedings of the Massachusetts Historical Society* 2, 3 (2d ser., 1886–87): 11–40, 18–19. "A catalogue of Priestley's library compiled after his death includes 27 titles specifically on Biblical prophecy, plus uncounted items within the 121 volumes of theological tracts," according to Clarke Garrett, "Joseph Priestley, the Millennium, and the French Revolution," *Journal of the History of Ideas* 34 (1973): 51–66, 53.

18. Joseph Priestley, *An Outline of the Evidences of Revealed Religion* (Philadelphia: T. Dobson, 1797); I have used W. 21:170–87.

to collect materials for a comparison of the Hindus and Moses, to some degree as a consequence of reactions to discourses 3 and 4 of the 1796 *Discourses*. Dedicated to a longtime patron, the Duke of Grafton, and dated 1 November 1799, the *Comparison of the Institutions of Moses with those of the Hindoos* was written to show the superiority of Mosaic institutions and independence from the Hindu.[19]

A rambling preface explained the juxtaposition of disjointed subjects in the volume; praised the work of a former student; announced the continuation of his church history and his notes on the Scriptures; reprinted the *Theological Repository* plan for a new translation of the Bible; defended himself from John Robison's claim that he belonged to subversive societies; and referred to the prophecies. It also claimed that we were now provided with ample materials for a study of Hindu religious institutions—and that there *had* been some progress since 1777. With the help of Dr. Ross, who had been much in the East, Priestley put together a list of some twenty-five volumes relating to the Hindus.

Unfortunately, his authorities differed so much that he had to provide a glossary of different names for the same Hindu deities, while his *Comparison* was confused by differing interpretations. Periodically he used Louis-Mathieu Langlès's preliminary discourse to a translation of *Hitopades* as an example of exaggerated claims, and depended heavily on the work of Sir William Jones, especially his translations of the *Padmapuran* and the *Institutes of Menu*, for correct information. But he quoted from works and persons who disagreed with one another, disavowed some of what was said, and then cited them again.[20] The confusion was most obvious in connection with the age and number of Hindu sacred books. Agreements between Hindu religious beliefs and those of other peoples were "beyond the effect of accident" (22). Any agreements with the Pentateuch, however, merely testified to the truth of Mosaic history. The Hindu account of creation was

19. Twining, *Travels in America*, 48. Priestley to Lindsey, 29 May 1797, to Thomas Belsham, 28 Dec. 1798, Wms. Joseph Priestley, *A Comparison of the Institutions of Moses with those of the Hindoos and Other Ancient Nations; with Remarks on Mr. Dupuis's Origin of All Religions; the Laws and Institutions of Moses Methodized, and An Address to the Jews on the Present State of the World and the Prophecies relating to It* (Northumberland: for the author, 1799). Copies were sent to James Freeman and William Bentley; Priestley to George Thatcher, 20 Feb. 1800, *Proceedings of the Massachusetts Historical Society* 3 (2d ser., 1886): 32–33.

20. Marshall, *British Discovery of Hinduism*, esp. intro., 20, 34, 39, and 43. Priestley once described the accounts of Holwell and Dow as differing so much from recently translated writings of the Hindus "that I am not disposed to pay much regard to them," and then he continued to use them.

an arbitrary and fanciful supposition compared to the Mosaic system, with a universe progressively developing toward perfection (63).

Hindu philosophy introduced the notion of dualism and contempt for the body. The caste system, so important to the Hindu religion, was missing from the Hebrew, and, in its European guise of nobility, also from America and France (111–47). Though sublime in concept, Hindu devotional rites, practices, and ceremonies were extravagant in practice and resulted in apathy and insensibility. They could not compare with decent and solemn Hebrew worship. Hindu food restrictions, unlike the rational principles of Hebrew diet, were arbitrarily rooted in religious beliefs irrelevant to nourishment.

Almost every activity customary to day-to-day living was a sin to the Hindu, requiring a variety of penances or preventatives. Many were disgusting and others licentious, obscene, or lascivious. Even Langlès, however much he admired the system, forbore to translate some passages of the *Hitopades* as too gross. The institutions of the Hebrews treated all this with contempt, escaping false philosophies and superstitions because their sacred books, liturgies, and prayers were free of them, teaching instead a spirit of pure and rational devotion. The Hindu idea of a future state was superior to that of any other heathen nation, but there was no way that the Hebrew system could have derived from this or any other Oriental system.

In "Remarks on Mr. Dupuis's Origin of all Religions," with an appendix on the "Allegorizing Talents of Mr. Boulanger" (301–722), Priestley returned to the discussion of Dupuis begun in the third edition of his *Observations.* If Langlès was obsessed with the Hindus, Dupuis was obsessed with Egypt. When he derived dates of 14,000 to 15,000 years B.C. for a cultured Egyptian society, Priestley asked, what were the Egyptians doing during the ten thousand years intervening between the known dates of their achievements? Dupuis's work bore more marks of deep erudition, more ingenuity, and more labor, with less judgment than anything that had appeared before. It was an experiment on how far confident assertion could go in imposing on the world. Given that neither cuneiform nor hieroglyphics had yet been translated, Priestley can hardly be faulted for his conservative response to Dupuis's assertion of man's antiquity.

Transferring his animus from Judaism to Christianity, Dupuis also transferred his allegiance to Persia and the Chaldeans. Again there were the elaborate analogies, and this time a curious analysis of Christ's supposed horoscope. Like Boulanger's allegories, these were easy to refute. "Much has been said of the credulity of Christians, but what is it compared to that of many unbelievers?" (370).

References to the various laws and rules from the *Pentateuch* were distributed into parts and subsections in "The Laws and Institutions of Moses methodized" (373–91). And, finally, in "An Address to the Jews" (393–428), dated 1 October 1794, Priestley declared his respect for Jews, said that the *Comparison* was an attempt to vindicate the honor of their religion, and noted that he had previously addressed them. The Book of Daniel (which could be supplemented by Revelation) had foretold the termination of the Jews' present dispersion.

Early in 1801 Priestley went to Philadelphia with his son Jos and daughter-in-law. There he had a bout of pleurisy and never quite recovered, after repeated bleedings by Dr. Rush with the concurrence of Dr. Wistar. As no Unitarian place of worship was open, he generally attended the Episcopal church, Dr. White, Bishop of Pennsylvania, preaching. "Knowing the Dr. to be dull of hearing, Bishop White always spoke much louder than usual when Dr. P was present."[21] Returning to Northumberland, continued weakness and illness kept him from any occupation except occasional visits to his laboratory, his reading, and especially his writing. Early fruits of this enforced leisure were two minor publications: *An Inquiry into the Knowledge of the Ancient Hebrews* and *A Letter to an Antipaedobaptist*.[22] He sent the manuscript of the first to London, where it was published with a preface by Lindsey. It was a short pamphlet going from presumptive arguments to inferences from the Old Testament to prove that Jews believed in a future state.

In the second, Priestley returned to arguments favoring infant baptism, addressed, by inference, to his old friend Joshua Toulmin, who was soon to be his successor at New Meeting. The relevant volumes in his library had been destroyed in the riots, but he had William Wall's *History of Infant Baptism* (1705) and his own work, first published as "Liberius" in the *Theological Repository* of 1771 and repeated in his *Institutes of Natural and Revealed Religion* (1772–4) to support his contention that primitive Christians had baptized infants. Baptism had no mystical value; it was merely a public admission of religious commitment of the baptized or their parents; any method answered the purpose if the commitment was there.

---

21. Smith, *Priestley in America*, 139; Thomas Cooper wrote of the illness to Jefferson, 17 March 1801, photostat, Edgar Fahs Smith Collection, Library, University of Pennsylvania; the Bishop White anecdote is from a letter to the Rev. Robert Asplund, in [Robert Asplund], "Memoir of the late Rev. Robert Aspland," *Christian Reformer* 1 (n.s., 1845): 358.

22. Joseph Priestley, *An Inquiry into the Knowledge of the Ancient Hebrews, concerning a Future State* (London: J. Johnson 1801); I have used W. 12:482–504, which lacks Lindsey's preface. Joseph Priestley, *A Letter to an Antipaedobaptist* (Northumberland: Andrew Kennedy, 1802); I have used W. 20:463–92. The preface is dated Feb. 1802.

Another development from the Philadelphia *Discourses* was Priestley's *Socrates and Jesus Compared* (1803).[23] Having taken on the Hindus and Muslims, Priestley now addressed those who would substitute Greek philosophy and Socrates for Revelation and Jesus. Dedicated to Joshua Toulmin and dated January 1803, *Compared* took the favorable accounts of Socrates from Xenophon and Plato (not always to be credited), matched by accounts of Jesus by the evangelists. Prince of heathen philosophers, Socrates was nonetheless a polytheist and public practitioner of divination. Priestley's comparison of the two showed Jesus superior in every regard.

This pamphlet led to Priestley's last public theological controversy. Priestley's letters to John Blair Linn show that the old master had not lost his touch. In his first controversy, he had lectured Venn on manners; he later lectured Horsley on the nature of evidence; now he was lecturing Linn on conducting an argument—stick to the point, avoiding irrelevancies. He accused Linn of having written too hastily and having missed the point of the comparison.[24]

Linn had underestimated Socrates and was manifestly unfair in censuring Socrates by rules derived from the Gospels, which could not apply to him. The conclusion set forth the real reason for Linn's attack on Priestley's *Compared;* he was seizing an opportunity to profess his faith in the articles of orthodoxy. Priestley admitted having spoken of Jesus as a man and ignored the doctrine of atonement, presenting his familiar arguments against the Trinity and insisting that atonement was an invention of Augustine. He cited his *Early Opinions, Corruptions,* and *Doctrine of Remission,* and declared his "dying testimony" of continued belief in the unity and perfect placability of God.

Of course, Linn answered with a second letter, to which Priestley replied with his *Second Letter to Linn.*[25] Linn's first letter had been written with

23. Priestley, *Socrates and Jesus Compared* (Philadelphia: P. Byrne, 1803), reprinted in London by J. Johnson, 1803. It was photo-reprinted as a "Rare Esoteric Book," with author's name misspelled as Priestly and title reversed: *Jesus and Socrates Compared* (Kila, Montana: Kessinger Publishing Company, 1994?), which is the version I have used.

24. Priestley, *A Letter to the Reverend John Blair Linn, A.M. Pastor of the First Presbyterian Congregation in the City of Philadelphia. In Defense of the Pamphlet, Intitled, Socrates and Jesus Compared* (Northumberland: Byrne; Philadelphia: Andrew Kennedy, 1803); I have used W. 21:188–220.

25. Joseph Priestley, *A Second Letter to the Revd. John Blair Linn D.D., Pastor of the First Presbyterian Congregation in the City of Philadelphia in Reply to His Defense of the Doctrines of the Divinity of Christ and Atonement* (Northumberland: P. Byrne; Philadelphia: Andrew Kennedy, 1803); I have used W. 21:221–46. Linn later "regretted some expressions, which on reflection, he perceived to be too acrimonious, and rather unbecoming his years; and what greatly added to his regret, was that the doctor departed this life before he received a letter of

modesty and respect; his second revealed the frustration of defending the "obvious" to someone who refused to recognize it. He acted as though Priestley was obstinately, disingenuously, and artificially attempting to support a belief he knew to be indefensible. Being used to such accusations, Priestley could excuse Linn's language of controversy, but he thought it revealed Linn's youth and inexperience. He declined to enter another controversy on the divinity of Christ or the atonement, citing his *Corruptions* and *Early Opinions,* which Linn had described as fables. To Linn's "boast of the great number of texts that you could produce in support of your hypothesis [of the divinity of Christ]," Priestley answered, "These texts, however, as you do not recite them, I consider as soldiers on a muster list, which never appear in the field" (237). With explanations drawn from *Familiar Illustrations* (1770), *Appeal to professors of Christianity* (1770), and *Arguments for the Unity of God* (1783), Priestley defended his assertion that the Athanasian Creed was much later than Athanasius, affirmed his victory over Horsley, and insisted again on the incredibility of the Trinity, whatever "the great end answered by it."

Priestley also determined, while in exile, to complete his original design for his history of the church, bringing it from "the Fall of the Western Empire" to the "Present Time." He wrote Lindsey in May 1795 that he had finished transcribing part of the continuation, in December that he had reached the Reformation, and in November 1797 that the whole was complete and transcribed for the press. This haste is revealed in misprints, incorrect dates, and a careless repetition of pronouns that often make the narrative hard to follow. He attempted to print it by subscription in Philadelphia but got only seven subscribers. Belsham successfully undertook to find subscriptions in England, writing, "the main design of the contribution is to make him happy for the remainder of his days, by enabling him . . . to prosecute an undertaking upon which his heart is set, and by convincing him, that his friends on this side the Atlantic . . . still retain the veneration due to his character, his merits, and his sufferings."[26]

---

apology, which had been prepared for conveyance." Lewis Leary, "John Blair Linn, 1777–1805," *William and Mary Quarterly* 4 (3d ser., 1947): 148–76, 171.

26. For the failure in Philadelphia, see Priestley to Benjamin Vaughan, 19 April 1798. Belsham's efforts were intended for the *Notes to the Scriptures* as well as the *History* and were successful to an amount exceeding £1,300; see Williams, *Memoirs of Thomas Belsham,* 506. One of the subscribers was John Law, Bishop of Elphin, who asked that his name be withheld, "as it would involve me with some acquaintance here, and do me more mischief than you can imagine"; Law to Theophilus Lindsey, in 1802, W. 9:iv. See also Hannah Lindsey to Timothy Kenrick, 31 March 1804, *Transactions of the Unitarian Historical Society* 5 (1931–34): 192–93.

With financial problems settled, the work was published in four volumes as *A General History of the Christian Church, from the Fall of the Western Empire to the Present Time* in 1802–3.[27] The dedication, dated July 1802, celebrated the importance of Thomas Jefferson. What friends of liberty in Europe could only support by their writings, Jefferson was achieving in a country on which the eyes of the civilized world were focused. Finally, Priestley added that personal note celebrating his delight in being, at last, in the favor of government. The preface is, among its characteristic rambling, a lesson in historiography. The first part of the *History* had been written from "original writers"; but this was no longer possible in a general history. Those writing general histories had to depend upon the fidelity of historians who preceded them—and that included the original writers. Priestley listed some of the authors on whom he had depended. The facts being theirs, the arrangement and the coloring was his and, as a Unitarian, he would differ from all preceding ecclesiastical historians.

What he actually added to their facts was the historical amplification of later parts of his *Corruptions* (1782), as *Early Opinions* (1786) had been the documentary evidence for the earlier. Priestley claimed that his history was uniquely candid respecting those who differed from him, and he willingly submitted to the "judgment of the impartial and of posterity" (xii). Allowance was due to the force of prejudice in the best-disposed minds and the absolute impossibility of access to truth in certain situations. Vice and folly were the most conspicuous in history because they were comparatively rare; common virtues passed unnoticed because they were common. Yet he would again dwell more on martyrdoms and violence to attract the attention of young readers.

Priestley's church history of 1790 had emphasized the miraculous spread of Christianity despite civil opposition; the growth of heresies and schisms; the futility of government interference in religion; and the Platonic nature of the Trinity. He now continued those themes, with the addition of attacks on the papacy. Controversies continued from 475 A.D. for all the imperial interferences, papal interventions, and councils. New heresies joined persistent old ones as theological speculation revived. Metaphysical speculation led some to a rejection of Christianity. Unbelievers, not interested in martyrdom, wrote of principles "true in philosophy, but not in religion." These controversies were countered by that wonderfully elaborate work by Thomas Aquinas, the *Summa*.

27. Priestley, *General History of the Christian Church;* incidentally, he had again underestimated the task; the title page of volume 1 declares the whole to be three volumes.

The text of volume 1 began at 475 A.D. and the fall of the Western Empire and went on to 1099 and the conquest of Jerusalem in the first crusade, now regarded as "foolish and ruinous in the extreme." The success of the first crusade led to others in which spiritual fervor was lost in the treacheries of emperors and venality of the crusaders, concealing the foolishness of the enterprises themselves. One section conventionally outlined the rise of Islam ("Mahometanism"), without even a reference his discourse in the 1797 *Discourses.* Papal infallibility was unknown in the early periods and some bishops denied the authority of the "infamous monsters" (339). When some of his ecclesiastical practices were questioned, Pope Gregory VII said that ancient custom was no model, as the "primitive church had dissembled many things, which were corrected afterwards, when religion was more confirmed, and extended" (461).

Volume 2 covered the period from 1099 to the unsatisfactory ending, in 1418, of the reforming Council of Constance. The volume was, intentionally or not, a history of the decline and fall of the Roman Church. Papal claims intensified, frequently leading to violence and even to schism and rival popes, long before the Great Schism of 1378. Priestley scarcely noticed the importance of national rivalries as a root cause for schisms. Volume 3 covered the period from 1418 to the Reformation, 1517. Attempts by secular princes, recalcitrant bishops, and the universities to control the papacy and reform the church failed. It was left much as it had been at Constance, for the popes rejected council decrees as "erroneous, detestable, null, contrary to the holy canons, hurtful to Christianity, and even ridiculous" (3). Persecutions against sectaries were now met with violence, but the cause of truth was never promoted by arms, and they should, in Priestley's view, have suffered persecutions without resistance (48).

In the longest continuous narrative of the *History* (156–340), Priestley followed the career of Martin Luther, raised up by divine providence for the great work of an effectual Protestant Reformation. In England, reform was provided by King Henry VIII, the country's most arbitrary monarch, whose ousting of papal power while retaining articles of Catholic faith achieved the absurdity of a layman at the head of the church. If the implacable opposition of Rome was not enough, with reformation achieved, Protestants had to deal with conflicts between reforming sects, which multiplied as the Roman Church predicted they would. Protestants now used the arguments that the Roman Catholics had used against them to justify their persecution of Unitarians, notably including John Calvin's burning of Michael Servetus, whose discovery of the lesser circulation of the blood was published in his *Christianismi Restitutio* of 1533. Priestley noted happily that many persons, both Catholic and Protestant, remarkable for their zeal as persecutors came to suffering and untimely ends.

The fourth volume of the *General History* commenced with a preface explaining that Priestley had included particulars giving an idea of the spirit of the times, which "is what is of the most real value in all history" (v). He submitted his history to the judgment of posterity (3:340–74), and posterity must then condemn him on at least three counts independent of his Unitarian biases. His failure to address growing nationalism is excusable given that the eighteenth century scarcely recognized the term. His failure sufficiently to emphasize the importance of wars during the period, especially those between the emperor and the king of France, is less excusable. He wrote that the concurrence of circumstances that assisted in bringing about the Reformation deserved the closest attention, but he omitted "merely civil transactions" of the period such as related to war and peace.

His discussion of the repercussions of the Reformation in the Germanies, Poland, Switzerland, etc., was incomplete given his exclusion of such events, for how could they be understood except in the context of the Thirty Years' War? Nor did events in France—the St. Bartholomew massacre, the Edict of Nantes, and its revocation—make sense in isolation from France's religious wars and the Thirty Years' War. And his view of the Council of Trent was also misleading. Priestley concluded that "this great council . . . called for to promote the unity of the Church, and the reformation of abuses, was terminated, without producing any effect of the former kind and but little of the latter" (3:374). Not until volume 4 did he admit that Trent achieved anything of a reform in the Roman Church.

The period covered in volume 4 went from the Council of Trent to the revocation of the Edict of Nantes (a "most egregious folly") and on to "the present time" (1802), with additions of a chronological table (421–37), a chart of the succession of popes, emperors of East and West, and kings of France and England (441–53), and an index to the whole (457–80). The text continues as before. Controversies within the Roman Church were allowed so long as they were not publicized. "Such is the boasted unity of the catholic church and the great utility of an infallible judge of controversies" (42). In France the immediate consequence of the revocation of Nantes was the suffering of Protestants (such as Lewis de Marolles, Isaac LeFevre, and Peter Maur, also described in their *History,* edited by Priestley). The long-term effect was an increase in Catholic anticlericalism, Protestantism, and an infidelity that flowered in the French Revolution, when church property was nationalized and general toleration declared.

Priestley naturally gave special attention to the progress of the Reformation in England and Scotland and particularly to the growth of Dissenting sects. He said little about the English Civil War except that it was admittedly a war of religion (186). The toleration promised at the restoration of the monarchy was promptly violated, and persecution continued, especially against Quakers and Unitarians. It appeared that the church by law established preferred the Roman Church to any other alternatives to itself. Priestley himself had lived through and previously discussed the development of Methodism and Deism in Great Britain and Ireland. He included some new material on the formation and insurrection of the United Irishmen and the Act of Union of 1800–1801, which was unlikely to solve the problem so long as Catholics were disabled (339).

Meanwhile, advancement of learning had demolished the authority of Aristotle, the true key to natural philosophy was announced by Lord Bacon, and the shackles of authority of every kind were being destroyed. Miscellaneous observations (382–418) were chiefly distinguished by allusion to developments in experimental philosophy (Newton, Franklin, and Herschel) and a conventional, but preachy, conclusion, with references to his *Corruptions*, but the true ending of this last volume was the section on the United States. This began with the standard Dissenting story of the religious peopling of North America and ended with a celebration of American toleration. "It is a glorious example . . . to the christian world, shewing . . . the perfect safety . . . [and] positive advantages . . . of universal toleration . . . [and] the exclusion of any establishment of religion whatever" (381). The many different sects lived in perfect harmony and acted together in any common cause, and yet there was as much real religion there as in any European country.

In April 1803 Priestley wrote Lindsey that his attention was directed more then ever to a future better world, but, sensible to the last, he continued working. In January 1804 he wrote that winter kept him from his laboratory; "reading and composing are my sole occupation and amusement." His debility growing steadily worse, he consulted with his son and his printer about unpublished works, but continued to add to them. The day before his death, he examined revisions of his notes on the Old and New Testaments. He had maintained, as early as his *Oratory and Criticism* (1777), that "mention of so many particular persons, places, and times, in the books of scripture affords . . . no small evidence of their genuineness and truth." His Sunday services at Leeds and especially at Birmingham had included regular expositions on the Scriptures that were so well received that he resolved to assemble and publish them, but the riots of 1791 destroyed most of what had been composed and transcribed by then. The dedication to William Russell and other members of his congregation at New Meeting suggests that, in the *Notes on all the Books of Scripture*, in his exile, loneliness, old age, and illness, Priestley had found time to reorganize and print those expositions.[28]

He explained that the *Notes* were not intended for critics and scholars but for liberal and intelligent Christians. He used the common English Bible but cited differences with the Hebrew, Samaritan, Greek (Septuagint), and occasional early manuscript versions, indicated some improvements by modern translators, and noted changes that could occur in copying (37). As usual, the *Notes* were repetitive, paraphrasing from previous publications and showing evidence of hasty preparation, with misprints and confusing syntax. As he had not at first intended to publish, he had not noted sources, here mentioning only the bishops Simon Patrick and Robet Lowth, Daniel Whitby, and, the only cited Dissenter, Philip Doddridge, but claimed that most of the notes were not borrowed from any specific writer. Most of the observations were standard to his time: glosses on obscure words and phrases, identification of people, tribes, and places. Priestley sometimes introduced citations from later books of Scripture and invariably included his personal coloring of some passages. Curiously, there seems to be no direct relationship between any of his *Notes* and those of the Bible he had edited in 1788–89.

Priestley took a conservative approach to Scripture. He admitted that he had given particular attention "to the circumstances which prove the genuineness and divine authority of the books of scripture" (xi). This theme was repeated throughout the four volumes, in the face of doubts expressed by contemporary scholars. He had, for example, no doubt that the Pentateuch was written by Moses—e.g., the lack of organization in Numbers was evidence of Moses' authorship.[29] Parallel passages from Exodus and Numbers were repetitions no editor would have made, showing that the books could not be artificial compilations. Joshua had the same internal marks of authenticity as the Pentateuch, with some interpolations. The narrative of Ruth had

28. Joseph Priestley, *Notes on all the Books of Scripture, for the Use of the Pulpit and Private Families,* 4 vols. (Northumberland: for the author, 1803–4). Although the first volume was published while Priestley still lived, the last three were posthumous.

29. By Priestley's day, scholars had questioned the authorship by Moses, and by 1753 the existence of duplicate and parallel narratives had led Jean Astruc to begin the analysis of different sources within the Pentateuch, which has developed into the present view that it is a composite of several sources from many different periods, all clearly later than the estimated thirteenth-century date for Moses. See, for example, *Abingdon Bible Commentary,* ed. Frederick Carl Eiselen et al. (Nashville: Abingdon-Cokesbury Press, 1929), and Frederick Gladstone Bratton, *History of the Bible* (Boston: Beacon Press, n.d.). Priestley was aware of the doubts of Mosaic authorship and repeatedly argued against the doubts; see his comments on 1 Kings, 563.

every mark of truth and none of fiction, but there was some indication that parts were not written near the time of the story. The "natural language of a pious heart" proved the authenticity of Nehemiah. The uncertainty in the dates of prophecies in Ezekiel was a "good proof" that the book was not a forgery. The Psalms were a collection of poems, chiefly by David, that showed the infinite superiority of the Hebrew religion to any other and represented a greater miracle than any recorded by Moses.[30]

Independent, nonscriptural references also testified to the reliability of the sacred books. Pliny described a theater similar to the temple Sampson supposedly brought down. The size of the sixteenth-century figure John Middleton showed that the description of Goliath was not unreasonable. Sir William Jones showed that the Afghans were descended from the Israelites, and Herodotus wrote about King Sennacherib.

Of course, Priestley's other enthusiasms were also present in force throughout the *Notes*. His obsession with miracles, for example, was supported by commentary on Exodus, where his lack of personal military experience left unquestioned the logistical problems attending two million people wandering in the desert for forty years. Priestley repeatedly mentioned prophecy as well. Following his commentary on Ezekiel, he gave an interpolated "General Observations on the subject of Prophecy" (513–18) in which, after a clumsily worded affirmation of his belief in prophecy, he declared that we should joyfully expect the coming of the kingdom of God, without demanding particulars. He quoted Newton's analysis of the prophecies in Daniel. And to the "predictions" of a Jewish people cursed when they broke their vows were added those of God's heavy judgment on the Christian and Mahometan powers who oppressed them (361).

Priestley addressed the question of atonement, obliquely, in Jeremiah's new covenant, where no person would suffer for the sins of ancestors but only for his own. Again he affirmed the superiority of the Hebrew religion. The first part of Genesis was probably a fable, Priestley thought, but it was still a more rational account of the origin of things than that of any heathen. His primary interest in Leviticus was its proof of the superiority of the laws of the Hebrew religion to those of any heathens. His notes on Numbers were followed by "A Dissertation in which are demonstrated the Originality and Superior Excellence, of the Mosaic Institutions," which was reprinted, with a preface, as *The Originality . . . of the Mosaic Institutions,* for the benefit of those who had not read the *Notes.* This text expanded on Priestley's

---

30. Priestley elaborately rationalized most of the psalms to relate to episodes in David's life, without concern for chronology or evidence from Samuel or Kings.

commentary on Leviticus and summarized the notes on the Pentateuch to compare to his earlier works on heathen institutions in general, Muslims, Hindus, and Greeks. He divided into twenty classes the items of his comparison of Mosaic religious and civil institutions with those of any other ancient nation, and showed the former to be unique and superior in every instance.[31]

Priestley leavened the first two volumes with comments on human nature and natural philosophy. He used his experience in the Birmingham Riots to illustrate the blaming of the victim. Proverbs represented Solomon's directions for a good life and was vastly superior to the wisdom literature of heathens. The whole showed that human nature has been the same in all ages and countries. It is surprising, given Priestley's view of the American Revolution, that he did not understand the northern kingdom's resentment of Solomon's excessive taxation and forced labor practices. Notes on 1 and 2 Chronicles explained the reluctance of some to end their exile and the inclination of those at their ease to continue where they were.

Priestley suggested scientific explanations for some early passages of Genesis: rotation of fluid becoming an oblate spheroid, operation of chemical affinities, etc. Whatever came to pass according to the usual laws of nature was frequently ascribed to God. Equivocal generation was absurd in a world so filled with design, but a continual creation, after the deluge, would answer any problem with the ark. Leviticus provided Priestley an opportunity to note his experiments on "green matter" and photosynthesis. He explained the stones falling upon the earth, mentioned in Joshua, as possibly the result of lunar volcanoes, and noted that the reference to the sun standing still was a quotation from a poem, the Book of Jashar, not a physical description.[32] A reference to mirrors in 1 Corinthians elicited a note on the physics of light reflected and absorbed in ancient mirrors.

Priestley was not at all happy with Ecclesiastes, supposedly composed by Solomon, but in his cynical, unhappy old age. Some passages were unclear and Priestley did not attempt to explain them, but those on the vanity of knowledge were unacceptable. The constant view of the wonders of nature as proofs of divine power as real and compelling as any miracles made no

---

31. Joseph Priestley, *The Originality and Superior Excellence of the Mosaic Institutions Demonstrated* (Northumberland: Andrew Kennedy, for P. Byrne; Philadelphia, 1803). I have used the version from *Notes*, without the preface. The twenty classes really condense to half that number, ranging from monotheism, purity of morals, design of temples, and rites of worship to the fact that the laws are fixed and written for all to consult.

32. The existence of meteors had been confirmed to Priestley in 1803 by communications via Andrew Ellicott from Robert Livingston, then in Paris; Livingston to Ellicott, 30 Sept. 1803, Catherine van Cortland Mathews, *Andrew Ellicott: His Life and Letters* (New York: Grafton Press, 1908), 210–11; Ellicott to Livingston, 20 Jan. 1804, *SciAuto.*, 178.

impression on the bulk of mankind. Bacon said that knowledge is power. "The more we understand of the laws of nature, the more we can avail ourselves of their operation in procuring the various conveniences of life." And their investigation was one of the most engaging of pursuits, affording endless satisfaction, as the subject was inexhaustible. Where there is an increase in knowledge, it may be presumed that, on the whole, there will be improvement in virtue.

Volume 1 included the Pentateuch, Joshua, Judges, Ruth, 1 and 2 Samuel, and 1 Kings. Priestley made an inexplicable aside in his notes on Exodus, maintaining the Phoenician origin of the ancient Irish nation (152–53). He was unhappy about Solomon's Song.[33] Written on the occasion of Solomon's marriage, the more erotic passages were not indelicate according to Eastern customs. Those who tried to find religion in the Song of Solomon made themselves ridiculous. Volume 2 of *Notes* encompassed the remaining books of the Old Testament, from 2 Kings to Malachi. Priestley drew attention to the acrostic nature of the poetry of Lamentations and the minor prophet Nahum.

The last two volumes of *Notes* concerned material in the New Testament, about which Priestley had been writing since his first theological publication, the *Doctrine of Remission* (1761). These volumes continued many of the themes of volumes 1 and 2 and added new ones: opposition to the papacy, denial of the divinity of Christ and of the second coming as prerequisite to eternal life. Priestley had, for example, no doubts that all the Epistles were written by the apostles.[34] Though Paul's letters lacked precision, they animated and affected his readers and provided the same evidence for truth as those of Cicero and others for Roman history (125). The pastoral Epistles, 1 Timothy and Titus, were separated from 2 Timothy by 2 Corinthians, Romans, and Ephesians in an effort to force the dates of writing into agreement with Acts. Priestley noted the "similarity" of parts of 2 Peter with passages in Jude, but he had no doubt its apostolic authenticity.

Miracles were not suited to our age; God did not routinely act upon nature or the mind of man. Paul was mistaken at the timing of parousia, mistaking a prophecy that moderns, better able to understand, took probably to mean the destruction of the papacy. Given Priestley's fascination with Daniel, it is no surprise to find that he was attracted by Revelation. It was

---

33. At least Priestley was not taken in by contemporary allegories that Solomon's Song represented the love of Christ for his church.

34. The authorship of several of the Epistles had been debated from very early, as Priestley was aware, for he had previously discussed the issue in his debates with Bishop Horsley.

written, he believed, by the apostle John, a conviction, he was pleased to note, shared by Sir Isaac Newton. We should observe the original sense of any passage in Scripture and not presume that it had a true different sense. Nevertheless, Priestley clearly relished the numbers game, loved matching prophecy to event, and delighted in the seven seals, trumpets, and vials and their esoteric meanings. He recognized that other commentators had indulged their imagination too freely. "We must proceed with great caution in the interpretation of prophecies not yet fulfilled, tho' it is probable that the accomplishment . . . is not very distant."

Although some of Jesus' discourses were "imperfectly recollected," his language was never that of a person who thought himself God. Divine worship of Christ, the Virgin Mary, and other dead men and women was idolatrous. The doctrine of atonement was unworthy of a divine being. His notes on Matthew 6.25 and 10.28 insisted that the doctrine of a soul subsisting independently of the body could not be found in Scripture but was borrowed from heathen philosophy. "All power depends upon *opinion,* and without the general opinion in their favour, magistrates are no more than single men."

Most of these comments can be found, in different words, in Priestley's earlier works, especially his *Corruptions of Christianity,* but this characteristic repetition is nowhere clearer than in the "Notes on the Harmony of the Four Evangelists" that began volume 3. The organization of topics, paraphrases by which the Gospels were "harmonized," and the notes, with some additions, were taken from his *Harmony of the Evangelists* (1777–80).[35] The remainder of volume 3 concerned "Notes on the Book of Acts," which, next to the Gospels, Priestley believed the most valuable part of the New Testament. The format of volume 4, on the Epistles, was very like that of the notes to the Gospels, without the harmonization of parallel accounts. There were constant cross references to Acts to confirm persons, places, and implied dates in the letters. And after quoting many of the Epistles at length, Priestley paraphrased them in language more intelligible to the modern reader. Of much less consequence than other books of the scriptural canon, these were nevertheless the oldest records of Christianity and preserved early apostolic attitudes and personalities.

35. He wrote Lindsey, 1 Jan. 1798, that, having leisure, he was recomposing his exposition of the New Testament lost at the riots. Paraphrasing previous publications, especially his *Harmony of the Gospels,* J. T. Rutt claims, in his editor's preface to the first volume of reprinted *Notes* on the New Testament, that he had added more notes, "omitted, probably by accident," from the manuscript when it was originally printed, which he distinguished from those in the Northumberland edition, W. 31:iii. I have failed to find any of these that are significant.

"St. Paul's epistles abound with . . . abruptnesses and . . . show that he wrote from his heart, and dictated his real thoughts and sentiments at the time of their composition. They likewise throw considerable light upon the *natural* temper of the great apostle . . . a warm man, of a quick apprehension, of great ardour and vehemence in whatever he engaged in, and that he was inclined to be hasty." He also paraphrased 1 Peter, for, like Paul's, Peter's language was often confusing.

The three letters of John were written in a figurative and abrupt language similar to the the Gospel of John and emphasized John's opposition to the Gnostics. A note on Ephesians observed that "the greater refinement of manners of this age holds it a disgrace to christianity to hold slaves tho' slavery was permitted in Old Testament ages." Priestley also noted the spurious addition of the "three witnesses" passage in 1 John (5:7–8).

Priestley indulged himself throughout his notes in mini-sermons: Only God could look to the heart of man for the truth of his piety, to assess his punishment—but Priestley also gloated that Pilate was later accused of bad administration, banished to Gaul, and there killed himself. Faith in Christ must be accompanied by good works, Christians should regulate their lives by the fruits of the doctrines of Christianity. Christians ought to prize their Scriptures as the Jews prized theirs. All Christians agreed on the essentials, to which they should give their greatest attention and consider other articles as subservient. All Christians needed to reform their lives in a firm belief in the word of God.

Priestley started planning an *Index to the Bible* in mid-1800 to accompany his *Notes* and completed it by late 1803, but it was not published until 1804–5. The preface acknowledged that makers of indexes were not recognized for their brilliance, though they certainly required good judgment. He had indexed subjects of history and prophecy, added to those on morality, which he had extracted from "Mr. Pilkington's *Rational concordance, or Index to the Bible*" of 1749, and he believed his work would help draw attention to the Scriptures.[36]

On the morning of the day he died, Priestley dictated notices to be added to *The Doctrines of Heathen Philosophy, Compared with those of Revelation,*

---

36. Priestley to Lindsey, [Oct.] 1800, fragment, Wellcome Historical Medical Library, London. Joseph Priestley, *Index to the Bible: in which the various Subjects which occur in the Scriptures are alphabetically arranged: with accurate References to all the Books of the Old and New Testaments, designed to facilitate the Study of these invaluable Records* (London: J. Johnson, 1805). However much "judgment" was required to make his *Index*, I lack judgment fruitfully to analyze it.

each part of which had separately been transcribed and prepared for the press so his son could publish what was finished. Ostensibly an expansion of *Socrates and Jesus Compared* and produced at the urging of friends, *The Doctrines of Heathen Philosophy* also continued the general references to philosophers contained in discourses 7 and 8 of the 1796 *Discourses*.[37] Although it never mentioned Boethius (his comparisons excluded philosophers after the acceptance of Christianity by the Roman emperors), the book had the character of *The Consolation of Philosophy* turned on its head, for one by one, from Hesiod and Homer through to Epicurus, its purpose was to show that true consolation could not be found in philosophy but only in Christianity.

Dated (posthumously November 1804, it was dedicated to the Roman Catholic priest Joseph Berington, and the Episcopal bishop William White, because he believed they agreed on the essential articles of Christianity and would meet in heaven, though each held he was eternally damned. The logic, metaphysics, or physics of heathen philosophers, all equally trifling and absurd, did not concern him. He extracted only what could reasonably be compared to Revelation. Despite the partial destruction of his library at Birmingham, he had at hand the sources he needed: Homer and Hesiod for inferences of pre-Pythagorean philosophy, Pythagoras, Socrates, Plato, Aristotle, Marcus Aurelius (called here Marcus Antoninus) and Epictetus, supplemented by Seneca and Arian for the Stoics, and Diogenes Laertius and Lucretius for the Epicureans. The part on Socrates was a reprinting of *Socrates and Jesus Compared*, with the dedication to Joshua Toulmin added as an appendix by Jos, at his father's request.

Priestley's examination of his selected philosophers, with numerous quotations from their writings, demonstrated the infinite superiority of Revelation, and especially of Christianity, to their systems. The seven "systems" shared certain general traits. Each contained some excellent moral and commonsense precepts; each was polytheist in one way or another; each (except for the Epicureans), while contemptuous of the commonality, believed that the prosperity of the state depended upon public worship conforming to rites common to the country as the law directed; and none contained any sure notion of that future state and retribution that so comforted the Christian.

The pre-Pythagoreans appeared to believe that the earth, its places and things, preceded the gods responsible for them, the Stoics that the universe

37. Joseph Priestley, *The Doctrines of Heathen Philosophy, compared with those of Revelation* (Northumberland: John Binns, 1804).

was eternal, in perpetual cycles. The Epicureans maintained that the universe came together by "a fortuitous concourse" of preexistent atoms and would in time disintegrate as it had begun. The remaining four "systems" held that the Supreme Being or Intellect created the universe out of preexistent substance and ruled it through his agents. Plato had some unintelligible and mischievous speculations on the relation of God, the universe, and ideas in the divine mind, while Aristotle, superior to Plato and all other Greek philosophers in genius and good sense, was unspeakably tiresome in his disquisitions on theology and metaphysics.[38]

Virtue was rarely defined beyond truthfulness and prudence. Plato thought it was the contemplation of abstract ideas, Aristotle that anything reputable in the eyes of man was virtuous, vice anything disreputable—a practical definition, but hardly advancing theology or moral science. The Stoics declared that virtue lay in freeing oneself of feelings, a principle of disinterestedness beyond human ability, Priestley thought, while the Epicureans made enjoyment (complete, not sensual) the object and end of human life. In none of these systems was there any real motive for the practice of virtue. Better the Christians' joy at death than Stoic resignation or Platonic loss of self. It pleased God to console mankind, sending light to a particular nation and Jesus Christ on his divine mission.

Priestley intended to deliver another set of discourses (date not given), but did not do so, perhaps because of repeated illnesses, and they remained unpublished until after his death. These *Four Discourses* were unlike those of 1796 and 1797 in actually being in the form of sermons.[39] The first extolled mutual exhortation by Christians to resist insidious worldly influences and retain their true character and virtue, particularly in view of the approaching second coming of Christ. The second recommended patience, discipline, and delayed gratification in full faith of God's promises. The third and fourth saw, in the changes occurring in the apostles after Christ's Resurrection, a guarantee of his divine mission and an inspiration for Christians to follow.

On the morning of 6 February 1804, after dictating corrections for *The Doctrines of Heathen Philosophy*, Priestley declared: "That is right; I have now done," closed his eyes, and quietly died. His son left what Rutt describes

---

38. Analysis of the reprinting of *Socrates and Jesus Compared* has been skipped here as a repetition of that already given in Chapter 17. Priestley disliked Plato as the quasi-progenitor of the doctrine of the Trinity; see *Theological Repository* 4 (1784): 76–97, *Corruptions*, and *Early Opinions*.

39. Priestley, *Four Discourses intended to have been delivered at Philadelphia* (Northumberland: John Binns, at the desire of the author, 1806).

as an "affecting and edifying" account of Priestley's last days, including a pretty speech to his grandchildren on the evening of 5 February: "I am going to sleep as well as you; for death is only a good long sound sleep in the grave, and we shall meet again" (W. 1.2:530). He was buried in a Quaker burial ground and later removed to another. His epitaph reads: "Return unto thy rest, O my soul, for the / Lord hath dealt bountifully with thee. / I will lay me down in peace and sleep till / I awake in the morning of the resurrection." The American Philosophical Society held a memorial service in his honor. New Meeting, Birmingham, resolved on 15 April 1804 to wear mourning for two months starting on 22 April, and William Wood, Priestley's successor at Mill Hill Chapel, Leeds, preached from the text "He was a burning and a shining light; and ye were willing for a season to rejoice in his light."[40]

40. Thomas Cooper to Benjamin Rush, 6 Feb. 1804, Bolton, #97; to Benjamin Smith Barton, 6 Feb. 1804, Historical Society of Pennsylvania, Philadelphia; *SciAuto.*, 179; Gibbs, *Joseph Priestley*, 44.

Appendix: Family

Most of Priestley's family contemporaries broke with him over religious differences, though there are occasional indications of contact. Brother Timothy, a member of Lady Huntingdon's "connection" of Calvinistic Methodists, had a semi-antagonistic relationship with Priestley.[1] Timothy published religious works and edited a *Christian's Magazine* (1790–92) to counteract Unitarianism, and died in 1814 at age eighty, leaving at least one son. A sister, Mrs. Martha Crouch, corresponded with Joseph after the death of her husband in 1786; she died childless in 1812. A younger brother, Joshua, still living at age eighty in 1816, left children, grandchildren, and great-grandchildren, one of them, born about the time Priestley died, named Joseph. Priestley gave Joshua some canal shares, which allowed him and his wife to live independently and comfortably.[2]

Priestley's posterity is best described by Dr. Priestley Toulmin III, a descendent through Joseph Jr. and the compiler of the most complete family genealogy: "Physicians, writers, scientists, clergymen, statesmen, and others, a few nationally or internationally prominent and many of solid, recognized stature in their fields of endeavor, seem to be represented in unusually high proportions. Whether through nature or nurture—both valid forms of inheritance—his progeny seem particularly attracted to the life of the mind."[3]

The more immediate members of that posterity include Sarah (Sally) Priestley Finch, Joseph Priestley Jr., William Priestley, and Henry Priestley. Sally (1763–1803) married, in 1786, William Finch, who was not prepared to cooperate with Dr. Joseph in Sally's behalf, being "strangely wrong headed

1. He preached a curious funeral sermon: Timothy Priestley, *A Funeral Sermon occasioned by the Death of the late Rev. Joseph Priestley;* see Schofield, *Enlightenment of Priestley,* 3n3.

2. *Christian Reformer* 111 (1844): 264. Parkes, "Mr. Parkes's Account of a Visit to Birstal," Schofield, *Enlightenment of Priestley,* 4n5.

3. Priestley Toulmin III, "The Descendents of Joseph Priestley, LL.D., F.R.S.," *Proceedings of the Northumberland County Historical Society* 32 (Part 2, 1994): 5.

and obstinate, tho' kind, sober, and industrious." Sally died of consumption in 1803, after receiving treatment, along with Tom Wedgwood, Southey, and Coleridge, at Dr. Thomas Beddoes's Preventive Medical Institution, which had the support of many Lunar Society members.[4] She left five daughters and two sons. For the girls, little but dates and observations of school-mistress occupation is known. One son, John Finch (1791–after 1830), pub-lished *Travels in the United States of America and Canada* (1833), dedicated to the Marquis of Lansdowne. The book lists Finch as a corresponding member of the Natural History Society of Montreal, the Literary and Histor-ical Society of Quebec, honorary member of the West Point Lyceum, Dela-ware, West Chester, etc. It notes that Priestley's name had introduced him to agreeable society and valued friends, including Robert Hare (who told Finch he had exhibited his oxyhydrogen blowpipe to Priestley in 1801), and records his visit to Northumberland, describing Dr. Joseph, the house, and land.[5]

Joseph Priestley Jr. (Jos) (1768–1833), educated in Dissenting schools and in Geneva, worked in a mercantile house under the patronage of William Wilkinson and was to be adopted as heir by his uncle, John Wilkinson, until he married without Wilkinson's permission. Jos engaged in a partnership with a Mr. Ashworth in a Manchester cloth business that failed due to prej-udice against the Priestley name after the Birmingham Riots. His letters to James Watt Jr. indicate that in 1794 he was more republican than his father (on a par with Watt Jr.), and was doing his "mite toward rooting those rascals: Kings, Priests & Nobles from the face of the earth" and foreseeing, "with infinite pleasure, the downfall of proud England, the Establishment of the French republic, & the universal sphere of equal rights and equal laws."

When he emigrated to the United States, in October 1793, he intended to go into cotton manufacturing, but decided, after inspecting several of the factories in the country, that they were all badly conducted and would con-tinue to be unprofitable so long as the cost of labor was high and land so cheap. He engaged in abortive land speculations before concentrating on local commercial activities, including a brewery at Northumberland and a plant nursery for English garden plants and fruit trees (surely one of the first in America). In 1798 he sailed for England for an interview with John Wilkinson, though he was disinclined to leave Northumberland. He sent the American Philosophical Society's Committee on Trade, Navigations, etc.

4. Priestley to Wilkinson, 1 April 1797, Warr.; Schofield, *Lunar Society*, 372–77.
5. I. Finch, *Travels in the United States of America and Canada, containing some Account of their Scientific Institutions, and a Few Notices of the Geology and Mineralogy of those Coun-tries. To which is Added, An Essay on the Natural Boundries of Empires* (London: Longman, Rees, Orme, Brown, Green, and Longman, 1833), 88, 295, 314–15.

a recipe for the composition of enamel for kitchen utensils and, while in England, "assisted" Humphry Davy in experiments on nitrous oxide. These appear to be the only instances of his interest in science.[6] He returned to Northumberland, but letters to James Watt Jr. between 1794 and 1812 show increasing distaste for life in the United States. In 1811 he visited England on a business trip, was caught by the outbreak of the War of 1812, and never returned to the United States. He died on 2 September 1833.

His daughter Elizabeth married Joseph Parkes, the Birmingham radical political reformer. Bessie Rayner Parkes, their daughter, was an eminent feminist and editor of one of the first women's magazines in England before she married Louis Swanton Belloc. Her children, Hilaire Belloc and Marie Belloc Lowndes, are still more famous.

William Priestley (1771–c.1840) was too high-spirited to settle down. He traveled in Europe with his uncle, William Wilkinson, was in Paris at the start of the French Revolution, and emigrated to the United States before his father. He traveled about, particularly in New England, exploiting his relationship to Dr. Joseph, and was welcomed by James Freeman in Boston and William Bentley in Salem. His father expected him to join his brother Henry in farming, and he shared Henry's farm till the latter's death on 11 December 1795, when the whole devolved on him, but he was impatient and lamented the wastage of time. He married Margaret Foulke, the daughter of a reputable farmer. By 1800 William's uncertain temper and jealously of Jos and his family was causing trouble. In a letter to Lindsey dates 2 October 1801: Priestley wrote: "It must appear impossible that a Being of such unusual wisdom and power can bear the least ill will to any of his creatures. . . . It follows with a force that gives me . . . a satisfaction I cannot describe. The most refractory tempers must be [rectified] some time or other, and in the mean time they are not without their use here; and the worst dispositions must be reclaimed. You will know to what I refer." The Federalist newspapers gleefully printed reports that William Priestley, imbued with "French principles," had tried to poison his father by putting arsenic in the flour. The report was denounced in the *Aurora*, but denials by William and Dr. Joseph did not convince the already committed. Priestley wrote William Russell on 1 August 1799: "The behavior of my son William is likely to prove the

6. Schofield, *Lunar Society*, 426–27; Joseph Priestley Jr. to James Watt Jr., esp. 20 Nov. 1794, Birmingham City Archives, Reference Library; [Wansey], *Journal*, 74. For Joseph Jr.'s activities in the United States, see, among others, Richardson's "Current Interpretation," 22, nos. 8, 12, and Garrett, "Which Cooper?" 24–25. Archives, APS, APS506.73/Am4mc; [Humphry Davy], *Researches, Chemical and Philosophical, chiefly concerning Nitrous Oxide, or Dephlogisticated Nitrous Air, and its Respiration* (London: J. Johnson, 1800), 15, 317.

greatest [affliction]." William had, apparently in a drunken rage, put tartar emetic in the family's flour, which induced vomiting but was not dangerous. Priestley wrote George Thatcher on 10 May 1800, "there is no proof that any serious mischief was intended." About 1801 William and family moved to Louisiana, where Spain was giving land to settlers from the United States for the cost of official proof of ownership, about twenty-five cents an acre. William settled on land bordering the Mississippi River, which increased in value after 1806. He amassed a considerable fortune, for those days, of several hundred thousand dollars from sugar and land speculation. He died circa 1840 and was buried in Louisiana.[7]

His daughter, Catherine Caroline, born in Louisiana, married Henry Dickenson Richardson, who became a partner in the cotton business of Henry Hobson & Co. Their son, Henry Hobson Richardson, born on the Priestley plantation on 29 September 1838, graduated from Harvard in 1859, was sent to France by his father, studied at the École des Beaux Arts, and became a distinguished American architect.[8] Henry Hobson Richardson had two sisters and a brother, William Priestley Richardson, who served with distinction in the Confederate Army and may have become a member of the Louisiana legislature.

Henry (Harry) Priestley (1777–95) was born at Calne and educated by Mrs. Barbauld and John Prior Estlin, at Bristol, then for a time at Hackney New College. He was a favorite of his father, who hoped he might become a scholar, but he emigrated with his father in 1794, and eagerly began to work as a farmer.[9] By late 1794, he began to clear three hundred acres of cheap land, his father actively joining in removing the timber. He died of ague (possibly malaria) on 11 December 1795.

7. William Priestley to Jean Senebier, 8 Dec. 1785, MS Montagu d.18, Bodleian Library, Oxford; "Correspondence of Dr. William Bentley"; Priestley to John Vaughan, 21 July 1794, Historical Society of Pennsylvania; to Lindsey, 20 Dec. 1794, Wms.; to John Wilkinson, 24 July 1794, 17 Dec. 1795, Warr. Marriage noticed in the *American Advertiser*, 13 Feb. 1796, according to Smith, *Priestley in America*, 79. The *Reading Weekly Advertiser*, 30 April 1800, carried the story of the "poisoning." Priestley to George Thatcher, 10 May 1800, *SciAuto.*, 171; Priestley to William Russell, 1 Aug. 1799, Wms.; Lillian C. Bourgeois, *Cabanocey: The History, Customs, and Folklore of St. James Parish* (Gretna, La.: Pelican, 1957) has no index reference to Priestley or Richardson, but on p. 196, in list of taxpayers of St. James Parish, is the name William Priestley, and the endpapers map dated 1858 shows a piece of land along the Mississippi River with the name "Wm Priestley & heirs."

8. See Mrs. Schuyler Van Rensselaer, *Henry Hobson Richardson and His Works* (Boston: Houghton, Mifflin, 1888).

9. Priestley to Estlin, 22 Nov. 1787, 6 Aug. 1790, *W.* 1.1:420, 1.2:75–77 (Harry to learn French, if his Greek was sufficiently perfect); Priestley to Lindsey (he hoped to make a scholar of Harry), 2 June 1791, Wms.

Select Bibliography

WORKS BY PRIESTLEY

Books and Pamphlets

An Address to the Methodists. See Priestly edition: *Original Letters by the Rev. John Wesley*. 1791.

An Address to Protestant Dissenters of all Denominations on the Approaching Election of Members of Parliament, with Respect to the State of Public Liberty in General, and of American Affairs in Particular. London: J. Johnson, 1774.

An Address to the Unitarian Congregation at Philadelphia, delivered on Sunday, March 5th, 1797. Philadelphia: Joseph Gales, 1797. (W. 16:490–99.)

An Answer to Mr. Paine's Age of Reason. See *Letters to the Philosophers and Politicians of France*.

An AppeJal to the Public on the Subject of the Riots in Birmingham, to which are added, Strictures on a Pamphlet intitled "Thoughts on the late Riot in Birmingham." Birmingham: J. Thompson, for J. Johnson, 1791.

An Appeal to the Public on the Subject of the Riots in Birmingham, Part II. To which is added, A Letter from W. Russell, Esq. to the Author. London: J. Johnson, 1792. (W. 19:434–508, appendices 17–32.)

The Case of Poor Emigrants Recommended. Philadelphia: John Gales, 1797. (W. 16: 500–511.)

A Comparison of the Institutions of Moses with those of the Hindoos and Other Ancient Nations; with Remarks on Mr. Dupuis's Origin of All Religions; the Laws and Institutions of Moses Methodized, and An Address to the Jews on the Present State of the World and the Prophecies relating to It. Northumberland: for the author, 1799.

Conduct to be Observed (1789). See "Sermons."

Considerations for the Use of Young Men and the Parents of Young Men. London: J. Johnson, 1775.

Considerations on the Doctrine of Phlogiston and the Decomposition of Water. Philadelphia: Thomas Dobson, 1796. Reprinted, along with an answer by John Maclean, as *Considerations on the Doctrine of Phlogiston . . . And Two Lectures on Combustion . . .*, ed. William Foster. Princeton: Princeton University Press, 1929.

Observations on the Doctrine of Phlogiston, and the Decomposition of Water, Part II (Philadelphia: Thomas Dobson, 1797).

[Defences of Unitarianism for the Year 1786, containing] Letters to Dr. Horne, Dean of Canterbury; to the Young Men, who are in a Course of Education for the Christian Ministry, at the Universities of Oxford and Cambridge; to Dr. Price; and to Mr. Parkhurst; on the Subject of the Person of Christ. Birmingham: for the author, 1787. Second printing, 1788, adds bracketed heading.

Defences of Unitarianism for the Year 1787, containing Letters to the Rev. Dr. Geddes, to the Rev. Dr. Price, Part II. and to the Candidates for Orders in the Two Universities. Part II. relating to Mr. Howe's Appendix to his fourth Volume of Observations on Books, a Letter by an UnderGraduate of Oxford, Dr. Croft's Bampton Lectures, and several other Publications. Birmingham: for the author, 1788.

Defences of Unitarianism for the Years 1788 & 1789. Containing Letters to Dr. Horsley, Lord Bishop of St. David's, to the Rev. Mr. Barnard, the Rev. Dr. Knowles, and the Rev. Mr. Hawkins. Birmingham: for J. Johnson, n.d. [1790]. (W. 19: 3–110.)

Discourses on Various Subjects. See "Sermons."

Discourses on the Evidences of Revealed Religion. London: J. Johnson, 1794. 2d ed. adds "As *delivered at Hackney in 1793, 1794.*" London: J. Johnson 1794. (W. 15:191–362.)

Discourses relating to the Evidences of Revealed Religion Vol. I. Delivered at Hackney in 1793, 1794. London: J. Johnson, 1794. Another edition of the above.

Discourses relating to the Evidences of Revealed Religion, delivered in the Church of the Universalists, at Philadelphia, 1796. Philadelphia: John Thompson, 1796.

Unitarianism explained and defended, in a Discourse delivered in the Church of the Universalists at Philadelphia. Philadelphia: John Thompson, 1796. (W. 16: 472–89, with prior "Conclusion," 195–96.)

Discourses relating to the Evidences of Revealed Religion, delivered in Philadelphia. Vol. 2. Philadelphia: Thomas Dobson, 1797.

Disquisitions relating to Matter and Spirit. To which is added, The History of the Philosophical Doctrine concerning the Origin of the Soul and the Nature of Matter, and Its Influence on Christianity, especially with Respect to the Doctrine of the Pre-existence of Christ. London: J. Johnson, 1777.

Doctrine of Philosophical Necessity Illustrated: Being an Appendix to the Disquisitions relating to Matter and Spirit. To which is added, An Answer to several Persons who have controverted the Principles of it. 2d ed. Birmingham: for J. Johnson, 1782. In the first edition (London: J. Johnson, 1777), the additions are named: *An Answer to the Letters on Materialism, and on Hartley's Theory of the Mind.*

Doctrine of Phlogiston established and that of the Composition of Water refuted. Northumberland: for the author, 1800.

Doctrine of Phlogiston established and that of the Composition of Water refuted, with additions. 2d ed. Northumberland: P. Byrne; Philadelphia, 1803.

Observations on the Doctrine of Phlogiston, and the Decomposition of Water, Part II. Philadelphia: Thomas Dobson, 1797.

The Doctrines of Heathen Philosophy, compared with those of Revelation. Northumberland: John Binns, 1804.

The Duty of Forgiveness of Injuries: A Discourse intended to be Delivered soon after the Riots in Birmingham. Birmingham: for J. Johnson, 1791. (W. 15:475–93.)

The Evidences of the Resurrection of Jesus . . . To which is added, an Address to the Jews. Birmingham: J. Johnson, 1791.

An Examination of Dr. Reid's Inquiry into the Human Mind, on the Principles of Common Sense, Dr. Beattie's Essay on the Nature and Immutability of Truth, and Dr. Oswald's Appeal to Common Sense in Behalf of Religion. 2d ed. London: J. Johnson, 1775.

Experiments and Observations on Different Kinds of Air. 2d ed. London: J. Johnson, 1775.

Experiments and Observations on Different Kinds of Air II. 2d ed. London: J. Johnson, 1776.

Experiments and Observations on Different Kinds of Air III. London: J. Johnson, 1777.

Experiments and Observations relating to various Branches of Natural Philosophy, with a Continuation of the Observations on Air. London: J. Johnson, 1779.

Experiments and Observations relating to various Branches of Natural Philosophy, with a Continuation of the Observations on Air II. Birmingham: J. Johnson, 1781.

Experiments and Observations relating to various Branches of Natural Philosophy . . . III. Birmingham: for J. Johnson, 1786.

Experiments and Observations on Different Kinds of Air, and other Branches of Natural Philosophy, connected with the Subject. . . . Being the former Six Volumes abridged and methodized, with many additions. Birmingham: J. Johnson, 1790.

Experiments and Observations relating to the Analysis of Atmospherical Air; also farther Experiments relating to the Generation of Air from Water. Read before the American Philosophical Society, Feb. 5th & 19th, 1796, and printed in their Transactions. To which are added, Considerations on the Doctrine of Phlogiston, and the Decomposition of Water, addressed to Messrs. Berthollet, &c. London. Reprinted for J. Johnson, 1796.

Experiments on the Generation of Air from Water; to which are prefixed, Experiments relating to the Decomposition of Dephlogisticated and Inflammable Air, from the Philosophical Transactions, Vol. LXXXI, p.213. London: J. Johnson, 1793.

Familiar Letters addressed to the Inhabitants of the Town of Birmingham, in Refutation of several Charges, advanced against the Dissenters, by the Rev. Mr. Madan, Rector of St. Philip's, in his Sermon, entitled "The principal Claims of the Dissenters considered" preached at St. Philip's Church, on Sunday, February 14, 1790. Part I (II, III, IV, V). Birmingham: J. Thompson, 1790. (W. 19: 135–304, from the second printing of the collected editon.)

Forms of Prayer and other Offices for the Use of Unitarian Societies. Birmingham: for J. Johnson, 1783. (W. 21:474–558.)

Four Discourses. 1806. See "Sermons."

[A Lover of Peace and Truth]. *A Free Address to those who have Petitioned for the Repeal of the late Act of Parliament in Favour of Roman Catholics.* London: J. Johnson, 1780. (*W.* 22:499–516.)

A Free Discussion of the Doctrines of Materialism, and Philosophical Necessity. In a Correspondence between Dr. Price and Dr. Priestley. To which are added, by Dr. Priestley, An Introduction, Explaining the Nature of the Controversy, and Letters to Several Writers who have animadverted on his Disquisitions relating to Matter and Spirit or his Treatise on Necessity. London: J. Johnson and T. Cadell, 1778.

A General History of the Christian Church, to the Fall of the Western Empire. 2 vols. Birmingham: sold by J. Johnson, 1790.

A General History of the Christian Church, from the Fall of the Western Empire to the Present Time. 4 vols. Northumberland: for the author, by Andrew Kennedy, 1802–3.

A General View of the Arguments for the Unity of God; and against the Divinity and Pre-existence of Christ, from Reason, from the Scriptures, and from History. Birmingham: for J. Johnson, 1783.

A Harmony of the Evangelists in English; with Critical Dissertations, and Occasional Paraphrase, and Notes for the Use of the Unlearned. London: J. Johnson, 1780.

A Harmony of the Evangelists, in Greek, to which are prefixed Critical Dissertations in English. London: J. Johnson, 1777.

Hartley's Theory of the Human Mind on the Principle of the Association of Ideas, with Essays relating to the Subject of It. London: J. Johnson, 1775.

Heads of Lectures on a Course of Experimental Philosophy, particularly including Chemistry, delivered at the New College in Hackney. London: J. Johnson, 1794.

The History and Present State of Electricity. London: J. Johnson et al., 1767.

An History of Early Opinions concerning Jesus Christ, compiled from Original Writers; proving that the Christian Church was at first Unitarian. 4 vols. Birmingham: for the author, 1786.

An History of the Corruptions of Christianity. 2 vols. Birmingham: Piercy and Jones, for J. Johnson, 1782.

    A Reply to the Animadversions on the History of the Corruptions of Christianity, in the Monthly Review for June 1783; with Additional Observations relating to The Doctrine of the Primitive Church, concerning the Person of Christ. Birmingham: for J. Johnson, 1783. (*W.* 18:3–37.)

    Remarks on the Article of the Monthly Review for September, 1783, in Answer to the Reply to some Former Animadversions in that Work. (*W.* 18:117–24.)

    Defences of the History of the Corruptions of Christianity. Containing I. A Reply to the Animadversions in the Monthly Review for June 1783. II. Letters to Dr. Horsley, Part 1. III. Remarks on the Monthly Review of the Letters to Dr. Horsley. Part 1. IV. Letters to Dr. Horsley, Part 2, 3. London: J. Johnson, 1783–86. (*W.* 18:1–309.)

The Importance of Religion to Enlarge the Mind of Man. Birmingham: J. Belcher & Son, 1801.

An Inquiry into the Knowledge of the Ancient Hebrews, concerning a Future State. London: J. Johnson 1801. (*W.* 12:482–504, lacking Lindsey's preface.)

Index to the Bible: in which the various Subjects which occur in the Scriptures are alphabetically arranged: with accurate References to all the Books of the Old and New Testaments, designed to facilitate the Study of these invaluable Records. London: J. Johnson, 1805.

Institutes of Natural and Revealed Religion. 2d ed. Birmingham: for J. Johnson, 1782.

Lectures on History, and General Policy; to which is Prefixed, An Essay on a Course of Liberal Education for Civil and Active Life. 4th ed. Birmingham: for J. Johnson, 1788. (*W.* 24:1–438, with additional lecture on the Constitution of the United States, 251–59.)

[Author of the "Free Address to Protestant Dissenters, as Such"]. *A Letter of Advice to those Dissenters who conduct the Application to Parliament for Relief from certain Penal Laws.* London: J. Johnson, 1773.

[Anon.]. *A Letter to a Layman, on the Subject of the Rev. Mr. Lindsey's Proposal for a Reformed English Church, upon the Plan of the late Dr. Samuel Clarke.* London: J. Wilkie, 1774.

A Letter to an Antipaedobaptist. Northumberland: Andrew Kennedy, 1802. (*W.* 20: 463–92.)

A Letter to Jacob Bryant Esq. in Defence of Philosophical Necessity. London: J. Johnson, 1780.

A Letter to the Rev. Mr. John Palmer, in Defence of the Illustrations of Philosophical Necessity. Bath: R. Cruttwell, for J. Johnson, 1780.

A Second Letter to the Rev. Mr. John Palmer, in Defence of the Doctrine of Philosophical Necessity. London: J. Johnson, 1780.

A Letter to the Reverend John Blair Linn, A.M. Pastor of the First Presbyterian Congregation in the City of Philadelphia. In Defense of the Pamphlet, Intitled, Socrates and Jesus Compared. Northumberland: P. Byrne; Philadelphia: Andrew Kennedy, 1803. (*W.* 21:188–220.)

A Second Letter to the Revd. John Blair Linn D.D., Pastor of the First Presbyterian Congregation in the City of Philadelphia in Reply to His Defense of the Doctrines of the Divinity of Christ and Atonement. Northumberland: P. Byrne; Philadelphia: Andrew Kennedy, 1803. (*W.* 21:221–46.)

A Letter to the Right Honourable William Pitt, First Lord of the Treasury, and Chancellor of the Exchequer; on the Subjects of Toleration and Church Establishments; Occasioned by his Speech against the Repeal of the Test and Corporation Acts, on Wednesday the 28th of March 1787. London: J. Johnson and J. Debrett, 1787.

Letters to a Philosophical Unbeliever, containing an Examination of the Principal Objections to the Doctrines of Natural Religion, and especially those contained in the Writings of Mr. Hume. 2d ed., identified as *Part I.* Birmingham: Pearson and Rollason, for J. Johnson, 1787.

Additional Letters to a Philosophical Unbeliever, in answer to Mr. William Hammon. 2d ed. Birmingham: for J. Johnson, 1787.

Letters to a Philosophical Unbeliever. Part II. Containing a State of the Evidence of Revealed Religion, with Animadversions on the two last Chapters of the first Volume of Mr. Gibbon's History of the Decline and Fall of the Roman Empire. Birmingham: Pearson and Rollason, for J. Johnson, 1787. A "Correspondence with Mr. Gibbon." (*W.* 17, appendix 7, 533–36.)

Letters to a Young Man, occasioned by Mr. Wakefield's Essay on Public Worship; to which is added, a Reply to Mr. Evanson's Objections to the Observation of the Lord's Day. London: J. Johnson, 1792. (*W.* 20:303–51.)

Letters to a Young Man, Part II. Occasioned by Mr. Evanson's Treatise on the Dissonance of the Four Generally received Evangelists. London: J. Johnson, 1793. (*W.* 20:352–463.)

Letters to Dr. Horne, Dean of Canterbury. See *Defenses of Unitarianism for 1786.*

Letters to Dr. Horsley, in Answer to his Animadversions on the History of the Corruptions of Christianity. With Additional Evidence that the Primitive Church was Unitarian. Birmingham: for J. Johnson, 1783.

Remarks on the Monthly Review of the Letters to Dr. Horsley; in which the Rev. Mr. Samuel Badcock, the Writer of that Review, is called upon to Defend what he has advanced in it. Birmingham: J. Johnson, 1784. (*W.* 18:127–42.)

Letters to Dr. Horsley, Part II. Containing Farther Evidence that the Primitive Church was Unitarian. Birmingham: Pearson and Rollason, for J. Johnson, 1784.

Letters to Dr. Horsley. Part III. Containing an Answer to his Remarks on Letters, Part II. To which are added Strictures on Mr. Howe's Ninth Number of Observations on Books ancient and modern. Birmingham: Pearson and Rollason, 1786.

Tracts in Controversy with Bishop Horsley, with Notes by the Editor, to which is Annexed, an Appendix, containing a Review of the Controversy, in Four Letters to the Bishops . . . never before Published. London: for the London Unitarian Society, sold by J. Johnson and Co. and D. Eaton, 1815.

Letters to the Inhabitants of Northumberland. 2d ed. Philadelphia: John Conrad, 1801. (*W.* 25:109–87.)

Letters to the Jews; inviting them to an Amicable Discussion of the Evidences of Christianity. (Part I.) Birmingham: for J. Johnson, 1786. (*W.* 20:227–50.)

Letters to the Jews. Part II. Occasioned by Mr. David Levi's Reply to the Former Letters. Birmingham: for the author, 1787. (*W.* 20:251–74.)

"Address to the Jews," prefixed to "Discourse on the Resurrection of Jesus," in *Discourses on the Evidences of Revealed Religion.* London: J. Johnson, 1794. (*W.* 15:191–362.)

Letters to the Members of the New Jerusalem Church, formed by Baron Swedenborg. Birmingham: for J. Johnson, 1791. (*W.* 21:43–86.)

Letters to the Philosophers and Politicians of France, on the Subject of Religion. London: J. Johnson, 1793. (*W.* 21:87–108.)

Letters addressed to the Philosophers and Politicians of France, on the Subject of Religion, to which are Prefixed, Observations relating to the Causes of the General Prevalence of Infidelity. Philadelphia: Thomas Dobson, 1794.

A Continuation of the Letters to the Philosophers and Politicians of France, on the Subject of Religion; and of the Letters to a Philosophical Unbeliever; in Answer to Mr. Paine's Age of Reason. Northumberlandtown: Andrew Kennedy, 1794. (*W.* 21:109–27, 128–69.)

Letters to M. Volney, occasioned by a Work of his entitled Ruins, and by his Letter to the Author. Philadelphia: Thomas Dobson, 1797. (*W.* 17:111–28.)

Letters to the Rev. Edward Burn, of St. Mary's Chapel, Birmingham, in Answer to his, on the Infallibility of the Apostolic Testimony, concerning the Person of Christ. Birmingham: J. Thompson, 1790. (*W.* 19:305–44.)

Letters to the Right Honourable Edmund Burke, occasioned by his Reflections on the Revolution in France, &c. 2d ed. Birmingham: for J. Johnson, 1791.

[A Quaker in Politics]. "Maxims of Political Arithmetic applied to the Case of the United States of America." First published 26 and 17 February 1798 in the newspaper *Aurora,* included in *Letters to the Inhabitants of Northumberland.* Philadelphia: John Conrad, 1799. (*W.* 25:175–82.)

Memoirs of Dr. Joseph Priestley, to the Year 1795, written by himself: with a Continuation . . . by his Son, Joseph Priestley: and Observations on his Writings, by Thomas Cooper, President Judge of the 4th District of Pennsylvania: and the Rev. William Christie. To which are added, Four Posthumous Discourses. London: J. Johnson, 1807.

Notes on all the Books of Scripture, for the Use of the Pulpit and Private Families. 4 vols. Northumberland: for the author, 1803–4.

Observation on the Increase of Infidelity, to which are added, Animadversions on the writings of several Modern Unbelievers, and especially the Ruins of Mr. Volney. Philadelphia: Thomas Dobson, 1797. (*W.* 17:1–110, appendices 1–3, 520–27.)

The Originality and Superior Excellence of the Mosaic Institutions Demonstrated. Northumberland: Andrew Kennedy, for P. Byrne; Philadelphia, 1803. Reprinted, with a preface, from "A Dissertation in which are demonstrated the Originality and Superior Excellence, of the Mosaic Institutions," following the notes on the Pentateuch in *Notes on all the Books of Scripture* 1:373–400.

An Outline of the Evidences of Revealed Religion. Philadelphia: T. Dobson, 1797. (*W.* 21:170–87.)

Philosophical Empiricism: Containing Remarks on a Charge of Plagiarism respecting Dr. H——s, interspersed with various Observations relating to Different Kinds of Air. London: J. Johnson, 1775.

A Political Dialogue on the General Principles of Government. London: J. Johnson, 1791. (*W.* 25:81–108.) This source appears in Ronald E. Crook, *A Bibliography of Joseph Priestley, 1733–1804* (London: Library Association, 1966), PS/309; he had not seen a copy, and I doubt this is actually by Priestley.

"A Prayer respecting the present State of Christianity." In William Christie, *Discourses on the Divine Unity, or, A Scriptural Proof and Demonstration of the One Supreme Deity, of the God and Father of all: and of the Subordinate Character and Inferior Nature of Our Lord Jesus Christ: with a Confutation of the Doctrine of a Co-Equal and Consubstantial Trinity in Unity: and a Full Reply to the Objections of Trinitarians.* 2d ed., corr., 303–8. Montrose: David Buchanan, 1790.

The Present State of Europe compared with Ancient Prophecies. See "Sermons."

The Proper Objects of Education (1791). See "Sermons."

Prospectus: "A Plan to Procure a Continually Improving Translation of the Scriptures." [With the Society for Promoting Knowledge of the Scriptures.] (*W.* 27, appendix 6, 532.)

Remarks on the Monthly Review of the Letters to Dr. Horsley. See *Letters to Dr. Horsley.*

"Remarks on Two Letters, addressed to the Delegates from the Several Congregations of Protestant Dissenters, who met at Devizes, on Sept. 14, 1789." In John Aikin, *The Spirit of the Constitution and that of the Church of England, compared...*, 15–42. London: J. Johnson, 1790.

Socrates and Jesus Compared. Philadelphia: P. Byrne, 1803. Reprint, London: J. Johnson, 1803. It was photo-reprinted as a "Rare Esoteric Book," with author's name misspelled as Priestly and title reversed: *Jesus and Socrates Compared* (Kila, Mont.: Kessinger Publishing Co., [1994?]).

Some Considerations on the State of the Poor (1787). See "Edited Works."

The Theological and Miscellaneous Works of Joseph Priestley, LL.D. F.R.S. &c., ed. John Towill Rutt. New York: Kraus Reprint Co., 1972. 25 vols. The great debt Priestley scholars owe to J. T. Rutt for his work in collecting this material is mitigated by his failures (in contemporary eyes) in exact scholarship. His editions of these writings, which are based on the London edition of 1817–31, are not uniform, or without sometimes conflating different editions, omissions, variation in paragraphing, etc. I have used materials from this edition only when access to original editions was difficult, and have cited them separately as *W.*, volume number, page number(s). Volume 1 is in two parts; citations of that volume contain as well a part number, e.g., *W.* 1.1:56–57.

Tracts in Controversy with Bishop Horsley. See *Letters to Dr. Horsley.*

Two Letters to Dr. Newcome, Bishop of Waterford. On the Duration of our Saviour's Ministry. Birmingham: J. Johnson, 1780.

A Third Letter to Dr. Newcome, Bishop of Waterford, on the Duration of our Saviour's Ministry. Birmingham: J. Johnson, 1781.

Unitarianism explained and defended. See *Discourses relating to the Evidences of Revealed Religion.* 1796.

Correspondence (Published Collections)

Memoirs and Correspondence, 1733–1787; Life and Correspondence (1787–1804). In [Joseph Priestley], *The Theological and Miscellaneous Works of Joseph Priestley, LL.D. F.R.S. &c.*, ed. John Towill Rutt, ed. New York: Kraus Reprint Co., 1972. Vol. 1, parts 1 and 2, containing letters (primarily from Priestley to Theophilus Lindsey and Thomas Belsham); herein cited as *W.* 1.1:pp. and *W.* 1.2:pp. Rutt was a disciple, not a historian, and his edition of the letters is faulty, sometime badly so. When possible and necessary, I have used the originals preserved in Dr. Williams's Library, London, and have cited these as Wms. and date.

"On some Correspondence of Dr. Priestley, preserved in the Warrington Municipal Library." J. F. Marsh, *Remains Historical and Literary connected with the Palatine Counties of Lancaster and Chester* (1855), 65–81. These are extracts from some twenty-five letters, chiefly from or to John Wilkinson, from some thirty-six or more letters, herein cited as Warr.

Scientific Correspondence of Joseph Priestley: Ninety-Seven Letters . . . edited by Henry Carrington Bolton. New York: privately printed, 1892. Herein cited as Bolton and letter number.

A Scientific Autobiography of Joseph Priestley: Selected Scientific Correspondence. Ed. Robert E. Schofield. Cambridge: MIT Press, 1966. Herein cited as *SciAuto.*

Correspondence (Other Published and Manuscript Letters)

There are substantial collections of manuscripts preserved in the archives or libraries of the Royal Society of London; the American Philosophical Society, Philadelphia (APS); the Birmingham Reference Library; the Bowood Papers, Bodleian Library, Oxford; Dickinson College Library, Carlisle, Pennsylvania; and the Massachusetts Historical Society, Boston. And there are separate items, manuscript and published, scattered in locations in Britain, Europe, and the United States. These are all listed in the footnotes, but I have not listed them in this bibliography as I hope soon to have published a preliminary checklist of all of Priestley's manuscripts and letters compiled in the process of writing the two volumes of this biography.

Scientific Papers (chronological)

"Observations on different Kinds of Air." *Philosophical Transactions* 62 (1772): 147–264.

"On the noxious Quality of the Effluvia of putrid Marshes." *Philosophical Transactions* 64 (1774): 90–95.

"An Account of further Discoveries in Air." *Philosophical Transactions* 65 (1775): 384–94.

"Observations on Respiration and the Use of the Blood." *Philosophical Transactions* 66 (1776): 226–48.

"Experiments relating to Phlogiston, and the seeming Conversion of Water into Air." *Philosophical Transactions* 73 (1783): 398–434.

"Experiments and Observations relating to Air and Water." *Philosophical Transactions* 75 (1785): 279–309.

"Experiments and Observations relating to the Principle of Acidity, the Composition of Water, and Phlogiston." *Philosophical Transactions* 78 (1788): 147–57.

"Additional Experiments and Observations relating to the Principle of Acidity, the Decomposition of Water, and Phlogiston. With Letters . . . on the Subject by Dr. Withering and James Keir, Esq." *Philosophical Transactions* 78 (1788): 313–30.

"Objections to the Experiments and Observations relating to the Principle of Acidity, the Composition of Water, and Phlogiston, considered; with farther Experiments and Observations on the same Subject." *Philosophical Transactions* 79 (1789): 7–20.

"Experiments on the Phlogistication of Spirit of Nitre." *Philosophical Transactions* 79 (1789): 139–49.

"Experiments on the Transmission of Vapour of Acids through an hot Earthen Tube, and further Observations relating to Phlogiston." *Philosophical Transactions* 79 (1789): 289–99.

"Observations on Respiration." *Philosophical Transactions* 80 (1790): 106–10, emending *Philosophical Transactions* 66 (1776): 226–38.

"Farther Experiments relating to the Decomposition of dephlogisticated and inflammable air." *Philosophical Transactions* 81 (1791): 213–22.

"Experiments and Observations relating to the Analysis of Atmospherical Air." Read 5 Feb. 1796, *Transactions of the American Philosophical Society* 4 (1799): 1–11.

"Further Experiments relating to the Generation of Air from Water." Read 19 Feb. 1796, *Transactions of the American Philosophical Society* 4 (1799): 11–20.

"An Appendix to the two Articles in this Volume." Read 23 Nov. 1798 as a letter to B. S. Barton, *Transactions of the American Philosophical Society* 4 (1799): 382–86.

"An Interesting Letter from Dr. Priestley, concerning the principles of the New Theory of Chemistry," 20 Dec. 1797. *Monthly Magazine* 5 (1798): 159–60.

"A Letter to Dr. Mitchill, in reply to the preceding [Attempt to accommodate the Dispute among Chemists concerning Phlogiston]." *New York Medical Repository* 1 (1798): 511–12.

"A Second Letter from Dr. Priestley to Dr. Mitchill," 14 June 1798. *New York Medical Repository* 2 (1799): 48–49.

"On Red Precipitate of Mercury as favourable to the Doctrine of Phlogiston," 20 July 1798. *New York Medical Repository* 2 (1799): 163–65.

"Objections to the Antiphlogistic Doctrine of Water," 23 August, 1798. *New York Medical Repository* 2 (1799): 166–67. (Essentially repeated in "A Letter to the Editor," 22 Aug. 1798, *Monthly Magazine* 6 [1798]: 237–38.)

"Experiments relating to the Calces of Metals, communicated in a fifth Letter to Dr. Mitchill," 11 Oct. 1798. *New York Medical Repository* 2 (1799): 263–68. (Substantially repeated in "A Letter to the Editor," *Monthly Magazine* 7 [1799]: 261–64.)

"Of some Experiments made with Ivory Black and also with Diamonds," 11 Oct. 1798. *New York Medical Repository* 2 (1799): 269–71. (Also in *Monthly Magazine* 7 [1799], 353–54.)

"On the Phlogistic Theory," 17 Jan. 1799. *New York Medical Repository* 2 (1799): 383–87. (Substantially repeated in "A Letter to the Editor," 17 Jan. 1799, *Monthly Magazine* 7 [1799], 354–56.)

"On the same Subject," 1 Feb. 1799. *New York Medical Repository* 2 (1799): 388–89.

"Dr. Priestley's Reply to his Antiphlogistian Opponents, No. 1," 18 July 1799. *New York Medical Repository* 3 (1800): 116–21.

"Dr. Priestley's Reply to his Antiphlogistian Opponents, No. 2," 24 July 1799. *New York Medical Repository* 3 (1800): 121–24.

"Dr. Priestley's Reply to his Antiphlogistian Opponents, No. 3," 26 July 1799. *New York Medical Repository* 3 (1800): 124–27.

"Experiments on the Transmission of Acids, and other Liquors, in the form of Vapour, over Several Substances in a hot earth tube." Read 20 Dec. 1799, *Transactions of the American Philosophical Society* 5 (1802): 1–13.

"Experiments relating to the Change of Place in different kinds of Air through several interposing Substances." Read 20 Dec. 1799, *Transactions of the American Philosophical Society* 5 (1802): 14–20.

"Singular Effects of Gaseous Oxyd of Septon (dephlogisticated Nitrous Air)," 30 Jan. 1800. *New York Medical Repository* 3 (1800): 305. (Also in *Monthly Magazine* 9 [1800]: 409.)

"Priestley's Sentiments on the Doctrine of Septon." Quoted from a letters of 24 July 1799. *New York Medical Repository* 3 (1800): 307.

"Air produced, without Limitation, from Water by freezing." *New York Medical Repository* 3 (1800): 422–23.

"Experiments on the Production of Air by the Freezing of Water." *New York Medical Repository* 4 (1801): 17–21. (Also in *Journal of Natural Philosophy, Science and the Arts* 4 [1801]: 193–96, and substantially the same as that read 18 April 1800 and printed in *Transactions of the American Philosophical Society* 5 [1802]: 36–41.)

"To the Editor of the Medical Repository." Correcting a review of his tract on phlogiston, 6 July 1800, *New York Medical Repository* 4 (1801): 103.

"Experiments on heating Manganese in Inflammable Air." *New York Medical Repository* 4 (1801): 135–37.

"Experiments tending to show that Azote is a Compound of Hydrogen and Oxygen." *New York Medical Repository* 4 (1801): 192–94.

"Some Observations relating to the Sense of Hearing," 8 May 1800. *New York Medical Repository* 4 (1801): 247–48.

"Experiments relating to the Absorption of Air by Water." *Transactions of the American Philosophical Society* 5 (1802): 21–27.

"Miscellaneous Experiments relating to the Doctrine of Phlogiston." *Transactions of the American Philosophical Society* 5 (1802): 28–35.

"Experiments on Air exposed to Heat in Metallic Tubes." Read 15 Aug. 1800, *Transactions of the American Philosophical Society* 5 (1802): 42–50.

"Remarks on the Work entitled 'A Brief History of Epidemic and Pestilential Diseases,'" 4 May 1801. *New York Medical Repository* 5 (1802): 32–36.

"Some Thoughts concerning Dreams." *New York Medical Repository* 5 (1802): 125–29.

"Observations and Experiments relating to the Pile of Volta," 16 and 29 Sept. 1801. *New York Medical Repository* 5 (1802): 153–59. (Substantially repeated in *Journal of Natural Philosophy, Chemistry, and the Arts* 1 [n.s., 1802]: 198–204.)

"Miscellaneous Observations relating to the Doctrine of Air," 30 July 1801. *New York Medical Repository* 5 (1802): 264–67.

"A Reply to Mr. Cruickshank's Observations in Defence of the New System of Chemistry, in the fifth volume of Mr. Nicholson's Journal p. 1, &c.," 21 Nov. 1801. *New York Medical Repository* 5 (1802): 390–92. (Substantially the same as *Journal of Natural Philosophy, Chemistry, and the Arts* 1 [n.s., 1802]: 181–84.)

"Additional Remarks on the Same." *New York Medical Repository* 5 (1802): 393.

"On the Theory of Chemistry," 20 Feb. 1802. *Journal of Natural Philosophy, Chemistry, and the Arts* 2 (n.s., 1802): 69–70.

"A Letter to the Editor." *Monthly Magazine* 14 (1802): 2–3. (Substantially repeated in "Remarks on Mr. Cruickshank's Experiments upon Finery Cinder and Charcoal," 12 April 1802. *New York Medical Repository* 6 [1803] 24–26.)

"Observations on the Conversion of Iron into Steel," 22 May 1802. *Journal of Natural Philosophy, Chemistry, and the Arts* 2 (n.s., 1802): 233–34. (Also in *New York Medical Repository* 6 [1803]: 158–59, and *Medical and Physical Journal, containing the earliest Information on Subjects of Medicine, Surgery, Pharmacy, Chemistry and Natural History* 20 [1808], 347.)

"Additional Remarks on Mr. Cruickshank's Experiments on Findery Cinder and Charcoal," 15 Nov. 1802. *New York Medical Repository* 6 (1803): 271–73.

"On Air from Finery cinder and Charcoal with other Remarks on the Experiments and Observations of Mr. Cruickshank." *Journal of Natural Philosophy, Chemistry, and the Arts* 3 (n.s., 1803): 52–54.

"Answer to the Observations of Mr. William Cruickshank upon the Doctrine of Phlogiston." *Journal of Natural Philosophy, Chemistry, and the Arts* 3 (n.s., 1803): 65–69.

"Observations and Experiments relating to equivocal, or spontaneous Generation." Read 18 Nov. 1803, *Transactions of the American Philosophical Society* 6 (1809): 119–29.

"Observations on the Discovery of Nitre, in common Salt, which had been frequently mixed with Snow." Read 2 Dec. 1803, in a letter to Caspar Wistar, *Transactions of the American Philosophical Society* 6 (1809): 129–32.

Theological Papers (chronological)

["Liberius"]. "Essay on the Harmony of the Evangelists," and "Observations on the Harmony of the Evangelists." *Theological Repository* 2 (1770): 38–59, 98–122, 230–47, 313–27; 3 (1771): 462–69.

[Editor]. "Introduction." *Theological Repository* 4 (1784): iii–xvi.

["Pamphilus"]. "Observations on Inspiration." *Theological Repository* 4 (1784): 17–26.

———. "Observations relating to the Inspiration of Moses." *Theological Repository* 4 (1784): 27–38.

["Hermas"]. "Of the Island on which the Apostle Paul was shipwrecked." *Theological Repository* 4 (1784): 39–49.

["Pelagius"]. "Remarks on Dr. Taylor's Key to the Apostolic Writings." *Theological Repository* 4 (1784): 57–69.

["Beryllus"]. "A Query relating to the Rise of the Arian Doctrine." *Theological Repository* 4 (1784): 70–72.

["Biblicus"]. "A Conjectural Emendation of Exod. xxiii:23." *Theological Repository* 4 (1784): 73–74.

["Hermas"]. "An Addition to the Paper, signed HERMAS, relating to the Island on which Paul was shipwrecked." *Theological Repository* 4 (1784): 75.

["Josephus"]. "A Query relating to the Doctrine of Plato, concerning the Divine Essence." *Theological Repository* 4 (1784): 76.

["Pelagius"]. "Of the Doctrine of Plato concerning God, and the general System of Nature." *Theological Repository* 4 (1784): 77–97.

["Pamphilus"]. "Observations on the Prophets of the Old Testament." *Theological Repository* 4 (1784): 97–122.

["Josephus"]. "Animadversions on the Preface to the new edition of Ben Mordecai's Letters." *Theological Repository* 4 (1784): 180–86.

[Editor]. "A Proposal for correcting the English Translation of the Scriptures." *Theological Repository* 4 (1784): 187–88.

["Pamphilus"]. "Observations on the Inspiration of the Apostles." *Theological Repository* 4 (1784): 189–210.

["Ebionita"]. "Observations on the Miraculous Conception." *Theological Repository* 4 (1784): 245–305.

["Beryllus"]. "The History of the Arian Controversy." *Theological Repository* 4 (1784): 306–37.

["Photinus"]. "An Attempt to shew that Arians are not Unitarians." *Theological Repository* 4 (1784): 338–44.

["Biblicus"]. "An Illustration of the Promise made to Abraham." *Theological Repository* 4 (1784): 361–63.

["Pelagius"]. "A View of the Principles of the later Platonists." *Theological Repository* 4 (1784): 381–407.

———. "Of the Platonism of Philo." *Theological Repository* 4 (1784): 408–20.

["Pamphilus"]. "Observations on the Inspiration of Christ." *Theological Repository* 4 (1784): 433–61.

["Biblicus"]. "Observations on the Prophecy concerning Shiloh." *Theological Repository* 4 (1784): 473–76.

["Josephus"]. "Of the Pre-existence of the Messiah." *Theological Repository* 4 (1784): 477–83.

["Ebionita"]. "Observations on the Roman Census, mentioned Luke ii.1, unfavourable to the miraculous Conception." *Theological Repository* 5 (1786): 90–99.

———. "Miscellaneous Observations of the same Nature." *Theological Repository* 5 (1786): 100–108.

["Biblicus"]. "A Supplement to the Illustration of the Promise made to Abraham." *Theological Repository* 5 (1786): 108–10.

["Scrutator"]. "Observations on the Prophecies of the Old Testament quoted in the New." *Theological Repository* 5 (1786): 111–23.

["Pamphilus"]. "Observations on the Quotation of Isaiah, ix.1, 2. by the Evangelist Matthew." *Theological Repository* 5 (1786): 123–28.

———. "Observations on the Prophecies relating to the Messiah, and the future glory of the House of David." *Theological Repository* 5 (1786): 210–42, 301–16.

["Hermas"]. "An Attempt to prove the perpetual Obligation of the Jewish Ritual." *Theological Repository* 5 (1786): 403–44.

———. "Of the Perpetuity of the Jewish Ritual (continued from Vol. V, p. 444)." *Theological Repository* 6 (1788): 1–21.

["Pamphilus"]. "Difficulties in the Interpretation of some Prophecies not yet fulfilled, and Queries relating to Them." *Theological Repository* 6 (1788): 203–8.

[Editor]. "An Account of the Rev. John Palmer, and of some Articles intended by him for this Repository." *Theological Repository* 6 (1788): 217–24.

["Pamphilus"]. "Observations on Christ's Agony in the Garden." *Theological Repository* 6 (1788): 302–22.

———. "Postscript to the Article signed PAMPHILUS, relating to a Case of bloody Sweat." *Theological Repository* 6 (1788): 347–48.

["Josephus"]. "A Query relating to the Origin of the low Arian Doctrine." *Theological Repository* 6 (1788): 376–82.

["Scrutator"]. "Queries relating to the Religion of Indostan." *Theological Repository* 6 (1788): 408–14.

["Hermas"]. "The Observance of the Lord's Day vindicated." *Theological Repository* 6 (1788): 465–83.

["Josephus"]. "Of the Origin of the Arian Hypothesis." *Theological Repository* 6 (1788): 484–90.

[Editor]. "To the Public." *Theological Repository* 6 (1788): 491–93.

Sermons (chronological)

The Doctrine of Divine Influence on the Human Mind, considered in a Sermon, published at the Request of many Persons who have occasionally heard It. Bath: R. Cruttwell, for J. Johnson, 1779.

A Sermon [on John 17:16] *preached December the 31st, 1780, at the New Meeting in Birmingham, on undertaking the Pastoral Office in that Place.* Birmingham: Pearson and Rollason, for J. Johnson, 1781. (*W.* 15:28–45.)

The Proper Constitution of a Christian Church, considered in A Sermon [on Revelation 3:2], *preached at the New Meeting in Birmingham, November 3, 1782,* &c. Birmingham: Pearson and Rollason, 1782. (*W.* 15:45–69.)

The Importance and Extent of Free Inquiry in Matters of Religion: A Sermon [on Matt. 13:9] *preached before the Congregation of the Old and New Meeting of Protestant Dissenters at Birmingham. November 5, 1785. To which are added, Reflections on the Present State of Free Inquiry in this Country; and Animadversions of some passages in Mr. White's Sermons at the Bampson Lectures; Mr. Howe's Discource on the Abuse of the Talent of Disputation in Religion; and, a Pamphlet entitled "Primitive Candour."* Birmingham: for J. Johnson, 1785. (*W.* 15:70–82.)

Discourses on Various Subjects, including Several on Particular Occasions. Birmingham: J. Johnson, 1787. (*W.* 15:1–182.)

A Sermon [on Luke 10:36–37] *on the Subject of the Slave Trade; delivered to a Society of Protestant Dissenters, at the New Meeting, in Birmingham: and published at their Request.* Birmingham: for the author, sold by J. Johnson, 1788.

The Conduct to be Observed by Dissenters, in Order to Procure the Repeal of the Corporation and Test Acts, recommended in a Sermon [on 1 Cor. 7:21], *preached before the Congregations of the Old and New Meetings, at Birmingham, November 5, 1789. Printed at the request of the Committee of the Seven Congregations of the Three Denominations of Protestant Dissenters, in Birmingham.* Birmingham: for J. Johnson, 1789. (*W.* 15:387–404.)

Reflection on Death: A Sermon [on Matt. 24:46], *on Occasion of the Death of the Rev. Robert Robinson, of Cambridge, Delivered at the New Meeting in Birmingham,*

June 13, 1790. And published at the Request of those who heard it, and of Mr. Robinson's family. Birmingham: sold by J. Johnson, 1790. (*W.* 15:404–19.)

A View of Revealed Religion; A Sermon, preached at the Ordination of the Rev. William Field of Warwick, July 12, 1790. . . . With a Charge, delivered at the same Time, by the Rev. Thomas Belsham. Birmingham: J. Thompson, for J. Johnson, 1790. Reprinted as Discourse XII in *Discourses on the Evidence of Revealed Religion.* London, 1794.

The Evidence of the Resurrection of Jesus considered, in a Discourse first delivered in the Assembly-room at Buxton, on Sunday, September 19, 1970. To which is added, an Address to the Jews. Birmingham: J. Thompson, for J. Johnson, 1790. Reprinted as Discourse XI in *Discourses on the Evidences of Revealed Religion.* London, 1794.

The Proper Objects of Education in the present State of the World Represented in a Discourse delivered on Wednesday, April 27, 1791. At the Meeting-House in the Old-Jewry, London; to the Supporters of the New College at Hackney. London: J. Johnson, 1791. (*W.,* 15:420–40, from the 2d ed. of 1791.)

A Discourse [on Luke 20:38] *on Occasion of the Death of Dr. Price; delivered at Hackney, on Sunday, May 1, 1791.* London: J. Johnson, 1791.

A Particular Attention to the Instruction of the Young recommended, in a Discourse [on 2 Cor. 8:9], *delivered at the Gravel-Pit Meeting, in Hackney, December 4, 1791, on entering on the Office of Pastor to the Congregation of Protestant Dissenters, assembling in that Place.* London: J. Johnson, 1791. (*W.* 15:458–75.)

The Duty of Forgiveness of Injuries: A Discourse [on Luke 23:34], *intended to be delivered soon after the Riots in Birmingham.* Birmingham: J. Thompson, for J. Johnson, 1791. (*W.* 15:475–93.)

A Sermon [on Psalm 46:1] *Preached at the Gravel-Pit Meeting in Hackney, April 19, 1793. Being the Day appointed for a General Fast.* London: J. Johnson, 1793. (*W.* 15:494–518.)

The Present State of Europe compared with Antient Prophecies; A Sermon [on Matt. 3:2], *preached at the Gravel Pit Meeting in Hackney, February 28, 1794, being the Day appointed for a General Fast. With a Preface, containing the Reasons for the Author's leaving England.* London: J. Johnson, 1794. Portions included in an anthology: *Wonderful Prophecies, being a Dissertation on the Existence, Nature and Extent of the Prophetic Powers in the Human Mind.* London: 1795.

The Use of Christianity, especially in Difficult Times; a Sermon [on Acts 20:32] *delivered at the Gravel Pit Meeting in Hackney, March 30, 1794, being the Author's Farewell Discourse to his Congregation.* London: J. Johnson, 1794. Bound into *The Present State of Europe,* 4th ed., 66–100. London, 1794.

Four Discourses intended to have been delivered at Philadelphia. Northumberland: John Binns, at the desire of the author, 1806.

Edited by Priestley

An Account of a Society for Encouraging the Industrious Poor. With a Table for Their Use. Birmingham: Pearson and Rollason, 1787. Priestley contributed a preface, "Some Considerations on the State of the Poor in General," but the bulk of the publication consists of interest tables, perhaps prepared originally by Francis Maseres.

An History of the Sufferings of Mr. Lewis de Marolles, and Mr. Isaac LeFevre, upon the Revocation of the Edict of Nantz. To which is Prefixed, A General Account of the Treatment of the Protestants in the Gallies of France. Translated from the French and now republished. Birmingham: for J. Johnson, 1788.

The Holy Bible, containing the Old and New Testaments; also the Apocrypha; translated out of the Original Tongues, with Annotations. Birmingham, Pearson and Rollason, 1788–89.

Original Letters by the Rev. John Wesley and his Friends, illustrative of his Early History, with other curious Papers, communicated by the late Rev. S. Badcock. To which is Prefixed an Address to the Methodists, with a Preface. Birmingham: for J. Johnson, 1791. (*W.* 25:325–36.)

Collins, Anthony. *A Philosophical Inquiry concerning Human Liberty, Republished with a Preface by Joseph Priestley.* 1790. Reprint, Bristol: Thoemmes Antiquarian Books, 1990.

Psalms and Hymns for the Use of the New Meeting in Birmingham, comp. William Hawkes and Joseph Priestley. Birmingham: J. Thompson, 1790.

The Theological Repository; Consisting of Original Essays, Hints, Queries, &c. calculated to Promote Religious Knowledge. Vol. 4 (1784); 5 (1786); 6 (1788). Birmingham: for J. Johnson. Priestley's personal contributions are noted separately.

Ellwall, Edward. *The Triumph of Truth.* 2d ed. Birmingham: Pearson and Rollason, 1789.

OTHER PRIMARY SOURCES

[Adams, John]. *The Works of John Adams, Second President of the United States.* Ed. Charles Francis Adams. 1850–56. Reprint, New York: Books for Libraries Press, 1969.

[Adams, John, and Thomas Jefferson]. *Correspondence of John Adams and Thomas Jefferson: 1812–1826.* Ed. Paul Wilstach. Indianapolis: Bobbs-Merrill, 1925.

[Adams, John Quincy]. "The Diary of John Quincy Adams." *Proceedings of the Massachusetts Historical Society* 16 (2d ser., 1902): 431, 441.

[Aukland, William, Lord]. *Journals and Correspondence of Ld. Aukland.* Vol. 2. London: Richard Bentley, 1860–62.

Baily, Francis. *Journal of a Tour in Unsettled Parts of North America in 1796 & 1797, with a Memoir of the Author.* London: Baily Brothers, 1856.

[Banks, Sir Joseph]. *The Banks Letters: A Calendar of the Manuscript Correspondence of Sir Joseph Banks preserved in the British Museum, the British Museum (Natural History) and other Collections in Great Britain.* Ed. Warren R. Dawson. London: Trustees of the British Museum, 1958.

Beattie, James. *Essay on the Nature and Immutability of Truth, in Opposition to Sophistry and Scepticism.* Edinburgh: A. Kincaid & J. Bell, 1770. Facsimile reprint, New York: Garland, 1983.

[Bentham, Jeremy]. *Collected Works of Jeremy Bentham.* Ed. John Bowring. London:

Simkin, Marshall Co., 1838–43. Reprinted in the United States as *The Works of Jeremy Bentham*. New York: Russell & Russell, Inc., 1962.

———. *Correspondence of Jeremy Bentham*. Ed. Timothy L. S. Sprigge. London: University of London Press, 1968.

Bentley, William. "Correspondence of Dr. William Bentley." *New-England Historical & Genealogical Register* 27 (1873): 352, 356–57.

Biblioteca Lansdowniana: A Catalogue of the Entire Library of the late Most Noble William Marquis of Lansdowne, which will be sold by Auction. London: Mundell and Sons, etc., 1806.

Biblioteca Lansdowniana: A Catalogue of the Entire Collection of Manuscripts, on paper and vellum, of the late Most Noble William Marquis of Lansdowne, which will be sold by Auction. London: Mundell and Sons, etc., 1807.

Bolton, Henry Carrington. See *Scientific Correspondence of Joseph Priestley*, above.

[Bretland, Joseph]. *Sermons, by the late Rev. Joseph Bretland. To which are prefixed, Memoirs of his Life, With an Appendix, &c*. Ed. W. B. Kennaway. Exeter: Hedgeland; London: Longman, Hurst, Rees, Orme, and Brown, 1820.

[Brissot de Warville, J.-P.]. *J.-P. Brissot Mémoires (1754–1793)*. Ed. Cl. Perroud. 2 vols. Paris: Librairie Alphonse Picard & Fils, 1911.

Burke, Edmund. *Correspondence of Edmund Burke*. Vol. 5, ed. Holden Furber; vol. 6, ed. Alfred Cobban and Robert A. Smith. Cambridge: Cambridge University Press, 1967.

Cavendish, Henry. "An Account of a New Eudiometer." *Philosophical Transactions* 73 (1783): 106–35.

[Channing, William Ellery]. *Memoirs of William Ellery Channing*. Boston: Wm. Crosby and H. P. Nichols, 1848.

[Coleridge, Samuel Taylor]. "Religious Musings." In *Poems of Samuel Taylor Coleridge*. London: Oxford University Press, 1912.

Cooper, Thomas. *A View of the Metaphysical and Physiological Arguments in Favor of Materialism*. Philadelphia: A. Small, 1823.

[Custis, G. W. P.]. "Letters from G. W. P. Custis to George Washington, 1797–1798." *Virginia Magazine of History and Biography* 20 (1912): 296–311.

[Curwen, Samuel]. *Journal and Letters of the late Samuel Curwen, Judge of Admiralty, etc., A Loyalist-Refugee in England, during the American Revolution. To which are added, Illustrative Documents and Biographic Notices of many Loyalists and other Prominent men of that Period*. Ed. George Atkinson Ward. London: Wiley and Putnam; New York: Leavitt, Trow, and Co., 1844.

Dalton, John. *Meteorological Observations and Essays*. London: W. Richardson, 1793.

———. "On the Tendency of Elastic Fluids to Diffusion through Each Other." *Memoirs of the Literary and Philosophical Society of Manchester* 1, 2d ser. (1805): 259–70.

[Davy, Humphry]. *Researches, Chemical and Philosophical, chiefly concerning Nitrous Oxide, or Dephlogisticated Nitrous Air, and its Respiration*. London: J. Johnson, 1800.

———. *Collected Works of Sir Humphry Davy*. London: Smith, Elder & Co., 1839–40.

———. *Fragmentary Remains, Literary and Scientific, of Sir Humphry Davy*. Ed. John Davy. London: J. Churchill, 1858.

[Davy, W.]. "Mr. Davy's Diary 1794," ed. Normal B. Wilkinson. *Pennsylvania History* 20 (1953): 123–41, 258–79.

DeLuc, Jean André. *Idées sur la Météorologie*. Paris: Veuve Duchesne, 1786.

[Dickinson, John]. "Four Letters addressed to John Dickinson," *Pennsylvania Magazine* 29 (1905): 226–27.

Ellis, Daniel. *An Inquiry into the Changes induced on Atmospheric Air by the Germination of Seeds, the Vegetation of Plants, and the Respiration of Animals*. Edinburgh: Wm. Creech; London: J. Murray, 1807.

Ellis, Henry, and Francis Douce, eds. *Catalogue of the Lansdowne Manuscripts in the British Museum*. London: British Museum, 1819.

[Emerson, Ralph Waldo]. *The Journals and Miscellaneous Notebooks of Ralph Waldo Emerson*. Cambridge: Belknap Press of Harvard University Press, 1960.

Faraday, Michael. "Speculations touching Electrical Conduction and the Nature of Matter." *Philosophical Magazine* 24 (3d ser., 1844): 136–44.

Finch, I. *Travels in the United States of America and Canada, containing some Account of their Scientific Institutions, and a Few Notices of the Geology and Mineralogy of those Countries. To which is Added, An Essay on the Natural Boundries of Empires*. London: Longman, Rees, Orme, Brown, Green, and Longman, 1833.

[Foljambe, F. J. Savile]. *The Manuscripts of the Right Honourable F. J. Savile Foljambe of Osberton*. London: Her Majesty's Stationery Office, Historic Manuscripts Commission, 1897. Fifteenth Report, Appendix, Part 5, 149.

[Franklin, Benjamin]. *The Papers of Benjamin Franklin*. New Haven: Yale University Press, 1962–.

A Full and Accurate Report of the Trials of the Birmingham Rioters, at the late Assizes for the County of Warwick; containing Sir Richard Perryn's Charge to the Grand Jury, the Speeches of the Counsel at length, and the Whole of the Evidence. London: J. Walter, T. Longman, W. Richardson, 1791.

An Appendix to the Account of the Birmingham Riots; containing interesting Papers omitted in that Work, or since Published. With the Damages claimed by, and Allowed to, the Sufferers. N.p., n.d. (1792–93?).

[George, Prince of Wales]. *The Correspondence of George, Prince of Wales, 1770–1812*. Vol. 2, 1789–1794. Ed. Arthur Aspinall. London: Cassel, 1964.

[George III, King]. *Correspondence of King George the Third: From 1760 to December 1783*. Ed. Sir John Fortescue. London: Frank Cass & Co., 1967.

———. *The Later Correspondence of King George the Third*. Ed. Arthur Aspinall. Cambridge: Cambridge University Press, 1962.

Graham, Thomas. "A Short Account of Experimental Researches on the Diffusion of Gases through each other, and their Separation by mechanical Means." *Quarterly Journal of Science and the Arts* 28 (1829): 74–83.

———. "On the Law of the Diffusion of Gases." *Philosophical Magazine* 2 (1833): 175–90, 269–76, 351–58.

———. *Elements of Chemistry, including the Applications of the Science in the Arts*. London: Hippolyte Bailliere, 1842.

———. "Speculative Ideas respecting the Constitution of Matter." *Proceedings of the Royal Society* 12 (1863): 620–23.

Grenville Papers. *Her Majesty's Historical Manuscript Commission Report*. 14th Report, Appendix 2.

[Guyton de Morveau, Louis-Bernard]. *A Scientific Correspondence during the Chemical Revolution: Louis-Bernard Guyton de Morveau and Richard Kirwan, 1782–1802*. Ed. Emmanuel Grison, Michelle Goupil, and Patricer Bret. Berkeley: Office for History of Science and Technology, University of California at Berkeley, 1994).

Hales, Stephen. *Statical Essays: Containing Haemastiticks; or An Account of some Hydraulic and Hydrostatical Experiments made on the Blood and Blood Vessels of Animals . . .* Vol. 2. 1773. Reprint, New York: Hafner Publ. Co., N.Y. Academy of Medicine, 1964.

———. *Vegetable Staticks, or An Account of some Statical Experiments on the Sap in Vegetables: Being an Essay towards a Natural History of Vegetation. Also, a Specimen of An Attempt to Analyse the Air, By a great Variety of Chymio-Statical Experiments . . .* 1727. Reprint, London: Oldbourne, 1961.

Harrington, Robert. "A New Year's Gift to Dr. Priestley, on the Subject of the Generation of Air from Water." *Gentleman's Magazine* 63 (1794): 36–40, 133–38.

[Hazlitt, William]. "The Hazlitt Papers." *Christian Reformer* 5 (1838): 505–12, 697–705, 756–64; and 6 (1839): 15–24, 373–74.

[Henderson, John]. "Two Letters from Mr. Henderson to Dr. Priestley, communicated by Dr. P. to the Gentleman's Magazine, April 1788." *Monthly Repository* 7 (1812): 286–92.

[Hill, Thomas Wright]. *Remains of the late Thomas Wright Hill, Esq. F.R.S.A., together with Notices of his Life, &c*. London: Richard T. Benbow, 1859.

Historical Manuscripts Commission. *Report on Manuscripts in Various Collections*. Vol. 6. Dublin: H. M. Stationery Office, 1909.

[Hobbes, Thomas]. *English Works of Thomas Hobbes*. London: John Bohn, 1839.

Hume, David. *Dialogues concerning Natural Religion*. With an introduction by Bruce M'Ewen. Edinburgh: William Blackwood and Sons, 1907.

Ingenhousz, Jan, "Remarques sur l'Origine et la Nature de la Matière verte de M. Priestley . . ." *Journal de Physique théorique et appliquée* 25 (1784): 3–122.

[Jefferson, Thomas]. *The Works of Thomas Jefferson*. Ed. P. L. Ford. New York: G. P. Putnam's Sons, 1904–5.

[Jervis, Thomas], "Veritas." "On Dr. Priestley's Connection with the Marquis of Lansdowne," *Monthly Repository* 6 (1811): 17–19.

Jervis, Thomas. *Remarks on some Passages in the Literary Recollections of the Rev. Richard Warner*. London: R. Hunter, 1831–32.

Kant, Immanuel. *Critique of Pure Reason*. Trans. Francis Haywood. London: William Pickering, 1848.

Laplace, Paul Simon, Marquis de. *A Philosophical Essay on Probabilities*. Trans. Frederick Wilson Truscott and Frederick Lincoln Emory. 1902; 1917. Reprint, New York: Dover Publications, 1951.

[Latrobe, Benjamin Henry]. *The Virginia Journals of Benjamin Henry Latrobe, 1795–1798*. Vol. 2. Ed. Edward C. Carter II. New Haven: Yale University Press, 1977.

Lavoisier, Antoine-Laurent. *Elements of Chemistry, in a New systematic Order, containing all the modern Discoveries.* Trans. Robert Kerr. 1790. Reprint, New York: Dover Publications, 1965.

——. *Oeuvres de Lavoisier: Correspondence.* Fasicules 2 (1957) and 3 (1964). Ed. René Fric, with Maurice Daumas and Douglas McKie. Paris: Editions Albin Michel.

[Lichtenberg, George Christoph]. *Lichtenberg's Visits to England: as described in his Letters and Diaries.* Trans. and annot. Margaret L. Mare and W. H. Quarrell. Oxford: Clarendon Press, 1938.

[Madison, Rev. James]. "Letters of Rev. James Madison, President of William and Mary College, to Thomas Jefferson." *William and Mary College Quarterly* 5 (2d ser., 1925): 145–51.

Melville, Herman. "Bartleby, the Scrivener." In *Great Short Works of Herman Melville*, 39–74. New York: Harper & Row, 1969.

[Mill, John Stuart]. *The Collected Works of John Stuart Mill.* Ed. F. E. L. Priestley. Toronto: University of Toronto Press, 1969.

Monboddo, James Burnett, Lord. *Antient Metaphysics: or, The Science of Universals.* London: T. Adell; Edinburgh: J. Balfour and Co., 1782.

[Morellet, Abbé]. *Mémoirs inedits de l'Abbé Morellet . . . Sur le Dix-Huitième Siècle et dur la Revolution.* Paris: De l'Advocat, 1872.

——. *Lettres de l'Abbé Morellet à Lord Shelburne.* Paris: E. Plon, Mourrit et Cie, 1898.

[Newton, Isaac]. *Sir Isaac Newton: Theological Manuscripts.* Ed. Herbert J. McLachlan. Liverpool: Liverpool University Press, 1950.

Parliamentary History of England from the earliest Period to the Year 1803. Ed. J. Wright. Vol. 29. London: T. Hansard, for Longman, Hurst, Rees, Orme & Brown, 1817.

Percival, Thomas. *The Works, Literary, Moral, and Medical of Thomas Percival, M.D.* London: J. Johnson, 1807.

[Price, Richard]. *The Correspondence of Richard Price.* Ed. D. O. Thomas and Bernard Peach. Durham: Duke University Press, 1983.

——. "The Price Letters." *Proceedings of the Massachusetts Historical Society* 17 (2d ser., 1903): 262–339; and 23 (1909): 624–25.

[Quincy, Josiah Jr.]. "Journal of Josiah Quincy, Jun., during his Voyage and Residence in England from September 28th 1774 to March 3d. 1775." *Proceedings of the Massachusetts Historical Society* 50 (1917): 433–70.

[Reid, Thomas]. *Thomas Reid's Inquiry into the Human Mind.* Ed. Timothy Duggan. Chicago: University of Chicago Press, 1970.

Robison, John. *System of Mechanical Philosophy.* Edinburgh: J. Murray, 1822.

Rochefoucauld-Liancourt, Duc de La. *Travels through the United States of North America, the Country of the Iroquois and Upper Canada in the years 1795, 1796 and 1797; with an Authentic Account of Lower Canada.* London: R. Phillips, 1798.

[Rush, Benjamin]. "Four Letters addressed to John Dickinson." *Pennsylvania Magazine* 29 (1905): 226–27.

——. *Letters of Benjamin Rush.* Ed. L. H. Butterfield. Princeton: American Philosophical Society, 1951.

[Russell, Catherine]. "Journal relating to the Birmingham riots, by a young lady of one of the persecuted families." Dated 14 July 1791. *The Christian Reformer* 2 (1835): 293–304, 295–97.
Saint-Fond, Barthélemy Faujas de. *Travels in England, Scotland, and the Hebrides.* London: James Ridgway, 1799.
[Scheele, Carl Wilhelm]. "Chemical Treatise on Air and Fire." In *Collected Papers of Carl Wilhelm Scheele,* trans. and ed. Leonard Dobbin. London: G. Bell & Sons, 1931.
[Sinclair, Sir John]. *The Correspondence of the Right Honourable Sir John Sinclair, Bart.* London: Henry Colburn and Richard Bentley, 1831.
[Stiles, Ezra]. *The Literary Diary of Ezra Stiles, D.D. LL.D. President of Yale College.* 3 vols. Ed. Franklin Bowditch Dexter. New York: Charles Scribner's Sons, 1901.
[Talleyrand, Charles M., de]. *Memoirs of the Prince de Talleyrand.* New York: G. P. Putnam's Sons, 1891.
[Thatcher, George]. "Letters to George Thatcher." *Proceedings of the Massachusetts Historical Society* 2, 3 (ser. 2, 1886–87): 11–40, 18–19.
Toulmin, Joshua. "Note to Mr. Urban." *Gentleman's Magazine* 64 (1794): 495.
Twining, Thomas. *Travels in America 100 Years Ago, being Notes and Reminiscences.* New York: Harper & Bros., 1893.
Unitarian/Universalist World, 15 March 1976, pp. 1–2; 15 Oct. 1977, p. 9.
Wansey, Henry. *The Journal of an Excursion to the United States of North America in the Summer of 1794.* New York: Johnson Reprint Corporation, 1969.
Watson, Richard. *Chemical Essays* (Cambridge: J. Archdeacon for T. and J. Merrill et al., 1781.
Watson, William Jr. *A Treatise on Time.* London: J. Johnson, 1785.
[Watt, James]. "James Watt's Letter to Joseph Priestley, 26 April 1783." *Annals of Science* 10 (1954): 294–300.
[Webster, Noah]. *Letters of Noah Webster.* Ed. Harry R. Warfel. New York: Library Publishers, 1953.
[Wesley, John]. *The Journal of the Rev. John Wesley, A. M.* 8 vols. Ed. Nehemiah Curnock. London: Robert Culley/Chas. H. Kelly, 1909–16.
Wilkes, John. *The Correspondence of the late John Wilkes, with his Friends, printed from the Original manuscripts.* Vol. 5. Ed. John Almon. London: Richard Phillips, 1805.
Willard, Joseph. "Willard Letters." *Proceedings of the Massachusetts Historical Society* 43 (1909–10): 609–11.
Wyvill, Christopher. *Political Papers, chiefly respecting the Attempt of the County of York . . . to effect a Reformation of the Parliament of Great-Britain.* Vol. 4. York: J. Johnson et al., 1802.

Manuscript Collections

Archives de l'Académie des Sciences, Institut de France. Le départ de M. Le Président de Virly. Letter of Antoine Lavoisier, 30 April 1785: minute.
Adams Papers. Massachusetts Historical Society, Boston. Microfilm.
American Philosophical Society Archives, Philadelphia.

Bowood Papers, Bowood Archives, Bowood, Calne.

Certificate Books of the Royal Society, Archives. Royal Society of London.

First Unitarian Church of Philadelphia Archives. Unidentified newspaper clipping about its centenary, 1876, also brochure of the First Unitarian Church of Philadelphia, n.p., n.d., p. 6 has organization document dated 12 June 1796.

Journal Book of the Royal Society. Vols. 27–28 (1774–77); vol. 29 (1777–78); vol. 30 (1778–80). Royal Society of London.

Koninklijke

Hollandsche Maatschappij der Wetenschappen, Haarlem. Minutes.

Minutes of the New Meeting Sunday School, Birmingham City Archives, Central Library, Birmingham.

Petition of Birmingham citizens to King George III thanking him for sending troops to put down riot: draft, n.d. [1791], JWP/W/13/3 Birmingham City Archives, Reference Library.

Benjamin Rush Papers, Historical Society of Pennsylvania, Philadelphia.

SECONDARY SOURCES

Aall, Anathon. *The Hellenistic Elements in Christianity.* London: University of London Press, 1931.

The Abingdon Bible Commentary. Ed. Frederick Carl Eiselen, Edwin Lewis, and David G. Downey. Nashville: Abingdon-Cokesbury Press, 1929.

Abrahams, Harold J., and Wyndham D. Miles. "The Priestley-Levi Debates." *Transactions of the Unitarian Historical Society* 12 (1959–62): 111–29.

Adams, C. K. *A Manual of Historical Literature.* New York: Harper & Bros., 1882.

Adams, James F., and Arnold A. Hoberman. "Joseph Buchanan, 1785–1839, Pioneer American Psychologist." *Journal of the History of the Behavioral Sciences* 5 (1969): 340–48.

Adams, M. Ray. *Studies in the Literary Background of English Radicalism.* Lancaster: Franklin and Marshall College Studies, No. 5, 1957.

Adelung, John Christopher. *Elements of the Critical Philosophy* . . . Trans. from the German by A. F. M. Willich. London: T. N. Longman, 1798.

Aikin, Lucy. *Memoir of John Aikin, M.D., with a Selection of his Miscellaneous Pieces, Biographical, Moral and Critical.* Vol. 1. London: Baldwin, Cradock, and Joy, 1823.

Aldridge, Alfred Owen. "Benjamin Franklin and Philosophical Necessity." *Modern Language Quarterly* 12 (1951): 292–309.

[Asplund, Robert]. "Memoir of the late Rev. Robert Aspland." *Christian Reformer* 1 (n.s., 1845): 358.

Bakewell, William. "Some Particulars of Dr. Priestley's Residence at Northumberland, America." *Monthly Repository* 1 (1806): 393–97, 504–8, 564–67, 622–25.

Badash, Lawrence. "Joseph Priestley's Apparatus for Pneumatic Chemistry." *Journal of the History of Medicine* 19 (1964): 139–55.

Baines, Edward. *History of the County Palatine and Duchy of Lancaster.* London: Routledge and Sons, 1870.

Barclay, John. *An Inquiry into the Opinions, Ancient and Modern, concerning Life and Organization*. Edinburgh: Bell & Bradfute, Waugh and Innes; London: G. & W. B. Whittaker, 1822.

Barnes, Sherman B. "Historians in the Age of Enlightenment." In *Historiography Under the Impact of Rationalism and Revolution*, ed. Sherman B. Barnes and Alfred A. Skerpan. Kent: Kent State University Press, 1952.

Beer, John J. "The Chemistry of the Founding Fathers," and "Woodhouse." *Journal of Chemical Education* 53 (1976): 405–18.

Bell, Herbert C., ed. "Northumberland." In *History of Northumberland County, Pennsylvania* (1891). Reprinted in *Proceedings and Addresses, Northumberland County Historical Society* 32 (1994): 35–59.

Belsham, Thomas. *A Vindication of Certain Passages in a Discourse, on the Death of Dr. Priestley &c.; to which is annexed the Discourse on the Death of Dr. Priestley*. Boston: T. B. Wait & Co., 1809.

———. *Memoirs of the late Reverend Theophilus Lindsey*. London: Johnson and Co., 1812.

———. "Mr. Belsham on the Controversy between Dr. Priestley and Bp. Horsley; in Reply to the strictures of the Rev. H. Horseley, on the Calm Inquiry." *Monthly Repository* 8 (1813): 172–77, 240–44, 294–97, 383–88, 450–54, 583–88, 723–31.

Bennett, Charles A. *History of Manual and Industrial Education up to 1870*. Peoria, Ill.: Charles A. Bennett Co., 1926.

Beranek, Leo L. "Acoustic Properties of Gases." In *American Institute of Physics Handbook*. New York: McGraw-Hill, 1957.

Black, Eugene Charlton. *The Associations: British Extraparliamentary Political Organization, 1769–1793*. Cambridge: Harvard University Press, 1963.

Bonwick, Colin. "English Dissenters and the American Revolution." In *Contrast and Connection: Bicentennial Essays in Anglo-American History*, ed. H. C. Allen and Roger Thomson. Athens: Ohio University Press, 1976.

———. *English Radicals and the American Revolution*. Chapel Hill: University of North Carolina Press, 1977.

———. "Joseph Priestley, Emigrant and Jeffersonian." *Enlightenment and Dissent* 2 (1983): 3–22.

Boorstin, Daniel J. *The Lost World of Thomas Jefferson*. Boston: Beacon Press, 1960.

Boulton, James T. *The Language of Politics in the Age of Wilkes and Burke*. London: Routledge & Kegan Paul, 1963.

Bourgeois, Lillian C. *Cabanocey: The History, Customs, and Folklore of St. James Parish*. Gretna, La.: Pelican, 1957.

Boyce, Anne Ogden. *Records of a Quaker Family: The Richardsons of Cleveland*. London: Samuel Harris & Co., 1889.

Bradley, James E. *Religion, Revolution, and English Radicalism: Nonconformity in Eighteenth-Century Politics and Society*. Cambridge: Cambridge University Press, 1990.

Brandon, S. G. F. "Tübingen Vindicated." *Hibbert Journal* (1920): 41–47.

Bratton, Frederick Gladstone. *History of the Bible*. Boston: Beacon Press, n.d.

Brazier, Mary A. B. *A History of Neurophysiology in the Seventeenth and Eighteenth Centuries: From Concept to Experiment*. New York: Raven Press, 1984.

Bronk, Detlev W. "Joseph Priestley and the Early History of the American Philosophical Society." *Proceedings of the American Philosophical Society* 86 (1942): 103–7.

Brooke, John Hedley. "'A Sower Went Forth': Joseph Priestley and the Ministry of Reform." In *Motion Toward Perfection: The Achievement of Joseph Priestley*, ed. A. Truman Schwartz and John G. McEvoy, 21–56. Boston: Skinner House Books, 1990.

Broussais, F. J. V. *On Irritation and Insanity*. Trans. Thomas Cooper (Columbia: S.C.: S. J. M'Morris, 1831.

Brown, Alexander Crum. "Note on the Phlogistic Theory." *Proceedings of the Royal Society of Edinburgh* 5 (1866): sec. 5, 328–30.

Brown, Ford K. *Life of William Godwin*. London: J. M. Dent, 1926.

Brown, Peter. *The Chathamites: A Study in the Relationship Between Personalities and Ideas in the Second Half of the Eighteenth Century*. London: Macmillan; New York: St. Martin's Press, 1967.

Brown, Philip A. *The French Revolution in English History*. 1918. Reprint, London: George Allen & Unwin, 1923.

Buchanan, Joseph. *The Philosophy of Human Nature*. Gainsville, Fla.: Scholars' Facsimiles & Reprints, 1969; Weston, Mass.: M. & S. Press, 1970.

Buckley, Jessie K. *Joseph Parkes of Birmingham and the Part which He played in the Radical Reform Movements from 1825 to 1845*. London: Methuen & Co., 1916.

Bultmann, Rudolf. *Primitive Christianity in Its Contemporary Setting*. New York: Meridian, 1956.

Burns, R. M. *The Great Debate on Miracles: From Joseph Glanvill to David Hume* (Lewisburg: Bucknell University Press, 1981).

Burr, Alex. C. "Notes on the History of the Experimental Determination of the Thermal Conductivity of Gases," *Isis* 21 (1934): 169–86.

Bushrod, Emily. "The History of Unitarianism in Birmingham from the Middle of the Eighteenth Century to 1893." Master's thesis, University of Birmingham, 1954.

["Cambriensis"]. "Other Reasons assigned for a certain Reverend Philosopher's leaving this Country." *Gentleman's Magazine* 64 (1794): 428–30.

Cappe, Catherine. *Memoirs of the Life of the late Mrs. Catherine Cappe*. London: Longman, Hurst, Rees, Orme, and Brown, 1822.

Carpenter, J. Estlin. *The Bible in the Nineteenth Century*. New York: Longmans, Green, & Co., 1903.

Casey, Robert P. "Clement of Alexandria and the Beginnings of Christian Platonism." *Harvard Theological Review* 18 (1925): 39–101.

Cassirer, Ernst. *Essay on Man: An Introduction to a Philosophy of Human Culture*. New Haven: Yale University Press, 1944.

———. *The Platonic Renaissance in England*. Austin: University of Texas Press, 1953.

Chadwick, Henry. *The Early Church*. New York: Dorset Press, 1967.

Chadwick, John W. "Theology of the Century." In John W. Chadwick, *Sermons, Addresses and Essays*. Philadelphia: by the Society, 1896.

Chapin, Lloyd W. "The Theology of Joseph Priestley: A Study in Eighteenth-Century Apologetics." Th.D. diss., Union Theological Seminary, 1967.

Chard, Leslie F. II. *Dissenting Republican: Wordsworth's Early Life and Thought in Their Political Context.* The Hague: Mounton, 1972.

Christian Reformer: "R. W.," Examination of Arguments adduced by Dr. Priestley to prove the identity of the Nazarenes and Ebionites," 4 (1837): 604–9, 651–58; "Critical Notices: The Miscellaneous Writings of F. W. P. Greenwood, D.D.," and "Obituary: Thomas Clark," 3 (n.s., 1847): 170–72, 759–60.

Christian Repository (1820): 157. "The Rev. T. H. Horne's Obligations to Unitarian Authors."

Christie, Ian R. "Economic Reform and 'the Influence of the Crown,' 1780." *Cambridge Historical Journal* 12 (1956): 144–54.

Clark, John Ruskin. *Joseph Priestley: "A Comet in the System."* Northumberland, Pa.: Friends of Joseph Priestley House, 1994.

——. "Joseph Priestley's Contribution to Unitarian Theology." Manuscript seen through the courtesy of Dr. Clark.

Clayden, P. W. *Early Life of Samuel Rogers.* Boston: Roberts Brothers, 1888.

Clifton, Charles S. *Encyclopedia of Heresies and Heretics.* Santa Barbara, Calif.: ABC-Clio, 1992.

Cloyd, E. L. *James Burnett: Lord Monboddo.* Oxford: Clarendon Press, 1972.

Cole, G. D. H. *The Life of William Cobbett.* New York: Harcourt, Brace, 1924.

Colie, Rosalie L. "Spinoza and the Early English Deists." *Journal of the History of Ideas* 20 (1959): 23–45.

Cone, Carl B. *The English Jacobins: Reformers in Late Eighteenth-Century England.* New York: Charles Scribner's Sons, 1968.

Conybeare, F. C. *History of New Testament Criticism.* New York: G. Putnam's Sons, 1910.

Cornforth, John, "Bowood, Wiltshire: The Seat of the Marquess of Lansdowne, Revisited—I, II, III." *Country Life* 151 (8, 15, 22 June 1972): 1448–51, 1546–50, 1610–13.

——. "The Making of the Bowood Landscape." *Country Life* 152 (6 Sept. 1972): 546–49.

Cowan, Helen I. *Charles Williamson: Genesee Promoter—Friend of Anglo-American Rapprochement.* Rochester, N.Y.: Rochester Historical Society, 1941.

Crane, Verner W. "The Club of Honest Whigs: Friends of Science and Liberty." *William and Mary Quarterly* 23 (3d ser., 1966): 210–33.

Creasey, John, ed. "The Birmingham Riots of 1791." *Transactions of the Unitarian Historical Society* 4 (1927–30): 417–29; and 13 (1963–66): 111–17.

Creed, John Martin. *The Divinity of Jesus Christ: A Study in the History of Christian Doctrine Since Kant.* Cambridge: Cambridge University Press, 1938.

Cromwell, Thomas. "Justice to Priestley—Dr. Scholten on Materialism, the Soul and the Future Life." *Christian Reformer* 8 (n.s., 1861): 33–36.

Crook, Ronald E. *A Bibliography of Joseph Priestley, 1733–1804.* London: Library Association, 1966.

Cross, R. Nicol. "The Blessed Trinity." *Hibbert Journal* 55 (1956–57): 231–40.

Curtis, Mattoon Monroe. "Kantian Elements in Jonathan Edwards." In *Philosophische Abhandlungen: Max Heinze sum 70 Geburtstage.* Berlin: E. S. Mittler und Sohn, 1906.

Cuvier, Georges. "Eulogy on Dr. Priestley." Translated in the *Monthly Repository* 1 (1806): 216–19, 328–34.

Dangerfield, George. *Chancellor Robert R. Livingston of New York, 1746–1813.* New York: Harcourt, Brace, 1960.

Daumas, Maurice, and Denis Duveen. "Lavoisier's Relatively Unknown Large-Scale Decomposition and Synthesis of Water, February 27 and 28, 1785." *Chymia* 5 (1959): 113–29.

Davies, J. G. *The Early Christian Church.* New York: Holt, Rinehart and Winston, 1965.

Davis, David. "Obituary." *Monthly Magazine* 1 (n.s., 1827): 693–95.

Davis, Richard W. *Dissent in Politics, 1780–1830: The Political Life of William Smith, M.P.* London: Epworth Press, 1971.

Dictionary of the Bible. Ed. James Hastings, revised by Frederick A. Grant and H. H. Rowley. New York: Charles Scribner's Sons, 1963.

Dictionary of the History of Ideas. Ed. Philip P. Weiner. New York: Charles Scribner's Sons, 1973. S.v. "Free Will and Determinism" (by Bernard Berofsky); "Free Will in Theology" (by Austin Farrer); "Association of Ideas" (by Robert M. Young).

Dictionary of National Biography. London: Smith, Elder & Co., 1896–1900. Reissued 1908–9.

Dictionary of Scientific Biography. Ed. Charles Coulston Gillispie. New York: Charles Scribner's Sons, 1972. S.v. "Antoine Lavoisier" (by Henry Gurelac).

Disraeli, Benjamin. *Sybil, or the Two Nations.* 1926. Reprint, Oxford: Oxford University Press, 1956.

Donovan, Arthur. *Antoine Lavoisier: Science, Administration, and Revolution.* Oxford: Blackwell, 1993.

Drummond, William. *Academical Questions.* London: W. Bulmer and Co., 1805.

Drury, John, ed. *Critics of the Bible, 1724–1873.* Cambridge: Cambridge University Press, 1989.

Duveen, Denis I., and Herbert S. Klickstein. "The Introduction of Lavoisier's Chemical Nomenclature into America." *Isis* 45 (1954): 278–92.

Edinburgh Encyclopaedia. Ed. David Brewster. American ed., Philadelphia: Joseph & Edward Parker, 1832. S.v. "Metaphysics" (by James Esdaile).

Edwards, Eliezar. *Sir Rowland Hill, K.C.B.: A Biographical and Historical Sketch, with Records of the Family to which He belonged.* London: Frederick Warne and Co., 1879.

Eichorn, J. G. "Biography of J. S. Semler." *General Repository and Review* 1 (1812): 58–72, 277–96; and 2 (1812): 38–65, 213–40.

Ellis, Grace A. *A Memoir of Mrs. Anna Laetitia Barbauld, with many of her Letters.* Boston: James R. Osgood and Co., 1874.

Encyclopedia Britannica, 11th ed. S.v. "Edward Gibbon" (by J. B. Bury), 927–36.

Encyclopedia of Philosophy, ed. Paul Edwards. New York: Macmillan, 1967. S.v. "Thomas Reid" (by S. A. Grave); "James Beattie" (by Elmer Sprague).

[English, David]. "A Brief Description of Joseph Priestley in a letter of David English to Charles D. Green, Princeton June 20, 1794." *Journal of the Presbyterian Historical Society* 38 (1960): 124–27.

Eyles, V. A. "The Evolution of a Chemist: Sir James Hall, Bt., F.R.S., P.R.S.E. . . . (1761–1832), and his relations with Joseph Black, Antoine Lavoisier, and other scientists of the period." *Annals of Science* 19 (1963): 153–82.

Faurot, J. H. "The Development of Reid's Theory of Knowledge." *University of Toronto Quarterly* 21 (1951–52): 224–31.

———. "Reid's Answer to Joseph Priestley." *Journal of the History of Ideas* 39 (1978): 285–92.

Fenn, W. W. "Biblical Authority During the Century." In W. W. Fenn, *Sermons, Addresses, and Essays.* Philadelphia: by the Society, 1896.

———. "Concerning Natural Religion." *Harvard Theological Review* 4 (1911): 460–76.

Field, William. *Memoirs of the Life, Writings, and Opinions of the Rev. Samuel Parr . . .* London: Henry Colburn, 1828.

Fitzpatrick, Martin. "Joseph Priestley and the Cause of Universal Toleration." *Price-Priestley Newsletter* 1 (1977): 3–30.

———. "William Godwin and the Rational Dissenters." *Price-Priestley Newsletter* 3 (1979): 4–28.

Foote, Henry Wilder. *The Religion of Thomas Jefferson.* Boston: Beacon Press, 1947.

Fox, Robert. *The Calorique Theory of Gases from Lavoisier to Regnault.* Oxford: Clarendon Press, 1971.

Frank, Willard C., Jr., "'I shall Never be Intimidated': Harry Toulmin and William Christie in Virginia, 1793–1801." *Transactions of the Unitarian Historical Society* 19 (1987–90): 24–37.

Fructman, Jack, Jr. "The Apocalyptic Politics of Richard Price and Joseph Priestley: A Study in Late Eighteenth-Century English Republican Millennialism." *Transactions of the American Philosophical Society* 73 (1983): part 4.

Fuller, Reginald H. *The New Testament in Current Study.* New York: Charles Scribner's Sons, 1962.

Garrett, Clarke. "Joseph Priestley, the Millennium, and the French Revolution." *Journal of the History of Ideas* 34 (1973): 51–66.

———. "Which Cooper? The Site of Coleridge's Utopia on the Susquehanna." *John and Mary's Journal* 5 (1979): 17–28.

Gascoigne, John. "The Royal Society and the Emergence of Science as an Instrument of State Policy." *British Journal for the History of Science* 32 (1999): 171–84.

Gerstner, Patsy A. "James Hutton's Theory of the Earth and His Theory of Matter." *Isis* 59 (1968): 26–31.

Gibbs, F. W. *Joseph Priestley: Adventurer in Science and Champion of Truth.* London: Thomas Nelson and Sons, 1965. Published in the United States as *Joseph Priestley: Revolutions of the Eighteenth Century.* Garden City, N.Y.: Doubleday, 1967.

Gilbert, George Holley. "From John Mark to John the Theologian: The First Great Departure from Primitive Christianity." *Harvard Theological Review* 16 (1923): 235–58.

Gill, Conrad. *History of Birmingham.* London: for the Birmingham City Council, by Oxford University Press, 1952.

Glaiser, James. "On Scientific Experiments in Balloons." *Proceedings of the Royal*

Institution of Great Britain 39 (1962–63): 641–50 (from the *Proceedings* of 1863).

Glover, Willis B. *Evangelical Nonconformists and Higher Criticism in the Nineteenth Century.* London: Independent Press, 1954.

Goodwin, Albert. *Friends of Liberty: The English Democratic Movement in the Age of the French Revolution.* Cambridge: Harvard University Press, 1979.

Gordon, Alexander. *Cheshire Classis Minutes.* London: Chiswick Press, 1919.

Gottschalk, Louis. "Reflections on Burke's *Reflections on the French Revolution.*" *Proceedings of the American Philosophical Society* 100 (1956): 417–29.

Graham, Jenny. "Revolutionary Philosopher: The Political Ideas of Joseph Priestley (1733–1804)." *Enlightenment and Dissent* 8 (1989): 43–68 (Part 1); and 9 (1990): 14–46 (Part 2).

———. "Revolutionary in Exile: The Emigration of Joseph Priestley to America, 1794–1804." *Transactions of the American Philosophical Society* 85 (1995): i–xii, 1–213.

Grant, Robert M. *Historical Introduction to the New Testament.* New York: Simon & Schuster, 1972.

Gray, Mike. "Joseph Priestley in Hackney." *Enlightenment and Dissent* 2 (1983): 107–10.

Gregory, Olinthus. "A Correspondent." "A Review of some leading Points in the Official Character and Proceedings of the late President of the Royal Society." *Philosophical Magazine* 56 (1820): 161–74, 241–57.

Griffith, William P., "Priestley in London. "*Notes and Records of the Royal Society of London* 38 (1983): 1–16.

Grimaux, Edouard. *Lavoisier, 1743–1794.* Paris: Felix Alcan, 1896.

Guignebert, Charles. *Ancient, Medieval, and Modern Christianity: The Evolution of a Religion.* 1927; New Hyde Park, N.Y.: University Books, 1961.

Guerlac, Henry. "Lavoisier, Antoine-Laurent." In *Dictionary of Scientific Biography,* ed. Charles Coulston Gillispie. New York: Charles Scribner's Sons, 1972.

Haakonssen, Knud, ed. *Enlightenment and Religion: Rational Dissent in Eighteenth-century Britain.* Cambridge: Cambridge University Press, 1996.

Hall, Courtney R. *A Scientist in the Early Republic: Samuel Latham Mitchill, 1764–1831.* New York: Columbia University Press, 1934.

Hampsher-Monk, Iain. "The Writings and Speeches of Edmund Burke. . . . Vol. VIII, The French Revolution 1790–1794 . . ." *History of Political Thought* 12 (1991): 179–83.

Haraszti, Zoltan. *John Adams and the Prophets of Progress.* Cambridge: Harvard University Press, 1952.

Harms, Ernest. "The Origins and Early History of Electrotherapy and Electroshock." *American Journal of Psychiatry* 111 (1955): 933–34.

Harnack, Adolph. *History of Dogma.* 7 vols. in 4. 1894; 1900; New York: Dover Publications, 1961.

Hartog, Sir Philip. "Joseph Priestley and his Place in the History of Science." *Proceedings of the Royal Institution* 26 (1931): 395–430.

Hartog, Sir Philip, A. N. Meldrum, and Sir Harold Hartley. "The Bicentenary of Joseph Priestley." *Journal of the Chemical Society* (1933): 896–920.

Hatch, Ronald B. "Joseph Priestley: An Addition to Hartley's *Observations.*" *Journal of the History of Ideas* 36 (1975): 548–50.

Heimann, P. M. "Faraday's Theories of Matter and Electricity." *British Journal for the History of Science* 5 (1971): 235–57.

Heinemann, F. H. "John Toland and the Age of Enlightenment." *Review of English Studies* 28 (1944): 125–46.

Hiebert, Erwin N., and Hans-Günther Köber. "Ostwald, Friedrich Wilhelm." In *Dictionary of Scientific Biography* (supplement), ed. Charles Coulston Gillispie. New York: Charles Scribner's Sons, 1972.

Hennell, Charles C. *An Inquiry concerning the Origin of Christianity.* 3d ed. London: Trübner and Co., 1870.

Henry, William. "Tribute to the Memory of the late President of the Literary and Philosophical Society of Manchester." *Memoirs of the Literary and Philosophical Society of Manchester* 3: (2d ser., 1819).

Hepburn, Joseph Samuel. "The Pennsylvania Associations of Joseph Priestley." *Journal of the Franklin Institute* 244 (1947): 63–72, 95–107.

Herbert, A. S. *Historical Catalogue of Printed Editions of the English Bible: 1525–1961.* London: British and Foreign Bible Society; New York: American Bible Society, 1968.

Hill, Joseph. *Bookmakers of Old Birmingham: Authors, Printers, and Booksellers.* Birmingham: Cornish Bros. Ltd., 1907.

Holmes, Frederic L. "The 'Revolution in Chemistry and Physics': Overthrow of a Reigning Paradigm or Competition Between Contemporary Research Programs?" *Isis* 91 (2000): 735–53.

Holt, Anne. *A Life of Joseph Priestley.* London: Oxford University Press, 1931.

Holt, Raymond V. *Unitarian Contributions to Social Progress in England.* London: George Allen & Unwin, 1938.

Honeywell, R. J. *The Educational Work of Thomas Jefferson.* Harvard Studies in Education, vol. 16. Cambridge: Harvard University Press, 1931.

Horberger, Theodore. *Scientific Thought in the American Colleges, 1638–1800.* Austin: University of Texas Press, 1945.

Hunt, Leslie B., and Peta D. Buchanan. "Richard Knight (1768–1844): A Forgotten Chemist and Apparatus Designer." *Ambix* 31 (1984): 57–67.

Hutton, W. *An History of Birmingham, to the End of the Year 1780.* Birmingham: Pearson and Rollason, 1781.

Hutton, William. *The Life of William Hutton, F.A. S.S., including a Particular Account of the Riots at Birmingham in 1791.* London: Baldwin, Cradock, and Joy, 1816.

Huxley, Thomas Henry. "Joseph Priestley." In Thomas Henry Huxley, *Science and Education.* New York: D. Appleton & Co., 1897.

Hyde, Edward, Earl of Clarendon. *The History of the Rebellion and Civil Wars in England.* Oxford: Clarendon Press, 1717.

Ihde, Aaron J. "European Tradition in Nineteenth-Century American Chemistry." *Journal of Chemical Education* 53 (1976): 741–44.

Index to Religious Periodical Literature. Becomes *Religious Index, One: Periodicals.* Vol. 1 (1949–52)–vol. 15 (1981–82).

Institut de France. *Index Biographique des Membres et Correspondents de L'Académie des Sciences du 22 Décembre 1666 au 15 Novembre 1954.* Paris: Gauthier, Villars, 1954.

The International Standard Bible Encyclopedia, ed. Geoffrey Bromiley et al. Grand Rapids, Mich.: William B. Eerdmans, 1986.

Jackson, Foakes. *A History of Church History: Studies of Some Historians of the Christian Church.* Cambridge, Eng.: W. Heffner & Sons, 1939.

[Jeffrey, Francis]. "Memoirs of Dr. Joseph Priestley." *Edinburgh Review* 9 (1806): 136–61.

Jeremy, D. J. "Henry Wansey and His American Journal, 1794." *Memoir of the American Philosophical Society* 82 (1970).

Jungnickel, Christa, and Russell McCormmach. *Cavendish.* Philadelphia: American Philosophical Society, Memoir 220, 1996.

Kargon, Robert Hugh. "William Rowan Hamilton and Boscovichean Atomism." *Journal of the History of Ideas* 26 (1965): 137–40.

Kelley, Maurice W. "Thomas Cooper and Pantisocracy." *Modern Language Notes* (April 1930): 218–20.

[Kenrick, Mrs. W. Byng], ed. *Chronicles of a Nonconformist Family: The Kenricks of Wynne Hall, Exeter and Birmingham.* Birmingham: Cornish Brothers, 1932.

Kiernan, Colm. *The Enlightenment and Science in Eighteenth-Century France.* Banbury: Voltaire Foundation, Studies on Voltaire and the Eighteenth Century, No. 59A, 1973.

Koch, G. Alfred. *Religion of the American Enlightenment.* New York: Thomas Y. Crowell, 1968.

Kramnick, Isaac. "Republican Revisionism Revisited." *American Historical Review* 87 (1982): 629–64.

———. "Eighteenth-Century Science and Radical Social Theory: The Case of Joseph Priestley's Scientific Liberalism." In *The Scientific Enterprise: The Bar-Hillel Colloquium: Studies in History, Philosophy, and Sociology of Science,* vol. 4, ed. Edna Ullmann-Margalit. Dordrecht: Kluwer Academic Publishers, 1992.

Knight, David. *Atoms and Elements: A Study of Theories of Matter in England in the Nineteenth Century.* London: Hutchinson, 1967.

Knight, Frida. *The Strange Case of Thomas Walker.* London: Lawrence & Wishart, 1957.

———. *University Rebel: The Life of William Frend (1757–1841).* London: Victor Gollancz, 1971.

Kümmel, Werner Georg. *The New Testament: The History of the Investigation of Its Problems.* Nashville: Abingdon Press, 1972.

Langford, John Alfred, ed. *A Century of Birmingham Life: or, A Chronicle of Local Events, from 1741 to 1841.* 2 vols. Birmingham: E. C. Osborne; London: Simkin, Marshall & Co., 1868.

Laprade, William Thomas. *England and the French Revolution, 1789–1797.* Baltimore: Johns Hopkins University Press, 1909.

Laqueur, Thomas Walter. *Religion and Respectability: Sunday Schools and Working-Class Culture, 1780–1850.* New Haven: Yale University Press, 1976.

Leary, Lewis, "John Blair Linn, 1777–1805." *William and Mary Quarterly* 4 (3d ser., 1947): 148–76.

Lebreton, Jules, and Jacques Zeiller. *The History of the Primitive Church.* London: Burns Oates & Washbourne, 1944.

Lenz, John W. "Hume's Defense of Causal Inference." *Journal of the History of Ideas* 19 (1958): 559–67.

Levere, Trevor H. "Dr. Thomas Beddoes at Oxford." *Ambix* 28 (1981): 61–67.

Lightfoot, Robert Henry. *History and Interpretation in the Gospels.* London: Hodder and Stoughton, 1935.

Loewenfeld, Kurt. "Contributions to the History of Science." *Memoirs of the Manchester Literary and Philosophical Society* 57 (1912–13): 45–96.

Lukehart, Peter M., ed. *Joseph Priestley in America, 1794–1804.* Exh. cat. for the bicentennial of Priestley's arrival in the United States. Carlisle, Pa.: Trout Gallery, Dickinson College, 1994.

Mack, Mary. *Jeremy Bentham: An Odyssey of Ideas, 1748–1792.* New York: Columbia University Press, 1963.

Maddison, R. E. S., and Francis R. Maddison. "Joseph Priestley and the Birmingham Riots." *Notes and Records of the Royal Society of London* 12 (1957): 98–113.

Mardon, B. "Memoirs of the Rev. Thomas Fyshe Palmer." *Christian Reformer* 4 (1837): 275–81, 337–42.

Marsh, A. E. W. *A History of the Borough and Town of Calne and some Account of the Villages, etc. in its Vicinity.* Calne: Robert S. Heath; London: Lamb & Storr, 1907.

Marsh, Herbert. *Lectures on the Criticism and Interpretation of the Bible: . . . To which are added, Two Lectures on the History of Biblical Interpretation.* London: J. G. and F. Rivington, 1838.

Marsh, Robert. "The Second Part of Hartley's System." *Journal of the History of Ideas* 20 (1959): 264–73.

Marshall, Herbert. *Immunological Psychology and Psychiatry.* Tuscaloosa: University of Alabama Press, 1977.

Marshall, Peter J., ed. *The British Discovery of Hinduism in the Eighteenth Century.* Cambridge: Cambridge University Press, 1970.

Martineau, Dennis. "Playing Detective: The Priestley Riots of 1791." *Birmingham Historian*, nos. 12–13 (1997): 15–18; 11–16.

Martineau, Harriet. *Illustrations of Political Economy.* Vol. 8. London: Charles Fox, 1834.

Martineau, James. "The Life and Works of Dr. Priestley." In James Martineau, *Essays, Reviews, and Addresses.* London: Longmans, Green and Co., 1890.

[Marum, Martinus van]. *Martinus van Marum: Life and Work.* Vol. 4. Ed. E. Lefebvre and J. G. De Bruijn. Leyden: Noordhoff, 1969–76.

Mather, C. *High Church Prophet: Bishop Samuel Horsley (1733–1806) and the Caroline Tradition in the Later Georgian Church.* Oxford: Clarendon Press, 1992.

Mathews, Catherine Van Cortland. *Andrew Ellicott: His Life and Letters.* New York: Grafton Press, 1908.

McCalman, Iain. "New Jerusalems: Prophecy, Dissent, and Radical Culture in England, 1786–1830." In *Enlightenment and Religion: Rational Dissent in*

Eighteenth-century Britain, ed. Knud Haakonssen. Cambridge: Cambridge University Press, 1996.

McCloy, Shelby T. *Gibbon's Antagonism to Christianity.* London: Williams & Norgate, 1933.

McEvoy, John G. "Joseph Priestley, 'Aerial Philosopher': Metaphysics and Methodology in Priestley's Chemical Thought, from 1772 to 1781." *Ambix* 25 (1978): 1–55, 93–116, 153–75; and 26 (1979): 16–38.

——. "Joseph Priestley and the Chemical Revolution: A Thematic Overview." In *Motion Toward Perfection: The Achievement of Joseph Priestley,* ed. A. Truman Schwartz and John G. McEvoy, 129–60. Boston: Skinner House Books, 1990.

McEvoy, John G., and J. E. McGuire. "God and Nature: Priestley's Way of Rational Dissent." *Historical Studies in the Physical Sciences* 6 (1975): 325–404.

McKie, Douglas. "Joseph Priestley (1733–1804), Chemist." *Science Progress* 109 (1933): 17–35.

——. *Antoine Lavoisier: The Father of Modern Chemistry.* Philadelphia: J. B. Lippincott, 1935.

——. "A Note on Priestley in America." *Notes and Records of the Royal Society of London* 10 (1952): 51–59.

——. "Priestley's Laboratory and Library and Other of his Effects." *Notes and Records of the Royal Society of London* 12 (1956): 114–36.

McLachlan, Herbert J. "More Letters of Theophilus Lindsey." *Transactions of the Unitarian Historical Society* 3 (1923–26): 363–64.

——. "The Old Hackney College 1786–1796." *Transactions of the Unitarian Historical Society* 3 (1923–26): 185–205.

——. *The Unitarian Movement in the Religious Life of England: Its Contributions to Thought and Learning, 1700–1900.* London: George Allen and Unwin, 1934.

——. "Warrington Academy." *Chetham Society: Remains* 107 (n.s., 1943).

——. *Essays and Addresses.* Manchester: Manchester University Press, 1950.

——. *Sir Isaac Newton: Theological Manuscripts.* Liverpool: Liverpool University Press, 1950.

——. *Socinianism in Seventeenth-Century England.* Oxford: Oxford University Press, 1951.

——. "Mary Priestley: A Woman of Character." In *Motion Toward Perfection: The Achievement of Joseph Priestley,* ed. A. Truman Schwartz and John G. McEvoy. Boston: Skinner House Books, 1990.

McLachlan, John. "Joseph Priestley and the Study of History." *Transactions of the Unitarian Historical Society* 19 (1987–90): 252–63.

Mendelsohn, Everett. *Heat and Life.* Cambridge: Harvard University Press, 1964.

Metzger, Bruce M. *The Text of the New Testament: Its Transmission, Corruptions, and Restoration.* New York: Oxford University Press, 1968.

Micklewright, F. H. Amphlett. "Some Prolegomena to the History of Protestant Dissent in England." *Notes and Queries* 187 (9 Sept. 1944): 117.

Miles, Wyndham, "Early American Chemical Societies." *Chymia* 3 (1950): 95–113.

——. "Benjamin Rush, Chemist." *Chymia* 4 (1953): 37–77.

Miller, Samuel. *A Brief Retrospect of the Eighteenth Century.* 1805. Reprint, London: J. Johnson, 1805.

Milner, Mary. *The Life of Isaac Milner, D.D. F.R.S.* London, John W. Parker; Cambridge: J. and J. J. Deighton, 1843.

Moffatt, James. *The Approach to the New Testament.* London: Hodder and Stoughton, 1921.

Moillet, A. *A Sketch of the Life of James Keir.* London: for private circulation, by Robert Taylor, [1868?].

Money, John. *Experience and Identity: Birmingham and the West Midlands, 1760–1800.* Montreal: McGill-Queens's University Press, 1977.

———. "Joseph Priestley in Cultural Context: Philosophic Spectacle, Popular Belief, and Popular Politics in Eighteenth-Century Birmingham." *Enlightenment and Dissent* 7 (1988): 57–81 (Part 1), and 8 (1989): 68–89 (Part 2).

The Monist. Articles on Monism by Paul Carus, 1890–1919, on determinism, 1892–93, 1917; Reid issues—61 (1978): 165—344; 70 (1987): 382–526.

Monthly Repository. Article critical of Samuel Badcock, 6 (1811): 202; republication of Badcock's lauditory poem on Priestley, 1819; "R. W.," "Clerical Fees from Dissenters," "T. C. H.," on Priestley's hasty translations of Greek and Latin, 15 (1820): 138–39, 335–36; Edward Burn's apology, 20 (1825); editorial notes: on secret clause in renewal of charter for Birmingham's King Edward Free Grammar School, "Sir Isaac Newton an Antitrinitarian," 5 (n.s., 1831): 68–72, 153–59.

Monthly Review. Reviews of Priestley's works—51 (1774): 136ff.; 52 (1775): 289–96; 53 (1776): 380–90; 54 (1776): 41–47, 107–14, 411–12, 425–35; 58 (1778): 60–68, 89–95, 347–53, 354–62; 64 (1781): 81–90, 161–73; 68 (1783): 132–36, 462–63, 515–26; 69 (1783): 89–105, 215–48; 78 (1788): 266, 269–70, 383–87, 457–59; 80 (1789): 1–8; 16 (n.s., 1795): 271–76 (by John Leslie).

Morgan, E. S. *Gentle Puritan: A Life of Ezra Stiles, 1727–1795.* New Haven: Yale University Press, 1962.

Muirhead, John H. *The Platonic Tradition in Anglo-Saxon Philosophy: Studies in the History of Idealism in England and America.* New York: Macmillan, 1931.

Munck, J. "Jewish Christianity in Post-Apostolic Times." *New Testament Studies* 6 (1960): 103–16.

Nangle, Benjamin Christie. *The Monthly Review, First Series 1749–1789: Indexes of Contributors and Articles.* Oxford: Clarendon Press, 1934.

Nash, Henry S. *History of the Higher Criticism of the New Testament.* New York: Macmillan, 1900.

Neill, Stephen. *The Interpretation of the New Testament, 1861–1961.* London: Oxford University Press, 1964.

Newell, Lymon C. "Peter Porcupine's Persecution of Priestley." *Journal of Chemical Education* 10 (1933): 151–59.

Nichols, John. *Illustrations of the Literary History of the Eighteenth Century.* London, 1817–18.

Nisbet, H. B. *Herder and the Philosophy and History of Science.* Cambridge: Modern Humanities Research Association, 1970.

Norris, John. *Shelburne and Reform.* London: Macmillan, 1963.

[Norton, Andrews]. "Anon." "An Account of the Controversy between Dr. Priestley and Dr. Horsley, the Monthly Reviewer, and Others." *The General Repository and Review* 1 (1812): 26–58, 229–77; 2 (1812): 7–38, 257–88; 3 (1813): 142, 250–99. Author identified as Norton by Earl Morse Wilbur in *A History of Unitarianism, in Transylvania, England, and America.* Cambridge: Harvard University Press, 1952.

Odling, William. "Revived Theory of Phlogiston." *Popular Science Monthly* 9 (1870): 560–69.

Oesper, Ralph E. "Priestley, Lavoisier, and Trudaine de Montigny." *Journal of Chemical Education* 13 (1936): 403–12.

O'Higgins, James. *Anthony Collins: The Man and His Works.* The Hague: Martinus Nijhoff, 1970.

Park, Mary Cathryne. "Joseph Priestley and the Problem of Pantisocracy." *Proceedings of the Delaware County Institute of Science* 11 (1947): 1–60.

Partington, James R. *A History of Chemistry.* Vol. 3. London: Macmillan, 1962.

Partington, James R., and Douglas McKie. "Historical Studies on the Phlogiston Theory. I. The Levity of Phlogiston." *Annals of Science* 2 (1937): 361–404; "II. The Negative Weight of Phlogiston." *Annals of Science* 3 (1938): 1–58; "III. Light and Heat in Combustion." *Annals of Science* 4 (1938): 337–71; "IV. Last Phases of the Theory." *Annals of Science* 5 (1939): 113–49.

Peacock, George. *Thomas Young.* London: John Murray, 1855.

Peardon, Thomas P. *Transition in English Historical Writing, 1760–1830.* New York: Columbia University Press, 1933.

Pearl, Leon. "Hume's Criticism of the Argument from Design." *The Monist* 54 (1970): 270–84.

Peaston, A. E. "The Revision of the Prayer Book by Dr. Samuel Clarke," and "Theophilus Lindsey's Prayer Book Revision compared with Clarke's." *Transactions of the Unitarian Historical Society* 12 (1959–62): 27–38.

Perrin, Carleton. "Early Opposition to the Phlogiston Theory: Two Anonymous Attacks." *British Journal for the History of Science* 5 (1970): 128–44.

Petty, Edmund George, Lord Fitzmaurice. *Life of William, Earl of Shelburne, afterwards first Marquess of Lansdowne: with Extracts from his Papers and Correspondence.* London: Macmillan, 1875–76.

Pevsner, Nikolaus. *The Buildings of England: Wiltshire.* Hammondsworth: Penguin Books, 1963.

Pfleiderer, Otto, "The Christ of Primitive Christian Faith in the Light of Religio-Historical Criticism." *The Monist* 14 (1904): 323–54, 672–710.

Philosophical Magazine 10 (3d ser., 1837): 357. "Editorial Note on Boscovich, Michell, and Priestley."

Piper, H. W. *The Active Universe: Pantheism and the Concept of Imagination in English Romantic Poets.* London: Athlone Press, 1962.

Popkin, Richard H. "Joseph Priestley's Criticism of David Hume's Philosophy." *Journal of the History of Philosophy* 15 (1977): 437–47.

Price, James L. *Interpreting the New Testament.* New York: Holt, Rinehart and Winston, 1961.

The Priestley Memorial at Birmingham, August 1874. Birmingham: Longman, Green, Reader, and Dyer, 1875.

Ramsey, Sir William. *Life and Letters of Joseph Black, M.D.* London: Constable and Co., 1918.

Reardon, Bernard M. G. *From Coleridge to Gore: A Century of Religious Thought in Britain.* London: Longman Group Ltd., 1971.

Reitzel William. "William Cobbett and Philadelphia Journalism: 1794–1800." *Pennsylvania Magazine of History and Biography* 5 (1935): 223–44.

Richards, Graham. *Mental Machinery: The Origins and Consequences of Psychological Ideas. Part 1: 1600–1850.* Baltimore: Johns Hopkins University Press, 1992.

Richardson, R. D. "The Doctrine of the Trinity: Its Development, Difficulties, and Value." *Harvard Theological Review* 36 (1943): 109–34.

Richardson, William N. "The Current Interpretation of the Joseph Priestley House." In *Joseph Priestley in America, 1794–1804,* ed. Peter M. Lukehart, 20–28. Exh. Cat. for the bicentennial of Priestley's arrival in the United States. Carlisle, Pa.: Trout Gallery, Dickinson College, 1994.

———. "Joseph Priestley's American Home." *Proceedings and Addresses of the Northumberland County Historical Society* 32 (1994): 60–70.

Richey, Russell. "Theophilus Lindsey: Some Manuscript Sermons and an Intellectual Vignette." *Transactions of the Unitarian Historical Society* (London) 14 (1967–70): 134–46.

Riddle, Donald Wayne. "Factors in the Development of Modern Biblical Study." *Church History* 23 (1933): 211–26.

Robbins, Caroline, "Honest Heretic: Joseph Priestley in America, 1794–1804." *Proceedings of the American Philosophical Society* 11 (1962): 60–76.

Robinson, Daniel N. *The Enlightened Machine: An Analytical Introduction to Neuropsychology.* 1973. Reprint, New York: Columbia University Press, 1980.

Robinson, Eric. "The English 'Philosophes' and the French Revolution." *History Today* (Feb. 1956): 116–21.

———. "An English Jacobin: James Watt, Junior, 1769–1848." *Cambridge Historical Journal* 3 (1960): 349–55.

———. "New Light on the Priestley Riots." *Historical Journal* 3 (1960): 73–75.

———. "Priestley's Library of Scientific Books: A New List." *Studies in History and Philosophy of Science* 1 (1970): 145–60.

Rodgers, Betsy. *Georgian Chronicle: Mrs. Barbauld and Her Family.* London: Methuen & Co., 1958.

Roscoe, Henry E., and Arthur Harden. *A New View of the Origin of Dalton's Atomic Theory.* 1896. Reprint, New York: Johnson Reprint Corp., 1970.

Rose, R. B. "The Priestley Riots of 1791." *Past and Present* 18 (1960): 68–88.

Rosen, George. "Noah Webster: Historical Epidemiologist." *Journal of the History of Medicine and Allied Sciences* 20 (1965): 97–114.

Rousseau, Andre Michel. "L'Angleterres et Voltaire III." *Studies on Voltaire and the Eighteenth Century* 147 (1976): 844–46.

Rowley, H. H., ed. *A Companion to the Bible.* 2d ed. Edinburgh: T. & T. Clark, 1963.

Royle, Edward. *Victorian Infidels: The Origins of the British Secularist Movement, 1792–1866.* Manchester: Manchester University Press, 1974.

Ruckstuhl, Annette. "Thomas Graham's Study of the Diffusion of Gases." *Journal of Chemical Education* 28 (1951): 594–96.

Rudé, George. *Paris and London in the Eighteenth Century.* New York: Viking Press, 1971.

——. *Protest and Punishment: The Story of the Social and Political Protesters Transported to Australia, 1788–1868.* Oxford: Clarendon Press, 1978.

Rupp, George. "The Idealism of Jonathan Edwards." *Harvard Theological Review* 62 (1969): 209–26.

Ruston, Alan. "Joseph Priestley at the Gravel Pit Chapel, Hackney: The Collier MS." *Enlightenment and Dissent* 2 (1983): 111–19.

——. "Joseph Priestley and the Gentleman's Magazine." *Transactions of the Unitarian Historical Society* 18 (1983–86): 9–13.

Ryle, Gilbert. *Concept of Mind.* New York: Barnes & Noble Books, 1949.

Salvatorelli, Luigi. "From Locke to Reitzenstein: The Historical Investigation of the Origins of Christianity." *Harvard Theological Review* 22 (1929): 263–363.

Schaffer, Simon. "Priestley's Questions: An Historiographic Survey." *History of Science* 22 (1984): 151–83.

[Schimmelpennick, Mary Anne (née Galton)]. *Life of Mary Anne Schimmelpennick.* Ed. Christiana C. Hankin. London: Longman, Green, Longmans, and Roberts, 1853.

Schofield, Robert E. "Joseph Priestley's American Education." In *Early Dickinsoniana: The Boyd Lee Spahr Lectures in Americana, 1957–1961.* Carlisle, Pa.: Library of Dickinson College, 1961.

——. *The Lunar Society of Birmingham: A Social History of Provincial Science and Industry in Eighteenth-Century England.* Oxford: Clarendon Press, 1963.

——. "Still More on the Water Controversy." *Chymia* 9 (1964): 71–76.

——. *Mechanism and Materialism: British Natural Philosophy in an Age of Reason.* Princeton: Princeton University Press, 1970.

——. "The Counter-Reformation in Eighteenth-Century Science—Last Phase." In *Perspectives in the History of Science and Technology,* ed. Duane H. D. Roller, 39–53. Norman: University of Oklahoma Press, 1971.

——. "Joseph Priestley on Sensation and Perception." In *Studies in Perception: Interrelations in the History of Philosophy and Science,* ed. Peter K. Machamer and Robert G. Turnbull, 336–54. Columbus: Ohio State University Press, 1978.

——. "Joseph Priestley, Eighteenth-century British Neoplatonism, and S. T. Coleridge." In *Transformation and Tradition in the Sciences: Essays in Honor of I. Bernard Cohen,* ed. Everett Mendelsohn. Cambridge: Cambridge University Press, 1984.

——. *The Enlightenment of Joseph Priestley: A Study of His Life and Work from 1733 to 1773.* University Park: Pennsylvania State University Press, 1997.

Scholten, Jan Hendrik. "Modern Materialism and Its Causes." In *The Progress of Religious Thought as Illustrated in the Protestant Church of France, being Essays & Reviews, Bearing on the Chief Religious Questions of the Day,* trans. and ed. John Relly Beard. London: Simkin, Marshall & Co.; Boston: Walker, Wise & Co., 1861.

Schwartz, A. Truman, and John G. McEvoy, eds. *Motion Toward Perfection: The Achievement of Joseph Priestley.* Boston: Skinner House Books, 1990.

Scott, Ernest Findlay. *The Literature of the New Testament.* New York: Columbia University Press, 1932.

Seed, John. "'A set of men powerful enough in many things': Rational Dissent and Political Opposition in England, 1770–1790." In *Enlightenment and Religion: Rational Dissent in Eighteenth-century Britain,* ed. Knud Haakonssen, 140–68. Cambridge: Cambridge University Press, 1996.

Sellers, Ian. "Unitarians and Social Change. Part I. Varieties of Radicalism 1795–1815." *Hibbert Journal* (Oct. 1962).

Shaffer, E. S. *"Kubla Khan" and the Fall of Jerusalem: The Mythological School in Biblical Criticism and Secular Literature, 1770–1880.* Cambridge: Cambridge University Press, 1975.

Sheps, Arthur. "Public Perception of Joseph Priestley, the Birmingham Dissenters, and the Church-and-King Riots of 1791." *Eighteenth Century* 13 (1989): 46–64.

Short, H. L. "From Watts to Martineau." *Transactions of the Unitarian Historical Society* 10 (1951–54).

Short, L. Baker, "Thomas Fyshe Palmer: From Eton to Botany Bay." *Transactions of the Unitarian Historical Society* 13 (1963–66): 37–68.

———. "William Christie and the First Unitarian Church in Scotland." *Transactions of the Unitarian Historical Society* 14 (1967–70): 10–27, 78–92.

Siegfried, Robert. "Lavoisier's Table of Simple Substances: Its Origin and Interpretation." *Ambix* 29 (1982): 29–48.

Siegfried, Robert, and Betty Jo Dobbs. "Composition: A Neglected Aspect of the Chemical Revolution." *Annals of Science* 24 (1968): 275–93.

Silliman, Vincent Brown. "An Early Unitarian Society in Portland, Maine." *Transactions of the Unitarian Historical Society* (U.S.) 2 (1931): 31–34.

Smeaton, W. A. "Is Water Converted into Air? Guyton de Morveau Acts as Arbiter Between Priestley and Kirwan." *Ambix* 1 (1968): 75–83.

Smith, Edgar Fahs. *Priestley in America, 1794–1804.* Philadelphia: P. Blakiston's Son & Co., 1920.

———. "Early Science in Philadelphia." *Pennsylvania Magazine of History and Biography* 51 (1927): 15–26.

Smith, James Morton. *Freedom's Fetters: The Alien and Sedition Laws and American Civil Liberties.* Ithaca: Cornell University Press, 1966.

Smith, J. W. Ashley. *The Birth of Modern Education: The Contribution of the Dissenting Academies, 1660–1800.* London: Independent Press, Ltd., 1954.

Snow, Lewis Franklin. *The College Curriculum in the United States.* New York: Columbia University, Teachers College, 1907.

Stephen, Leslie. *History of English Thought in the Eighteenth Century.* 2 vols. London: Smith, Elder & Co., 1876.

Stephens, John. "Samuel Horsley and Joseph Priestley's *Disquisitions Relating to Matter and Spirit.*" *Enlightenment and Dissent* 3 (1984): 103–14.

Stephenson, H. W. "Hackney College and William Hazlitt." *Transactions of the Unitarian Historical Society* 3 (1923–26): 185–205, and 4 (1927–30): 219–47, 376–411.

Streeter, Burnett Hillman. *The Primitive Church: Studied with Special Reference to the Origins of the Christian Ministry.* London: Macmillan, 1929.

Stromberg, R. N. "History in the Eighteenth Century." *Journal of the History of Ideas* 12 (1951): 295–304.

Stuhlmacher, Peter. *Historical Criticism and Theological Interpretation of Scripture: Toward a Hermeneutics of Consent.* Trans. and with an introduction by Roy A. Harrisville. Philadelphia: Fortress Press, 1977.

Tapper, Alan. "The Beginnings of Priestley's Materialism." *Enlightenment and Dissent* 1 (1982): 73–81.

Teich, Mikuláš. "Circulation, Transformation, Conservation of Matter, and the Balancing of the Biological World in the Eighteenth Century." *Ambix* 29 (1982).

Thomas, D. O. "Francis Maseres, Richard Price, and the Industrious Poor." *Enlightenment and Dissent* 4 (1985): 65–82.

Thompson, James Westfall, with Bernard J. Holm. *A History of Historical Writing.* Vol. 2, *The Eighteenth and Nineteenth Centuries.* New York: Macmillan 1942.

Thorpe, T. E. *Joseph Priestley.* London: J. M. Dent; New York: E. P. Dutton, 1906.

Toulmin, Joshua. *Memoirs of the Revd. Samuel Bourn, for many years, one of the Pastors of the United Congregations of the New Meeting in Birmingham, and of the Meeting in Coseley . . .* Birmingham: J. Johnson, 1808.

Toulmin, Priestley, III. "The Descendents of Joseph Priestley, LL.D., F.R.S." *Proceedings of the Northumberland County Historical Society* 32 (Part 2, 1994): 1–105.

Toulmin, S. E. "Crucial Experiments: Priestley and Lavoisier." *Journal of the History of Ideas* 18 (1957): 205–20.

Travers, Morris W. *The Experimental Study of Gases.* London: Macmillan, 1901.

Turnbull, Paul. "Gibbon's Exchange with Joseph Priestley." *British Journal for Eighteenth-Century Studies* 14 (1991): 139–58.

Van Rensselaer, Mrs. Schuyler. *Henry Hobson Richardson and His Works.* Boston: Houghton, Mifflin, 1888.

Verbruggen, F. "How to Explain Priestley's Defense of Phlogiston." *Janus* 59 (1972): 47–69.

Vielhauer, Philipp, and Georg Strecker. "IV Jewish-Christian Gospels." In *New Testament Apocrypha.* Vol. 1, *Gospels and Related Writings,* ed. Wilhelm Schneemelcher, 134–78. London: James Clarke & Co.; Westminster: John Knox Press, 1991.

[Wansey, Henry]. "Henry Wansey and His American Journal, 1794." Ed. D. J. Jeremy. *Memoir of the American Philosophical Society* 82 (1970).

Ward, A. W. "Historical and Political Writers. II: Bolingbroke." In *Cambridge History of English Literature,* vol. 9, ed. A. W. Ward and A. R. Waller. Cambridge: Cambridge University Press, 1912.

Warren, Charles. *Jacobin and Junto, or, Early American Politics as Viewed in the Diary of Dr. Nathaniel Ames, 1758–1822.* Cambridge: Harvard University Press, 1931.

Watts, Michael R. *The Expansion of Evangelical Nonconformity.* Vol. 2 of *The Dissenters.* Oxford: Clarendon Press, 1995.

Webb, R. K. "Rational Piety." In *Enlightenment and Religion: Rational Dissent in Eighteenth-century Britain, ed.* Knud Haakonssen. Cambridge: Cambridge University Press, 1996.

Weisinger, Herbert. "The Middle Ages and Late Eighteenth-Century Historians." *Philological Quarterly* 27 (1948): 63–79.

Weiss, Johannes. *Earliest Christianity: A History of the Period A.D. 30–150.* 2 vols. 1937; Gloucester, Mass.: Peter Smith, 1970.

Wellek, René. *Immanuel Kant in England, 1793–1838.* Princeton: Princeton University Press, 1931.

Wells, G. A. *Who Was Jesus: A Critique of the New Testament Record.* LaSalle, Ill.: Open Court, 1989.

Wells, George. "Stages of New Testament Criticism." *Journal of the History of Ideas* 30 (1969): 147–60.

Werkmeister, Lucyle. *The London Press, 1772–1792.* Lincoln: University of Nebraska Press, 1963.

Westfall, Richard S. *Never at Rest: A Biography of Isaac Newton.* Cambridge: Cambridge University Press, 1980.

Wheatley, Christopher J. "Polemical Aspects of Hume's Natural History of Religion." *Eighteenth-Century Studies* 19 (1986): 502–14.

Whitney, Lois. *Primitivism and the Idea of Progress.* Baltimore: Johns Hopkins University Press, 1934.

Wigmore-Beddoes, Dennis G. *Yesterday's Radicals: A Study of the Affinity Between Unitarianism and Broad Church Anglicanism in the Nineteenth Century.* Cambridge: James Clarke & Co. Ltd., 1971.

Wilbur, Earl Morse. *A History of Unitarianism, in Transylvania, England, and America.* Cambridge: Harvard University Press, 1952.

Williams, John. *Memoirs of the late Reverend Thomas Belsham, including A Brief Notice of his Published Works, and Copious Extracts from his Diary, together with Letters to and from his Friends and Correspondents.* London: for the author, 1833.

Wilson, A. N. *Paul: The Mind of the Apostle.* New York: W. W. Norton, 1976.

Winkler, Henry R. "The Pamphlet Campaign Against Political Reform in Great Britain, 1790–1795." *The Historian* 15 (1952): 23–40.

Wright, Conrad. "Edwards and the Arminians on the Freedom of the Will." *Harvard Theological Review* 35 (1942): 241–61.

———. *The Beginnings of Unitarianism in America.* Boston: Beacon Press, 1955.

Yalton, John W. *Thinking Matter: Materialism in Eighteenth-Century Britain.* Minneapolis: University of Minnesota Press, 1983.

Young, Robert M. "David Hartley." In *Dictionary of Scientific Biography,* ed. Charles Coulston Gillispie. New York: Charles Scribner's Sons, 1972.

Young, Thomas. *Course of Lectures on Natural Philosophy and the Mechanical Arts.* 2d ed. London: Taylor and Walton, 1845.

Zeitlin, Solomon. "The Duration of Jesus's Ministry." *Jewish Quarterly Review* 55 (1965): 181–200.

Zelazny, Roger. "Home Is the Hangman." In Roger Zelazny, *My Name Is Legion.* New York: Ballentine Books, 1976.

Index

Académie Royale des Sciences, 151
action-at-a distance, 68, 83
  affirmed in Newton's *Opticks*, 84
Adams, John, 236, 318, 333, 379, 381
  ambivalence toward Priestley, 335
  esteemed by Priestley, 337–38
Adams, John Quincy, 259
Adet, Pierre, 355, 357
Aepinus, Franz U. T., 68
agriculture, Priestley on, 370–71
Aikin, Arthur, 305, 305 n. 26
Aikin, John, Jr., 271, 355
Aikin, Anna Laetitia. *See* Barbauld, Anna
  Laetitia
air
  alkaline (ammonia), 94, 98, 103, 104, 117
  dephlogisticated (oxygen), 113, 188; early
    experiments on, 105, 157; "discovered,"
    106–7, 107 n. 27, 111–14; not acidic, 139,
    158, 181, 181 n. 20; revealed to the
    French, 105
  fixed (usually carbon dioxide), 186, 188
  fluor acid (silicon tetrafluoride), 116–17
  inflammables, 102, 103, 114, 115, 163,
    174–75, 176, 180, 186, 186 n. 33, 188,
    180, 190, 192, 307–8, 359, 363, 365–68
  nitrous (nitric oxide), 98, 104, 107, 112; test
    by (eudiomitry), 112, 137–39, 137 n. 31
  vegetable acid, disavowed, 111
  vitriolic (sulphur dioxide), 105, 106, 110,
    110 n. 35
airs (gases), 98
  adsorption of, 110, 110 n. 35
  diffusion of, 99, 158, 182
  sensible properties of, 102, 119
  specific constitution of, 179, 179 n. 18
Alexander, John, 68, 147

Alien and Sedition Acts, 334, 334 n. 42
  "particularly unwise," 338
alkalies, different, 117
American Chemical Society, 372
American colonies
  British on, 6 n. 7, 16, 18, 19
  independence of, 22
American Philosophical Society, 351, 352
  Priestley's membership, and its respect for
    him, 354
anti-phlogistonists
  errors of, 183, 192, 357, 358, 362, 363, 367
  ignore Priestley's arguments, 356
apparatus
  scientific, 11, 11 n. 20, 95, 96, 97, 97 n. 11,
    109–10; in U.S., 350; posthumously
    given to Dickinson College, 372
  various: air pump, Smeaton's, 114;
    bladders, 130 n. 13, 134; earthenware,
    154; ground-glass stoppers, 110; lutes,
    110, 134; pneumatic trough, 94, 94 n. 4,
    95, 158; pyrometer, 161
Aquinas, Thomas, 217, 218, 389
Arden, Richard, 121
Ashworth, Mr., of Manchester, 317–18
associationism, 3, 38, 38 n. 27, 49, 51, 53
  physiological analogue, 55
Athanasian Creed, 15, 15 n. 29
atonement, doctrine of, 252
attraction and repulsion
  spheres of, 55, 62, 63, 67, 68, 132, 140, 140
    n. 36, 166
  powers and principles of, 67, 69, 83–84,
    302, 307, 369–70
Augustine ("Austin"), St., 217, 218
  Priestley on, 262
Averroes, 219

Bacon, Francis, 396
Badcock, Rev. Samuel, 224 n. 17
  critical of Priestley, 224–25, 233
  early admiration, 73, 224, 224 n. 17
Bain, Alexander, 52
Bakewell, Robert, 371
balloons, 163, 163 n. 29
Banks, Sir Joseph, 275, 275 n. 30, 31, 300, 353
baptism, infant, 386
Barbauld, Anna Laetitia Aikin, 318–19, 321
Barclay, John, critical of materialism, 74
Barré, Isaac, 5
Barton, Benjamin Smith, 351, 352, 354, 355
  borrowed Priestley's copy of Pallas's
    comparative vocabularies, 351
Bayen, Pierre, 170
Beattie, James, 44, 46–47
Beccaria, Cesare, *Essay on Crime and
  Punishment,* 256
Beccaria, Giambatista, 122
Becket, Thomas à, 268, 268 n. 13
Beddoes, Thomas, 405
  factitious airs, medicinal uses of, 358
  Preventive Medical Institution, 404
Belcher, James, 321
Belsham, Thomas, 3 n. 2, 215–16, 230, 346,
  383
    arranges subscription for Priestley's
      works, 388
    criticisms of Bishop Horsley, 227, 227
      n. 25, 230–31
Belloc, Hilaire, 405
Bengel, Johann Albricht, 210
Bennet, Abraham, 164
Bentham, Jeremy, 123–24, 123 n. 6, 130
Bentley, Thomas, 4
Bentley, William, 374
Bergman, Torbern, 122
Berington, Joseph, 61
Berthollet, Claude Louis, 190
Bewley, William, 71, 115, 119, 159
Birmingham
  character of, 195–96
  1780 description of, 148
  commercial committee, 265, 265 n. 9
Birmingham Riots, 284–89
  affadavits on, 297
  destructions from, 284–85
  Establishment role in, 285, 288
  indemnities for, 297–99, 299 n. 9

  predictions of, 273, 284
  Priestley and, 213, 284–89, 295, 295 n. 6,
    296, 296 n. 7, 297, 298 n. 12, 299, 300,
    300 n. 7, 322
Birrell, Augustine, 246
Black, Joseph, xiii, 101, 115, 127, 166
  gravimetric techniques, 96
Blackburne, Archdeacon, 15
"Black Wadd." *See* substances, pyrolousite
Blagden, Charles, 173
Blasphemy, Act Against (1698), 264
Blyth, Samuel, 195–96
Boerhaave, Hermann, 101
Boethius, Consolation of Philosophy, 399
Bois-Reymond, Emil de, 57
Book of Common Prayer, revised, 27
Boscovich, Roger Joseph, 63, 132, 194
  atomism of, 71
  attacks materialism, 72–73
  continued interest in, 71, 73–74
  Whewell on, 71
Bostock, John, 305, 305 n. 26
Boullanger ("Boulanger"), Mr., 385
Boulton, Matthew, 104, 123, 150, 196
Bowood, Wiltshire, 4, 8
Bowyer, William, 209
Bradlaugh, Charles, 75
Bretland, Joseph, 3 n. 2, 247
Brewster, David, 73
Brocklesby, Richard, 124, 125, 126
Brooke, John, 285, 289
Brougham, Henry, Ld., xi
Bryant, Jacob, 86–87, 87 n. 13
Buchanan, Joseph, materialist, 74
Bull, Bishop George, 233
Burgess, James B., reports gossip from Paris,
  323
Burke, Edmund, 12, 19, 246
  conservatism, 278
  early friendship with Priestley, 279, 305,
    312
  reactions to, 278–79, 278 n. 37
  reflections on the French revolution, 278,
    278 n. 36
Burnes, Edward, 272, 272 n. 25, 273

Calder, Sir John, 108, 122
Calne, Wiltshire, 8
Calvin, John, 390
Calvinist heritage, 79, 79 n. 4

Canton, William, 163–64
Cappe, Newcome, 11
  defends Priestley's Greek translations, 229
carbon monoxide. *See* air, inflammables
Carles, Joseph, 285, 288
Carlisle, Anthony, 366
caste system, European nobility, example of, 385
Catholic Relief Act, 22, 267, 267 n. 12
cause and effect, 79, 368
  validity of, 41–42
Cavendish, Henry, xii, xiii, 12, 101, 113, 121
  composition of water, 172–73
  "Experiments on Air," 172
Chadwick, John W. 237
Channing, William Ellery. 236
Chatham, Lord, 6 n. 7, 16
Chathamites, 19
Chemical Revolution, 169–94. *See also* Lavoisier
  based on inferences, 368
  established, 191–92
  new nomenclature, 186, 191
  specifics of, 180–81, 181 n. 20
Christianity. *See also* corruptions of Christianity
  evidences of, 380–81
  incorruptible, 221
  primitive, 218, 260
  not popery, 376
  system of, 218–19
Christie, William, 215
chronology, biblical, 34–35, 34 n. 20, 35 n. 22
Chrysostom (John of Antioch), 262
church and state
  civil interference, invited, but futile, 228, 262, 389
  relations of, 219–20, 221, 223, 312
  unnatural, corrupting, and obstructive alliance, 246, 252, 260, 262
Church of England. *See* Established Church
Church, Roman
  "decline and fall of," 390
  papacy praised, 256
  Priestley criticizes, 389
Clark, John Ruskin, 237, 237 n. 44
Clark, Thomas, 286
Clarke, Samuel, 27, 70, 148
Cobbett, William ("Peter Porcupine"),
  attacks Priestley, 329, 329 n. 31, 335, 337

Cobden, Richard, 343
Colden, Cadwallader, 86
Coleridge, Samuel Taylor, 51, 52, 236, 319
Collins, Anthony, 70, 78, 247
compounds, chemical, 102
  nature of, 178, 178 n. 16
  variations with combinations, 104, 114, 115, 190
  variations with same constituents, 357, 362
Constable, William, 175
Constantine, Emperor, 260 261
Constitution of the United States, Priestley's praise of, 338, 343
consumption (illness), 114, 114 n. 38
convictions
  criminal, of innocents, a civil sacrifice, 256
  moral, must bear the consequences of, 311
Conybeare, F. C., 239
Cooke, Charles, 270
Cooper, Robert, 75
Cooper, Thomas, 74, 318, 333–34, 338
  candidacy to Royal Society rejected, 275
Copley Medal of the Royal Society, 5, 94
Council of Trent, 391
councils and synods, 262
corruptions of Christianity, various, 67, 68, 218, 219, 221
Crawford, Adair, 130, 169, 308
creation, continuous not equivocal, 395
Creed, John Martin, 239
Cressener, G., 6 n. 8
criticism, biblical
  eighteenth-century Dissenter criticism, 201–2
  principles of, 32, 32 n. 14
Cromwell, Thomas K., 75
Cruickshank, William, 357, 366–68
Crusades, "foolish and ruinous," 390
Cudworth, Ralph, 78
Curtis, Rev. Charles, 285, 298
Cuvier, Georges, xii

D'Alembert, Jean, 376
Dalton, John, xii, 135, 168
Darwin, Erasmus, 52, 150, 160, 369, 370
Daventry Academy, move to Northampton, 245
Davis, Rev. David, "jeu d'esprit," 73
Davy, Humphry, xii, 353, 363, 364, 366, 405
  Priestley's influence on, 189

Dawson, Benjamin, 15
Deane, Silas, 16 n. 31, 275
Deiman, J. R., 189
DeLuc, Jean André, 166
Descartes, Rene, 61
  his dualism, 48
design
  argument from, 64
  of nature unchanged since Moses, 369
determinism, 79
  scientific, 81
diffusion, gaseous, 136, 308, 359, 360, 360
    n. 31, 365
  through bladders or water, 177, 177 n. 14
  through earthenware, 166–68, 167 n. 42
Disney, John, 215
Dissenters, 12, 12 n. 33
  organizations in London, 12, 288
  united by Birmingham riots, 321
divine essence, 64
Dodddridge, Philip, 43, 68
Drummond, William, 73
dualism, 48
  not scriptural, 218, 397
Dundas, Henry, 289, 320
Dupuis, Charles François
  erudite, ingenious, lacking judgment, 385
  mocked, 376–77

Ebionites and Nazarenes, 232–35, 235
    n. 37
Eden, William (Lord Auckland), 324
Edict of Nantes, "a most egregious folly,"
    391
Edinburgh Encyclopedia, 73
Edwards, Jonathan, 78, 84 n. 10
Eason, Dr., 127
East India Company, 17
electricity, 121, 308
  animal, 308
  capacitance, 140
  electrometer, 164
  shock, 163–64, 164 n. 34
  studies of, 68
elements, 307, 365
  Lavoisier's list of, 178
  operational definition of, 192
emanations, 66
Emerson, Ralph Waldo, 236, 259
  transcendental theology of, 236

emigration to the United States (1794), 322
energy, 193–94
Enfield, William, 44
entities, vain multiplication of, 49
equivocal (spontaneous) generation, 369
Essex Street Chapel. *See* Lindsey, Theophilus
established church, 14
  abuses in, 221–22, 267, 275
  attacks Birmingham Sunday schools and
    library, 270, 268 n. 16, 270 nn. 19, 20
  attacks Priestley, 272–73
  defeats repeal, 273, 264–5
  enforced by civil power, 267
  inconsistencies in, 274–75
  prefers Roman Church to Dissent, 392
  Priestley's friends in, 212
  snobbery of, 264, 264 n. 4
establishments, 96, 185, 202, 249, 269, 269
    n. 28, 271
  been supported by Dissenters, 271
  futility of, 261, 271
Evanson, Edward, 310–11, 313–14
evidence, prejudice against new, 251
experiments, need interpretation, 133, 179

Faraday, Michael, xii
  read Priestley, 772
Feather's Tavern petition, 14, 14 n. 27, 25,
    228
Fenn, W. W., 237
Ferguson, James, 31
fish, 117
  need air in water, 157
fluids, imponderable, 178
Fontana, Felice, 118, 132
force hypotheses, 70
forms and qualities, Aristolelian substantial,
    70
Fothergill, Dr. John, 17
Fox, Charles James, 271
Franklin, Benjamin, 4, 5, 7, 17, 18, 93, 95, 95
    n. 8, 124, 130, 150, 188
Freeman, James, 374, 378
  on bigotry in the U.S., 327
French Revolution, 255 n. 29
  initial approval in England, 277
  sign of Millenarian restoration, 277
  used against reform, 276–77
Frend, William, 215, 320
Fromond, Mr., 5

Galton, Samuel, Jr., 151, 163, 352, 353, 361
Galvani, Luigi, 308
Garbett, Samuel, 20, 148, 287
Garrick, David, 116
gases. *See* airs
Gassicourt, Cadet de, 170
Gay, Rev. John, 52
Gentleman's Magazine, 297, 303
George III, King, 21, 320
  Royal Proclamations: August 1775, 18, 18
    n. 34; May 1792, 321
George, Prince of Wales, 185
Gerrald, Joseph, 321
Gibbon, Edward, 207, 221–22, 221 n. 13, 250
  challenged, 252
Gibelin, Jacques, 108, 122, 130
Gillray, James, 1790s in pay of Pitt
    administration, 282
Girtanner, Christoph, 369
Gnostics, 67, 69, 261
  opposed in New Testament, 398
God, evidences of
  from design, 38– 39
  from nature, 67–68
  from science, 41
Godwin, William, 293–94
  defends Priestley's Corruptions of
    Christianity, 229
Gordon Riots, 267, 296
Grafton, Duke of, on conciliation of
    American colonies, 19
Graham, Jenny, 338, 343
Graham, Thomas, xii, 132, 132 n. 18, 168
Graham, William, 67
gravimetrics, 132, 135
  of calces, 105
  Priestley's early indifference to, 133
  subsequent uses of, 359
gravity, 83
"Green Matter." *See* photosynthesis
Griesbach, Johann Jacob, 210
Grotius, Hugo, 210

Hackney (suburb of London), Gravel-Pit
    Meeting of, 293, 309
  influence of Priestley on, 305, 305 n. 26
  Literary and Philosophical Society, 306
  New College, 216, 246, 293
  students at, 305
Hales, Stephen, 132, 170, 186

  his *Vegetable Staticks,* 69
  influence on Priestley's science, 95, 95 n. 8,
    96
Halhed, Nathaniel Brassey, 207
Hamilton, William Rowan, 71
Hampden, R. D., 238
Hanover, Dissenters loyal to, 274
Hardinge, Georg, 298, 298 n. 10
Hare, Robert, 351, 404
Harrington, Robert, 303–4, 303 n. 22
Hartley, David, 43, 48–49, 68, 364
  on evaluating evidence, 254
  Observations on Man, 51, 53
Harvard College, 373
Hawkes, William, 195
Hazlitt, William, 373
heat, 308
  animal, 130, 308
  chemical reaction, 193
  conductivity in gases, 159, 159 n. 22
  intensity of, 114
  latent and sensible, 158
Helmholtz, Herman von, 57
Henderson, John, 73
Henry VIII, King, "absurdity of lay
    leadership of church," 390
Henry, Thomas, 105, 123
Herschel, William, 71
hermeticism, 67
Higgins, Bryan, 124, 125, 126, 128
Hill, Thomas Wright, 245, 286
  fiancé on Birmingham riots, 286
  got start by teaching at New Meeting
    Sunday School, 245
historiography, 389
Hobbes, Thomas, 70, 78
Holbach, Baron d', 37, 39
Horne, Thomas Hartwell, 238
Horsley, Samuel, 86, 88–89
  anti-Newtonian, 89, 89 n. 18
  influence on Monboddo, 88–89
  criticisms of: attack on Origen, 231;
    fictitious church at Aelia, 230, 232, 261;
    mistranslations, 231–32; poor
    chronologies, 231, 232; Priestley's
    criticisms of: choice of authorities, 233;
    edition of Newton, 230, 230 n. 31;
    grammar, 229; logic, 230; misrepre-
    sentations and lies, 275
Howard, John, 256

human nature, same in all ages, 395
Hume, David, 37, 47, 51, 78
    on *Natural Religion,* 40
Humphreys, George, 288, 298
Hurd, Bishop Richard, 222
Hutcheson, ("Hutchinson") Francis, 44, 47
Hutton, William, 148
hypotheses, order facts, 99

immaterialism, 64–65
imponderables
    light, 308
    light, heat, and phlogiston, 357
    pass through glass, 357, 362
indeterminism, Darwinian, relativity,
    quantum physics, thermodynamics, 82
Ingenhousz, Jan, 139, 154–56, 156 nn. 17, 18,
    363, 369
    belief in equivocal generation, 188
    mistakes of, 157
Institute Royale de France, xii
intellectuals, conceit of, 315

Jacobite clergy, 274
Jefferson, Thomas, 236, 259
    praises Priestley, 339
    Priestley praises, 343, 389
Jeffrey, Francis, xi, 3, 3 n. 1
Jervis, Thomas, 5, 10–11, 73
Jews, 251–60
    belief in future state, 386
    excellence of, 380
    favored of God, 260
Johnson, Joseph, 51, 247, 293, 317, 321
Johnson, Robert Augustus, 151, 164
Jones, Sir William, 207, 384
Joyce, Jeremiah, 321
Judaic religion, evidences of, 380–81

Kant, Immanuel, 47, 81–82
Keir, James, 140, 150, 162, 284
Kames, Lord, 78
Kelvin, William Thompson, Lord, 71
Kenrick, William, 86–87
kinetic theory of gases. *See* diffusion
Kippis, Andrew, 246
Kirwan, Richard, 156, 172, 180, 353
Knight, Richard, 305, 305 n. 26
knowledge, as power, 396
Knox, William, 6 n. 8

Lamb, Charles, 51
land speculation, Pennsylvania, 329–30
Landriani, Marsiglio, 109, 118, 122
Langlès, Louis-Mattiew, 384
Lansdowne, Marquess of. *See* Shelburne,
    Lord
Laplace, Pierre Simon, 81, 130, 173
Lardner, Nathaniel, 68, 217
    Letter on the Logos, 68
Latrobe, Benjamin, 373, 376 n. 9
Lavoisier, Antoine Laurent, xiii, 105, 111,
    115, 118, 122, 123, 162, 170, 171, 301
    character of, 169–70
    false claims, 133, 133 n. 20, 363–64
    first responses to, 166
    mistakes of, 134
    new chemistry of, 169, 170, 170 n. 3, 178,
        180
    operational definition of element, 130, 131,
        134, 135, 169–70, 170 n. 2, 178
    sustained attack on phlogiston, 180
laws of nature
    various, 88
    general principles, 109
    comprehensive, 54
Lee, John, 7, 18
LeRoy, C., 105
Leslie, John, 159, 304 n. 24, 305, 307, 308
Lichtenberg, Georg Christoph, 56
lightning rods, 121
Lindsey, Theophilus, 4, 7, 15, 18, 26, 27,
    28–29, 215, 346, 351, 392
    defends Priestley's competence in religion,
        229
    opens chapel in Essex Street, 25, 25 n. 5
    supported by Priestley, 27–28, 28 n. 8
Linn, John Blair, 387, 387 n. 25
Lister, Mr. Ambassador, 381
Livingstone, Robert R., 339
    new paper-making process, 371, 371
        n. 45
    writes about steam engines, 371
Locke, John, 43, 51, 67–68, 78
Lowndes, Marie Belloc, 405
Ludewig, German translator, 109
Luther, Martin, "raised up by divine
    providence," 390
Lunar Society of Birmingham, Priestley's
    early contacts with, 150
    becomes member, 151, 160

guests and correspondents, 153, 153 n. 13, 265
is useful to, 160–63, 164

Maclean, John, 355, 356, 356 n. 27
Macquer, Pierre J., 101, 127
Madan, Rev. Spencer, 274–75, 274 n. 27
Madison, Bishop James, 259
Magellan (Magelhaens), John Hycinth, 7, 122, 127
magnetism, animal, 164
Mann, Nicholas, 33
Marcellinus, 262
Marshall, Wallace, 57
Martineau, Harriet, 237 n. 42
Martineau, James, 237
Marum, Martinus van, 165, 177, 189
Mascoti, P., 122
Maseres, Francis, 266, 266 n. 11
Massotti, Ottaviano F., 71
materialism, 39–40, 55–56, 67
   atheistic consequences of, 72
   criticisms and defences of, 74–76, 76 n. 21
   early, 70, 70 n. 8
   dismissed, 76
   system of, 65
matter, 62–63, 68–69, 237, 176
   Boscovichean, 71
   changes in properties of, 306
   functional definition, 67, 83
   Jonathan Edwards on, 84 n. 10
   hylozoic, 87
   spiritualized, 71, 84, 87
   systems of, 63–64, 85
   theories of, 70, 194
Maxwell, James Clerk, 71
Merivale, Samuel, 44
Michaelis, Johann David, 31, 210
Michell, John, 63, 69, 114, 123, 132, 194
Mill, James, and John Stuart, 52, 81
millenarianism, 210, 314, 383
Milner, Isaac, 183
miracles, 249, 250, 369, 382, 394
   Christianity spread by, 260
   evidences of, 315
miraculous conception, 206, 206 n. 24
Mitchill, Samuel Latham, 352, 360–61
Moffatt, James, 239
Monboddo, James Burnett, Lord, 88–89

monism, 49, 56, 65, 67, 84–85, 226
   chemical, 100
   Hebrew roots, 210
   Leibnizean, 70
   mechanistic, 70
   Scholten's, 75
   in theology and science, 193, 218, 226–27, 250
Montesquieu, 256
Montigny, Trudaine de, 7, 105, 122
Moravians, reaction to Priestley, 373
More, Henry, 68
Morellet, Abbé, 5 n. 6, 20
Morgan, William, 353
Muir, Thomas, 321, 321 n. 13

nationalism, 391
natural religion, incomplete without revelation, 250
nature
   constitution of, 116
   simplicity of, 49, 54
   system of, 156
Nazarenes. See Ebionites
necessity, doctrine of, 77, 78
   defense of, 78
   optimism of, 80
neo-Platonists, Cambridge, 78
Neptunist (geological), 163
Neuman, Caspar, 101
New College, Hackney. See Hackney
New Meeting, Birmingham, 147, 195
   damaged in early riots (1714–15), 263
   destroyed in 1791 riots, 284–85
   grant from King's purse, 320
   governance, 196
   Sunday School, 243–45, 243 n. 6
   Sunday Society and "Cast-iron Philosophers," 245
Newcome, William (Bishop of Waterford), 36–37, 36 n. 23, 37 n. 24
Newton, Sir Isaac, 132, 308
   chronology, 254, 254 n. 28
   directions for research, 136
   forces, 67–68, 83
   Opticks, 54
   optical Queries, 98
   Principia, 54
   "Rules of Reasoning," 67
   studies in theology, 381, 394, 397

New York Medical Repository, 355–56
Nicholson, William, 121, 366
Nooth, Dr. John M., 118
Norris, John, 78
North, ministry of, 18
Northumberland, Pennsylvania, 345–47,
    375
    college in, 330–31, 331 n. 35, 339–40, 340
    n. 50
    Unitarians in, 374
Norton, Andrews, on Horsley-Priestley
    controversy, 231 n. 33, 232–33
nutrition, plant and animal, 156–57

Old Meeting, Birmingham, 148
Oliver, Andrew, 122
organic chemistry, 115
Oriental systems, 67
    "Indian philosophy," 68
Origen, 261, 261 n. 41
Oswald, James, 44, 46
Oxnard, Thomas, 374
oxygen. See air, dephlogisticated

Paine, Thomas, 294, 305
    Age of Reason attacked, 377–78
Palmer, John, 86, 89, 148
Palmer, Thomas Fyshe, 321, 323
pantheism, 249
Parker, W., and Sons, glassmakers, 97
Pennsylvania, University of, chemical
    professorship at, 351
Percival, Thomas, 119
persecution
    by Christians, 261–62
    by pagans, 260
Petty, William. See Shelbourne, Lord
Philadelphia, Chemical Society of, 351
phlogiston, 99–100, 191
    defended, 102, 103
    in respiration, 129–30
    surviving supporters of, 361
    the unknown cause of known effects,
    99–101
    varying characteristics of, 110
photosynthesis, 116, 139, 154–55, 363
physiopsychologists, 56
Pickering, Timothy, 334, 335, 335 n. 44
Pitt Administration
    block inquiry into Birmingham riots, 289

control of press, 282
    stirs fears of Jacobins, 282, 282 n. 45, 283
Pitt, William (the Younger), 271, 275,
    276–77, 282–83, 320–21, 324
plagiarism, charges of, 304
Platonic theology, 233–34, 261
pluralism, 70
Plutonist (geological), 163
politics
    Dissenter interest in, 296
    new alignments in, 265
    war with France, 312
    "white terror" campaign against dissent and
    reform, 319–23
postivism, scientific, 42
posterity, faith in, 90; judgment of, 391
pre-existence, 60, 62, 66–67, 217
prejudice, force of, 48
prescience, God's, 80, 86
Price, Richard, 5, 7, 13, 20, 54, 78, 106, 199–
    200, 200 n. 14, 216, 246–47, 277, 311
    on Newtonianism and matter, 82–86
    praise of Priestley, 371
Priestley, Joseph
    at Birmingham (1780–91): early contacts
    with, 147–48; home (Fairhill), 142, 148,
    286; move to (a happy event), 142–47;
    New Meeting, 147, 195, 197, 242–43,
    309; library, 243; Lunar Society, 150,
    151. See also Birmingham Riots,
    Priestley and
    at Bowood/Calne (1773–80): house at
    Calne, 8, 8 n. 13; librarian-companion,
    10; occasional preaching at, 25, 25 n. 2;
    and Shelburne (Lansdowne) requests
    return, 141–43, 147, 265; teaching maths
    and science to Shelburne sons, 10–12;
    visits from friends, 4, 9
    at Clapton/Hackney (1791–94): decision
    to leave England, 314, 316, 319 n. 7, 324;
    house in, 293; called to Gravel-Pit Meet-
    ing, 309, lectures at New College, 304–5;
    re-establishes laboratory, 300
    family: Harry (son), 317, 348, 406; Joseph
    Jr. (Jos, son) and children, 245, 317, 318,
    404–405; Joshua, Martha Crouch, and
    Timothy (brothers and sister), 403;
    Mary (wife) (see Priestley, Mary); Sarah
    (Sally, daughter, Mrs. William Finch)
    and children, 284, 316, 403–4; William

(son) and children (*see* Priestley, William)

finances, 346, 349–50; funds, 299, 299 n. 14, 349 n. 11; salary and pension from Shelburne, 5; subscription for researches, 151, 151 n. 8, 300, 353

on France: visits and dislikes (1774), 6; correspondents in, 3 n. 2; supports French revolution (1791), 246; invited, and declined, to settle there, 296, 318; named citizen and delegate to National Convention, 318, 318 n. 3; reacts to excesses of (1798, 1799), 301, 335, 337; considers visit to settle affairs (1797), 333

memberships: American Philosophical Society, 152; Academie Royale des Sciences, 151; Club of Honest Whigs, 18; list of seven other scientific societies, 151–52; Royal Society of London (1766), 122; Society for Promoting Knowledge of Scripture, 202

politics: denies concerns with, 23–24, 265; activities in, 329, 331–32, freedom of speech, 255, innocents sacrifice for society, 256, literacy for poor, 266, poor laws, 255, 266, surplus taxation, 255, support American colonists, 17, 18, Test and Corporation Acts, 13–15. called "gunpowder Joe," 273; utilitarianism, 20; on Home Office list of disaffected and seditious persons (1792), 323; colony in U.S. for liberal Dissenters (Pantisocracy?), 329–30, 330 n. 2; respecting American citizenship, 323, 336; sides with Jeffersonians, 332, 334, 337; abused by Federalists, 333–37

natural philosopher: read chemistry but not a chemist, 101, 103, 124, 140–41, 157, 193, received Copley Medal, 94, discursive writing style, 118; powers of observation, 98, 135, 138; poor memory, 134–35, attacked as plagiarist, 124, 126, 27, mistranslations and misrepresentations, 118, procedural errors in experiments, xiii, 356–61, nonscientific publications not interfere, 175, 241; in U.S.: anticlimatic, 354; promotes by experiments, 350, influence on American chemistry, 372, 372 n. 46

teaching, education, and metaphysics: not perform secular historical research, 257–58, influence on American education, 342, metaphysics influences science, 108; spiritualism (ghosts), 73, spiritualization of matter, 71, 84, 87

theology: his primary concern, 266–67; most honorable employment, 197, antislavery, 198–200, 198 n. 11; controversy with Samuel Horsley, 230–34, arguments confirmed by nineteenth- and twentieth-century scholars, 234–35; revived Theological Repository (1784), 31, 202–7, 217–18

in United States (1794–1804): arrives New York, 324; arrives Philadelphia, 325; death, 400; early contacts with Americans, 18 n. 34, 326; epitaph, 401; house in Northumberland, Pennsylvania, 347, 347 n. 8, 370; invited to preach, 374–75, 375 n. 6, 378–81; Jefferson's government first friendly to live in, 343; last illness commences (1801), 386, 392

Works

Address to Protestant Dissenters . . . on Approaching Election, 1774, 15–17, 16 n. 30, 22–23

"Address to the Jews," annexed to Discourses relating to Evidences of Revealed Religion, 1796, 211 n. 34

Address on the Lord's Supper to Children, 1773, 25

"Address to Methodists" (*see* Priestley edited, *Original Letters by the Rev. John Wesley*)

Advice to Dissenters conducting application against certain penal laws, 1773, 13–15,22

Answer to Mr. Paine's Age of Reason. See *Letters to Philosophers & Politicians, Continuation of*

Appeal to Public on ... the Riots in Birmingham, 1791, 213 294–97, 295 nn. 4, 6

Appeal to Public, Part II, 1792 (*W.* 19:435–508, Appendices 17–32), 297

Case of Poor Emigrants, 1797 (*W.*16:500–511), 332–33, 333 n. 39

Comparison of Moses with Hindoos, 1799, 384–86

Priestley, Joseph *(continued)*
  Considerations for Young Men, 1775,
    28–29
  Considerations on Doctrine of Phlogiston,
    1796, 355
  Defenses of Unitarianism, 1786, 1787; 1788
    & 1789(*W.*19:3–110) , 228
  Discourses relating to revealed religion,
    1796, 380–81
  Discourses, Vol. II, 1797, 381–82
  Disquisitions on matter and spirit, 1777,
    59–61
  Doctrine of Philosophical Necesssity, 1772,
    77–81
  Doctrine of Phlogiston Established, 1800;
    with *Additions*, 1803, 361–64; *Obser-*
    vations on the Doctrine of Phlogiston,
    Part II, 1797, 355
  Doctrines of Heathen Philosophy, 1804,
    399–400
  Examination of Scottish Common Sense
    Philosophy, 1774, 43–51
  Exp. & Obs., 1775, 95–105; *Exp. & Obs.*
    II, 1776, 108–19; *Exp. & Obs. III*, 1777,
    131–37
  Exp. & Obs. Nat. Phil., 1779, 12, 137–41;
    Exp. & Obs. Nat. Phil. II, 1781, 153–60;
    Exp. & Obs. Nat. Phil., 1786, 175–78
  Experiments and Observations on Differ-
    ent Kinds of Air . . . being the former Six
    Volumes, 1790, 185–89
  Experiments and Observations . . . on
    atmospherical air, reprinted from Trans-
    actions Of the American Philosophical
    Society, 1796
  Experiments on the Generation of Air from
    Water, 1793, 302–3
  Familiar Letters addressed to the
    Inhabitants of Birmingham, 1790
    (*W.* 19:135–304), 274, 274 n. 27, 275
  Forms of Prayer, 1783 (*W.* 21:474–558),
    200
  Four Discourses, 1806, 400
  Free Address to those petitioning for repeal
    of act favouring Roman Catholics, 1780
    (*W.* 22:499–516), 267, 267 n. 12
  Free Discussion of materialism and
    necessity, 1778, 82–86
  General History of Christian church to the
    Fall of the Western Empire, 1790, 228,

    259–60, 259 n. 36; *General History from*
    the Fall of the Western Empire to the
    Present, 1802–3, 388–92, 388 n. 26
  General View . . . for the unity of God,
    1783, 226
  Harmony of the Evangelist in Greek, 1777;
    in English, 1780, 30–31, 31 n. 13, 32, 32
    n. 14, 33, 33 nn. 18, 19, 34, 34 nn. 20, 21,
    35, 35 n. 22
  Hartley's Theory of the Human Mind,
    1775, 52, 53
  Heads of Lectures on natural philosophy,
    1794, 304–8, 304 n. 24
  History of Early Opinions, 1786, 226–28
  History of optics, 1772, 69
  History of the Corruptions of Christianity,
    1782, 216–23, 216 n. 6; *Defences of the*
    History of Corruptions, 1782–783 (*W.*
    18:1–309); *Reply to the Anamadversions*
    . . . in the Monthly Review, 1783 (*W.*
    18:3–37; Remarks *on the Monthly*
    Review, 1783 (*W.* 18:117–24)
  "Hints concerning public education," ms,
    1800, 340–42
  Importance of Religion, 1801
  Index to the Bible, 1805, 398–99
  Inquiry into the Knowledge of ancient
    Hebrews, 1801 (*W.* 12:482–504), 386
  Institutes of Natural and Revealed
    Religion, 1774, 25
  Lectures on History, 1788, 11, 253–58, 253
    n. 26; "Of the Constitution of the
    United States," in Lectures on History,
    Philadelphia edn., 1803 (*W.* 24:1–438),
    343
  Lectures on Oratory and Criticism, 1777, 10
  Letter to a Layman, on Lindsey's church,
    1774, 27–28
  Letter to an Antipaedobaptist, 1802
    (*W.* 20:463–91), 386
  Letter to Jacob Bryant, 1780, 86, 86 n. 11
  Letter to the Inhabitants of Birmingham,
    1791, 294, 294 n. 3
  Letter to the Rev. John Palmer, Second
    Letter, to Palmer, 1780, 86, 86 n. 11
  Letter to the Rev. John Blair Linn, Second
    Letter to Linn, 1803 (*W.* 21:188–220,
    221–46), 387, 387 n. 25, 388
  Letter to the Right Honourable William
    Pitt, 1787, 268, 268 n. 17

Letters to a Young Man, 1792, 310–11; Part II, 1793 (*W.* 20:303–51, 352–463), 313–14

Letters to . . . New Jerusalem Church, Swedenborg, 1791 (*W.* 21:43–86), 213–14, 213 n. 40

Letters to Dr. Horsley, I, 1783; II, 1784; III, 1786; IV, 1790, 225–26, 229–34; *Remarks on the Monthly Review,* 1784 (*W.* 18:127–42)

Letters to M. Volney, 1797, 377

Letters to the Inhabitants of Northumberland, 1799, 336

Letters to the Jews, Part I, Part II, 1786, 1787 (*W.* 20: 227–50, 251–74), 210–11

Letters to philosophers and politicians, 1793, 37–42, 37 n. 25, 311–12; *Continuation . . . and Letters to philosophical unbeliever,* III, 1794 (*W.* 231:109–27, 128–69, 377

Letters to a philosophical unbeliever, 1787, 37–42, 64; *Additional Letters . . . ,* 1787, 248–49, 248 n. 19; *Letters . . . ,* Part II (*W.* 17: Appendix 7, 533–36), 1787, 249–52

Letters to the Rev. Edward Burn, 1790 (*W.* 19: 305–14), 272–73, 272 n. 25

Letters to the Right Honourable Edmund Burke, 1791, 279–82, 279 n. 38

"Maxims of Political Arithmetic," in *Aurora,* 16–27 February 1798, reprinted in *Letters to Inhabitants of Northumberland,* 1799 (*W.* 25:175–82), 333–34

Miscellaneous Observations relating to Education, 1778, 10–11

Notes on . . . on books of scripture, 1803–4, 393–98

"Observations on infidelity," prefixed to *Letters to Philosophers and Politicians,* Philadelphia edn., 1794, 375

Observations on the increase of infidelity, 1797 (*W.* 17: 1–110), 376, 376 n. 9

Originaliity . . . of the Mosaic institutions, 1803, 394–95

Outline of the Evidences of Revealed Religion, 1797 (*W.* 21:170–87), 383

Philosophical Empiricism, 1775, 124–29

Political Dialogue on general principles of government (doubtfully ascribed to Priestley), 1791 (*W.* 25:81–108), 282 n. 43

"Remarks on Two Letters addressed to the Delegates . . . ," in John Aikin's *Spirit of the Constitution,* 1790, 271, 271 n. 22

"Short View of ... opinions ... concerning the proposed test," MS, 1773, 13

Socrates and Jesus Compared, 1803 (reprinted as Jesus and Socrates Compared), 387

"Some Considerations on the State of the Poor" see Priestley edit., *An Account of a Society for encouraging the . . . Poor,* 1787

Theological and Miscellaneous Works of Joseph Priestley, LL.D. F.R.S. &c., edit. John Towill Rutt, 25 vols., 1972 edition of 1817–31 edition

Two Letters to Dr. Newcome, 1780, 36–37

Third Letter to Dr. Newcome, 1781, 36

Unitarianism explained, 1794 (*W.* 16:472–59, with prior conclusion, 195–96), 327–28, 381

Scientific Papers in the Philosophical Transactions: 1774, 94–95; 1775,106–7; 1776, 129–30; 1783, 165–68, 171–72, 171 n. 4; 1785, 174; (1) 1788, 181–83; (2) 1788, 182; (1) 1789, 182–83; (2) 1789, 183–84; (3) 1789, 184; 1790, 184, 184 n. 29; 1791, 190–91

Scientific Papers in the Transactions of the American Philosophical Society: 3 papers, 1799, 355; 6 papers, 1802, 359–60; 2 papers, 1809, 368–70

Scientific Papers in the Monthly Magazine: 1798, 355, 3556 n. 26; four papers essentially repeating those in the New York Medical Repository, 1798–99, 357 n. 28; one of 1800, 361 n. 33, and a summary of those on carbon monoxide, 1802, 361 n. 34

Scientific Papers in the New York Medical Repository: 1797, 356 n. 26; 1799, 355–56; nine papers 1799–1800, 357–59, 357 n. 28; four 1800–1801, 359–61, 359 n. 30, 361 n. 33; 1801, on hearing, 364, 365 n. 37, 1802, on pestilential diseases, 364, 365 n. 37, 1802, on dreams, 364–65, 365 n. 37; 1802, "voltaic" experiments, 366–7; and five, 1802–3, on carbon monoxide, 367–68

Priestley, Joseph (*continued*)
Scientific Papers in Nicholson's Journal of
Natural Philosophy, Science and the
Arts: seven papers 1800–1803, essential
repeating N.Y. Medical Repository
papers, 359 n. 30, 360 n. 31, 366 n. 38,
367 n. 39
Sermons: 1779, 29–30; 1781, 198; 1782,
198 n. 10; 1785 (*W.* 15:70–82); 1788,
198–200, 198 n. 11; 1789 (*W.* 15:387–
404), 271, 1790, 199 n. 13; (1) 1791, 200,
200 n. 14; (2) 1791 (*W*.15:420–440), 246;
(3) 1791, 309, 310; (4) 1791, 310; 1793,
312–13; 1794, 314–15; (2) 1794, 316;
1797, 328; six collected in *Discourse on
Various Subjects*, 1787 (*W.* 15:1–182);
twelve collected in *Discourses on the
Evidences of Revealed Religion*, 1794
(*W.* 15:191–362), 315, 315 n. 38; "A
Prayer respecting the present State of
Christianity," in William Christie's
Discourses on the Divine Unity, 1790
Theological Repository, 31, 202–7; papers
in: on inspiration, 203–4; on prophecy,
204; against Arianism, 204–5; on Plato
and Platonism, 205; minor papers, 206
Priestley, Joseph, edited
*An Account of a Society for encouraging
the industrious Poor*, 1787; tables of
interest, perhaps prepared by Francis
Maseres, 266, 266 nn. 10, 11
Bible, reprinted Baskerville Bible, 1788–89,
with Priestley notes, 208–9; references
for, 209–10
Anthony Collins, *Philosophical Inquiry
concerning Liberty*, 248
Edward Elwall's Triumph of Truth, 211
*An History of the Sufferings of Mr. Lewis
de Marolles and Mr. Isaac LeFevre*,
transl. *from the French and now
republished*, 1788, 211
Original Letters by the Rev. John Wesley,
1791, 212–13, 213 n. 39
*Psalms and Hymns for the Use of the New
Meeting in Birmingham* (with William
Hawkes), 1790, 201
Theological Repository, 4 (1784), 5 (1786),
6 (1788)
Priestly, Mary (wife), 8, 293, 309, 345, 346
death, 348

determination to leave England, 318
dislike of cities, 346
mourned, 348–49, 349 n. 10
in poor health, 329
Priestley, William (son) and children, 277,
317, 318, 405–6
accused poinoner, 405–6
named French citizen, 318, 318 n. 3
Pringle, John, 94
his Copley Medal Address, 94
processes
airs: absorption by water, 151, 187;
agitating, 99, 116, 134, 186; animal substances perserved in, 138; decomposition
on charcoal, 180; for balloons,163;
generation of, 98, 302; heat conductivity
of, 159; heat expansion of, 136, 136 n.
26, 158, 158 n. 19; indices of refraction,
117, 136; intensity of sound, 258; on
metals, 174, 174 n. 16, 368; by mice, 112;
by nitrous air test, 112; purity, 137–39,
137 n. 31
other: deliquence, 135; electrolysis, 365–
66, 366 n. 38; galvanic ("voltaic"), 366;
Meniscus/adhesion test for mercury, 188
proofs, nature of, 38
prophecy, 381, 394
numbers game, 397
Protestant Dissenters Relief Bill, 22, 22 n. 45
Prout, William, 159
putrefaction, 156

Quincy, Josiah, Jr., 18

Reeves, John, 320
Reid, Thomas, 44, 45 n. 4, 47, 48–49, 50–51
Reign of Terror, 277
Reimarus, Johann A. H., 57
Reformation, Protestant, 390–92
religions, non-Christian, 3, 252
heathen, vices of, 380
Greek (with philosophies): philosophical
gentiles, 66–67; Platonism, 67; superiority of Christianity, 387, 399–400
Hindu ("Hindoo"), 66, 252; confusing
evidences, 383–84, 384 n. 20; practices
gross, 385; worship not equal Hebrew,
385
Moslem ("Mahometism"), 390; praise of,
256; Koran contrasted to Scriptures, 282

religious persecution by Protestants, 390
religious wars, 391
respiration
    oxidation process, 130, 188
    phlogistic process, 129–30
resurrection, intensive investigation of, 315
Revelation, Christian, 61, 250
    apostolic accounts, 260
    divine, 382
    ensures future state, 377
    evidences for, 383
Rhode Island College (Brown), 259
Richardson, Henry Hobson, 406
Rittenhouse, David, 326, 326 n. 24
Robertson, William, 51
Robson, John, 337
Rockingham Whigs, 18, 19
Rogers, Samuel, 293–94
Romanticism from rationalism, 82
Romantics, reject Enlightenment, 281, 343
Rotherham, Caleb, 121, 130, 247
Rowning, John, 67, 69
Royal Society of Dublin, 353
Royal Society of London, 5, 12, 122, 301, 301
        n. 19, 353
    access to library, 21
    guests and Fellow nominations, 122 n. 2,
        153
    politics in, 275
Rozier's Observations sur la Physique, 94
Rumford, Benjamin Thompson, Count, 159,
        363
Rush, Benjamin, 106, 330, 351, 353, 379
Russell, Catherine, 284
Russell, Martha, 196
Russell, William, 268, 271, 272, 317–18, 320
Rutt, John Towill, 3 n. 3

Saussure, Nicolas T. de, 139
Savile, Sir George, 21
Scheele, Carl Wilhelm, 112, 116, 157, 364
schisms, early Christian, 261
Scholefield, Radcliffe, 148, 197
Scottish Common Sense philosophers, 70
scriptures
    authenticity of Old Testament, 382, 393,
        393 n. 29, 394
    authenticity of New Testament, 313, 383,
        396, 396 n. 34, 398
    new translation of, 207–8

no impostures, 252
not superseded by tradition, 220, 220
        nn. 11, 12
parousia foretold in, 386
synoptic problem, 33
willful ignorance of, 251
scriptures, books of
    Genesis, scientific explanations for, 395
    Leviticus, photosynthesis in, 395
    Joshua, meteors in, 395, 395 n. 32; standing
        sun reference from poem, not
        observation, 395
    Ecclesiastes, rejects pessimism of, 395–96
    Song of Solomon not religious, 396
    prophecies in Daniel, 210
    Acts most valuable of New Testament
        books, Epistles the oldest record of
        Christianity, 397
    Corinthians, physics of light in, 395
    Revelation of St. John, 210
    "three witnesses" passage spurious, 398
Semon, Richard Wolfgang, 57
Senebier, Jean, 139
Sequin, Armond, 130, 161
Servetus, Michael, 390
'sGravesande, Willem, 67
Shelburne, Lord, 19–20, 20 nn. 36, 37, 38,
        21–22
    and American colonies, 16
    break with Priestley, 141–43
    Chathamites, leader of, 142
    house at Bowood, 8
    library, 10 n. 17
    remarries, 142
    son, Ld. Fitzmaurice, 11–12
    try engage again, 143
    visitors, 9–10
Shipley, Jonathan, Bishop of St. Asaph, 22
Shore, Samuel, 260
Sinclair, Sir John, 370
slavery, 270
    disgrace though permitted in Old
        Testament, 398
Small, Dr. William, 104, 150
Smith, William, M. P., 288
Socinian. See Unitarianism
Sparkes, Alexander, 374
specific gravity, 128, 158
soul, sleep of, 68
Spencer, Dr. Benjamin, 285, 288–89

Spencer, Herbert, 52, 81
Spinoza, 78
spirit, nature of, 63, 64
spontaneous generation, 188
steam engine, gases substitute for steam, 160, 161
Stephen, Leslie, xi, xi n. 1, 1
Stiles, Ezra, 14, 374
substance, 63
    differences in, 303, 365
    different forms of, 119
    diverse properties of, 69, 188, 307
    in form of air, 131, 131 n. 17, 132 n. 18, 187
    immaterial, 64–65
substances, 70
    general: ordered by physical form
        (airiform, liquid, solid) 307, 307
        n. 28, 308
    specific: acetylides, 161, 177, 177 n. 13;
        anthrocite ("black substance"), 164;
        chlorine, 157, Derbyshire spar (Blue
        John), 123; finery cinder (ferrosopheric
        oxide), 357; fixed air (carbon dioxide),
        113, 115, 128; hydrocarbons, 367;
        hydrofluoric acid, 107, 116; mercurius
        calcinatus per se (mercuric oxide), 105,
        105 n. 24; mercury, volitile, 157; minium
        (red lead), 111, 113; nitrosyl chloride,
        135; phosphorus acid (phosphine), 138;
        pyrolucite (black wadd), 163
suppression of ideas, failure of, and back-
    fires, 296–97
Symonds, Dr. John, 258

T.A.S. on Parmenides, 229
Test and Corporation Acts, 14
    New Meeting, Birmingham, on, 268
    occasional conformity, 268
    Priestley sermon on, 271–72
    repeal, 270–71, 272
Thatcher, George, 334–35, 351, 353, 374, 378, 383
"Theodosius," 275, 275 n. 29
theory
    with experiments, 98
    interpretation by, 133
Thirty-nine Articles, 15
    Bentham on, 15 n. 28
    subscription to, 228, 269, 269 n. 18
Thomson, J. J., 71

thought
    physiological theory of, 70
    principles of, 63–64
Toland, John, 70
toleration
    Act of 1689, 264
    in America, 392
    Priestley's, 212
Tooke, John Horne, 294
Toplady, Augustus, 51, 73
Toulmin, Joshua, 3 n. 2
transmutation, 124
trials, abortive treason (1794), 324, 330
Trinity, 15, 15 n. 29, 217, 232–34, 261, 262
Troostwick, Paets van, 189
truth
    by argument, 15, 27, 27 n. 7, 37, 38, 38
        n. 27, 59, 61, 90, 118, 118 n. 42, 261, 269
    nature of, 65
Turgot, A. R. J., 7
Turner, Matthew ("William Hammond"),
    158, 248 n. 19
Twining, Thomas, 371, 383

unexpected, cause of, 157
Unitarianism, 3, 5
    early, by inference. 227, 227 n. 25
    Jewish Christian, 216
    Society of Unitarian Christians,
        Philadelphia (1796), 328
    in U.S., 236
Unitarians
    rational piety of, 198
    Relief Bill (1813), 262–63
    repudiate Priestley (c. 1850), 75, 235–39
Universalists
    eternal torment indefensible, 381
    First Church of, Philadelphia, 378, 378
        n. 13
utilitarianism, 3, 81
    naturalistic Christian versus normative, 20

Vaughan, Benjamin, 247, 346, 350, 370
Vaughan, John, 330, 349, 351, 378
Vaughan, Samuel, 7, 18, 20, 352
Vaughan family, 293
Venn, Rev. Henry, xii
vibrations, doctrine of association, 53–55, 70
    Hartley's, 63
vibratiuncles, 55, 57

Virginia, University of, 259
Volney, C.F. deC., Comte de, his Ruins, 376–77
Volta, Alessandro, 94, 122, 131, 308
Voltaire, 376, 380

Wakefield, Gilbert, 310–11, 321
Walker, Adam, 121, 147
Walker, George, 44
Warltire, John, 11, 105, 159, 172
Warner, Richard, 73
Warrington Academy, moves, 245
Warwick Assizes (1791), 288, 288 n. 52
Warwickshjire Constsitutional Society, 283
Washington, G. W. P., 259
water
    composition of, 172–73, 189, 192, 362
    discovery of, 159, 160, 173 n. 6, 176
    polluted in experiments, 95
    Priestley on, 182–83, 183–85, 184 n. 29, 190–91
Watson, Richard, 101
Watson, William, Jr., 247
Watt, James, 150, 161, 166, 172, 317, 353
    use of factitious airs, 358, 361
Watt, James, Jr., 317, 404
Watts, Isaac, 43, 67–68
Webster, Noah, 364
Wedgwood, Josiah, 4, 97, 147, 150, 161, 163, 166, 353
    his pyrometer, 161
Wedgwood, Thomas, 177, 301
    experiments on light and heat, 162
weights and measures, standardization of, 163

Wesley, Rev. John, 212–13
Wettstein, Johann Jacob, 209
Whigs, Club of Honest, 18, 18 n. 33
Whitbread, Samuel, 288
White, Bishop of Pennsylvania, 386
Whitehead, John, 86–87
Wilkes, John, 12
Wilkins, Sir Charles, 207
Wilkinson, John, 142, 164, 177, 299, 317, 348, 349, 350, 350 n. 12
Wilkinson, William, 277, 317–18
Willard, Joseph, 373
William and Mary, College, 259
Williams College, 259
Williamson, Charles P.
    diary of temperatures, 371
    source of sulphur, 371
Wilson, Benjamin, 109, 109 n. 32
Winterbotham, William, 321, 323, 323 n. 17
Withering, William, 104, 150, 161, 163, 164, 301, 330, 353
Woodhouse, James, 351, 358–59, 359 n. 29
Wollaston, William, 70
Wordsworth, William, 52, 319
Wyvill, Christopher, 265, 322, 343

Yale College, 259, 374
Yorkshire Association, 265
Young, Arthur, 174
Young, Thomas, xii, xii n2

Zelazny, Roger, 57 n. 25
Zuicker, 230